RANKING, SPICER AND PEGLER'S

EXECUTORSHIP LAW
AND ACCOUNTS

Twenty-first edition

by

K. S. CARMICHAEL, F.C.A., F.T.I.I.

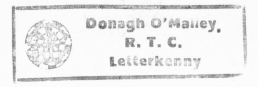

H F L (PUBLISHERS) LTD
9 BOW STREET, COVENT GARDEN,
LONDON WC2E 7AL

First published ..	..	..	..	*1895*
Twenty-first Edition	..	..	..	*1971*
(Second impression) revised	..	..	*1972*
(Third impression)	..	..	..	*1974*

ISBN 0 372 01622 7

Printed in Great Britain at

THE STELLAR PRESS, HATFIELD, HERTS

PREFACE

Ten years have passed since this book was last revised and unfortunately in that period both Mr. H. A. R. J. Wilson and Mr. A. E. Langton have died. Consequently, a new author has had the task of introducing ten years' legislation and cases, including the major changes in the Finance Act 1969.

The entire book has been recast. In particular the former chapter on Estate Duty has been broken down into a number of chapters. At the beginning of each chapter, with the exception of Chapters XV and XVI, there is an introductory paragraph. This summarises the contents of the chapter and readers may like to read these, before studying the text in detail, to obtain a comprehensive view of the entire subject. This feature has been introduced to help those who are using the book to study for professional examinations.

Unfortunately, due to the period which has elapsed since the last edition, it is necessary to continue to state law which does not apply to deaths on or after 16th April, 1969, but many readers have to apply such law. I have set out the law which has been surpassed.

This revised impression of the twenty-first edition contains the provisions of the Finance Acts 1971 and 1972 (the latter mainly in Appendix VII). If any reader has any constructive comments on improving future editions, I shall be happy to hear from him.

117 NEWBERRIES AVENUE,   K. S. CARMICHAEL
RADLETT, HERTS.

TABLE OF CONTENTS

Chapter I

THE DEVOLUTION OF PROPERTY ON DEATH

Chapter II

EXECUTORS AND ADMINISTRATORS

vii

Chapter II (*continued*)

EXECUTORS AND ADMINISTRATORS

Chapter III
THE DEATH DUTIES

Chapter IV
VALUATION OF PROPERTY FOR ESTATE DUTY PURPOSES

Chapter X
CONTROLLED COMPANIES

Chapter XI
APPORTIONMENT

Chapter XII
POWERS AND DUTIES OF THE PERSONAL REPRESENTATIVE

Part III – ACCOUNTS (*continued*)

THE INVESTIGATION AND AUDIT OF EXECUTORS' AND TRUSTEES' ACCOUNTS

APPENDICES

Appendix I

Appendix II

Appendix III

Appendix IV

Appendix V

Appendix VI

Appendix VII

TABLE OF CASES

TABLE OF REFERENCES

ABBREVIATIONS USED IN CITATIONS, ETC.

Abbreviation	Reference
A. & E.	Adolphus and Ellis
A.C.	House of Lords and Privy Council Appeal Cases
Acct. L.R.	Accountant Law Reports
Add.	Addams
A.E.A.	Administration of Estates Act 1925
A.E.R.	All England Reports
Ambl.	Ambler
App. Ca(s)	House of Lords and Privy Council Appeal Cases
Atk.	Atkyns
B(arn) & Ald.	Barnewall and Alderson
B. &. C.	Barnewall and Cresswell
Beav.	Beavan
Bingh.	Bingham
Bing. N.C.	Bingham's New Cases
Bligh, N.S.	Bligh, New Series
Brownl.	Brownlow and Goldesborough
Broc. C. C.	Brown's Report of Cases in Chancery
Burr.	Burrow
Cas. t. Finch	Finch
Cas. temp. Lee	Lee
C.B.	Common Bench
Ch.	⎫ Chancery Division
C(h).D.	⎭
Ch. App.	Chancery Appeals
Chanc. Cas.	Chancery Cases
Cl. & F.	Clark and Finnelly
C.L.R.	Common Law Reports
C.P.	Common Pleas
Co.	Sir Edward Coke
Coll.	Collyer
Cox	Cox
Cr. & J.	Crompton and Jervis
Curt.	Curteis' Ecclesiastical
De G. F. & J.	Die Gex, Fisher & Jones
De G. M. & G.	⎫ De Gex, Macnaghten and Gordon
D.M. & G.	⎭
De G. & S(m).	De Gex and Smale
Dick.	Dickens
Dow	Dow
Drew.	Drewry
Dr. & Sm.	Drewry and Smale

Abbreviation		Reference
Dyer	.. ..	Dyer
East	.. ..	East
Eq. ..	.. ..	Equity
Ex. ..	.. ..	Exchequer
F.A...	.. ..	Finance Act
F. (Ct. of S.) ..	.. ..	Fraser (Scottish Session Cases)
Freem.	.. ..	Freeman
Giff...	.. ..	Giffard
H. &. C.	.. ..	Hurlstone and Coltman
Hagg.	.. ..	Haggard
Hagg. Eccl. ..	.. ..	Haggard's Ecclesiastical Reports
Ha(re)	.. ..	Hare
H. & M.	.. ..	Hemming and Miller
H. & N.	.. ..	Hurlstone and Norman
H.L.(C).	.. ..	House of Lords
Ir. ..	.. ..	⎫
I (r.) R.	.. ..	⎬ Irish Reports
I.C.T.A.	.. ..	Income and Corporation Taxes Act 1970
J(ac). & W. ..	.. ..	Jacob and Walker
Joh.	.. ..	Johnson
J. & H.	.. ..	Johnson and Hemming
Jur., N.S.	.. ..	Jurist, New Series
K.B.	.. ..	King's Bench
K(ay) & J. ..	.. ..	Kay and Johnson
Keen.	.. ..	Keen
L.J. ..	.. ..	Law Journal
L.P.A.	.. ..	Law of Property Act 1925
L.P.U.S.P. ..	.. ..	Law, Practice and Usage in the Solicitor's Profession
L.R...	.. ..	Law Reports
L.T...	.. ..	⎫
L.T. Jour.	.. ..	⎬ Law Times
Lev...	.. ..	Levinz
Madd.	.. ..	Maddock
Macq.	.. ..	Macqueen
Mac. & G. ..	.. ..	Macnaghten and Gordon
M. & G(r.). ..	.. ..	Manning and Granger
M. & S.	.. ..	Maule and Selwyn
M. & W.	.. ..	Meeson and Welsby
Mer(iv).	.. ..	Merivale
Mod.	.. ..	Leache's Modern Reports
Moo. P.C. ..	.. ..	Moore's Privy Council Cases
Moore	.. ..	Moore
Morrel	.. ..	Morrel's Bankruptcy Reports
My. & Cr. ..	.. ..	Mylne and Craig
M(y). & K. ..	.. ..	Mylne and Keen

Abbreviation		Reference
Notes of Cas...	..	
N.C.	..	} Notes of Cases
N.C.P.R.	..	Non-Contentious Probate Rules, 1954
N. Ir.	..	Northern Ireland Law Reports
N.R.	..	New Reports
P. ..	..	Probate, Divorce and Admiralty
P.D...	..	Probate Division
P. & D.	..	Perry and Davison
Palm.	..	Palmer
Paton, Sc. App.	..	Paton, Scotch Appeals
Phil. Ch. C. ..	..	
Phillim.	..	} Phillimore
Price	..	Price
P. Wms.	..	Peere Williams
Q.B...	..	Queen's Bench
Q.B.D.	..	Queen's Bench Division
R. & M.	..	Russell & Mylne
R.R.	..	Revised Reports
Robt.	..	
Robert.	..	} Robertson
Roll. Rep.	..	Sir H. Rolle
R.S.C.	..	Rules of the Supreme Court
Russ.	..	Russell
Russ. & M.	..	Russell and Mylne
Salk.	..	Salkeld
S.C.	..	Supreme Court
Sc.	..	Scotch Reports
Sch. & Lef.	..	Schoales and Lefroy
Sel. Cas Ch. (T. King)	..	Select cases in Chancery temp. King
Sid. ..	..	Siderfin
Sim.	..	Simons
Sim. & St.	..	Simons & Stuart
Sir T. Raym. ..	..	Sir T. Raymond
S.J. ..	..	Solicitor's Journal and Reporter
S.L.T.	..	Scots Law Times
Sm. & G.	..	Smale and Giffard
Str. ..	..	Strange
Sw. ..	..	Swabey
S(w). & Tr.	..	Swabey and Tristram
S.R. & O.	..	Statutory Rules and Orders
T.C.	..	Tax Cases
T.L.R.	..	Times Law Reports
Term Rep.	..	Durnford and East's Term Reports
Turn. & Russ.	..	Turner and Russell
Vaugh.	..	Vaughan
Vent.	..	Ventris
Vern.	..	Vernon

Abbreviation			Reference
Ves.	..	..	Vesey
Ves., Jun.	..	..	Vesey, Junior
s., Sen.	..	..	Vesey, Senior
Wightw.	..	..	Wightwick
Wils.	..	..	George Wilson
W.L.R.	..	..	Weekly Law Reports
W.N.	..	..	Weekly Notes
W.R.	..	..	Weekly Reporter
Y. & C.	..	..	Younge and Collyer
Y. & J.	..	..	Younge and Jervis
Younge	..	..	Younge

AUTHORITIES CITED

RULES

TABLE OF STATUTES

CHAPTER I

THE DEVOLUTION OF PROPERTY ON DEATH

§ 1. Introduction

A major difficulty in attempting to understand the law applicable to the administration of the estate of a deceased person is the mass of detail which must be assimilated from several Acts of Parliament and many hundreds of decided cases spread over four centuries. Unlike Income tax there is no basic Act on which an explanation can be based. Nevertheless, an overall picture of the administration from the death of the deceased to the final distribution of his or her's estate must be obtained. In an attempt to help readers, the first section of each Chapter gives a simplified and brief synopsis of the contents of the chapter so that if the reader reads initially the first sections of each chapter he will appreciate the principles involved. He can study the detailed rules by reading the remainder of the chapter. In addition to the illustrations contained in each chapter explaining individual problems, there is an illustration covering administration.

Any person may be called upon to administer the estate of a deceased person, either by virtue of statute or by the expressed wish of the deceased person. Whether he undertakes the administration, depends upon the circumstances, thus an infant will not be allowed to administer the estate until he is of full age. The consent of the person in question will be necessary, either expressly or by implication.

Broadly speaking, the deceased's estate will be administered either as his will directs, or if there is no valid will, in accordance with the rules laid down in the Administration of Estates Act 1925, as subsequently amended by the Intestates Estates Act 1952, and the Family Provision Act 1966. It should be noted from the outset that complete freedom of disposition of property upon a death is no longer permitted in England, as the law recognises the fact that certain duties with regard to maintenance of the dependants of a deceased person cannot be disregarded by him in his will.

1

When the deceased names the person in his will whom he wishes to administer his estate after death, i.e. his executor, the authority to deal with the estate will vest in that person immediately upon death. In any other case, however, the authority will only vest when probate or letters of administration, i.e. formal acknowledgement of that right, have been obtained.

If the deceased has left a will, the first duty of the executor (after burying the deceased) will be to obtain probate of the will, which means that the will is acknowledged to be in order, insomuch as it apparently satisfies the legal requirements. Until Estate Duty on the personal property of the deceased has been paid, probate will not usually be granted and thus the executor will be bereft of the 'formal recognition' which will be necessary if he wishes to deal with the deceased's property, e.g. transfer stocks and shares in limited companies.

The will, to be valid, must be signed by the testator, or on his behalf, and the signature must be witnessed by two competent persons, who should sign in the presence of the testator a statement to that effect, such statement being embodied in the will itself.

It follows that if the will is subsequently altered in any material respect, the alteration should be effected in the clearest possible manner *and* it must be signed by the testator and attested by two witnesses.

The possibility of the will being 'revoked', i.e. negatived by the testator, must not be overlooked as the right to revoke a will subsists until death. Any effective revocation must be made by, or with the authority of, the testator, who must have the intention to revoke the will; the most usual method of effecting revocation is by reciting a clause to that effect in any subsequent will made. If it is the intention to change part of the will, the latter need not be revoked, as an addition to the existing will, termed a codicil, can be made which will suffice to effect the alteration. The codicil is read with the original will and must be effected with the same formalities.

The essential requirements necessary to execute a valid will are that the testator is of full age and has the mental capacity and soundness of mind, so that any presumption which may be made that at the relevant time he failed to have a complete understanding of the effect of the document he was signing, may be rebutted. One class of persons has a privileged position, this class consisting of members of the armed forces and merchant seamen, who may effect a valid will, though still under age and though the will is made orally or informally. These wills are known as nuncupative wills and certain conditions must be complied with for the privileges to apply (see § 3 (*f*)).

There are many safeguards which have the effect of preventing a person from disposing of his possessions in a manner to which he does not subscribe. Thus any will which is executed under force, fear or undue influence, or obtained by fraud is of no effect. Likewise, bequests to witnesses of the instrument in which the bequest is made, are invalid, except in a few circumstances, e.g. a witness who is also a creditor is not deprived of the amount of the debt owing to him.

By virtue of the Inheritance (Family Provision) Act 1938 (as amended), where the deceased leaves a spouse, a daughter who has not married, an infant son, or a daughter or son who is incapable of maintaining herself or himself because of a mental or physical disability, and the sum provided for the mainten-ance of such a person is deemed to be insufficient, the court may make such order as to payment on account of maintenance from the estate as it thinks fit. The dependant must make the application for the order, and the court must take into account all relevant facts, e.g. the income of the applicant and his future prospects. Upon cesser of the disability or marriage or the attainment of majorities as the case may be, the order will be determined.

Frequently a person dies without executing a valid will, or if he executes such a will, fails to dispose of the whole of his property. He is then said to be intestate or partially intestate and in such a case the undisposed of property falls to be distributed in accor-dance with a formula which is contained in the Administration of Estates Act 1925 (as amended). This attempts to share the property amongst those relatives of the deceased, in the order of priority and in such amounts as it is presumed that the testator would have bequeathed had he disposed of all of his property by will. Thus, under the laws of intestacy, it will be seen that the surviving spouse is entitled (after payment of all debts) to the personal chattels, the amounts of £8,750 or £30,000 (depending upon whether or not there are surviving children or children of a deceased child of the intestate) plus interest from the date of death to date of payment at the rate of 4% per annum, if the death is after the 1st January, 1967. The remainder of the property is also subject to the various interests of the widow, depending upon the circumstances of the particular case. The emphasis is on giving the spouse a far greater share of the intestate's property as the class(es) of the survivors becomes more remote relatively speaking from the deceased, so far as blood relationship is concerned. An example of the operation of the law is where the intestate leaves a spouse, but no issue, i.e. children or children of a deceased child, and no parent, brother or sister of the whole blood, or issue of the brother and sister of the whole blood; here the property is held in trust for the surviving spouse absolutely. Had there been issue of the marriage, and if the death had taken place after the 1st January, 1967, the spouse would have received the personal chattels and cash of £8,750 plus 4% per annum interest on that sum from the date of death to the date of payment, together with a life interest in one half of the balance. The remaining half would have been held on the 'statutory trusts' for the issue, i.e. an appropriate proportion of the property would become vested in the issue upon their attaining the age of twenty-one years, or marrying before that date. Upon the death of the surviving spouse, the property which produced the life interest will fall into the same 'statutory trusts' as above.

Legally adopted children and legitimated children, i.e. children born out of wedlock, whose parents subsequently marry, are in the same position as children of the whole blood of the adopter parents. However, if the child is only adopted by one of the spouses to the marriage, it is not treated as a child of the other spouse. Adopted children have no claims in the intestacy of their natural parent, and the word 'child' or 'children' in a will of the natural parent does not include them.

§ 2. Preliminary Considerations

The person authorised to deal with and distribute the property of a deceased person is styled his 'personal representative'. If the deceased left a will, the personal representative is normally the person named therein as 'executor', who obtains probate of the will. If the deceased did not leave a will, i.e. if he dies 'intestate', (or if he made a will but did not appoint an executor willing or able to act) the personal representative is the 'administrator', i.e. the person to whom 'letters of administration' are granted.

Property may broadly be classified as 'real' and 'personal'. Real property (or realty) consists of freehold land and the buildings erected thereon. Personal property (or personalty) comprises all other forms of property, including certain interests in land known as 'chattels real' (e.g. leasehold property).

A personal representative has an absolute power of disposition over all the personal estate of the deceased whom he represents and also over the real estate to which the deceased person was entitled to an interest not ceasing on his death. It follows that the power and authority to deal with and dispose of the property of a deceased person is vested exclusively in his personal representatives, whether as executors appointed under a will of which they obtain 'probate', or as administrators deriving their authority from 'letters of administration' granted by the court. In any case, the exercise of his powers by the personal representative will be governed by the intentions of the deceased, so far as they are expressed in or can be construed from his will, and by the rules devised by law, where those intentions are not effectively expressed in a valid will, and an 'intestacy', total or partial, arises.

Devolution of property takes place either by will or on intestacy. An intestate includes not only a person who has died without making a will, but also a person who leaves a will but dies without having disposed by the will of some beneficial interest in his estate (A.E.A., s. 55 (1)). In other words, intestacy includes partial intestacy. Thus:

X dies leaving £10,000. He bequeaths legacies of £3,000, £1,000 and £4,000 to C, D and E, and there is no clause contained in the will disposing of the residue of his estate. X will be intestate as to £2,000.

§ 3. The Will

A will is a written instrument by which a person signifies his wishes as to the devolution of his property after his death.

It must be in writing, but no particular form of document or of words is necessary; it need not be in the English language or in the testator's own handwriting. Any instrument properly executed may be admitted to probate, provided that it was revocable during the lifetime of the executant, and executed *animo testandi*, that is, only intended to come into operation after his death. Thus, orders on a banker, or on savings banks, or a letter and directions sent to an executor or devisee, having been duly executed, have been admitted as testamentary dispositions (*In the goods of Robinson* [1867]; *Cock* v. *Cooke* [1867]). The Wills Act 1837, as amended in 1852 and 1963 contains the law relating to wills.

If the testator so elects, his will may be deposited for safe custody with the authorities at Somerset House under regulations made in accordance with the provisions of the Judicature Act 1925, Section 172, but the will once deposited cannot be withdrawn. This does not imply that a further will cannot be executed but it is wise to see that any subsequent will or codicil is similarly deposited.

Under the Wills Act 1963, which came into force on 1st January, 1964, a will is treated as properly executed if its execution conforms to the internal law of the territory:

(1) where it was executed; or

(2) where the testator was domiciled or had his habitual residence either –

    (*a*) at the time of execution; or

    (*b*) when he died; or

(3) of which the testator was a national either –

    (*a*) at the time of execution; or

    (*b*) at the time of his death.

Under the same Act a will executed on board a vessel or aircraft is treated as properly executed if validly executed in accordance with the territory with which the vessel or aircraft is taken to be most closely connected.

The construction of a will is not altered by any subsequent change of domicil by the testator (Wills Act 1963, s. 4).

Immovable property (e.g. land) can only be transferred in accordance with the *lex situs*, i.e. the law of the place where the property is situated. For the purpose of transfer, leaseholds are regarded as immovable property, and therefore a will of English leasehold should primarily speaking be executed according to

English law. Thus, a Frenchman who desires to dispose of English leaseholds must make his will according to English law (*Pepin* v. *Bruyere* [1902]).

(a) Form of Will

The following is the form of a simple will:

Illustration

This is the last Will and Testament of me Alan Brown of Wokingham in the County of Berkshire. I hereby revoke all Wills at any time heretofore made by me.

I appoint Henry Smith to be the Executor of this my Will.

I direct that all my just debts and funeral and testamentary expenses shall be paid as soon as conveniently may be after my decease.

I give and bequeath to Clive Dunn the sum of five hundred pounds.

I give and bequeath the residue of my estate to Edward Fisher for his sole use and enjoyment.

Dated this First day of December, One thousand nine hundred and sixty-seven.

(Signed) Alan Brown

Signed and declared by the said Alan Brown the Testator as and for his last Will in the presence of us present at the same time, who at his request, in his presence, and in the presence of each other, have hereunto subscribed our names as Witnesses.

(Signed) George Henry
(Signed) John Knight

The Lord Chancellor may from time to time prescribe and publish statutory will forms to which a testator may refer in his will, and give directions as to the manner in which they may be referred to, but these forms are not deemed to be part of any will unless so referred to (L.P.A., s. 179). Forms were prescribed in the Statutory Will Forms, 1925, but these do not seem to be used to any great extent.

(b) The Essentials of Execution

The essentials of a valid execution of a will are:

(1) The signature of the testator, or of some other person in his presence and by his direction.

The signature must be made or acknowledged by the testator

in the presence of two or more witnesses, present at the same time (Wills Act 1837, s. 9), and made before the witnesses sign. The signature must be so placed 'at or after, or following, or under, or beside or opposite' the end of the will that it is apparent on the face of the will that the testator intended to give effect, by such signature, to the writing (Wills Act Amendment Act 1852, s. 1). Where an illiterate testator pressed his thumb, which had been smeared with ink, at the foot of the will, such 'signature' being duly attested by two witnesses, the court held that the will was duly executed, though the method of making the testator's mark did not commend itself to the court (*In the Estate of Finn* [1935]).

Where a will is signed on the first page only, but is continued on the next page, the second page is not admitted to probate unless there is also a reference above the signature on the first page which effects incorporation (Registrar's Direction [1953] 1 W.L.R. 689) as there was in *Palin* v. *Ponting* [1930].

Where a testator signed at the head and on the right hand side of his will with the signatures of the attesting witnesses underneath his signature the court held that the will was not validly executed (*in the Estate of Bercovitz* (1962)).

The words 'your loving Mother' were accepted as sufficient attestation of a will otherwise complying with the Wills Act 1837 (*Re Cook* [1960]).

(2) The signature and attestation of the witnesses.

The witnesses must actually sign in the presence of the testator. Although both witnesses must be present when the testator makes or acknowledges his signature, and must attest it in his presence, it is not essential that they attest in the presence of each other (*Brown* v. *Skirrow* [1902]).

Where a testator wrote the date, a clause purporting to dispose of her estate and her signature on one side of a piece of paper and two signatures in different handwriting were on the reverse side, the document was held to be a duly executed will (*in the Estate of Denning* (1958)).

It is not essential that the witnesses should know that it is the will of the testator they are attesting; it is his signature that they acknowledge (*In re Benjamin's Estate* [1934]). An acknowledgment by a witness of his signature previously made is not sufficient (*Moore* v. *King* [1842]).

Subject to the following comments anybody can be a witness. A blind person cannot be a witness (*In the Estate of Gibson* [1949]). Persons of unsound mind and very young persons are not competent witnesses, as they cannot understand the nature of the proceedings, and, therefore cannot 'attest' the signature within the meaning of the Act but there is no rule that a minor cannot be a witness. Illiterate witnesses should be avoided, since if the will were impeached, their evidence would be received with caution (*see Pearson* v. *Pearson* (1871)). Persons beneficially interested under a will and their husbands or wives should not act as witnesses, since, though the will would stand, a witness, or the husband or wife of a witness, loses all interest under the will (Wills Act 1837, s. 15). This rule, however, has no application in the case of a will which requires no attestation, e.g. a Nuncupative Will (see § 5 of this chapter) (*re Limond* [1915]. Examples of decisions affecting attestations by witnesses are:

A creditor who acts as witness is not deprived of the benefit of any charge or direction in the will for the payment of debts (Wills Act 1837, s. 16).

An executor can be a witness but cannot then take any bequest made to him in the will.

Where the will provides that the trustees are to be paid fees for their services, a trustee appointed by the will who attested the will cannot take the fees, but an attesting witness who is appointed later by the other trustee(s) can do so, because he had no beneficial interest at the time the will was attested (*Re Royce's Will Trusts* [1960]).

Where a legacy is given to a class, and a member of that class attests the will, the bequest to the class is still valid, but the attesting party cannot take any benefit under the gift (*Fell* v. *Biddolph* [1875]).

If a legatee attests a codicil under which he does not benefit, a bequest in the will or earlier codicil is not vitiated, since he does not witness the actual instrument which provides for that bequest; nor will a residuary legatee lose his rights in similar circumstances where the subsequent codicil revokes legacies to other persons, thereby increasing the amount of the residuary estate (*Gurney* v. *Gurney* [1855]; *Tempest* v. *Tempest* [1856]).

In another case a testatrix had made two wills in favour of her son, under the second of which he could claim no interest, as his wife attested it. That will, however, disclosed no general intention to revoke the earlier one, and it was held that the son remained entitled to his interest under the first will in so far as its dispositions were not inconsistent with the terms of the second (*Re Robinson; Lamb* v. *Robinson* [1930]).

Where a will provides for a legacy to one of the attesting witnesses, and is subsequently confirmed by a codicil witnessed by other persons, the codicil has the effect of republishing and incorporating the original will so as to validate the legacy, notwithstanding the fact that the legatee was a witness of the will (*Anderson* v. *Anderson* [1872]).

(c) The Attestation Clause

The attestation clause, the usual form of which will be found at the foot of the will given above, is a clause declaring that the formalities required by the Wills Act were observed. Though this clause is not essential it is most desirable that it should be inserted, since it raises the presumption that the will was properly executed, even if the witnesses are dead, or if they do not recollect its execution. Unless there is an attestation clause, the executor cannot get probate on his own oath alone, but must produce an affidavit from one of the attesting witnesses, or some other satisfactory evidence, showing that the formalities required by statute have been observed. If such an affidavit cannot be obtained, the Registrar may require evidence or affidavit from any person he may think fit, to show that the signature on the will is in the handwriting of the deceased or to confirm any other matter which may raise a presumption in favour of the due execution of the will (N.C.P.R., R. 10).

(d) Alterations, Interlineations, and Erasures

Any alterations, interlineations, or erasures in the will which existed at the time of execution, form a part of the will. They should be recited and identified in the attestation clause. Any made after execution must themselves be executed and attested by the signatures of the testator and two witnesses placed at or near the alterations (Wills Act 1837, s. 21). Obliterations, unless attested, will be inoperative if the original words can be made out, even though mechanical aid, such as magnifying glasses may be necessary (*In the goods of Ibbetson* [1838]); and even where paper had been pasted over the words to obliterate them (*In the goods of Gilbert* [1893]). Original words which can only be made out by infra-red photography are treated as obliterated because the photograph is a new document (*Re Itter* [1950]). In this case, however, it was held on the facts that the doctrine of dependent relative revocation (*see* (g) *below*) applied and the original words were admitted to probate. If there is complete obliteration the will is admitted to probate as if there were blanks in it (*In the goods of Ibbetson* [1838]).

(e) *Contingent Will*

A contingent will is one intended by the testator to come into operation only upon the happening, or not happening, of an event (other than, of course, the event of death), such as a mariner's will beginning 'Instructions to be followed if I die *at sea or abroad*'. If the condition is not satisfied, the will is void. Where the will is made absolutely dependent upon the happening of an event, that event must occur before the will can become operative; but if the possibility of an event happening is merely stated as a reason for making the will, the will becomes operative whether the event happens or not.

(f) *Privileged and Nuncupative Wills*

The wills of soldiers, airmen, etc., on active military service and seamen at sea can be made without the formalities required by the Wills Act 1837 (see § 5 of this Chapter).

(g) *Revocation of Will*

Till the death of the testator, a will is said to be *ambulatory*, that is, capable of revocation. Even if expressed to be irrevocable it may still be revoked (*Vynior's Case* [1609]).

A will may be revoked by 'burning, tearing, or otherwise destroying'. The act of destruction must be done by the testator himself, or by someone in his presence and by his direction, and it must be done with the intention to revoke (Wills Act 1837, s. 20), i.e. there must be *animus revocandi*. A portion of a will can be revoked in this way upon proof of intention. Merely striking through the will with a pen will not of itself operate to cancel it (*Stephens* v. *Taprell* [1840]). A will destroyed in the testator's lifetime, without his authority, may be established upon satisfactory proof being given of its destruction and its contents (*Sugden* v. *Lord St. Leonards* [1876]). Destruction made under a mistake, either of fact or of law, does not revoke a will. If the testator destroys his will with the specific object of making, establishing or reviving some other testamentary document, but never makes the other document, or makes it invalidly, or fails to revive it, the revocation has no effect, as the testator had no intention to revoke the will unless the other document took effect, and since the other testamentary document fails, he is deemed never to have intended to revoke at all. The act of destruction in such cases is known as *Dependent Relative Revocation*.

Illustrations

(1) A testator, having made a good first will, makes an ineffectual second will, and then, under an impression that the second will is valid, destroys the first will. The destruction will not revoke the first will, because the intention to revoke it was dependent on the second will being good (*Re Perrott* [1811]).

(2) A wife, under the mistaken idea that her husband would take all her property if she died intestate, destroyed a will which she had made in his favour; the terms of the will destroyed were admitted to probate (*Re Greenwood* [1930]).

(3) A testator erased words in his will, intending to revoke a legacy by substituting a different sum, but the substituted legacy was not effectively given; the original legacy stood (*Brooke* v. *Kent* [1841]).

The will may be expressly revoked by a subsequent will, codicil or other writing declaring an intention to revoke it and executed in the manner in which a will must be executed (Wills Act 1837, s. 20). A properly executed document sufficiently showing an intention to revoke a will operates as a revocation, even if it does not expressly revoke it (*Re Spracklan's Estate* [1938]). In this case a document executed and attested like a will contained a request to destroy a will and was held to revoke it.

Even a subsequent will entitled a 'last will and testament' does not of itself revoke a previous will unless the subsequent will disposes of the whole of the testator's property, in which case it will be presumed that earlier wills are revoked; but when there are two or more documents, the intention of the testator must be sought from the dispositions of property which he has made (*Simpson* v. *Foxon* [1907]). Two wills can stand together so far as they are not in conflict with each other; and if a subsequent testamentary paper is only partially inconsistent with one of earlier date, the former will only be revoked as to such parts as are inconsistent. If a testator intends to revoke a former will, he should insert in the subsequent instrument an express clause of revocation.

It has been held that verbal declarations made by a testator after the execution of a will which has been lost are admissible to show that the will contained a revocation clause revoking an earlier will (*Barkwell* v. *Barkwell* [1928]).

If a contingent will contains a clause revoking a previous will, that clause is void if the contingency never happens, and the previous will stands.

Marriage at once revokes a will (Wills Act 1837, s. 18), except that a will expressed to have been made in contemplation of marriage with a particular person is not revoked by the solemnisation of marriage with that person (L.P.A., s. 177). A reference in a will to marriage generally (the words used being simply 'made in contemplation of marriage') is not enough; the reference must be made expressly to marriage with a particular person and be followed by the solemnisation of that marriage (*Sallis* v. *Jones* [1936]). The principle on which these rules are founded is that on marriage the testator is presumed to wish to make provision for his wife and issue. But a will made in exercise of a power of appointment is not revoked by subsequent marriage, if in default of appointment the property appointed would not have passed to the executor, administrator, widow or widower (*In the goods of Gilligan* [1949]) or of the next-of-kin (Wills Act 1837, s. 18). Where a married man, whose wife had left him, made a will in favour of a woman with whom he was cohabiting, describing her as his 'wife', and afterwards married her on the expiration of several years after the disappearance of the first wife, it was held that the second marriage, being *primâ facie* valid, the will was in contemplation of marriage and was valid (*Pilot* v. *Gainfort* [1931]).

Revocation of one mutual will (i.e. a will made in favour of a person who has made his own will in favour of the person who made the first will) does not revoke the other (*Hinckley* v. *Simmons* [1798]). Mutual wills made *pursuant to an arrangement* between two persons, whereby the survivor is to take a life interest in the other's estate, impose a contractual obligation upon the survivor, where one has died without having revoked, to observe the terms of that arrangement, if he takes the benefit thereof. Hence the personal representatives of the survivor, notwithstanding any revocation by him, take his property upon trust to perform the arrangement originally made between the mutual testators (*Dufour* v. *Pereira* [1769]). But if the survivor takes an absolute interest, no such trust is imposed, and he is free to dispose both of the property which he inherits and of his own property (*Re Oldham* [1925]).

A will deposited at Somerset House can only be revoked by the execution of another will or codicil, since it cannot under any circumstances be delivered out of the registry.

A revoked will can only be revived by being again executed in the original manner, or by a codicil, duly executed, declaring an intention to revive it. This intention to revive must appear from the codicil itself (Wills Act 1837, s. 22) and the will must still be in existence (*In the Goods of Reade* [1902]). If the will has been intentionally destroyed, it cannot be revived by a subsequent codicil, but must be re-executed. Thus, if a man executes a will, which he ultimately destroys after revoking it by a subsequent will, and later executes a codicil purporting to revive the first will, such codicil is ineffective, and the second will must be admitted to probate (*In the goods of Steele* (1868)).

(*h*) Codicil

A codicil is an instrument made by the testator subsequently to the will, to explain or alter or to add to, or subtract from, the dispositions in the original will. It is to be read as one with the will.

The following is the form of a simple codicil:

Illustration

This is a Codicil to the Will of me Alan Brown which Will bears date the First day of December, One thousand nine hundred and sixty-seven.

I appoint Maurice Norman to be the Executor of my said Will jointly with Henry Smith the Executor named herein, and in all other respects I confirm my said Will.

Dated this First day of January, One thousand nine hundred and sixty-eight.

(Signed) Alan Brown

Signed and declared by the said Alan Brown as
    and for a Codicil to his Will in the presence
    of us, present at the same time, who at his
    request in his presence, and in the presence
    of each other, have hereunto subscribed
    our names as Witnesses.

(Signed) Oliver Park
(Signed) David Roberts

A codicil properly executed will render valid a previous will the execution of which is defective, if it clearly refers to and identifies that will (*Allen* v. *Maddock* [1857]). A codicil purporting to confirm an earlier will brings the earlier will down to the date of the codicil; and the two must be read as if the testator made the same dispositions of his property as in the earlier will, with the alterations made by the codicil (*Re Fraser; Lowther* v. *Fraser* [1904]).

It would appear that the revocation of a will does not revoke a codicil thereto unless it can be shown that the testator intended to revoke the latter as well (*In the goods of Bleckley* [1883]; *Gardiner* v. *Courthope* [1887]).

(i) *Forgery*

The forgery of a will, codicil, or other testamentary document whether of a dead or a living person, or of any probate or letters of administration, with intent to defraud, is punishable with imprisonment for life.

Such forgery consists in knowingly making a false document in order that it may be used to put forward as a genuine document (Forgery Act 1913, ss. 1, 2).

§ 4. Ability to make a Will

Any person who is *sui juris* and of sound understanding can make a will. Testamentary incapacity exists, therefore, only in the following cases:

(*a*) INFANTS, i.e. persons under the age of eighteen years, cannot make a valid will (Family Law Reform Act 1969), except when sailors at sea, soldiers or members of the Air Force in active military service (*ibid.* s. 11; Wills (Soldiers and Sailors) Act 1918). An individual reaches the age of eighteen years on the first moment of the eighteenth anniversary of his birth (*Re Shurey; Savory* v. *Shurey* [1918]).

An infant like any adult can if sixteen years of age or over nominate any person to receive any sum due to him at his death in respect of a holding of National Savings Certificates or a deposit in the Post Office Savings Bank or any stock or bonds held on the Post Office Register (except Premium Savings Bonds). The nomination in writing must be sent to the Post Office Savings Bank Department during his lifetime and must be witnessed by one attesting witness. The witness cannot benefit under the nomination (Post Office Savings Bank Act 1954, s. 7; P.O.S.B. Regulations 1938 (s. I., 1938), No.556).

Similar nominations may be made in the case of a deposit in a Trustee Savings Bank and of shares in an Industrial and Provident Society up to £500 in each case and provided this limit is not exceeded it is not necessary to produce probate or other grant of representation (Trustee Savings Bank Act 1954, s. 21). Industrial and Provident Societies Act 1965, ss. 23-27; Friendly Societies Act 1896, ss 56-58; Friendly Societies Act 1955, s. 5; Administration of Estates (Small Payments) Act 1965).

The nomination is revoked by the subsequent marriage of the nominator or by written notice of revocation sent to the appropriate department, but not by will (Reg. 32).

A nomination by a person over eighteen which is invalid to any extent, e.g. because it is for more than £500, where appropriate can be proved as a will if there are two attesting witnesses (*In the goods of Baxter* [1903]).

Should the nominee predecease the nominator, the nomination lapses (*Re Barnes*, *Ashenden* v. *Heath* [1940]).

A PERSON NOT OF SOUND MIND, MEMORY OR UNDERSTANDING cannot make a valid will during the time of his incapacity. This includes incapacity arising from idiocy, general insanity, senility, excessive drunkenness which deprives a person of his reason and understanding, etc.

In all cases the burden of proof is on those seeking to upset the will.

Wills obtained by force, fear, fraud, or undue influence are void.

§ 5. The Privileged Wills of Members of Her Majesty's Forces and Merchant Seamen

The statutory formalities required by the Wills Act 1837, in relation to wills generally are relaxed in the case of wills made by soldiers in active military service or by seamen or marines at sea (*ibid*. s. 11; Wills (Soldiers and Sailors) Act 1918). Members of the Air Force are regarded as soldiers for this purpose.

The privilege extends to the wills of seamen (including merchant seamen) and marines at sea, from the moment the ship is joined, whether in peace or war; and to the wills of marines and seamen who are members of her Majesty's naval or marine forces and so circumstanced that if they were soldiers they would be in active military service.

The effect of this relaxation is that wills made by persons of the classes and in the circumstances contemplated by the statutory exemptions are valid and effective although made by:

(1) an infant;

(2) informal writing; or

(3) oral declaration, called a 'Nuncupative Will', so long as it is clear that the declaration was intended to have testamentary effect (*In the Estate of Donner* [1917]).

A person falls within the category of soldier, sailor or airman in active military service if he is actually serving with the armed forces at a time when military operations in a theatre of war are taking place, have been taking place or are imminent (*Re Wingham; Andrews* v. *Wingham* [1949]).

A will made by a Red Cross nurse while on a hospital ship was treated as privileged (*In the Estate of Stanley* [1916]).

The term 'marine or seamen' also includes a *female* typist employed on a liner (*In the goods of Hale* [1915]); the purser of a man-of-war (*Re Hayes* (1839)), and a naval surgeon (*In the goods of Saunders* [1865]).

A will made informally while in actual military service is not revoked by a return to civilian life, unless so expressed (*In the goods of Coleman* [1920]), but is revoked by marriage, unless made in contemplation of that marriage. A formal will can be revoked while on active service, etc., by a letter or other informal act showing an intention to revoke it (*In the estate of Gossage; Wood* v. *Gossage* [1921]).

The will may be actually executed on shore either during the course of a voyage or between voyages. *In the goods of Lay* (1840) it was held that a will made in the course of a voyage need not be witnessed.

When, however, the property of a deceased seamen has come into the hands of the Board of Trade (as the master of the ship is bound to hand it over) under the Merchant Shipping Act 1894, s. 177 (1), the Board may refuse to recognise any will made at sea unless it is in writing signed or acknowledged by the testator in the presence of, and attested by the master or first or only mate. If the will was not made on board ship (except where the person claiming under the will is related to the testator by blood or marriage) the will must be in writing, and signed or acknowledged by the testator in the presence of, and attested by, two witnesses, one of whom is a superintendent, or is a minister of religion, or a justice, British consular officer, or an officer of customs. Wherever the Board refuse to pay or deliver the residue to a person claiming under a will, the residue is to be dealt with as if no will had been made.

§ 6. Married Women

A woman is entitled to hold, as her separate estate, all real and personal property belonging to her at the time of her marriage and all property acquired subsequently to the marriage, and may dispose of it by will or otherwise, as if she were a *feme sole* (Married Women's Property Act 1882, ss. 2, 5). The whole of the estate of a married woman devolves on her personal representatives, as in the case of any other deceased person.

§ 7. Inheritance (Family Provision) Act 1938

In most countries, other than England, a man can dispose of the whole of his property only if he dies without a wife or issue. English law does not impose any direct restriction upon a testator in the disposal of his property by will, which may validly exclude his wife and children from all benefit. The Inheritance (Family Provision) Act 1938, as amended by the Intestates' Estates Act 1952, and subsequently by the Family Provision Act 1966, whilst not creating any such direct restriction, is designed to enable dependants to make application to the court to rectify, in some measure, any apparent injustice done to them by the testator in the disposition of his property. The Act (as subsequently amended) applies to England and Wales only.

An application under the Act may be made to the appropriate County Court where it is shown to the satisfaction of the court that the value of the deceased's net estate does not exceed £5,000. (Family Provision Act 1966, s. 7).

Where a person dies domiciled in England and the court, upon application made by a dependant, is of the opinion that the will or the law of intestacy or a combination of the will and the law of intestacy does not make reasonable provision for the maintenance of that dependant, the court may order that such reasonable provision, as it thinks fit and subject to such conditions or restrictions as it may impose, shall be made out of the testator's net estate for the maintenance of that dependant.

The expression 'dependant' is confined to:

(1) a wife or husband;

(2) a daughter who has not been married, or who is, by reason of some mental or physical disability, incapable of maintaining herself;

(3) a son who has not attained twenty-one years; or

(4) a son who is, by reason of some mental or physical disability, incapable of maintaining himself.

The terms 'son' and 'daughter' respectively include a male or female child adopted under the provisions of the Adoption Act 1958, and also a posthumous child. They do not include an illegitimate child.

If the provision for maintenance is to be by way of periodical payments of income, the order must provide for their termination not later than:

(*a*) in the case of a wife or husband, her or his re-marriage;

(*b*) in the case of a daughter who has not been married, or who is under disability, her marriage or the cesser of her disability, whichever is the later;

(*c*) in the case of an infant son, his attaining the age of twenty-one years;

(*d*) in the case of a son under disability, the cesser of his disability; or,

(*e*) in any case, his or her earlier death.

The court has power to make an order providing for maintenance, in whole or in part, by way of a lump sum payment. Where it appears to the court that the applicant is in urgent need and that property is available in the estate the court may make an interim order.

In making any order, the court must have regard to the present or future financial resources of the dependant, to his or her conduct in relation to the deceased, to the nature of the property representing the deceased's estate and to any other relevant circumstances. The court is not to make an order which would necessitate a realisation that would be improvident, having regard to the interests of the deceased's dependants and of the person who, apart from the order, would be entitled to that property.

The court must also have regard to the deceased's reasons, so far as they are ascertainable, for making the dispositions by his will (if any), or for not making provision or any further provision, as the case may be, for a dependant. The court may accept such evidence of those reasons as it considers sufficient, including any statement in writing signed by the testator and dated. In estimating the weight to be attached to any such statement the court must have regard to all the circumstances from which any inference can reasonably be drawn as to its accuracy.

The court is not to assume that the law relating to intestacy makes reasonable provision in all cases.

Any application by a dependant for provision for maintenance must be made within six months from the date on which representation in regard to the deceased's estate is first taken out or obtain the permission of the court.

The right of application to the court does not render the personal representatives liable for having distributed any part of the estate of the deceased after the expiration of the said period of six months on the ground that they ought to have taken into account the possibility that the court might exercise its power to extend that period. If the application succeeds the dependant will have the usual rights to recover any part of the estate so distributed.

In considering the question when representation was first taken out, a grant limited to settled land or to trust property is to be left out of account and a grant limited to real estate or to personal estate is to be left out of account unless a grant limited to the remainder of the estate has previously been made or is made at the same time.

The court may vary an order or add another dependant, on application.

§ 8. Devolution of Property on Intestacy

Upon the death of an intestate his real and personal estate vests in the President of the Probate, Divorce, and Admiralty Division of the High Court until administration is granted, whereupon it vests in the personal representative (A.E.A. 1925, s. 9). After the debts, funeral and administration expenses have been paid, the distribution of the remainder (the 'residue') of the estate will depend upon whether or not the intestate leaves a spouse and/or issue surviving. The possible cases are separately considered below. These rules apply in the case of persons dying intestate on or after 1st January, 1967.

(A) WHERE THE INTESTATE LEAVES A SURVIVING SPOUSE

If the intestate:

(1) leaves:

   (*a*) no issue, and

   (*b*) no parent, or brother, sister of the whole blood, or issue of a brother or sister of the whole blood

The residuary estate is to be held in trust for the surviving husband or wife absolutely.

(2) leaves issue (whether or not persons mentioned in (1) (*b*) above also survive)

The surviving husband or wife takes the personal chattels absolutely. In addition, the residuary estate of the intestate (other than the personal chattels) stands charged with the payment of a net sum of £8,750, free of death duties and costs, to the surviving husband or wife, with interest thereon from the date of the death at the rate of £4 per cent. per annum until paid or appropriated. Subject to providing for that sum and the interest thereon, the residuary estate (other than the personal chattels) is to be held:

(*a*) as to one half, upon trust for the surviving husband or wife during his or her life, and, subject to such life interest, on the statutory trusts for the issue of the intestate, and

(*b*) as to the other half, on the statutory trusts for the issue of the intestate.

(3) leaves one or more of the following, i.e. a parent, a brother or sister of the whole blood, or issue of a brother or sister of the whole blood, but leaves no issue.

The surviving husband or wife takes the personal chattels absolutely. In addition, the residuary estate of the intestate (other than the personal chattels) stands charged with the payment of a net sum of £30,000, free of death duties and costs, to the surviving husband or wife, with interest thereon from the date of the death at the rate of £4 per cent. per annum until paid or appropriated. Subject to providing for that sum and the interest thereon, the residuary estate (other than the personal chattels) is to be held:

(A) WHERE THE INTESTATE LEAVES A SURVIVING SPOUSE (*cont.*)

> (*a*) as to one half in trust for the surviving husband or wife absolutely, and
>
> (*b*) as to the other half:
>
> > (i) where the intestate leaves one parent or both parents (whether or not brothers or sisters of the intestate or their issue also survive) in trust for the parent absolutely or, as the case may be, for the two parents in equal shares absolutely,
> >
> > (ii) where the intestate leaves no parent, on the statutory trusts for the brothers and sisters of the whole blood of the intestate.

The interest on the net sum of £8,750 or, as the case may be, £30,000 to a surviving husband or wife is payable primarily out of income.

The amount of £8,750 or £30,000 payable to the surviving spouse is commonly called a statutory legacy.

(B) WHERE THE INTESTATE LEAVES NO SURVIVING SPOUSE

  (i) If the intestate leaves issue, the residuary estate is to be held on the statutory trusts for the issue of the intestate;

 (ii) If the intestate leaves no issue but both parents, then the residuary estate is to be held in trust for the father and mother in equal shares absolutely;

(iii) If the intestate leaves no issue but one parent, then the residuary estate is to be held in trust for the surviving father or mother absolutely;

(iv) If the intestate leaves no issue and no parent, then the residuary estate is held in trust for the following person living at the death of the intestate, and in the following order:

> *First*, on the statutory trusts for the brothers and sisters of the whole blood of the intestate; but if no person takes an absolutely vested interest under such trusts; then
>
> *Secondly*, on the statutory trusts for the brothers and sisters of the half blood of the intestate; but if no person takes an absolutely vested interest under such trusts; then
>
> *Thirdly*, for the grandparents of the intestate and, if more than one survive the intestate, in equal shares; but if there is no member of this class; then
>
> *Fourthly*, on the statutory trusts for the uncles and aunts of the intestate (being brothers or sisters of the whole blood of a parent of

(B) WHERE THE INTESTATE LEAVES NO SURVIVING SPOUSE (*cont.*)

the intestate); but if no person takes an absolutely vested interest under such trusts; then

Fifthly, on the statutory trusts for the uncles and aunts of the intestate (being brothers or sisters of the half blood of a parent of the intestate).

(v) In default of any person taking an absolute interest under the foregoing provisions, the residuary estate of the intestate is to belong to the Crown or to the Duchy of Lancaster or to the Duke of Cornwall for the time being, as the case may be, as *bona vacantia*, and in lieu of any right to escheat.

The Crown or the said Duchy or the said Duke may, out of the whole or any part of the property devolving on them respectively, provide, in accordance with the existing practice, for dependants, whether kindred or not, of the intestate and other persons for whom the intestate might reasonably have been expected to make provision.

A husband and wife for all purposes of distribution or division under the foregoing provisions are treated as two persons.

Where the intestate and the intestate's husband or wife have died in circumstances rendering it uncertain which of them survived the other and the intestate's husband or wife is by virtue of Section 184 of the Law of Property Act 1925, deemed to have survived the intestate, the above rules, nevertheless, have effect as respects the intestate as if the husband or wife had not survived the intestate.

The 'personal chattels' comprise carriages, horses, stable furniture, and effects (not used for business purposes), motor cars and accessories (not used for business purposes), garden effects, domestic animals, plate, plated articles, linen, glass, books, pictures, prints, furniture, jewellery, articles of household or personal use or ornament, musical and scientific instruments and apparatus, wines, liquors and consumable stores, but do not include any chattel used at the death of the intestate for business purposes, nor money or securities for money (A.E.A. 1925, s. 55). A stamp collection (*Re Reynolds Will Trust* [1966]) and racehorses kept as a hobby are personal chattels (*Re Hutchinson* [1955]).

The 'statutory trusts' for issue upon which the residuary estate of an intestate is, in appropriate circumstances, directed to be held, are defined (A.E.A. 1925, s. 47) as creating trusts in that residue 'in equal shares, if more than one, for all or any the children or child of the intestate, living at the death of the intestate, who attain the age of eighteen years or marry under that age, and for all or any of *the issue* living at the death of the intestate who attain the age of eighteen years or marry under that age, *of any child* who predeceases the intestate such issue, if more than one, to take in equal shares, the share which their parent would have taken if living at the death of the intestate'. The term 'child' includes a posthumous child, and a child adopted under the provisions of the Adoption Act 1958.

Where the statutory trusts are for relatives other than issue, the definition is the same, with the substitution of 'members or member of that class' for 'children or child of the intestate'.

Two aspects of these 'statutory trusts' require especially to be noticed, namely:

(i) The interest of any beneficiary is contingent upon his or her attaining the age of eighteen years or marrying: upon the happening of either of those events the interest vests absolutely, but if the beneficiary should die before the occurrence of one or other of those events, the interest will fail and its subject matter will devolve as if that beneficiary had predeceased the intestate.

(ii) Where a person who would have been entitled to an interest in the residuary estate had he survived the intestate, in fact predeceased him, but left issue (of any degree) surviving, such issue will take as representing their parent and will become entitled to share equally the interest which that parent would have acquired had he survived. This principle of representation *per stirpes* does not confer any *independent benefit* upon issue, but merely invests them with the interest to which their parent would have been entitled had he been alive at the date of death of the intestate. Where their parent in fact survives the intestate, the issue cannot take *per stirpes*, there being no occasion to 'represent' the beneficiary.

If the trusts in favour of the issue [or relatives] should fail by reason of *no* child or other issue [or relative] attaining an absolutely vested interest, then the residuary estate, including accumulations and the income thereof, devolves and vests as if the intestate had died without leaving issue [or relatives of the class concerned] at the death of the intestate (A.E.A. 1925, s. 47 (2); Intestates' Estates Act 1952).

It follows that where a member of a class of beneficiaries (children, brothers and sisters, uncles and aunts, and so on) dies without attaining an interest which has vested absolutely, the class will be regarded as if it had never included that beneficiary; while if *all* the members of a given class die before their interests have vested absolutely, the trust for that class will fail, and the statutory trust for the class next entitled will come into operation.

It must not be supposed that the attainment of majority, or marriage of a beneficiary denotes the termination of the statutory trusts. Subject to the demands of beneficiaries who are *sui juris* and who may therefore require their share of the *corpus* to be transferred to them, the trusts will persist.

Once an absolutely vested interest is acquired, it will devolve upon death of the beneficiary as part of his estate and not so as to enlarge the interests of his co-beneficiaries.

In determining the 'equal shares' to which issue may be entitled, account must be taken of moneys paid to, or settled upon a child by way of advancement or upon marriage during the life-time of the intestate. This matter is dealt with fully in Chapter XIV, § 18. Illegitimate persons are not generally entitled to share in the estate of an intestate (but see § 9 of this Chapter).

Illustrations

(1) X died intestate after 31st December, 1966, leaving a wife and two infant sons.

The widow receives (*a*) the personal chattels absolutely, (*b*) £8,750 and 4% interest thereon from the date of X's death to the date of payment (the interest being payable primarily out of income), and (*c*) a life interest in half the residuary estate. The other half is held on the statutory trust for the two infant sons of X in equal shares, each son acquiring a vested interest in his share on attaining the age of eighteen or marrying under that age. On the death of the widow, the half of the residue in which she enjoyed a life interest will also be divided equally between the two sons. If, after reaching the age of majority or marrying, either son predeceases the widow, the share to which he would have become entitled on the widow's death had he lived will go to his personal representative, to be dealt with as part of his estate passing under his will or intestacy. Should one of the sons die before acquiring a vested interest, his share of both halves of the residue will be added to the share of the surviving son. In the event of *both* sons dying without acquiring a vested interest, the statutory trust for the children will fail and the whole estate will devolve as if X had left a surviving spouse and no issue. If, therefore, no parent or brother or sister of the whole blood, or issue of a brother or sister of the whole blood, had survived X, the widow would take the *whole estate* absolutely. If one or more relatives in the above mentioned classes had survived X, the widow would become entitled to a further £21,250 (to make up the £30,000) and to half the residue *absolutely*. The other half would go to the parents, or brother or sisters of the whole blood, or their issue, as the case may be.

(2) Y died intestate leaving a wife, an adult brother and sister, and two infant sons of a deceased brother.

The widow takes the personal chattels, together with £30,000 with 4% interest from date of Y's death till payment, and half the residue absolutely. The remainder goes as to one-third to the brother, one-third to the sister and one-third on statutory trusts for the infant sons of the deceased brother.

An agreement can be made by all those entitled to share in an intestate's estate to allow a more remote next-of-kin to share, but if the arrangement is not agreed to by all, it does not bind any of the parties to it (*In re Morton; Morton* v. *Morton* [1932]).

Where a person dies leaving a will effectively disposing of only part of his property, the rules governing distribution upon intestacy apply as regards the part of his property not disposed of by the will, *subject to the provisions contained in the will* (A.E.A. 1925, s. 49), but where the deceased leaves a husband or wife who acquires any beneficial interests under the will of the deceased (other than personal chattels specifically bequeathed) the net sum of £8,750 or £30,000 (as appropriate) payable to a surviving husband or wife, is diminished by the value at the date of death of the said beneficial interests other than personal chattels. Interest is payable on the diminished sum only (Intestates' Estates Act 1952, s. 3 (2)).

The personal representative must employ a duly qualified valuer where necessary.

See Chapter XIV, § 3, (*g*), *re* the effect of renouncing a right to a share on an intestacy.

SUMMARY OF RULES GOVERNING DISTRIBUTION OF INTESTATE ESTATE

Intestate dies leaving:	*Distribution of Estate:*
(1) Husband or wife; no issue and no parent or brother or sister of the whole blood or issue of a brother or sister of the whole blood.	Surviving spouse takes everything absolutely.
(2) Husband or wife, no issue but a parent or brother or sister of the whole blood, or issue of brother or sister of the whole blood.	Surviving spouse takes: (*a*) Personal chattels absolutely. (*b*) £30,000 free of death duties and costs, and interest at 4% per annum. (*c*) Half the residue absolutely. The parent or brother, etc., takes the other half of the residue.
(3) Husband or wife and issue.	Husband or wife takes personal chattels, £8,750 and interest at 4% per annum and a life interest in half the residue. Subject to this interest the property is held on the statutory trusts for the issue. If all the issue die in the life-time of the husband or wife without acquiring a vested interest, then the estate devolves as in (1) or (2) above.
(4) Issue, but no husband or wife.	The whole estate is held on the statutory trusts for the issue.
(5) Parents, but no issue or spouse.	Father and mother take the whole estate in equal shares absolutely.
(6) One parent, but no issue or spouse.	The surviving parent, i.e. father or mother, takes the whole estate absolutely.
(7) Relatives, other than parents, but no spouse or issue.	Relatives take in the following order: 1. Brothers and sisters of the whole-blood and the issue of deceased brothers and sisters of the whole-blood. 2. Brothers and sisters of the half-blood and the issue of deceased brothers and sisters of the half-blood. 3. Grandparents in equal shares. 4. Uncles and aunts (brothers and sisters of intestate's parent) of the whole-blood and the issue of deceased uncles and aunts of the whole-blood.

SUMMARY OF RULES GOVERNING DISTRIBUTION OF
INTESTATE ESTATE (*continued*)

Intestate dies leaving:	Distribution of Estate:
	5. Uncles and aunts (brothers and sisters of intestate's parent), of the half-blood and the issue of deceased uncles and aunts of the half-blood.
	In cases 1, 2 and 4 to 7, the statutory trusts operate in favour of members of the class who do not die under eighteen and unmarried.
(8) No husband or wife or relatives who make take.	The Crown, Duchy of Lancaster or Duke of Cornwall takes as *bona vacantia* and may provide for dependants or kindred of the intestate and any other persons for whom he might reasonably have been expected to make provision.

§ 9. Legitimation

A child born out of wedlock whose parents subsequently marry is legitimated from the date of the marriage or 1st January, 1927, whichever is the later date (Legitimacy Act 1926), unless the marriage was before 29th October, 1959, and the father or mother was married to a third person when the illegitimate child was born (*ibid.*, Legitimacy Act 1959).

The father must, at the date of the marriage, be domiciled in England or Wales. A declaration of legitimacy may be obtained from the High Court or from the County Court, by a person claiming that he or his parent or any remoter ancestor became legitimated.

A legitimated person and his spouse or descendants are entitled to take any interest:

(*a*) in the estate of an intestate dying after the date of legitimation;

(*b*) under any disposition coming into operation after the date of legitimation;

(*c*) by descent under an entailed interest created after the date of legitimation;

in like manner as if the legitimated person had been born legitimate. When the right to any property, real or personal, depends on the relative seniority of the children of any person, and those children include one or more legitimated persons, the latter rank as if they had been born on the day upon which they had become legitimated by virtue of the Act (i.e. from 1st January, 1927, or the date of the marriage of their parents, whichever is later). Persons who became legitimated at the same time rank as between themselves in order of seniority.

The death of an illegitimate person before the marriage of the parents, does not adversely affect the rights of his or her spouse or descendants in respect of taking interests in property. Their position will be the same as if the illegitimate person had lived and become legitimated upon the marriage of the parents.

If a legitimated person, or a child or descendant of his, dies intestate, the rules as to succession apply as if the intestate had been born legitimate.

Where the mother of an illegitimate child, who has not been legitimated, dies intestate as respects all or any of her property, and does not leave any surviving legitimate issue, the illegitimate child, or if he is dead, his issue, will succeed as if such child had been born legitimate. Conversely, if the mother survives the child, who dies intestate, the interest of the mother in the intestate estate of the child will be determined as if the child had been legitimate.

In the event of a gift by will to 'children', 'grandchildren', or 'issue' the word 'lawful' is presumed to precede such words, so that an illegitimate child will not share, unless it appears in the true construction of the will that the intention of the testator was to include illegitimate children.

Moreover, as from 29th October, 1959, where the father of a child is domiciled in England at the time of its birth, or, if he died before the birth, was immediately before his death so domiciled, the child is treated as legitimate notwithstanding that it was a child of a void marriage, if at the time the child was conceived (or at the date of marriage, if later), either the father or the mother reasonably believed that their marriage was valid. If the title to an honour or property settled to go therewith is involved this applies only to a birth on or after the above date (Legitimacy Act 1959, s. 2).

An illegitimate child is given the same rights as a legitimate child to inherit on the death intestate of his parent. Similarly the parents are entitled to inherit on the illegitimate child's death as if he had been legitimate (Family Law Reform Act 1969).

§ 10. Adopted Children

An adopted child is treated as though he is the natural legitimate child of his adopter(s) and not of his natural parents. The only exception to this rule relates to property settled to devolve along with a dignity or title of honour, in which case the property or any interest therein is not to be severed from the dignity or title, whether the property devolves through the child's adoptive or natural relatives.

A child may be adopted by a single adopter or by both spouses. If adopted by a single adopter, he or she counts as a half brother or half sister of children or other adopted children of that adopter, and does not count as a child at all of the adopter's spouse; but if adopted by both spouses, he or she is treated as a brother or sister of the whole blood of children or adopted children of both spouses, but still only as a half brother or half sister of children or other adopted children of one of the spouses only.

Thus, an adopted child inherits on the death intestate of his adopter or either of them, and also on the death intestate of any relative of his adopter or either of them to whom he would be next-of-kin if he were a natural legitimate child. He does not inherit on the death intestate of his natural parents or any of their relatives. On the death intestate of an adopted child without issue attaining a vested interest, it is his adopter or adopters or their relatives who inherit, and not his natural parents or their relatives.

In a will, codicil or settlement *inter vivos* made on or after 1st January, 1950, and after an adoption order, references to a child or children of the adopter include an adopted child, and references to the child or children of his natural parents do not include him. References to a relative of the adopted child include those who would be his relatives if he were the natural legitimate child of his adopter or adopters and not the child of his natural parents. These rules are subject to any contrary intention appearing in the will, codicil or settlement.

The above provisions apply to an adoption order made anywhere in the United Kingdom, the Isle of Man and the Channel Islands but not to an order made under a foreign jurisdiction (see *Re Wilson, Grace* v. *Lucas* [1954]; *Re Wilby* [1956]). The provisions do not apply to provisional adoptions. A trustee or personal representative who has distributed the property in trust or estate without having ascertained that no adoption order has been made is not liable to anyone of whose claim he had not had notice at the time, but an adopted child can follow the property into the hands of any person, other than a purchaser, who received it.

Where an illegitimate child had been adopted by his father and mother before 29th July, 1960, and is legitimated under the provisions of the Legitimacy Act 1959, by their marriage, the court may revoke the adoption order, but the revocation is not to affect any disposition made or intestacy occurring before the revocation (Adoption Act 1960).

§ 11. Law of Commorientes

When two or more persons die in circumstances rendering it uncertain which of them survived the other or others, the deaths are (subject to any order of the court) for all purposes affecting the title to property under a will, presumed to have occurred in order of seniority, and accordingly the younger is deemed to have survived the elder (L.P.A. 1925, s. 184). The principle involved is known as the LAW OF COMMORIENTES. The words 'subject to any order of the court' mean that the presumption as to the order of death is rebuttable and the court is entitled to receive evidence on the subject which may displace the statutory presumption (*Re Lindop; Lee-Barber* v. *Reynolds* [1942]), but if it is impossible by legal proof to demonstrate that two persons died at precisely the same moment of time, and if it cannot be said for certain which of them died first, it must be assumed that the elder died first; all that is necessary to invoke the statutory presumption is the presence in the circumstances of an element of uncertainty as to which of the deceased survived the other(s) (*Hickman* v. *Peacey* [1945]). See Chap. VII, § 16, as to relief from Estate Duty given by the Finance Act 1958.

A testator in his will left his estate to his wife, but directed that 'in the event of the decease of my wife preceding or coinciding with my own decease' it should go to other relatives. Both lost their lives in a shipwreck, and there was no evidence to show whether the wife's death preceded or coincided with her husband's. The testator was aged thirty-seven and the wife twenty-eight. The Court of Appeal held that in the context, 'coinciding' meant coinciding in point of time and was not a reference to the deaths having occurred on the same occasion or in the same calamity. The testator's estate would therefore pass to his wife's estate by virtue of Section 184 of the Law of Property Act 1925 (*Re Rowland, Smith* v. *Russell* [1962], 2 All E.R. 837 (C.A.)).

If an intestate and the intestate's wife or husband both die after 31st December, 1952, in circumstances rendering it uncertain which of them survived the other, the intestate's estate is to be administered as if the wife or husband had not survived the intestate. If both husband and wife die intestate, the estate of each will be administered as if the other spouse had not survived (Intestates' Estates Act 1952, s. 1 (4)).

Unlike the 1958 amendment, the 1952 amendment affects the devolution of property as well as Estate Duty.

CHAPTER II

EXECUTORS AND ADMINISTRATORS

§ 1. Introduction

It has already been seen that the essential preliminary to administrating the estate, is to obtain a grant of probate of the will if the person died testate, or to obtain letters of administration in any other case. Apart from the legal technicalities as to whom such a grant should be made, and the differing time element involved as to when effective control can be exercised, there would appear to be little difference between the offices of administrator and executor.

A grant of probate or administration in England does not give formal control of the whole of the assets of the deceased; primarily the grant is only effective for English realty and for personalty located in Great Britain, thus, if land in Scotland is comprised amongst the assets, a Scottish grant must be obtained. In the case of foreign wills, the English court will usually grant probate if valid probate has been obtained from the proper court of the country where the deceased was domiciled.

An executor is appointed by the will either because he is expressly named as such, or by virtue of the duties which the testator imposes upon him. Thus, if a person is asked in the will to collect the debts, discharge the liabilities and legacies, etc., then that person is said to be an 'executor according to the tenor'. A practice which is becoming more prevalent, is to appoint a trust corporation to act as executor. An advantage claimed for such appointment is that there is less chance of a break in the continuity of office, thus ensuring a more efficient administration.

Probate cannot usually be obtained until seven days have elapsed since the death. Whilst there is no rule that probate has to be taken out within a specified time, since there are various penalties which may be incurred if Estate Duty on personalty is not paid within six months from the date of death, indirectly it is necessary for probate to be obtained in this period.

The grant may be obtained by application being made at one

of the Probate Registries, i.e. in 'common form', or by an action in the court where all parties interested are cited to appear, i.e. 'in solemn form'. The latter form is by no means common, and is usually instanced where certain irregularities are suspected in the will itself, or in the circumstances surrounding the will, e.g. where the testator is suspected of being under duress when he signed the will. The first method of obtaining probate necessitates the production of the death certificate, the will, the *Inland Revenue Affidavit* together with the payment of the Estate Duty on personalty and the executor's oath to carry out his duties properly. He will also swear that he believes the will to be the true and last will of the testator.

Any number of executors may be appointed, but probate will not be granted to more than four in number. A person so appointed is under no obligation to act as executor, and he may renounce the office either by formal renunciation or by refusing to carry out the necessary formalities. Once he has accepted office, and obtained probate, he cannot renounce and, furthermore, cannot accept office subject to his own conditions, excepting for the payment of reasonable remuneration in the case of trust corporations. If he dies before completing the administration, and appoints an executor of his own estate, then if he was the sole surviving executor, his own executor, if he accepts office as such, must carry out the administration of the first estate together with the administration of the executor's own estate.

A person who interferes with the administration of an estate, unless the interference is an act of necessity or kindness, or is done with relevant authority, is termed an executor *de son tort*, until he takes out probate. This term also includes a personal representative of an intestate's estate up to the date he obtains the grant of administration.

Where the deceased dies intestate or partially intestate, i.e. fails to dispose of the whole of his estate, the right to obtain letters of administration or probate devolves upon those persons whom the law recognises as having a prior claim to the grant. In the case of a person who dies wholly intestate, the grant is made to those persons in the same order as to their priority in sharing the estate under the rules of devolution. Creditors are the last class to which a grant will be given. In a partial intestacy, the same broad principle is followed, executors having the first claim to the grant, persons having no vested interests by statute or otherwise, being the last in the order of priority. The will, if there is one, and the Inland Revenue Affidavit together with the Estate Duty on the personalty, the death certificate and a bond from two sureties or a guarantee society, together with the oath which must be sworn by the administrator that he will administer the estate faithfully, must be produced before letters of administration will be granted. The latter will not usually be granted where there is no will, until fourteen days have elapsed since the death.

It will be seen later, that there are different forms of grants which can be made, depending on the circumstances appertaining to the particular case. Thus, some forms of grant are limited in time, e.g. a grant limited to the period during which the named executor is abroad, or a grant for a specific purpose, e.g. to collect the goods of the deceased.

A grant of probate or administration may be revoked by the occurrence of subsequent events. Thus, a later will may be found which names a different executor, or it may be discovered that probate was granted to the wrong person. In any event, transactions entered into and carried out in the period by a previous executor, if of a *bona fide* nature, will not be affected by any subsequent revocation. Such transactions include the conveyance of both real and personal property.

§ 2. Dealing with the Estate

On the death of any person, the first questions that will arise are 'How is the estate of the deceased person to be distributed, and who is to undertake the distribution?'

The answer to these questions will depend on whether the person has died testate or intestate. If he has left a will, and in that will has appointed an executor, the executor so appointed is the proper person to administer the estate and, if he accepts office, he must act in accordance with the terms of the will, of which he must seek probate. If a will has been made, but no executor has been named or the named executor cannot or will not act as such, or from any cause the chain of executorship has been broken, then an administrator will be appointed *cum testamento annexo* (i.e. with the will annexed), to distribute the estate as required by the will.

If the person has died intestate, the estate will be administered according to law by an administrator appointed by the Probate Division of the Court.

The functions of the Probate Division only extend to deciding who is the person entitled to a grant of administration, or whether a will should be admitted to probate. That court has nothing to do with the actual administration of the estate, or with the interpretation of the will further than is necessary to decide whether it should be admitted to probate. All questions of interpretation and administration are matters for the Chancery Division.

The court has jurisdiction to grant probate or administration affecting real property in England and personal property in Great Britain or even if the deceased left no estate. But if the deceased died domiciled in Scotland, the English grant will not extend to Scottish property, and in any event it does not extend to Scottish land.

Just as an English probate extends only to assets within the jurisdiction of the English court (and usually to Scottish personalty), so a foreign probate has no intrinsic operation in this country, but on production of a copy of the probate validly issued by the proper court in the country where the deceased was domiciled at his death, the court in this country will grant its own probate to the same person. Otherwise representation will be granted to the person entitled by the law of the place where the deceased died domiciled, or if there is no such person, to such person(s) as the Registrar directs (N.C.P.R., R. 29).

An English grant of representation can be resealed in Scotland or Northern Ireland or vice versa only where the deceased was domiciled in the country which issued the original grant (Judicature' Act 1925, s. 168). If the deceased was not so domiciled, a separate grant is needed, except that a Northern Ireland grant or a colonial grant can be resealed in England (*ibid.*, s. 169, N.C.P.R., R. 41). Grants in the Republic of Ireland cannot be resealed in England.

Where a will is not available owing to its being retained in the custody of a foreign court or official, a duly authenticated copy of the will may be admitted to proof, without any special order (N.C.P.R., R. 53).

§ 3. The Executor

(a) The Appointment of Executor

An executor can only be appointed by will or codicil. He may be appointed either expressly or by implication. An express appointment involves the naming of the executor in the will, or the naming in the will of a delegate by whom the appointment of an executor is to be made (*In the goods of Ryder* [1861]).

A person will be executor by implication, or 'according to the tenor', if it appears to be the testator's intention that, though not expressly appointed, he should act as executor, e.g. if it appears that the person indicated was to collect the assets, pay the debts and funeral expenses, and discharge the legacies (*In the goods of Adamson* [1875]). The implication might be good even though the direction to administer the estate is in general and not in explicit terms, but the court will not grant probate to an executor not expressly appointed unless there is in the will a requirement for the person to pay the debts and generally to administer the estate (*In the Estate of Mackenzie* [1909], P. 305).

Executors may be named in the alternative or in succession, e.g. where the deceased by codicil directed that in the event of a 'vacancy' occurring 'in the office of the individual executor and trustee' one of two named persons, in the order named, should fill the vacancy and the executors named in the will refused to act or prove the will, and the first named person renounced, the court granted probate to the second named of the substituted executors (*In the Estate of Freeman* [1931]).

A trust corporation may be named either solely or jointly with another person as executor of the will of a deceased person. A TRUST CORPORATION is the Public Trustee or a corporation either appointed by the court in any particular case to be a trustee, or entitled by rules made under the Public Trustee Act 1906, to act as custodian trustee.

Rules so made provide that any corporation constituted under the law of the United Kingdom or of any part thereof and having a place of business there and empowered by its constitution to undertake trust business, and being either:

(a) a company incorporated by special Act or Royal Charter, or

(b) a company registered (whether with or without limited liability) under the Companies Act, having a capital (in stock or shares) for the time being issued of not less than £250,000, of which not less than £100,000 shall have been paid up in cash; or

(c) a company registered without limited liability under the Companies Act, whereof one of the members is a company within any of the classes hereinbefore defined,

shall be entitled to act as a custodian trustee.

Any corporation constituted under the law of the United Kingdom or of any part thereof and having its place of business there, and being either

(a) a company established for the purpose of undertaking trust business for the benefit of Her Majesty's Navy, Army, Air Force or Civil Service, or of any unit, department, member, or association of members of any one or more of those services and having among its directors or members any persons appointed or nominated by the Admiralty Board, the Army Board, the Air Force Board, or any Department of State or any one or more of those Departments, or

(b) a company authorised by the Lord Chancellor to act in relation to any charitable, ecclesiastical, or public trusts as a trust corporation,

shall be entitled to act in relation to such business or trusts as a custodian trustee.

'Trust corporation' also includes, *inter alia*, trustees in bankruptcy and trustees under deeds of arrangement, the Treasury Solicitor, the Official Solicitor, and any person holding any other official position prescribed by the Lord Chancellor. As a trust corporation can act alone, trustees in bankruptcy and under deeds of arrangement are not under the necessity of securing the appointment of a further trustee for the purpose of making any conveyance of land. As will be seen later, at least two trustees are otherwise necessary for this purpose. On application for probate or administration by a trust corporation other than the Public Trustee, the officer authorised by the corporation to act on its behalf must in every case lodge in the registry a certified copy of the resolution appointing him, and must depose in the oath to lead to the grant that the corporation is a trust corporation within the meaning of the Act, and that it has power to accept a grant (N.C.P.R., R. 34). The acts of the authorised officer of a trust corporation are binding on the corporation (Judicature Act 1925, s. 161), and he is entitled to be kept indemnified by the corporation as regards the matters so authorised. No surety is required on application for a grant of administration by a trust corporation (N.C.P.R., R. 38).

Where an ordinary corporation, as distinct from a trust corporation, applies for a grant, it will be made to its nominee, or if its principal place of business is outside England to its nominee or lawfully constituted attorney expressly appointed by the company for the purpose (N.C.P.R., R. 34). Such a nominee is commonly called a 'syndic'.

If there is an infant beneficiary, or a life tenancy, the grant of administration must be made either to a trust corporation or to not less than TWO individuals. If in such a case there is only one individual representative, the court may, on the application of any person interested, or of the guardian, committee or receiver of any such person, appoint one or more additional representatives (Judicature Act 1925, s. 160). Representation must not be granted to more than FOUR persons in regard to the same property (*ibid.* s. 169 (1)).

In the case of 'settled land' (i.e. land vested in the deceased which was settled previously to his death and not by his will and which remained settled land notwithstanding his death) the court may appoint a special or additional personal representative in respect of that settled land (A.E.A., 1925, § 23 (2)). The special executors in regard to settled land constituted by A.E.A. 1925, Section 22, have a prior right of grant of probate limited to the settled land otherwise the person or persons entitled to a grant of administration limited to settled land are determined in accordance with the following order of priority:

 (i) the trustees of the settlement at the time of the application for the grant;

 (ii) where there are no such trustees and the settlement arises under a will or intestacy, the personal representative of the settlor;

(iii) the personal representative of the deceased.

Where the persons entitled to a grant in respect of the free estate are also entitled to a grant of the same nature in respect of settled land, a grant expressly including the settled land may be issued to them. Where there is settled land and a grant is made in respect of the free estate only, the grant must expressly exclude the settled land (N.C.P.R., R. 28).

If a firm is appointed, probate will be granted individually to those who were members of the firm at the date of the will, not exceeding four in number, even if the firm has been dissolved (*In the goods of Fernie* [1849]).

An infant may be appointed executor, but during minority can neither obtain probate nor act in any way as a personal representative. If an infant be sole executor, administration *cum testamento annexo et durante minore ætate* will be granted to his guardian or such other person as the court may think fit (Judicature Act 1925, s. 165 (see this Chapter § 5, (*c*)). If one of two or more executors is an infant, probate may be granted to the other executor(s) not under disability, with power reserved to making a like grant to the infant on his attaining his majority. If the other executors renounce or do not take out probate, administration may be granted *durante minore ætate* (N.C.P.R., R. 32).

An alien can be appointed executor. If a person entitled to a grant resides outside England, administration may be granted to his attorney (see this Chapter, § 5) after notice to any other executors unless the Registrar dispenses with such notice (N.C.P.R., R. 30).

A married woman can be appointed, and can accept the office without her husband's consent, and act as if a *feme sole* (Married Women's Property Act 1882, ss. 1, 18, 24; L.P.A., 1925, s. 170).

If an executor is by reason of mental or physical incapacity incapable of managing his affairs when application for probate becomes necessary the court will appoint some other person as administrator (N.C.P.R., R. 33).

A person is not debarred, by reason of insolvency alone, from acting as executor, particularly if the deceased knew of his financial position when he appointed him; but in the interests of the estate the court may refuse probate to a bankrupt or insolvent executor, or, if probate has been granted, restrain him from acting, and appoint a receiver. A receiver will not, however, be appointed where there is another executor willing to act.

The court may, in any other proper case, remove an executor and appoint a judicial trustee (Judicial Trustee Act 1896, s. 1).

The Public Trustee may be appointed as executor. A testator need not obtain his consent to act as such when so appointing him, though the Public Trustee has a discretion as to whether he will act, but he may not refuse to act only by reason of the small value of the estate. After probate, the court may transfer the administration to the Public Trustee (Public Trustee Act 1906; Public Trustee Rules, 1912, 1916).

Only the executor may prove (*Wankford* v. *Wankford* [1704]), and any person having an interest may apply to the court for a citation, calling on the executor to prove the will or renounce. Every will referred to in a citation must be lodged in a registry before the citation is issued, except where the will is not in the citor's possession and the Registrar is satisfied that it is impracticable to require it to be lodged (N.C.P.R., R. 45). The court may make an order to any person suspected of having a will in his possession directing him to bring it into the registry. If there are reasonable grounds for supposing that, though not in his possession, he has knowledge of such instrument, then he may be directed to attend for the purpose of being examined in open court or upon interrogatories respecting it (Court of Probate Act 1857, s. 26).

(b) Qualification or Limitation of Appointment

The appointment of an executor may be qualified or limited in various ways.

(1) *As to time.* The office may be made to commence after a certain period, or may be limited as to duration. The court may in this case appoint an administrator during the vacancy.

(2) *As to place.* Different executors may be appointed for property in different countries.

(3) *As to subject-matter.* Different executors may be appointed for different parts of the property, e.g. one for stock, one for furniture, etc.; but these are all executors and may be sued as one.

(4) *Conditional.* To commence upon fulfilment of a condition precedent, e.g. of the giving of security; or subject to a condition subsequent, e.g. the office to terminate if the executor goes abroad.

(c) Transmission of Office

Since he owes his office to the confidence reposed in him by the testator the executor cannot assign his office, but the sole or last surviving executor who has proved the will of the original testator can transmit his office to his own executor. The executor of an executor thus becomes the personal representative of the original testator. If there are several executors, only the last of these remaining alive can transmit the office to his own executor. If one or more executors appointed by the original testator have not proved the will they must be cited to do so before the executor of the last surviving executor who did prove is entitled to act for the original testator. So long as the chain of representation is unbroken, the last executor in the chain is the executor of every preceding testator.

The chain of such representation is broken by:

(*a*) the intestacy of the sole or last surviving executor, or

(*b*) the death of the sole or last surviving executor without having appointed an executor, or

(*c*) the failure of the executor of the sole or last surviving executor to obtain probate of the will,

but is not broken by a temporary grant of administration if probate is subsequently granted, e.g. the administrator *durante minore ætate* of the executor of an executor is the representative of the first testator (A.E.A. 1925, s. 7).

If the original executor dies without having proved the will, an administrator *cum testamento annexo* will have to be appointed, but where a sole executor, having proved the will dies intestate, administration *de bonis non administratis* must be taken out; the office of executor of the original testator is not transmitted to the executor's administrator.

(*d*) *Renunciation of Office*

A person named as executor is not bound to act, but may renounce the office, even if he has agreed in the testator's lifetime to accept it. The renunciation should be in writing, filed in the registry, but may be evidenced by his not appearing when cited to take out probate (A.E.A. 1925, s. 5).

An executor cannot renounce after he has once accepted office; that is to say, after he has done any act which shows an intention of exercising the authority of an executor. The executor cannot accept in part and renounce in part, except that an executor may renounce his office as regards settled land without renouncing as regards other property, unless he is a Settled Land Act trustee (A.E.A. 1925, s. 23).

So long as he has not administered in any way, the court will allow him, on his own application, to renounce, even though he has taken the usual oath (*Jackson* v. *Whitehead* [1821]); but he cannot renounce after he has taken probate (*In the goods of Veiga* [1863]). A person who renounces in one capacity is not allowed to take representation in another capacity unless the Registrar directs that he may. The Registrar may allow renunciation to be retracted, but only exceptionally will retraction be allowed if a grant has been made to some other person (N.C.P.R., R. 35).

(e) *Executor de son tort*

Any person who, not being appointed executor of a will either expressly or by implication, intermeddles with the goods of the deceased in such a manner as to show an intention of exercising the authority of an executor, may make himself liable as an executor *de son tort* (i.e. of his own wrong).

Very slight acts of intermeddling will make a person executor *de son tort*; for example, advertising for claims to be sent in, receiving debts, carrying on a business (*Hooper* v. *Summersett* [1810]); but not simple acts of kindness or necessity, such as feeding animals; or acts done with the authority of the rightful representative, or as agent of an executor who subsequently proves the will (*Sykes* v. *Sykes* [1870]).

It does not follow that the position of an executor *de son tort* arises only upon occasions of unauthorised interference. If an executor acts under a will in which he has been appointed, and which, upon application for probate, is declared invalid, he is an executor *de son tort*, for if the will fails so does his appointment. Where a person dies intestate, the person to whom a grant of letters of administration is subsequently made will doubtless have taken steps to protect and administer the estate, e.g. by carrying on the business of the deceased, but until the grant is made, he has no legal authority so to act, and in the meantime is in the position of an executor *de son tort*. If the grant is made in his favour, it will relate back to the date of death and his acts for the benefit of the estate will be thereby validated, e.g. under the doctrine of relation back, a sale of goods by an executor *de son tort* was held to be valid upon his obtaining a grant of administration (*Kenrick* v. *Burges* [1583] Moore 126), but he will be under obligation to account to the appointed administrator if the grant for some reason is made to some other person.

The executor *de son tort* is liable to be sued by the rightful executor or administrator, or by a creditor or a legatee; he is liable for due payment of Estate Duty (under penalties which may amount to as much as twice the duty, where it is not paid in due time) but only to the amount of the assets which have come into his hands, and he cannot be forced to take out administration. He must account to the personal representative, and will thus put an end to his liability except as regards outstanding legal actions (*Hill* v. *Curtis* [1866]). All payments by him *bonâ fide*, when acting as executor, are binding on the personal representative (*Padget* v. *Priest* [1787]).

A limited company registering a transfer of shares out of the name of a deceased member without production of probate or letters of administration, runs the risk of being held an executor *de son tort*, and liable thereby for death duties (*Attorney-General* v. *New York Breweries Co.* [1899]).

§ 4. Probate

(a) Nature of Probate

Proof or probate of a will may be defined as the process of obtaining formal recognition of the validity of the will. This process may be either administrative, resulting in 'proof in common form', or judicial, whereby the instrument is proved in 'solemn form'. There is no essential difference between the operation of one and the other mode of proof, each representing the exercise of jurisdiction vested by statute in the Probate Division of the High Court; but solemn form of proof is resorted to where the validity of the instrument propounded is a matter of contention or doubt, so that judicial investigation is necessary.

Probate cannot issue until after the lapse of seven days from the death of the testator, unless by leave of two of the Registrars (N.C.P.R., R. 5).

No time is prescribed within which probate of a will must be obtained, but persons dealing with the estate of a deceased render themselves liable to statutory penalties if Estate Duty on personalty is not paid within six months from the death.

The executor of a will proved in common form may at any time be compelled by a person having an interest, to prove it in solemn form. The next-of-kin are not barred by the receipt of a legacy or other evidence of past acquiescence to proof in common form, from requiring the executor to prove in solemn form (*Bell* v. *Armstrong* [1822]).

For proof in solemn form it would be necessary to have the witnesses to the execution of the will examined in open court, and if the witnesses were dead, and no record of their evidence could be obtained, the whole will might be endangered. If the will is once proved in solemn form, the executor cannot be compelled to prove it again. The executor should always prove the will in solemn form if there are any doubts as to the validity of the will, or a codicil, or if there is any likelihood that the validity of the will may be contested at some future date.

Under the Administration of Estates (Small Payments) Act 1965 small estates (not exceeding £500) can be disposed of on death without the necessity of taking out a grant of probate to persons appearing to be beneficially entitled thereto. A legal discharge can only be given by a personal representative, however, and so there must be an element of risk in transferring property belonging to a deceased person to anyone other than his personal representative. If there is any doubt a grant of probate or letters of administration should always be taken out.

(b) Proof in Common Form

Application for probate in common form may be made through a solicitor at the Principal Probate Registry or at any one of the District Registries.

If it is desired to obtain probate or administration without the intervention of a solicitor, application must be made in person at the Personal Application Department, Room 111, South-West Wing, Bush House, Strand, London WC2, or to the clerk in charge of personal applications at the District Registry, by the executors named in the will or by the persons entitled to a grant of administration. The applicant should take with him the Registrar's certificate of death, or an official certificate of burial, and the will, if there is one. The Personal Application Department will usually prepare the affidavits mentioned below and will charge fees on an *ad valorem* scale based on the amount of the net estate.

If the personal representative prepares the documents he must prepare them away from the Registry and swear them before an outside commissioner. There is, however, little point in his preparing the documents since the department acts for him in the same way as a solicitor would do. Once, however, the grant of representation has been obtained the personal representative can complete the administration of the estate without incurring further fees.

If death cannot be proved, application must be made for leave to presume death; at common law this may be presumed after the lapse of seven years from the time when the person was last heard of as living, but the court will only admit the presumption after sufficient inquiries have been made, and there is no presumption of death at any particular date.

An application for leave to swear to the death of any person is made to a Registrar either of the Principal or of a District Registry. It has to be supported by an affidavit setting out the grounds of the application, and containing particulars of all policies of insurance on the life of the presumed deceased (N.C.P.R., R. 52).

The application for a grant must be supported by the oath of the executor contained in an affidavit that he will execute the office well and faithfully. To this affidavit must be annexed the original will, which the executor must swear he believes to be the true and last will of the testator, and the will must be marked by the signatures of the executor and the person before whom he is sworn (N.C.P.R., RR. 6 & 8). The Registrar may require evidence as to alteration, date of execution, appearance of attempted revocation, etc. (N.C.P.R., RR. 12, 13).

If the deceased left personal property in Scotland (e.g. shares in a Scottish company) or Northern Ireland there should be included in the oath a statement that the deceased died domiciled in England if such is the case. If the deceased died domiciled outside England the oath should state where the deceased died domiciled (N.C.P.R., R.6).

If there is no attestation clause, or an imperfect attestation clause, an affidavit of at least one of the attesting witnesses is required to state that the requirements of the Wills Act 1837, as regards execution, were complied with; unless both witnesses are dead or otherwise not available, when the Registrar can accept affidavits as to the handwriting of the deceased or other matters raising a presumption of the due execution of the will (N.C.P.R., R. 10).

Where the testator appears to have been blind or illiterate, or where the will has been signed for him, the Registrar must satisfy himself that the testator knew the contents of the will (N.C.P.R., R. 11).

The affidavit for Estate Duty purposes must be sworn, stating the gross amount of the personal property of the deceased, wherever situated, and the real estate in Great Britain and Northern Ireland, in the proper Inland Revenue form.

The Inland Revenue affidavit may be lodged at the Principal Probate Registry or District Probate Registry without prior reference to the Estate Duty Office, where the property passing is under £4,500 (net) value.

Affidavits so presented direct to the registry are examined after the grant has been made.

These various documents are to be delivered to the proper officer at the Principal or District Registry, as the case may be, the Estate Duty in respect of all PERSONAL property of which the deceased was competent to dispose having first been paid. If all is in due form, the official certificate of probate will be annexed and notice will be given to the executor to attend and take it up.

(c) Proof in Solemn Form

The courts having solemn form jurisdiction are:

(1) The Probate Division of the High Court of Justice (Judicature Act 1925, s. 150).

(2) Assizes, where so ordered by the Registrar if it will save expenses in respect of witnesses (Tristram and Coote's *Probate practice* 22nd Ed., p. 742).

(3) The County Court having jurisdiction in the place of abode of the deceased, where the Registrar is satisfied that the net estate (after allowing for funeral expenses, debts and incumbrances) beneficially owned by the deceased was under £1,000 (County Courts Act 1959, s. 62). Applications for probate may also be remitted by the principal Probate Registry to the appropriate County Court where the Registrar is satisfied that in any contentious matter arising out of the application, the state of the property and place of abode of the deceased were such as to give jurisdiction in the matter to a County Court.

Proceedings are by action. All parties interested are cited to appear; the witnesses are examined on oath (one of the attesting witnesses must always be called by the party propounding the document (*Oakes* v. *Uzzell* [1932]), and the court decides on the validity or otherwise of the will. If the will is declared valid, probate will issue in the registry on the executor taking the usual oath, after paying the Estate Duty on personalty.

(d) Probate of Lost Will

Probate of a lost will may be granted, provided there is clear proof that the will was in existence after the testator's death, or that it was destroyed in his lifetime without his privity or consent; or there is satisfactory evidence of its having been duly executed, and of its contents, e.g. if there is a draft of the will in existence, or witnesses can be brought who saw and read the will; and evidence can be given to show that the testator did not revoke the will. Proof will normally be by action, unless all the persons who would be interested on intestacy consent to its being on motion, i.e. by a simple application to the judge or court.

(e) Double Probate

If there is more than one executor to a will, they need not all prove; one or more may do so, power being reserved to the others to come in and prove at a subsequent time, so long as they do not renounce or fail to appear on a citation. When another or others apply, what is called 'DOUBLE PROBATE' is granted to them. The additional executors are sworn; the probate granted to them recites the original grant, and a copy of the will is annexed. Since not more than four persons can act at a time, double probate cannot be granted where more than four persons would then hold probate.

It should be noted that where two or more executors are appointed, upon the death of one of them the powers of the survivor or survivors are not terminated, but full powers devolve upon those remaining (Trustee Act 1925, s. 18 (1)).

(f) Caveats and Citations

Any person who wishes to prevent a grant of probate or administration from being issued may lodge a CAVEAT, i.e. a caution entered in the Probate Court to stop probates, administration, etc., from being granted without the knowledge of the person entering it. A *caveat* may be entered either at the Principal or at a District Registry; it remains in force for six months, and may be renewed. When a *caveat* against a grant is issued, the person applying for the grant must 'warn' the *caveator*.

The form of warning is obtained from the Principal Registry, and states the name and interest of the party applying. The warning will be signed by the Registrar, and sent by post to the person who entered the *caveat*. The *caveator* must enter appearance, when proceedings will commence (Judicature Act 1925, s. 154; N.C.P.R., R. 44).

CITATIONS are issued, by those desiring to obtain a grant of probate or letters of administration, to all who have a prior claim. They are issued from the Principal Registry, and personal service must be made, unless the Registrar otherwise directs (N.C.P.R., RR. 45–48). A citation has the effect of compelling those entitled in priority to take out representation or, if they do not do so, operates as a renunciation of their rights. Where a person appointed executor by a will is cited to take out probate and does not appear to the citation, his rights in respect of the executorship wholly cease, just as if he had died after the testator without taking out probate, or had renounced probate; and the administration devolves as if no executor had been named (A.E.A. 1925, s. 5).

§ 5. The Administrator

(a) *The Appointment of Administrator*

When a person leaves a will but no executors are able or willing to act, or if he dies intestate, administration of his estate must be granted to some one or more of the persons interested in the residuary estate if they make application for the purpose, except where the estate is insolvent, and the court thinks it necessary or expedient to grant administration to some other person. Where land has been settled previously to the death of the deceased and remains settled after his death, administration is to be granted to the trustees of the settlement if they will act (Judicature Act 1925, s. 162, as amended by Administration of Justice Act 1928, s. 9).

(1) WHERE THERE IS A WILL

Where the deceased died on or after the 1st January, 1926, the person or persons entitled to a grant of probate or administration with the will annexed are determined in accordance with the following order of priority (N.C.P.R., R. 19):

   (i) The executor;
  (ii) Any residuary legatee or devisee holding in trust for any other person;
 (iii) Any residuary legatee or devisee for life;
  (iv) The ultimate residuary legatee or devisee or, where the residue is not wholly disposed of by the will, any person entitled to share in the residue not so disposed of (including the Treasury Solicitor when claiming *bona vacantia* on behalf of the Crown) or, the personal representative* of any such person:

   Provided that where the residue is not in terms wholly disposed of, the Registrar may, if he is satisfied that the testator has nevertheless disposed of the whole or substantially the whole of the estate as ascertained at the time of the application for the grant, allow a grant to be made† to any legatee or devisee entitled to, or to a share in, the estate so disposed of, without regard to the person entitled to share in any residue not disposed of by the will;

   (v) Any specific legatee or devisee or any creditor or the personal representative* of any such person or, where the estate is not wholly disposed of by the will, any person who, notwithstanding that the amount of the estate is such that he has no immediate beneficial interest therein, may have a beneficial interest in the event of an accretion thereto;

(vi) Any legatee or devisee, whether residuary or specific, entitled on the happening of any contingency, or any person having no interest under the will of the deceased who would have been entitled to a grant if the deceased had died wholly intestate.

* Unless a Registrar otherwise directs, administration shall be granted to a living person in preference to the personal representative of a deceased person who would, if living, be entitled in the same degree and to a person not under disability in preference to an infant entitled in the same degree (N.C.P.R., R. 25).

† If the Crown might be interested, notice must be given to the Treasury Solicitor and the Registrar may order delay (N.C.P.R., R. 37).

(2) ON INTESTACY

Where the deceased died on or after the 1st January, 1926, wholly intestate, the persons having a beneficial interest in the estate are entitled to a grant of administration in the following order of priority (N.C.P.R., R. 21):

(i) The surviving spouse;

(ii) The children of the deceased (including any persons entitled by virtue of any enactment to be treated as if they were the children of the deceased born in lawful wedlock), or the issue of any such child who had died during the lifetime of the deceased;

(iii) The father or mother of the deceased or, in the case of an illegitimate person who died on or after the 1st January, 1927, without having been legitimated, his mother;

(iv) Brothers and sisters of the whole blood, or the issue of any deceased brother or sister of the whole blood who has died during the lifetime of the deceased.

If no person in any of the classes mentioned in (ii) to (iv) above has survived the deceased, then, in the case of:

(*a*) a person who died before the 1st January, 1953, wholly intestate, or

(*b*) a person dying on or after the 1st January, 1953, wholly intestate without leaving a surviving spouse,

the persons hereinafter described, if they have a beneficial interest in the estate, are entitled to a grant in the following order of priority:

  (i) Brothers and sisters of the half blood, or the issue of any deceased brother or sister of the half blood who has died during the lifetime of the deceased;

 (ii) Grandparents;

(iii) Uncles and aunts of the whole blood, or the issue of any deceased uncle or aunt of the whole blood who has died during the lifetime of the deceased;

(iv) Uncles and aunts of the half blood, or the issue of any deceased uncle or aunt of the half blood who has died during the lifetime of the deceased.

In default of any person having a beneficial interest in the estate, the Treasury Solicitor is entitled to a grant if he claims *bona vacantia* on behalf of the Crown.

If all persons entitled to a grant under the foregoing provisions have failed to obtain a grant if cited or are not available, a grant may be made to a creditor of the deceased or to any person who, notwithstanding that he has no immediate beneficial interest in the estate, may have a beneficial interest in the event of an accretion thereto.

The personal representative of a person in any of the above classes of relatives or the personal representative of a creditor has the same right to a grant as the person whom he represents except that children and other relatives are preferred to the personal representative of a spouse who has died without taking a beneficial interest in the whole estate of the deceased as ascertained at the time of the application for the grant.

The provisions of the Adoption Act 1958 apply in determining the entitlement to a grant as they apply to the devolution of property on intestacy.

There being no idea of confidence on the part of the deceased connected with the office, the administrator is required to enter into a bond for the due performance of his office. No person incapable of executing a bond can be administrator; therefore, minors and persons of unsound mind are excluded.

The court may take 'special circumstances' into account (Judicature Act 1925, s. 162 (1), as amended by Administration of Justice Act 1928, s. 9), e.g. where the next-of-kin were unable to agree on the administration of the estate by any one or more of themselves, the court granted letters of administration to two nominees of the next-of-kin (*Re Morgans* [1931]).

In the case of an intestate dying without any persons entitled being alive, the residuary estate goes as *bona vacantia* to the Crown or to the Duchy of Lancaster, or to the Duke of Cornwall; but the Crown, the Duchy or the Duke may provide for dependants of the deceased and other persons for whom he might have been expected to provide (A.E.A. 1925, s. 46 (1)).

A grant will not be made to a person residing out of England. In such a case administration may be granted to his attorney acting under a power of attorney limited until he obtains a grant himself or in such other way as the Registrar directs (N.C.P.R., R. 30). Where a named executor or other person to whom administration could be granted is a foreign national not resident in England, and has not applied for a grant through a resident attorney, a grant may be made to a consul of the foreign state (Consular Conventions Act 1949, s. 1). These provisions apply only to countries with which a convention in that behalf has been made.

The grant may be made to a creditor or even to the nominee of a person about to commence proceedings against the estate, e.g. the court made a grant in order that the administrator might be made a defendant in an action in which the applicant sought to be indemnified out of a third party insurance policy (*In the estate of Simpson; In the estate of Gunning* [1936]).

In the winding-up of a company the liquidator may take out administration of the estate of a deceased contributory; for this purpose, money due to the company is deemed to be due to the liquidator himself (Companies Act 1948, s. 245 (2) (*f*)).

Where there is a will, letters of administration with the will annexed will not be granted within seven days from the date of death; in other cases, letters of administration cannot issue within fourteen days after the deceased's death, unless it is otherwise ordered by two Registrars (N.C.P.R., R. 5).

Administration will not be granted to more than four persons in respect of the same property. If there is a minority or a life interest, administration will only be granted to a trust corporation or to not less than two individuals (Judicature Act 1925, s. 160). The person entitled to a grant may authorise a trust corporation to take the grant on his behalf, but only with the consent of all members of the same class, and of the class ultimately entitled to the residue.

(b) The Administrator's Oath and Bond

The administrator must swear an oath faithfully to administer the estate; and stating whether, and if so, how all those with a prior right to a grant have been cleared off, and whether any minority or life interest arises under the will or intestacy (N.C.P.R., R. 6).

Administrators are required to enter into a bond with sureties that they will make a true inventory of the estate, and exhibit it in the registry; that they will well and truly administer the estate according to law; and will make a true and just account whenever required by law to do so; and that, if it should afterwards appear that the deceased made a will, they will exhibit it to the court. The bond is to be given to the Principal Probate Registrar. The penalty is to be double the amount under which the estate is sworn, but the court or a Registrar has power to reduce this amount.

There must generally be two or more sureties and they may be required to justify, i.e. produce evidence to show that they are good for the amount of the bond. They will become liable on the breach of any of the conditions of the bond. The bond of a guarantee society is accepted instead of sureties.

No surety is required where application for the grant is made by a trust corporation, by trustees of settled land, a Crown servant in his official capacity, by a nominee of a public department or local authority, or where the deceased left no estate, while only one surety is necessary where the gross estate is sworn to be under £500 (N.C.P.R., R. 38).

If a trust corporation and an individual are joint administrators, the bond is given by both without sureties.

(c) *Special and Limited Grants*

A grant may be either general, that is, giving full power to deal with the whole of the estate; or limited, either as to time, amount of estate to be dealt with, or in both particulars. Where there is an intestacy, and no special features, a general grant is made. In certain cases, a special grant is necessary, as will be seen below.

(1) CUM TESTAMENTO (with the will annexed)

This grant is made when a will exists, but:

(*a*) no executor has been named in it, or

(*b*) the will directs that the named executor is not to act until after the expiration of a certain time, or

(*c*) the executor named has died without proving the will, or has renounced, or has been cited and has not appeared, or is not competent to take probate, or is resident out of Great Britain, or

(*d*) when the chain of executorship is in any way broken.

It is usually made to the person who would have been entitled to an original grant (see Table in § 5 (*a*)), although the court has a discretionary power to make a grant in favour of some person who may, in the circumstances, have a greater interest in the estate than the person ordinarily entitled (Judicature Act 1925, s. 162). Any of the following grants (2) to (12) inclusive will also be *cum testamento annexo* if there is a will.

The grant may also be made where the duly appointed executor is adversely interested in the estate or is otherwise unsuitable, probate being refused (*In the goods of Ray* [1927]). The will must be proved in a similar manner to that in which an executor proves.

(2) DE BONIS NON ADMINISTRATIS (of the goods not administered)

This grant is made when the executor of a will dies without having transmitted the executorship, or where an administrator dies without completing administration, and the assets of the original testator or intestate have not been fully administered. The grant is usually made to a person who would have been entitled originally to seek it if there were no executor able and ready to act.

(3) DURANTE ABSENTIA (during absence)

(*a*) Where at the time of the deceased's death, the named executor or the person entitled to take out letters of administration, as the case may be, is abroad, administration may be granted to an attorney of the person entitled to representation, limited until that person becomes resident and applies for a grant (N.C.P.R., R. 30).

(*b*) Where the executor to whom probate has been granted, or the administrator to whom letters have been granted, is residing out of the jurisdiction of the court at the expiration of twelve months from the testator's death, the court on the application of any creditor, or person interested in the estate, may grant a special administration (Judicature Act 1925, s. 164). The grant is limited 'until further order of the court', and the person holding the original grant cannot act until the limited grant is recalled or revoked (A.E.A. 1925, s. 15).

In a case where a grant of administration *cum testamento annexo* had been made to the universal legatee, and he became bankrupt, and, at the expiration of twelve months from the death of the testatrix, he was out of the jurisdiction, the court made a grant to his trustee in bankruptcy (*In re Rosse* [1934]).

(4) FOR THE USE OF INFANTS

Where a person otherwise entitled to a grant is an infant a grant of administration (with the will annexed where relevant) will be made to his parents jointly or his guardian, or such other person as the court thinks fit, limited until the infant attains the age of eighteen years, when the grant expires (Family Law Reform Act 1969). If no guardian is able or willing to act, a child of sixteen years of age or over may nominate any next-of-kin to act. An infant married woman may nominate her own or her husband's next-of-kin (N.C.P.R., R. 31). Where two representatives are required, the person so entitled can nominate the other (*ibid.*).

If the infant does not take out probate after attaining the age of eighteen, a new grant of administration will have to be made, as the original grant expires on his eighteenth birthday, and the quondam infant cannot act unless and until he takes out probate (Family Law Reform Act 1969).

(5) FOR THE USE OF A PERSON UNDER DISABILITY

When the sole executor or administrator is or becomes of mental or physical incapacity either before or after obtaining a grant, the court may appoint an administrator at its own discretion. Such a grant is not given until all persons equally entitled have been cleared off (N.C.P.R., R. 33).

(6) PENDENTE LITE (pending litigation)

This grant is made when any legal proceedings are pending touching the validity of the will, or for obtaining, recalling, or revoking any grant of probate or administration. The person appointed will have all the powers of a general administrator, except that of distributing the residue. His functions cease on the conclusion of the suit. He is subject to the immediate control of the court and acts under its direction. The court may assign to any administrator so appointed reasonable remuneration out of the estate of the deceased (Judicature Act 1925, s. 163). The appointment can only be made after the proceedings have commenced, i.e. after the writ has been issued.

(7) AD LITEM (limited to an action)

When the proper representative will not qualify to act, and it is necessary in the interests of the estate of the deceased that it should be represented at some suit or proceedings in the Chancery Division affecting those interests, the Probate Division or the Chancery Division may appoint a person to represent the estate.

(8) AD COLLIGENDA BONA DEFUNCTI (to collect the goods of the deceased)

This grant may be made when no person entitled, creditor, or other person applies for administration, and there is danger to the estate by reason of its being of a perishable nature. Application is to a Registrar (N.C.P.R., R. 51).

(9) CÆTERORUM (of the rest)

If a grant is limited in the first instance to a portion of the estate, and a subsequent grant is made for the administration of the residue, this is called a grant *cæterorum*.

(10) 'SAVE AND EXCEPT'

This grant is made when a certain portion of the estate is excepted, and general administration of the residue, excepting that particular portion, is granted.

Where, owing to there being a life interest, a grant of administration is given to a trust corporation alone, the grant is limited 'until further representation be granted', unless all persons interested in the residue have consented. There may also be a grant limited until the will can be found or produced.

(11) SPES SUCCESSIONIS (in expectation of succeeding)

Where the beneficial interest in the whole estate of the deceased is vested absolutely in a person who has renounced his right to a grant and has consented to administration being granted to the persons who would have been entitled to his estate if he had himself died intestate administration may be granted to such persons. Such a *spes successionis* grant will only be given to persons not exceeding four in number, who apply jointly for the grant (N.C.P.R., R. 27).

(12) CESSATE (on cessation)

A fresh grant made when a limited grant has come to an end, e.g. where the person entitled to a grant had it made to his attorney and now wants it made direct, or a lunatic becomes of sound mind.

(13) TILL A WILL BE FOUND

This may be granted where a will is known to have been made but cannot be found.

A grant made to the nominee or attorney of a corporation is limited 'for the use and benefit of the company and until further representation is granted'.

§ 6. Revocation of Probate or Administration

Probate may be revoked:

(1) where it appears to the High Court that probate or administration either ought not to have been granted, or contains an error (Admin. of Justice Act 1956, s. 17);

(2) upon appeal to a higher tribunal against the decision whereby probate was granted; this appeal will lie against a grant
from the Probate Division of the High Court to the Court of
Appeal, and (with permission) from that Court to the House
of Lords;

(3) by a suit in which the executor who obtained probate is cited
to prove in solemn form and, upon such citation, fails
sufficiently to prove the will.

Citation for this purpose may be made where the will has not
previously been proved in solemn form. Where it has been so
proved, the executor cannot be called upon by persons who were
parties to the original proceedings to prove the will again except
upon the ground:

(a) that probate was obtained by fraud (*Birch* v. *Birch* [1902]);

(b) that there has been discovered a later will or a codicil revoking the will proved or changing the executors;

(c) that probate has been granted in error, e.g. where the testator
is found to be alive (*In the goods of Napier* [1809]), or the
executor is found to be under full age;

(d) that one of the several executors has become of unsound
mind, when a new grant will be made to the sane executors.

Letters of administration may be revoked:

(1) as in (1) or (2) above,

(2) when granted less than fourteen days (seven days if there is a
will) after the deceased's death, or where the proper parties
have not been cited;

(3) where the person to whom it has been granted becomes in
any way incapable through insanity or continued ill-health;
mere old age or infirmity is not a sufficient ground (*In the
goods of Morris* [1862]);

(4) where it has been made to the wrong person, e.g. where made
to an 'unmarried wife' (*Re W. Moore* [1845]) or where made
to the next-of-kin, but there is a residuary legatee entitled
under a will; or where a will is produced after a grant was
made as on an intestacy;

(5) if granted pending a caveat or even where the caveat has expired (*Trimlestown* v. *Trimlestown* [1830]), when notice has not been given to the adverse party.

If an executor has failed to take out probate and letters of administration *cum testamento annexo* have been granted but it is subsequently discovered that the executor had, prior to the grant, dealt with the estate, the grant may be revoked and the executor cited to prove the will.

Where the grantee has disappeared, or being a creditor, he has paid his own debt and taken no further interest in the estate, revocation is now unnecessary; the court can make a grant in respect of the estate not administered.

Where a grant is revoked, persons having made or permitted any payment or disposition in good faith under it are indemnified and protected and all payments and dispositions made to a personal representative in good faith before the revocation are a valid discharge to the person making them; the personal representative who acted prior to the revocation may retain and reimburse himself in respect of payments or dispositions which the person to whom representation is ultimately granted might have properly made (A.E.A., 1925, s. 27).

Moreover, all conveyances of any interest in real or personal estate to a purchaser by a person to whom probate or letters of administration have been granted remain valid, notwithstanding any subsequent revocation or variation of the probate or administration and such property cannot be recovered from the purchaser (*ibid*. s. 37).

§ 7. Probate Copies

To facilitate the administration of estates, copies of grants of probate or administration can be obtained at the Principal or District Probate Registries, so as to obviate delay in circulating the original document to companies, etc., as the executor's or administrator's authority to deal with the shares or other property held by the deceased. The copies are prepared photographically, and sealed with the small seal of the court; one shilling each is charged for copies. Companies, etc., are bound to recognise the authenticity of such copies (Lord Chancellor's circulars, December, 1933 and April, 1934).

CHAPTER III

THE DEATH DUTIES

§ 1. Introduction

Duty on property, which is left or is deemed to pass on the death of a person, is levied under the provisions contained in the Finance Act 1894, as amended by subsequent Finance Acts. The duty on deaths prior to 16th April, 1969, is a graduated stamp duty, and is calculated by reference to the scale set out on p. 86. For deaths on or after that date, the duty is calculated on a slice of the assets at varying rates, see p. 86 and Appendix VI.

The duty is calculated from the information shown in the Inland Revenue Affidavit. The details required for the preparation of the affidavit can be divided into four distinct categories:

(1) The valuation of the whole of the property, both real and personal, wherever situated, at market value, which has been left by the deceased;

(2) The valuation of property which is defined as passing on the death;

(3) The valuation of settled property in which the deceased had an interest;

(4) The ascertainment of all allowable deductions, including liabilities of the deceased due at the date of death.

The date of death is the usual date for valuation purposes and the valuation must be based on the price which the property can be expected to realise if sold on the open market at that date. In some cases this valuation is provisional only and may be upset if subsequent events prove it to have been incorrect.

It is obvious from an examination of the four categories, that there is little avenue for the avoidance of Estate Duty, but nevertheless, by many ingenious schemes, the payment of duty has been avoided in the past, and the complexity which now attaches itself to the subject is the result of such schemes. However, not all property which falls into one of the above categories will be liable to duty, for the statutes make numerous exemptions (see this Chapter, § 3). Amongst the most important of these, is that which applies to property which has already borne Estate Duty on the death of the first spouse to a marriage, if that property was settled on the surviving spouse and the latter had no powers to appoint the property to himself or herself.

While certain property is exempt from duty, other types of property are not so exempt, but some relief may be afforded since the property is not subject to aggregation with the other assets passing on death. As Estate Duty is calculated on a graduated scale, which increases as the aggregate value of property passing on death rises, an increase in the principal value of the estate's property, may increase the rate of duty. It follows, therefore, that if funds are placed into non-aggregable property, whilst the latter may suffer duty, since it is treated as a separate estate there will be an overall saving of duty. These exemptions are of the greatest importance, as the effect of failing to claim them might have far reaching effects on the amount of duty payable, e.g. the relief given where the 'unsettled' estate is less than £15,000 and there are settled funds (see this Chapter, § 7).

The value of realty should be separately stated from that of personalty. There are two important reasons for maintaining the division; in the first place, interest at 3% per annum is chargeable on the Estate Duty payable on personalty, from the date of death to the date of payment, whilst interest on realty does not become payable until after one year has elapsed since the death or from the date of sale, if earlier. Furthermore, the duty on realty can be spread rateably over eight years, providing that the property is not sold in the intervening period. Realty, as between the estate and the devisee, usually bears its own Estate Duty, unless it is expressed by some direction in the Will itself to be payable out of some other fund. As between the Inland Revenue and the personal representative, however, the duty is a charge on the realty, ranking after any other encumbrances.

Circumstances must arise where, if the rules for calculating duty were strictly adhered to, the result would operate most harshly against the estate. A system of marginal relief has therefore evolved, and this can be applied in three circumstances.

Firstly, where the death was prior to 16th April, 1969, and

the net estate only slightly exceeded in value the sum on the scale at which the rate increased, then if the higher rate was applied, it might be that the excess over the highest amount covered by the lower scale rate, was much less than the increase in duty which became otherwise payable. Marginal relief had the effect of restricting the total duty payable to the rate on the highest amount under the lower scale, plus the excess over the highest amount in that scale. A simple illustration will readily show the extent of the relief. If a person died prior to 16th April, 1969, leaving a net estate of £1,000,500 the amount of duty payable without marginal relief would be at the scale rate of 80%, i.e. £800,400, but if relief is claimed, the duty payable will be at the scale rate of 75% on £1,000,000, i.e. £750,000 plus the excess of the principal value over £1,000,000, i.e. £500, giving a total of £750,500 which provides a saving of some £49,900. For deaths on or after that date, this system of marginal relief does not apply.

Secondly, marginal relief is also provided, whenever the date of death, for cases where the 'unsettled' property does not exceed £15,000 or only slightly exceeds that figure, and there is settled property which also passes on the death. If the 'unsettled' property is less than £15,000, then both that property and the settled property are treated as separate estates. Where the unsettled property is slightly in excess of £15,000, there is an aggregation of total property passing, so that the scale rate can be ascertained for the settled property. The duty payable on the 'unsettled property' will not exceed that payable on an estate of £15,000, i.e. nothing, or if the death was prior to 16th April, 1969, £400, plus in each case the excess of the value of such property over the initial £15,000.

Lastly, regardless of the date of death, in cases where there is an exemption from Estate Duty if the amount involved does not exceed a stated amount, e.g. gifts not exceeding £500. Whilst the full value of the gift is subject to aggregation (with any necessary adjustment to be claimed under section 64 (i) of the Finance Act 1960), the Estate Duty payable must not exceed the excess of the value of the gift over £500.

Generally speaking, the personal representative is responsible for the payment of Estate Duty on all property left by the deceased, wherever situated, except property of which the deceased was *not* competent to dispose at the date of his death. The latter includes gifts *inter-vivos, donationes mortis causa* and settled property of which the deceased was life tenant. Whilst the Estate Duty on this property is leviable on the trustees and donees, the personal representatives must disclose the existence and valuation of such property, in the affidavit. As with the Estate Duty chargeable on realty, the testator can direct that such gifts be duty free, and in that case, if the estate is in a position to pay the duty, it will become the responsibility of the personal representative.

Allowable deductions include all those liabilities of a *bonâ fide* nature which have been entered into for full consideration by the deceased. Funeral expenses of a reasonable nature are allowable, but other debts contracted after the death by the personal representative are not. Estate Duty which has been charged by another country, on foreign property situated abroad, is allowed as a credit against the Estate Duty charged in this country on the same property.

The actual payment of duty can be effected in several different ways besides the normal method of payment by cash. A benefit can be derived from payments in kind. Thus, works of art of historic etc. interest are not only exempt from aggregation, if offered to the nation, thereby saving the estate from duty, but are also accepted as payment for duty in lieu of cash. Whilst some adjustment is made to the valuation for these purposes, to take into account the duty which would be paid if the works of art were sold on the open market, there is still a considerable 'profit' to the estate. Likewise, certain government securities can be surrendered at their par value, including acrued interest, in satisfaction of the duty, and where the securities are quoted below par on the date of death, a benefit accrues to the estate.

§ 2. Property subject to Estate Duty

Estate Duty is a graduated stamp duty, payable on the net principal value, after deducting debts, encumbrances and reasonable funeral expenses, of all unsettled property, both real and personal, and certain classes of settled property, which passes on death (F.A. 1894, s 1.).

The rates of Estate Duty are set out in § 5 of this Chapter. It should be noted for deaths on or after 16th April, 1969, the

Estate Duty payable is determined by ascertaining the net principal value of the Estate and levying duty on the successive slices of the value, which slices are charged at increasing rates in accordance with the table set out in Part I, 17th Schedule, Finance Act 1969.

Property which does not *actually* pass on death but is deemed so to pass by virtue of express provisions contained in various Finance Acts is also subject to the charge (see (B)) below.

(A) ALL PROPERTY, REAL OR PERSONAL, SETTLED OR NOT SETTLED

Property is said to be 'settled' when it is held in trust to be enjoyed by different persons in succession.

It is necessary to distinguish between realty and personalty, as will be seen later in this chapter.

Any interest in land less than freehold is considered to be personalty, e.g. leaseholds are personalty; a share in a partnership is personalty, even if the whole of the partnership assets are real property (Partnership Act 1890, s. 22).

If a person has contracted to sell real property and dies before the title is conveyed to the purchaser, the proceeds of sale are regarded as personal estate of the deceased at the date of his death (*Lysaght* v. *Edwards* [1876]). It is the right to the proceeds and not the land that passes.

(B) PROPERTY 'PASSING ON THE DEATH'

Property is regarded as 'passing on the death' of a person where the beneficial ownership, possession or enjoyment of that property is diverted by the event of death, whether:

(*a*) immediately upon the death, or

(*b*) at a time determinable by reference to the death (Section 1, Finance Act 1894).

Whether the passing is absolute (i.e. whatever the circumstances obtaining at the time of death), or contingent (i.e. providing certain other facts concur apart from the fact of death), makes no difference.

Where the death was before 16th April, 1969, under (*b*) will be included property in which the deceased did not himself have an interest, and with which he was unconnected, save by reason of the fact that his death was the event that determined when an interest in that property was transmitted from one person to another. This situation will not occur in respect of deaths on or after that date since duty will be chargeable when the person interested in the property dies and not when the property passes on the death of the unconnected person.

Property passing on the death of the deceased is defined in Section 2, Finance Act 1894, as amended, as:

(*a*) property in which the deceased was at the time of his death competent to dispose;

(*b*) property in the case of which at any time during the period of seven years ending with the date of the deceased's death was comprised in a settlement and the deceased was entitled to a beneficial interest in possession of that property as, or as successor to an interest of, a beneficiary under the settlement;

(*c*) property which at any time during the period of seven years ending with the date of the deceased's death was comprised in a settlement and in which the deceased had at a time before that period been entitled to a beneficial interest in possession from which he was not entirely excluded prior to that seven year period;

(*d*) property being, or having after 15th April 1969, been included in settled property, subject to a discretion conferred on trustees or some other person as to the application of the combined income of the property (not being a discretion only as to the amount of annuity or as to the provision of maintenance for a person under age) and

   (i) the deceased immediately before the date of his death was eligible to benefit as a result of the discretion and had benefited at any time during a period of seven years prior to his death and which falls after 15th April, 1963, or

   (ii) having ceased to be eligible the deceased had benefited during that period, or

   (iii) the deceased had ceased to be eligible outside the seven year period but had not been entirely excluded from possession or enjoyment of the property throughout that period, then if the deceased had benefited during that period, providing that some part of that period falls after 15th April, 1963, or

(e) the property was at the date of the deceased's death comprised in settled property held by trustees under a settlement made by the deceased whereby that settled property was held on trust to accumulate or with a power for the trustees at the discretion of the trustees or some other person to accumulate the whole or part of any income of that settled property, and that trust for or power of accumulation determined at the death;

(f) gifts *inter vivos* – see Chapter VI;

(g) property consisting of an interest of the deceased as a partner under a partnership agreement, being an interest to which under the terms of that or some other agreement, some person other than the deceased's executor becomes entitled to the interest on the deceased's death otherwise than by the exercise of an option to acquire that interest;

(h) property subject to an option to purchase granted otherwise than by the deceased's Will and exercisable by reference to the deceased's death, if the property would have passed on the deceased's death had there not been an option to purchase it.

Thus property is, for Estate Duty purposes, 'deemed to pass' on death, notwithstanding that the death does not operate directly to shift the beneficial possession. Such cases include property of which the deceased was competent to dispose, certain gifts *inter vivos* and *donationes mortis causa*, life policies, interests arising on death, property in which life interests were determined prior to death, and property which had been transferred to 'controlled' companies.

Illustration

The above analysis of the embracing character of the phrase 'property passing on death' is exemplified by the following dispositions in which the death of A. causes an interest in property to 'change hands'.

(i) A. by his will devises Blackacre to B., but if B. should predecease A. then to C. for life.

The property in Blackacre shifts to B. *immediately* and *absolutely* upon A.'s death if B. survives him. If B. does not survive A., the *original grant* of the interest to B. necessarily fails and the *substitutive limitation* to C. takes effect.

(ii) The income of property is settled by deed upon D. for a period to end twenty-one years after the death of A., the corpus and income then to vest in E. if she be unmarried or a widow, but if she be then married or dead, to go to D. absolutely.

The disposition to E. takes effect at a time *determinable by reference to A.'s death* and is *contingent* upon E.'s being alive and unmarried at that time.

(iii) Settlement on G. for the life of A. and then to H. An estate *pur autre vie* is vested in G., the property in which he enjoys that interest passing upon A.'s death, although A. has himself no interest in that property. For deaths before 16th April, 1969, duty would have been paid on A's death; for deaths after that date on G's death.

Where property is settled, and the interest of any person under the settlement fails or determines by reason of his death *before it becomes an interest in possession*, the property is not deemed to pass at his death before 16th April, 1969, by reason only of the failure or determination of that interest (F.A. 1894, s. 5 (3)), provided the subsequent limitations continue (F.A. 1938, s. 48). Thus:

(i) The contingent interest in the estate of an intestate enjoyed by an infant under the statutory trusts fails if the infant dies unmarried; the property is accordingly not chargeable to Estate Duty by reason of the infant's death before 16th April, 1969, even where the infant has received maintenance out of income. For deaths after that date, see below.

(ii) In a marriage settlement, A. settled property upon trust to pay the income to herself during the joint lives of herself and her husband, and on the death of either, to the survivor, and on the death of the survivor, upon trust for the issue, and in default of issue, in trust to herself, if she survived her husband, absolutely. The husband died before the wife and there were no issue. No Estate Duty was payable upon the husband's death, as his interest had never fallen into possession and the subsequent limitations remained effective, even though the ultimate gift was one in remainder (*Attorney-General* v. *Wood* [1897]). For this exemption to remain effective if the death is on or after 16th April, 1969, the husband must not receive any enjoyment in the income of the trust in the seven years prior to his death.

The definition of 'settled property' has been amended and extended by the Finance Act 1969 so that for deaths on or after 16th April, 1969, the term will include:

(*a*) any disposition whereby property is held by trustees on trust to accumulate the whole or part of any income of that property or with a power for the trustees to make payments out of that income at the discretion of the trustees or some other person with or without the power to accumulate surplus income (s. 36 (5) (a) (i) (aa));

(*b*) any disposition regulated by the law of a territory outside Great Britain which would constitute a settlement within the meaning of Section 22 (1) (i) of the Finance Act 1894 if it had been regulated by the law of England, or, as the case may require, of Scotland (s. 36 (5) (a) (i) (bb));

(*c*) a lease of property which is for a life or lives or for a period ascertainable only by reference to a death or which is terminable on, or at a date ascertainable only by reference to, a death, that property being treated as the property comprised in the settlement (s. 36 (5) (a) (ii)).

The following property is deemed to pass upon the death of a deceased person (F.A. 1894, s. 2):

(i) *Property of which the deceased was at the time of his death competent to dispose,* whether he actually disposed of it by his will or not. This includes property over which the deceased had a general power of appointment, and property which he could appoint to himself under a special power.

> A person is deemed competent to dispose of property if he has such an estate or interest therein, or such general power as would, if he were *sui juris*, enable him to dispose of the property. The expression 'general power' includes every power or authority enabling the donee or other holder thereof to appoint or dispose of property as he thinks fit, whether exercisable by instrument *inter vivos*, or by will, or both, but exclusive of any power exercisable in a fiduciary capacity under a disposition not made by himself, or exercisable as tenant for life of settled land, or as mortgagee (*ibid.* s. 22 (2) (*a*)).

Money which a person has a general power to charge on property is deemed to be property of which he has power to dispose (*ibid.* s. 22 (2) (*c*)).

A legatee is competent to dispose of the legacy as soon as the testator dies. Disclaiming the legacy disposes of it (*Re Parsons, Parsons* v. *Attorney-General* [1943]). See also Chapter XIV, § 3 (*g*).

(ii) *Donationes mortis causa* (i.e. gifts made in expectation of death but conditional on the death occurring).

(iii) *Gifts inter vivos made within seven years of death* with certain exceptions (see Chapter VI).

(iv) *Gifts inter vivos made at any time, if the donee did not assume bona fide possession to the immediate and entire exclusion of the donor.* Similar gifts where a BENEFIT, whether charged upon the property or not, was RESERVED or secured TO THE DECEASED by contract or otherwise.

If, however, a benefit or interest so retained by the deceased was surrendered to his entire exclusion seven years (or in the case of a gift for public or charitable purposes, one year) before the death, such property is not deemed to pass at his death (F. (1909-10) A. 1910, s. 59; F.A. 1968, s. 35).

If the gift consisted of a house, provided the donee took possession and became the head of the house, the donor could reside there as a guest without attracting duty under this provision (*Attorney-General* v. *Seccombe* [1911]).

On the death of a donor after 28th July, 1959, property which he had given away but which had not been possessed and enjoyed by the donee to the entire exclusion of the donor, will escape Estate Duty on the death of the donor if he has been given full consideration in money or money's worth for the possession or benefit (F.A. 1959, s. 35, (2)).

(v) *Property to which the deceased had been absolutely entitled but had caused to be vested in himself and some other person jointly,* so that the other person takes BY SURVIVORSHIP.

(vi) *The deceased's severable share of property of which he was a joint tenant or joint owner with another or others.* The charge of duty will be limited to the deceased's share of the joint property unless the whole is dutiable under (v) above by reason of the deceased having been originally entitled to the whole.

In the case of REAL AND LEASEHOLD PROPERTY held in the joint names of a husband and wife, on the death of the husband (by concession) or of the wife (*Dunbar* v. *Dunbar* [1909]), Estate Duty is payable on one-half IF THE PROPERTY WAS PURCHASED OR PROVIDED BY THE HUSBAND unless the husband dies within seven years of completing the purchase, when the whole is liable. If provided by the wife, Estate Duty is payable on her death on the whole property, but none is payable on the husband's death. In the above remarks it is assumed in each case that the other spouse survives. In the case of other property, duty is only payable on the death of the party to the marriage who provided the property.

Where the property has been contributed by the joint tenants, duty is charged on the share provided by the deceased, or of which he was competent to dispose, if greater.

Savings or property purchased out of housekeeping moneys belongs to the spouses in equal shares, in the absence of any agreement to the contrary, if provided by the husband as such in the first instance (Married Women's Property Act 1964, s. 1).

(vii) *Property which the deceased had enjoyment of or interest in for life, or for some period determinable by reference to his death,* under an express or implied trust in a settlement made by himself.

Even if the life tenant surrenders his interest to the remainderman, or otherwise deals with it so that the property does not pass on the life tenant's death, the property is nevertheless 'deemed to pass' on his death, whether the disposition was for value or not, unless the death takes place more than seven years from the date of the surrender (on a surrender for public or charitable purposes the period is twelve months), and *bona fide* possession and enjoyment were immediately assumed by the person entitled (F. (1909-10) A. 1910, s. 59; F. A.1969, 17th Sch. Part III, Part 6; (see § 19, Chapter IV).

(viii) A slice of the company's assets which the deceased had transferred to a controlled company coming within the

Finance Act 1940, s. 46 *et seq.*, from which he derived benefits (see Chapter X).

(ix) Gifts by way of creation of a burden or release of a right (F.A. 1940, s. 45).

(x) Sums of money which become payable to the deceased's estate by reason of his death, and for the recovery of which there lies an action in law. This includes the repayment of contributions made to a group life assurance and pension scheme, as well as the assurance monies. Note that if the latter are payable by the exercise of a discretionary power of the trustees only, so that no legal right exists, then Estate Duty will not be leviable thereon. (Re Miller's Agreement, see p. 74.)

(xi) Damages awarded for loss of expectation of life under the Law Reform (Miscellaneous Provisions) Act 1934, but NOT damages recovered under the Fatal Accidents Acts as these are intended to compensate members of the family of the deceased (see § 7 (g), Chapter XII).

(xii) *Property of which the deceased or any other person had an interest ceasing on the death of the deceased providing that death was before 16th April, 1969,* to the extent to which a benefit accrues or arises by the cesser of such interest; but exclusive of property, the interest in which of the deceased or other person was only an interest as holder of an office, or recipient of the benefits of a charity, or as a corporation sole. This includes a cessation of a limited interest in unascertained residue (F.A. 1938, s. 47) (see Chapter IV, § 16).

At one time it was possible to avoid duty, chargeable upon the death of a life tenant on the trust funds, by providing for a limited interest extending beyond the death (Re Ralli's Settlements), so that the interest did not *cease* on the death of the life tenant. This operation is now provided for by virtue of the Finance Act 1966, s. 40, so that such property is now liable to Estate Duty.

Section 1, Finance Act 1894, imposes Estate Duty on all property passing on death and Section 2 states the property which is deemed to pass. Section 1 imposes the charge to Estate Duty in general terms and Section 2 defines by inclusion and exclusion the precise area of that charge (*Public Trustee* v. *C.I.R.* [1960]). In this case the testator left a gift in his will of a share of the income of the residuary estate to one of his trustees 'as long as he shall act as executor and trustee'. On the death of the trustee, the Crown claimed estate duty on the slice of the estate of which the trustee enjoyed the income, at the rate found by aggregation with the trustee's own estate. The trustee's executors claimed that no duty was payable because the trustee was only interested in the income as the holder of an office, and the House of Lords agreed. A similar decision had been made in respect of the cessation on his death of an annuity to a trustee as remuneration for his service (*Attorney-General* v. *Eyres* [1909]).

It will be appreciated from the provisions of Section 2, Finance Act 1894 set out in § 2 above, that for deaths on or after 16th April, 1969, the provisions relating to cessers of interest will be inapplicable.

(xiii) ***Annuities or other interests which the deceased*** (either alone or by arrangement with any other person) ***purchased or provided,*** to the extent of the beneficial interest accruing or arising on the death of the deceased prior to 16th April, 1969 (no deduction being allowed for any interest in expectancy the beneficiary may have had therein before the death (F.A. 1934, s. 28)). Annuities purchased or provided by some person who was at any time entitled to any property derived from the deceased (F.A. 1939, s. 30), where the principal interest arises on the death prior to 16th April, 1969.

A single annuity not exceeding £52, or the first granted of two or more such annuities, is not deemed to pass upon the death. A marginal relief is provided where the annuity exceeds £52, but is less than £104, in which case it is chargeable with duty as if it amounted to twice the excess of the annuity over £52, e.g. an annuity of £90 is chargeable on the *capitalised* value of $2 \times (£90 - £52) = £76$ (F.A. 1894, s. 15 (1); F.A. 1935, s. 33). If the deceased purchased annuities for two or more different persons, each can claim the relief.

It will be appreciated that the annuities referred to above

are annuities purchased or provided by the deceased in his lifetime, to arise or accrue on his death prior to 16th April, 1969, and not annuities given by his will. Such provisions have been repealed in respect of deaths on or after 16th April, 1969.

For duty to be attracted in respect of the beneficial interest accruing or arising on the death of the deceased it must be an interest which the beneficiary can claim by law. Thus, in *Re Miller's Agreement* [1947], a partner on retiring from his firm sold his interest therein to his co-partners in consideration, *inter alia*, of their agreement with him to pay annuities to his daughters for their lives as from the date of his death. On his death two years later duty was claimed from the daughters on the value of their annuities, but it was held that it was not leviable as the daughters had no right to the annuities which the law would protect. They were strangers to the contract between their father and his co-partners, and so could not sue on the contract at common law, and no trust had been created in their favour giving them any equitable rights as beneficiaries. Similarly, if the granting of a widow's pension is entirely at the discretion of the trustees of a pension fund to which the deceased was not a contributor, no Estate Duty is payable on the pension (*Re J. Bibby & Sons, Ltd, Pension Trust Deed, Davies* v. *C.I.R.* [1952]). In the case of such pensions, the Revenue practice is to regard the pension as provided by the deceased if he contributed to the pension fund, either by direct payment or by deduction from his salary. If he has not made such contributions he is not regarded as having provided the pension by service alone. The position may be different if the annuitant is the executor of the deceased partner (*Beswick* v. *Beswick*).

Where the deceased contracted for and paid for an annuity in favour of a nominee, duty will only be payable on the saleable value of the annuity at the deceased's death if the contract was completed within the seven years prior to death (subject to the reduction in value provided by the Finance Act 1960, s. 64, where the death occurred in the fifth, sixth or seventh year after the gift described above). The annuity will be an estate by itself not subject to aggregation, since the deceased never had an interest in it.

§ 3. Exemptions from Estate Duty

The following exemptions must be noted:

(i) *Settled property, in respect of which Estate Duty has been paid* (or would have been paid had the estate not been below

£15,000) *on the death of one party to a marriage, is free from Estate Duty on the death of the other party to the marriage* provided the latter was not at any time during the continuance of the settlement competent to dispose of the property (F.A. 1894, s. 5 (2); F.A. 1914, s. 14; F.A. 1954, s. 32 (2)).

This includes the property passing by reason of the death of the spouse who had a life interest in a deceased intestate's estate.

Where the estate had no value, or was insolvent at the first death but subsequently appreciates so that property passes on the second death, the exemption applies (F.A. 1956, s. 36). A similar exemption will apply where on the first death, the property was exempt because of the provisions relating to persons dying on war service, see (iv) below.

Where Estate Duty has been paid in Northern Ireland on the death of a party to a marriage, relief is given on the death of the other party in Great Britain as if the duty had been charged in Great Britain (F.A. 1936, s. 25). In practice, the exemption covers the cesser of an annuity on the death of the surviving spouse.

If duty on the first death was paid only on a portion of the property, proportionate relief is given on the second death.

Property settled on trust to pay an annuity to A. for life with remainder to B. who settles the reversionary interest on A.'s wife will be exempt from duty on the death of A.'s wife if she survives him and duty was paid on A.'s death.

Where the husband and wife were both beneficiaries under the same discretionary trust, the surviving spouse exemption will apply in respect of the duty on the settled property. A full explanation of the provisions will be found in Chapter IV, § 15.

(ii) *All property situate outside Great Britain where the deceased owner was domiciled outside Great Britain at the time of his death.* If the deceased was merely tenant for life, the property will be dutiable if the proper law governing the settlement was English or Scottish. But if the proper law was foreign, the property will escape if either the deceased died domiciled abroad or the settlement was made by a foreign domiciled settlor otherwise than out of funds provided by a person domiciled in England or Scotland (F.A. 1949, s. 28 (2) as amended by F.A. 1962, s. 28).

(iii) *Property passing under or by virtue of transactions for full money consideration* (F.A. 1894, s. 3). Where the transaction was for partial consideration in money or money's worth paid to the vendor or grantor for his own use or benefit, the value which corresponds to the consideration is allowed as a deduction from the value of the property (*ibid.*). (But see § 19 of Chapter IV as to dispositions in favour of relatives.)

(iv) *Estates of members of the Armed Forces killed on active service.* Estate Duty is not chargeable on the death of a person certified by the Admiralty, Air Council or the Secretary of State to have died from a wound inflicted, accident occurring or disease contracted at a time when the deceased was a member of the armed forces of the Crown, or of the women's services, or subject to the law governing any of those forces by reason of association with or accompanying any body of those forces and (in any case) was either:

(*a*) on active service against an enemy, or

(*b*) on other service of a warlike nature which the Treasury consider to involve the same risks.

The exemption also applies to the death of such a person from disease contracted at some previous time if the death is due to or hastened by aggravation of the disease during a period the deceased satisfied the conditions.

In practice the relief applies to the estates of civilians dying from injuries caused by the operations in Malaya, Korea, Kenya and Cyprus.

The exemption given to the settled property passing on the death of a surviving spouse will still operate as if Estate Duty had been paid on the death in active service of the spouse who died first, notwithstanding the above exemption on the death of the latter (F.A. 1952, s. 71).

The above exemption applies to all property passing on the death, including settled property, reversions, etc., and timber, works of art, etc., sold.

(v) *Certain specific property not exceeding £100 transferable without grant of representation,* under the Regimental Debts

Act 1893, the Navy and Marines (Property of Deceased) Act 1865, and the Merchant Shipping Act 1894, and compassionate allowances and pensions granted by the British Government to the widows and children of members of Her Majesty's Naval, Military and Air Forces, and the gratuities awarded to the representatives of deceased civil servants under the Superannuation Acts. A death gratuity payable to the deceased's representatives under the Teachers (Superannuation) Act 1925, is liable (*Attorney-General* v. *Quixley* [1929]). Duty is not claimed in respect of pensions, allowances, etc., paid direct to the widows and dependants of deceased police officers, under the Police Pensions Act 1948, but payments to the personal representatives, as such, of deceased officers are liable to duty. No Estate Duty is payable in respect of pensions under the Widows, Orphans and Old Age Contributory Pensions Acts.

(vi) *Property held by the deceased as trustee for another:*

(*a*) under a disposition not made by the deceased; or

(*b*) under a disposition made by the deceased more than seven years before his death, or such part of that period as falls after 19th March, 1963, where possession and enjoyment were *bona fide* assumed by the beneficiary immediately upon the creation of the trust, and thenceforth retained to the entire exclusion of the deceased, or of any benefit to him by contract or otherwise (*ibid*), s.2 (3); F.A. 1969, 17th Sch. Part III, para 6 (*b*), or where full consideration was paid in respect of the benefit (F.A. 1959, s. 35).

(vii) *Property saved from lapse by virtue of the operation of s. 33, Wills Act 1837* (F.A. 1958, s. 29). Prior to the F.A. 1958, property which passed to a deceased child's estate on the subsequent death of his parent was subject to a double charge for duty. Such property will now be liable to duty by reference to the parent's death only.

(viii) *Works of art not yielding income whether settled or not regarded by the Treasury as of national, scientific, historic or artistic interest,* i.e. pictures, prints, books, manuscripts, works of art, scientific collections or other things; duty in these cases is only to become payable when they are sold, and then only in respect of the last death on which the property passed (F.A. 1930, s. 40).

This exemption only applies if an undertaking is given to the Treasury that the objects will be kept permanently in the U.K. and will not leave it temporarily except with their consent, that reasonable care will be taken for their preservation and reasonable facilities are given for their examination. If these undertakings are not complied with, Estate Duty becomes chargeable on the value at that time of those objects in respect of the death on which the exemption was given (F.A. 1950, s. 48).

If, however, such property is sold to the National Gallery, the British Museum, or other similar national institution, any University, any County Council, any Municipal Corporation in Great Britain, the National Art Collections Fund, 'the Friends of the National Libraries', or to the Minister of Works under the Historic Buildings and Ancient Monuments Act 1953 (F.A. 1956, s. 34) the exemption from death duties will still apply (F.A. 1930, s. 40 (2) (*proviso*); F.A. 1936, s. 26). Appropriation to a beneficiary as part of his share of the estate is not a sale. See also Appendix VII.

A purchase by a national institution at an auction does not give exemption; the sale must be by private treaty (F.A. 1958, s. 31).

The foregoing exemptions in respect of sales of works of art of historic etc., interest to an individual Institution have been unaffected by the Finance Act 1969. But where the sale is not to that specified Institution or the Institution acquires the property at an Auction or there has been a non-observance of an undertaking given regarding the works of art etc., the provisions of Section 39, Finance Act 1969, bring the proceeds of sale in charge to duty.

If the disposal occurs within a period of three years beginning with the date of death, the principal value of the object at the date of death will be aggregated with all other property passing on the death as though such principal value had never been exempted from duty. The total duty payable on the entire Estate will thereby be increased so

that the proceeds of sale of the work of art will be chargeable to duty and the Estate Duty payable on the other
property will be increased. If the event occurs after the
expiration of three years following the death, the proceeds
of sale will be aggregated with all other property passing
on the death to determine the duty which is chargeable on
the proceeds of sale of the work of art. The Estate Duty
payable on the other property will not, however, be
increased. It should be noted that where the sale is within
three years, the figure to be brought into the computation
is the principal value at the date of death which may not
be the proceeds of sale. Of course, if the painting is sold
within a few weeks or months of the death, then the
proceeds are likely to be regarded as the principal value.
If, however, the Estate has been finalised before the period
of three years has elapsed and then the sale occurs, it is
the principal value which must be taken and not the
proceeds of sale. If the sale is outside the three year
period, then the proceeds of sale represent the amount
to be brought into the computation of the net principal
value at the date of death.

Illustration

James died on 31st May, 1969. Estate Duty was payable on the 1st
January, 1970 as follows:

Principal Value

Free estate – personalty	..	..	..	£45,000
realty	..	..	..	17,000
Gifts	..	..	..	6,000
				£68,000

The Estate Duty payable will be:

On £40,000	..	..	..	..	£10,125
On £28,000 at 60%	..	..	..	..	16,800
					£26,925

The value of the estate above did not include a painting valued at
£20,000. On 1st July, 1970, this painting was sold for £26,000.
Since this sale is within three years of death, the value of the estate

will be increased to £88,000. The Estate Duty payable will become:

On £80,000	..	..	..	..	£34,125
On £8,000 at 65%	..	..	..	..	5,200

£39,325

Since both the amount and rate increase, the increase in the estate of £20,000 gives rise to an increased liability of £12,400.

It will be noted that the recipients of the gifts will be affected by the sale, viz.

Original Estate Duty on gifts $\frac{6,000}{88,000} \times £26,925 = £2,376$

Revised Estate Duty $\frac{6,000}{88,000} \times £39,325 = £2,681$

If the painting had been sold in August, 1973, the liability on the original estate would have been unaffected, but the duty on the painting would have been based on the proceeds of sale, viz.

Original estate	..	..	..	..	£68,000
Proceeds of sale	..	..	..	..	26,000

£94,000

Estate Duty on an estate of £94,000 is:

On £80,000	..	..	..	..	£34,125
On £14,000 at 65%	..	..	..	..	9,100

£43,225

Estate Duty on painting $- \frac{26,000}{94,000} \times £43,225 = £11,956$.

If there is more than one sale after the expiration of the three years, separate calculations will be made as if each sale were the only sale outside that period except where the articles being sold constitute a set and the sales are either to the same person or persons, or to persons who are connected or acting in concert, as defined for the purposes of Capital Gains tax. In these circumstances, the earliest sale or disposal of any of the objects within the set is treated as the date of sale of all of them. This has the effect that if the first sale of the part of a set occurs within the three year period following the date of death, the value of the set at the date of death will be liable to aggregation and not the proceeds of sale.

(ix) *Timber,* until sold (see § 9 of Chapter IV).

(x) *Any estate or interest in land given, devised or bequeathed absolutely to the National Trust* is subject to prescribed conditions, and is exempt from death duties. The exemption operates even where a life interest in favour of the disponor or his spouse or child is created, or life interests in favour of the disponor *and* his spouse or child are created, so as to intervene between the date when the gift is made and the time when it vests in possession of the National Trust (F.A. 1937, s. 31). The Treasury may remit the duty on any estate or interest in land given, devised or bequeathed either to the National Trust immediately for the public benefit, or to the Commissioners of Works or a local authority, and accepted by them under s. 2, Ancient Monuments Consolidation and Amendment Act 1913. Such estate or interest must be the deceased's whole interest in the land (F.A. 1931, s. 40; F.A. 1936, s. 27).

The exemption extends to maintenance funds accompanying such a gift of land to the National Trust (F.A. 1949, s. 31).

The exemption is extended to objects given with or subsequently to the gift of the building, for preservation and use in it and to a maintenance fund in connection with these objects. Exemption applies also, where the Treasury so direct, to a gift of a house, land or other building for the public benefit to or to trustees for:

(*a*) a government department;

(*b*) a local authority; or

(*c*) any other body not established or conducted for profit.

Objects kept in such a house, etc., and maintenance funds are treated likewise. The house, land, or building, must have outstanding historic architectural or aesthetic interest and the body be an appropriate one to preserve it (F.A. 1951, s. 33; F.A. 1963, s. 54). See Appendix VII.

(xi) Securities issued free of taxation while in the beneficial ownership of persons neither domiciled nor ordinarily resident in Great Britain or Northern Ireland (F. (No. 2)

A. 1915, s. 47; F.A. 1966, s. 41), e.g., $3\frac{1}{2}\%$ War Loan, 4% Funding Loan, 4% Victory Bonds, 3% Savings Bonds, 1965-75, 6% Exchequer Loan, 1970, $5\frac{1}{2}\%$ Funding Stock, 1982-84, $8\frac{1}{2}\%$ Treasury Loan 1980-82.

The conditions of domicile and residence operate by reference to the persons in beneficial ownership of the securities immediately before the death (F.A. 1969, 17th Sch., para. 8). The exemption extends to such securities in the hands of a donee of a gift *inter vivos* made within seven years of the donor's death if still in the donee's ownership.

(xii) Damages or compensation moneys payable under the Fatal Accidents Acts 1846 and 1959, the Workmen's Compensation Acts, the Carriage by Air Act 1932, the National Insurance (Industrial Injuries) Act 1946, and the National Insurance Acts, and pensions under the Widows', Orphans' and Old Age Contributory Pensions Acts.

(xiii) Settled property in which the deceased's interest failed before it became an interest in possession; e.g., X. settled property on A. for life, with remainder to B. for life, with remainder to C.: if B. dies in A.'s lifetime, no Estate Duty is payable on B.'s death. However, if there is an unfettered right to the income with a contingent right to the capital, then the latter will not escape liability to Estate Duty.

(xiv) Property which was settled on the deceased for life and which reverts on his death to the settlor, in the latter's lifetime (F.A. 1896, § 15), provided that no other interest is created by the settlement, e.g.

   A. settled property on his mother for life with remainder to himself absolutely. On his mother's death in A.'s lifetime, no Estate Duty is payable. If, however, A. pre-deceased his mother, then on her death Estate Duty would be payable on the property reverting to A.'s estate, and duty would also be payable on the property in respect of A.'s death.

(xv) Premium Savings Bonds owned by persons who die domiciled in the Channel Isles, the Isle of Man or Northern Ireland are not treated for Estate Duty purposes as situate in Great Britain (Inland Revenue Press Notice, 2nd July, 1951).

(xvi) Interests enjoyed by virtue of an office or by a charity. In practice the property of Roman Catholic religious communities whose purposes are charitable is treated as trust property held for charitable purposes even where there is no enforceable trust, with the result that Estate Duty is not claimed on the death of one of the nominal owners of the property.

(xvii) Income tax post-war credits not encashed before the death (F.A. 1941, s. 7).

(xviii)Advowson (F.A. 1894, s. 15 (4).

(xix) The part of any trust property required to produce an annuity which represents reasonable remuneration for services rendered on the death of a trustee (see Inland Revenue Statement 5a, May 1971).

§ 4. Aggregation

To ascertain the rate at which Estate Duty is payable 'all property passing on the death' on which Estate Duty is leviable is to be aggregated, as if it formed one estate. Property is not to be aggregated more than once, nor is Estate Duty in respect thereof to be levied more than once, on the same death (F.A. 1894, s. 7 (10)).

There are, however, the following EXEMPTIONS FROM AGGREGATION:

(1) All property which is exempt from Estate Duty.

(2) Property in which the deceased NEVER had any interest (*ibid.* s. 4) and providing he died prior to 16th April, 1969; such property forms an estate by itself, and duty is charged on its principal value at the rate appropriate thereto. Where there is more than one such property, each is in practice treated as an estate by itself, except rights under nomination life policies which may have to be aggregated among themselves (see § 4 of Chapter IV). The general principle that property in which the deceased never had an interest is exempt does not apply for deaths on or after 16th April, 1969, except in respect of nomination policies (see below).

Property in which the deceased never had an interest, includes (*inter alia*):

(1) Annuities and other interest purchased or provided by the de-

ceased, to commence or come into existence on his death, and not charged on any property belonging to him.

(2) Rights under policies of insurance effected by the deceased before 20th March, 1968, on his own life, under the Married Women's Property Act 1882, for the benefit of his wife or children. This limited relief continues in respect of nomination policies, even though death occurs after 15th April, 1969 (s.40 (2)(c) F.A. 1969).

(3) Property passing under a contract approved by the Commissioners of Inland Revenue providing for the payment of an annuity to a surviving spouse or dependant under the retirement pensions' provisions allowed by the Finance Act 1956. Such property will, however, be aggregated with rights under nomination policies as in § 4 of Chapter IV (s. 35, F.A. 1956).

(4) Where the property passing on the death includes settled property as well as other property and the other property does not exceed a net value of £15,000, the other property is not to be aggregated with the settled property.

For this purpose, 'settled property' does not include any property included in a settlement made by the deceased himself, or made, directly or indirectly, at his expense or out of funds provided by him; nor does it include property of which he has been competent to dispose and has disposed by the exercise by will or otherwise of a power conferred by the settlement, or which devolves as assets for payment of his debts. Property which devolves upon the deceased life tenant from the settlement in which his life tenancy subsisted, by reason of the death of the reversioner, is treated as settled property notwithstanding that it is received into his estate, and is therefore tantamount to property of which he was competent to dispose (*Rivington* v. *I.R.E.* (1964)).

The 'other property' does not include property on which Estate Duty neither is payable on the death, nor would be if duty were payable on estates of however small a value, i.e. it excludes property which is exempt from duty for some reason other than that its value does not exceed £15,000.

(5) Timber (see § 9 of Chapter IV).

(6) When works of art, etc., exempted from Estate Duty while they are enjoyed in kind, are sold or taken abroad without

permission, Estate Duty on the proceeds (or value) is payable in respect of the last death on which the objects passed, at the rate appropriate to the principal value of the estate passing on that death. They are not, however, to be aggregated with other property in arriving at the principal value. Where the sale is to a national institution, see this Chapter, § 3 (viii) (F.A. 1930, s. 40; F.A. 1950, s. 48). The duty is assessed on the net proceeds, i.e. gross proceeds less expenses of the sale (*Tyser* v. *Attorney-General* [1938]).

(7) Settled property on which Estate Duty has been commuted during the deceased's lifetime (*Attorney-General* v. *Howe* [1925]), i.e. paid in advance by arrangement with the Estate Duty Office (see § 15, Chapter IV).

Subject to the above-mentioned exceptions, settled property is aggregated with the free and other aggregable property of a deceased tenant-for-life to find the rate of Estate Duty. The persons succeeding to the unsettled property may thus suffer at a very high rate owing to the aggregation, in spite of the fact that the deceased had no power of disposal over the capital of, the settled property, and possibly enjoyed the income from it for a short period only. Similarly, the person taking settled property may find it subject to a rate of Estate Duty considerably augmented by the aggregation with the deceased life tenant's free property, in spite of the fact that none of such free property goes with the settled property. To correct some anomalies, the relief in respect of duty on unsettled property was introduced.

Duty is not leviable more than once in respect of the same property in connection with the same death (F.A. 1894, s. 7 (10)). Accordingly, if A. had settled property on B. for life, with remainder to C. for life, with remainder to B. absolutely, on B.'s death the property passes as settled property, and the duty payable on the settlement covers B.'s reversionary interest.

§ 5. Rates of Estate Duty

In the case of persons dying on or after the 4th April, 1963, and before 16th April, 1969, the following are the rates of Estate Duty (F.A. 1949, s. 28 and the 7th Schedule as amended by F.A. 1963, s. 52).

Where the Principal Value of the Estate		General Scale		'Agricultural' and 'Business' Scale (see § 11 (a) and (g) below)	
Exceeds	and does not exceed	Rate % of E.D.	Margins	Rate % of E.D.	Margins
£	£		£ s. d.		£ s. d.
	5,000	Nil		Nil	
5,000	6,000	1	5,050 10 1	0·55	5,027 13 1
6,000	7,000	2	6,061 4 6	1·10	6,033 7 4
7,000	8,000	3	7,072 3 4	1·65	7,039 2 11
8,000	10,000	4	8,083 6 8	2·20	8,044 19 10
10,000	12,500	6	10,212 15 4	3·30	10,113 15 1
12,500	15,000	8	12,771 14 10	4·40	12,643 16 7
15,000	17,500	10	15,333 6 8	5·50	15,174 12 1
17,500	20,000	12	17,897 14 7	6·60	17,706 2 1
20,000	25,000	15	20,705 17 8	8·25	20,359 13 6
25,000	30,000	18	25,914 12 9	9·90	25,457 16 6
30,000	35,000	21	31,139 4 10	11·55	30,559 12 10
35,000	40,000	24	36,381 11 7	13·20	35,665 6 6
40,000	45,000	28	42,222 4 6	15·40	41,040 3 10
45,000	50,000	31	46,956 10 6	17·05	45,895 2 5
50,000	60,000	35	53,076 18 6	19·25	51,362 4 7
60,000	75,000	40	65,000 0 0	22·00	62,115 7 9
75,000	100,000	45	81,818 3 8	24·75	77,740 17 4
100,000	150,000	50	110,000 0 0	27·50	103,793 2 1
150,000	200,000	55	166,666 13 4	30·25	155,913 19 7
200,000	300,000	60	225,000 0 0	33·00	208,208 19 2
300,000	500,000	65	342,857 2 11	35·75	312,840 9 4
500,000	750,000	70	583,333 6 8	38·50	522,357 14 6
750,000	1,000,000	75	900,000 0 0	41·25	785,106 7 8
1,000,000		80	1,250,000 0 0	44·00	1,049,107 2 11

In the cases of the agricultural value of land and of land or premises and machinery or plant used in business, the rates are reduced by 45% of themselves as shown in the above tables (see §§ 7 and 10 of Chapter IV). The effect on marginal relief limits should be noted.

In the case of deaths on or after 22nd March, 1972, duty is levied on successive slices of the aggregate of net principal value of the estate.

Slice		Rate per cent.	Aggregate	Estate Duty on Aggregate
On the first	£15,000	Nil	£15,000	Nil
On the next	£5,000	25	£20,000	£1,250
,, ,, ,,	£20,000	30	£30,000	£4,250
,, ,, ,,	£10,000	35	£40,000	£7,750
,, ,, ,,	£40,000	40	£50,000	£11,750
,, ,, ,,	£10,000	45	£60,000	£16,250
,, ,, ,,	£20,000	50	£80,000	£26,250
,, ,, ,,	£20,000	55	£100,000	£37,250
,, ,, ,,	£50,000	60	£150,000	£67,250
,, ,, ,,	£50,000	65	£200,000	£99,750
,, ,, ,,	£300,000 .	70	£500,000	£309,750
Excess over	£500,000	75		

The scales of Estate Duty for deaths on or after 16th April, 1969 and before 22nd March, 1972 will be found in Appendix VI. The 'margins' indicated in the first table in this paragraph will no longer arise.

Where it is necessary to ascertain the duty applicable to a specified proportion of the estate, the estate rate will be found by expressing as a percentage the proportion which the total Estate Duty payable bears to the net principal value of the estate.

§ 6. Interest on Estate Duty

Interest is payable on the Estate Duty on PERSONALTY at 3 (accruing prior to 30th May, 1970, 2) per cent. per annum from the day after death to the date of delivery of the affidavit, and is recoverable as if it formed part of the duty (F.A. 1970 s.30). Income tax cannot be deducted from the interest. For Surtax purposes the amount of the interest can be grossed up as if it were a net sum after deduction of Income tax at the standard rate and treated as an annual charge.

Estate Duty on REALTY carries interest from the expiration of one year after the death. No discount is allowed for earlier payment. If the real estate is sold before the end of the year, interest becomes payable as from the date of the completion of the sale (F.A. 1894, § 6 (8)).

In the case of timber and works of art, etc., interest runs from the date of sale.

So far as the beneficiaries are concerned, interest on Estate Duty is a charge against income (*re Howe, Howe* v. *Kingscote* [1903]), but so far as the Revenue are concerned it is part of the duty, and therefore charged on the property.

§ 7. Marginal Relief

(*A*) *Marginal Relief in computing Estate Duty in connection with property passing on the death, which includes settled property and 'other property', slightly in excess of £15,000.*

Where the 'other property' (see § 4 of this Chapter), exceeds the sum of £15,000, it must be aggregated with the settled property so that the relevant scale rate of duty can be ascertained for the latter. However, there is a marginal relief, in that if the 'other property' is of a net value exceeding £15,000, the duty payable in respect of it is not to exceed the amount of the excess together with the duty which would have been so payable if the net value of the other property had been reduced rateably by the amount of the excess (but this is not to affect any marginal relief in the duty payable on the settled property).

In arriving at the above-mentioned £15,000, there must be included not only the deceased's free estate, but also all other property liable to Estate Duty on his death, exclusive of 'settled property' defined in § 4; e.g. the 'other property' must include: property over which he had and exercised a general power of appointment by his will or otherwise, *donationes mortis causa*, gifts *inter vivos* subject to duty, rights under policies on his life kept up by the deceased for the benefit of a donee, and other unsettled property (although, for the purpose of arriving at the rate payable, the property is treated as an estate by itself).

Illustrations

(1) Property passing on A.'s death:

(a) Free estate	£2,500
(b) Property settled by A. and liable as a gift *inter vivos* ..	7,000
	£9,500

(c) Property settled by A.'s deceased wife's will on A. for life	£20,000
(d) Property settled by A.'s mother on A. for life	£40,000

Since the sum of (a) and (b) does not exceed £10,000 and (c) is exempt from duty (being settled property which has borne duty on the death of one party to a marriage), the rate of duty if death was before 16th April, 1969 on (a) + (b) is 4 per cent and the rate of duty on (d) is 24 per cent. For deaths after that date, no duty is payable on the unsettled property and on (d) duty is £10,125.

Were it not for the exemption from aggregation, (a), (b) and (d) would be aggregable, so that duty would be payable on £49,500.

(2) Property passing on B's death after 21st March, 1972

(a) Free estate	£9,000
(b) Property settled by B. and liable as a gift *inter vivos* ..	6,100
	15,100
(c) Property settled by another person	20,000
	£35,100

Here the 'other property' exceeds £15,000 and is not therefore exempt from aggregation with the settled property. Were it not for marginal relief on the unsettled property, the duty would be $\frac{15,100}{35,100} \times £6,035 = £2,596$, but the duty on the other property, (*a*) and (*b*), is not to exceed:

On £10,000	..	..	..	..	..	—
Excess over £10,000	..	..	..	..	..	100
						£100

This will be split rateably between (*a*) and (*b*), viz. $\frac{9,000}{15,100} = £59$ to (*a*) and $\frac{6,100}{15,100} = £41$ to (*b*).

The duty on the settled property is:

On £35,000	..	..	..	..	..	£4,250
Excess over £30,000	..	..	..	..	..	1,785
						£6,035

$$\frac{20,000}{35,100} \times £6,035 \quad .. \qquad .. = \underline{£3,439}$$

It will be seen that where marginal relief is given on 'other property' it does not benefit or prejudice the duty on the settled property.

(3) Property passing on C.'s death:

(*a*) Free estate	..	..	..	..	..	£3,100
(*b*) Gift *inter vivos*	..	..	..	..	..	6,200
(*c*) Estate by itself (exempt from duty as being under £15,000)						1,050
(*d*) Settled property	..	..	..	..	..	34,050
						£44,400

Since the 'other property' exceeds £10,000 each item is deemed to be reduced by its proportion of the excess of £350, viz.:

					Reduced Amount £
(*a*) $\frac{3,100}{10,350} \times £350 = £105$	..	..	..	..	2,995
(*b*) $\frac{6,200}{10,350} \times £350 = £210$	..	..	..	..	5,990
					8,985
(*c*) $\frac{1,050}{10,350} \times £350 = £35$	..	..	..	..	1,015
£350					£10,000

(c) is exempt, so the duty payable on (a) and (b) is restricted to:

On £8,985	..	..	..	=	—
Excess over £10,000	..		..	=	350
					£350

This is borne rateably by (a) and (b), viz. £117 by (a) and £233 by (b).

Had (a) and (b) been aggregated with (d), the total would have been £43,350, attracting duty of £12,135. Duty on (a) and (b) would have been $\frac{9,300}{43,350} \times £12,135 = £2,603$. As it is, duty on (d) will be at

$\frac{34,050}{43,350} \times £12,135 = £9,531$ but (a) and (b) attract the marginal relief and bear only £350.

The margin where the settled property attracts duty at 80 per cent is no less than £48,000.

(4) Property passing on D.'s death prior to 16th April, 1969:

(a) Free estate	..	..	..	..	..	£6,240
(b) Gifts *inter vivos*	..	..	..	..	..	600
(c) Estate by itself	..	..	..	..	..	5,160
(d) Settled property	..	..	..	..	..	96,000

In this case the 'other property' exceeds £10,000 by £2,000, but includes non-aggregable property of £5,160. Only (a), (b) and (d) would therefore be aggregated, giving a total of £102,840, on which the rate of duty is 50 per cent. However, marginal relief is claimed under s. 13, F.A. 1914, thus the duty to be borne by (d) will be ascertained as follows:

Total duty chargeable on aggregated estate, i.e. (a), (b) and (d):

45% of £100,000	..	..	=	£45,000
Add: excess over £100,000	..	=		2,840
				£47,840

Proportion attributable to settled property:

$$\frac{£\ 96,000}{£102,840} \times £47,840 \quad .. \qquad .. \qquad = \qquad £44,658$$

The 'other property' is rateably reduced by its proportion of the excess of £2,000, viz.:

Reduction of (a)	$\frac{£\ 6,240}{£12,000} \times £2,000$	..	=	£1,040	=	£5,200
,, ,, (b)	$\frac{£\ 600}{£12,000} \times £2,000$	..	=	100	=	500
,, ,, (c)	$\frac{£\ 5,160}{£12,000} \times £2,000$	..	=	860	=	4,300
				£2,000		£10,000

The duty payable on (*a*), (*b*) and (*c*) is restricted to:

(*a*) 1% on £5,200	..	..	..	£52
(*b*) 1% on £500	..	..	..	5
(*c*) NIL being under £5,000	..	..		—
Excess over £10,000	..	..	..	2,000
		Total Duty		£2,057

This is instead of at the rate found by aggregating (*a*), (*b*) and (*d*), which would make the duty:

$$\text{on } (a) \; \frac{\text{£} \quad 6,240}{\text{£}\,102,840} \times \text{£}47,840 \quad = \quad \text{£}2,903$$

$$\text{on } (b) \; \frac{\text{£} \quad 600}{\text{£}\,102,840} \times \text{£}47,840 \quad = \quad 279$$

$$\text{on } (c) \; 1\% \text{ on £}5,160 \;\; .. \quad = \quad \underline{\quad 52}$$

$$\underline{\underline{\text{£}3,234}}$$

The Act gives no indication as to the manner in which the duty on the 'other property' is to be apportioned where different rates are involved. It is understood, however, that the official view is that in such a case the full amounts of the duty as shown above are to be rateably reduced to the 'ceiling', thus:

$$(a) \; \frac{2,057}{3,233\cdot4925} \times \text{£}2,902\cdot775 \quad = \quad \text{£}1,850$$

$$(b) \; \frac{2,057}{3,233\cdot4925} \times \text{£}279\cdot1175 \quad = \quad 174$$

$$(c) \; \frac{2,057}{3,233\cdot4925} \times \text{£}51\cdot6 \quad = \quad \underline{\quad 33}$$

$$\underline{\underline{\text{£}2,057}}$$

This reduces the duty in the same proportions as the values of the items.

In computing the 'duty' on the gifts for the purposes of the computation of the marginal relief, it will be noted that no reduction is made for the fact that the total duty borne by the gift *inter vivos* will be restricted to the excess of the original gift over £500, i.e. £100 (F.A. 1957, s. 38). This follows the wording of Section 38 (ii), *ibid.*, which states that such restriction is not to affect any reduction of duty on other property.

(B) Marginal Relief in computing Estate Duty where maximum of any one scale is slightly exceeded and the date of death is before 16th April, 1969

Where the net value of an estate for Estate Duty purposes exceeds by a small margin a step in the scale of duties, the estate would

be prejudiced but for the principle of MARGINAL RELIEF. By
this relief the amount of Estate Duty payable is, where necessary,
reduced so as not to exceed the highest amount of duty which
would be payable at the next lower rate, with the addition of the
excess of the value of the estate over the value on which the
highest amount of duty would be payable at the lower rate
(F.A. 1914, s. 13 (1)). As is shown in the Table on p. 86 the
margins are considerable in the higher ranges of rates.

Illustration (1)

In the case of an estate where the death occurred prior to 16th April, 1969,
amounting to exactly £40,000 for Estate Duty purposes, the Estate Duty at
24 per cent would be £9,600.

In the case of an estate amounting to £40,001, the Estate Duty would be
£9,601, since, although estates exceeding in value £40,000 but not exceeding
£45,000 are subject to Estate Duty at the rate of 28 per cent, the amount
payable must not exceed 24 per cent on the maximum amount subject to
that rate, viz. £40,000, plus the amount by which the estate exceeds that
sum, viz. £1. But for the principle of marginal relief, the duty would have
been £11,200.

After the turning point is reached the higher rate of duty is more
advantageous. Thus, where the estate exceeds £40,000, but does not exceed
£42,222, relief is obtained in every case, but immediately the estate exceeds
that amount, it is more advantageous to pay the higher rate of duty, viz. 28
per cent.

Where it is necessary to compute Estate Duty in respect of
several aggregated properties, and marginal relief applies to the
aggregated estate, the total duty thus found is apportioned
between the several units making up the aggregate.

Illustration (2)

An estate consists of £20,200 personalty and £10,100 realty.
Applying marginal relief the total duty payable is:

18% on £30,000	..	..	..	..	£5,400
Add: 'Margin'	..	..	..	..	300

Total Duty	£5,700

This duty is apportioned as to:

$\frac{20,200}{30,300}$ of £5,700 = £3,800 to personalty.

and

$\frac{10,100}{30,300}$ of £5,700 = £1,900 to realty.

But for marginal relief the duty payable would have been 21 per cent on
£30,300, i.e., £6,363.

§ 8. Responsibility for the Payment of Estate Duty and the Incidence of Estate Duty

(a) Responsibility for payment of Estate Duty

The Estate Duty on personalty is due on the delivery of the Inland Revenue affidavit or six months from the death, whichever date is earlier (F.A. 1894, s. 6).

Estate Duty on realty is due twelve months from the death or on previous sale of the property (*ibid.* § 6).

The account is delivered to the Estate Duty Office, and after formal assessment of the duty, payment may be made personally at the Accountant-General's Office, or may be sent there by cheque payable to the 'Commissioners of Inland Revenue, Death Duties, *re* .... deceased, or Bearer', and crossed 'Bank of England – Inland Revenue'. A money order may be obtained free of commission and sent similarly drawn and crossed. A cheque for the estimated amount of the duty and interest may be sent with the Estate Duty Affidavit to the Estate Duty Office.

Where the Commissioners are satisfied that Estate Duty cannot without excessive sacrifice be raised at once, they may allow payment to be postponed for such period, to such extent, and on payment of such interest, not exceeding 4 per cent, or any higher interest yielded by the property, and on such terms, as they think fit (F.A. 1894, s. 8 (9)). The Commissioners are also empowered to stamp the affidavit on credit, if satisfied that the applicant has no funds of his own or of the deceased to pay the duty; they then retain the grant until the duty and interest are paid, but the Solicitor of Inland Revenue will produce the grant in evidence at the cost of the executor or administrator (Stamp Act 1815, ss. 45-49; Customs and Inland Revenue Act 1881, s. 26 (3); F.A. 1894, ss. 6 (1), 8 (1)). The exercise of these powers is exceptional. Normally, an advance can be obtained from bankers to meet the duty. The duty can be paid out of a Post Office Savings Bank account in the name of the deceased. The deposit book and a covering letter should accompany the Estate Duty Affidavit.

Deferment of payment under the F.A. 1894, s. 6, (3), is in practice allowed in respect of unascertained compensation for loss of medical goodwill, also for duty on property overseas which is frozen by currency restrictions or other overseas legislation, until receipt of the asset.

An executor is accountable for the Estate Duty in respect of:

(*a*) all personal property wherever situated, on immovable property situated abroad if the deceased was competent to dispose at his death (F.A. 1894, ss. 6 and 8; F.A. 1962, s. 28). (See § 14 of Chapter IV);

(*b*) all land in England and Wales, including settled land, which may devolve upon him by virtue of any statute or otherwise (L.P.A. 1925, s. 16).

In the case of real property devolving on the executor, he is accountable for the duty, and if he assents to the property vesting in a beneficiary, that beneficiary becomes jointly accountable with him. Where the executor is not accountable for the Estate Duty in respect of land in England and Wales, e.g. land over which the deceased had no control, but which passes on his death, the estate owner (other than a purchaser who acquires a legal estate after the charge for death duties has attached and free from such charge) is accountable (L.P.A. 1925, s. 16 (2)).

He may also pay the duty in respect of other property passing at the death which by virtue of any testamentary dispostion of the deceased is under his control; or in respect of property not under his control, if the persons accountable request him to make the payment (F.A. 1894, s. 6 (2)). Where the executor, although not responsible for the payment of Estate Duty on certain property, nevertheless pays such duty, he may recover what he pays from the donees or trustees of the property, or he may by sale or mortgage raise the amount paid by him out of the property. Though the executor will not pay the Estate Duty on property of which the deceased was not competent to dispose, such as gifts *inter vivos* made within seven years before the death, or *donationes mortis causa*, he must include such property in his Estate Duty Affidavit, showing who has taken it, and the party liable will pay the Estate Duty on an account.

If property is subject to a limited (special) power of appointment, the deceased life tenant is not deemed competent to dispose of it (unless he himself was one of the objects of the power), and consequently the executor is only responsible for disclosure of the property in his affidavit, unless, in default of appointment, the remainder vests in the deceased, in which case it will form part of the free estate.

The executor is not liable for any Estate Duty in excess of the assets (including land) which he has received as executor, or might, but for his own neglect or default, have received (F.A. 1894, s. 8 (3); L.P.A. 1925, s. 16 (6); Land Registration Act 1925, s. 73 (14)).

Where the executor is not accountable, the person to whom any property passes as a beneficial interest in possession is accountable for the duty on that property. Likewise, to the extent of the property actually received or disposed of by him, every trustee, guardian, committee or other person in whom any interest in the property so passing, or the management thereof, is at any time vested, and every person in whom the property is vested in possession, is accountable for the Estate Duty on the property. The accountable person must deliver to the Commissioners and verify an account, to the best of his knowledge and belief, of the property (F.A. 1894, s. 8 (4)). A person is not accountable for duty if he acts merely as agent or bailiff for another person in the management of property.

As a result of the passing of the Trustee Investments Act 1961, it is understood the Commissioners of Inland Revenue have instructed the Estate Duty Office that where a certificate of the prospective amount of the duty has been issued under Section 44 (3) of the Finance Act 1950, or Section 28 (7) of the Finance Act 1958, and the amount is invested in a manner authorised by Section 1 of the Trustee Investments Act 1961, the liability of the trustees will be limited to the amount certified or to the sum realised on the sale of the investments, whichever is less, provided that the provisions of the Act have been complied with regarding advice and restricting wider-range investment.

Where under the former practice the amount certified has already been invested in securities issued by the British Government or authorised by statute for the investment of trust funds, the liability of the trustees will be similarly limited whether they retain those securities or re-invest in accordance with the Act as indicated above.

In the case of property transferred to a controlled company being deemed to pass on a death for Estate Duty purposes under s. 46, Finance Act 1940, the company is accountable for the duty (F.A. 1940, s. 54).

Where the proceeds of sale of objects of national, etc., interest become chargeable with Estate Duty, the person by whom or for whose benefit the objects were sold is accountable for the duty (F.A. 1930, s. 40 (2)) unless they were bequeathed 'free of duty' when the duty is payable out of residue (*Re Bedford, Russell* v. *Bedford* [1960]). (See § 9 of Chapter IV as to timber.)

A *bona fide* purchaser for valuable consideration without notice is not liable to or accountable for duty (F.A. 1894, s. 8 (18)). In the case of land (not registered land – see Land Registration Act 1925, s. 73) passing on a death, a purchaser acquiring a legal estate takes free from any charge of death duties except where a charge in respect thereof has been registered as a land charge (L.P.A. 1925, s. 17 (1)).

Any person against whom a claim has been made by the Crown for death duties or who has reasonable grounds for apprehending that such a claim may be made against him, may apply in a summary manner to the High Court to have it determined whether he is accountable for or chargeable with, or is or may thereafter become liable to pay those duties, and, if so, to have the extent of his liability determined (Administration of Justice (Miscellaneous Provisions) Act 1933, s. 3).

Where a full and true account, containing all the material facts, for the ascertainment of the rate and amount of duty, has been settled, no person is liable for the payment of any death duties after the expiration of six years from the date of such settlement of account (F.A. 1894, s. 8 (2)). The Commissioners are empowered to remit all or any duty or interest remaining unpaid after the expiration of twenty years from a death on which the duty became payable (F.A. 1894, s. 8 (11); F.A. 1907, s. 13).

A person accountable for Estate Duty can apply to the Estate Duty Office for a certificate of discharge under the Finance Act 1894, s. 11 (2) (as amended by F.A. 1907, s. 14) if he has delivered a full statement to the best of his knowledge and belief of all property passing on the death of the deceased and all persons entitled thereto; and, on payment of the duty at that rate, the property in question and the applicant (so far as regards that property) are discharged from any further claim for Estate Duty, a certificate to that effect being issued. In order to afford the maximum protection, all accountable persons should join in the application. It must be remembered that the advertisement under the Trustee Act 1925, s. 27 (see Chapter XIII, § 3) does not afford complete protection.

In practice, if a clearance certificate is received in which the only qualification is 'on the facts at present before the office', the Inland Revenue have informed the Law Society that it may be assumed that the values returned in the Inland Revenue Affidavit for assets which have not a determined market value at the date of death have been accepted and will not subsequently be questioned. A certificate of discharge will not be issued unless all values have been accepted and such certificates can be applied for and will be issued even where the value of the estate is such that no Estate Duty will be payable (*Law Society Gazette*, Vol. 56, No. 7, July, 1959, p. 479). There is a restriction on re-opening cases on the ground of legal mistake. If duty was originally paid and accepted as the right amount, any duty found to be payable or repayable later must be calculated on the same view of the law (F.A. 1951, s. 35).

The provisions referred to in this book, for the payment of Estate Duty to the British Exchequer, apply only to Great Britain (i.e. England, Wales and Scotland). They do not apply to Northern Ireland, the Republic of Ireland, the Channel Islands or the Isle of Man.

The duty in respect of unincorporated businesses and duty payable in respect of shares valued under Section 55, Finance Act 1940, may be payable, if so required by the executors, by eight equal yearly instalments or sixteen half-yearly instalments. The same spread may also be claimed in respect of Estate Duty on leasehold property. If the executors can show that undue hardship will be suffered if the duty is payable immediately on unquoted shares (valued other than under Section 55) is not deferred, they may with the agreement of the Commissioners of Inland Revenue, pay the duty by eight yearly or sixteen half yearly instalments. Interest will be payable on unpaid sums due.

(b) Duty on Real Estate

The person delivering the account may elect to pay the duty due on real property by eight equal yearly instalments, or sixteen half-yearly instalments, with interest at the rate of 3* per cent. per annum from the date at which the first instalment is due,

*The rate was 2 per cent for interest on unpaid Estate Duty accruing before 30th May, 1970.

without deduction of Income tax. The first instalment is due on the first anniversary of the death. The balance of the duty can be paid, with interest to date, at any time. If the property devolves on another death, the duty can continue to be paid by instalments. If the estate is sold, the duty for the time being unpaid must be paid on completion of the sale (F.A. 1894, s. 6 (8)).

A personal representative may, as a condition of giving an assent or making a conveyance, require security for the discharge of the Estate Duty, but is not entitled to postpone the giving of an assent merely because of the subsistence of any such duties if reasonable arrangements have been made for discharging them. But an assent or conveyance does not, except in favour of a purchaser of a legal estate, prejudice the right of the personal representative or any other person to recover the estate or interest to which the assent or conveyance relates, or to be indemnified thereout against any duties, debt, etc., to which it is subject (A.E.A. 1925, s. 36). The personal representative, on payment of the duty, can obtain a certificate from the Commissioners of the duty paid; this certificate is conclusive evidence that the duty is a first charge on the property after debts and encumbrances allowed in assessing the duty. In the case of real property, the duty may be paid to a personal representative (with interest) by the trustees or owners of the land, by the same instalments as might have been paid to the Revenue (F.A. 1894, s. 9).

The Commissioners may, if they think fit, on the application of any person liable, accept real or leasehold property in satisfaction of the duty payable. The conveyance to the Commissioners will be exempt from stamp duty (F. (1909-10) A. 1910, s. 56; F.A. 1946, s. 51).

§ 9. The Incidence of Estate Duty

Estate Duty on personalty passing to the executor as such is payable out of the residue. Although the personal representative is held accountable for all death duty on land, including settled land, which may devolve upon him in his representative capacity, this does not disturb the liability of persons beneficially interested in the land in respect of the duty (L.P.A. 1925, s. 16). In consequence, realty bears its own estate duty (*Re Morris, Skinner* v. *Sanders* [1927]). The duty is a first charge on the property (after allowing for the incumbrances) included in the assessment. If a beneficiary is given and exercises an option under the will to take realty as part of his share of residue, he must bear the duty thereon (*Re Jolley, Neal* v. *Jolley* [1901]), but if the executors simply appropriate realty on account of a share of residue, the duty is payable out of residue generally. A person who exercises an option given by will, to buy real property, takes it as a purchaser and is not liable for the duty (*Re Fison's Will Trusts, Fison* v. *Fison* [1950]). Legacies payable out of real property bear their proportion of the Estate Duty on realty, and if a mixed fund of real and residuary personal estate is created by will with a direction that duties and legacies shall be paid out of the proceeds indiscriminately, then so far as it appears that legacies have been paid out of proceeds of real estate they must bear their own proportion of the Estate Duty on realty (*Re Spencer Cooper; Poe* v. *Spencer Cooper* [1908]; *Re Owers; Public Trustee* v. *Death* [1941]).

Upon property not passing to the executor as such, the rateable part of the Estate Duty attaches as a first charge, except as against a *bona fide* purchaser for valuable consideration without notice. An exception is made, however, by the Finance Act 1894, s. 20 (2), which provides that nothing in the Act shall create a charge on any property situate in a British possession while so situate.

Property not passing to the executor as such includes (1) free realty, (2) property outside Great Britain, (3) property over which the deceased exercised a general power of appointment, (4) entailed property, (5) gifts *inter vivos*, including gifts of rights under policies kept up by the deceased for the benefit of donees, (6) *donationes mortis causa*, (7) property passing under settlements created otherwise than by the will or intestacy of the deceased, (8) joint property passing by survivorship, and (9) property passing under a nomination by the deceased (e.g. under the Post Office or Trustee Savings Banks Regulations). All these must bear their own duty. But in the case of personal property outside Great Britain or other personal property of which the deceased was competent to dispose, the executor must pay the duty, even if it absorbs all the estate in this country. Property subject to a general power of appointment, even where the deceased has exercised the power by his will, does not pass to the executor *as such*, and the duty thereon is a charge on the property itself and is not payable out of residue (*O'Grady* v. *Wilmot* [1916]). In the case of a partial intestacy, the Estate Duty is payable primarily out of property undisposed of by the will, and only out of residue in so far as the property undisposed of is insufficient.

A person authorised or required to pay the Estate Duty in respect of any property has power to raise the amount by the sale or mortgage of or on a terminable charge on that property or any part of it (F.A. 1894, s. 9 (5)).

Any person with power to sell any property in order to raise Estate Duty, may agree with the Commissioners of Inland Revenue for the property to be accepted in payment of the duty in pursuance of any enactment authorising its acceptance by the Commissioners; the transaction will be regarded as a sale (F.A. 1958, s. 32).

The Postmaster General will allow encashment of Premium Bonds before probate for the purpose of paying Estate Duty (Parliamentary answer 3-12-59).

In certain cases, the Commissioners may compound or commute the duty, e.g. where by reason of the number of deaths on which the property has passed, or of the complicated nature of the interests of different persons, or from some other cause, it is difficult to ascertain the exact amount of duties (F.A. 1894, s. 13); or on an interest in expectancy after the executor's right of election to commute has not been exercised (*ibid.* s. 12).

The Commissioners are authorised to accept land (F. (1909-10) A., 1910 s. 56; F.A. 1946, s. 49) or 4% Funding Loan (valued at 80%) or 4% Victory Bonds (at par) (see § 11 *post*) or any work of art which the Treasury are satisfied is pre-eminent for its aesthetic merit or historical value (F.A. 1956, s. 34), in satisfaction of Estate Duty. Differences of opinion between the executors and the Treasury as to the value of works of art accepted in satisfaction of Estate Duty may be referred to an independent panel set up by the Chancellor of the Exchequer. In determining the prices offered for articles which are exempt from duty until sold the policy of the Treasury and the Ministry of Works is to deduct from the full value 75 per cent of the value of the exemption from duty (i.e. of the duty which would be payable on an ordinary sale). Where certain buildings are accepted in payment of duty, the Commissioners may accept in (part) payment of Estate Duty objects kept in the buildings which the Treasury regard as desirable to remain there. The buildings in question are those accepted in payment of duty, or belonging to Her Majesty or to a Government Department, or a building of which the Minister of Works is guardian under the Ancient Monuments Consolidation and Amendment Act 1913, or one vested in the National Trust. Such acceptance is exempt from stamp duty and will not be regarded as a sale depriving the objects of any exemption which might apply to works of art, etc. (F.A. 1953, s. 30).

§ 10. Disclosure

The executor of the deceased is, to the best of his knowledge and belief, to specify in appropriate accounts annexed to the Inland Revenue Affidavit all the property in respect of which Estate Duty is payable upon the death of the deceased, whether he is or is not accountable for the duty thereon. Where the executor does not know the amount or value of any property which has passed on the death, he may state in the Inland Revenue Affidavit that such property exists, but that he does not know the amount and value thereof, and that he undertakes, as soon as the amount and value are ascertained, to bring in an account thereof, and to pay both the duty for which he is or may be liable, and any further duty payable by reason thereof.

Estate Duty, so far as not paid by the executor, is collected upon an account setting forth the particulars of the property. It is to be delivered to the Commissioners of Inland Revenue within six months after the death, by the person accountable for the duty. The Commissioners may call upon any person accountable for Estate Duty to deliver verified particulars to them. Every person thought to have taken possession of or administered property liable to Estate Duty may be asked for similar details. The penalty for non-compliance is £100, or double the amount of Estate Duty unpaid, as the Commissioners elect (F.A. 1894, s. 8).

For this purpose, the term 'executor' includes not only a duly authorised executor or administrator, but also an executor *de son tort* (F.A. 1894, s. 22 (1) (*d*)). A person who takes possession of or in any way administers any part of the personal estate of a deceased person, without obtaining probate or letters of administration within six months from the death (or two months from the termination of any suit respecting the will or grant) is also liable, either:

(*a*) to deliver an account of the estate and pay such duty as would have been payable if a grant had been obtained (Crown Suits, etc., Act 1865, s. 57);

(*b*) to pay the duty with a penalty of £100 plus 10 per cent on the amount of the duty (Stamp Act 1815, s. 37); or

(*c*) to pay double the amount of the duty (Customs and Inland Revenue Act 1881, s. 40).

An executor *de son tort* who is not entitled to take out a grant, must therefore see that the Estate Duty is paid, to avoid incurring penalties. If he is entitled to take out a grant he must, of course, pay the Estate Duty before he can obtain the grant. Any representative who fails to take out a grant is also liable to the penalties if he does not pay the Estate Duty.

§ 11. Government Securities in satisfaction of Estate Duty

The duty (including interest) may be paid by the surrender of 4% Victory Bonds at par, and/or 4% Funding Loan, 1960-90 (issued at 80) at 80; plus, in either case, the gross interest accrued on the stock since the date of the last interest payment. If, however, the stock is quoted *ex div.* at the date of surrender, from the amount so arrived at must be deducted the full (i.e. gross) amount of the interest receivable by the estate. It is a condition that the securities must have been held by the deceased for at least six months prior to his death (F.A. 1917, s. 34).

Where the securities form part of the assets of a partnership, they may be tendered to an extent equivalent to the ratio that the share of the deceased bears to the aggregate partnership capital (as determined for the purpose of death duties). The securities must likewise have been held continuously by the partnership for a period of not less than six months preceding the death of the partner concerned.

Funding Loan Stock or Bonds will not be accepted to a value, including the appropriate interest, in excess of the duty payable, but arrangements will be made by the Commissioners of Inland Revenue under which Victory Bonds in excess of the duty payable (e.g. bonds of large denomination) may be exchanged for Victory Bonds of smaller denomination. Stock or Registered Bonds will only be accepted, as regards capital, in amounts of £5, or multiples of £5. Bonds to Bearer must have all coupons not yet due attached.

It must be noted that all securities must be brought into the Estate Duty Account at the market values ruling at the date of the death, irrespective of the basis upon which they may be surrendered in payment of such duty.

If, at the request of the trustees of settled property, the executor has paid the Estate Duty thereon, he is entitled to be refunded the full amount of the duty, notwithstanding that he has used Victory Bonds belonging to the free estate for settling the duty and has thus obtained more than their market value for the bonds (*Re Ticehurst's Settlement, Wyatt* v. *Ticehurst* [1930]).

When Victory Bonds are surrendered in payment of Estate Duty at their face value with the addition of accrued interest, the personal representatives are not assessable to income tax in respect of such accrued interest (*Monks* v. *Fox's Exors.* [1928]). This decision would also apply in the case of 4% Funding Loan.

Illustration

A. died on 31st May, 1970. The Estate Duty payable amounted to £4,560, and was paid sixty days later. His estate included £4,000 Victory Bonds, then quoted ex dividend, which were surrendered in part payment of the duty. Calculations to nearest £.

					£
The duty is therefore satisfied as follows:					
Estate Duty ..,	..	..	..	..	4,560
Interest at 3% for 60 days	..	..	..		23
					———
Total	..	..	..	..	£4,583
					═══

				£
£4,000 Victory Bonds at par	..	..	..	£4,000
Interest accrued from 2nd September to 11th February inclusive, 163 days, $\frac{163}{181}$ of £80 (gross)			..	72
				———
				4,072
Deduct: 6 months interest (gross) (because of transfer *ex div.*)	..	..	..	80
				———
Total value at which the bonds are accepted		..		3,992
Cash	..	..	..	..	591
				———
				£4,583
				═══

§ 12. Deductions for Estate Duty purposes

In calculating the amount on which Estate Duty has to be paid, deduction may be made for reasonable funeral expenses, and for certain debts and incumbrances (F.A. 1894, s. 7). No allowance is to be made for debts incurred or incumbrances created by the deceased unless they were incurred or created *bona fide* for FULL CONSIDERATION in money or money's worth wholly for his own use and benefit, and take effect out of his interest. Since death terminates employment, any redundancy pay due at death is a deductible debt. Dismissal must occur within eight weeks of death; if this is not within that period, the personal representatives will be deemed to have re-employed the employee and redundancy pay will not be payable. No deduction is allowed in respect of gaming debts, debts of honour, or other debts not enforceable at law. Since an executor is not bound to plead the Limitation Act, however, debts which would be enforceable but for that Statute can be deducted if they are actually paid in the course of administration. Nor is any allowance made for any debt with regard to which there exists a right of indemnity or reimbursement against some other estate or person unless that right proves abortive. A debt or incumbrance cannot be deducted more than once, e.g. where it is charged on several portions of the estate (F.A. 1894, s. 7). Incumbrances, including mortgages and terminable charges, can be deducted from the value of the property liable thereto.

If the deceased had contracted to pay an annuity and had received adequate consideration, the capital value may be deducted; but if the agreement was voluntary, no deduction is allowable (*H.M. Advocate* v. *Alexander's Trustees* [1905]). Moreover, no deduction can be made in respect of a voluntary bond undertaken by the deceased to pay money to a charity (*H.M. Advocate* v. *Gunning's Trustees* [1902]). No deduction is allowable for a debt or incumbrance for which the consideration was derived from the deceased as laid down in Finance Act 1939, s. 31.

Liabilities due at future dates, e.g. on bills of exchange, should be discounted. In the case of servants' wages and tenancy agreements, there can be deducted the minimum cost to the estate of terminating the deceased's liability. The full amount of local rates for the period in which the deceased died, is deductible unless the death occurred before the rate was made or payable.

Income tax and Capital Gains tax payable is deductible. Under Schedule B, the assessment is apportionable on a day-to-day basis; other assessments must be calculated on the basis of the cessation of the source,* and the Income tax payable computed, having regard to the deceased's allowances and reliefs. Any Income tax paid in advance (e.g. on the apportioned part of the assessment under Schedule B falling after death), must be brought in as an asset along with any Income tax recoverable. The position may not be the same in respect of Capital Gains tax, but see Chapter V. Surtax is calculated on the statutory total income for the year of death, at the rates for that or the previous year, whichever are lower. Any arrears are proper deductions, e.g. additional assessments for the penultimate year and Surtax not yet paid for the year prior to death. In the case of the death of a married woman who was at the time of her death living with her husband, Income tax (including Surtax) can be deducted from her estate if they were separately assessed, or if her husband exercises his right, under the Income and Corporation Taxes Act 1970, s. 41, to disclaim liability for tax in respect of her income.

Debts due to persons not resident in Great Britain can only be deducted from the value of any property of the deceased situated outside Great Britain, on which Estate Duty has been paid, unless they have been contracted to be paid in Great Britain, or are charged on property situated here. If the property of the deceased situated outside Great Britain is shown to be insufficient for the payment of debts due to persons not resident here, a repayment of Estate Duty can be claimed (F.A. 1894, s. 7 (2)). Any foreign duty payable is allowed as a credit against the Estate Duty payable on that foreign property in this country, unless there is an agreement for the avoidance of double death duties. (F.A. 1962, s. 29).

In practice, where the death terminates a settlement, any withdrawal fee payable to the Public Trustee or any other trust

---

* If a deceased trader's business is carried on by his widow, the cessation provisions are only applied in practice if claimed; but losses and capital allowances cannot be carried forward from before the death against subsequent income.

corporation in respect of the trusteeship may be deducted from the value of the settled property as an incumbrance.

Whether or not the funeral expenses are reasonable depends on the position of the deceased and the amount of his estate. Funeral expenses do not, for Estate Duty purposes, include the expense of bringing the body from abroad, though in practice, where the deceased died abroad or away from his family burying place, reasonable expenditure in embalming and transporting the body is usually allowed. No deduction is allowed for the cost of a tomb or monument, or of putting the family or servants into mourning (*Goldstein* v. *Salvation Army Assurance Society* [1917]), although a small amount for mourning *may* be allowed in practice if the deceased was the head of the household and the cost came out of his estate. A death grant under the National Insurance Act is not liable to Estate Duty and does not have to be deducted from the funeral expenses. Funeral expenses of a married woman are payable out of her separate estate and are not recoverable from her husband (*Rees* v. *Hughes* [1946]). The position where the wife leaves no estate is not clear; it may be that the husband is liable under common law, but that has not been decided.

No deduction is allowed in respect of testamentary expenses, Estate Duty, executorship or administration expenses, legacies or devises, since these are not liabilities at the date of death.

CHAPTER IV

VALUATION OF PROPERTY FOR
ESTATE DUTY PURPOSES

§ 1. Introduction

Having determined the assets which pass on death and, there-
fore, require valuation, the next stage in computing the Estate
Duty liability is to value each asset. The provisions of the Finance
Act 1894 require the value shall be the principal value.

The principal value for the purposes of valuing property at
death is defined in Section 7 (5), Finance Act 1894, as 'the price
which, in the opinion of the Commissioners, such property
would fetch if sold in the open market at the time of the death
of the deceased'. It is necessary to assume that the sale could be
effected on the date of death, that all preliminary arrangements
had been made and the sale was subject to such conditions as
might reasonably be calculated to obtain for the vendor the
best price for the property. Since this sale is to be made on the
open market the Act requires the assumption that the property
is offered under conditions enabling every person desirous of
purchasing to come in and make an offer. It, therefore, presup-
poses that proper steps have been taken to advertise the property and let all likely purchasers know that the property is for
sale (*C.I.R.* v. *Clay*, *C.I.R.* v. *Buchanan*). Obviously, it must be
assumed that the transaction takes place between a willing seller
and a willing purchaser so that the vendor must be assumed to
be inclined to sell and the purchaser must not be under an urgent
necessity to buy. Nevertheless, in view of the requirement that
the property shall be valued on the basis of a sale in the open
market, the possibility of a person desirous of acquiring the
property at a substantially higher price than others may be
willing to pay must not be ruled out. The price obtainable from
such a buyer will be the value for Estate Duty.

In determining the market value the executors must not assume that it is necessarily the price at which the property could
be sold to a single purchaser. If the property would yield a
greater sum on a division of that property into lots, it is to be

assumed that a division into lots was made (*Buccleuch* (*Duke*) v. *C.I.R.*). Since the valuation is to be made at the date of death variations arising by reason of subsequent events are to be ignored. It has been decided that the words 'at the time of death' mean immediately after death. This was the decision in the House of Lords in *Commissioners of Inland Revenue* v. *Graham's Trustees*, a case dealing with the valuation of land occupied by a partnership and owned by one of the partners. Clearly if a sale at arm's length takes place shortly after death this will usually be the value as at death. If either the Revenue or the Executors claim that this value is not the value at the date of death it will be necessary for them to demonstrate why the price at the date of death should be different.

This basis of valuation applies to all property listed in this chapter except where a different basis is specifically provided. No allowance is made for the costs of sale in estimating the market value. If the death of the deceased caused the value of the property to depreciate, such depreciation may be taken into account F. (1909-10) A. 1910, s. 60 (2)).

Thus in making any valuation of assets it is necessary to take into account the following factors:

(1) a hypothetical sale at the time of the death of the deceased,
(2) the price which the properties would fetch on this hypothetical sale,
(3) the hypothetical sale must be made on the open market,
(4) it is to be assumed that all preliminary arrangements for the sale had been made prior to the time of death so that the sale takes place at the time of death.

In an adjournment debate in May 1965 the question was raised that the District Valuer, using the above basis, suggested that in the case of a property which was a house it should be valued on the basis that it would form an excellent site for a small block of flats. This gave a higher value and since the house remained in the possession of the deceased's widow the balance of the estate would naturally be reduced by the additional duty. Clearly every such case must be decided on its own facts but it is suggested that so far as possible the valuation should be made on the basis of the property as it exists at the date of death. In any case if there is to be a change in use a deduction should be allowed for the betterment levy which would have been payable.

The basis of the valuation of individual assets is set out in the following paragraphs.

§ 2. Stocks and Shares

Stocks and shares should be valued and included in the Estate Duty Account on the basis of published quotations, or, if unavailable, on the basis of brokers' certificates or letters from the secretaries of the companies showing the market price at the date of death. Where there is a published quotation, one quarter of the difference between the official closing prices is added to the lower quoted price; e.g. where the closing prices were 98-100, the price for Estate Duty purposes is taken to be $98\frac{1}{2}$. Where the death occurred on a Sunday or other day for which no prices are available, the price for the day before or day following should be taken, whichever is the more beneficial to the estate. Where bargains are recorded, the valuation may be based on them instead of on the quotation; the price to be taken being midway between the lowest and highest prices. If there is only one bargain the price of that bargain applies. In the case of unit trusts, the valuation of the 'units' will be based on the manager's buying prices.

Dividends and interest declared and accrued due to the date of death must be included in the Estate Duty Account; but it should be noted that if the market price is cum dividend (cum div.) this price includes the dividend or interest accrued to the date of death, and consequently no further sum need be included in respect thereof. If quoted ex dividend, the shares must be valued as above and then the FULL AMOUNT of the next dividend received must be aggregated with such value. Where $3\frac{1}{2}\%$ War Loan and similar stocks, in respect of which income tax is not deductible at source from the interest paid thereon, are quoted ex dividend (ex div.), it is the practice of the Estate Duty office to allow income tax to be deducted from the amount of the next interest payment, whether the stock is held in registered, inscribed or bearer form.

Certain stocks such as short-dated gilt-edged stocks are quoted excluding the accrued interest, which must be added to arrive at the cum div. value.

Where National Development Bonds are held by the deceased and the latter has been owner for a period in excess of six months they are subject to redemption at par, upon one month's notice being given, together with any accrued interest. Where they are held for less than six months no interest is allowed so that any received by the deceased must be deducted from the par value.

In the case of Defence Bonds, the value is the amount of cash that would have been received if demanded on the date of death, i.e. the par value plus any premium then payable, plus accrued interest, less interest for the period of notice (usually six months, as in the case of the 5 per cent. Bonds) that must be given if such a deduction is a condition of immediate encashment. The fact that no deduction of interest for the normal period of notice is required if the encashment is for the purpose of winding-up the deceased's estate is now ignored.

Where securities have been valued according to the official list of a provincial stock exchange a copy of that list should be attached, but where there is no official market quotation, the estimate of the principal value should be supported by other published quotations, or brokers' certificates, or letters from the secretaries of the companies. Any such certificate or letter should show either the date, price and amount of recent sales in the open market, or particulars of the last three years' dividends and of the amounts carried forward in those years, as well as the basis of the valuation. If there have been no such recent sales, the date, price and amount of the last sale in the open market should be given.

Where a bonus has been distributed, the facts should also be stated.

An 'open market' valuation is essential, even if, in fact the shares are not freely marketable or subject to restrictions on transfers as will be the case with unquoted shares.

When submiting the Estate Duty Affidavit, a certificate from the Company's secretary or auditors should be attached stating the value or an estimated figure should be inserted with the note that a revised valuation will be submitted. The Share Valuation division have a standard form which they send to executors requesting details of the type of business conducted, copies of the accounts and directors' reports for the three periods of account immediately preceding death, details of dividends paid in the period and details of recent transactions in the company's shares. When replying to this questionairre it is advisable to submit details of the value of the shares indicating the basis of and reasons for the valuation.

If shares are held subject to restrictions on transfer imposed by the Articles of Association, including a right of pre-emption in favour of existing holders of shares, the valuation for Estate Duty purposes is not necessarily the price fixed by the Articles at which they would have to be sold to any existing holder under the pre-emption clause, but is to be estimated at the price which they would fetch if sold in the open market on the terms that the purchaser would be entitled to be registered as holder of the shares and should take them subject to the Articles. A price arrived at because of a special demand for a particular purpose from a particular buyer is not the open market value, though it may affect it (*C.I.R.* v. *Crossman & Mann.*) The effect of restrictions in the Articles is only taken into account as a factor in arriving at the price which a purchaser would pay to ensure being registered as the holder of the shares, so as to stand in the shoes of the deceased and to hold the shares subject to those restrictions (*Salvesen's Trustees* v. *C.I.R.*)

An allowance should be made in valuing the shares for any loss which can reasonably be expected to accrue from the cessation of the deceased's services and personal prestige, i.e. the valuation must be made on the footing that he is already dead; death causes the property to pass, and the cause precedes the effect (*Re Magan*).

The principles of valuation were extensively discussed in *Holt* v. *C.I.R.* A minority interest is valued by reference to estimated dividend yield, prospective dividend and the possibility of capital appreciation having regard to the information that would be known to the vendor and purchaser. Information that would only be known to directors is relevant to the extent to which the directors would have given such information in reply to the appropriate question while the history of the company and its hazards are obviously relevant (*Lynall* v. *C.I.R.*)

It is sometimes suggested by the Estate Duty Office, in the case of a minority holding, that the assets basis of valuation of shares may be relevant. Such suggestion may be made where a company has valuable assets, but cannot show adequate profits.

The suggestion is made on the assumption that a buyer could expect other shareholders to concur in turning the assets to the best advantage. Every case must be decided on its own facts. Normally it is possible to refute the suggestion since it may be obvious that the other shareholders, who are members of a family, would never agree to such suggestion. If such an assumption were accepted, the valuation would be based on the break-up value, i.e. what the assets would fetch, less liabilities and expenses of realisation and winding-up (*McConnel's Trustees* v. *C.I.R.*).

Where a conclusive value of the shares has been agreed for the purpose of the Capital Gains tax liability arising on death, it will be conclusive for Estate Duty purposes.

· Where shares are valueless, and there is a liability for unpaid calls or uncalled capital, that liability, estimated at the amount it would be necessary to pay a transferee to take them over, may be deducted in arriving at the value of the estate.

Shares in certain companies of which the deceased had the control are to be valued according to the provisions of Section 55, Finance Act 1940, as to which see Chapter X. In such cases restrictions on alienation are irrelevant.

§ 3. Household Goods, Pictures, China etc.

In estates of any size such property should be valued by an expert, and the valuation annexed to the Estate Duty Account with a detailed inventory. Details and individual values of items valued at £50 and upwards should be given. In small estates, a valuation by the executor is usually accepted. Where works of art etc., are exempt from Estate Duty on the grounds of national interest, etc., a separate schedule is required.

§ 4. Life Policies

Liability can arise in respect of:

(*a*) Policies on which all premiums have been paid by the deceased and which are on the life of the deceased;

(*b*) Policies which were taken out by the deceased on his life but which were later assigned by him prior to his death; and

(c) Policies in which the deceased never had an interest, but which were taken out on his life and in respect of which he paid the premiums.

Where a person takes out a policy on the life of another and pays all the premiums, no estate duty liability will arise on the death of that other person. But if the person who effected the policy dies before the other person, the estate of the first person will include such policy which must be valued at its saleable value at the date of the first person's death. The saleable value is not necessarily the same as the surrender value, and is determined actuarially.

In respect of policies in (a) above, the full amount received from the Insurance Company must be included in the Estate Duty Account.

No liability to Estate Duty can arise in respect of a policy on which no premiums were paid by the deceased in the seven years prior to his death, provided that the deceased has had no beneficial interest in the policy in that period. If, therefore, the deceased assigned the policy more than seven years before his death and did not pay any premiums after assignment, no Estate Duty liability will arise on his death. If after assignment the deceased paid premiums, but no payments were made in the seven years prior to death, there will be no Estate Duty liability on his death. The payment of premiums after assignment within the seven years preceding death and/or the assignment within the same period may give rise to a liability. The computation of that liability will be made in the same manner as for those in which he never had an interest (for illustration, see p. 195).

Policies affected and kept up by the deceased for the benefit of others, i.e. those in (b) and (c) above, are valued for Estate Duty purposes as follows:

(i) If the deceased, within seven years of his death, voluntarily assigned a life assurance policy on his own life, he is regarded as having made a gift of a value equal to the proportion of the value of the policy (even if it is not still in force at his death) that the total amount of the premiums paid up to the time for the assignment bears to the total amount of the premiums paid to the date of the maturity of the policy, or its earlier assignment of surrender by the donee.

(ii) Where any premiums were paid by the deceased after such an assignment but within seven years of death, each premium so paid is treated as a gift of rights under the policy (whether the policy is still in force at the death or not) of an amount equal to the proportion of the value of the policy which the amount of the premium bears to the aggregate amount of all premiums paid to the date of the maturity of the policy or of its earlier assignment of surrender by the donee.

(iii) Where the policy was not assigned, but from its commencement the deceased never had an interest, each premium paid by him is treated as a gift of rights under the policy so that the value of the policy must be allocated to each premium on the basis that the amount of that premium bears to the aggregate amount of all premiums paid to the date of the maturity of the policy or its earlier assignment or surrender by the donee.

The 'value of the policy' in (ii) and (iii) above is the amount received at its maturity, or on its surrender or sale for value, or, if the donee had given it away or disposed of it for less than its market value, the market value when he did so.

It will be noted that the amount to be included in the Estate Duty Account is computed on the basis that the payment of each premium is a gift by the deceased. If the payment of the premiums can be regarded as part of the normal expenditure of the deceased, there will be no liability to Estate Duty since a gift will not have been made. Similarly, should the gift be claimed to be exempt from duty because its total value does not exceed £500 (£100 if the policy was settled) it may be valued at its market value at the date of gift instead of at the date of death or surrender etc. Each premium paid by the deceased in the seven years prior to death will be valued at the proportion of such market value that the amount of the premium bears to the aggregate amount of all premiums previously paid on the policy. There is marginal relief where the aggregate of the gifts exceeds £500 (F.A. 1959, s. 34) (see Chapter VI).

By s. 11 of the Married Women's Property Act 1882 a policy of assurance effected by a man on his own life, and expressed to be for the benefit of his wife or child, or by a woman on her own life, and expressed to be for the benefit of her husband or child (commonly called a 'nomination policy') creates a trust in favour of the beneficiary named therein, and the monies payable under the policy will be paid to the beneficiary. The amount receivable will be liable to duty in so far as it can be treated as a gift, see (iii) above. The term 'child' includes an adopted, illegitimate and legitimated child. Where death occurred prior to 20th March, 1968, the amount liable to duty was not aggregable with other property passing on the insured's death, for the purpose of fixing the rate of Estate Duty, as it represented property in which the insured never had an interest. Where a parent took out four nomination policies for the benefit of a particular child, if that child was living at the parent's death, or if not, for the benefit of the deceased's two other children equally, or to the survivor of them, but if all three children pre-deceased the parent, the moneys were to be paid to 'the estate of the last to die' of the three children, the policies were held to be non-aggregable as the ultimate limitation to the last surviving child gave the children a fully vested interest in the policy moneys; there being no distinction between the moneys going to a named individual absolutely and the same moneys going to the estate of such persons (*Walker and others* v. *C.I.R*). All such policies (or interests in such policies passing on the death, to which, immediately after the death any one person is absolutely and indefeasibly entitled, are aggregated (so far as liable to Estate Duty) among themselves. It should be noted that there can be more than one interest in such a policy. Thus the policies and policy moneys may be held for the widow for life with remainder to the children. The widow's life interest will be actuarily valued and will form a separate estate of its own, as will the value of the children's interest in remainder. Thus, if more than one person is interested in such a policy, the total value of the interests will be equal to the value of the policy. Policies in which no one person is absolutely or indefeasibly entitled are aggregated with all the policies and interests in policies in which the deceased never had an interest, including those allocated to individual beneficiaries, but only to find the rate applicable to the policies in which no one person is absolutely, etc., entitled and death is before 16th April, 1969.

The taking out of a policy for the benefit of some person

other than the wife, husband or child of the person effecting it does not confer any legal right to the policy monies on that other person, but they will belong to the estate of the person who provided the policy unless by express words that person had declared himself a trustee for the person in whose name the policy was taken out. If a person enters into a trust to take out an insurance policy on his own life for the benefit of another, the same affects can be obtained as if the policy were taken out for the benefit of spouse or child if the trust is properly drawn. Some insurance companies have draft deeds for the purpose.

In respect of policies taken out and deaths after 19th March, 1968, and before 16th April, 1969, the exemption from aggregation of nomination policies with the remainder of the estate does not apply and, *to the extent the amount of such policies is liable to duty as a gift inter vivos*, that amount will be aggregated with the remainder of the estate to find the rate of duty on the gift and the remainder of the estate.

There is a transitional relief in respect of policies taken out before 20th March, 1968, but the death giving rise to the claim to duty is on or after that date. The circumstances in which this relief is given are:

(i) the policy must be on the life of the deceased;

(ii) property comprised in a gift of the policy or rights under the policy must pass on death;

(iii) such property must have been property in which the deceased never had an interest; and

(iv) the proceeds of all such policies must not exceed £25,000. If (i) to (iv) apply, the proceeds of such policies or that part liable to duty will not have to be aggregated with the remainder of the estate passing on death. As already indicated, the values of the individual policies may have to be aggregated to find the rate of duty thereon because the same person is interested after death in the proceeds of the policies.

If the aggregate value of policies made before 20th March, 1968, exceeds £25,000, the exemption from aggregation with the remainder of the deceased's estate will apply only to that proportion of the value of the policy which £25,000 bears to the aggregate value of all policies. It should not be forgotten that the value of the policy is the sum payable on death (including accrued bonuses). On that part of the value of each policy which is exempt from aggregation, the rate of duty is not to be less than it would have been, if instead of only treating a proportion of the policy exempt from aggregation, the whole amount liable in respect of that policy had been treated as a separate estate. To compute the duty payable in respect of such policies it is necessary –

(a) to compute the total value of the deceased's estate (using the normal rules relating to aggregation but excluding the value of nomination policies);

(b) to ascertain the aggregate value of all nomination policies;

(c) to decide if the aggregate value of the policies in (b) exceeds £25,000 since if it does the 'exempt' proportion of each policy must be ascertained;

(d) to compute the rate of duty on such policies including them at their full value, i.e. the value before computing the exempt proportion; and

(e) to aggregate the 'non-exempt' proportion (found in (c)) with the total value of the remainder of the estate (found in (a)) to compute the rate of duty on the 'non-exempt' proportion and the remainder of the estate.

As will be seen in Chapter VI, § 6, the amount on which duty is payable will be affected by the date on which premiums are paid. Such dates will determine whether the amount applicable to each policy can be reduced by 15 per cent, 30 per cent, or 60 per cent. In the following illustrations since the discussion of gifts is left until a later chapter, this factor has been ignored.

Illustration

An individual died on 30th September, 1968 and his estate (excluding nomination policies) was £70,000. At the date of death there were the following nomination policies:

(a) A policy valued at £30,000 in favour of his wife;

(b) A policy valued at £20,000 in favour of his eldest son; and

(c) A policy valued at £10,000 in favour of his second son.

The aggregate value of such policies is £60,000. The 'exempt' and the 'non-exempt' proportions of such policies are:

Policy	Total Value		Exempt	Non-exempt
Wife's policy	£30,000	£30,000 $\times \dfrac{25,000}{60,000} =$	£12,500	£17,500
Eldest son's policy	£20,000	£20,000 $\times \dfrac{25,000}{60,000} =$	£8,333	£16,667
Second son's policy	£10,000	£10,000 $\times \dfrac{25,000}{60,000} =$	£4,167	£5,833

The rates of duty will be:

Wife's policy   18* per cent. of £12,500.
Eldest son's policy 12* per cent. of £8,333.
Second son's policy 4* per cent. of £4,167.

*Rates applicable to estates of £30,000, £20,000 and £10,000.

These provisions apply in respect of deaths after 15th April, 1969 (s.40 (2) (c) F.A. 1969). Duty payable on wife's policy would be $\dfrac{12,500}{30,000} \times £4,250 = £1,771$; on the eldest son $\dfrac{8,333}{20,000} \times £1,250 = £521$; no duty on second son – estate under 15,000.

Where policies are written under s. 11, Married Women's Property Act 1882, and all the relevant premiums are paid outside the seven year period before the date of death of the settlor, and the beneficiary has an absolute interest which is subject to defeasance if she fails to live one month longer than the settlor, no duty is chargeable on the death of the latter as there has been no ascertainable change in character of the interest in the one month period, *Re Kilpatrick's Policies Trusts.*

For deaths after 16th April, 1969, see § 15 below.

An annuity becoming payable on a death to a widow(er) or other dependant of the deceased under an approved retirement annuity scheme is to be treated as if it arose under a nomination policy.

If a retirement annuity under the provisions for self-employed persons in the Finance Act, 1956, passes on the death prior to 16th April, 1969, it must be aggregated with any nomination policies passing to the same person (F.A. 1956, s. 35).

Liability continues for deaths after 15th April, 1969, where deceased has not exercised general power of appointment or payments are made to deceased's legal personal representatives. Other payments of pensions under superannuation schemes do not normally give rise to a charge to duty on death of deceased or annuitant.

§ 5. Copyrights

A detailed valuation by the publisher or literary agent should be submitted.

§ 6. Ships and Shares in Ships

These will be valued by a ship's valuer, and the detailed valuation must be annexed to the affidavit.

§ 7. Businessess

If the deceased owned a business, each of the assets must be valued as at the date of his death, at their market value and must include the goodwill valued according to the nature of the trade carried on. Liabilities are deductible as usual. As in the case of unquoted shares, the basis of and reasons for the valuation should be sent to the Estate Duty Office.

If the deceased was a partner, his executors will be entitled to his share of the partnership assets calculated according to the terms of the partnership agreement, and it is only upon such share that they will be called upon to pay Estate Duty. A balance sheet signed by the surviving partners is required. The Commissioners will usually, at a later date, ask for the partnership agreement, or a full copy of it for perusal, where goodwill, by agreement, accrues to the surviving partners, it is property in which the deceased had an interest ceasing on his death and chargeable with Estate Duty, unless no donative element is present. Where, by terms in the partnership deed, the goodwill was to pass to the sons of the deceased partner on his death, and in the meantime the sons were to devote their time to the business and not to be concerned in any other business, it was held that the obligations thus placed on the sons paid for the goodwill in money's worth, and no Estate Duty was payable (*A.G.* v. *Boden*). The *Boden* decision was criticised, however, in *Perpetual Executors and Trustees Assn. of Australia* v. *Commissioners of Taxes of Commonwealth of Australia* on the ground that the goodwill did not pass to the son on the father's death, but to the executors, from whom the son had the right to buy it. It seems, therefore, that the consideration must pass before the death, if no liability to Estate Duty is to arise. In *A. G.* v. *Ralli* by an agreement, reserves necessary for the purpose of the partnership were held as joint tenants and it was held that the obligations of the partners under the agreement consituted full money consideration.

Where a business or an interest in a business passes on a death, any Estate Duty chargeable in respect of industrial land or buildings used in and occupied for the purposes of the business or in respect of machinery or plant so used is to be charged (in the same way as the agricultural value of property) (see § 10 post) at 55 per cent. of the rate of duty normally applicable. If the machinery or plant is not used exclusively in the business such part of the relief is given as appears to the Commissioners of Inland Revenue to be just and reasonable. Land or premises used in a business are treated as industrial if so treated for the purpose of a rating valuation or, in the case of land or premises outside Great Britain, would fall to be so treated if situated in England. In the case of land or premises used partly for industrial purposes and partly for other purposes, the value is to be apportioned between those purposes except where it does not exceed £1,000.

A share in a partnership gives a proportionate interest in each asset, on which the reduced rate of duty is payable (*Burden-Coutts* v. *C.I.R*).

The above relief does not apply to:

(*a*) a business carried on in the exercise of a profession or vocation, or carried on otherwise than for gain;

(*b*) a business for sale of which a binding contract has been entered into other than a sale to a company formed for the purpose of carrying it on made in consideration wholly or mainly of shares in that company (F.A. 1954, s. 28).

§ 8. Freehold and Leasehold Properties

These should be valued by a competent valuer on the basis of a reasonable number of years' purchase of the net annual value, and the valuation annexed to the affidavit. To arrive at net annual value for this purpose, the gross rental, if let, or the estimated gross rental if unlet and occupied by the deceased, is diminished by the annual outgoings paid by the owner, e.g. repairs, insurance premiums, ground rents, etc. The method of sale that would fetch the best price must be adopted, i.e. sale as one lot or divided into several lots all particulars should be furnished as are requisite to arrive at the principal value.

If the real property includes unlet fishing or sporting rights, unlet building land, mines or other property which has not an annual value, or the annual value whereof is an insufficient criterion of the principal value, full details should be given. Where the property is licensed, it should be expressly so stated, and the particulars of the lease or other lettings should be fully set out.

The value of land is agreed with the District Valuer and the agreed value assessed to Estate Duty.

An appeal against the valuation of land (including freehold property) may be made to the Lands Tribunal (Lands Tribunal Act 1949, s. 1). From their decision, an appeal on a point of law may be taken to the Court of Appeal. An appeal against the valuation of other property can only be made by petition to the Chancery Division of the High Court; (if the value in question does not exceed £10,000 it may be taken in the County Court). Leave of the Court or of the Court of Appeal is needed for any appeal from the decision of the High Court, but no leave is necessary for an appeal from the County Court. An appeal to the House of Lords may follow, with the usual leave (F.A. 1894, s. 10 (5), F.A. 1896, s. 22).

It is important to remember that leasehold property is personalty. Debts charged on leaseholds are included in the schedule of debts.

Freehold property is realty, and entered in a separate section and incumbrances thereon are included in a schedule set apart for that purpose. Income arising from realty prior to the death and owing to the deceased at that time is personalty.

Where the deceased had entered into a binding contract for the sale of real estate, his interest in such contract is part of his personal estate. If he had entered into a contract for the purchase of real estate, the property would form part of his realty, subject to the burden of the unpaid purchase money. If the contract for sale or purchase was conditional, or was an option only, the above principles would not apply, and the estate would be valued as if the conditional contract or option did not exist. If the property is sold at arm's length a short time after death, the

gross sum realised will usually be admitted as the value for
Estate Duty purposes, subject, where relevant, to variations in
circumstances since the death. In the case of an onerous leasehold, the negative value, i.e, what would have to be paid to get
rid of the lease, may be deducted from the value of the estate.

§ 9. Timber

Where land, on which timber, trees, wood or underwood are
growing, is chargeable to estate duty, the value of such timber,
trees, wood or underwood is not to be taken into account in
estimating the principal value of the estate or the rate of Estate
Duty. No duty is payable at the time of death on the value of
timber. When timber, trees or wood are felled and sold, Estate
Duty is payable on the net monies received (after deducting all
necessary outgoings since the death of the deceased). Such outgoings would include, *inter alia*, the cost of replanting and maintaining trees. Duty is levied on such monies at the rate applicable
to the principal value of the estate, without aggregating the sums
received on sale of the timber. The rate of duty is determined by
the value of the property passing on the death of the last person
whose death attracted duty on the land carrying the timber (F.A.
1912, s. 9). Marginal relief does not apply (Dymond). Underwood does not attract duty, whether sold or not. In no case will
duty be payable on a larger amount than the value of the whole
timber of the estate at the date of the last death. Interest at
three per cent. per annum is charged on the amount of duty
payable from the date of receipt of the proceeds to the date of
payment.

If the timber, trees, or wood are sold standing either with or
apart from the land on which they are growing, the Estate Duty
becomes payable on the principal value as on the date of the
death of the deceased (whatever price it fetches) after allowance
of the Estate Duty (if any) paid on the net monies as above (F.
(1909-10) A. 1910, s. 61 (5). If part is sold unfelled, the principal
value is apportioned.

In effect, therefore, the value of growing timber is ignored,
and Estate Duty is only payable as and when such timber is sold.
The person who is entitled to the proceeds of sale being charged
with the payment of the duty.

Illustration

Value of estate excluding timber, on last death	£90,000
Value of timber, at that date	£15,000

The estate is regarded as one of a value of £90,000, not £105,000. If the death was before 16th April, 1969, duty was payable at 45 per cent. on £90,000. Since that date the duty would be:

On £80,000..	£34,125
On £10,000 at 65%	6,500
	£40,625

If there was a partial felling bringing in £5,000, duty would be paid before 16th April, 1969, duty is payable at 45 per cent. on £15,000 only, as and when the monies are received. If that death is after 15th April, 1969, the duty payable will be: $\frac{40.625}{90.000} \times £15,000 = £6,771$.

If there was a partial felling bringing in £5,000, duty would be paid at the above rates on that sum and on further realisations until duty had been paid on £15,000 or a further death occurred, which would give rise to a fresh liability by reference to that death.

If 60 per cent. of the timber was sold unfelled, duty on 60 per cent. of £15,000 = £9,000, would be payable.

In the case of land passing on the death of one man (A) to another (B) for life with remainder to a third person (C)., on the death of the reversioner (C), the value of the reversion in standing timber must be taken into account for the purposes of aggregation and assessment. Moreover, as a general rule, the death of the reversioner, before his interest falls into possession, has no effect on the liability to duty on sales of timber. The practice relating to the charging of duty changed in August, 1955. For the transitional arrangements readers are referred to the 20th edition, page 82.

§ 10. Agricultural Property

Special provisions apply to the valuation of agricultural property and to the rate of Estate Duty payable thereon. 'Agricultural property' means agricultural land, pasture and woodland, cottages, farm houses and buildings and a mansion house as are of a character appropriate to the property, and it includes agricultural land etc. situated abroad. Broiler houses, glasshouses used for commercial growing of tomatoes, intensive mushroom cultivation and intensive rearing of livestock for human consumption are by concession treated as agricultural property.

Growing crops (including unexhausted manures) are regarded

as agricultural property in the case of deceased owner occupiers and tenant farmers. Fishing rights are only regarded as agricultural property if the water is part of an agricultural estate and not primarily for use for fishing. Sporting rights are normally agricultural unless not held with agricultural property.

The rates of duty payable on the agricultural value are 55 per cent. of the normal rates. 'Agricultural value' means what the property would fetch if subject to a perpetual covenant prohibiting its use otherwise than as agricultural property, decreased by the value of any timber, etc. growing on it. In determining the amount on which a reduced rate of duty is payable, the property is valued in the ordinary way to ascertain the principal value. Next the property is valued subject to the perpetual covenant previously mentioned. In both valuations the value of timber is ignored. The full rate of duty is payable on the excess of the principal value over the agricultural value, while the reduced rate is charged on the latter. Mortgages on the land are to be apportioned rateably between the agricultural value and the excess of the principal value over the agricultural value (F.A. 1925, s. 23). Unsecured debts are a charge against personalty not agricultural land.

A share in a partnership gives a proportionate interest in each asset so that if agricultural property is held by the partnership the reduced rate of Estate Duty applicable to such property can be claimed on that part of the share in the partnership (*Burdett-Coutts* v. *C.I.R*).

Where a sale of agricultural property is subject to a binding but uncompleted contract for sale at the date of death of the vendor, the reduced rate is claimable in respect of the unpaid purchase monies, providing the contract of sale is binding on all the parties concerned.

Illustration (1)

A died leaving estate valued for probate at £30,000 which included agricultural property valued at £15,000. The agricultural value of the property was £10,000, the excess of £5,000 being an assessment of its presumptive value for building development.

Estate Duty if the death were before 16th April, 1969, would be payable at 18% at normal rates, but the agricultural rate is 55% of 18%=9.90%. Estate duty would be at 18% on £20,000 and at 9.90% on £10,000. If the death were on or after that date, the duty payable would be:

Duty on £30,000   £5,625

Duty on agricultural property, 55% of $\frac{5.625}{30.000}$ × 10,000 = £1,031
Duty on remainder of estate, $\frac{5.625}{30.000}$ × 20,000 =   3,750

                                                         £4,781

Where marginal relief applies in respect of deaths before 16th
April, 1969, the duty payable on the non-agricultural value is a
proportionate part of the total duty on the whole estate calculated by reference to the normal rate, and the duty chargeable
on the agricultural value is a proportionate part of the total
duty on the whole estate calculated by reference to the agricultural rate, since it is not the amount of duty on the agricultural
value, but the scale of rates which is reduced by 45 per cent.

Illustration (2)

The principal value of an estate is £30,030, the agricultural value included
therein being £10,010. Duty on £30,030 at 21 per cent. would be £6,306
but marginal relief applies. Death occurred on 1st February, 1969.
At normal rates, duty on an estate of £30,030 is:

18% on £30,000   ..   ..   £5,400
Add excess of estate over £30,000   30

                                                                 £5,430

Proportion applicable to non-agricultural value
$\frac{20,020}{30,030}$ × £5,430   =   £3,620

At agricultural rates, without marginal relief, the duty on an estate of
£30,030 is 55 per cent. of 21 per cent = 11·55 per cent. = £3,468. Applying
marginal relief the duty would be:

55% of 18% = 9·90% on £30,000   ..   ..   ..   £2,970
Add excess of estate over £30,000   30

                                                                 £3,000

Proportion applicable to agricultural value
$\frac{10,010}{30,030}$ × £3,000   £1,000

Total duty £3,620 plus £1,000   £4,620

It may happen that marginal relief would apply to one scale and
not to the other.

Illustration (3)

The principal value of the estate is £30,900 of which £10,300 is agricultural value. Death occurred on 1st January, 1969.

Duty on £30,900 at 21 per cent. would be £6,489, therefore marginal relief applies. In respect of the non-agricultural value, the duty would be:

18% on £30,000	£5,400
Add excess of estate over £30,000	900
	£6,300

Proportion applicable to non-agricultural value

$$\frac{20,600}{30,900} \times £6,300 \qquad\qquad £4,200$$

If the marginal relief calculation were applied to the agricultural value the duty would be:

9·90% on £30,000	£2,970
Add excess of estate over £30,000	900
	£3,870

But the duty at 55 per cent. of 21 per cent. = 11·55 per cent. on £30,900 is only £3,569 therefore 11·55 per cent. on £10,300 = £1,190 would be payable.

See § 7 *ante* for a similar lower rate in respect of certain business assets.

§ 11. Property subject to a compulsory purchase, demolition or clearance order

Relief can be claimed where Estate Duty has been paid, or is payable, in respect of an interest in land in Great Britain and, in pursuance of a notice to treat served, or of an agreement or order made, not more than five years after the date at which the interest was valued for the purposes of that duty, that interest is compulsorily acquired by, or sold to, a public authority possessing compulsory purchase powers. The conditions are set out in F.A. 1956, s. 33 and F.A. 1958, s. 33. The amount of duty payable in respect of such interest is to be the amount payable if the principal value of the interest had been equal to the amount of the compensation (or price payable for the purchase thereof) including, in the case of compensation, any additional compensation payable under Part III of the Town and Country Planning Act 1954 or Part III of the Town and Country Planning

(Scotland) Act 1954. Where the site is retained by the owner the site value will be included in the value of such interest. The effect of these provisions is to prevent the valuation at death exceeding the compensation monies.

§ 12. Underwriting interests

The executor, in practice, has the option of paying Estate Duty on an estimated valuation of future profits or on those profits as they are received. In the latter case, he must give an undertaking to account for the duty as the profits are received. In computing the amount of the profits, the tax liability thereon is deductible. The Special Reserve Fund of a Lloyd's underwriter is an asset of his estate.

§ 13. Securities quoted in Foreign Currency

In the case of holdings of foreign currency, and deposits in banks abroad, where the rate of exchange is quoted at a range of prices, the extreme of the quotation giving the lowest value in sterling is adopted. The former practice of deducting a quarter of the difference from the higher of the two quotations is in abeyance owing to exchange restrictions.

Where dollar securities are quoted in the official list in London, the usual 'quarter-up' rule applies (whether in sterling or in 'London dollars', i.e. at 5 dollars to the £); otherwise the value of U.S.A. securities is the sterling equivalent of the New York price (taken at the mid-price of dealings, or at the bid if no dealings) at the official rate of exchange as above, plus the premium ruling on the date of valuation. However, in the case of deaths after 7th April, 1965, the premium can only be realised on three-quarters of the value of such assets, the other quarter being valued at the official rate of exchange. The value of the asset will be the aggregate of one quarter of the value converted at the official rate and three-quarters of the value converted at the rate including the premium. The rate and premium are shown in the Stock Exchange Daily Official lists. The Foreign Exchange Market was closed from 20th to 22nd November, 1968, inclusive. Where death occurred on one of those dates, the prices in the Daily Official List should be used but the amount of twenty-five per cent. of the premium surrendered should be calculated by reference to the spot rates on 25th November, 1968.

Canadian stocks are similarly valued at the Canadian price converted at the current official rate of exchange, plus the premium.

Where foreign securities are quoted on the local market in currency, the mid-price method of valuation must be followed to arrive at the price of the bonds; the currency will be converted into sterling at the London buying rate (subject to the above comments regarding premiums).

§ 14. Property situate outside Great Britain

In this paragraph on property situated outside the United Kingdom, the word 'foreign' or 'abroad' is used as relating to any country, whether British or not, except England (including Wales) and Scotland, which comprise Great Britain.

Although the Acts do not extend to other countries, nevertheless it is a general rule that property passing or deemed to pass on a death, whether that property is in Great Britain or abroad, is liable to Estate Duty in Great Britain, unless it can be brought within the scope of one of the exemptions, e.g. the deceased died domiciled abroad.

Property abroad is not liable to Estate Duty if:

(a) the proper law regulating its devolution or disposition is foreign; *and*

(b) either:

(i) the deceased died domiciled abroad, or

(ii) the property passed under a disposition made by a person domiciled abroad and not made on behalf of, at the expense of, or out of funds provided by, a person domiciled in Great Britain (F.A. 1949, s. 28 (2)).

Property owned in the United Kingdom by a person domiciled abroad is liable to Estate Duty unless exempt by reason of its nature (e.g. certain Government securities) or by reason of a Double Taxation Relief agreement.

Property situated abroad is not termed 'personal property' and 'real property', but is classified as 'movable' and 'immovable' property. Immovable property comprises broadly, interests in land, whether freehold or leasehold and movable property any other property (i.e. the equivalent of 'pure personalty' in English law).

The following summary of rules and illustrations explains the statutory provisions outlined above:

(1) Property abroad is in all cases liable to Estate Duty if the 'proper law' regulating its devolution or disposition is English or Scottish. The question of 'proper law' is chiefly of importance in relation to property passing under settlements. In general, proper law is the law which the parties choose or intend to govern the settlement, and if they have not expressed their choice or intention, it is a question of fact to be decided in the light of all the circumstances, particularly the form in which the settlement is drafted. But parties cannot make any law they chose apply to the settlement; for example, a domiciled Englishman settling English securities on beneficiaries domiciled in England could not make Chinese the proper law of the settlement simply by saying so; there must be sufficient factual connection with the country in question.

(2) Immovable property abroad, as such, was exempt from Estate Duty in respect of deaths before 1st August, 1962, because the proper law governing immovables is always the *lex situs*, i.e. the law of the country where it is situated (*Philipson-Stow* v. *C.I.R*). But interests in immovable property abroad could be governed by the law of this country; for example, if the property were settled on trust for sale according to English law, then the rights of the beneficiaries in the proceeds would be regulated by English law. The question of whether property is movable or immovable may be important for deaths after that date in view of the various Double Taxation Relief agreements.

(3) Property abroad in the absolute ownership of the deceased is liable to Estate Duty if the deceased died domiciled here, but not if he died domiciled abroad, for *mobilia sequuntur personam* (movables follow the person, i.e. the law regulating movable property is that of the owner's domicil).

(4) Property abroad the subject of a settlement, of which the proper law is foreign, escapes Estate Duty if the deceased life

tenant (or other limited owner) was domiciled abroad at the date of his death. It also escapes, even if the deceased was domiciled here at the date of his death if the settlor was domiciled abroad at the date of the settlement, provided that the funds were not provided, etc., by a person domiciled in Great Britain. In all other cases, the settled property will be liable to Estate Duty. These possible combinations are illustrated as follows (assuming in each case that the proper law of the settlement is foreign):

(i) A father domiciled in New York makes a settlement of American securities on his daughter for life on the occasion of her marriage to a domiciled Englishman. She dies domiciled in England. No Estate Duty is payable, because the settlement was made by a settlor domiciled abroad out of his own funds. But if the husband had put the American father into funds to make a similar settlement, Estate Duty would have been payable on the daughter's death.

(ii) A father domiciled in England makes a settlement of American securities on his daughter for life on the occasion of her marriage to an American. The daughter dies domiciled in New York. No estate duty is payable, because the deceased died domiciled abroad.

The liability to duty in respect of gifts *inter vivos* of foreign property is subject to special rules. They are exempt from Estate Duty if the donor was domiciled abroad at the date of the gift, or at the date of his death. Otherwise, they are liable to Estate Duty regardless of the domicil of the donee. Their value for the purposes of computing the duty will be computed as for English law (see Chapter VI).

Where, owing to the Defence Regulations or the Exchange Control Act 1947, bearer securities situated outside the United Kingdom have been converted into, or exchanged for, registered securities in Great Britain, they are treated as situated outside Great Britain. The section applies only if, between the conversion or exchange and the death, the securities neither have been disposed of nor have passed on the death of a person competent to dispose of them (F.A. 1947, s. 51).

Premium Savings Bonds held by persons who are domiciled

in the Channel Isles, the Isle of Man or Northern Ireland are treated for Estate Duty purposes as property situate outside Great Britain.

Where a person domiciled in this country dies leaving property abroad as well as property in this country, Estate Duty is payable in respect of the whole of the property, wherever situate, but the personal representative is not liable for any duty in excess of the amount of the assets which he has received, or might have received but for his own neglect or default (F.A. 1894, s. 8 (3)). Where, by Section 9 (1) of the Finance Act 1894 (under which a rateable part of the Estate Duty on an estate, in proportion to the value of any property which does not pass to the executor as such, is a first charge on that property) a charge in respect of a rateable part of the Estate Duty on an estate is imposed on property situate abroad, the charge extends to assets which form the proceeds of any disposition of the property, or for the time being directly or indirectly represent it. A *bona fide* purchaser thereof for valuable consideration without notice is protected from the charge (Finance Act 1962, s. 28 (3)).

The fact that the deceased appointed separate executors in connection with the property abroad does not affect the liability of the English executors; to the extent of the assets in this country Estate Duty can be claimed from them (*Consuelo, Dowager Duchess of Manchester; Duncannon* v. *Manchester*).

Personal or movable property situate abroad which is not saleable or transferable in Great Britain is included in the Estate Duty Account in the appropriate section, but property abroad which is saleable or transferable in Great Britain should be included with the personal property situate in Great Britain.

In computing the value of property situate outside Great Britain, debts due to persons abroad are allowed as deductions (Finance Act 1962, s. 28 (5)). There can be deducted the amount of the ADDITIONAL expense incurred in administering or realising such property by reason of its being situate out of Great Britain but such deduction cannot exceed 5 per cent. of the value before deducting debts of the property (F.A. 1894, s. 7 (3). The expense that would have been incurred had the property been in Great Britain is estimated and only the excess over that amount is allowed as a deduction.

Any foreign death duty payable on property abroad is not

deductible from the value of the property in calculating the amount on which Estate Duty is chargeable but is allowed as a credit against the Estate Duty payable in respect of that property on the same death. This general provision may be over-ruled by the double taxation relief agreement with the government of the territory in which the property is situated (Finance Act 1962, s. 29 (1)).

It is necessary to aggregate property abroad (even where the duty paid there is deductible from the duty payable in this country) for the reason that the net value of the property, fixing the percentage of Estate Duty, may be varied thereby to the extent of throwing the estate into a higher scale for Estate Duty.

To obtain relief for Estate Duty payable abroad a certificate showing details of the property charged and the duty paid. Any duty payable abroad in excess of that payable on the same property in the United Kingdom cannot be relieved. Although no duty may be payable in the United Kingdom because of the duty paid abroad, the value must be included to determine the rate of Estate Duty in the United Kingdom.

Relief from double Estate Duty has now been provided for by agreements between this country and a number of overseas countries. A list of the agreements will be found in Appendix II.

The broad effect of a double taxation relief agreement is to identify the locality of certain assets with the domicil of the deceased, so that Estate Duty will only be payable in one or other of the two countries. Thus, under the agreement with the U.S.A. debts due to the deceased are deemed to be situated in the country where the deceased was domiciled at his death, and Estate Duty thereon will only be payable in that country. Stocks and shares, on the other hand, are deemed to be situated at the place in which the corporation was constituted. In the case of other assets, on which a double charge for duty arises, a deduction is allowed from the duty payable in the country of the deceased's domicil for any duty payable on the same property in the other country to the agreement.

Probate fees paid in India or Pakistan are in practice treated as if they were Estate Duty paid in those countries and allowed as a credit against Estate Duty payable in Great Britain on the same property.

In the case of the Republic of Ireland, reciprocal arrangements have been made to allow the duty paid in each country to be deducted from the duty payable in the other. Similar provisions apply in the case of Northern Ireland.

Illustration

A, domiciled in Great Britain, died on the 1st September, 1968, and an examination of his affairs reveals the following facts:

	£
(1) Gross Personal Property situate in Great Britain or saleable or transferable there	28,500
Funeral expenses and debts of deceased due to persons in Great Britain	300
(2) Gross Personal Property abroad, not saleable or transferable in Great Britain	18,200
Debts of deceased due to persons outside Great Britain ..	200
Duty was paid abroad on £18,200 amounting to	720
(3) Real Property in Great Britain	6,000
Encumbrances on Real Property	3,000

The Estate Duty on the personalty was paid exactly four months after the death of the testator. The amount of the duty payable would be ascertained as follows:

Property	Gross Value of Property	Deductions	Net Value of Property Personal	Realty
1	£28,500	300	£28,200	—
2	18,200	200	18,000	—
3	6,000	3,000	—	3,000
Total net value of aggregable personalty and realty respectively ..			46,200	3,000
Net value of realty			3,000	
Net value of property fixing amount of Estate Duty at 31%			£49,200	

Duty	£
Estate Duty @ 31% on net personal property £46,200	14,322
Less duty payable abroad	720
	13,602
Add interest at 2% per annum for 4 months	91
Carried forward £13,693	

				£
Total Duty and Interest (personalty)	..	..	..	13,693
Estate Duty @ 31% on net realty £3,000	..	..	..	930
Total Duty and Interest	..	..	..	£14,623

If A had died on 1st September, 1969, the duty payable would have been:

Estate as above	..	..	..	..	..	£49,200
Estate Duty: On £40,000	..	..	..	..	10,125
9,200 at 60%	..	..	..	..	5,520
					£15,645

Estate Duty on net personal property, $\frac{15.645}{49.200} \times 46,200 =$	£14,691
Less duty payable abroad	720
	13,971
Add interest at 2% for 4 months	93
	14,064
Estate Duty on net realty, $\frac{15.645}{49.200} \times 3,000 =$	954
	£15,018

§ 15. Settled Property

Where the life tenant of settled property dies so that an interest in that property is deemed to pass, duty is payable on the value of that property, including all income arising from the property including any outstanding or accrued due at the date of the death (F.A. 1894, s. 6 (5)). Where a life tenant dies, there must be included in his estate the accrued income on the settled property to the date of his death; such accrued income is deductible from the value of the settled property. However, if the 'surviving spouse' exemption clause applies (see Chapter III, § 3 (i)) such income is deemed to be part of the settled funds and thus avoids the charge for duty (*I.R.C.* v. *Coutts & Co*).

The law relating to the assessment of duty in respect of settled property was substantially amended by the Finance Act 1969.

(a) Duty will be chargeable on settled property in respect of deaths after 15th April, 1969, where:

(a) the deceased was the life tenant of a settled estate and his interest ceases on his death;

(*b*) at any time during the period of seven years ending on the deceased's death, the property was comprised in a settlement in which the deceased had a beneficial interest in possession (even though the trust is for a period not determinable by reason of his death) or as successor to an interest of a beneficiary in that settlement, e.g. such interest would occur where within the seven years prior to his death, the deceased purchased an interest in expectancy in the property and retained it until his death or the interest was assigned to him;

(*c*) the deceased was not entirely excluded from enjoyment in the seven years before his death even though the interest had been determined or disposed of outside that period;

(*d*) the deceased held the property at death *per autre vie* (for the life of another) under a settlement even though the other person remains alive or died within the seven years prior to the deceased's death (there will be no charge on the death of the other person);

(*e*) the deceased had benefited in the income of a discretionary trust during any part of the seven year period ending on his death as falls after 15th April, 1963;

(*f*) the deceased had not benefited in the income of the discretionary trust in the period of seven years mentioned in (*e*) but had received an advance out of the capital funds of the trust and had enjoyed benefits from that advance within the seven years prior to his death, in so far as that period fell after 15th April, 1963;

(*g*) the deceased had ceased to be eligible in or the discretionary settlement had ceased prior to his death, but he had benefited or had not been entirely excluded from enjoyment of any part of the property in or originally in the settlement in that part of the seven years prior to his death as falls after 15th April, 1963; and

(*h*) the property was comprised in an accumulation settlement made by the deceased and such accumulation ended on his death.

It should be noted that in determining the deceased's interest in a discretionary settlement, annuities under the settlement even if variable and sums spent on his maintenance while under full age are ignored.

Where there is a charge to duty, the general principle is to charge to duty that part of the assets of the settlement which the benefits to the deceased bear to the actual income in the seven year period prior to the deceased's death and after 15th April, 1963. Thus, if the deceased was entitled to all the income during that period, the principal value of the assets comprised in the settlement at the date of death will be the amount on which duty will be payable. To cope with other situations the Act provides:

(i) where the deceased was entitled to a stated proportion of the income of a settlement, duty will be levied on that proportion of the principal value of the assets of the settlement at the date of his death;

(ii) where the deceased was entitled to an annuity chargeable on some particular part of the property comprised in the settlement, the value of such property will be chargeable to duty; if such annuity requires only part of the income from that property, the amount chargeable is reduced proportionately;

(iii) where under (i) or (ii) above, the passing of the property does not occur on death but by reason of an earlier disposition or determination within the seven years prior to his death, the proportions in (i) and (ii) will be calculated on the value of the assets at the date of earlier disposition or determination;

Liability may arise where property has been taken out of the settlement within the 7 years immediately preceding death except:

(a) where the property is disposed of for the purpose of paying any tax or duty (including foreign taxes and duties) for which the trustees are accountable and which is properly payable out of capital. This will cover payment of such U.K. taxation as Estate Duty, Capital Gains tax, Income tax payable on gains assessable under Schedule D, Case VII, Betterment Levy and Special Charge; or

(b) where the settlement (or party of it) has come to an end by reason of the deceased's having become absolutely and indefeasibly entitled to the property or that part of it. This prevents a double charge to duty in that the property vested in the deceased absolutely will have augmented his free estate liability either under Section 2 (1) (*a*) or possibly have been the subject of a subsequent gift by him which would be assessable under Section 2 (1) (*c*).

Illustration

The income of a settlement created in 1961 is payable to A and B in equal shares. On 1st July, 1965, with the consent of A and B the trustees made an advancement of £5,000 to one of the remaindermen. A died on 1st September, 1970, when the settled fund was valued at £60,000.

The amounts chargeable to Estate Duty in respect of the above will be:

A's life interest – ½ × £60,000			£30,000
A's share of advance to remaindermen–			
½ × £5,000	£2,500		
Less 30% reduction			
(3 to 4 years)	750		
	———		1,750
			———
			£31,750

(iv) where the subject-matter of the settlement does not yield income, but simply the right to use and enjoy property, the proportion of the value of the property at death chargeable to duty is that proportion of the full principal value which the annual value of the deceased's interest bore to the aggregate of his interest and the annual value of the interests of the other people using and enjoying that property;

(v) where the deceased's interest in the income of the settlement was variable, the amount to be included in calculating the value of his estate will be the proportion of the total assets of the estate which the actual benefits received in the seven year period prior to death (or the date of the earlier disposition or determination) and after 15th April, 1963, bear to the total income of the settlement in the same period;

(vi) in the case of discretionary trusts, duty will be charged on the proportion of the value of the assets at the date of death, which the income received by the deceased since

15th April, 1963, and within the seven years prior to his death bears to the aggregate income of the trust in that period. If there were advances to beneficiaries other than the deceased, these are dutiable gifts if made within the seven years prior to his death. The charge is on the proportion of the advance which the income received since 15th April, 1963, and within the seven years prior to his death and to the date of the advance bears to the total income within that period. Income paid for maintenance during infancy is ignored. The annual value of property enjoyed by the deceased is added to the actual income received and to the total income of the settlement in determining the proportions mentioned in this paragraph.

If the deceased receives out of trust funds a sum of money or other distribution of funds stated to be a capital distribution, such amount is deemed to be income for the purposes of determining the deceased's share of the discretionary income, except to the extent the sum exceeds the trust income in the period beginning 16th April, 1963, and ending with the date when the sum in question was paid, or where the death occurs after 16th April, 1970, the first day of the seven year period ending with the date of death. Such periods are known as 'relevant periods'.

Unless the whole of the income of a relevant period was received by the deceased, the 'slice' principle is applied here by comparing the sums paid to or applied for the benefit of the deceased in the relevant period with the whole of the combined income of all the property subject to the trust arising during that period. There is, however, a complicated provision to cover the possibility that some of the income may be accumulated and later distributed as capital. Thus on the occasion of a purported distribution of capital it is necessary to consider whether in the period between 16th April, 1963, and that date the total available income has exceeded the total amount of the discretionary payments of income to or for the beneficiaries. If it has, the difference, up to the amount of the capital payment or payments, is regarded as an application of income, being apportioned pro rata when there has been more than one capital payment at the same time.

The calculation of available income always commences on 16th April, 1963 (or on the commencement of the trust, if later) even though in the case of deaths after 16th April, 1970, this will be earlier than the commencement of the relevant period. This may result in the amounts treated as payments of income during the relevant period exceeding the available income of that period; in that event the income of the trust for that period is to be treated as increased by the excess.

Where all the available income is distributed as it arises and there are no capital payments out of accumulated income (there may still be advances not of the original capital of the trust) or in any case where there has been no payments of a capital nature the major complications disappear.

Illustration

Under a discretionary trust set up in 1960 the income has been divided annually between several beneficiaries of whom P was one. P died on 1st April, 1970. The total income of the trust during the period 16th April, 1963, to 1st April, 1970, was £12,000 and the total of the payments made to or for the benefit of P during the same period was £2,000. One-sixth of the value of the fund on 1st April, 1970, will pass on P's death as settled property in which he was eligible to benefit immediately before his death.

If in addition advances out of capital had been made of £5,000 to P on 1st May, 1969, and £8,000 to Q on 1st June, 1969:

(a) no liability arises (under s. 2 (i) (b)) in respect of the £5,000 because this vested in P himself and is exempted by Sch. 17, Pt. II, para. 2;

(b) the £8,000 is property which ceased to be subject to the trust within seven years before P's death. If the total income of the trust for the period 16th April, 1963, to 1st June, 1969, was £10,000 and the total paid to P in the same period was £1,800 there will be a further liability to estate duty on
$\frac{1,800}{10,000} \times £8,000 = £1,440$.

If two or more persons share in distributions and it is necessary to deem part of the amounts paid as income payments, each person will be deemed to receive income in proportion to the sums received.

Where the capital distributed, together with the income distributed, exceeds the income for the period up to the date at which the capital distribution has been made, the excess of that distribution over the available income will be treated as a distribution of capital and will not therefore form part of the fraction under this particular rule. Sums of money paid away in satisfaction of any tax or duty for which the trustees are accountable, will not be deemed to be a distribution of income or capital for these purposes.

Apart from the foregoing paragraphs, income is defined as being the income from the property, after the deduction of any costs, expenses or fees properly payable out of *income*.

The Finance Act 1970 has provided that liability can also arise if cash is retained within the discretionary trust and asset distributions are made instead.

(vii) where the settlement was made by the deceased and the income from the property was to be accumulated and the period of accumulation was determined by the death Section 37 (4) provides that where the whole of the income has not been accumulated the slice of the property passed under this provision is to be calculated by reference to a fraction of which the numerator is –

the total income of the trust during the period of accumulation less the income not accumulated

and the denominator is the total income for the whole period.

It will sometimes happen that a husband and his wife will both be beneficiaries under the same discretionary trust. The 'surviving spouse' exemption which applies to settled property which has already been liable to Estate Duty on the earlier death of the other party to the marriage is extended to interests in discretionary trusts.

A proportion of the property passing on the later death is treated as having passed on the earlier death equal to whichever is the less of –

(*a*) the proportion of the property so comprised which was treated as passing on the earlier death; or

(*b*) the proportion of the property so comprised which is treated as passing on the later death less the proportion of that property which would have been treated as passing on the later death if the later death had occurred at the same time as the earlier death (Sch. 17, Pt. II, para. 6).

Illustration

Mr and Mrs M were both beneficiaries of a discretionary trust created by M's father on 1st June, 1966. Mr M died on 1st May, 1969, when the fund was valued at £50,000 and Mrs M on 1st March, 1970, when the value was £42,000.

In the period 1/6/66 to 1/5/69, Mr M received £2,000 and Mrs M £500 out of a total income of £10,000.

In the period 1/5/69 to 1/3/70, Mrs M received £1,500 out of a total income of £2,000.

On Mr M's death the settled property passing will be
$\frac{2,000}{10,000} \times £50,000 = £10,000$.

Estate Duty will be paid on this at Mr M's estate rate, by the trustees out of capital.

The proportion of the property treated as passing was $\frac{2,000}{10,000}$ or 1/5th.

On Mrs M's death the property passing before applying the surviving spouse exemption is $\frac{500 + 1,500}{10,000 + 2,000} = \frac{2,000}{12,000}$ or 1/6th of £42,000 = 7,000

The proportion exempt as having passed on the earlier death
of Mr M is the lower of:

(a) 1/5th

(b) $1/6th - \frac{500}{10,000} = 1/6th - 1/20th = 7/60ths$.

(b) being lower than (a) the exemption is 7/60ths of £42,000   = 4,900

Liable to Estate Duty on Mrs M's death   £2,100

The surviving spouse exemption illustrated above does not depend upon the two deaths occurring within any limited time.

(b) Duty will be chargeable on settled property in respect of deaths before 16th April, 1969, where:

(i) there is settled property charged with an annuity; or

(ii) where there is a cesser of interest (see § **16** below); or

(iii) where there is a disposition, determination or enlargement of life interest (see § **19** below).

The liability under (i) will arise, where:

(a) any settled property (other than property comprised in a settlement made by the deceased or made, directly or indirectly, at his expense or out of funds provided by him) passes on the death by reason of the termination of an interest limited to cease on the death; and

(b) at the time of the death there is payable out of the income of the settled property so passing an annuity not so limited, but limited by the settlement to cease on another death;

then that part of the value of the settled property equal to the value of the annuitant's interest is deemed, for the purposes of Estate Duty on that or any subsequent death, not to pass on that death by reason of the termination of the interest limited to cease on that death. The annuitant's interest is the benefit which would be treated as accruing or arising by the cesser of the annuity immediately before the death. This does not apply to any settled property of which the deceased has been competent to dispose and has disposed by the exercise of a power conferred by the settlement. For these purposes the extent of the annuitant's interest in the settled property, where the annuity is so limited as to be reduced in amount (but not to cease) on the death, is determined by reference to the reduced amount of the annuity, as if the reduction had taken effect before the death. Where, immediately before a death, an annuity limited by a settlement to cease on that death, or any part of such an annuity, is payable out of the income of the settled property, and is so payable for his own benefit to a person who on the death becomes beneficially entitled in possession to some other interest in the settled property or the income thereof, the above applies in relation to the passing of the settled property on that death as if the annuity or that part of it had been an annuity not limited to cease on that death, but limited by the settlement to cease on a subsequent death. There is a proviso, that the proportion of the settled property which by reason of that annuity is deemed not to pass on the death, is not to exceed the proportion of the income to which, if the interest subsisting at the time of the death had been the same interest as subsisted immediately after the cesser of the annuity, the said person's interest would have been treated as extending for purposes of Estate Duty, had it been he who died.

Settled property which is to any extent deemed not to pass on a death by reason of the termination of an interest limited to cease on that death will not in consequence be deemed to pass on that death by reason only of the deceased's having been competent to dispose of it. Where, however, an interest in settled property devolves on the deceased's personal representatives as assets for the payment of his debts, duty is chargeable in respect of that interest. Where, on the death of a tenant in tail in possession within the meaning of the Settled Land Act 1925, any settled property passes to the heir under the entail or, in default of such an heir, to a person entitled in remainder under the settlement, the foregoing provisions apply as if the property passed by reason of the termination of an interest limited to cease on the death.

The above provisions apply to property which is deemed to pass on a death by reason of a disposition or determination of an interest limited to cease on that death within the meaning of Section 43, F.A. 1940, as if that property passed on the death by reason of the termination of that interest; but save as aforesaid they do not apply to reduce the extent to which any property not passing on a death is, apart from these provisions, to be deemed to pass on that death (F.A. 1956, s. 32).

See Appendix IV for Revenue's views on income of trusts.

§ 16. Cesser of Interest

Where the death is after 15th April, 1969, the provisions relating to cessers of interest will not apply in view of the provisions relating to settled property and described above.

A cesser of interest represents the value of the benefit accruing or arising to an estate by reason of a charge or burden thereon ceasing to be operative. Thus, if A charged certain property with the payment of an annuity for the life of B upon B's death before 16th April, 1969, the property was freed from the charge, and Estate Duty was payable in respect of the consequential benefit to the property.

The calculation of the benefit was as follows:

(a) if the interest which had ceased extended to the whole income of the property, it was the principal value of that property;

(b) if the interest extended to less than the whole income of the property, it was the principal value of an addition to the property equal to the income to which the interest extended (F.A. 1894, s. 7 (7));

(c) if the interest was a limited interest in the residue of the
estate of a testator or intestate and the administration of the
estate had not been completed, it was the value of the interest
in the unadministered estate of the testator or intestate as for
the time being held by his personal representatives, subject
to outstanding charges on residue (any sum payable out of
residue under the law of intestacy was deductible (F.A. 1956,
s. 41)) and to any adjustments between capital and income
remaining to be made in due course of administration and
in the property (if any) representing ascertained residue. The
interest was deemed to have become an interest in possession
on the date as from which the income of the residue would
have been attributable to that interest if the residue had been
ascertained immediately after the death of the testator or intestate (F.A. 1938, s. 47, F.A. 1956, s. 41).

Illustrations
(1) A fund had been set aside to provide an annuity of £300 per annum,
and the fund yielded that exact amount. On the annuitant's death,
prior to 16th April, 1969, there was a cesser of interest extending to the
whole fund, and the principal value of the whole property comprising
the fund was liable to Estate Duty.
(2) Where the benefit was the cesser of an annuity of £30 which is charged
upon property producing £120 per annum, the value of the cesser was
one-fourth of the principal value of the property charged.

If the annuity was 'free of Income tax', the gross equivalent
had to be taken into account in valuing the cesser of interest.

In the case of a continuing annuity given to persons in succession, it was the value of the annuity to the successors which
passed on the death of one annuitant and not the capital fund
supporting it (*Re Duke of Norfolk's Will Trusts*). It was this value
which was subject to Estate Duty, not a proportion of the capital
fund. On the death of the last survivor the annuity ceased and
duty was leviable on the appropriate slice of the capital fund.
Where income from residue was divided in shares between various
persons with accrual of such shares to survivors, on each death
an aliquot part of the capital passed proportionate to the income
enjoyed by the deceased, and Estate Duty was payable on the
principal value of that share, and not on the actuarial value of
the income (*Re Northcliffe, Arnholz v. Hudson*).

If, however, the income of settled estate was held on trusts to
pay an annual payment of a fixed sum or an annuity (whether

the annuity is or is not charged on any part of the estate) and subject thereto to pay the income to another person, then on the death of the latter the whole property passed on the death (F.A. 1894, s. 1, *Cowley* v. *C.I.R. Re Lambton's Marriage Settlement, May* v. *C.I.R*). unless he was only interested in the income as the holder of an office, e.g. where he was to have the income so long as he acted as executor (*Public Trustee* v. *C.I.R*). If a terminable annuity was payable to the same person both before and after the life tenant's death, Estate Duty was payable on the life tenant's death on the whole fund, less the actuarial value of the annuity (*Re Longbourne's Trusts, Warren* v. *C.I.R*).

Where a life tenant and remainderman joined in mortgaging settled property, only the equity of redemption passed on the death of the life tenant, and estate duty was payable on its value only (*Cowley* v. *Commissioners of Inland Revenue*).

Where, on the death of an assured person, premiums ceased to be payable on policies for the benefit of beneficiaries in remainder under a trust, so that the life tenant became entitled to the whole trust income, there was held to be no cesser of interest so as to attract Estate Duty. The real 'interest' of the beneficiaries in remainder was not in the premiums but in the sums assured. Their interest did not cease when the premiums ceased to be paid; they gained by the addition to the trust property of the sums assured, but their 'interest' remained unchanged (*Coutts & Co.* v. *C.I.R*).

Where two or more persons have a concurrent right to reside on any specific property, the cesser of the right on the death of one of them was treated as not capable of measurement so long as the right was to enjoy it in specie; if, however, the deceased would have been entitled to a share of the income if the property had been let or sold, Estate Duty was payable on the slice of the property appropriate thereto. On the death of the survivor, the property passed and was liable to Estate Duty in either case.

If the court orders maintenance to be paid under the Inheritance (Family Provision) Act 1938, as amended by the Family Provision Act 1966, Estate Duty was normally payable on the cesser of interest on the death of a beneficiary other than a spouse while in receipt of such maintenance. Exemption arises on the death of the spouse because of Estate Duty having been paid on the 'settled' property on the death of the testator.

As to life interests etc., disposed of or determined within seven years of death, or where the disposition did not exclude the deceased; see § 19 of this chapter.

§ 17. Reversions

Where an estate includes an interest in expectancy, Estate Duty in respect of that interest may be paid, at the option of the executors, either with the duty on the other property passing on the death or when the interest falls into possession. For the purpose of determining the rate of Estate Duty payable on such other property the interest in expectancy is to be valued at the date of death of the deceased and aggregated therewith. If payment of duty on the interest in expectancy is postponed until after it falls into possession, the rate of Estate Duty payable on that interest when it falls into possession is found by adding the value of the property then received to the value of the rest of the estate as previously ascertained (F.A. 1894, s. 7 (6)). If there are two or more such reversions in the estate and a decision is made to defer payment of the duty on all of them, when the second and subsequent reversions fall in, the values of reversions which have previously fallen in, are to be taken as they were at the date of death, for the purposes of calculating the duty chargeable on the former class of reversions, i.e. those subsequently falling in. The executors must elect whether they will pay duty on the reversion at once or when it falls in, when delivering the Estate Duty Account or a Corrective Account.

The market value of an interest in expectancy should take into account the age of the life-tenant, any contingencies other than the expectation of life of the life-tenant which would affect the deceased's interest and the cost of covering such contingencies by insurance; the Estate Duty and costs payable when the interest falls in; the nature of the assets and whether they are likely to fall in value; the rate of interest; and mortality tables. The common method of valuation by taking the principal value of the property, less the capitalised value of the life tenant's interest therein, and the discounted estimated amount of any duties and costs that will be payable on the life tenant's death under the title which created the reversion will often produce a value in excess of the market value.

If the duty on the reversion is paid at the same time as the duty on the rest of the estate it will be upon the value at the date of death. Interest will run from the date of death. If the duty on the reversion is not paid until the interest falls into possession, it will be paid on the actual value which falls into the estate on the life tenant's death. Interest on the duty on the reversion is payable from the date when the reversion falls in to the date of payment.

If property, to which the deceased is ultimately entitled is held by trustees to pay an annuity to a third party, the personal representatives can either pay duty on the whole of the funds as valued at the date of the reversioner's death, or pay duty on the part of the funds not required for the annuity, i.e. an immediate payment in both cases. In the latter case, upon the death of the annuitant, the value of the interest which then falls in will be the aggregate value of the funds required to pay the annuity and any unabsorbed income.

A policy on the life of another person is not regarded by the Inland Revenue as a reversionary interest for this purpose. Property which will 'fall in' on the determination of a lease is not a reversionary interest (F.A. 1894, s. 22 (1) (j)), but for deaths after 15th April, 1969, a lease determinable on a death will be liable (F.A. 1969, s. 36 (5) (b)). The duty on such assets must be paid at once on their market value as determined by the Commissioners.

It should be observed that where payment of Estate Duty on the reversionary interest is deferred until the interest falls in, the aggregate value of the estate may be increased or reduced to an extent which would cause a higher or lower rate of duty to become payable. Such increase or reduction only affects the duty on the reversionary interest, and does not disturb the duty paid on the other property passing on the death.

It is possible that the aggregate value of the estate where the death occurred before 16th April, 1969, would be of such an amount that marginal relief can be claimed, in which case, where the duty on the reversionary interest is not paid at once the duty on the other property would be a proportionate part of the duty payable on an estate including the reversionary interest. Similarly when marginal relief applies on the reversionary interest falling in, the duty on the reversionary interest will be the proportion of the duty payable which the value of the interest falling in bears to the aggregate value of the estate (including the reversionary interest) (see illustration (2) below).

Illustration (1)

A. died on the 31st October 1968, and part of his estate consisted of an outstanding reversionary interest in property settled by X. upon Y. for life, with remainder over to A. absolutely.

At the date of A's death, Y. being still living, the outstanding reversionary interest and the rest of the property of which A. died possessed, subject to Estate Duty, were valued at £12,800 and £86,300 respectively.

The Estate Duty payable in respect of A's estate, if the whole of the property consisted of personalty, and

(a) assuming the Estate Duty on the outstanding reversionary interest was paid at once will be £44,595, or

(b) assuming the Estate Duty on the outstanding reversionary interest was not paid till it fell in, when its value was £25,000, will be £51,335.

These figures are computed, as follows:

(a) *Where the Estate Duty on the Reversion was Paid on the Death:*

Net value of A's estate, excluding outstanding reversionary interest	£86,300
Value of outstanding reversionary interest at A's death ..	12,800
Total present value of estate, fixing Estate Duty at 45% ..	£99,100

45% on £99,100   = £44,595

(b) *Where the Estate Duty on the Reversion was Not Paid until the Interest fell in:*

Net value of estate for Estate Duty purposes, apart from the value of the outstanding reversionary interest	£86,300
Value of outstanding reversionary interest at A's death ..	12,800
	£99,100

Estate Duty payable on A's death 45% on £86,300 = £38,835

On the falling in of the outstanding reversionary interest:

Value of A's estate at date of his death, excluding the outstanding reversionary interest	£86,300
Actual value of property comprised in reversionary interest at the date when it fell in	25,000
Total value, fixing Estate Duty at 50%	£111,300

Estate Duty payable on reversionary interest 50% of £25,000 = £12,500

Illustration (2) .

Taking the facts as in illustration (1) except that the value of the outstanding reversionary interest at the date of A's death was £20,000, and the value on its falling in was £22,700.

Estate Duty would be payable as follows:

Net value of A's estate, excluding outstanding reversionary interest	£86,300
Value of outstanding reversionary interest at A's death ..	20,000
Total present value of estate	£106,300

Estate Duty on £106,300 at 50 per cent. would be £53,150, therefore marginal relief applies,

Amount of Estate Duty applicable to the whole estate:

45% on £100,000	£45,000
Add excess of estate over £100,000	6,300
	£51,300

Estate duty payable on A's death:

$$\frac{86,300}{106,300} \times £51,300 \quad .. \quad .. \quad .. \quad = \quad £41,648$$

On the reversionary interest falling in Estate Duty would be payable thereon as follows:

Net value of A's estate, excluding outstanding reversionary interest	£86,300
Actual value of property comprised in reversionary interest at the date when it fell in	22,700
Total value	£109,000

Estate Duty on £109,000 at 50 per cent. would be £54,500, therefore marginal relief again applies:

45% on £100,000	£45,000
Add excess of estate over £100,000	9,000
	£54,000

Estate Duty payable on reversionary interest

$$\frac{22,700}{109,000} \times £54,000 \quad .. \quad .. \quad .. \quad = \quad £11,246$$

Illustration (3)

Same facts as in illustration (1) except that death occurred on 31st October, 1969. The Estate Duty payable under (*a*) would be:

Present value of estate .. .. =	£99,100

Duty on first £80,000	..	..	..	.. =	34,125
,, ,, next 19,000 at 65 per cent.		..	.. =		12,415
					£46,540

The Estate Duty payable under (b) would be:

On that part of the estate other than the reversionary interest–

$$\frac{86,300}{99,100} \times £46,540 \quad .. \quad .. \quad .. \quad .. \quad .. \quad = \quad £40,528$$

On falling in of reversion:

Total estate	..	..	..	.. =	£111,300
Duty on first £80,000	..	..	..	.. =	34,125
Duty on next 31,300	..	..	..	.. =	20,345
					£54,470

Proportion applicable to reversionary interest

$$\frac{25,000}{111,300} \times £54,470 \quad .. \quad .. \quad .. \quad .. \quad = \quad £12,235$$

Total duty – £40,528 + 12,235   ..   ..   .. =   £52,763

It may happen that the executors, after deciding to defer payment of duty on the reversion until it falls in, at a later date wish to commute the duty in order to facilitate a sale or mortgage of the reversionary interest. In such a case, they can apply to the Commissioners of Inland Revenue for permission, which is usually given, unless the life tenant is not in good health (F.A. 1894, s. 12).

By virtue of Section 2 (1) (b) Finance Act 1894, as amended, personal representatives of a deceased person who has purchased an interest in an expectancy in an estate in which he was interested may elect either to have the interest valued on the basis of the purchase consideration given, or the interest may be valued in accordance with the normal 'open market' method of valuation. The election to pay the duty on the interest in expectancy either on the relevant date or when the interest falls into possession if the settlement subsists beyond the death of the reversioner, can only be made if the interest is valued in an 'open market' manner. The option as to the manner in which the interest is to be valued must be exercised within twelve months after the date of death by notice in writing given to the Board of Inland Revenue.

§ 18. Annuities

The Estate Duty on an annuity or other definite annual sum purchased or provided by the deceased, in respect of which a beneficial interest arises on his death, before 16th April, 1969, may, at the option of the person delivering the account, be paid by four equal yearly instalments. The first instalment is due one year after death and interest on the unpaid portion from the anniversary of death is added to each instalment. At any time, however, the duty for the time being unpaid, with interest to date, may be paid (F.A. 1896, s. 16).

Illustration

A. purchases an annuity payable during the joint lives of his sister and himself, and on the death of either of them, to the survivor.

A. dies. The Estate Duty on the annuity to the sister may be paid by instalments.

Annuities can be valued according to the tables contained in the Succession Duty Act 1853, but these tables are not obligatory for Estate Duty purposes, any proper valuation being sufficient (cf. § 2 of Chapter III). Where the annuity is to terminate on the remarriage of a widow the normal valuation is based on a two-year purchase of the annuity, but this is subject to increase in certain circumstances, e.g. if the widow is over the age of 65 years or the annuity is guaranteed for a definite period regardless of remarriage.

Where an annuity has been given by will, a benefit accrues to the estate of the testator upon the annuitant's death, since the annuity is a charge upon the residue and the death of the annuitant releases such charge. Even though the annuitant dies only two days after the testator who gave the annuity, Estate Duty is payable by reason of the cesser of interest in respect of the portion of the testator's estate required to produce the annuity (*Attorney-General* v. *Watson*, see § 16 post).

§ 19. Disposition, Determination or Enlargement of Life Interests

As has already been shown, the death of the life tenant of settled property gives rise to a liability for Estate Duty on that property, since the determination of the life interest causes a passing of the property within the meaning of s. 2 (1) of the Finance Act 1894. For deaths on or after 16th April, 1969, the following provisions have been superseded by those set out in § 15 of this Chapter. For deaths on or before that date, the fact that the life tenant may have disposed of his life interest will make no difference, so long as the disposition was made to a stranger to the settlement, since the property will still pass on the death of the original life tenant. Where, however, the life tenant disposes of his life interest to the person who, under the settlement, is entitled to the property on the death of the life tenant, the life interest is immediately determined by the disposition, and there will be no passing of the property on his death. It is provided, however, that if, on such a disposition, *bona fide* possession and enjoyment of the property was not assumed by the remainderman to the entire exclusion of the life tenant (i.e. he must receive no further benefit from the property) more than seven years prior to the life tenant's death, the property will be deemed to pass by reference to his death, and Estate Duty will be payable (F.A. 1940, s. 43, F.A. 1968, 14th Sch.). Moreover if at any time after the life tenant has disposed of his interest to the remainderman the life tenant receives a benefit by virtue of any operation associated with the disposition the remainderman will not be deemed to have assumed possession of the property to the entire exclusion of the life tenant, and Estate Duty will be payable on the property on the life tenant's death (F.A. 1950, s. 43).

Illustrations

(1) X. surrenders his life interest in settled property to the remainderman Y., for a cash consideration. With such consideration, or part thereof, X. purchases an annuity from Y. If, as is probable, it can be established that the surrender of the life interest and the purchase of the annuity are associated operations, or that the annuity is payable out of the consideration or the income therefrom, the settled property will be deemed to pass on X's death.

(2) A settlor during her life settled property so that the whole net income was payable to her three children equally and if a child died leaving issue, the issue took equally *per stirpes;* if he left no issue, his share accrued to the surviving children and on the settlor's death, the capital was to be divided under similar provisions. The claim of the children, that each was entitled to exactly the same rights as before, viz. to one-third of the income failed;

they had exchanged interests in income for an absolute interest in capital and Estate Duty was payable on the settlor's death on the whole trust fund (*Coats' Trustees* v. *Lord Advocate*).

A purchase by a life tenant of the reversionary interest is regarded as an enlargement of the life interest, and there is no liability to Estate Duty on the life tenant's death in respect of the life interest. The property will, of course, form part of the life tenant's free estate. If the life tenant dies within seven years after the purchase of the reversion, duty will normally be chargeable on the amount of the consideration paid, and in respect of deaths on or after 16th April, 1969, this provision is extended to cover the purchase of an interest of a person who, after the determination of the life interest could be a discretionary beneficiary of the trust. Should the remainderman die within seven years of the purchase, duty will be payable on any element of gift in the transaction, i.e. to the extent that full consideration was not given for the reversion.

Where the deceased had an interest in property limited to cease on his death any other interest belonging to him is to be deemed to belong to another person so that duty can be claimed in respect of the cessation of his life interest on his death under the provisions of Section 2 (1) (b), F.A. 1894.

§ 20. Repayments of Income Tax

Since the payment of the Income tax and Surtax in his wife's income is the responsibility of a husband, in the absence of a claim for separate assessments, he will receive any repayment whether it arises in respect of his income or his wife or both. If the husband has died, the amount of that repayment which relates to a source of her income will be treated as being held by his personal representatives as on trust for his wife, so that no duty will be payable on that part on his death. This exclusion from liability only applies to tax which has not been met by the husband out of his own pocket. If the wife has died, but not the husband, duty will be payable of the part of the repayment which is attributable to a source of her income (see Inland Revenue Press Release, 11th August, 1967)

CHAPTER V

CAPITAL GAINS TAX AND DEATH

The comments below relate to deaths before 31st March, 1971. For deaths after that date, property is revalued at the market value at death for Capital Gains tax purposes, but Capital Gains tax is not chargeable on the deceased's personal assets as a consequence of his death.

§ 1. Introduction

The death of a taxpayer does not give rise, of itself, to any liability to Income tax and Surtax under Schedule D, Case VII (the short term gains tax). Death is deemed to be a disposal of assets of which the deceased is competent to dispose for Capital Gains tax purposes and, the personal representative will always have to bear in mind the provisions relating to that tax. Such assets are deemed to have been sold by the deceased and acquired by his personal representative at their market value at the date of death. The deceased is treated as having been competent to dispose of all assets which he could, if of full age and capacity, have disposed of by his will, assuming that all assets were situated in England. Assets over which the deceased had a power of appointment or the testamentary power conferred by statute to dispose of entailed interest is not property of which he is competent to dispose. Property situated outside England will be treated as disposed of by the deceased on his death providing that he was resident or ordinarily resident in the United Kingdom in the year of assessment in which he died. It does not matter whether he is domiciled in the United Kingdom. In Scotland a deceased person who was an heir of entail in possession of an entailed estate, whether *sui juris* or not, or a proper liferenter of an estate is treated as having been competent to dispose. It will be noted that the law has been so framed that an infant and/or mental defective is treated as being competent to dispose of property so that Capital Gains tax liabilities may arise on their death.

Readers requiring a full explanation regarding the assets passing on death are referred to *Capital Gains Tax* by the author.

Briefly, the disposal of certain assets, whether by the deceased in his lifetime or by his personal representatives after his death, will not give rise to a Capital Gains tax liability.

These exemptions include:

(*a*) the personal house of the deceased (but only that which he has elected to be his principal residence if he has more than one residence;

(*b*) motor vehicles used commonly as private vehicles;

(*c*) savings certificates and similar non-marketable securities issued under the National Loans Act 1939;

(*d*) proceeds of Insurance policies (except where the deceased purchased a policy in respect of which premiums were paid by another);

(*e*) the gain, within certain limits, arising on the disposal of certain Government securities listed in the Ninth Schedule, F.A. 1965, where the death occurred before 6th April, 1969. In respect of the following securities, Nyasaland Government 3 % Guaranteed Stock 1954/74, Sudan Government 4 % Guaranteed Stock 1974, Sudan Government $4\frac{1}{2}$ % Guaranteed Stock 1939/73 and Tanganyika Government 4 % Guaranteed Stock 1952/72 these limits continue to exist for deaths after that date but all gains (where the security has been held for more than one year) on the sale of other Government securities is exempt from Capital Gains tax.

(*f*) tangible moveable wasting assets, e.g. boats;

(*g*) chattels under £1,000 in value;

(*h*) works of art; and

(*i*) timber.

§ 2. Valuation of Property

Where the asset has to be valued at the price which the asset might reasonably be expected to fetch on a sale in the open market, the valuation for the purposes of Capital Gains tax is conclusive for the purposes of Estate Duty. In other cases, the values for Capital Gains tax and Estate Duty may be different, e.g. where the deceased owned shares in a controlled company which must be valued on a 'net assets' basis for Estate Duty purposes but which will be valued for Capital Gains tax purposes at the price the shares might fetch on a sale in the open market.

Illustration

The deceased died owning 5 per cent. of the shares in XY. Limited, a controlled company. His shares fell to be valued on the 'net assets' basis under Section 55, Finance Act 1940, for Estate Duty purposes. Such valuation might give a value of £1 per share whereas the 'open market' value of a 5 per cent. holding might be 6/– per share.

Personal representatives and their advisers will be concerned when negotiating values with both Capital Gains tax and Estate Duty. The full value will be included in the computation of the Estate Duty, while only the gain in value since acquisition (and if the acquisition by the deceased were prior to 7th April, 1965, only part of that gain) will be included for Capital Gains tax purposes. It will thus normally be advantageous in negotiating with the Inland Revenue to contend for the lowest possible value.

Circumstances may arise when a Capital Gains tax assessment has become conclusive but another assessment is made based on a revised market value, e.g. where an additional assessment is raised. If this occurs, the value for Estate Duty purposes is similarly revised except where prior to the issue of the new assessment a certificate discharging any further claim for estate duty on the asset in question has been given (see Chapter III, § 8), or the Commissioners of Inland Revenue are otherwise precluded from re-opening the estate duty position.

In estimating the value of any settled property to be included in the computation of the Estate Duty liability, the Capital Gains tax liability will be deductible so far as such tax falls to be paid out of the property passing or which falls to be borne by any person who will obtain a beneficial interest in possession in the property.

In computing the gain arising on the deemed disposal on death, there may be deducted incidental costs incurred by the personal representatives or other persons on whom assets devolve.

§ 3. Interrelationship of Capital Gains tax and Estate Duty

Subject to any relief which has been given under the retirement provisions of Section 34, Finance Act 1965, the first five thousand pounds of chargeable capital gains are exempt from Capital Gains tax. The chargeable gains which may be included for this purpose are those arising on the 'deemed' disposal on death and those arising in respect of *donationes mortis causa*, after deducting allowable losses similarly arising.

The deceased may have made chargeable gains in the part of the year of assessment prior to his death and may have made allowable losses. In computing the liability for the year of assessment in which he dies, these items cannot be treated as being part of the chargeable gains covered by the '£5,000 exemption'. But if the gains arising on death exceed £5,000, the excess is aggregated with those arising in the period prior to death to ascertain the chargeable gains of that year. This aggregation may affect the rate of Capital Gains tax since the excess may prevent the other capital gains being taxed on the alternative basis.

Illustration (1)

AB. died on 1st January, 1970. During the period 6th April, 1969, and 31st December, 1969, both dates inclusive, he had carried out transactions on which chargeable gains of £1,000 and allowable losses of £460 had arisen. On the deemed disposal on death, the chargeable gains were £12,200. His other income in the year of death was £10,000 all unearned.

The liability to Capital Gains tax for 1969/70 would be:

Chargeable gains arising prior to death	..	£1,000	
Less allowable losses		460	£540
Chargeable gains arising on death		12,200	
Less standard deduction		5,000	7,200
			£7,740

Liability to Capital Gains tax, 30 per cent. of £7,740 = £2,322.

Illustration (2)

Same facts as in Illustration (1) except that the other income was £3,600 all earned. Calculations to nearest £.

Without the aggregation of the chargeable gains arising on death, the liability would have been on the alternative basis provided for in Section 21, Finance Act 1965.

Earned Income ..	..	..		£3,600		£3,600
Chargeable gains – ½ of £540	..			—		270
				3,600		3,870
Less E.I.R. ..	..	..	£800		£800	
P.R.	..	..	340		340	
C.R.	..	..	115	1,255	115	1,255
				£2,345		£2,615

				£		£
Reduced rate ..	..	..	300	80	300	80
Standard rate..	..	..	2,045	844	2,315	955
				£924		£1,035

Additional tax on capital gains (£1,035 – £924 =) £111.

This compares with the basic charge of £162.

After aggregating the 'excess' capital gains arising on death, the rate of 30 per cent. applies.

Earned income			£3,600		£3,600
Chargeable gains £7,740 but only ½ of £5,000 + £2,740 to be included			—		5,240
			3,600		8,840
Less E.I.R.	£800			£800	
P.R.	340			340	
C.R.	115			115	
		——	1,255	——	1,255
			£2,345		£7,585

				£		£
Reduced rate ..	..	..	300	80	300	80
Standard rate..	..	..	2,045	844	7,285	3,005
				£924		£3,085

SURTAX:

Income as above		8,840
Less E.I.R.	£800	
P.R.	120	
Excess of E.I.R. over £2,000	800	
C.R.	115	
	——	1,835
		£7,005

SURTAX: £1,114.

Additional tax is, therefore, £3,085 + £1,114 = £4,199.

Additional tax is, therefore, £3,085 + £1,114 = £4,199 – £924 = £3,275.

This compares with 30 per cent. of £7,740 = £2,322 so that the latter amount would be payable.

Illustration (2) affords an example of the need for personal representatives, when negotiating valuations with the Inland

Revenue, to consider not only the amount of the valuation but its effect on the rates of Capital Gains tax. The importance of this factor will decrease as the rate of Estate Duty increases.

Illustration (3)

CD. died and left an estate, subject to the liability for capital gains, of £1,000,000. EF. died and his estate, computed on the same basis, amounted to £10,000. The Capital Gains tax payable by CD. was £20,000, by EF. £200. The rate of duty on the slice of an estate from £750,000 to £1,000,000 is 85 per cent; on an estate of £10,000 is Nil. The liability to Capital Gains tax in the case of CD. reduces the Estate Duty payable by 85 per cent. of £20,000 or £17,000 so that the net estate bears only 15 per cent. of the Capital Gains tax liability while in the case of EF. the Estate Duty saving is Nil, leaving the net estate to bear 100 per cent. of liability.

Of course, the beneficiaries of the estate where death occurred before 16th April, 1969, may be sufficiently fortunate to find that the Government pays the full amount of the liability to Capital Gains tax as will occur when the amount of the estate before and after the deduction of that liability falls within the marginal value for duty purposes.

Illustration (4)

The estate of GH deceased before the deduction of the liability to Capital Gains tax amounted to £81,000. The tax liability is £6,000.

The Estate Duty on £75,000 is 40% of £75,000 =	..		..	£30,000
Excess	..	..	..	..	..	6,000
					£36,000

The Estate Duty on £75,000 is 40% of £75,000 = £30,000

Thus the payment of the aggregate of the Estate Duty of £30,000 and the Capital Gains tax of £6,000 does not exceed the duty payable if Capital Gains tax had never been introduced.

In preparing the Estate Duty Affidavit, the legal personal representative should deduct an estimated amount for the Capital Gains tax liability arising on death as a debt due to a creditor resident in Great Britain from the assets forming the personalty of the estate. If no deduction is made the Estate Duty overpaid when ascertained will be repaid but without interest. There is not, in such circumstances, any need to file a corrective affidavit.

Capital Gains tax can be paid by instalments where there is a deemed disposal on the deceased's death and the chargeable gains arise in respect of:

(i) the disposal of land or an estate or interest in land;

(ii) the disposal of shares in a company where the valuation of those shares is made under Section 55, Finance Act 1940 (the 'net assets' basis);

(iii) a disposal of shares in a company not covered by (ii) above and not quoted on a recognized stock exchange in the United Kingdom or elsewhere and where the Commissioners of Inland Revenue are satisfied that the tax cannot be paid at once without undue hardship.

Payment can, in these circumstances, be made by eight equal yearly instalments or sixteen half-yearly instalments with interest at 4 per cent. per annum (without deduction of income tax) on the outstanding balance. The first instalment is due twelve months after the date of deemed disposal. Although the personal representatives may have elected to pay the tax by instalments, they can at any time change their minds and pay the unpaid tax. If the property in respect of which the payments are being made is sold, the unpaid tax becomes due and payable at once (para. 4, Tenth Schedule, F.A. 1965).

In deciding the proportion of the relief for the initial five thousand pounds of chargeable gains which is appropriate to property in (i) to (iii) above, the relief is to be divided between such property and other property on the basis of the tax on the respective gains on the two types of property.

It is understood that at the time of writing, the Estate Duty Office have not made a decision as to whether the full amount of the tax or a discounted amount can be deducted in the Estate Duty Affidavit when a claim is made to make payments by instalments.

Section 26 (1), F.A. 1965, provides that, in determining the value of the estate for Estate Duty purposes, the amount due in respect of Capital Gains tax arising because of the deemed disposal on death, is to be deducted. Any Capital Gains tax arising on transactions in the year of assessment in which death occurs and any unpaid tax for previous years may also be deducted. Except for settled property passing on the death, there is no provision for such tax to be paid out of any specific part of the estate or out of the proceeds of the asset in respect of which it arises. The deceased can provide for the payment out of the proceeds of specified assets but if he does not do so or such proceeds are insufficient, the residue of the estate must bear the tax. Where the deceased makes specific bequests on which substantial chargeable gains may arise (e.g. where a bequest of shares in a family company is made) he should appreciate the effect Capital Gains tax may have on the residue.

Illustration (5)

MN. died on 1st February, 1970, and under the terms of his will he left his shareholding in KL. to his son and the residue of his estate to his wife.

No chargeable gains arose prior to death but on death the chargeable gain in respect of that shareholding, after deducting the relief for £5,000 was £45,000. His only assets at death were:

Shares in KL Limited	£60,000
Insurance policy, proceeds	60,000
House	10,000
Cash at bank	16,000

Apart from the Capital Gains tax liability, the other debts due at death, funeral expenses etc. were £2,400.

Shares		£60,000
Insurance policy		60,000
House		10,000
Cash at bank		16,000
		146,000
Less Debts etc. 2,400		
Capital Gains tax 30% of £45,000 13,500		15,900
		£130,100

Estate Duty payable:

On £80,000	£34,125
On £50,100 at 65%	32,565
	£66,690

The amounts payable out of the residue will be:

Debts etc.	£2,400
Capital Gains tax	13,500
Estate Duty	66,690
	£82,590

The residue is £86,000 so that the widow will enjoy only £3,410 while the son will have his specific legacy valued at £60,000. The problems of providing for one's spouse while passing on the ownership of the family company to a later generation have been substantially increased. In the above case it would seem advisable to leave the whole estate to the wife for life with remainder to the son, so that the widow can receive any dividends on the shares.

§ 4. Loss relief on death

A taxpayer can set off against chargeable gains any allowable losses incurred in the same year of assessment and any allowable losses incurred in previous years and not relieved against chargeable gains of previous years. Allowable losses arising on disposals deemed to occur on death can be set off against chargeable gains arising on such deemed disposals. This set off must be deducted in arriving at the chargeable gains against which the 'death' relief of £5,000 may be set. In so far as the set off has not been made, the allowable losses arising on death may be set against chargeable gains arising on transactions occurring in the year of assessment in which death occurs but before that death.

In some cases, however, the losses arising on disposals deemed to occur on death may exceed the chargeable gains arising on such disposals and those arising prior to death in the year of assessment in which the taxpayer dies. Alternatively, the taxpayer may occur losses in that year which exceed the chargeable gains arising in that year and on death. In both circumstances, a form of terminal relief is provided. Such losses may be set off against the chargeable gains accruing to the deceased in the three years of assessment preceding the year of assessment in which death occurs. Relief for these losses is to be given against chargeable gains of a later year before those of an earlier year; the usual L.I.F.O. method adopted by the Inland Revenue.

Illustration

JK. died on 1st April, 1970. On his death, there were no chargeable gains, while the allowable losses amounted to £15,000. In 1969/70 and prior to his death he had made chargeable gains of £2,580 while in the years 1966/67, 1967/68 and 1968/69 the chargeable gains were £2,000, £2,460 and £3,150. There would be no tax liability on any of these gains, viz.

Gains arising in year of death, 1969/70		..		..	..	£2,580
,,	,,	,,	1968/69	..	..	..	3,150
.,	,,	,,	1967/68	..	..	..	2,460
,,	,,	,,	1966/67	..	..	..	2,000
						£10,190

The balance of the unrelieved losses £(15,000 – 10,190)= £4,810 would be lost. Relief could not be claimed for 1965/66 since chargeable gains arose outside the three year period.

It will be noted that Section 24 (2) states that only gains in excess of £5,000 arising on death will be treated as chargeable gains. Circumstances may arise in which such gains after deducting losses arising on death do not exceed £5,000. There will be no liability arising on such gains nor will there be any relief available for the unused balance of the amount of five thousand pounds (except a limited relief in respect of settled property for which see Chapter XIII, § 31). Where the taxpayer has incurred allowable losses prior to death but in the year of assessment in which death occurs, allowable losses may be set off against chargeable gains in the three preceding years on the basis exemplified in the illustration above. The legal personal representatives will become entitled to repayments of tax paid for the earlier years. Such repayments will form part of the free estate of the deceased and be liable to Estate Duty. The benefit of such repayments will be partially lost in a similar manner to the liability for Capital Gains tax being partially relieved because of the reduction in Estate Duty (see § 3 above).

§ 5. Interrelationship of Retirement relief and the 'Death' exemption

Section 34, F.A. 1965, provides for a retirement relief where an individual, who has attained sixty years of age, disposes of shares in a family trading company which shares he has owned in the ten years prior to the disposal and of which company he has been a full time working director throughout that period. The maximum retirement relief is:

If he has attained 60 years but not 61 years of age　£2,000

,, ,, ,,　,,　61 ,, ,,　,, 62 ,, ,,　,,　£4,000

,, ,, ,,　,,　62 ,, ,,　,, 63 ,, ,,　,,　£6,000

,, ,, ,,　,,　63 ,, ,,　,, 64 ,, ,,　,,　£8,000

,, ,, ,,　,,　65　　　　　　　　　　£10,000

For any part of a year by which the taxpayer exceeds the lower age he is entitled to a proportionate part of £2,000.

Illustration

OP. disposes of shares when aged 60 years and 4 months – max. relief £667
PQ.   „   „   „   „   „   62   „   „   8 months – „   „   £5,333
QR.   „   „   „   „   „   66   „   „   „   „ £10,000

A similar relief may be claimed where:

(a) the taxpayer disposes of the whole or part of a business which he has owned throughout the ten years prior to disposal; or

(b) the taxpayer disposes of shares in a family trading company and in the ten year period he has either owned those shares or the whole or part of the business formerly carried on by him and at the time of disposal owned by the family trading company; or

(c) the taxpayer disposes of the whole or part of a business which he owned and in the ten year period, he owned either the whole or part of the business or sufficient shares in the family trading company which carried on that business. Full details of such relief will be found in *Capital Gains Tax* by the same author. Readers should appreciate that there is no need for the taxpayer to retire, merely to dispose of a particular type of asset which he has held for a specified time and be of a certain age.

It is provided that where retirement relief has been claimed, the amount of the exemption on chargeable gains arising on death shall be reduced by the excess of the retirement relief over £5,000 (Section 34 (4), F.A. 1965). This provision has the effect of limiting the aggregate retirement relief and exemption on death to £10,000. In deciding the effect of retirement relief a taxpayer must consider his potential Estate Duty position as well as the Capital Gains tax liability for the year of assessment in which disposal is made. He will have to determine or estimate:

(i) the amount of the chargeable gain and the maximum liability to Capital Gains tax in that year of assessment;

(ii) the assets which he is likely to own at his death and the extent to which capital gains are likely to arise thereon;

(iii) the rate of Estate Duty likely to be levied on death and whether the amount of the estate will fall within the 'marginal' limits;

  (iv) the effect on the dispositions under his will of increasing the Capital Gains tax liability at the time of his death;

  (v) his existing resources to pay the tax in his lifetime and provide for his needs during his life;

  (vi) the loss of relief by his failing to claim any retirement relief and only obtaining exemption on death in the sum of £5,000 and

(vii) the future rates of Capital Gains tax.

There is no provision whereby the taxpayer can only claim such retirement relief as he personally wishes. It 'shall be given'. He can only limit the retirement relief for making such disposals as only gives him partial relief. Normally, it will be advantageous to obtain the maximum retirement relief since –

(*a*) relief on £10,000 at the present time must be worth more than relief on £5,000 at some future date;

(*b*) if in respect of deaths before 16th April, 1969, the value of the estate falls into the 'marginal fields' (see illustration (4) in § 3), the Government gains no additional sum by increasing the Capital Gains tax liability arising at death; even if the amount of the estate does not fall into the marginal areas, the larger the estate the lower the percentage of the Capital Gains tax which will be borne by residue; and

(*c*) the retention of the cash which would be expended on the tax must be beneficial to the taxpayer himself.

The retirement relief is given against chargeable gains arising on the disposal of chargeable business assets where the whole or part of a business is sold or otherwise disposed of to another person. For these purposes, 'chargeable business asset' means –

'An asset (including goodwill but not including shares or securities or other assets held as investments) which is, or is an interest in, an asset used for the purposes of a trade, profession, vocation, office or employment carried on by the individual, other than an asset on the disposal of which no chargeable gain accrues.'

Where the disposal is of shares or securities in a family trading company, a chargeable business asset is –

'An asset (including goodwill but not including shares or securities or other assets held as investments) which is, or is an interest in, an asset used for the purposes of a trade carried on by the individual's family company, other than an asset on the disposal of which no chargeable gain accrues or on the disposal of which no chargeable gain would accrue if the family company disposed of the asset at the time of the disposal of the shares or securities.'

A 'family company' means, in relation to an individual, a company the voting rights in which are –

(*a*) as to not less than twenty-five per cent., exercisable by the individual, or

(*b*) as to not less than seventy-five per cent., exercisable by the individual or a member of his family, and, as to not less than ten per cent, exercisable by the individual himself.

'Family' means, in relation to an individual, the husband or wife of the individual, and a relative of the individual or the individual's husband or wife.

'Relative' means brother, sister, ancestor or descendant.

Illustration

ST. died on 1st February, 1968, aged 69 years. His estate consisted of –

Shares in ST. & Son Limited, valued at	£40,000
Private House	15,000
Shares in quoted companies	16,000
Insurance policies	10,000
Cash at bank	3,000
His liabilities were:	
Debts due at death..	1,900
Funeral expenses	100
His chargeable capital gains were:	
Shares in ST. & Son Limited	3,000
Shares in quoted companies	1,500

In the year 1966/67 ST. had disposed of shares in ST. & Son Limited and a chargeable gain of £5,000 had arisen thereon. ST. did not pay any Capital Gains tax on that sum since he was, by reason of his age, entitled to retirement relief of more than £5,000. Since that relief did not exceed £5,000 the exemption at death would not be reduced. The Estate Duty liability at death would be (the possible benefits of reduced rate of duty on shares in controlled companies has been ignored): ˙

Shares in ST. & Son Limited	..	..	..	.. £40,000
Private House	..	..	..	.. 15,000
Shares in quoted companies	..	..	..	.. 16,000
Insurance policies	..	..	..	.. 10,000
Cash at bank	..	..	..	.. 3,000

				84,000
Less debts due at death	..	..	.. 1,900	
funeral expenses	..	..	.. 100	
Capital Gains tax –				
Chargeable gains	..	.. 4,500		
Less exemption ..	..	.. 5,000	NIL	2,000

Fixing rate of duty at 45 per cent.   ..   £82,000

Estate Duty £36,900.

If retirement relief had been £6,500 the exemption at death would have been £3,500, thereby creating a liability at death of £1,000 at 30 per cent. which would have reduced the net estate to £81,700. On an estate of this size the duty would be 40 per cent. on £75,000, namely £30,000 plus £6,700 or a total of £36,700.

In 1966/67, assuming the alternative charge basis did not apply, the relief against Capital Gains tax on the excess of the retirement relief over £5,000 would have been – 30 per cent. of £1,500 or £450. At death, the loss of that relief increased the Capital Gains tax liability by £1,500 at 30 per cent. or £450, but the latter liability was partially met by a reduction in Estate Duty of £(36,900 – 36,700 =) 200. Therefore, by obtaining retirement relief ST. saved himself £450 at the time of disposal and £200 at the date of death; the net charge to the estate being £250.

If death had occurred after 15th April, 1969, the Estate Duty payable on £82,000 would have been £35,425. If the estate had been reduced to £81,700 the total Estate Duty payable would have fallen by £195 to £35,230. There would thus have been a benefit to the estate similar to that previously described but of smaller amount due to the lower Estate Duty payable under the new system.

A taxpayer cannot avoid the restriction of the exemption of the first five thousand pounds of chargeable gains arising on death by the excess of the retirement relief by giving away shares immediately before his death, if that gift can be shown to be a *donatio mortis causa*. The latter is defined as a gift on account of death; a gift of personal property intended to become effective only on his death made by a person who apprehends that he is in danger of death. He may, however, be able to get additional relief by obtaining the maximum relief of £10,000 under the retirement provisions and foregoing his 'death' exemption. It clearly will not be advisable for a taxpayer to 'drop dead' but rather to remain alive, if lingering, while the potential personal representatives compute whether the retirement relief will apply and, if so, the taxpayer must make gifts of shares in family businesses or family trading companies prior to death. Perhaps major shareholders in such companies or partners should have proper deeds of gift drafted to which they can append their signature at any time.

§ 6. Personal Representatives

In respect of their dealings with the estate of a deceased person the personal representatives are treated as a single continuing body of persons so that changes in personal representatives will not give rise to an acquisition or disposal for either the purposes of Schedule D, Case VII (Section 12 (7), F.A. 1962) or Capital Gains tax (Section 24 (6), F.A. 1965). For Case VII purposes the personal representatives are treated as being resident and ordinarily resident in the United Kingdom, unless the general administration of the estate is ordinarily carried on outside and the majority of such representatives are not resident or not ordinarily resident in the United Kingdom. For Capital Gains tax purposes the personal representatives are treated as having the deceased's residence, ordinary residence and domicile at the date of death. The distinction may be important since Case VII liabilities cannot arise on a person who is not resident *and* ordinarily resident whereas Capital Gains tax liabilities can arise when a person is resident without necessarily being ordinarily resident.

'Personal representatives' means, in relation to the estate of a deceased person, his personal representatives in England and Wales as defined by Section 55, of the Administration of Estates Act 1925 (i.e.· the Executor (including a person deemed to be appointed executor as respects settled land) original or by representation, or administrator for the time being of the deceased) and persons having in relation to the deceased under the law of another country any functions corresponding to the functions for administration purposes under the law of England and Wales of personal representatives as so defined, and references to personal representatives as such shall be construed as reference to the personal representatives in their capacity as having such functions as aforesaid) (s. 423 (4), I.T.A. 1952).

Thus it is the residential status of the personal representatives rather than that of the deceased person which determines this matter but there is one exception to the rule in that if the personal representative is a 'body corporate carrying on a business which consists of or includes the management of trusts, and acting as trustee of a trust in the course of that business' it will be treated as not resident in the United Kingdom if the deceased, at the time of his death, was not domiciled, resident or ordinarily resident in the United Kingdom.

The taxation liabilities affecting personal representatives under wills or intestacies may be considered in relation to a number of successive periods.

(a) *Before the date of death:* These are personal Income tax and Capital Gains tax liabilities of the deceased. To the extent that they had not been assessed and paid during his lifetime they must be ascertained and paid by the personal representatives. Such liabilities, whether accrued before the date of death or not, are payable as debts out of the capital of his free estate and are allowable deductions for Estate Duty purposes. Any necessary claims for carrying back allowable losses against assessments to Capital Gains tax in the preceding three years should be made and the amounts repayable agreed.

The duty of agreeing assessments for the year in which the death occurred (proportion up to date of death) and, in many cases, for the year preceding that, is likely to fall on the personal representatives. Details of the method of agreement of Income tax and Surtax liabilities in respect of sources of income other than those falling within Schedule D, Case VII, is outside the scope of this book. Readers are referred to *Income Tax* (Spicer and Pegler) edited by the same author.

Liability under Schedule D, Case VII, cannot arise unless there has been both an acquisition and a disposal of a chargeable asset, within the relevant period. Acquisition and disposal are much wider expressions than purchase and sale; it may be necessary to consider gifts and bargains not made at arm's length. But liability will not arise because of the death of the deceased. In some cases a potential liability under Case VII may be reduced or avoided by an appropriate election under the provisions of the Ninth Schedule, Finance Act 1962. It is obvious that the personal representatives, or their professional advisers, may be faced with a wide field of enquiry which is not made any easier by the death of one of the principal parties to the relevant transactions. This field may be narrowed by considering some of the more important exemptions, as follows:

(i) Non-chargeable assets need not be considered. These are defined in s. 11, F.A. 1962, as amended by the Twenty-second Schedule, F.A. 1965, and include motor cars, chattels worth less than £1,000 each, works of art of historic etc. interest, a dwelling-house or part of a dwelling house which was the only or main residence of the deceased, and patent rights.

(ii) Assets acquired by the deceased before April 10th, 1962, or as a legacy need not be considered as the subsequent disposal of them will not give rise to a chargeable gain.

(iii) Assets owned by the deceased at the date of his death need not be considered because, however recently they have been acquired, there has been no disposal of them. It is specifically provided that the vesting of a deceased's property in his personal representatives does not constitute an acquisition or disposal (s. 12 (7), F.A. 1962).

When all the foregoing have been eliminated there may remain to be considered a large volume of transactions in stocks and shares. If the deceased has not kept complete records of his dealings, particulars will have to be obtained from stockbrokers and bankers of all the relevant transactions. The possibility and effect of option and contango transactions should not be overlooked, the relative provisions of the Ninth Schedule (*ibid.*) being applied to these and for the purpose of identifying disposals with acquisitions where they have been several transactions in the same kind of investment. It will be remembered that sales of bonus shares or 'rights' are disposals but the dates of acquisition are fixed by reference to the purchases of the holdings which gave rise to them.

A similar procedure must be adopted in respect of the Capital Gains tax liabilities except that death will be deemed to be a disposal so that the assets in (iii) above cannot be ignored.

(*b*) *During the Administration Period:* Assessments under Schedule D, Case VII, on personal representatives during the administration period (that is, from the date of death to the date on which the residue is ascertained) may arise if in the course of administering the estate they acquire and dispose of chargeable assets within the relevant time limit. If the disposal is more than twelve months after the date of death or after the acquisition by the personal representatives who acquired the asset otherwise than on death, any chargeable gain will be liable to Capital Gains tax. If the personal representatives dispose of an asset within twelve months of the acquisition by the deceased, Capital Gains tax will be payable on any chargeable gains, since the personal representatives will not have made any acquisition. The vesting of the deceased's property is not treated as an acquisition and disposal (Section 12 (7), F.A. 1962).

Personal representatives will only be liable to assessment under Schedule D, Case VII, when, in the course of administration, they acquire and dispose of chargeable assets within twelve months. Such liabilities might arise from the temporary investment of surplus funds or from the acquisition (and subsequent disposal) of an asset with the object of protecting the value of existing assets. In the latter connection, it should be noted that the 'enhancement' provisions of Section 13 (5), F.A. 1962, do not apply to 'land acquired as legatee'.

Illustration (1)

VW acquired on 1st June, 1968, the freehold of 10 acres of land which were valued for probate, on his death on 12th December, 1968, at £20,000. In June, 1969, VW's executors were able to acquire a neighbouring plot of 1 acre with access to a public road at a cost of £30,000 and they sold the whole 11 acres for £130,000.

It is agreed that:

(i) the value of the 10 acres immediately before the acquisition of the additional 1 acre was £72,000.

(ii) the proceeds may be apportioned as to £90,000 for the original 10 acres and £40,000 for the 1 acre.

Subject to deduction for the relevant expenses of acquisition and disposal the personal representatives will be assessed under Case VII on £40,000 – £30,000 = £10,000.

If VW had survived and had completed the transaction himself, the profit would have been calculated as follows:

Proceeds of 1 acre	£40,000
Add Enhancement in value of 10 acres £90,000 – £72,000 ..	18,000
Carried forward	£58,000

	Brought forward	£58,000
Less Cost of 1 acre		30,000
Chargeable gain (subject to expenses)		£28,000

Note–for the sake of simplicity, the effect of the Betterment Levy has been ignored.

Where the personal representatives are assessable under Schedule D, Case VII in respect of any chargeable gain made during the administration period, their liability will be to Income tax alone. Surtax liability, if any, is a matter affecting the residuary lagatees. Where a legatee has an absolute interest, the Schedule D, Case VII, liability created by the personal representative must be regarded as part of the income of that legatee for the year of assessment in which the liability arises. Where the legatee has a limited interest, e.g. a life interest, no part of the liability will be his income for Surtax purposes since he does not have any interest in capital.

Personal representatives may not have to worry unduly regarding the provisions of Schedule D, Case VII, having ascertained any outstanding liabilities at death. But the problems of Capital Gains tax must be considered on every disposal, including those made to provide for Estate Duty payments. Capital Gains tax will always be payable by the personal representatives at 30 per cent. The alternative charge basis laid down in Section 21, F.A. 1965, does not apply. If a disposal is made to a legatee, the latter acquires the asset as at the date of death at the value fixed at that date for Capital Gains tax purposes. If the personal representative acquires an asset to satisfy the legacy, the legatee is treated as acquiring the asset on the date the personal representative acquired it, at the price paid by him. Different values may be appropriate for different legatees following the provision that a legatee takes the shares at the Capital Gains tax value at death.

Illustration (2)

JM owned sixty per cent. of the issued share capital of OM Limited at the date of his death. These shares were valued at that date at £6 per share. He left each of his six sons, one-tenth of his holding. His wife was killed in the same car accident and at her death, she held ten per cent. of the issued share capital of OM Limited and this holding was valued at £2 per share.

She left her shares to the eldest of the six sons. The eldest son thus holds twenty per cent. of the issued share capital, of which one half is valued at £6 per share and the other half at £2 per share.

The transfer by the personal representative to the legatee is not treated as a disposal by the personal representative.

If the disposal is not to a legatee, the personal representatives will pay Capital Gains tax on any chargeable gain, which will be the difference between the proceeds of disposal and the aggregate of the costs of disposal, the value at the date of death and any expenditure on enhancement between the date of death and disposal provided that the enhancement remains in the state of affairs of the asset at the date of disposal. If the personal representatives make losses on disposal, they may set these off against the chargeable gains assessable on them for the same year of assessment as that in which the loss arises. They cannot set them against chargeable gains assessable on them for previous years of assessment. But in respect of deaths on or before 5th April, 1969, any losses which accrue to them in the period of three years from death they may, if they cannot otherwise obtain relief, deduct from them the chargeable gains accruing to the deceased in the year of assessment in which death occurs or in the three years of assessment preceding the year in which death occurred. They set off the losses against chargeable gains of later years before those of earlier years.

Illustration (3)

PD died on 1st December, 1967. The chargeable gains arising on the deemed disposals on death were £8,600. The chargeable gains arising in 1967/68 prior to death were £600. In 1965/66 and 1966/67 the chargeable gains were respectively £900 and £1,200.

In 1967/68 the personal representatives made chargeable gains of £860. In 1968/69 their chargeable gains were £1,700 but in the last year of their administration they made allowable losses of £6,200 and chargeable gains of £100.

The amounts assessable would be:

Personal representatives –					£
1967/68 Chargeable gains	..	..	..	..	860
1968/69 ,, ,,	..	..	..	..	1,700
1969/70 ,, ,,	£100				
Less allowable losses	6,200				NIL
Allowable losses unused	£6,100				

In respect of the deceased –

1967/68 chargeable gains arising on deemed disposal	..		£8,600
Less exemption relief under Section 24	..	..	5,000
			3,600
Less allowable losses of personal representative		..	3,600
			——— NIL
1967/68 Chargeable gains prior to death	..	..	600
Less allowable losses of personal representatives		..	600
			——— NIL
1966/67 Chargeable gains		..	1,200
Less allowable losses of personal representatives		..	1,200
			——— NIL
1965/66 Chargeable gains		..	900
Less allowable losses of personal representatives		..	700
			——— 200

Notes

(1) Section 24 (3) provides that chargeable gains arising on death are to be treated as gains accruing to the deceased in the year of assessment in which death occurs. Where section 24 (8) provides for the losses of personal representatives to be set against chargeable gains arising to the deceased in the year of assessment in which death occurs, it would seem that such gains must include those arising on deemed disposals on death. This is the view of the Inland Revenue (see paragraph 169) of the booklet on Capital Gains tax issued in February 1966).

(2) Since losses cannot be set against gains arising in previous years of assessment the personal representatives must pay Capital Gains tax in 1967/68 and 1968/69.

In respect of deaths occurring after 5th April, 1969, the comments above relating to losses accruing in the three years before death have been amended by paragraph 5, 19th Schedule, Finance Act 1969. In future losses or gains arising in the three years beginning with the death in respect of assets of which the deceased was competent to dispose will not accrue to personal representatives. Instead the gains or losses are to be deemed to have arisen to the deceased at the time of his death. Although Capital Gains tax will be computed for the purposes of assessing the original Estate Duty without regard to these provisions the computation will have to be amended at the end of the three year period or the end of the period of administration whichever occurs first. Personal representatives will have to be particularly careful regarding sales in this period since the losses will reduce the Capital Gains tax burden at death while sales will increase the Capital Gains tax liability. Sales which are deemed to accrue on the date of death may change the basis of assessment to 30 per cent. from the alternative charge basis. If the personal representatives do not make a disposal within this three year period gains or losses will be chargeable on them or allowable to them on the basis set out above.

In view of the foregoing amendments the rights of personal representatives to set their losses against those arising to the deceased in the three years of assessment prior to death cease in respect of deaths after 5th April, 1969. This loss of relief is unimportant since the losses deemed to arise on death will constitute allowable losses which may be deducted from the chargeable gains accruing to the deceased in the three years of assessment preceding that in which death occurs.

For death after 6th April, 1969, in determining the relief of £5,000 mentioned in § 5 above, if the chargeable gains arising in the three years following death exceed the allowable losses in that period the excess is to be ignored in determining whether any part of the relief of £5,000 is available to trustees where the deceased died having an interest in settled property but if the allowable losses exceed the chargeable gains these may be added to the sum of £5,000.

If personal representatives set off losses made by themselves against chargeable gains made by the deceased, there will be a repayment of tax. The amount repaid may not be at the rate of 30 per cent., since the alternative basis of charging tax may have been appropriate in the years prior to death. The amount of tax repaid in such circumstances is not an asset at the date of death and cannot be liable to Estate Duty. If the figures for the years prior to death had not been agreed and the personal representatives make the claims illustrated above, the amount deductible for Estate Duty purposes is the amount before deducting relief for losses. Since these arose by reason of events occurring after death, they cannot affect the computation of the Estate Duty liability.

Personal representatives must be particularly careful which assets they dispose of to pay Estate Duty, debts, legacies and administration expenses to limit the further burden of Capital Gains tax. They will need to decide whether to realise property within the three years subsequent to death or outside that period, remembering that disposals within that period will be deemed to occur on death, while those outside that period will be their responsibility and will be borne by the residuary legatee(s). Where gains are inevitable they must, as far as possible, ensure that they incur losses before gains or in the same year of assessment. Furthermore they should appreciate that if they assent to a legacy so that the beneficiary becomes absolutely entitled to the subject matter of the legacy, any gain arising on the disposal of that subject matter after assent will be a liability of the beneficiary not that of the personal representatives. Since the majority of legatees receiving assets from the personal representatives will want the asset treated as being acquired by them at the highest possible value, to limit the chargeable gain assessable on them on a later disposal (which chargeable gain will be the full amount of the difference between the proceeds of disposal and the transfer value) care will have to be taken in distributing assets in specie. Non-residents and charities will not be concerned as to the values at which assets are transferred to them. To assist in revising the bequests of the deceased so as to give the greatest advantage to beneficiaries, it is provided that if not more than two years after death any of the dispositions of the deceased's property, whether under the provisions of his will or the law relating to intestacies, are varied under a deed of family arrangement or similar instrument, the deceased will have been deemed to have disposed of his assets in accordance with that deed. The variations provided in the deed will not be treated as disposals.

(c) *At the end of the Administration Period:* When the personal representatives have paid all duties and taxes due, all debts, funeral expenses, all specific, demonstrative and general legacies and administration expenses, they will dispose of the residue of the estate in accordance with the provisions of the deceased's will or the law relating to intestacy. The transfers of assets to the residuary legatees will not, of themselves, constitute a disposal by the personal representatives. The legatee will take the assets at their values at death for Capital Gains tax purposes and will be deemed to have acquired them at that date and for those values. He cannot suffer any Schedule D, Case VII, liability on the disposal of such assets since he will receive them as a legatee.

If the personal representatives had acquired the assets after death, he will be treated as acquiring them on their date of acquisition and at the cost to them. Since the assets will also form part of his legacy, Schedule D, Case VII, cannot apply to any future disposal by him.

If the deceased's will or the law of intestacy requires the residue to be transferred to trustees for life tenants or for other beneficiaries with limited interests, the transfer to such trustees will not be treated as a disposal by the personal representatives. Prior to giving their assent, the personal representatives should consider the position regarding the gains and losses arising during the administration period, as once they have assented the assets will belong to a different body of persons, namely the trustees for the life tenant or other beneficiary. In many cases the personal representatives may be the same persons as the trustees. The moment of assent should be determined so as to avoid arguments in the future.

CHAPTER VI

GIFTS INTER VIVOS

§ 1. Introduction

Gifts made within a relatively short period before the death are subject to Estate Duty under the provisions of Section 2 (1) (c) of the Finance Act 1894, together with numerous amendments which have been contained in ensuing Finance Acts.

A donor will not be treated as having made a gift unless he has ceased to retain any benefit in the property. The property must be enjoyed by the donee to the entire seclusion of the donor. If this condition is not satisfied, the property is dutiable whenever given. A similar result will follow where the donor fails to make the gifts effective by his own mistake.

All gifts made by the deceased within the seven years preceding his death, are dutiable as if they had formed part of his property at the date of his death, but there are exceptions which are as follows:

(a) Gifts made for public or charitable purposes more than twelve months before the death;

(b) Gifts made in consideration of marriage, including certain wedding gifts providing that the property comprised in the gift is limited to the spouses to the marriage, their issue, and the spouses of such issues and subject to certain maxima;

(c) Gifts which are part of the normal expenditure of the deceased providing they are reasonable and have been paid out of the deceased's income;

(d) Unsettled property not exceeding £500 in total, or settled property not exceeding £100 in total, which has been given to the same donee in the seven years prior to the date of death;

(e) Gifts which are expressed to be applied in reduction of the National Debt, either immediately or at some time in the future.

Gifts *inter vivos* which have been made during the seven year period, or which otherwise became liable to Estate Duty may change by description and in value between the date of the gift and the death of the donor. Various rules have been laid down by Section 38 of the Finance Act 1957, with a view to regulating the position, and these will be dealt with in detail in § 5 below.

Relief is afforded by the Finance Act 1960, where the death occurs within the fifth, sixth or seventh year after the gift has been made since the value of the gift for Estate Duty purposes is reduced by 15%, 30% and 60% respectively. This relief is not restricted to gifts *inter vivos*, but is available to other dispositions deemed to have been made in relation to the death, which can be classified generally as being of the same nature, e.g. determination of life interests, premiums paid on life policies. The reduction in value of the gift made in consequence of the above relief, is not to be taken into account in determining whether a gift is exempt from duty, on the ground that it does not exceed £500 in value; thus if a gift of £700 is made in the sixth year prior to the death, for aggregation purposes it will be treated as a gift of £490, but it would not on this account be exempt from duty, the maximum duty payable thereon being the excess of the value of the gift before the reduction, i.e. £700 over the sum of £500 so that relief is £200.

Generally speaking, the Estate Duty chargeable on gifts *inter vivos* is normally leviable on the donee. The testator by inserting the appropriate clause in his will, can give directions that the duty payable on such gifts be paid out of the residue of his estate, or some other fund put aside by him for that purpose.

§ 2. Definition

The primary requirement in determining whether a gift has been made is that there should be an element of bounty. Dispositions of property which are made for full consideration fall outside the scope of the definition and there can be no gift. If dispositions are made for partial consideration, the parties to the transaction must be unrelated, and the contract must be a valid contract within the normal rules of contract if the transaction is not to involve a gift. The consideration must arise either at present time or in the future; past consideration is of no account. The parties to the contract must acquire all the rights and liabilities which are accorded to the parties of normal contracts. Where there is a disposition of property to a stranger and the consideration falls short of the true value of the property contained in that disposition, the Inland Revenue, in order to substantiate a claim for duty on that property, must be able to prove that there was a bounteous desire on the part of the disponor. Disposition made to relatives, however, are automatically treated as gifts, and hence dutiable, unless full and adequate consideration has proceeded from the donee. The onus of justifying the adequacy of the consideration in this instance rests entirely on the donee of that property; the proof necessary in both circumstances shifts with regard to the relationship of the donor to the donee

Gifts *inter vivos* which are made prior to the seven year period before the donor's death are not liable to Estate Duty, providing the property taken under the gift has been assumed by the donee immediately after the gift was made or, assumed outside the seven year period if not assumed immediately, and the donor has been excluded from any benefit proceeding from that gift, either by way of contract or otherwise. If the gift is made subject to any reservation of benefit for the enjoyment of the donor, the exemption does not run until such reservation has been surrendered. If, by chance, during the seven year period prior to the date of the donor's death, the donor has been in a position to obtain any benefit from the subject matter of the gift, the exemption will be lost. Thus, in one instance, property had been given outside the statutory period by the deceased to his son. This property subsequently formed part of the partnership assets in which both the deceased and his son were partners. It was held that the donor of the property had not been entirely excluded from enjoyment of the property, and hence the exemption was lost (*Chick* v. *Commissioner of Stamp Duties*). If the gift of a share in a partnership is given as a *bona fide* transaction outside the seven-year period, it is unusual for the Revenue to claim the deceased retained an interest in the share given away, *New Law Journal*, November 1966. Where property is given by the donor, and he subsequently becomes the trustee of that property for the donee, the condition as to exclusion of the donor is still satisfied and the exemption will not be lost. There is one important exception to this general rule provided by Section 35 (2), Finance Act 1959, whereby if the property is an interest in land or consists of chattels and the deceased donor had received full consideration from the partnership for the right to use such land or chattels, the gift will be exempted from the charge for duty.

If there is the slightest possibility of the gift, or some part of it, reverting back to the donor, it will become subject to duty, even if such reversion occurs indirectly, e.g. where as a result of an imperfect gift the Inland Revenue are able to claim that there is a resulting trust in favour of the donor.

Where property is purchased in another's name, it is necessary to ensure that the Inland Revenue cannot claim that the donor had the right to exercise a lien on the property in respect of the purchase monies. Such a presumption can only be rebutted upon the production of satisfactory evidence, which is frequently shown by reciting in the deed of gift, if cne has been executed, that no such lien exists. Such declaration must be made where life policies have been effected by the deceased upon his own life for the benefit of others, as in such cases the Inland Revenue have successfully contended in the past that the donor has had a lien upon the policy monies in respect of the payment of the premiums over the *full* life of the policy.

Debts due to the deceased which were extinguished by him before the date of his death, without receiving adequate consideration, are treated as dutiable gifts if they were extinguished in the statutory seven year period while 'artificial debts' (i.e. those created by the deceased where he has received no consideration at all) are disallowable as a liability for Estate Duty purposes. If the donor dies insolvent, gifts *inter vivos* liable to Estate Duty are assessed without any deduction for his debts; no allowance can be made for debts beyond the value of the assets out of which they are payable (*Re Barnes*).

Joint property presents complexities not of valuation, but in determining the beneficial interest of the deceased. The prime requisite is one of evidence, in as much as there may be no formal agreement between the parties as to their respective interests in the property.

Where land is involved, there may be a joint tenancy in which case, on the death of one party to the transaction, the survivor acquires the whole interest in that property, or it may be a conveyance in which the parties are stated to be beneficial tenants in common, in which case the share of the deceased will pass to his personal representatives. Usually, when one person provides the whole of the money for the purchase of the property and has it conveyed into joint names, when that person dies the whole of the property passes for Estate Duty purposes, unless there is a presumption of advancement. Such presumption will arise between a husband and his wife and/or children, or persons to whom the donor stands in *loco-parentis*, i.e. there is a moral obligation to support the other person. If this presumption can be substantiated the person to whom the property is advanced takes an immediate absolute interest.

The most common occurrence with joint property is that held by husband and wife, and in cases where there is little evidence to support any other contention the courts treat the purchase money has having been provided by husband and wife equally. A similar situation arises with joint bank accounts, but in this instance both must operate the account, which means in effect that there must be joint contributions of receipts in that bank account and not only joint withdrawals. Where the husband alone contributes the receipts to the account, it is usually inferred that the ability of both spouses to draw cheques on the account is an arrangement of convenience only. The balance on the Account remains the husband's property. By virtue of Section 1 of the Married Women's Property Act 1964 property which has been purchased out of house-keeping money is deemed to belong to husband and wife in equal shares, in the absence of any agreement to the contrary. It should not be overlooked that in practice husband and wife may operate a joint bank account into which will be transferred or credited, monies in respect of the house-keeping allowance. In this case the above rule as to the apportioning of the bank balance will not apply, and any balance thereon at the death of either party to the marriage will be divided equally. The husband could agree to give away his share of any savings, in which case the balance would belong to the wife. Such gifts should be evidenced in writing. Estate Duty is unlikely to be assessable on the gifts since they will usually be out of income.

When investments are purchased by one person, and placed in the names of that person and another, it is usually inferred that the purchaser intended the other to obtain an interest in such funds only if the purchaser pre-deceased the other person. For example, if a husband makes investments in the names of himself and his wife and the wife pre-deceases the husband, there would appear to be no charge for Estate Duty as there would be a resulting trust to the husband. The argument for such assumption would be strengthened where the income has been used generally by husband and wife. Conversely, if the husband pre-deceases the wife, upon his death Estate Duty will be leviable on the full value of the investments at the date of death.

§ 3. Date of Gift

The date of effectively making the gift is clearly important since the preliminaries leading to the vesting of the gift may ensue sometime outside the statutory seven-year period, but the actual date of vesting is maybe inside the seven-year period. The gift is not completed until it is irrecoverable from the point of view of the donor. This does not mean that the entire formalities necessary to effect the vesting have to be completed; all that is necessary is that the donor has done everything necessary from his side to effect the gift, e.g. in a transfer of shares, if the donor has completed the transfer the fact that the transfer has not been registered in the books of the company or that the share certificate has not been issued in the name of the donee is immaterial.

Where a person entitled to shares in a company on the sale of a business issued a direction to the company to allot specified numbers of shares to his children, it was held that the direction was an equitable assignment of rights and a perfect gift on the day the direction was given. Although the actual issue of shares was within five years of death, Estate Duty was not payable, since the direction was outside the five years (*Letts* v. *C.I.R.*)

The period of five years which applied when the case was decided is now seven years.

§ 4. Exemptions

From the list of exemptions set out in the introduction to this chapter, it can be seen that there are numerous exemptions from duty in respect of gifts made within the statutory seven-year period. These will now be examined in detail.

[a] **Gifts made for public and charitable purposes, more than twelve months before the date of death are subject to complete**

exemption. The term 'public or charitable purposes' has been held to include gifts made for political purposes. 'Charitable' will include gifts for the relief of poverty, advancement of education and/or religion and for any purpose beneficial to the community. Whether or not an intended gift falls within the ambit of this provision, can be ascertained from the Inland Revenue before the gift is made.

[b] **Dispositions of property in consideration of marriage** providing they benefit a fixed class of persons (s. 53, F.A. 1963) and do not exceed a prescribed amount (s. 36, F.A. 1968). The limitation in the amount which can be given applies only to gifts after 19th March, 1968, and deaths after that date. To be exempt, regardless of the amount involved, the persons to whom the property is given must be restricted to:

(1) In the case of an outright gift, the spouses of the marriage.

(2) In the case of other property, the following persons:

 (i) the parties to the marriage, their issue, or a wife or husband of any such issue;

 (ii) persons becoming entitled on the failure of trusts for any such issue under which trust property would vest indefeasibly on the attainment of a specified age or on some earlier event; or persons becoming entitled on the failure of any limitation in tail;

 (iii) a subsequent wife or husband of a party to the marriage, or any issue, or the wife or husband of any issue, of a subsequent marriage of either party;

 (iv) persons becoming entitled under protective trusts under Section 33 (1) of the Trustee Act 1925, where the principal beneficiary is a person falling within (i) or (iii) above;

 (v) as respects a reasonable amount by way of remuneration, the trustees of the settlement (Finance Act 1963, s. 53).

In order for the gift to be exempt, the marriage for which it is expressed to be made must be contemplated to take place in a reasonable time, and the parties thereto must be in a position to effect a valid marriage; thus the pre-requisite of a divorce before the relevant parties can get married will not exempt the gift. The gift may be made before or after the marriage, but in the latter instance there must be an agreement in existence before the marriage took place. Gifts made in consideration of the disponor's own marriage are not exempt from Estate Duty (s. 53 (2), Finance Act 1963).

Where a gift is made in consideration of marriage the stamp duty on the gift will be 10/- (s. 64, Finance Act 1963). Gifts in money do not attract stamp duty.

In respect of gifts after 19th March, 1968 and deaths after that date, Estate Duty will be levied on the excess of the value of the gift over the figures mentioned in (vi) to (ix) below. It will be noted that the amount exempt depends on the relationship of donor and donee. The term 'child' includes an illegitimate child, an adopted child and a step-child,

(vi) where the gift is an outright gift to a child or remoter descendant of the donor, the exempted sum is £5,000.

(vii) where the donor was the parent or remoter ancestor of either party to the marriage and the gift was either an outright gift to the bride or bridegroom or the property comprised in the gift was settled by the gift, the exempted sum is £5,000.

(viii) where the donor was either the bride or bridegroom and either the gift was an outright gift to the bridegroom or bride or the property comprised in the gift was settled by the gift, the exempted sum is £5,000.

(ix) in any case not covered in (vi) to (viii), the exempted sum is £1,000.

It will be appreciated that the value of the gift will be determined by the rules set out in § 4 above. The value of the gift and whether it exceeds £5,000 or £1,000 is before allowing any reduction in value dependent on the time which elapses between the date of the gift and death (see § 6 below). The sums of £5,000 and £1,000 are the maxima for any one marriage. If a donor has many relatives, the amount which may be distributed and still gain exemption can be considerable.

[c] **Gifts which form part of the normal expenditure of the deceased made out of income so that the deceased has sufficient income left after making the gift to maintain his usual standard of living.** In determining whether the donor had sufficient income left after

making the gifts, the effect of Income tax and Surtax should presumably be considered. It is considered Capital Gains tax being a charge on disposals of capital assets should be ignored. The standard of living which has to be considered is that of the donor not a reasonable man. Each case must be decided on its own facts. Many premiums paid on life policies taken out under the Married Women's Property Act 1882 will rank under this heading thereby giving exemption from Estate Duty on the value of the policy on the death of the donor. Premiums paid in respect of such policies or any nomination policies which were taken out in conjunction with the purchase of an annuity cannot be treated as within this exemption.

[d] **Gifts of settled property or gifts where the donor reserves an interest, not exceeding £100 in value, and gifts of unsettled property where there is no reservation, not exceeding £500.** These amounts are the aggregate amount of all such gifts made in the seven years prior to the donor's death to any one donee. If the gifts of settled property together with gifts of unsettled property are not in aggregate in excess of £500 the exemption can be claimed. The difference in treatment between the two classes of property will readily be appreciated, when it is realized that property which has some benefit reserved for the donor, is normally caught for Estate Duty irrespective of the time which has elapsed between the date of the gift and date of the donor's death. Where the aggregate value of gifts is only slightly in excess of the £500 limit the duty payable is limited to the excess of the value of the gift over £500. There is no marginal relief in respect of the £100 limit for settled property; if the value is £105, duty is payable on the full value. The value of the gift for these purposes is its value either at the date of gift or at the date of death whichever the donee chooses but the basis chosen must be applied to all gifts.

[e] **Gifts to be held in trust for immediate accumulation and ultimate transfer to the National Debt Commissioners or absolute gifts for the reduction of the National Debt.** Such gifts include land or an interest in land given to the National Trust or the National Trust of Scotland providing that the gift comprises

the entire interest of the donor in that land. Such gifts can be made subject to one or more life interests. Any person interested in making such gifts should study s. 31, F.A. 1937. This exemption is extended to chattels kept at the time of gift on the land and any maintenance fund. If the amount of the maintenance fund is greater than is required in the opinion of the Commissioners of Inland Revenue, the exemption is restricted to the amount required. This exemption is also available, if the Treasury so directs, to gifts of buildings and land of outstanding architectural, historic, scenic or scientific interest to a Government department, local authority or other body not established or conducted for profit.

§ 5. Valuation

The rules of valuation, appropriate when a gift *inter vivos* becomes liable to the charge for Estate Duty, are complex. The basis of valuation depends on the action taken by the donee in respect of the subject matter received.

[a] **If the donee disposes of the property prior to the donor's death in substitution for other property, that other property will be valued on the date of the donor's death.** A gift of money, however, will never change its value. The rules relating to settled property are explained in [e] below. Property received in exchange for original property will include:

 (*a*) in relation to property sold, exchanged or otherwise disposed of by the donee, any benefit received by the donee by way of consideration for the sale, exchange or other disposition; and

 (*b*) in relation to a debt or security, any benefit received by the donee in or towards satisfaction or redemption thereof; and

 (*c*) in relation to any right to acquire property, any property acquired in pursuance of that right.

Illustration (1)

John Smith died in 1970. Two years before his death, he had given 1,000 5/– shares in P. Ltd. quoted at that time at £2 per share to Alf Smith. Any Capital Gains tax arising in respect of this gift is to be ignored. Prior to John Smith's death, these shares had been the subject of a takeover by Q. Ltd. under which Alf Smith received 2,000 shares in Q. Ltd. at a market value of 50/– per share, in exchange for his holding. At the date of John

Smith's death, these shares were still held by Alf Smith and were quoted at 55/– per share. Their value for Estate Duty purposes will amount to £5,500 being the value at the death of John Smith of the property received in exchange for the original gift.

Because the shares in Q. Ltd were exchanged for those in P. Ltd duty was not assessed on the value of P, Ltd shares as at the date of the takeover bid, nor the value at that date of the consideration in Q. Ltd shares received in respect thereof. If there had been a sale for cash with a re-investment of that cash duty would have been assessed on the sale proceeds of the gift received.

Illustration (2)

John Smith died in 1970. Two years before his death, he had given 1,000 shares of 5/– each in P. Ltd. quoted at that time at £2 per share to Alf Smith. Any Capital Gains tax arising in respect of this gift is to be ignored. Prior to John Smith's death, the shares had been the subject of a take over by Q. Ltd. Alf Smith had decided not to accept the offer and sold his shares immediately before the last date for acceptance for £4,350. Ignore any Capital Gains tax on this disposal. Following a subsequent fall in value of Q. Ltd. shares he had purchased 2,000 shares in that company for £3,750. These shares were valued at John Smith's death at £4,000.

In this case, there is no exchange, but a sale. Consequently, death duties would be payable, subject to Capital Gains tax, on £4,350.

[b] If the donee has given away any of the property or disposed of it for less than its full value, he will be treated as continuing to have possession and enjoyment of the property, which will be valued at its full value on the date when it was given away or disposed of, without any deduction for the consideration [if any] received for it. The donee will be treated as voluntarily divesting himself of property where any interest in it is merged or extinguished in another interest held or acquired by him in the same property. The Solicitor-General in the debate on the 1957 Finance Bill pointed out that without the latter provision, the donor might sell to the donee the reversion in a long lease, leaving just one day in the reversion, and then give the long lease to the donee. The long lease would merge in the reversion, and without this provision duty could not be charged on the gift as the subject matter thereof had ceased to exist.

Illustration (3)

John Smith also gave 1,000 ordinary shares in T. Ltd valued at 16/– per share to Flossie Pitt-Dragen. Prior to John Smith's death the donee had transferred her holding to her son for £400 (at that date the market value was 20/– per share). At the date of John Smith's death the shares were quoted at 12/– per share. For Estate Duty purposes the shares will be valued at £1,000 which is the market value at the date of disposition for less than full value. There will not be any relief for the consideration received by Mrs Pitt-Dragen.

[c] Bonus shares and shares received on a rights issue are treated as part of the original gift. Where any shares or debentures are comprised in a gift *inter vivos* and the donee is issued with shares in or debentures of the same or any other body corporate otherwise than by way of exchange (these are already caught under (a) above), such shares or debentures are to be deemed to be included in the original gift. Bonus shares are, therefore, to be treated as part of the gift. Where the donee has the right to apply for shares or debentures on a 'rights' issue, the shares or debentures received will be deemed to be part of the gift, but in valuing the gift any consideration *given by the donee* is to be deducted. The donee cannot treat sums capitalized by the company out of reserves and applied in extinguishing any liability of the donee as consideration given by him.

Illustration (4)

John Smith had made a gift to Miss Jamjoy, his secretary, of 1,000 10/– shares in R. Ltd which at the date of the gift were quoted at 22/– per share. Subsequently, R. Ltd made a bonus issue of 1 share for every 2 held. At the date of John Smith's death, the shares, which were still retained, were valued at 15/– per share. The value for Estate Duty purposes would be £1,125, i.e. 1,000 + 500 = 1,500 shares at 15/– per share.

[d] Where the donee predeceases the donor, the former's personal representatives may have to withhold distribution of the donee's estate. Where a donee has predeceased the donor, and included in the property deemed to pass on death is property given to the deceased it is to be assumed the donee had not died. The acts of his personal representative are to be deemed to be his acts. If the donor has not died by the date of the death of the donee, the personal representatives of the latter may be faced with a charge for Estate Duty arising on the donor's death. As they will be unable to ascertain the amount of the charge, for their own protection they should withhold an adequate portion of the estate unless they receive an indemnity from the beneficiaries.

[e] **The gift may be by way of a settlement of assets on the donee or the donee may have settled the assets comprised in the gift.** Where property comprised in a gift *inter vivos* is deemed to pass on the donor's death (i.e. the gift was made within the seven years preceding death) and the property is settled (either by donor or donee), Estate Duty will be levied on the property comprised in the settlement at the donor's death, providing such property consists of the property originally given (i.e. bonus shares, etc., will be included). If the settlement comes to an end before the donor's death, Estate Duty is payable on the value, as at the date on which the settlement came to an end, of the property comprised in the settlement. From the preceding wording it is clear that where the trust deed relating to the settlement provides for income to be accumulated, the accumulations are not treated as derived from the original gift.

Similar treatment is accorded where property which was formerly comprised in a gift to the donee has been settled by the donee before the donor's death. Such property may be settled by the donee either by the normal method of settlement by his will, or by the effect of the rules applicable to intestacies

For the purposes of aggregation, any property which is to be treated as comprised in a gift *inter vivos* made by the deceased is to be deemed to be property in which the deceased had an interest, unless derived from property in which he never had an interest.

§ 6. Graduation in Value of Gifts

Where a person dies on the seventh anniversary of the making of a gift, the gift is not treated as dutiable. For the period to commence to run, it is necessary that the donor be excluded entirely from benefit to the property and the donee's title become final. For deaths before 19th March, 1968, the period of seven years was only five years. But, if the gift was made more than five years before 19th March, 1968, it will not be liable to duty since there is a specific exclusion for gifts made on or before

19th March, 1963. The provisions of the Finance Act 1960, as amended by the Finance Act 1968, provide that the value of the gift, for the purpose of aggregation to find the rate of duty, is to be reduced in each of the last three years of the seven year period. Where, therefore the gift is made:

More than four years but less than five years before death, the value of the gift is reduced by 15 per cent.

More than five years but less than six years before death, the value of the gift is reduced by 30 per cent.

More than six years but less than seven years before death, the value of the gift is reduced by 60 per cent.

If the donor died on or before 19th March, 1968, the 15 per cent. reduction applied where the gift was made more than two years but less than three years before death; the 30 per cent. reduction applied where the gift was made more than three years but less than four years before death; while the 60 per cent. reduction applied where the death occurred in the last of the five years.

But, for the transitional provisions of sub-section (4) of Section 35, many donees would have had to pay additional Estate Duty because the donor's death occurs on or after 20th March, 1968, instead of on or before 19th March, 1968. Sub-Section (4) provides that the provisions are not to apply so as to give a lesser percentage than would have applied assuming the donor died on 19th March, 1968, instead of the later date on which death actually occurred. Once a rate of relief has arisen under the rules for deaths on or before 19th March, 1968, it will not be lost because the rules applying for deaths after that date do not provide for relief at that rate but the rate of relief will not increase until the rules applying after 19th March, 1968, give a greater rate of relief. At the present time this provision may not be of importance but it will become a material factor during the coming years. Legal personal representatives are required in completing the Inland Revenue Affidavit to give details of gifts in the extended period of two years.

The effect of the reliefs can be seen in the illustration given overleaf

Illustration

Henry Jones died on 12th August, 1968, and during the seven years commencing on 12th August, 1961, made the following gifts –

(i) to Barry Jones £14,000 on 1st December, 1961.

(ii) to Cynthia Jones, £6,000 on 1st August, 1963.

(iii) to David Jones, £8,000 on 1st December, 1964.

(iv) to Edward Jones, £2,000 on 1st January, 1966.

(v) to Francis Jones, £15,000 on 1st April, 1968.

The rate of Estate Duty appropriate to Henry Jones' estate was 80 per cent.

Estate Duty will be payable on the following amounts:

(i) There will be no liability on the gift to Barry since the gift was made before 19th March, 1963.

(ii) The gift was made more than five years but less than six years before death. The amount on which liability would be assessed is 40 per cent. of £6,000 = £2,400. The rules for death before 19th March, 1968 would apply since the reduction is not to be less than it would have been if death had occurred on 19th March, 1968. Without this provision the reduction would have been 30 per cent. and not 60 per cent.

(iii) The gift was made more than three years but less than four years before death. Under the rules for deaths prior to 19th March, 1968, the rate of the reduction in the principal value would have been 30 per cent. while under the rules for deaths after that date there would have been no reduction. Estate Duty would be payable on 70 per cent. of £8,000 or £5,600.

(iv) The gift was made more than two years but less than three years before death. Under the rules there would be a reduction in value of 15 per cent. Estate Duty will be payable on £1,700.

(v) Both the gift and the death occurred after 19th March, 1968, so that the transitional rules cannot apply. Estate Duty would be payable on £15,000.

The effect of the rules can be illustrated by leaving the dates of the gifts unchanged but having the donor die on 12th August, 1970.

(i) As before there will be no liability, but the reason in these circumstances will be that the gift was made more than seven years before the donor's death.

(ii) Exempt gift having been made more than seven years before death; the transitional relief arrangements will not apply since they would have given relief by way of a reduction in value of sixty per cent.

(iii) Gift made more than five years but less than six years before the donor's death. The reduction would normally be 30 per cent. of the value. But regard must be had to the transitional arrangements. If the donor had died on 19th March, 1968, the gift would have been made more than three years but less than four years. The transitional relief would provide the same rate so that the reduction will be 30 per cent. of the value.

(iv) Gift made more than four years but less than five years before the donor's death. The reduction would be 15 per cent. Under the transitional arrangements the gift would have been made more than two years but less than three years before 19th March, 1968, so that there would have been a similar relief.

(v) The transitional relief could not apply and the gift being more than two years but less than three years there would be no reduction in value.

Legal personal representatives acting in the winding-up of an estate where the deceased died after 19th March, 1968, must determine the answers to the following questions before they can advise the donees of the amount of Estate Duty payable.

(a) What was the date of the gift?

(b) If the gift was before 19th March, 1968, will the transitional reliefs give greater relief than the rules for deaths after that date.

(c) The rate of Estate Duty payable after including the amount of the gift at the sum determined under (b).

Since the value of the gift of a life policy is computed on the basis of the premiums paid in the seven years prior to death (see Chapter IV, § 4), it will be appreciated that the part of the proceeds applicable to premiums in the last three years of the seven year period will be subject to the reductions in value described. Transitional relief will apply where appropriate.

Instead of making a gift of cash or an item of property, a donor may decide to assign a life policy taken out on his life to the person he wishes to benefit; or he may take out a policy on his life and immediately assign the benefit of the proceeds to the beneficiary; or he may take out the policy under the provisions of the Married Women's Property Act 1882; or form a trust and give to the trustees the benefit of a life policy on his life. In each case, the donor will be making a gift. The valuation of that gift will be as follows:

(1) If the deceased, within seven years of his death, voluntarily assigned a life policy on his own life, he is regarded as having made a gift of a value equal to the proportion of the value of the policy (even if it is still not in force at his death) that the total amount of the premiums paid up to the time of assignment bears to the total amount of the premiums paid

to the date of the maturity of the policy, or its earlier assignment or surrender by the donee.

(2) Where any premiums were paid by the deceased after such an assignment but within seven years of death, each premium so paid is treated as a gift of rights under the policy (whether the policy is still in force at the death or not) of an amount equal to the proportion of the value of the policy which the amount of the premium bears to the aggregate amount of all premiums paid to the date of the maturity of the policy or of its earlier assignment or surrender by the donee.

(3) Premiums paid in respect of policies taken out by a man on his own life for the benefit of his wife and/or children under the provisions of the Married Women's Property Act 1882, are treated as gifts as in (2) (such policies are commonly called 'nomination policies').

(4) Premiums paid in respect of a policy for the benefit of some person other than the wife, husband or child of the person effecting it (policies for the benefit of such persons are covered by (3)), do not rank as gifts since the policy remains an asset of the estate of the person providing it, unless the person paying the premiums puts the policy into trust. Insurance companies can usually provide draft deeds for this purpose If the policy is put into trust, so that it is not part of the estate of the person paying the premiums, the provisions of (2) above will apply.

(5) If the deceased assigned the policy more than seven years before his death and paid no premiums after assignment or ceased to pay premiums more than seven years before death, providing the deceased had no beneficial interest in that policy in that period, no liability to Estate Duty will arise on his death.

The value of the policy for the purposes of (1) and (2) above is the amount received at its maturity, or on its surrender or sale for value, or if the donee had given it away or disposed of it for less than its market value, the market value when he did so.

It must be remembered that a claim for Estate Duty based on premiums paid may be resisted on the grounds that the payment of the premiums was part of the normal and reasonable expenditure of the deceased.

Since each premium constitutes a gift, that part of the value of the policy appropriate to those paid in the fifth, sixth and seventh years preceding death will be reduced by 15 per cent., 30 per cent., and 60 per cent. respectively.

Illustration (1)

Walters who died in September, 1968 gave to Muir in June, 1963 a with-profits policy taken out by Walters on his own life in 1952, on which an initial premium of £4,000 and eleven subsequent annual premiums of £1,200 each had been paid, i.e. a total of £17,200. The premiums were due in February, and after assignment Walters paid five further premiums of £1,200 each.

The policy and the bonuses realised £34,800.

The value of the gifts would be:

(i) Value of policy assigned in June, 1963 (within the sixth year prior to death)

$$\frac{17,200}{23,200} \times 34,800 = £25,800$$

(ii) Value appropriate to premium paid Feb. 1964 (within the fifth year prior to death).

$$\frac{1,200}{23,200} \times 34,800 = £1,800$$

(iii) Value appropriate to premium paid Feb. 1965 (within the fourth year prior to death).

$$\frac{1,200}{23,200} \times 34,800 = £1,800$$

(iv) Value appropriate to premium paid Feb. 1966 (within the third year prior to death).

$$\frac{1,200}{23,200} \times 34,800 = £1,800$$

(v) Value appropriate to premium paid Feb. 1967 (within the second year prior to death).

$$\frac{1,200}{23,200} \times 34,800 = £1,800$$

(vi) Value appropriate to premium paid Feb. 1968 (within the year prior to death).

$$\frac{1,200}{23,200} \times 34,800 = £1,200$$

Estate Duty would be payable on an aggregate amount of:

(i)	£25,800 less 60 per cent. of £25,800 =	£10,320
(ii)	£1,800 less 60 per cent. of £1,800 =	720*
(iii)	£1,800 less 30 per cent. of £1,800 =	1,260
	Carried forward	£12,300

		Brought forward	£12,300
(iv)	£1,800 less 15 per cent. of £1,800 =		1,530
(v)	£1,800		1,800
(vi)	£1,800		1,800
			£17,430

*The transitional provisions relating to the graduation in value in the last three years of the seven (formerly five) year period will apply.

To summarise the rules which apply for gifts made after 19th March, 1968, and to deaths which occur after that date –

(1) Complete exemption will only apply where the gift was made more than seven years before the death and the donor was entirely excluded from possession and enjoyment of the property and of any benefit to him by contract or otherwise more than seven years before his death.

(2) A reduction of the principal value of the gift will not occur until four years have elapsed from the date of the gift.

(3) After four years the reduction in value will be in accordance with the following table –

If the gift was made more than *four* years but less than *five* years before death,	The value of the gift will be reduced by 15 per cent.
If the gift was made more than *five* years but less than *six* years before death,	The value of the gift will be reduced by 30 per cent.
If the gift was made more than *six* years but less than *seven* years before death,	The value of the gift will be reduced by 60 per cent.

The relief applies also to various dispositions within the seven year period, viz. dispositions in favour of relatives, the determination of life interests, benefits in settled property etc. and to premiums paid on life policies for the benefit of donees or nominees (§ 15 of Chapter IV).

The reduction in value of a gift made in the fourth, fifth or sixth year prior to the death is not to be taken into account in determining whether a gift is exempt from duty on the ground that it does not exceed £500 in value, or if so, whether marginal relief applies (F.A. 1960, s. 64 (5)). For example, if a gift of £600 were made in the sixth year prior to the death, for Estate Duty purposes it would be treated as a gift for £240, but it would not on this account be exempt from duty as being a gift of not more than £500 in value, and the maximum amount of duty payable on the gift would still be the excess of the original value of the gift over £500, viz. £100.

When making a gift prior to his death, the donor will have paid any Capital Gains tax payable. But as mentioned above, the incidence of estate duty is on the donee. The donee may be placed in financial difficulty, therefore, if the rate of Estate Duty applicable to the value of the gift is 80 per cent. and the donee disposes of the subject matter of the gift prior to or after the donor's death and he has to pay Capital Gains tax on the chargeable gain at 30 per cent. Relief from the double charge is given under the provisions of Section 42, Finance Act 1966. The relief granted to the *donee* or his estate depends on whether he disposes of the subject matter before or after the donor's death.

(1) If the donee of a chargeable asset disposes of it between the date of the gift and the date of the donor's death he will be liable to Capital Gains tax if he disposes of it (or is deemed to dispose of it, e.g. where he in turn makes a gift of it) at a price or value in excess of that at which he was deemed to acquire it. The chargeable gain if the gift was given to him after 6th April, 1965, will be the full amount of that excess. If the gift was received by him on or before that date, the chargeable gain will be a proportion of the excess or, if lower, the excess of the value at disposal over the value at 6th April, 1965. On the subsequent death of the donor within seven years of the date of the gift the donee will become liable to Estate Duty thereon. The Capital Gains tax paid or payable on his disposal will be allowed as a deduction from the principal value of the property in the computation of Estate Duty payable. This deduction is made before any reduction in value under Section 64 of the Finance Act 1960 (see § 6 above).

Illustration (1)

In August, 1965, John Davis gave Edward Davis a holding of shares worth £12,000. Edward sold the shares in May, 1968, for £20,000. The amount of Capital Gains tax payable was 30 per cent. of £8,000 = £2,400. John died in September 1969 and the value of his estate (other than the subject of the gift) was £750,000. The Estate Duty payable on his death was £547,341.

The Estate Duty payable by Edward will be:

Proceeds of sale	..	..	..	..	.. £20,000
Less Capital Gains tax ..	..	..	..	..	2,400
					17,600

Less reduction in value due to date of gift (death more than 4 years but less than 5 years – 15%) 2,640

£14,960

Estate Duty payable $-\dfrac{14,960}{764,960} \times$ £547,341 .. .. = £10,704

(2) Where the donee does not dispose of the property until after the death of the donor, so that the liability to Estate Duty arises first, for the purposes of computing the gain or loss on the subsequent disposal, a proportion of the Estate Duty payable on the gift will be allowed as part of the cost of the property in computing the gain or loss. This proportion is the amount by which the principal value of the property at the date of death of the donor (before any reduction under Section 64 of the Finance Act 1960, see § 6 above) exceeded its notional cost to the donee, expressed as a fraction of that principal value.

Illustration (2)

Assuming the same facts as in illustration (1), but that Edward did not sell the shares. The value of the shares at John's death was £28,000. Since Edward did not dispose of the shares prior to John's death, he will not have suffered Capital Gains tax at that date. Consequently, it is necessary to compute the proportion of the Estate Duty to be added to the cost of the asset in computing the chargeable gain on a subsequent disposal.

Estate Duty payable by Edward:

Value of the shares at John's death	..		..	.. £28,000
Less reduction in value due to date of gift		..	..	4,200
				23,800

Estate Duty payable $\dfrac{23,800}{773,800} \times$ £554,855 .. .. £17,996

Proportion to be added to cost

$$£28,000 - £12,000 = \frac{£16,000}{28,000} \times £17,996 = £10,283$$

On a subsequent disposal by Edward the amount to be deducted from the sale proceeds to compute the chargeable gain will be £12,000 + £10,283 = £22,283.

Further details concerning Capital Gains tax will be found in *Capital Gains Tax* by the editor.

Where in respect of a gift made more than seven years prior to the death, Estate Duty would be payable by reason of the donor not being entirely excluded from possession and enjoyment of the property, if he became so excluded at some time within the seven year period and continued to be so until his death, the section will apply by reference to the period between the date on which he became so excluded and the date of death.

§ 7. Incidence of Duty

The duty on gifts will normally be borne by the donee of the gift, unless there is some pre-existing arrangement which was entered into before the donor's death, but which is to take effect after the death, e.g. the donor may recite in his will, the fact that certain gifts which he has made should be duty-free, and hence the duty will be borne by the residuary beneficiaries. If the estate should prove insolvent, however, the person ultimately responsible for the payment of the duty will be the donee notwithstanding anything to the contrary in the will itself. In a case where the donee has pre-deceased the donor, the normal rules which have already been detailed will apply and the duty will be payable by the donee's personal representative. If, therefore, the property comprised in the gift accrues under the donee's will or intestacy to a beneficiary of his, Estate Duty will be payable by reference to the donee's death, on the value of the property at the date of the donee's death as if he had given it away at that date. Where the property is sold by the donee's personal representative before the donor's death in the course of administering the donee's estate, the duty will be payable on the cash proceeds.

§ 8. Dispositions in Favour of Relatives

Any disposition of property by the deceased in favour of a relative of his is treated for the purposes of Estate Duty as a gift *inter vivos* unless:

(*a*) the disposition was made for full money or money's worth paid to him for his own use or benefit; or

(b) the deceased was concerned only in a fiduciary capacity imposed on him otherwise than by a disposition made by him.

Where the disposition was made for partial consideration, the value of the consideration will be allowed as a deduction from the value of the property for the purposes of Estate Duty (F.A. 1950, s. 46 (1). An annuity or life interest granted to the deceased by the relative cannot be treated as consideration in money's worth for the disposition so as to exempt the property from Estate Duty. Associated operations effected to pay or facilitate the payment of annuities have the same effect.

The expression 'relative' includes the wife or husband, father, mother, children, uncles and aunts of the deceased, and any issue of any of those persons (F.A. 1940, s. 44).

The expression 'annuity' includes any series of payments, whether interconnected or not, whether of the same or varying amounts and whether payable at regular intervals or otherwise. Dividends on shares and interest on debentures in a company may be treated as annuities if the payments are liable to cease or be reduced on the death.

If the deceased has made in favour of a controlled company a disposition which, if it had been made to a relative of his, would have fallen within the above provisions, the disposition will be regarded as having been made to a relative, unless no relative was, at the time of the disposition, or subsequently during the life of the deceased, a member of the company (F.A. 1940, s. 40).

For the above purposes, the creation of a debt enforceable against the deceased personally or charged on his property will be treated as a disposition of property made by him and will not be allowed as a deduction from the property liable to Estate Duty on his death (F.A. 1940, s. 45).

Where the payments made to the deceased on account of the annuities, etc. have exceeded the income of the property comprised in the disposition made by him the amount of such excess, together with simple interest at 2 per cent. per annum, may be deducted from the value of the property deemed to pass on the death (F.A. 1944, s. 40). It is thought that where the actual income from the property gives a normal return and the property is retained by the donee, the actual income would probably be taken by the Commissioners, instead of 2 per cent.

CHAPTER VII

QUICK SUCCESSION RELIEF

§ 1. Introduction

Where Estate Duty becomes payable on property on which Estate Duty was paid on an earlier death occuring within five years before the later death, relief is given against the *amount* of the Estate Duty payable on the second death. The relief is granted by reducing the amount of the Estate Duty payable on the second death on the property where the earlier death occurred:

within three months before the later	– by 75 per cent.
„ one year before the later	– „ 50 „ „
„ two years „ „ „	– „ 40 „ „
„ three „ „ „ „	– „ 30 „ „
„ four „ „ „ „	– „ 20 „ „
„ five „ „ „ „	– „ 10 „ „

It will be noted that the percentages decrease as the later death becomes more remote from the earlier death.

The relief is given on the lower of the value at the later death or the net value at the earlier death. Net value for this purpose has a special meaning for which see § 4 of this chapter. Although the Act grants relief only in respect of the same property, provision is made for identifying property passing on the second death with property which passed on the previous death. Identification is necessary because the term 'same property' is not necessarily taken literally, since the relief is not confined to property which is still held in the same state as that in which it devolved upon the former death. The Eighth Schedule, Finance Act 1958, contains provisions relating to the tracing of property through the deaths (see § 3 of this chapter). Where specific assets were received and retained, identification is simple. Where the person dying at the later date received sums out of the proceeds of dutiable assets on the first death, the rules provide for the identification of the sums with the assets. If that person received a sum of money and can show that at all times since the earlier death he has held property at least to the amount received the relief may be claimed in full on property to that value on the later death. However, if it is apparent that the property left by the deceased has not been acquired by reference to that left upon the earlier death, the relief will be restricted to that amount of the property left at the earlier death which is still deemed to be in existence at the later death. Thus, if a person is left £8,000 at the earlier death and at the later death he leaves £10,000, but during the intervening period he has won a sum of money amounting to £4,000, at any one time the total property held by the deceased from the earlier death amounted to only £6,000 and the relief would be restricted to that figure.

Under the Law of Commorientes, where two persons die in circumstances which render it uncertain which died first, the younger is deemed to survive the elder. If the elder had left property to the younger, Estate Duty would be payable on both deaths. It is provided, however, that both are assumed to have died at the same instant, so that no Estate Duty will be payable on the same property on the death of the younger.

The essentials to claiming Quick Succession Relief are:

(i) The second death must occur within five years of the earlier death,

(ii) Estate Duty must be payable on both deaths,

(iii) The Estate Duty in (ii) must be that appropriate to the same property,

(iv) Relief is given on the value of the property at the earlier death or on the value at the later death, whichever is the lower,

(v) The amount of Estate Duty against which relief is given is that payable on the *later* death, so that the relief cannot exceed the duty on that death.

§ 2. Rate of Relief

Quick succession relief will be given against the Estate Duty payable on a death where any property passes or is deemed to pass in relation to that death, provided that the Commissioners of Inland Revenue are satisfied that Estate Duty has been payable on the same property on an earlier death occurring within five years before the death for which relief is being claimed and that the person entitled to the property immediately before that death did not acquire his title to the property by purchase for consideration in money or monies worth (F.A. 1958, 30). Estate Duty must have been payable on the property at the earlier death. If no duty was payable on that property, for example, by reason of the fact that the net principal value did not exceed £10,000, relief cannot be claimed against duty payable on the later death.

The rate by which the duty is to be reduced, is stated in the introduction to this chapter, but it must be emphasised that it is the duty payable on the later death which is reduced by the appropriate percentage, and therefore it may be necessary to apportion any duty payment over the relevant property at the later death by reason of the fact that marginal relief under Section 13, Finance Act 1914, may have been claimed. If the second death is on the first anniversary of the earlier death, it is within one year of the earlier death and so on with each.

It should be noted that the earlier death need not be that which immediately precedes the death giving rise to the claim for quick succession relief. The personal representatives can select the earlier death, if there is more than one within the preceding five years, which will entitle them to the greatest relief. For example, if on the death of A in 1969, shares in a limited company formed part of his estate so as to become liable to Estate Duty and within the preceding five years the same shares had been subject to Estate Duty on the death of B in 1965 and on the death of C in 1967, quick succession relief would be available on A's death by reference to the death of either B or C, but not both. If the value of such shares fluctuated so that in 1965 the value was higher than in 1967, A's personal representatives would claim relief by reference to the value at B's death and not that at C's death. As can be seen in § 4 of this chapter, the 'value' of property for this purpose can vary by reason of a number of factors other than actual valuation.

For relief to be claimed there is no need for the property passing on the second death to have been property derived by the second deceased from the first deceased. A donor may find that having given property to the donee, the latter dies first. If the donor dies within five years of the donee, the same property will have suffered Estate Duty twice within that period and the donor's personal representatives can claim quick succession relief.

§ 3. The same property

Since relief can only be claimed if duty is being levied on the same property, the Eighth Schedule, Finance Act 1958, contains rules for determining whether the property passing or deemed to pass on the second death is the same property as that which passed or was deemed to pass on the earlier death. To understand these rules, it is necessary to appreciate the circumstances in which and the types of property which can be liable to duty on both deaths.

(a) The person dying at the earlier date may have given by will a specific asset to the person dying later. To determine whether the same property is suffering duty on the second death, it is only necessary to see whether that property is one of the assets forming part of the estate liable to duty on that death. This rule will cover specific bequests and devise.

(b) The personal representatives of the person dying at the earlier date may have appropriated a specific asset of that estate to satisfying the bequest to a residuary legatee. If such asset is one of those forming part of the estate of the second deceased, relief can be claimed.

(c) In many cases, however, the personal representatives of the person dying at the earlier date will have had to sell assets liable to duty on that death. Part of the proceeds may have been used to pay the debts of that estate, in which case the proceeds clearly cannot have passed to the second deceased. The remainder of the proceeds may have been reinvested in the course of administration of that estate. Alternatively, assets dutiable on the first death may have been sold by that person's legal personal representatives and reinvested. The assets representing the reinvestments will have transferred to the person who died later. The assets transferred if still amongst the assets liable to duty on the second death will be regarded as having been liable to duty on the first death. This rule means that although the assets existing at the second death may not have formed part of the estate of the first deceased at his death, by a system of 'relating-back' relief can be claimed on the later death.

(*d*) The second deceased may have received a legacy of money on the earlier death. It is unlikely that such sum would remain in the form of money at the date of the second death. Any rules which required the tracing of the money would have proved impractical to administer. Consequently, relief will be granted on the second death, if it can be shown to the satisfaction of the Commissioners that property at any time paid away or otherwise disposed of by the second deceased since the death of the first deceased was property other than that representing the cash received. If the estate at the second death has a greater value than the cash received, relief will be given in respect of the cash received. If the estate is valued at an amount lower than the amount of the cash received, then the relief will be restricted to that appropriate to the value of the estate on the second death. After the earlier death, the second deceased may have made gifts or settlements which are liable to duty on his death (e.g. because they were made in the seven years prior to his death). In so far as the cash received exceeded the value of the deceased's estate at his death, the excess is treated as being applied rateably in making the gifts or settlements. The value of the gifts or settlements will be the amount chargeable to Estate Duty. If this amount is less than the excess, there can be no relief in respect of the balance.

(*e*) The asset received by the second deceased may have formed the subject matter of a gift *inter vivos* liable to duty on the earlier death. The rules for identifying the property passing at the second death with the subject matter of that gift are the same as in (*d*). Following the earlier death, the second deceased may have received a bonus issue of shares. These will be treated as the same property as the shares forming the original gift. If there has been a 'rights' issue, only the proportion of the value of the shares received on the rights issue which can be attributed to the rights element at the time of issue can be treated as the same property as the original shares.

(*f*) Where an interest in a settlement is liable to duty on both deaths, the assets included in that settlement at the two deaths are regarded as the same assets. If the settlement comes to an end, the assets received by the second deceased will be identified as in (*c*) above. The assets received on a distribution under a settlement will be identified as in (*d*) above.

(*g*) The property passing on the first death may have been a life policy. The proceeds of that policy will be regarded as the same as the policy. Thus, the personal representatives of the recipient of the policy monies can claim that these were the same property as the policy and obtain quick succession relief.

(*h*) Quick succession relief in the case of discretionary trusts, where a liability arose on an earlier death on or after 16th April, 1969, may apply where one beneficiary dies not more than five years after another. In such a case there is to be treated as the same property passing on each of the deaths a proportion of the part of the property comprised in that settlement which passed on the earlier death equal to the proportion which the part of the property so comprised passing on the later death bears to the whole of the property so comprised (Sch. 17, Pt. II, para. 7, F.A. 1969).

Illustration

R and S were both beneficiaries of a discretionary trust, R died on 1st June, 1969, and 1/5th of the fund valued at £50,000 passed on his death. His estate rate was 12 per cent. Estate Duty paid by trustees on R's death 1/5th of £50,000 = £10,000 at 12 per cent. = £1,200.

S died on 1st April, 1970, and 1/4th of the fund, then valued at £48,000, passed on his death. His estate rate was 25 per cent.

Estate Duty payable by trustees on S's death
1/4th of £48,000 = £12,000 at 25%   ..   ..   .. = £3,000

Less Quick Succession Relief –
1/5th of 1/4th of £48,000 = £2,400 at 25%   ..   .. =   600
                                                                  ———
                                                                £2,400
                                                                  ═══

In (*a*) to (*g*) above, it has been assumed that the second deceased retained the assets which suffered or can be deemed to have suffered estate duty on the earlier death. But the second deceased may have disposed of his interest in such assets. If he has given them away, relief can only be claimed to the extent that the gift is liable to duty on the second death when relief is available under (*d*) above. The second deceased may have disposed of the assets, however, in such a manner as to receive money or money's worth. In these circumstances his personal representatives can still claim relief, which will be based on the lower of the net value of the asset passing on the earlier death or the asset received in substitution (for further details see § 4 below).

In deciding whether assets are to be treated as the same property, it must never be forgotten that relief cannot be claimed in any case where the deceased acquired his interest in the settlement by purchase.

§ 4. Value on which relief claimable

As has already been stated relief is given on the lower of the value at the later death or the net value at the earlier death. The value at the later death is the amount which has to be included for the purpose of assessing duty on that death.

If the value is reduced at both deaths as in the case of gifts made in the fifth, sixth and seventh years prior to death (see Chapter VI, § 6), it is the reduced value which is included as the value at both dates; the reduced value at the earlier death will be the amount from which the allowable deductions are made. But where the reduced value applies on one death and the full value on the other, it is not necessary to make any adjustment; the value is treated as being the reduced value on the one death and the full value on the other. Particular care should be taken where the second deceased's estate includes assets received by way of gift from the first deceased, since the quick succession relief may be severely restricted by this rule.

For the purposes of a claim to quick succession relief, the ascertainment of the value at the later death will not be unduly difficult. But the value at the earlier death will have to be determined by the following rules:

(a) If the property formed part of the estate of the first deceased at his death and was transferred to the second deceased as the person specifically entitled thereto, the net value at the earlier death is the amount on which Estate Duty was paid on the earlier death less the aggregate of the amounts payable out of that property in respect of death duties on that death and liabilities of the first deceased. In computing the amount of the death duties there is to be taken into account the Estate Duty payable in Great Britain and any similar duties under the laws of any other country or territory. There is *not* to be deducted from the amount on which Estate Duty was paid any duties or liabilities which are met in the course of administration out of or by means of other property passing on the death. Thus, the actions of the personal representative of the first person dying may affect the relief on the second death. Debts or liabilities specifically chargeable on the asset deducted in arriving at the amount assessable to Estate Duty will, of course, have been already deducted. This rule relating to the net value will apply to cases falling within §3 (*a*) and (*b*) above.

(b) Where property is appropriated by the personal representatives of the first deceased to satisfying a legacy in the circumstances in § 3 (*c*) above, or there is a payment of money (as in § 3 (*d*) above), or a settlement comes to an end (as in §3 (*f*) above), the net value is the value at the time of payment or appropriation, after allowing for any charge or incumbrance subject to which it was paid or appropriated.

(c) Where the property comprised a life policy (as in § 3 (*g*) above, the net value is the value for Estate Duty purposes on the earlier death less any death duties payable out of the proceeds on that death. It should be noted that the life policies covered by this rule do not include policies whose proceeds formed part of the deceased's free estate. The value of the latter policies will be ascertained as in (*b*).

(d) In respect of all other property, which is deemed to be the same property, the net value is the value on which duty was payable on the earlier death less any death duties paid out of that property on that death. Such property would include gifts (as in §3 (*e*) above), property settled by the first deceased which remains settled at the death of the second deceased, and joint property accruing by survivorship.

Where the property chargeable with duty on the later death is or has been settled property, it will be recalled the property at any time comprised in the settlement is to be regarded as the same property, notwithstanding any substitution of one item for another. The net value at the earlier death will be based on the assets in the settlement at that date and the value at the second death will depend on the assets therein at that date.

Where on the second death before 16th April, 1969, duty was charged under Section 43, Finance Act 1940 (*see* Chapter IV, § 19) on the determination of a life interest, and the settlement came to an end before the second death, the relief was restricted to cases where the first death after the end of the settlement was either the death of the settlor, or the death of a person who received property under the settlement when it ended, and did not acquire his title by purchase (*see* Illustration (4) *post*).

Where the donee has died before the donor, relief will not be allowed by reference to any death subsequent to that of the donor. Property is to be regarded as being the same property if duty would have been paid on it if the donor had died immediately before the donee. The net value after the donee's death is to be taken to be the value on which Estate Duty is payable on the donee's death. Thus the duty leviable on the donor's death has to be ascertained in order to discover the net value of the property for the purpose of claiming relief.

So that the relevant amount upon which the relief may be claimed, can be ascertained, the use of a formula is necessary, this being:

$$\frac{V1 - (V2 \times R1)}{1 + R2 - R1}$$

V1 is the value at the earlier death before the deduction of duty chargeable on the later death but after deduction of any administration expenses on that later death.

V2 is the value for Estate Duty purposes on the later death.

R1 is the effective rate of duty on the later death before quick succession relief but after all other allowances.

R2 is the effective rate after taking into account all allowances on the later death including quick succession relief.

It will be seen that the calculation is based upon a hypothetical situation inasmuch as the death of the donor is deemed to have occurred before the death of the donee.

Illustration

Humble died on 31st July, 1968. The rate of duty on his death was 40 per cent. On 30th September, 1965, Humble had made a gift to his doctor of £5,000 in cash. The doctor was unfortunately killed in a car crash on 31st May, 1966, leaving an estate of £40,000, including the amount of £5,000 which had been deposited with a building society. The building society deposit had been specifically bequeathed to the doctor's grand-daughter.

Using the formula mentioned above, the duty chargeable on the gift by Humble would be:

$$\frac{£5,000-(£5,000 \times 40\%)}{1+(40\%-30\% \text{ of } 40\%)-40\%} = \frac{3,000}{1+(28\%)-40\%} = £4,412$$

Estate duty at 40% on gift of £5,000	£2,000
Less allowance for quick succession relief, 30% of 40% of £4,412	529
Duty payable on gift in relation to death of donor ..	£1,471

Similar provisions apply for the substitution of other property of the donee, for the subject matter of the gift where the latter is no longer in existance, as is the case with other specific bequests which are made in normal circumstances (see Illustration (5)).

Where a donee has disposed of the property comprised in the gift for partial consideration, this will not be regarded as a 'purchase for consideration in money or money's worth' so as to preclude the application of quick succession relief, but where such relief is given in respect of the property comprised in the gift, the 'net value after the earlier death' must be abated in the same proportion as that in which the value on which Estate Duty is payable on the later death is abated by reason of the consideration (see Illustration (3) post).

In some cases, the second deceased will have disposed of the asset he received from the first deceased. As indicated in §3 of this Chapter relief can still be claimed but the computation of the two values requires re-consideration. The value at the earlier death will be ascertained in the manner already described. The value at the later death is the amount or value of that which he received in substitution, at the time when he ceased to have possession and enjoyment.

§ 5. Claims for Relief

Details enabling the Estate Duty Office to check claims are usually given either when submitting the Estate Duty affidavit or in subsequent correspondence. In preparing details of the claims, the principles set out in the foregoing paragraphs must be adopted. In an examination, care should be taken and if it is thought there is such possibility, the computation of quick succession relief is always based on the lower of the two values and is at the rate on the second death. The following illustrations incorporate the principles set out in the preceding paragraphs, and apply to deaths before and after 16th April, 1969, except in latter case the figures apply to the estate rate.

Illustration (1)

X., by his will, bequeathed to Y. a freehold house valued at X.'s death prior to 16th April, 1969, at £6,000. The rate of Estate Duty payable on X.'s death was 21 per cent., Y died 18 months after X., possessed (*inter alia*) of the house received from X., then valued at £5,500. The rate of Estate Duty payable on Y.'s death was 18 per cent.

Since Estate Duty on realty is payable out of that property, the net value after X.'s death was £6,000 *less* 21% of £6,000 = £1,260 Estate Duty = £4,740. As this is less than the value of the property on Y.'s death, the duty payable thereon on Y.''s death will be:

	£
18% on £5,500	990
Less Quick Succession Relief, 40% of 18% on £4,740 ..	341
	£649

Illustration (2)

Facts as in Illustration (1), except that the house was left to Y. 'free of duty'. Consequently, the Estate Duty thereon would have been met out of other property passing on X.'s death, so that no deduction for Estate Duty would be made in calculating the net value after X.'s death, which would be £6,000 (see § 4 (*a*) of this Chapter). Quick Succession Relief on the death of Y. would have been 40% of 18% on £5,500 = £396, reducing the duty payable to £594.

Illustration (3)

Under the will of P., Q. received legacies of 2,000 shares in a company, valued as in § 4 (*a*) at £4,000, and £5,000 in cash. Estate Duty was paid on P.'s death at 15 per cent. Q. sold the shares for £3,500.

On his death, 2½ years after that of P., and before 16th April, 1969, Q. left net estate of £9,000, of which £1,000 was cash and £8,000 other personalty.

Quick succession relief will be available on Q.'s death at 30 per cent. of 4 per cent. on £3,500 in respect of the shares (the amount received in substitution being less than the value after P.'s death) (see last paragraph of § 4 above), and 30 per cent. of 4 per cent. on £5,000 in respect of the cash. Although Q.'s estate includes only £1,000 cash, the net amount thereof, exclusive of the £3,500, on which relief is otherwise given, is greater than the 'value at the earlier death' of £5,000, and will, therefore, be deemed to include the 'same property' as the cash received from P. Estate Duty is not deducted in computing the 'net value after the earlier death' as the duty on legacies of personalty is payable out of the general residue, and not out of the property comprised in the legacies.

Illustration (4)

During his lifetime M. made a gift to N. of shares valued at £8,000. N. disposed of the shares to his son O. for £2,000, when their principal value was £10,000. M. died within two years of the gift to N. and after the transfer of the shares to O. At the date of M.'s death the shares were valued at £20,000. N. died nine months after M. At the death of N. the shares were valued at £25,000. Estate duty was paid at 35 per cent. on the death of M. and at 40 per cent. on the death of N.

Since N. had disposed of the shares comprised in the gift for less than their principal value, he is treated as continuing to have possession of them (see Chapter VI, § 5) and Estate Duty is payable on M.'s death on the value of the shares at the date on which N. disposed of them, viz. £10,000 without any deduction for the £2,000 consideration received. The duty will be at 35 per cent., and the net value after M.'s death will thus be: £10,000—£3,500 = £6,500.

N. having disposed of the shares for partial consideration within seven years of his death, estate duty is payable on the value of the 'gift' to O. Since the price paid by O. for the shares was one-fifth of their principal value at the date of transfer, duty will be payable on N.'s death on four-fifths of their value at that date – four-fifths of £25,000 = £20,000 (*Re Bateman, A. G.* v. *Wreford Brown*). For the purposes of quick succession relief the net value after M.'s death will be abated in the same proportion as the value on which duty is abated on N.'s death by reason of the consideration (F.A. 1958, 8th Schedule (5)). The duty payable on the shares, on N.'s death, will therefore be:

40% on £20,000	£8,000
Less Quick Succession Relief, 50% of 40% of four-fifths of £6,500	1,040
	£6,960

Illustration (5)

A gratuitously settled property on B. for life with remainder to C. B then surrendered his life interest, without consideration, to C. A. died within seven years of the settlement, but after the release of the life interest. Estate Duty was payable on the property comprised in the settlement as a gift within seven years of the death. B. died within seven years of the release of the life interest to C. and of the death of A.

On B.'s death, before 16th April, 1969, Estate Duty is payable under s. 43, Finance Act 1940, on the property released from the settlement, as he had disposed of his life interest without consideration to the remainderman within seven years of his death, thereby merging the two interests and bringing the settlement to an end, Chapter IV, § 19. Quick succession relief will apply by reference to the death of A., since his was the first death after the end of the settlement, and he was the settlor.

If, after the release of the life interest, C. had sold the property for full consideration to D. and D. had predeceased A. and B., relief would not be available in respect of the duty payable under s. 43, Finance Act 1940, on B.'s death, since the first death after the end of the settlement was neither that of A. (the settlor) nor C. (the person who received property under the settlement when it ended).

§ 6. Relief from Estate Duty where persons die simultaneously

Where two or more persons have died in circumstances rendering it uncertain which of them survived the other or others, the property chargeable with Estate Duty on each death is to be ascertained as if they had died at the same instant and all relevant property had devolved accordingly (F.A. 1958, s. 29). The effect of this provision is to prevent a double charge of Estate Duty where, by the law of commorientes, the younger person is deemed to have survived the elder. Although the estate of the younger may become entitled to property under the will or intestacy of the elder, this property will not now be deemed to pass, for Estate Duty purposes, by reason of the death of the younger.

This rule applies equally where a husband and wife have died simultaneously and intestate. (Intestates' Estates Act 1952, s. 1 (4)).

CHAPTER VIII

ILLUSTRATIONS

§1. Introduction

In the foregoing chapters, the steps to be taken in obtaining probate or, in the case of intestacy letters of administration, the provisions relating to determining the property liable to estate duty and the valuation of that property and the various reliefs which may be claimed have been described. For probate to be granted, the Estate Duty Office will require the preparation and submission of the Inland Revenue Affidavit, and a prerequisite to the preparation of the latter is the collation of the relevant information.

In order to obtain this information the following procedure can be adopted:

(1) The personal records of the deceased, bank statements and other private papers should be thoroughly examined, and if books of account have been kept these should be written up to the date of death.

(2) All securities, which are in the house of the deceased, such as cash, negotiable securities and insurance policies should be listed and placed in safe custody as soon as possible.

(3) Enquiries should be made of the business associates of the deceased and his professional advisers (e.g. accountant, solicitor, broker or banker) to glean further information with regard to assets which the deceased may hold or may have held in the seven-years prior to the date of his death.

(4) The liabilities owed by the deceased should be listed, together with sufficient evidence to justify their inclusion in the Inland Revenue Affidavit. Furthermore, insertions should be made in the London Gazette and local papers, for all claims outstanding against the deceased, to be submitted within not less than two months from the date of the notice.

(5) The assets left by the deceased will have to be valued and the valuer's report must be available for submission. It is not

essential to provide valuations when a preliminary application is being made in the case of assets which are subject to difficulty in so far as valuation is concerned. An agreed valuation may be obtained later, and the necessary Corrective Affidavit submitted in due course (see Chapter IX).

In preparing the Estate Duty account, great care must be taken to ensure that a strict division is maintained between the differing classes of property, e.g. the separation of realty from personalty and the chargeable gifts *inter vivos* from the free estate. Failure to observe this basic requirement could lead to a miscalculation of the Estate Duty payable and to a failure to attribute the incidence of duty to the right person. Furthermore, if the Estate Duty on personalty has been miscalculated to the benefit of the estate, the balance of the duty payable when the mistake is rectified, will be increased by the charge for interest of 3 (formerly 2) per cent. per annum. A similar mistake but in favour of the Revenue will result in a repayment of an excess interest paid but there will be a loss of interest which could have been earned on the money overpaid.

Having considered all available information the preparation of the Estate Duty Account should follow the following lines:

(1) All free personalty in Great Britain, i.e. personal assets which devolve upon the personal representative and which are available for the payment of the deceased's debts should be listed and valued in accordance with the rules described in Chapter IV.

Because of the relief which may be claimed on plant and machinery in certain types of businesses, any valuation for a business as a whole, or shares in such a business, should show the relevant amount applicable to those particular assets.

(2) From the total of the free personalty should be deducted the liabilities of the deceased which may be deducted for Estate Duty purposes. These will include the funeral expenses and other creditors (normally listed-on a supporting schedule), but will *not* include mortgages on property which are properly payable out of realty.

(3) Gifts *inter vivos* which are deemed to pass on the death should be individually listed. The amount to be included

will be that liable to assessment (but details of the gifts must be given). The aggregate of such amounts is added to the net free personalty (i.e. 1–2).

(4) A similar procedure as in 1 and 2 above, will be followed for personalty situated outside Great Britain. Debts due abroad and the additional expenses of realising such property (limited to 5 per cent. of the gross value of the property) should be deducted.

(5) The values of all freehold properties in Great Britain, less any mortgages charged thereon, should be listed; the same treatment being accorded to free realty situated abroad. Interest on mortgages which has accrued up to and including the date of death should be included amongst the deductions in this section.

(6) Finally, all interests of the deceased in settled property and all property in which the deceased never had an interest, but which is deemed to pass on the death, must be listed and valued. A strict division between the individual trusts involved must be maintained, as each trust will bear its own duty. Furthermore property in which the deceased never had an interest, will *not* be subject to aggregation, but will form an estate by itself, bearing its own rate of duty.

The values disclosed by the above lists and schedules will be summarised and the total value of the property subject to aggregation found (called the 'Net Principal Value' of the estate), from which the appropriate rate of Estate Duty can be ascertained. At this stage particular attention should be given as to whether or not the various reliefs are available.

Until the Estate Duty Account has been filed with the Inland Revenue Authorities, probate or letters of administration will not be granted. In the absence of probate an executor has no authority to deal with the assets of the deceased. To pay the duty shown to be due by the account, the executor usually arranges a temporary loan from the deceased's bankers.

§ 2. Illustrations of Estate Duty Accounts

There are several different forms of Estate Duty Account, according to the nature of the property passing. Readers who wish to study the forms in detail can obtain copies from the

Estate Duty Office or a Head Post Office. In the official form, investments are shown first, followed by cash and then the other assets broadly in the order of realisability, as in the following illustrations:

Illustration (1)

A. died on 17th February, 1969, leaving the following estate:

£15,000 2½% Consols valued at 38.

100 Ord. Shares of £1 each fully paid in J. Andrews & Co. Ltd. @ £2 *ex div.* of 12%.

Cash in house, £45.

Cash at Bank, £500.

Cash on Deposit Account, £563, including interest accrued.

Book Debts, £1,210.

Loan on Mortgage, £5,500.

Interest thereon (net), £72.

Life Insurance policy, £5,000.

Household furniture, etc., valued at £1,500.

Goodwill of business, £4,000.

Capital in a partnership business £8,000, including half-share (valued at £3,000) in plant and machinery used in the business.

Current Account in partnership, including profits to date of death, less drawings, £700.

Leasehold Flat Property valued at £2,800.

Rents of leasehold property paid to previous Christmas @ £70 per quarter.

Real property in England, £6,500 (in occupation of deceased).

Mortgage thereon, £1,000. Interest paid to date of death.

Sundry debts due at death and payable out of personalty in the United Kingdom, £320 (including income tax).

Funeral expenses, £65.

Loan to the local *Times*, in a Commonwealth country, £2,500, secured on book debts.

Loan to Isak Meyer, in a foreign country, £2,000, secured on personal guarantee of A. Hirsch.

Death duty on property situated abroad was levied at the rate of 5%.

Estimated additional expense in realising foreign property, £50.

Freehold farms in foreign countries, valued at £6,000.

From the above particulars prepare an Estate Duty Account and show the exact amount of duty payable, the affidavit being presented on 1st July following the death.

Income Tax to be taken into account at 8s 0d in £. All calculations are to be the nearest £ ignoring shillings and pence.

ESTATE DUTY ACCOUNT

PERSONALTY IN GREAT BRITAIN

		£
£15,000 2½% Consols at 38		5,700
100 Ordinary Shares in J. Andrews & Co. Ltd at £2 *ex div.*		200
,, ,, ,, ,, ,, ,, ,, Dividend at 12% *less* tax		8
Cash in house		45
Cash at bank—Current Account		500
Deposit Account with interest to date of death		563
Book Debts		1,210
Loan on Mortgage	£5,500	
Interest thereon, *less* tax	72	
		5,572
Life insurance policy		5,000
Household furniture, etc.		1,500
Goodwill of Business		4,000
Capital in Partnership Business, including profits, *less* drawings ..		8,700
Leasehold Flat property		2,800
Rents accrued thereon, 54 days		42
Gross Personalty		35,840
Deduct Creditors	£320	
Funeral Expenses	65	
		385
Net Personalty in Great Britain ..		**£35,455**

MOVABLE PROPERTY OUTSIDE GREAT BRITAIN

		£
Loan in Commonwealth country		2,500
Loan in foreign country		2,000
		4,500
Less Additional Expenses of realisation		50
Net Movable Property outside Great Britain ..		**£4,450**

REAL PROPERTY IN GREAT BRITAIN

		£
Realty in England		6,500
Less Mortgage		1,000
Net Realty in Great Britain		**£5,500**

IMMOVABLE PROPERTY OUTSIDE GREAT BRITAIN

Freehold farms in foreign countries	**£6,000**

SUMMARY

	£
Net Personalty in Great Britain	35,455
Net Movable Property outside Great Britain	4,450
Net Realty in Great Britain	5,500
Net Immovable Property outside Great Britain	6,000
Total, fixing estate duty at 35 per cent.	**£51,405**

but, marginal relief applies (except to the reduced rate on the partnership plant, etc. (see Note)).

31% on £50,000	15,500
Excess over £50,000	1,405
	£16,905

Amount payable on personalty (other than business plant and machinery) in Great

Britain: $\dfrac{35,455 - 3,000*}{51,405} \times £16,905$ .. .. | 10,673

* If the marginal relief is applied to the industrial plant rate, the duty on the plant will be

55% × 31% = 17·05% on £50,000 .. 8,325	485
Add Margin 1,405	
£9,930	

Carried forward	**£10,673**

ESTATE DUTY ACCOUNT (*Continued*)

								Brought forward	£10,673
Applicable to plant, etc.: $\frac{3,000}{51,405} \times £9,930 =$									485
On Movable property outside Great Britain: $\frac{4,450}{51,405} \times £16,905$								£1,463	
Less duty paid abroad								225	
									1,238
									12,396
Interest for 134 days at 2%									91
									£12,487
On Immovable Property outside Great Britain: $\frac{6,000}{51,405} \times £16,905$								£1,973	
Less duty paid abroad								300	
									£1,673
Estate Duty on realty in Great Britain: $\frac{5,500}{51,405} \times £16,905$									£1,808

Illustration (1a)

If A had died on 17th February, 1970, the Estate Duty payable and its incidence on the various types of property would have been:

Total estate, as above **£51,405**

Duty thereon **£16,968**

Amount payable on personalty (other than business plant and

machinery) in Great Britain: $\frac{32,455}{51,405} \times £16,968$ .. = 10,713

Amount payable on business plant and machinery:

$\frac{3,000}{51,405} \times \frac{55}{100} \times £16,968$ .. .. .. = 545

Amount payable on movable property outside

Great Britain: $\frac{4,450}{51,405} \times £16,968 =$ 1,469

Less duty paid abroad 225

.. .. 1,244

12,502

Interest for 134 days at 2% from 17th February, 1970 to 30th
May, 1970; 3% onwards 103

12,605

Amount payable on immovable property outside

Great Britain: $\frac{6,000}{51,405} \times 16,968$ .. .. = 1,980

Less duty paid abroad 300

1,680

Amount payable on realty in Great Britain: $\frac{5,500}{51,405} \times 16,968$ = 1,815

£16,100

Illustration (2)

W. Jones died on 17th October, 1969, leaving the following property:
Freehold House and Land, valued at £6,000, let at £480 per annum, rent paid to preceding 29th September.
House furniture and effects, valued at £1,500.
£3,000 2½% Stock, quoted at 34–38.
£5,000 4% Loan, quoted at 86–90 *ex div.*
£4,000 5½% Dominion Stock, quoted at 82–86.
£1,000 Loan at 6% (Interest paid to 30th September, 1969).
Policy of Assurance on Testator's life, with bonuses, £5,885.
Cash at Bank, on Current Account £2,365.
Cash in the House, £15.

Jones had a life interest in the residue of the estate of his father, which, at the date of Jones's death, comprised the following investments:

£20,000 2½% Stock, quoted at 34¾—35¾. (Interest payable 5th January, 5th April, 5th July, 5th October.)
£5,000 3½% Loan quoted at 40–44. (Interest payable 1st June and 1st December.)
£20,000 2½% Birmingham Corporation Stock, quoted at 39–43. (Interest payable 1st January and 1st July.)
Cash held by trustees pending re-investment, £2,988.

The trustees of the settlement had paid to Jones the income received up to the previous 30th June.
In July 1964 the deceased had given £2,000 to his son James, £1,000 to the Birmingham Hospital, and £200 to his friend, John Williams.
At the date of his death, Jones owed £415 to sundry creditors, and £259 for Income tax. The funeral expenses amounted to £120.
There was a mortgage on the freehold house and land of £3,000 at 8% interest (payable half-yearly on 30th June and 31st December).
Compute the amount of Estate Duty payable, the affidavit being made on 15th April, 1970, when duty on all the properties was paid.
Income Tax is taken into account at 8s in the £. Any necessary apportionments are to be made to the nearest half-month. Calculations are made to the nearest £.

FREE PERSONALTY

	£	£
£3,000 2½% Stock @ 35		1,050
£5,000 4% Loan @ 87 *ex div.*		4,350
£4,000 3½% Dominion Stock @ 83		3,320
½ year's Interest, *less* tax, on £5,000 4% Loan		60
Income due to deceased from father's settlement:		
Cash in Trustee's hands:		
2 quarters' interest on 2½% Stock received 5th July and 5th October,		
less tax £150		
½ year's interest on Birmingham Stock, received 1st July, *less* tax 150		
	300	
Carried forward	£300	£8,780

FREE PERSONALITY (*Continued*)

				Brought forward	£300	£8,780
Accrued Income, *less* tax, on settled investments:						
£20,000 2½% Stock—½ month ..			..	£12		
£5,000 3½% Loan—4½ months ..			..	39		
£20,000 2½% Birmingham Corporation Stock—3½ months ..				87		
					138	
						438
Cash in House ..	..	..	..	..	..	15
Cash at Bank ..	..	..	..	..	..	2,365
Loan at 6% ..	..	..	..	..	1,000	
Interest accrued thereon, *less* tax, ½ month ..	..	..	..	..	1	
						1,001
Policy of Assurance and Bonuses ..	..	..	..	..		5,885
Household Furniture and Effects ..	..	..	..	..		1,500
Rent accrued on Freehold Property—½ month ..	..	..	..			20
						20,004
Deduct Debts ..	..	..	..	..	415	
Income Tax ..	..	..	..	..	259	
Funeral Expenses ..	..	..	..	..	120	
						794
Net Personalty ..	..	..	..	..		£19,210

FREE REALTY

						£	£
Freehold House and Land ..	..	..	..	.	..		6,000
Deduct Mortgage ..	..	..	..	..	..	3,000	
Interest accrued thereon at 8% per annum, *less* tax—3½ months..						42	
							3,042
Net Realty ..	..	..	..	..	..		£2,958

SETTLED PERSONALITY

							£
£20,000 2½% @ 35 ..	..	..	..	..	..	..	7,000
£5,000 3½% Loan @ 41 ..	..	..	..	..	..	..	2,050
£20,000 2½% Birmingham Corporation Stock @ 40 ..	..	..	..	..		..	8,000
Cash ..	..	..	..	..	..	..	2,988
							20,038
Deduct Accrued Income included in above and payable to deceased life tenant's estate ..	..	..	..	..	..	..	138
							£19,900

GIFT *INTER VIVOS*

Gift to son James in fifth year before death—£2,000 less 30% (F.A. 1960, s. 64) (as amended)	£1,400

SUMMARY

							£
Net Free Personalty ..	..	..	..	..	..	..	19,210
Net Free Realty ..	..	..	..	..	..	..	2,958
Settled Personalty ..	..	..	..	..	..	..	19,900
Gift *inter vivos* ..	..	..	..	..	..	..	1,400
Total ..	..	..	..	..	..	..	£43,468
Estate Duty payable thereon..	..	..	..	..	..	..	£12,206

	Amount of Estate Duty and Interest		Payable by
	£	£	
Net Personalty	5,394		Jones's Executor
Interest thereon at 2% per annum for 6 months	54		
		5,448	
Net Realty		830	ditto (but recoverable from the devisee (if any)
Settled Personalty	5,588		
Interest thereon at 2% per annum for 6 months	56		
		5,644	Trustees of the Settlement
Gifts *inter vivos*	394		
Interest thereon at 2% per annum for 6 months	4		The Donee
		398	
Total duty and interest		£12,320	

Notes:

(1) Income accrued to the date of Jones's death on the settled property in which he has a life interest represents a debt due to him, and as it is included in the *cum. div.* values of these investments, it must be deducted therefrom and included in Jones's free estate.

(2) The gift *inter vivos* to the Birmingham Hospital is exempt from duty as it is a gift for charitable purposes made more than 12 months prior to the death. The gift made to John Williams is exempt, as it does not exceed £500. The gift made to James is reduced by 30% as it would have been deemed to have been made in the fourth year before death, had the latter occurred on the 19th March, 1968. (See transitional provisions contained in s. 35, Finance Act 1968, Chapter VI, § 6.)

The preceding two illustrations cover the type of problems occurring in professional examinations. The following illustration is more detailed. It covers the problems which may arise in practice where husband and wife die within one year of each other.

Illustration (3)

Peter Winter, an industrialist, died on January 1st, 1970. His will read as follows: 'I appoint Joseph Green and Cecil Carr to be the executors of my estate and trustees of the after mentioned settlement for my wife. I direct them to pay all my debts and direct that the Estate Duty on the settled property should be paid thereout and the duty on the agricultural estate and house out of the other assets. Equitable apportionments are to be disregarded.

'I leave to my wife Maureen for life my holding of £20,000 4 per cent. Victory Bonds, 10,000 10 per cent. Cumulative Preference shares of £1 each in Colne Manufacturing Industries Limited and £10,000 6 per cent. Debenture Stock in Tyne Transporters Ltd. After her death these holdings are to be transferred to my two children, John (a chartered accountant aged 30 years) and Diana (a fashion model aged 25 years). The residue of my estate I leave to my wife.'

The details of the Estate Duty Affidavit were:

	£	£
£20,000 4 per cent. Victory Bonds	18,900	
10,000 10 per cent. Cum. Pref. shares in Colne Manufacturing Industries Ltd.	15,000	
£10,000 6 per cent. Debenture stock in Tyne Transporters Ltd.	8,000	
Half-year's interest thereon 300		
Less income tax 124	176	
Business (including plant and machinery, £4,600) ..	16,000	
Bank balance	35,608	
Insurance policy	75,000	
Personal chattels	1,000	
Picture insured for	24,000	
	193,684	
Less Debts due at death 1,096		
Funeral expenses 64	1,160	
		192,524
Agricultural estate (agricultural value, £18,200) ..		33,520
Freehold house in Pinner		22,000
Freehold flat in Portugal	4,500	
Household furniture in the flat	820	
Bank balance at Bank of Portugal	284	
		5,604

There were no debts in Portugal. The picture was regarded by the Treasury as of national interest and the usual undertaking was given regarding its preservation and permanent retention in the United Kingdom.

In 1960 Mr Winter had effected a policy on his own life for £30,000 (annual premium £2,000 p.a. payable on 1st April in each year) which he had maintained for the absolute benefit of Maureen Winter, her executors and assignees and in which he never had an interest.

The assets in Portugal were disposed of in July, 1970, as follows: flat for £4,860, furniture £600, the costs of disposal being approximate to those which would have been incurred had the property been siutated in the United Kingdom, i.e. £140. The proceeds and the bank balance were remitted to the United Kingdom after accounting for estate duties of £562. It was agreed that the Estate Duty valuations need not be amended. The business was sold for £16,000 (including plant £4,600) on 1st April, 1970. The proceeds of the insurance policy were received on 1st March, 1970. The duty on personalty was paid on 31st January, 1970, by means of a bank overdraft. This was later reduced by the transfer of the balance on the deceased's account at his death, the proceeds of the life policy and business and the Portuguese assets.

The first duty of the executors would be to ascertain the Estate Duty payable on Peter Winter's death. In computing the duty the following matters must be borne in mind.

(1) The Estate Duty in respect of the business will, in so far as it is leviable on the value of plant and machinery, be at a reduced rate under the provisions of Section 28, Finance Act 1954 (see Chapter IV, § 7).

(2) No duty will be levied in respect of the picture (see Chapter IV, § 3).

(3) Agricultural property ranks as property on which a reduced rate of duty is chargeable (see Chapter IV, § 10).

(4) The flat in Portugal ranks as immovable property but is liable to duty (see Chapter IV, § 14).

(5) Since Mr Winter never had an interest in the policy taken out in 1960, it would be treated as a separate estate. The amount deemed to pass would be measured by reference to the premiums paid since the 20th March, 1963, to the date of death (not exceeding seven years (s. 35, Finance Act 1968) in their relationship with the sum assured, i.e. £30,000.

Thus, each premium would be valued at $\dfrac{£30,000}{10}$ = £3,000, the denominator representing the number of premiums paid over the term of the policy. Since the policy was written before 20th March, 1968, and the proceeds of the policy exceeded £25,000, the part of the policy monies chargeable to duty which may be treated as a separate estate will be restricted to $\dfrac{25,000}{30,000}$ ths of the dutiable amount.

The amount of the policy monies attributable to each premium, i.e. £3,000, will be treated as a separate gift made on the date on which the premium was paid, and accordingly such amounts rank for reduction under s. 64, F.A. 1960 (as amended).

The reduced value of the relevant proportion of the policy monies will be calculated as follows:

Date Premium paid	Amount £	% age reduction	Dutiable amount £
1st April 1969	3,000	—	3,000
1st April 1968	3,000	—	3,000
1st April 1967	3,000	—	3,000
1st April 1966	3,000	—	3,000
1st April 1965	3,000	15%	2,550
1st April 1964	3,000	30%	2,100
1st April 1963	3,000	60%	1,200
			£17,850

BUT under s. 38, F.A. 1968, only a proportion of such monies will be treated as an estate in which the deceased never had an interest, that proportion being determined by applying the fraction $\frac{25,000}{30,000}$ to the sum ascertained as dutiable, i.e. £17,850.

Therefore $\frac{25,000}{30,000} \times$ £17,850 = £14,875, which amount will be dutiable at the scale rate applicable to an estate of £17,850. The duty will be £1,980, so the estate rate is 11%. 11% of £14,875=£1,636.

The remainder, i.e. £(17,850—14,875)=£2,975, will be aggregated with the other property left by the deceased, and will be dutiable accordingly.

The liability for Estate Duty on Winter's estate will be computed as follows:

	£	£
Personalty		
£20,000 4% Victory Bonds	18,900	
10,000 10% Cum. Pref. shares in Colne Manufacturing Industries Ltd	15,000	
£10,000 6% Debenture stock in Tyne Transporters Ltd	8,000	
Add: half-year's interest thereon (net) ..	176	
	42,076	
Business	16,000	
Bank balance	35,608	
Insurance policy	75,000	
Personal chattels	1,000	
	169,684	
Less debts due at death 1,096		
funeral expenses 64		
	1,160	
		168,524
Aggregable amount of policy monies in which the deceased never had an interest		2,975
		171,499
Realty		
Agricultural estate	33,520	
House at Pinner	22,000	
		55,520
Property overseas		
Immovable property – flat	4,500	
Movable property – furniture .. 820		
bank balance .. 284		
	1,104	
		5,604
Total		£232,623

The duty payable would be:

On £150,000	..	..	..	..	£79,625
On £82,623 at 70 per cent.	..	..	..		57,836
£232,623					£137,461

This would be apportionable as follows:

	£	£
Personalty		
Total excluding value of plant and machinery ..	121,848	

Duty $\dfrac{121,848}{232,643} \times £137,461$ 72,002

Duty on plant and machinery

$\dfrac{4,600}{232,623} \times \dfrac{55}{100} \times £137,461$ £4,600   1,495

£73,497

Settled property

Duty $\dfrac{42,076}{232,623} \times £137,461$ £24,881

Aggregable amount of policy monies:	£	
Duty on £2,975 ..	..	..	..	1,758	
Duty on £14,875	..	..	..	1,636	
		£3,394

Realty

Total as above	..	..	..	..	55,520	
Less agricultural value	..	..	..	18,200	

Duty thereon $\dfrac{37,320}{232,623} \times £137,461$ £37,320   22,053

Duty on agricultural value

$\dfrac{18,200}{232,623} \times \dfrac{55}{100} \times £137,461$ 5,886

£28,939

Property abroad

Duty $\dfrac{5,604}{232,623} \times £137,461$ ..	..	..	3,311	
Less duty payable abroad ..	..	..	562	£2,749

The total duty payable in the United Kingdom is, therefore: £

Personalty	..	..	..	..	98,378
Policy for benefit of widow	..	..	..		3,394
Realty	..	..	..	..	28,939
Property abroad	..	..	..	..	2,749

£133,460

Interest on estate duty should be paid as follows:

(a) On personalty, at the rate of 2 per cent. per annum from the day after the death to the date of delivery of the affidavit;

(b) On realty, at the rate of 3 per cent. per annum from the first anniversary of the death to the date of payment of the duty or if the property is sold prior to the first anniversary, from the date of sale (the rate will be 3 per cent. since the interest would start after 29th May, 1970);

(c) On property abroad, the rules are the same as for property in the United Kingdom namely on movable property as if it were personalty; on immovable property as if it were realty.

The duty on the property settled by the will was to be paid out of the settled property, so that £24,881 would have to be found by selling some of the investments. Interest on the duty would be payable out of the income arising from the settled investments.

Mrs Winter died in a car accident on 1st August, 1970, having given £10,000 to Diana (paid out of the residue of her husband's estate), the agricultural estate to John on the occasion of his marriage in June, 1970. The settled property and her estate passed to John and Diana in equal shares. Mrs Winter's will provided that all duties including that on her gift to Diana, should be paid out of the residue of her estate. Apart from the property passing to her on her husband's death, Mrs Winter had the following assets:

	£
Balance in Deposit Account (being proceeds of life policy taken out by Mr Winter in 1960 (£30,000 — £3,394 estate duty)	26,606
Balance on Current Account (excluding the sum of £176 accrued on settled property at Winter's death)	5,779
Personal chattels	10,600
£15,000 3½% War Loan	5,700
Other relevant values were:	
Agricultural estate	35,000
(Agricultural value – £21,000)	
House at Pinner	24,000

Diana had prior to her mother's death bought investments with the gift which the latter had made, which at her mother's death were valued at £16,000.

Since Mrs Winter died within one year of her husband, quick succession relief under the provisions of Section 26 and 8th Schedule, Finance Act 1958, will be available in respect of the Estate Duty payable on her death on the assets received as part of the residue of her husband's estate.

Duty would be payable in respect of the agricultural estate on the death of Mrs Winter, even though it was the subject of a gift made in consideration of marriage and was made to a party to the marriage. An amount of £5,000 will be exempt, however, in respect of that gift, as it was made by a parent of one of the parties to the marriage.

Computation of duty payable on death of Mrs Winter

To compute the quick succession relief appropriate to the estate of Mrs Winter, her own assets should be distinguished from those receivable from her husband's estate. No duty will be leviable in respect of the property settled on her for life by her husband since it was settled property which had already borne duty on the death of one party to the marriage and the other party was not competent to dispose of the property during the continuance of the settlement. Similarly, since the picture has not been sold, no duty will be payable in respect thereof. As will be seen from the following computation the estate rate on Mrs Winter's death is $\frac{65,969}{128,990}$ or 51·1% compared to that on her late husband's death of $\frac{137,461}{232,623}$ or 59·1%. If the picture was sold by public auction in 1970 for £60,000, duty would be payable on the sale proceeds at the estate rate applicable to her estate.

The Estate Duty payable on Mrs Winter's death would be:

Own assets – personalty				£	£
£15,000 3½% War Loan	..	..	..	5,700	
Bank Deposit account	..	..	..	26,606	
Current account, balance	..	..	..	5,779	
Personal chattels ..	..	..	..	10,600	
					48,685
Assets received from husband's estate					
Personal chattels ..	..	..	..		1,000
Other personalty	..	..	..		
Business	..	..	..	16,000	
Bank balance ..	..	..	..	35,608	
Insurance policy	..	..	..	75,000	
Portuguese assets	..	..	..	5,744	
				132,352	
Less debts due at death ..	..	1,096			
costs of realising property abroad	140				
funeral expenses	..	..	64		
				1,300	
		Carried forward		£131,052	£49,685

		Brought forward		£131,052	£49,685

Less estate duty on all assets other than settled investments:

Personalty ..	..	..	£73,497		
Realty	..	..	28,939		
Property abroad	..	..	3,311		
				105,747	
				25,305	
Less gift to Diana	..	..	..	10,000	
					15,305
					64,990
House at Pinner ..	..	..	..		24,000
Dutiable part of gift made in consideration of marriage – John (£35,000 — 5,000) ..			..		30,000
Gift to Diana	..	..	..		10,000
Total ..	..	..	..	..	£128,990

Estate Duty Payable:

On £80,000 ..	..	..	..		£34,125
On £48,990 at 65 %	..	..	..		31,844
					£65,969

Apportionable as follows:

On own assets:

$$\frac{65,969}{128,990} \times £48,685 \qquad .. \qquad .. \qquad .. \qquad £24,898$$

  Less Quick succession relief – 50 per cent.

  of $\frac{65,969}{128,990}$ of £17,850 =   4,565

                              20,333

On personal chattels from husband:

$$\frac{65,969}{128,990} \times £1,000 \qquad .. \qquad .. \qquad .. \qquad 511$$

  Less Quick succession relief – 50 per cent.

  $\frac{65,969}{128,990}$ of £1,000   256

                              255

	Carried forward	£20,588

Brought forward				£20,588

On cash from husband's estate:

$\frac{65,969}{128,990} \times £15,305$ 7,827

Less Quick succession relief – 50 per cent.

$\frac{65,969}{128,990}$ of £15,305.. 3,913

                                                3,914

On house at Pinner:

$\frac{65,969}{128,990} \times £24,000$ 12,274

Less Quick succession relief – 50 per cent.

$\frac{65,969}{128,990}$ of £22,000 5,625

                                                6,649

On gift to Diana:

$\frac{65,969}{128,990} \times £10,000$ 5,114

Less Quick succession relief – 50 per cent.

$\frac{65,969}{128,990}$ of £10,000 2,557

Gift to John in consideration of his marriage: ..   2,557

Full value of estate £35,000
Agricultural value thereof .. £21,000
Relief restricted to £5,000 apportionable as to
   agricultural value:

$\frac{21,000}{35,000} \times £5,000 = £3,000$

Non-agricultural value:

$\frac{14,000}{35,000} \times £5,000 = £2,000$

Duty payable:

Non-agricultural property: £

On £(14,000 — 2,000), i.e. £12,000

$\frac{65,969}{128,990} \times £12,000$ 6,137

Less Quick succession relief – 50
    per cent. of $\frac{65,969}{128,990}$ of
   £12,000 3,068

                                             3,069

Carried forward   £3,069   £33,708

| | Brought forward | £3,069 | £33,708 |

Agricultural property:

On £(21,000 — 3,000), i.e. £18,000

$$\frac{65,969}{128,990} \times \frac{55}{100} \times £18,000 \quad .. \quad 5,062$$

Less Quick succession relief – 50
per cent. of 55 per cent. of

$$\frac{65,969}{128,990} \text{ of } £18,000 \quad .. \quad 2,531$$

		2,531	
			5,600
			£39,308

Mrs Winter's estate includes a sum received on the earlier death under the life policy which was a separate estate on her husband's death. The sum of money is regarded as being the same property as the policy. Since the policy was valued at £17,850 on the previous death, quick succession relief may be claimed on that sum.

Since Mrs Winter had given Diana the sum of £10,000 out of her late husband's estate, the value of the property passing on the second death must be reduced by that amount. Duty will only be leviable, however, on £10,000 and not the value of the investments purchased by Diana since the gift was a gift of cash.

Quick succession relief is available despite Mrs Winter giving the property away since Estate Duty is leviable on her death on the gift.

Administration expenses have been ignored, except in the case of the property abroad.

CHAPTER IX

CORRECTIVE AFFIDAVITS

In many cases during the administration of an estate, it will be found that the amount of Estate Duty paid when filing the original affidavit to obtain probate was incorrect.

A corrective account will be required where:

(1) assets or liabilities had been omitted from or wrongly included in the original Estate Duty Account;

(2) a provisional valuation was made;

(3) it is found that an incorrect basis of valuation was adopted originally;

but no adjustment would be made merely by reason of a profit or loss on realisation, provided the value of the assets as at the date of death had been correctly ascertained.

In the case of such assets as land and houses, furniture, etc., however, the sum realised on a sale within a few months of death will usually be an indication of their value at the date of death, and if it can be shown that nothing has arisen to cause a change in value in the meantime, the realised prices can usually be included in a corrective account. It is usually a matter for the party suggesting that the realised price should not be taken to prove their case.

A corrective account cannot be delivered for the purpose of reclaiming duty paid under a mistake of law (F.A. 1951, r. 35). Thus, where the Estate Duty was paid as the law was believed at the time to stand, but subsequently a judicial decision or change in the practice of the Commissioners indicates that the former view of the law was incorrect, no repayment will be allowed except where the duty is being paid by instalments so that it can be off-set against future instalments.

It must not be forgotten that any adjustment made by a corrective affidavit may involve the scale of duty being raised or lowered in respect of the whole estate, for deaths prior to 16th April, 1969. For deaths after that date, the rate of duty on the top slice of the estate may be varied. The 'estate rate' will be varied. Interest is payable on an increased amount of duty following from the filing of the corrective affidavit, in the case of personalty from the date of death or in the case of realty from the first anniversary of death or earlier sale (see Chapter III, § 6, for the full rules relating to interest on Estate Duty).

Frequently more than one corrective affidavit is necessary in the case of large estates.

Once a clearance certificate is received from the Estate Duty Office, in the absence of fraud, the personal representatives can distribute the estate to the beneficiaries.

Illustration (1)

A died 1st May, 1969, leaving net personalty valued for Estate Duty purposes at £25,000 and realty valued at £10,000. The duty on personalty paid on the following 1st July, 1969, amounted to £5,625 with £18·75 interest.

It was subsequently discovered that the deceased was the owner of shares in a private limited company, the certificates having been lodged with his bankers for safe custody. The value of these shares at the date of death was ascertained to be £3,500, and there was also a sum on deposit of £1,500. The Inland Revenue claimed taxes of £750 in respect of underpayments in respect of this deposit.

The assets scheduled in the original affidavit included a loan of £2,000 to a friend, but it was subsequently ascertained that the debtor had been adjudicated bankrupt without visible assets, and it was apparent that the debt had been irrecoverable at the date of death.

The debts due by the estate ultimately amounted to £600 instead of £400 originally scheduled, a claim for legal charges having been omitted.

Corrective affidavit was filed on the following 1st December, 1969.

PERSONAL PROPERTY

Items of Personal Property in Original or last Corrective Affidavit, *needing correction* (*) and omitted property and deductions (if any)	Value as last previously shown	Increase	Decrease	Value as now corrected†
	£	£	£	£
1. Assets:				
Shares in private limited company		3,500		3,500
Deposit at Bank		1,500		1,500
Loan	2,000		2,000	
Totals	£2,000	£5,000	£2,000	£5,000
2. Debts and Funeral Expenses:				
Legal charges	400	200		600
Inland Revenue		750		750

REAL PROPERTY

Items of Real Property in Original, or last Corrective Affidavit, *needing correction* (*) and omitted property and deductions (if any)	Value as last previously shown	Increase	Decrease	Value as now corrected†
	£	£	£	£
Totals				

* Items not needing correction should not be inserted.

† The circumstances should be here stated in which the corrections are considered to have become necessary.
     If the property has been sold, the gross amount realised and the date of completion of the sale should be stated.
     Annex a separate statement if the space is insufficient.
     Shillings and pence have been omitted.

The Duty payable is as follows:

	£
Personalty originally declared	25,000
Net Increase as per Corrective Affidavit	3,000
	28,000
Less Increase in Debts	950
Net Personalty	27,050
Realty	10,000
Total Estate	£37,050

	£
Duty on £30,000	5,625
„ „ 7,050 at 45%	3,173
	£8,798
On Net Personalty of £27,050	6,425
Less Duty already paid	5,625
Duty now payable	800
Interest thereon @ 2% for 7 months	9
Total	£809

The Duty on Realty of $\dfrac{10,000}{37,050} \times 8,798 = £2,373$ will be paid in due course.

Should the amount of the Estate Duty payable on a corrective affidavit be less than that previously paid, the difference can be reclaimed, together with interest which has been actually paid on the excess amount. A claim for interest on such excess for the period during which it has been in the hands of the Inland Revenue cannot be sustained except where over-payment was due to an over-valuation by the Commissioners (F.A. 1894, s. 8 (12)), or the court orders interest to be paid (*ibid.* s. 10 (3)). There is no time limit within which repayment must be claimed.

Illustration (2)

On submitting a corrective affidavit, it was found that the net estate was as follows:

		£
Net personalty originally declared		40,000
Decrease in assets	£5,000	
Increase in liabilities	1,000	
		6,000
Amended personalty		34,000
Realty		10,000
Total Estate		£44,000
Duty originally paid, 3 months after death – on personalty of £40,000		12,900
Duty now found to be payable – on £34,000		9,678
Duty repayable		£3,222

No matter at what interval the corrective affidavit is filed, the Revenue will only allow interest from the date of death to the date on which the original duty was paid, i.e. in this case, 3 months, unless the over-payment was due to their error, or they are ordered by the Court to pay interest for a longer period.

CHAPTER X

CONTROLLED COMPANIES

§1. Introduction

If property is to be liable to Estate Duty, it must pass or be deemed to pass, by relation to the death. It follows, that if by some means the deceased could transfer his property in his lifetime and more than seven years before his death, whilst leaving himself in a position to enjoy the income, Estate Duty would be avoided without detriment to the donor. One method of effecting such saving is based on the principle that the true owners of the limited company are its shareholders. If the deceased secured a position in relation to the company whereby he held an overall power over the income and assets of the company by, for example, entering into a long term service agreement or by an irrevocable clause in the articles of association of the company without owning any or only a relatively few shares, Estate Duty would be avoided or substantially reduced. The agreement or clause would enable the deceased to enjoy the income or assets of the company. Such avoidance has been restricted by the provisions of the Finance Act 1940, as amended by subsequent Finance Acts.

The anti-avoidance provisions which are concerned only with controlled companies are contained in Sections 46–59 of that Act; s. 46 dealing with companies to which property has been transferred by the deceased, and s. 55 dealing with the overall situation subsisting where the deceased, who had effective control has left shares in a company. In some cases there will be property, including shares, which will fall within the framework of both s. 46 and s. 55. The double charge for Estate Duty is avoided by offsetting the value of the property deemed to pass by virtue of the transfer under s. 46, against the value of the shares ascertained in accordance with s. 55. It would appear, however, that there is no set-off where property is deemed to pass because of benefits received which are not referable to the property which was transfered (see later).

The rules relating to a valuation under s. 46 are extremely complex but, broadly speaking, they apply where a person has transferred property of any value, to a 'controlled' company at any time, and where that person has received or could have received, by the exercise of his powers, benefits during the seven years preceding his death. Transitional provisions apply, as with gifts *inter vivos* in cases where the deceased died after 19th March, 1968, i.e. where the statutory period has been extended from five to seven years [s. 35, F.A. 1968]. A proportion of the net assets of the company to the extent that the deceased's aggregate benefits bear to the total aggregate income (including such benefits) of the company in the period, are deemed to pass on the death. Benefits in this context have a very wide meaning, and include remuneration in excess of 'reasonable' remuneration for services rendered, dividends, interest, and benefits in kind. In the case of the company, its net income is computed in accordance with the normal corporation tax principles. It is necessary to realise at this point, that two calculations are necessary, to determine the part of the slice of the assets ascertained as above which relates to the transfer of property, and the part which relates to benefits regarded as exceeding the amount properly attributable to that property; the latter, as already indicated, is not affected by any subsequent valuation of shares on the 'assets' basis under s. 55.

For shares and debentures to be valued in accordance with s. 55, further conditions to the general conditions stated above, must be satisfied. Thus, the deceased must have had voting control or a beneficial interest in more than half of the shares or debentures at some time in the immediately preceding seven years, or powers equivalent to control (no other person having control) in any two of those seven years, or the right to more than one half of the aggregate of all dividends and interest payable in any two years of the same period. For the Section to apply, in those cases other than where the deceased had voting control, the company must be controlled after the death by a person, with or without his relatives, and that person must have a beneficial interest in shares or debentures which pass, or the control of the company must remain in the same hands both before and after the death, by virtue of the shares and debentures giving a controlling interest being in the hands of trustees.

If these conditions are satisfied the net assets of the limited company, valued as a going concern, are apportioned rateably over the shares and debentures of the company in accordance with their respective rights.

In both types of valuation, the assets are valued on a 'going concern' basis, and the liabilities, which may include a reasonable amount for contingent liabilities, but which must exclude debentures, will be deducted from the valuation. The relief given to individuals in respect of property of an agricultural or industrial nature, is to be applied to the amount represented in such property, which has been included in the ascertained valuations. Similarly, both quick succession relief and the reduction in the valuation of gifts under Section 64 of the Finance Act 1960 (as amended), will be available in appropriate circumstances.

Finally, the duty made payable under a s. 46 valuation, is leviable directly on the company; that under s. 55 being leviable in accordance with the normal rules.

§2. Definition of a Controlled Company

A Controlled Company is one, wheresoever incorporated, which would be deemed to be under the control of not more than five persons, if the rules set out in (a) to (d) below applied.

A company is deemed to be one under the control of five or fewer persons, if any five or fewer persons:

(a) together exercise, or are able to exercise, or are entitled to acquire, control, whether direct or indirect over the company's affairs, or if they possess, or are entitled to acquire, the greater part of the voting power; or

(b) possess, or are entitled to acquire, the greater part of the share capital; or

(c) possess, or are entitled to acquire, such part of the share capital as would, if the whole of the company's income were distributed to the members, entitle them to receive the greater part of the amount so distributed; or

(d) on the assumption that the company is one to which these rules would apply, would receive directly (or indirectly via other companies to which the rules apply) more than half of the company's income.

In determining who consitutes the relevant five persons, the following are treated as a single person:

  (i) husband, wife, ancestor, lineal descendant, brother or sister,

  (ii) partners,

  (iii) nominee and the beneficial owner,

  (iv) bare trustee and the beneficial owner.

It should be noted that a company will remain a controlled company for Estate Duty purposes if it is under the control of five or fewer persons even though the public may be substantially interested.

§3. Property transferred to a Company

Where a person has, at any time, transferred property to a controlled company, and benefits accrued to him from the company in the seven years prior to his death, or from 19th March, 1963, to the death, whichever is the shorter period, a portion of the company's assets can be deemed to pass on his death. The portion of the assets is found by multiplying the total assets by the benefits received or receivable by him from the company and dividing by the net income of the company (F.A. 1940, c. 46).

The most common form of TRANSFER is the sale of property (land, investments, businesses, etc.) to a company in consideration of an issue of shares or debentures. The subscription for shares, etc., in cash is a transfer (F.A. 1952, s. 72). A purchase of shares, etc., from existing holders is not such a transfer. The term 'transfer' is comprehensive, and a transfer may be indirect or the result of associated transactions.

The only property excluded is an interest limited to cease on the death of the transferor, or property transferred in a fiduciary capacity imposed on him otherwise than by a disposition made by himself.

BENEFITS accruing to the deceased from the company include:

(*a*) actual benefits directly received by the deceased, e.g. dividends, interest, excessive remuneration, any beneficial occupation of land, etc.;

(b) benefits received indirectly, e.g. profits put to reserve and so increasing the value of his shares; dividends paid to another company controlled by him, etc.;

(c) any such income, payment or enjoyment, which the deceased was entitled to receive but did not receive, or which, by the exercise of any power, he could have been entitled to;

(d) interest at the 'average rate' on any payment, etc. (other than a periodical payment) which the deceased could have become entitled to, but did not receive.

The 'average rate' is the percentage ascertained by dividing the aggregate net income (profits less losses) of the company for the relevant accounting years, i.e. the accounting years involved in the computation of benefits, etc., viz. seven (unless the company has not existed so long) by the number of those years, and comparing the result with the principal value of net assets of the company deemed to pass on the death of the deceased as a result of Section 46.

The term 'payment' includes a transfer of property and the set-off or release of an obligation. It may be of income or capital, and the benefit may be direct or indirect; e.g. if the redemption of debentures out of income has enhanced the value of the shares, the deceased will be deemed to have received a benefit to that extent. Such 'periodical payments' as the Commissioners consider to be reasonable remuneration for the services rendered by the deceased to the company are *not* regarded as benefits. Temporary loans to the deceased by the company may be benefits (*A. G.* v. *Hon. Lionel Michael St. Aubyn* (No.2) [1950]) as also may be the repayment by the company of a loan made to it by the deceased (*cf. A. G. Jenkins* v. *C.I.R.* [1944]).

A surrender of a right to benefits is ineffective for the avoidance of duty unless made to the entire exclusion of the deceased more than seven years before the death. Transitional relief is given where the benefits were obtained or surrendered prior to 19th March 1963 (s. 35 and 14th Sec., F.A. 1968).

If, however, the death occurred on or after 20th March, 1968, and a surrender of title to benefits was made *bona fide* before the beginning of the four years before the death, the valuation of the surrendered benefits is reduced in the same way as gifts *inter vivos*, i.e. if the surrender took place during the fifth year before death, the value is reduced by 15 per cent., if within the sixth year by 30 per cent., and if earlier than the sixth year, by 60 per cent. It should be noted that the reduction applies not only to benefits surrendered within the years before the death, but also to benefits surrendered more than seven years before the death which have to be brought into account because the surrender was not to the entire exclusion of the deceased (Finance Act 1960, s. 65). This reduction in valuations is confined to benefits which have been surrendered by the deceased. It is important to note that the rate of relief is determined by the date on which the right to benefit was surrendered, not by the dates on which the benefits would, in fact, have risen. Thus, if a man gave away 20,000 6 per cent. £1 preference shares on 25th October, 1964, in the company's accounting year ended 31st January, 1965, and he died on 18th December, 1970, the surrender of the right to benefits was made in the sixth year prior to the death. The dividends received between 25th October, 1964 and 31st January, 1970, will have to be included in benefits, but will be reduced in value by 30 per cent., although actually received in the fifth, fourth, third, second or first year before the death. (The dividends received after 31st January, 1970, will not be included in benefits at all, since they were not received in the last seven accounting years of the company prior to death).

In determining what benefit the deceased could have received by exercising any power, he will be assumed to have acted in accordance with his greatest financial advantage, and the benefit will be deemed to accrue at the earliest time that the deceased could have received it.

Benefits are to be calculated without deduction of income tax. Land enjoyed in specie will be valued at the annual value for Income tax purposes. Dividends appear to be benefits of the year in which they are declared, not in which they are earned.

For any accounting year ending later than 5th April, 1966, the net income of a company for the purpose of calculating liability to Estate Duty under Section 46 of the Finance Act 1940 is to be computed as for Corporation tax purposes except that:

(a) franked investment income and group income is to be included, but not profits which are neither *bona fide* earned in the ordinary course of business nor produce of income producing assets, and

(b) no regard is to be had –

    (i) to any investment allowances, initial allowances or balancing charges; nor

    (ii) to any deduction falling to be made in respect of losses, allowances or expenses of management outside the period in which a deduction originally falls to be made in respect thereof; nor

    (iii) to any restriction on the deduction that may be made for directors' remuneration.

(c) Corporation tax borne by the company on its income for the year is deducted.

Remuneration of any person holding an office under the company is deductible only to the extent that the Commissioners are satisfied that it is reasonable; this applies to any person holding an office, not merely to the deceased. For accounting periods ending before 5th April, 1966, readers are referred to the twentieth edition.

No deduction is allowed for any loss sustained before the beginning of the year or of any annual payment which, under Section 177, Taxes Act 1970, would be treated as a loss sustained before the beginning of the year, or of capital allowances in respect of plant and machinery for any previous year.

The PROPORTION of benefits to net income is ascertained by comparing the *aggregate* of the benefits for the last seven accounting years with the *aggregate* of the net income of the company for those years, losses being deducted in arriving at such aggregate profits. If the company came into existence during the seven years prior to the death, the average of the available years is taken. Where a company has taken over a business, profits for any period prior to its incorporation cannot be included.

The extent to which the assets of the company may be deemed to pass on the death is the proportion, ascertained as above, of the value of the net assets of the company at the date of the death, but must not exceed the value of the assets transferred to the company, so far as that proportion is based on benefits received as consideration for the transfer.

The NET ASSETS of the company are valued on the basis of the sale of the business as a going concern, and include goodwill. Deductions are allowed for all liabilities (including a reasonable estimate for contingent liabilities) except (*a*) shares or debentures in the company, (*b*) liabilities not wholly incurred for the purposes of the business, and (*c*) remuneration disallowed as unreasonable. Where the death occurs after 5th April, 1967, and before 24th July, 1970, and the Company's assets include land which has a betterment value, but which is unrealised, the potential levy payable may be included amongst the contingent liabilities. The liability, which must be an estimation, will be based on the probable future utilisation of the land.

It is important to note that the term 'debenture' includes any obligation in respect of loan capital, *except* in consideration of a bank loan, or of a transfer of capital assets to the company otherwise than one in the ordinary course of the transferor's business.

An adjustment is allowed for any prospective balancing charge (or presumably for any balancing allowances) which will arise when assets are sold or scrapped, and a reasonable estimate should be deducted from the assets (*Re Sutherland*).

A deduction, of such amount as appears reasonable, may be claimed in respect of the Corporation tax payable on any capital gain which might arise if the company's assets were realised.

Provision is made for the inclusion of assets which have been disposed of or distributed by the company between the beginning of the relevant accounting periods and the death of the deceased, either in satisfying rights attaching to shares or debentures of the company, or otherwise. The following, however, are *not* to be included:

(*a*) assets disposed of for full consideration;

(*b*) payment of rates, taxes or other statutory liabilities, or in discharge of a fine or penalty for a tort;

(*c*) payments from which Income tax is deductible, or which were assessable to Income tax, but not exceeding, in respect of any accounting period, the income of the company for that period.

Where any distributed assets are included, the net income of the company for the periods subsequent to the distribution must be increased by interest at the 'average rate' from the date thereof. If any of the distributed assets were received by the deceased, the interest thereon which is included in the net income of the company must be treated as income of the company which the deceased was entitled to receive, and an equivalent amount must be added to the deceased's benefits. As, however, the value of such distributed assets received by the deceased will form part of his estate passing on his death, an amount equal to the value thereof must be deducted from the 'slice' of the company's assets on which Estate Duty is chargeable.

If the valuation of shares or debentures which have been surrendered within seven years of death (or longer if the deceased retained an interest in them) is reduced as explained above, the value of those assets is to be reduced in the proportion that the reduced value of the benefits in question bears to the amount of all benefits from such shares or debentures. Thus, if shares valued at £6,000 were surrendered in the seventh year before death, and the deceased received in that year, but before the surrender, dividends of £400, and the dividends included in the benefits for the period from the surrender to the end of the relevant seven accounting years, were £1,400, the latter would be reduced by 60 per cent. to £560, and the value of the shares would be reduced to:

$$\frac{£400 + £560}{1,800} \times £6,000 = £3,200$$

Conversely, in order to prevent the appropriate fraction of the company's assets being distorted by additions to the assets between the beginning of the first relevant accounting year and the date of death, where any such addition has been made to the assets of the company, interest at the 'average rate' on such addition from the beginning of the first relevant accounting year to the date of the addition must be added to the income of the company. If the addition was made by the deceased, his benefits must also be increased by the amount of such interest.

The DUTY payable is a liability of the company, who can

recover the appropriate portion on distributed assets from the recipient of those assets. The company must notify the Commissioners within one month of the date of death of the deceased, of the death and of the transfer of property and the accrual of benefits.

A limitation of the liability is imposed, for which purpose it is necessary to distinguish benefits accruing to the deceased by virtue of the transfer of property to the company (such as dividends on shares issued to him as consideration for the transfer) from other benefits. The value of the company's assets on which duty is charged by reason of the benefits accruing by virtue of the transfer of property to the company, is not, in any event, to exceed the value, as at the date of transfer, of the assets transferred by the deceased to the company, plus the excess (if any) of interest thereon at the 'average rate' from the date of transfer over the aggregate value of the benefits received by the deceased by virtue of the transfer. There is no such limitation on the duty attributable to the other benefits.

In order to prevent a double charge of Estate Duty where the deceased has disposed of shares or debentures in a company for consideration in money or money's worth paid to him for his own use or benefit, and benefits have accrued to him by virtue of a power exercisable by him in relation to those shares or debentures, it is provided that if the value of the said consideration is equal to or more than the proportion of the 'slice' of the company's assets which corresponds to the said benefits, or if such proportion, if ascertained, would not be substantially greater than the said consideration, duty on the proportion will not be payable. In any other case, the amount of the proportion will be reduced by the amount of the said consideration.

This provision will not apply where Estate Duty is payable on the deceased's death on the value of the shares or debentures, or would be so payable but for an exemption from Estate Duty (F.A. 1940, s. 51 (1)).

If exemption is claimed on the ground that shares or debentures have passed for full consideration in money or money's worth, exemption only applies if the Commissioners are satisfied that it would have done so on the hypothesis that the company held its assets on trust for its members, i.e. that the assets of the company were really the assets of the members. If, on this hypothesis, it appears that the property in question has not passed for full consideration in money or money's worth, exemption from Estate Duty cannot be claimed (F.A. 1940, s. 56).

If the aggregate value at the date of death of shares or debentures sold is greater than the value of the consideration paid for them, that aggregate value is to be allowed as a deduction from the proportion of the 'slice' of the company's assets instead of the value of the consideration. Lots disposed of separately are to be valued separately and the results aggregated. Artificial increases in value are to be ignored (F.A. 1940, s. 51; F.A. 1950, s. 47; F.A. 1952, s. 72).

Since the Acts require the slice of the company's assets to be aggregated with other property passing on the deceased's death, the appropriate privileges apply, e.g. reduced rates on agricultural property and on industrial land, buildings and plant and machinery; the right to pay duty on realty by instalments; payment of duty on the sale of timber; works of art; and quick succession relief.

Illustration

Eight years prior to his death X. had transferred to a controlled company, in consideration of shares, property then valued at £98,000. The dividends received by the deceased amounted in the aggregate to £2,000 during the first year and £35,000 during the next seven years following the date of the transfer. The deceased received £1,000 per annum as director's fees in each of the eight years, but in fact performed no duties. X. had no power over the rest of the company's income. The company's aggregate net income for the seven years immediately preceding X.'s death was £56,000. The net assets of the company were valued at £180,000 at the date of X.'s death.

The benefits received by X. during the seven years immediately prior to his death amounted to £42,000, viz. £35,000 dividends and £7,000 director's fees. Only the dividends can be regarded as accruing by virtue of the transfer.

Since the deceased performed no duties, the remuneration paid to him would not be regarded as reasonable, and would not be deductible in arriving at the company's net income, the total of which for the seven years would therefore be £56,000 + £7,000 = £63,000.

The 'slice' of the company's assets deemed, by virtue of Section 46, Finance Act 1940, to pass on X.'s death will be $\frac{42,000}{63,000} \times £180,000 = £120,000$, of which $\frac{35,000}{63,000} \times £180,000 = £100,000$ is attributable to benefits accruing by virtue of the transfer.

Since this exceeds the value of the assets transferred by X. to the company, it must be ascertained if the limitation imposed by Section 51 (1), Finance Act 1940, will operate.

The 'average rate' is $\frac{63,000}{7} \div 180,000 = 5$ per cent.

(a)	5% on £98,000 for 8 years = ...	£39,200
(b)	The aggregate of the benefits received by X. by virtue of the transfer for the 8 years = ...	37,000
	Excess of (a) over (b)	£2,200

The proportion of the assets on which Estate Duty is chargeable is therefore not limited since the amount computed under Section 51 is £98,000 + £2,200 = £100,200 in respect of benefits arising from the transfer, plus $\frac{7,000}{63,000} \times$ £180,000 = £20,000 in respect of other benefits, a total of £120,200.

If the value of any shares or debentures in the company on which Estate Duty is payable on the death of the deceased is equal to or greater than the proportion of the net assets of the company deemed to pass by reference to benefits accruing to the deceased in respect of the shares or debentures, duty on that proportion of the net assets is not payable. In any case where the value of the shares or debentures is less than the value of that proportion of the net assets, the amount of the 'slice' on which duty is to be charged is reduced by the value of the shares or debentures. The proportion of the 'slice' referable to other benefits is not reduced (F.A. 1944, s. 38).

As already indicated, where duty is assessed under Section 46 the amount payable can be recovered from the company. This potential liability can inhibit the disposal of shares either by way of sale or introduction to the public. The Board of Inland Revenue have indicated that a clearance may be obtained in such circumstances from the Controller, Estate Duty office.

The company requiring the clearance must supply the following information:

(a) The name and address of the registered office of the company.

(b) A copy of the original Memorandum and Articles of Association of the company with all amendments to date.

(c) The Trading & Profit & Loss Accounts of the company for each of the last seven years with Balance Sheets at the end of those years.

(*d*) Details as at seven years ago, with all subsequent changes of the Company's issued capital, the names of shareholders (indicating their relationship and/or whether they were trustees) and their shareholdings and the names and addresses of the directors.

The person whose death is being assumed for the purposes of the application:

(*a*) That person's name and address.

(*b*) The salary, commission, fees, pension and any other remuneration received by him from the company during each of the last seven years with details of any office held in the company.

(*c*) The services rendered in return for the remuneration in (*b*).

(*d*) Full statements for the seven-year period of any current or loan account with the company.

(*e*) All benefits in kind or assets of the company enjoyed by him during that period.

(*f*) Any income or capital of the company paid to him or for his benefit or to which he was entitled during the last seven years, e.g. dividends, interest payments, repayments of debentures and other distributions.

(*g*) Any other benefits to him in the last seven years, not mentioned above, arising directly or indirectly from his connection with the company, e.g. bonus issues, releases of debts made by the company in favour of other companies in whose shares the person was beneficially interested.

(*h*) Brief details of transactions within the last seven years which may have affected his title to receive any benefits from the company, e.g. gifts, sales, exchanges of shares, debentures or other interests in the company.

(*i*) Brief details of all agreements between him and the company and of all settlements made by him of shares, debentures or other interests in the company or its assets.

(*j*) Details of the transaction giving rise to the application for a clearance.

The Estate Duty office will not enter into any discussion in respect of its decision on the application.

§4. Valuation of Shares and Debentures under Section 55, Finance Act 1940 (as amended by Finance Acts 1946, 1954 and 1960)

In view of the complexities of the legislation contained in Section 46, the Estate Duty Office do not usually seek to invoke the section, unless they feel there has been a deliberate attempt at avoiding duty. More frequently they will try to value the shares under the provisions of Section 55. This section applies in the circumstances set out below and enacts that shares or debentures must be valued by reference to the net assets of the company and not by reference to the market price. As in the case of Section 46 what follows is an outline and a general guide only.

The section applies where shares or debentures of a company pass on the death of a person who had voting control of the company at any time during the seven years ended with his death.

It also applies where the deceased did not have voting control, but:

(*a*) where he had powers equivalent to control, e.g. as governing director, or the power to veto the appointment of directors, etc., for a continuous period of two years out of the seven; or

(*b*) where he received during a continuous period of two years out of the seven years immediately preceding his death over half the dividends and interest, (or if s. 46 had applied, more than half of them would have been treated as benefits); or

(*c*) where he had a beneficial interest in half or more of the nominal amount of shares or debentures issued and outstanding, and no other person controlled the company;

but in these three events, only to shares or debentures which satisfy one of the following conditions:

(1) that immediately after the deceased's death, a person having control or powers equivalent to control of the company (either alone or in conjunction with relatives), has a beneficial interest in possession in the shares or debentures;

(2) that immediately before and after the death, the shares or debentures are held by the trustees of a trust who then have control of the company by virtue of the shares or debentures held as trustees; or

(3) in the case of shares or debentures liable to Estate Duty as gifts *inter vivos* made by the deceased or by virtue of a disposition or determination of a life interest that the donee or other person entitled has control (or powers equivalent thereto) either alone or with relatives, immediately after the death or at any previous time since the gift or the determination of the life interest.

Relative here means spouse, ancestor, lineal descendant, brother or sister (F.A. 1954, ss. 30, 31).

Control in a fiduciary capacity under a disposition not created by the deceased is ignored (Finance Act 1940, s. 55 (5)).

The term 'debenture' includes any loan other than a temporary bank loan, obligation or debt not incurred in the ordinary course of business. There is no need for there to be any charge on any of the company's assets. The term does not include a building society mortgage.

The section does not apply to shares or debentures for which permission to deal has been granted by the committee of a recognised Stock Exchange in the United Kingdom, and ordinary deals have been recorded in the year preceding the death.

The value of the assets of a company, for the purposes of Section 55, Finance Act 1940, is to be on the footing that the notional sale of the business by reference to which the value is to be estimated is a sale where the assets are subject to an enforceable restriction that they are to be used only for the purposes of that business (Finance Act 1960, s. 66), i.e. they are to be valued on a going concern basis. This provision does not apply to securities, stocks, shares, land or buildings in so far as they are assets of a company whose business includes dealing in such assets or making or holding investments. In valuing these assets in the case of such companies, therefore, the break-up value is taken. When the provision applies it is not to reduce the value of shares or debentures below the lower of (a) an open market valuation or (b) a valuation under Section 55 on the basis of a sale at the best possible price. Since the profits of companies are charged on the basis of the actual profits in the accounting period, any taxes arising on profits earned in periods prior to death are deductible. Deductions will also be allowed, as discussed in connection with Section 46, for possible liabilities to tax on capital gains, balancing charges and betterment levy. From the value of the assets are deducted liabilities other than debentures to determine the net assets.

The whole of the outstanding issued shares and debentures are then regarded as equal in value to the net assets, and that value is apportioned among the shares and debentures, having regard to the rights attached to them. If any class is quoted and dealt in, that class is valued by reference to the market quotation, and the balance of the net assets apportioned to other classes.

As already stated, if the value of the 'slice' of the company's assets (so far as attributable to benefits in respect of the shares or debentures) determined under Section 46 exceeds the value of the shares and debentures passing on the death determined under Section 55, the value of the 'slice' will be reduced by the value of the shares and debentures. If the shares and debentures exceed in value that part of the 'slice' of the company's assets, no duty will be payable on that part, though the part of the 'slice' attributable to other benefits will be dutiable in full.

Illustration (1)

The issued capital of a controlled company consisted of 20,000 8% preference shares of £1 each and 50,000 £1 ordinary shares. There were also in issue £20,000 6% debentures.

At the date of his death, A. held 5,000 of the preference shares, 30,000 of the ordinary shares and £15,000 of the debentures. The assets were valued for the purpose of Section 55, Finance Act 1940, at £126,000, and the liabilities were £9,000 (excluding any accrued debenture interest or proposed dividends).

Assuming A. died 3 months after the date of the last payment of debenture interest and preference dividend, the shares and debentures passing on A.'s death might be valued as under:

	£	£
Value of £20,000 Debentures:		
Nominal	20,000	
Accrued interest 6% per annum for 3 months, *less* tax at 8s 3d in £..	176	
		20,176
Carried forward		£20,176

	Brought forward	£20,176

Value of 20,000 8% Preference Shares:

Nominal	20,000	
Accrued dividend, 8% per annum for 3 months, *less* tax at 8s 3d in £..	235	
		20,235
Balance, being value of 50,000 ordinary shares		76,589
Assets less liabilities		£117,000

Value of A.'s Holding:

	£
5,000 Preference Shares — $\frac{5,000}{20,000} \times$ £20,176	5,044
£15,000 Debentures — $\frac{15,000}{20,000} \times$ £20,235	15,176
30,000 Ordinary Shares — $\frac{30,000}{50,000} \times$ £76,589	45,953
	£66,173

If Section 46, Finance Act 1940, applied, and the amount of the 'slice' of the company's assets deemed to pass on A.'s death had been £90,000, of which the proportion applicable to the benefits derived from the shares and debentures issued to A. was £80,000, duty under Section 46 would be charged on:

	£
Proportion of 'slice' attributable to shares and debentures ..	80,000
Less value of shares and debentures	66,173
	13,827
Proportion attributable to other benefits	10,000
	£23,827

If the value of the proportion of the 'slice' applicable to the shares and debentures were less than £66,173, no duty would be payable thereon. Duty would, however, still be charged on the proportion of the 'slice' attributable to the other benefits, £10,000.

Should the assets of a company, the shares in which are valued in accordance with Section 55, Finance Act 1940, include industrial land or buildings or plant and machinery used in the business, the rate of duty applicable to the relevant proportion of the net value of the shares or debentures is to be reduced by 45 per cent. A similar reduction is given in respect of the agricultural value of land if the company is engaged in husbandry or forestry. If the land is used only partly for the purposes of agriculture or forestry, a just proportion is apportioned to those purposes (F.A. 1954, s. 28).

The 'relevant proportion' of the net value of shares or debentures means such part of that value as is attributable to the value of any of the following:

(*a*) Industrial premises (under the definition for rating purposes), used in and occupied for the purposes of the business. If used only partly for business purposes, apportionment is necessary unless the value does not exceed £1,000, in which event it will all be regarded as used for business purposes. Premises held as an investment do not qualify.

(*b*) Machinery and plant used in the business. If partly used for other purposes, such relief is given as the Commissioners regard as just and reasonable.

Relief is also given on the proportion of the value of the shares or debentures attributable to the value of industrial premises and machinery and plant used by or let to subsidiary companies or let by a subsidiary company to the company in question for the purposes of the business of that or any other subsidiary of the company.

In calculating the proportion, liabilities secured on the assets are deducted from the value of the assets charged. Otherwise the liabilities are applied first against other assets. Only liabilities deductible under Section 55 are taken into account.

Illustration (2)

If in Illustration (1), the net assets of the company were made up as follows:

	£	£
Factory, land and buildings	10,000	
Less Mortgage thereon..	6,000	
		4,000
Machinery and plant		30,000
Other assets		83,000
		£117,000

the proportion of the shares and debentures passing on A.'s death eligible for 45 per cent. reduction in rate of duty would be:

$$\frac{34}{117} \times £66,173 = £19,229.$$

Illustration (3)

Radlow Ltd manufactures branded shelving. The company's Balance Sheet as at 31st March, 1969, is shown below, while the 'memorandum' figures are the values estimated to be realised by sales of those assets on the open market, assuming their continued use in the trade. Where 'memorandum' figures are not given the assets are at their realisable value.

Share Capital Issued and fully paid	£	Fixed Assets:	£	Memorandum £
10% Cumulative Preference shares of £1 each	62,500	Freehold factory at cost	100,000	150,000
Ordinary shares of £1 each	100,000	Plant at cost, *less* depreciation ..	50,000	62,500
	162,500	Goodwill at cost ..	25,000	50,000
Reserves and undistributed profits ..	32,469			
	194,969		175,000	
8% Debentures ..	50,000	Quoted Investments at cost	11,250	
Corporation Tax Equilisation Account ..	7,500			

	£		£
Current Liabilities:		Current Assets:	
Trade creditors ..	61,281	Stocks and work in progress	45,000
Current taxation ..	8,750	Trade debtors ..	87,500
Corporation tax payable by Jan., 1970	16,250	Balance at bank ..	37,500
Proposed dividends for year (gross)	17,500		170,000
	103,781		
	£356,250		£356,250

(a) The market value of the quoted investments was £12,500.

(b) Each issued share carries one vote. There have been no changes in shareholdings in the seven years ending with Jones' death on 31st March, 1969. The Preference shares were held by the Estate Saving Trust (a publicly quoted company). The Ordinary shares were held as to 60 per cent. by Jones. The remaining shares were held by eight employees, each with 5 per cent.

(c) It is agreed that the preference shares are worth 22/- per share cum. div., while the debentures are worth par.

(d) The rate of Estate Duty on Jones' estate is 80 per cent.

(e) Contingent taxation liabilities in respect of balancing charges and capital gains are estimated at £1,500.

(f) The debentures were secured by a floating charge on all the assets.

JONES DECEASED

VALUATION OF ORDINARY SHARES IN RADLOW LTD

		Values for	
		Section 55 Finance Act 1940	Section 28 Finance Act 1954
Freehold factory		£150,000	£150,000
Plant		62,500	62,500
Goodwill		50,000	
Quoted Investments		12,500	
Stocks and work in progress		45,000	
Trade debtors		87,500	
Balance with Bank		37,500	
		445,000	212,500
Less Trade creditors	£61,281		
Current taxation	8,750		
Corporation tax	16,250		
Schedule F income tax	7,219		
Contingent tax liabilities	1,500		
		95,000	
Total value attributable to Debentures and Shares		350,000	212,500
Less Agreed Values:			
Debentures	50,000		30,357
Cumulative Preference shares	62,500		
		112,500	37,946
Value attributable to 100,000 Ordinary shares		£237,500	£144,197

Value per share, £2 7s 5d.

Estate Duty 80 per cent. on 60,000 shares at £2 7s 5d	£113,800
Less Relief under Section 28, 45 per cent. of 80 per cent. on $\frac{60,000}{100,000} \times £144,197$	31,146
	£82,654

The relief does not extend to:

(i) a profession or vocation; (it is doubtful if a company can carry on either activity, each of which denotes some individual skill, etc.).;

(ii) a business not carried on for gain;

(iii) a business which is the subject of a binding contract for sale unless the sale is wholly or mainly for shares in a company formed to acquire the business; or

(iv) a company in liquidation, otherwise than for the purpose of reconstruction or amalgamation.

Quick succession relief (see Chapter VII) applies to all shares or debentures caught twice in five years by Section 55.

If shares or debentures valued under Section 55 are sold within three years after the death by the persons accountable for the duty on them, or by the persons to whom they passed on the death, and the Commissioners are satisfied that the sale is a freely negotiated one at arm's length, and nobody concerned as seller or having an interest in the proceeeds was a relative of the purchaser or interested in the purchase, the sale price can be substituted for the Section 55 value, if the latter is higher (F.A. 1954, s. 30). An adjustment must be made for changes in circumstances, and if there has been a subdivision or consolidation of capital, or a bonus issue, the shares sold must be identified with those valued on the death by regarding the shares deriving from the original shares as part of them.

CHAPTER XI

APPORTIONMENT

§1. Introduction

Where interests in or arising out of property are vested in different persons entitled to severable rights (to be enjoyed in succession or otherwise), it may become necessary, for the purpose of enabling those persons independently to receive their due benefit and enjoyment, to divide the property, or the income thereof, in proportion to their respective rights and interests. This process is technically termed 'apportionment', the object of which is thus to secure due adjustment between different interests in the same property. Not only may it be necessary to apportion benefits arising out of property, but where its preservation involves expenditure or its existence creates liabilities, division of the burden also may be requisite.

If the different interests are identical in character and extent, apportionment consists in a simple division. So also where property yielding a uniformly accruing and continuous benefit is to be enjoyed by persons in succession, due apportionment is achieved by division according to the respective periods of enjoyment. Should the interests to which the various beneficiaries are entitled be dissimilar in nature, or the subject matter produce irregular and intermittent accruals of benefit, for an equitable result to be obtained the problem of apportionment may be more difficult. The principles of apportionment are to be deduced partly from statutory provisions ('statutory apportionment') and partly from rules conceived by the courts to produce an equitable distribution of interest ('equitable apportionment').

The term 'apportionment' is applied also in the case where accretions to property have to be allocated between income and capital so as to determine whether a life tenant is entitled to the accretions or whether they form part of the capital of the estate which will ultimately vest in the remainderman.

The current law as to statutory apportionments is contained in the Apportionment Act 1870, which provides that all rents, annuities, dividends and other periodical payments in the nature of income (whether reserved or made payable under an instrument in writing or otherwise) shall, like interest on money lent, be considered as accruing from day to day, and shall be apportionable in respect of time accordingly (s. 2).

The apportioned part is payable or recoverable when the entire portion of which such apportioned part forms part becomes due and payable and not before (*ibid.*, s. 3).

The word 'annuities' includes salaries and pensions; the word 'dividends' includes all payments made by the name of dividend, bonus (this would not include a capital bonus) or otherwise out of the revenue of companies, divisible between all or any of the members of those companies, whether usually declared at any fixed time or otherwise. Such dividends are deemed to have accrued by equal daily increment during the period for or in respect of which the payment is expressed to be made (*ibid.*, s. 5).

Nothing in the Act is to render apportionable any annual sums made payable on policies of assurance of any description (*ibid.*, s. 6).

So far as this work is concerned apportionment is necessarily dealt with:

(1)   for the purpose of assessment of Estate Duty;

(2)   for the purpose of allocating the income received between life tenant and remainderman, and between successive life tenants;

(3)   for the purpose of allocating expenditure between life tenant and remainderman, and between successive life tenants; and

(4)   for the purpose of adjusting the incidence of losses between life tenant and remainderman.

As will be seen in the later paragraphs of this chapter, where statutory apportionments of income arise:

(*a*)   for Estate Duty purposes, the value of any stocks and shares must be the *cum* dividend value;

(*b*)   between beneficiaries, the dividend is apportioned in the proportion which the number of days before death bear to the number of days after death of the period for which the dividend is paid or in the case of arrears of cumulative preference dividend in the proportion which the number of days before death bear to the number of days after death of the period of the Profit & Loss Account out of which the arrears are paid (interim dividends are treated as on account of the dividends for a year); and

(*c*) interest and rents are apportioned on a day to day basis.

The equitable apportionments are:

(*d*) *Howe* v. *Lord Dartmouth*

    (i) Where there is no power to postpone conversion, the life tenant is entitled to 4 per cent. per annum on the proceeds of unauthorised investments sold during the executor's year, from the date of death to the date of sale; and at the same rate on the aggregate value of the unsold unauthorised investments at the end of the year.

    (ii) Where there is power to postpone conversion, the life tenant is entitled to 4 per cent. per annum on the proceeds of unauthorised investments realised during the executor's year from the date of death to the date of sale; and at the same rate on the aggregate probate value of the unauthorised investments remaining unsold at the end of that year.

(*e*) *Earl of Chesterfield's Trusts*

The life tenant receives in one sum when the property is realised, the amount which, when added to the sum on which interest is accumulated at 4 per cent. less tax compound interest from the date of death to the date of realisation, will equal the amount realised.

(*f*) *Allhusen* v. *Whittell*

The life tenant is credited with all income but is charged with interest at either an agreed rate or the average rate less tax earned in each year from the date of death to the date of payment on the sum which with interest thereon would be equal to each payment when made.

(*g*) *Re Atkinson*

The life tenant is entitled to that part of the amount realised on any mortgaged security which arrears of interest to the date of realisation bear to the original loan and any unpaid interest accrued prior to death.

(*h*) *Re Perkins*
Where a testator has made himself liable during his lifetime to pay an annuity, on each payment of the annuity, capital is charged with the sum which at 4 per cent. per annum simple interest from the date of the testator's death to the date of payment will, together with the interest, equal the amount paid. The life tenant will suffer the balance of the payment.
Equitable apportionments are barred in most wills.

§2. Statutory Apportionments of Income

The personal representative must include as personalty in respect of which he is liable for Estate Duty, not only the personalty actually existing at death, but accruing income of every kind up to the date of death, such as rents, and income from all investments. Income *received* prior to death is not, however, apportionable even if a portion of it relates to the period after death.

Where it is expressly stipulated that no apportionment shall take place, the Apportionment Act does not apply so far as beneficiaries are concerned (§7). A clear intention to that effect must appear in the will or deed of gift (*Re Oppenheimer*). Such a stipulation is inoperative, however, as regards the Inland Revenue, and for Estate Duty purposes all necessary apportionments will have to be made (F.A. 1894, s. 6 (5)).

If income-producing property has been specifically devised or bequeathed, and the income for a period which commenced prior to the death of the testator has been paid to the specific legatee or devisee, the personal representative must claim so much as belongs to the estate unless the terms of the bequest give *all* accruing income (*Pollock* v. *Pollock*).

Illustration (1)

P. died on 19th March, 1970, and by his will devised the fee simple in Blackacre to Q. Blackacre is let to R. at an annual rent payable on 25th December in each year in arrear. P.'s executor must recover from Q. the proportion of the year's rent in respect of the period 26th December, 1969, to 19th March, 1970. The executor could not, however, recover if the devise were of 'Blackacre with all rents accruing'.

The dividends of all companies under any of the Companies Acts are apportionable (*Re Lysaght; Re Griffith*; Apportionment Act 1870, s. 5). The income from stocks and shares is not dealt with in apportionment of the dividend in computing the Estate Duty liability, as the value of the estate must include the market value of the stock or shares *cum div.* on the day of death, which includes not only the value of the investment but also any accrued dividend. If a stock is quoted *ex div.*, there must be added to the quoted value the full dividend or the next payment of interest, thus making up the *cum div.* value. Some stocks including certain short-dated government securities, are dealt with on the stock exchange on the basis of adding to the quoted price the accrued interest; it is then necessary to add the accrued interest for Estate Duty purposes. Relief is given to the residuary beneficiary for Surtax purposes for the Estate Duty appropriate to the accrued income included in the valuation of the estate for duty purposes (s. 430, Taxes Act 1970).

In the case of rents, interest on loans and similar income, accruing from day to day, the actual proportion up to and including the day of death must be accounted for and Estate Duty paid thereon by the personal representative.

The profits of a private partnership or of a voyage of a single ship company, are not apportionable (*Jones* v. *Ogle*) as it is not possible to ascertain the profits until the end of the period, and such profits are not periodical payments in the nature of income (*Re Robbins, Midland Bank Executors, etc., Co.* v. *Melville*). Any sum duly and properly paid in advance is not apportionable; thus, rent payable in advance is not apportionable (*Ellis* v. *Rowbotham*); and where a testator had agreed to pay a lump sum by instalments for the occupation of a house, and died before all the instalments were paid, it was held that the unpaid instalments were payable out of capital (*Re Hanbury*).

Reference should here be made to Chapter XV, §§ 1-8, to assist in a full appreciation of the entries in the books of account.

The income accrued at the date of death, which under the Apportionment Act forms part of the estate of the deceased and which is included in the Estate Duty Account for the purposes of Estate Duty, should be credited to the Estate Capital Account and debited to the capital column of the particular Asset Account as at the date of death, through the medium of the Journal. The portion of the income relating to the period after death is not recorded in the books at all until the actual cash is received. When the cash is received, the apportionment is made in the Cash Book, both capital and income being posted therefrom to the respective columns of the particular Asset Account. The proportion applicable to capital should be transferred to Estate Account, where the effect will be to leave on the capital columns, the asset at probate value (see the recommendations of the Institute of Chartered Accountants in England and Wales, in Chapter XV, § 2).

Illustration (2)

Date of death, 31st October, 1970. Assets: Loans on Mortgage, £5,000. Interest at 6% per annum receivable half-yearly, 30th June and 31st December, Apportionment to be made in months. Assume Income tax at 8s in the £ and all entries to nearest £.

JOURNAL

1970					£	£
Oct. 31	Sundries					
	To Estate Account	..	..	..		5,060
	Loan on Mortgage	..	..	*Dr.*	5,000	
	Interest accrued thereon to date (4 months)..		..	£100		
	Less Tax at 8/-	..	..	..	40	
					60	
	Being assets as per Estate Duty Affidavit					

LOAN ON MORTGAGE

Date		Income	Capital	Date		Income	Capital
1970		£	£	1970		£	£
Oct. 31	Estate A/c:			Dec. 31	Cash:		
	Loan ..		5,000		Interest at 6%		
	Interest £100				on £5,000 for		
	Less Tax at				half-year to date		
	8/- .. 40				£150		
			60		*Less* Tax at		
Dec. 31	Income A/c ..	30			8/- .. 60		
					Capital 4		
					months		60
					Income 2		
					months	30	
					Balance c/f ..		5,000
		£30	£5,060			£30	£5,060
1971							
Jan. 1	Balance b/f ..		£5,000				

CASH BOOK

Date	Particulars	Income	Capital	Bank	Date	Particulars	Income	Capital	Bank
1970 Dec. 31	Loan on Mortgage: Interest at 6% on £5,000 for half-year to date £150 *Less* Tax at 8/- 60	£	£	£ 90			£	£	£
	Capital 4 months		60						
	Income 2 months	30							

(a) *Income from Investments*

(1) CUM DIVIDEND AT DATE OF DEATH

Where the quotation of stocks or shares is *cum dividend* at the date of death, the proportion of dividend accrued to that date, as well as the capital value, is included in the quoted price, and consequently no further amount need be credited to the Estate Capital Account in respect thereof.

When the first dividend is actually received in cash, however, apportionment under the Apportionment Act is necessary, and the dividend so apportioned will be entered in the Cash Book in the income and capital columns respectively, and posted to the Asset Account in the usual way.

The balance carried down on the capital column will be the net principal value of the asset, and will differ from the amount shown in the Estate Duty Account by a sum equal to the capital apportionment of the dividend. Consequently the latter should be transferred to Estate Account.

Illustration (3)

Date of death, 19th February. Part of estate consists of 10,000 Ordinary shares of £1 each in AB Ltd valued at £8,400 *cum. div.* Show the ledger account of the holding, including the first dividend of 3 per cent. received for the quarter to 5th April, and bring down a balance. Assume Income tax at 40*p* (8/–) in the £.

ORDINARY SHARES OF £1 IN AB LTD

Date			Nom-inal	In-come	Capital	Date		Nom-inal	In-come	Cap
19.. Feb. 19	Estate A/c:	..	£ 10,000	£	£ 8,400	19.. Apl. 5	Cash: Dividend for quarter to date, £300	£	£	£
Apl. 5	Income A/c	..		90			Less tax 120			
	Estate A/c	..			90		Income 45 days		90	
							Capital 45 days			
							Balance c/f ..	10,000		8,4
		£	10,000	90	8,490		£	10,000	90	8,4
Apl. 6	Balance b/f	..	10,000		8,400					

Note: In practice, the estate books would be balanced either as at the date of distribution or at the expiration of one year from the date of death. Transfers to Income Account would not, therefore, be made until the balancing date. The amount of the dividend apportioned to capital has been transferred to Estate Account in accordance with the recommendations of the Institute of Chartered Accountants in England and Wales, see Chapter XV, § 2.

(2) EX DIVIDEND AT DATE OF DEATH

Where the quotation of stocks or shares is *ex dividend* at the date of the death of the deceased, the accrued dividend is not included in the price, and it must, therefore, be brought into the Estate Duty Account in addition to the quoted price.

The custom of the Stock Exchange is, upon first quoting an *ex dividend* price, to reduce the *cum dividend* price by the full amount of the next dividend, despite the fact that it may not be payable immediately; and despite the fact that the interest is not yet actually due for payment.

According to the rules of the Stock Exchange, Government and Corporation Securities (Inscribed, Registered Certificates or Bonds), are quoted *ex dividend* on the day after that on which the books are closed for the payment of the dividend. Consols, and similar Government Stocks dealt with in the Consols market of the Stock Exchange, will be found to be quoted *ex dividend* about one month prior to the actual payment of the interest. Due, presumably, to the large number of dividend warrants involved and the time required for their preparation, 3½ per cent. War Loan is quoted *ex dividend* about five weeks prior to the dividend date, whereas in the case of Victory Bonds the period is ten days.

Owing to the fact that not only the interest or dividend accrued to the date of death but also the amount accrued from the date of death to the due date of the interest or dividend has been deducted from the *cum dividend* valuation to arrive at the *ex dividend* price, the Inland Revenue Authorities require the full period's interest or dividend to be brought in for Estate Duty purposes in addition to the quoted price.

Illustration (4)

Assume a stock quoted at par paying regular quarterly dividends at the net rate of 12 per cent. per annum.

Stock issued 1st January.

Ignoring all factors which affect the price except the dividends:

On 31st January the stock should be quoted at £101, since one month's dividend has accrued.

On 28th February the stock should be quoted at £102, since two months' dividend has accrued.

On the 1st March the stock is quoted *ex div.*, and by the custom of the Stock Exchange a full quarter's dividend is deducted in spite of the fact that only two months' dividend has accrued. This reduces the *ex div.* value to £99, which is £1 below the true *ex div.* valuation.

In consequence for Estate Duty purposes the Inland Revenue Authorities require the full quarter's dividend, viz. £3 to be added to the fictitious *ex div.* value for Estate Duty purposes, thus restoring the price to the *cum. div.* equivalent of £102.

From the point of view of the Stock Exchange it is perfectly correct to deduct the full quarter's dividend, since a purchaser on 1st March would have to wait four months before he received his first quarter's dividend, and the seller receives one month's dividend which really accrues to the purchaser.

When the dividend is actually received on the due date, this must be apportioned under the Apportionment Act, that part of the dividend which accrued up to and including the date of death being treated as capital, and that part which accrued after the date of death as income.

Illustration (5)

Date of death, 21st March. Part of the estate consists of £10,000 Dominion Ltd Ordinary stock valued at £8,150 *ex div*. Show the ledger account of the stock, including the first dividend of 1½ per cent. received for the quarter to 5th April, and bring down a balance. Assume Income tax at 40*p* (8s) in the £.

DOMINION 3 PER CENT. STOCK

Date		Nom-inal	In-come	Capital	Date		Nom-inal	In-come	Cap
19.. Apr. 21	Estate A/c:	£ 10,000	£	£ 8,150	19.. Apl. 5	Cash:	£	£	£
Apl. 5	Income A/c ..		15			Dividend for quarter to date, £150 *Less* Tax 60 £90			
						Income 15 days ..		15	
						Balance c/f ..	10,000		8,1
		£ 10,000	15	8,150		£	10,000	15	8,1

DOMINION 3 PER CENT. STOCK DIVIDEND ACCOUNT

Date		Capital	Date		Capital
19.. Mar. 21	Estate A/c	£ 90	19.. Apl. 5 Apl. 5	Cash .. .. .. Estate A/c: Balance written off ..	£ 75 15

(3) INTERIM DIVIDENDS

An interim dividend which has been actually received during lifetime, being an anticipatory payment, is not to be apportioned (*Ellis* v. *Rowbotham*); but in ascertaining what portion (if any) of a final dividend received after death is to be treated as capital, any interim dividend already paid for the same period must be taken into account, the whole dividend for the period being deemed to accrue from day to day (Apportionment Act, 1870, s. 5). The interim dividend is not a dividend for a shorter period, but a payment on account of the dividend for the whole year.

Illustration (6)

Date of death, 30th April, 1970. Part of the estate consists of 1,000 shares of £1 each fully paid in the Economic Coffee Co., Ltd, valued at 25s per share for Estate Duty. An interim dividend at the rate of 5 per cent. per annum free of tax was declared in respect of the half-year ending 28th February, 1970, and received on the 5th April. A final dividend at the rate of 15 per cent. per annum free of tax was declared in respect of the half-year ending 31st August, 1970, making with the interim dividend 10 per cent. for the whole year free of tax. This dividend was received on the 25th October, 1970. Show the ledger account in the executor's books dealing with the above matters, and bring down a balance. Apportionments may be made in months and to the nearest £. Ignore Income tax.

ECONOMIC COFFEE CO. LTD, SHARES

Date		Nom-inal Value	In-come	Capital	Date		Nom-inal Value	In-come	Capital
1970		Shares	£	£	1970 Oct. 25	Cash:	Shares	£	£
.. 30	Estate A/c: 1,000 shares, £1 each, fully paid, at 25s per share ..	1,000		1,250		Final Dividend at 15% per annum free of tax for half-year ended 31st August, _re_ year then ended.. £75			
. 25	Income A/c ..		33			_Add_ Interim Dividend at 5% per annum free of tax for half-year ended 28th February, _re_ year ended 31st August .. 25			
	Estate A/c ..			42					
						Making 10% dividend for year ended 31st August £100			
						Capital, 8 months .. £67 _Less_ Int. Div. 25			42
						Income, 4 months Balance c/f ..	1,000	33	1,250
		1,000	£33	£1,292			1,000	£33	£1,292
. 26	Balance b/f ..	1,000		1,250					

It occasionally happens that this method of apportionment cannot be strictly adhered to, owing to the fact that interim dividends have been paid at a higher rate than can be maintained for the final dividend.

In no case can the tenant for life claim more than the actual amount of the dividend received after death, so that where no final dividend is paid, no apportionment of the interim dividend received before death takes place. Where only a small final dividend is paid, which is not sufficient to cover the proportion of the total dividend for the year applicable to income under the usual method of apportionment, as shown in the preceding illustration, income will be credited merely with the amount of the final dividend, irrespective of what it should be credited with theoretically.

Illustration (7)

Date of death, 31st May, 1970. Part of the estate consists of 1,000 shares of £1 each, fully paid, in the Economic Coffee Co., Limited, valued at 25s per share for Estate Duty. An interim dividend of 9 per cent. free of tax was declared in respect of the year ending 31st August, 1970, and received on 5th April, 1970. A final dividend at the rate of 1 per cent. free of tax was declared on 25th October, in respect of the year ending 31st August, 1970, making with the interim dividend 10 per cent. for the year, free of tax. Show the ledger account dealing with the above matters, and bring down a balance. Apportionments in months and to the nearest £.

ECONOMIC COFFEE CO., LTD, SHARES

Date		Nominal Value	Income	Capital	Date		Nominal Value	Income	Cap
		Shares	£	£			Shares	£	£
1970 May 31	Estate A/c: 1,000 shares, £1 each, fully paid, at 25s per share ..	1,000		1,250	1970 Oct. 25	Cash:			
						Final Dividend at 1% free of tax for year ended 31st August, *re* year then ended £10			
Oct. 25	Income		10			*Add* Interim Dividend at 9% free of tax *re* year ended 31st August.. 90			
						Making 10% dividend for year ended 31st Aug. ..£100			
						Capital, 9 months .. 75 *Less* Int. Dividend .. 90			
						—			
						Therefore Final Dividend is' all Income .. .. Balance c/f ..	1,000	10	1,2
		1,000	£10	£1,250			1,000	£10	£1,2
Oct. 26	Balance b/f ..	1,000		1,250					

Note to Illustration:

If the method of apportionment first explained had been strictly followed in this case, the result would have been as follows:

Dividend for the year at 10 per cent. per annum, free of tax, £100.

      Capital, 9 months £75

      Income, 3 months   25

                                £100

As the final dividend brought in only £10 in cash it would seem that income could claim £15 out of the interim dividend received on the 5th April, which already forms part of the capital of the estate. But the interim dividend is already impressed with the nature of capital, and income can therefore only claim to be satisfied out of the proceeds of the dividend received after death; if this is insufficient, income suffers loss to such extent. Thus, in the above illustration, income claims the whole amount of the final dividend of £10 but can claim no contribution from capital to make up the £25 accrued after death.

If an interim dividend is received after death, the period in respect of which it is declared must be ascertained, and if this period is one which is regularly adopted, it might be considered to be a periodical payment as referred to in the Apportionment Act, in which case, if the dividend was declared prior to the death of the testator, it would be treated entirely as capital, although received after death; otherwise the apportionment should be deferred as it would be unwise for the executor to pay to the life tenant income in advance, since the life tenant may die before the end of the period. If the interim dividend were apportioned at once over the full year, such a position might arise.

Illustration (8)

X. died on 31st August, 1970. A few days later an interim dividend of £6,000 was received on one investment, on account of the year to the 31st December, 1970. The executor should argue in this way: 'The worst that can happen is that no final dividend will be received; if so, the interim dividend will be the dividend for the year and will be apportionable as to 8 months (£4,000) to capital and 4 months (£2,000) to income. But I am not sure that the life tenant will live until the end of the year, and if I give him the full £2,000 at once, I may overpay him. There is nothing to prevent me, however, from giving him £500 at the end of each month if he needs the money. If a final dividend is ultimately received, I can apportion it 8 months to capital and 4 to income.

Of course, in many estates, the number of the investments is such that the executor can be reasonably sure that any immediate potential over-payment on one stock can be set against other income, and can apportion accordingly. Frequently, payments of round sums on account of income are made to the life tenant at intervals during each year, the exact balance remaining due being paid after the end of the year, when the accounts have been prepared.

Where stock is sold *cum div.* so that the final dividend is never received, any interim dividend received after death but before sale is apportionable over the full period in respect of which it is paid (*Bulkeley* v. *Stephens*). It is simply a payment on account of the full accounting period of the company, and when no final dividend is received, must be treated as if it were the dividend for the full period.

(4) ARREARS OF CUMULATIVE PREFERENCE DIVIDENDS

Arrears of cumulative preference dividends are only apportionable when they are declared out of the credit balance of the Profit and Loss Account of the particular period in which the deceased died. In such a case apportionment of the total dividend paid will be made in the usual manner.

Where there are arrears of dividend on cumulative preference shares, and a dividend is declared in the year in which the deceased died, but payable out of the credit balance of Profit and Loss Account of the preceding year, no apportionment will take place, the whole dividend, when paid, being credited to capital; and where such a dividend is declared payable out of the credit balance of the Profit and Loss Account of a year subsequent to that in which the deceased died, no apportionment will take place, the whole dividend being credited to income (*In re Wakley, Wakley* v. *Vachell,* supporting the decision in *re Taylor's Trusts*). The rule is not affected by the fact that a credit balance may have been brought forward into the relevant Profit and Loss Account, or a transfer from Reserve to the Profit and Loss Account been made; the period of the Profit and Loss Account out of which the dividend is declared is the determining factor.

Illustration (9)

Date of death, 1st March, 1969. Part of the estate consisted of 1,000 6 per cent. cumulative preference shares of £1 each, fully paid, in the X.Y.Z. Co., Limited, valued for Estate Duty at 15s per share. No dividend had been paid on these shares since the incorporation of the company on the 1st January, 1957. On the 25th February, 1970, a dividend on the preference shares of 30 per cent. was declared out of the profits of the year 1969, being dividend for the year 1969, at 6 per cent., and arrears to date, the cash being received on the 15th March, 1970.

Show the ledger account of the investment, including the receipt of the dividend. Assume Income tax at 8s in £, and apportion in months and to the nearest £.

THE X.Y.Z. CO. LTD, PREFERENCE SHARES

ate		Nom- inal	In- come	Capital	Date		Nom- inal	In- come	Capital
		Shares	£	£	1970 Mar. 15	Cash:	Shares	£	£
·69 ·r. 1	Estate A/c:					Dividend of 30% per annum declar- ed out of the pro- fits of the year 1969 being divi- dend for the year 1969 at 6%, and arrears to date £300			
	1,000 6% cum. pref. shares of £1 each, fully paid, valued for Estate Duty at 15s per share	1,000		750					
·70 ·r. 15	Income A/c ..		150			Less Tax £120			
	Estate A/c ..			30		Capital, 2 months			30
						Income 10 months		150	
						Balance c/f ..	1,000		750
		1,000	£150	£780			1,000	£150	£780
·r. 16	Balance b/f ..	1,000		750					

Notes to Illustration:

It is important to observe that:

(1) the date of declaration of the dividend is of no consequence;

(2) the date of payment of the dividend is only important in so far as it is used to record the entries in the books from a cash point of view; it has no reference whatever to the apportionment;

(3) the vital points on which the apportionment turns are the date of death and the period covered by the Profit and Loss Account out of which the dividend is declared;

(4) the amount paid is to be regarded as one dividend for the period, and not as a series of dividends relating to different periods.

Where, under a scheme of arrangement sanctioned by the court, preference shareholders waived their conditional right to arrears of dividend in consideration of their receiving in place of such dividend ordinary shares in the company provided by the ordinary shareholders, who surrendered two-thirds of their holdings for the purpose, it was held that the ordinary shares so received belonged to the person who would have been entitled to the arrears of preference dividend had the arrears been paid, i.e. they were income and not capital (*In re MacIver's Settlement; MacIver v. Rae*). In the case of another trust holding both preference and ordinary shares in the same company, it was held that ordinary shares allotted to the trustees under the arrangement came to them in exchange for the rights of the preference shareholders to arrears of dividend, and they held those shares as part of the income upon trust for the life tenants, although ordinary shares surrendered under the scheme were a diminution of capital (*Re Smith's Will Trusts, Smith* v. *Melville*).

(b) Apportionment on death of tenant for life

Upon the death of a tenant for life it will be necessary to apportion the income – that accrued to the date of the death of the tenant for life falling into his estate, and that accruing after the death of the tenant for life either belonging to the succeeding tenant for life, or to the remainderman.

Illustration (10)

W. Thompson had a life interest in the estate of J. Thompson deceased. W. Thompson died on 30th December, 1969, and his four children then became entitled to the estate in equal shares.

The following sums have been received by the Trustees of J. Thompson's estate. To whom and in what proportions would they be payable?

1970

Jan.   5.   A quarter's dividend on £1,000 2½ per cent. Consols.

Jan. 22.   Half-year's ground rent, £60, due this day.

Feb. 14.   Half-year's interest on mortgage, £3,000 at 3 per cent., due 10th Feb., 1970.

April 5.   Dividend on 100 £30 shares, £15 per share paid up, in the London and Northern Bank, Limited, at the rate of 4 per cent., making, with an interim dividend of 2 per cent. previously paid, 6 per cent. for the year ended 31st March, 1970.

Ignore Income tax and make apportionments to the nearest £.

Date	Particulars	Amount	No. of days	W. Thompson's Estate		W. Thompson's Children	
				Days to date of Death	Amount	Days after W.T.'s Death	Amount
1970		£			£		£
Jan. 5	Consols, quarter's Div. on £1,000 2½%	6	92	86	6	6	–
Jan. 22	Ground rent, half-year ..	60	184	161	52	23	8
Feb. 14	Mortgage, half-year's int. on £3,000 @ 3% to 10th Feb.	45	184	142	35	42	10
April 5	London and Northern Bank, final div., making with interim dividend already received, 6% for year to 31st March, 1970	90	365	274, *i.e.* $\frac{274}{365}$ of £90	68	91	22
		£201			£161		£40

Note:

The interim dividend received has not been apportioned until the final dividend was received, in order to avoid any possible over-distribution to the life tenant.

Following the general principle stated in § 3 below, if upon the death of the last tenant for life any investments are sold for the purpose of facilitating the division of the estate, and these investments are quoted *cum* dividend at the date of sale, the executors of the deceased tenant for life are not entitled to any part of the purchase money received from the sale. If the dividend had actually been received, the estate of the deceased would have been entitled to a proper proportion thereof; but the fact that it is never received prevents this being done (*Bulkeley* v. *Stephens*), even where the rules of the Stock Exchange require the accrued interest to be calculated separately (*re Walker, Walker* v. *Patterson*). It should be observed that, in *Bulkeley* v. *Stephens*, part of the sale price was in fact ordered to be paid to the tenant for life, but the court was careful to point out that it was only because of special circumstances in the case. The general rule was affirmed in *re Firth's Estate, Sykes and Lacey* v. *Hall*, where the judge pointed out the difficulties of apportioning, and indicated that only in special circumstances would an apportionment be ordered. If trustees consider that in any special case it would be desirable to apportion, they should therefore obtain the consent of all beneficiaries or apply to the court for approval. The law as it now stands was set out by Morton J. (*Re Henderson, Public Trustee* v. *Reddie*) as follows:

(*a*) if the investment is still held by the trustees of the will when the dividend becomes due and payable, they must pay over to the personal representative of the deceased life tenant the apportioned part of the dividend;

(*b*) if the investment has been transferred (e.g. appropriated) to a person absolutely entitled under the will, before the dividend became due and payable, the trustees ought first to have made arrangements to ensure that the deceased life tenant's estate will receive the apportioned part; if such an arrangement has not been made, the transferees must pay the appropriate sum to the estate;

(c) if the investment in question has been sold by the trustees *cum* dividend, the purchaser cannot be called upon for any part of the dividend, and there is no apportionment of the sale price of the investment.

On the death of one of two or more life tenants it is important to determine whether the share of the deceased accrues to the survivors or to the remainderman, e.g. where a testator left his residue upon trust to pay one-half of the net income to R. and the other half to T., and 'from and after their decease' to pay the principal and income to X., it was held that on the death of R. (even though he predeceased the testator), the surviving life tenant was entitled to the whole income (*In re Ragdale, Public Trustee* v. *Tuffill*).

These rules do not operate for Income tax purposes, as to which reference should be made to ss. 426 to 433, Income and Corporation Taxes Act 1970, and the decisions in *C.I.R.* v. *Henderson's Trustees* (1931), *Reid's Trustees* v. *C.I.R.* (1929), *Wood* v. *Owen* (1940) and *Stewart's Exors* v. *C.I.R.* (1952). (See Spicer and Pegler's *Income Tax* (28th Edn. by the author).

§ 3. Other Apportionments between Life Tenant and Remainder-man

(a) Variation of Securities

Where stocks and shares are bought or sold, the question of the accrued dividend in the purchase or sale price must be considered. If equitable principles were strictly followed, it might appear necessary to apportion this accrued interest. But the courts in England have taken the view that by enforcing this apportionment 'a grievious burden would be imposed upon the estates of testators by reason of the complex investigation which it would lead to. The gain to either party (i.e. life tenant and remainderman) would be far more than compensated by the expenses' (*Scholefield* v. *Redfern*), and apportionment of the purchase or sale price is not required for the purposes of English trust accounts, as will be seen from the following cases:

(1) INVESTMENTS BOUGHT CUM DIVIDEND

The Apportionment Act does not apply to a change of investments, so that where investments are sold, and the amounts received are re-invested, the life tenant is entitled to the whole income accruing on the new investment (*Re Clarke, Barker* v. *Perowne*) except where the investment is purchased *cum div.* after the dividend has been declared. The dividend in such a case will, when received, form part of the capital and will not go to the tenant for life (*Re Peel's Settled Estates*). It will be seen that there still is no apportionment.

(2)   INVESTMENT SOLD CUM DIVIDEND

Where stocks, shares, debentures or other securities are sold between two dividend dates, the life tenant is not entitled to any apportionment of the proceeds in respect of the accruing dividend, and the whole proceeds are capital (*Scholefield* v. *Redfern*). This rule applies equally where by the rules of the Stock Exchange the stock is sold at a fixed price plus accrued interest, as this is merely a formula to arrive at the *cum* dividend price (*Re Walker, Walker* v. *Patterson*).

Any course of action deliberately taken by the trustee whereby the changes of investment benefited the life tenant at the expense of the remainderman or vice versa would be a breach of trust, and restrainable by the court, or actionable by the injured beneficiary.

(3)   GOVERNMENT SECURITIES SURRENDERED IN PAYMENT OF DEATH DUTIES

In view of the above rules, it is considered that the accrued interest added to the surrender value of Government securities surrendered in settlement of Estate Duty and interest, is capital, i.e., it should not be credited to the life tenant. 'The machinery (of adding interest) was designed to put the matter on the same basis as that on which it would have stood if the executors had sold . . . on the market' (Rowlatt, J., in *Monks* v. *Fox's Exors.*), i.e. the addition is to arrive at a *cum div.* price.

(b) Executorship Expenses

The treatment of executorship expenses depends on the nature of the payments. All expenses incurred in realising and protecting the estate are chargeable to capital, whereas those incurred in carrying on the trust are chargeable to income.

(c) Charges in respect of Settled Estates

(1)   IMPROVEMENTS

Trustees of settled estates are given power by the Settled Land Act 1925, ss. 83 and 84, to expend capital money derived from settled land upon improvements thereto. The improvements authorised fall into three categories (*ibid.*, Third Sch.). Part I of the Schedule comprises improvements which are necessarily of permanent value to the land, such as drainage and irrigation works, where capital money applied to improvements of this kind cannot be recouped out of income. Part II contains improvements upon which capital money may be expended, but in respect of which the trustees are entitled, in their discretion, to require that the money shall be repaid out of the income of the settled land by not more than fifty half-yearly instalments. These improvements include, for example, the restoration of buildings damaged by dry rot. Part III lists improvements in respect of which the trustees are bound to provide for the recovery of the expenditure out of income by not more than fifty half-yearly payments. This Part deals with improvements which ought not to give rise to a permanent capital loss to the settled property, such as the purchase of lorries for farming purposes.

These powers (*inter alia*) are exercisable by personal representatives while any life interest in the estate of the deceased is subsisting or during the minority of a beneficiary. In these cases the personal representatives are endowed, as regards land vested in them in their representative capacity, with the powers of trustees under the Settled Land Act 1925, s. 39; L.P.A. 1925, s. 28.

The improvements authorised by Part I of the Third Schedule include *additions to* and *alterations in buildings* reasonably necessary or proper to enable them to be let, e.g. the construction of a new roof and a new entrance, the supply of water to the mansion house, etc., but not ordinary repairs (*Clarke* v. *Thornton*), or hot water pipes or other heating apparatus (*Re Gaskell*), nor alterations in sanitary arrangements (*Re Tucker*), or an electric light installation (*Re Blake*), but complete drainage of a mansion house is included (*Re Leconfield*).

These statutory powers are in addition to any powers specifically conferred by the settlement itself.

Improvements carried out under the Landlord and Tenant Act 1927, and any compensation paid to a tenant for an improvement or goodwill, are chargeable against capital (Landlord and Tenant Act 1927, s. 13).

Where the life tenant has obtained relief from Income tax under Section 68, Capital Allowances Act 1968, in respect of expenditure on improvements payable out of capital monies, he need not account therefore to the trustees of the settlement (*Re Pelly; Ransome* v. *Pelly*).

(2) REPAIRS TO FREEHOLDS

A tenant for life of freeholds is not bound to keep the property in repair unless so required by the trust instrument.

Where the tenant for life of an agricultural estate comprised in a settlement subject to the Settled Land Act, 1925, had expended on farm properties let and on cottages occupied by estate employees, sums in excess of the net rents received, it was held that the tenant for life could recoup from the trustees, out of capital, the money expended or to be expended by him in the execution of repairs specified in paragraph 23 of Part II of Schedule III of the Agricultural Holdings Act 1948, i.e. repairs to fixed equipment, being equipment reasonably required for the proper farming of the holding, other than repairs which the tenant is under an obligation to carry out (*In re Northumberland*). This does not apply to such repairs done before 1948 (*Re Sutherland Settlement Trusts*). Improvements are included and the cost thereof is recoverable, even if the tenant of the property is liable for repairs (*Re Brougham & Vaux's Settled Estates*).

As between tenant for life and remainderman, repairs within Part I or II, Schedule III, Settled Land Act 1925, ought in a proper case *prima facie* to be borne out of capital; as ought other repairs if they constitute permanent improvements. They ought more readily to be considered as permanent improvements if they are to remedy a bad condition of the property at the death of the previous owner (*Re Smith, Vincent* v. *Smith*). Casual repairs which fall to be carried out in the ordinary course by a person in possession of property and the cost of which is generally payable by the tenant for life, cannot be treated as permanent improvements (*ibid.*).

(3) REPAIRS TO LEASEHOLDS

As regards leaseholds, a life tenant of leaseholds is bound, as between himself and the lessor, to perform the covenant to repair contained in the lease, and he is liable for breach of the covenants to repair which occur in his lifetime (*Re Betty*). The estate of the deceased life tenant, however, is not liable to the remainderman for the repairs made necessary by the non-fulfilment during the life tenancy of these covenants (*Re Parry and Hopkins*).

(4) GENERAL RULES AS TO LIABILITY FOR OUTGOINGS

(i) In the absence of any special provision in the trust instrument (will or settlement), the tenant for life is not liable in respect of repairs which had become necessary before his interest vested in possession, and the cost of such repairs ought to be defrayed out of the corpus.

(ii) The income bears current expenses including the cost of complying with the covenants to repair contained in the lease (except so far as the breach occurred prior to the death of the settlor).

(iii) The cost of complying with notices from sanitary authorities and the like, to repair, depends on whether the repairs amount to a permanent improvement or not. If they do, then the costs fall on capital, but if the required repairs do not amount to a permanent improvement, then the cost ought to be borne by income.

(5) WASTE

Waste is such damage to land as produces permanent and lasting injury to the inheritance or alters the nature of the property. There are three kinds of waste:

(*a*) Voluntary waste is any positive act which alters the character of the land, e.g. cutting timber, opening mines, ploughing up pasture land, etc.

(*b*) Permissive waste consists in passive acts of omission, such as allowing land or houses to get out of repair.

(*e*) Equitable waste is wanton destruction, e.g. cutting down ornamental timber.

If a limited owner, e.g. a life tenant, is given power to commit voluntary waste, he is said to be 'unimpeachable for waste'. Impeachment for waste is the term given to the liability for committing waste. A tenant for life may not commit voluntary waste unless the trust instrument or will, under which he takes his title, expressly makes him unimpeachable. On the other hand, he is not responsible for permissive waste unless the instrument or will expressly makes him responsible. In the case of equitable waste, the life tenant is liable in equity, even if the settlement or will makes him unimpeachable for waste.

If the life tenant is unimpeachable for waste, he is entitled to keep three-quarters of the rent of any mining lease, and must pay one-quarter to the trustees; if impeachable, he is entitled to one-quarter, the remaining three-quarters going to the trustees. Where there is timber ripe for cutting, the life tenant, if unimpeachable, may cut and sell the timber (except timber planted for ornament or shelter) and keep the whole proceeds; but if he is impeachable he can only cut with the consent of the trustees, or by obtaining an order of the court, and even then he is entitled only to one-quarter of the proceeds, the remainder being taken to capital (Settled Land Act 1925, s. 66).

The tenant for life and all persons employed by or under contract with him may from time to time enter on the settled land, and without impeachment for waste by any remainder-man or reversioner, thereon execute any improvements authorised by the Settled Land Act 1925, or inspect, maintain and repair the settled land (Settled Land Act 1925, s. 89).

§4. The Equitable Apportionments

Apart from apportionments required by the Apportionment Act 1870, there are various equitable rules which are designed, in their appropriate application, to secure an equitable adjustment of burden and benefit between life tenant and remainder-man. The principal of these arise out of the judgments in the following cases:

>*Howe* v. *Earl of Dartmouth*, and *Re Fawcett, Public Trustee* v. *Dugdale*.
>*Re Earl of Chesterfield's Trusts*.
>*Allhusen* v. *Whittell*.
>*Re Perkins, Brown* v. *Perkins*.
>*Re Atkinson, Barbers' Co.* v. *Grose-Smith*.

The rules derived from these cases are based upon a presumed intention of the testator. They will not therefore apply where the terms of the will indicate directly or by implication that the apportionments and adjustments contemplated by the rules are inconsistent with the settlor's intention. Well drawn wills commonly bar equitable apportionments.

(a) Howe v. Earl of Dartmouth

The rule in *Howe* v. *Earl of Dartmouth* is based on the assumption that where a testator gives a general *residuary bequest* to persons in succession, he intends their successive interests to be derived from the same continuing subject-matter. Accordingly, where *the residue consists in part or in whole of wasting or hazardous property, such property must be converted* into money and the proceeds invested in authorised securities so as to ensure the preservation of the residue in a permanent form (*Howe* v. *Earl of Dartmouth*).

Property is said to be wasting when its enjoyment tends to exhaust its substance, e.g. a wine-cellar. Hazardous property includes all 'unauthorised securities,' whether of a wasting character or not (*Re Chaytor, Chaytor* v. *Horn*). It will be recalled that a security is 'authorised,' only when expressly permitted by the instrument creating the settlement or when approved by law and not prohibited by that instrument.

The principle of the rule, being founded upon the presumed intention of the testator, has no application where the terms of the will indicate an intention which renders the operation of the rule inappropriate. Moreover, the rule is not applied:

(1) in the case of authorised investments;

(2) where properties are specifically bequeathed, or settled by deed (*Vincent* v. *Newcombe; Re Straubenzee*);

(3) in the case of real estate (*Re Searle; Re Darnley*);

(4) in the case of properties situate outside the jurisdiction of the courts, if the foreign law allows them to be enjoyed in specie;

(5) to property passing on an intestacy, where the power to postpone conversion has been duly exercised (*Re Sullivan, Dunkley* v. *Sullivan*). In an intestacy the property of the intestate is held by the personal representatives on trust for sale with full power to postpone sale and conversion for such period as they think proper, without being accountable (A.E.A. 1925, s. 33 (1)). This does not exclude, however, the rule in *Howe* v. *Lord Dartmouth* in cases of intestacy

where there has been no positive exercise of the statutory power to postpone conversion (*In re Fisher; Harris* v. *Fisher*);

(6) to leasehold property, by virtue of the wide definition of land in L.P.A. 1925, s. 205 ('*land* includes land of any tenure') and s. 28 (2) and (5), which govern the application of the income of land held upon trust for sale (*Re Brooker; re Berton, Vandyk* v. *Berton*); see also *Re Gough, Phillips* v. *Simpson.*

The rule applies in respect of personalty not within (1) to (6) above (*Re Trollope's will Trusts, Public Trustee* v. *Trollope*).

The conversion of the wasting or hazardous property into authorised securities should be made within a reasonable time, and if possible during the executor's year; if the personal representative takes a longer period he may be called upon to justify the delay (*Grayburn* v. *Clarkson*). It is thought that following the passing of the Trustee Investments Act 1961, a personal representative who wishes to retain investments would be wise to obtain proper advice from a stockbroker etc. as to whether the investments are satisfactory and must make the apportionment of securities between narrow-range, wider-range and special-range during the executor's year.

The rule in *Howe* v. *Earl of Dartmouth*, being purely artificial, may tend to defeat the real wishes of the testator, and consequently the courts incline to exclude the rule where the intention to do so, either expressly or by implication, can be read into the will (*Hinves* v. *Hinves; Mackie* v. *Mackie*). The burden of proof rests on the party denying the application (*Macdonald* v. *Irvine*). Each case must be carefully and separately considered:

(a) the mere absence of directions to convert is not of itself sufficient evidence that the property is to be enjoyed by the life tenant in specie (*Morgan* v. *Morgan*);

(b) where an intention appears that some particular portion of the property shall not be converted, the rule will be excluded to this extent (*Blann* v. *Bell*); and

(c) an intention exhibited contrary to the conversion of the property until some particular date, will preclude any earlier conversion (*Alcock* v. *Sloper*).

Where there is no trust for conversion and express power is given to retain existing investments, no apportionment of income will be necessary. The whole of the revenue derived from the property will go to the tenant for life in accordance with the intention of the testator exhibited by the absence of direction for conversion coupled with the express power of retention (*Re Bates, Hodgson*, v. *Bates*). The position is similar where the trustee is specifically empowered to retain unauthorised securities (*Re Nicholson, Eade* v. *Nicholson*). A discretion to postpone conversion, however, does not prevent apportionment unless there is express provision that all income be paid to the life tenant (*Brown* v. *Gellatly*; *Re Owen*; *Re Parry; Brown* v. *Parry*). There must be in existence a specific and independent power to retain, not subsidiary and ancillary to a paramount trust for conversion, to render the life tenant entitled to the whole income (*ibid.*)

The question is one of construction; if the testator intends that the power to postpone should be exercised for the benefit of the life tenant, i.e., if it is a power permanently to continue or retain existing investments, the court makes no distinction between unauthorised securities of a wasting nature and those of permanent nature, and will give the whole income to the life tenant. On the other hand, if the power is conferred simply to permit a more convenient realisation of the estate when the trustees can sell advantageously, the court will apportion (*Re Inman, Inman* v. *Inman*).

The discretion of the trustees is to be exercised for the benefit of the estate, and not by any means necessarily with a nice consideration of how either life tenant or remainderman will be affected, but whether the property is likely to realise better if converted at once or in the future.

In all instances where the rule applies, the courts take the viewpoint that the life tenant is intended to enjoy the income from the fund that will ultimately go to the remainderman as capital. Accordingly, pending the realisation of the unauthorised investments, an equitable apportionment is required, resorting to capital where necessary, to maintain this relationship. A fair rate of simple interest is assumed; this is at present 4 per cent. (*Re Fawcett; Public Trustee* v. *Dugdale*). Income tax is deductible from the interest at the standard rate. The life tenant is to be credited with interest at that rate out of the income produced, any deficiency being made good out of subsequent surplus income or out of realisations of the unauthorised investments as these take place.

The method of apportionment is always in the discretion of the court (*Re Poyser, Landon* v. *Poyser*), but certain principles are followed which are explained below.

The principles of apportionment were conveniently summarised in *Re Fawcett; Public Trustee* v. *Dugdale* which clarified many points formerly in doubt. In this case the residue was settled on persons in succession, the will conferring on the executors no power to postpone conversion of unauthorised investments. The following are the rules as set out in the judgment.

Pending conversion of the unauthorised property, apportionment will proceed as follows:

(1) As regards unauthorised investments which are retained at the end of the executor's year, the life tenant is entitled to 4 per cent. per annum (less tax) on the aggregate value of these investments taken *at the end of that year*. Equity considers that to have been done which ought to have been done, and the interest is therefore payable from the date of death and runs to the date of realisation of the respective investments. In calculating the interest, the investments for the time being unsold are taken *en bloc* as one fund.

Where, however, the residue is left on trust for sale *with absolute power to postpone conversion*, and the executors retain assets in their existing condition they do so for the benefit of the estate as a whole, and, for the purpose of computing the amount of income due to the life tenant, the unauthorised investments, whether sold in or retained to the end of the executor's year, should be valued as at the date of the testator's death (*Re Parry; Brown* v. *Parry*).

(2) In respect of unauthorised investments realised during the executor's year, the life tenant is entitled to interest at 4 per cent. per annum on the net proceeds of sale, from the date of death to the respective dates of realisation.

Where there was a power to postpone sale in the case of a hotel business which was not an authorised investment and which was sold in the executor's year, it was held in *re Berry*, *Lloyds Bank Ltd* v. *Berry*, that the life tenant was entitled to 4 per cent. per annum on the proceeds from the date of the testator's death until the date of sale.

(3) The Apportionment Act 1870 is not to be applied, either at the death or any other date, in reference to the income from the unauthorised investments.

(4) If the actual income produced by the property in question is more than the amount found to be due to the life tenant under the above rules, the excess is to be invested in authorised securities. The life tenant will, of course, be entitled to the income from such authorised securities.

(5) If the actual income available is insufficient to pay the life tenant the interest, calculated as above, it must be paid out of the proceeds of any sale of unauthorised securities during the same accounting period. Any interest for the time being in arrear will then be made good out of (1) future excess income from the unauthorised investments still held, and (2) the proceeds of those investments, as and when realised. Pending such amounts becoming available, the life tenant cannot be paid more than the income available.

(6) A deficiency of income in any accounting period cannot be made good out of *past* excess income or *past* realisations, as these sums ought to have been invested in authorised securities.

Where there is no power to postpone conversion at the end of the executor's year, therefore, the life tenant is entitled to interest at 4 per cent. per annum.

(*a*) on the proceeds of unauthorised investments realised in the year, from the date of death to the date of sale; and

(*b*) on the aggregate value of the unsold unauthorised investments at the end of the year.

Thereafter, he is entitled, up to the date of realisation, to 4 per cent. per annum on the value at the first anniversary of death.

If there is power to postpone conversion at the end of the executor's year, the life tenant is entitled to interest at 4 per cent. per annum.

(*a*) on the proceeds of unauthorised investments realised in the year from the date of death to the date of realisation;

(*b*) on the probate value of investments unsold at the end of the year.

Thereafter, the life tenant is entitled, up to the date of realisation, to 4 per cent. per annum on the probate value. Where the income is insufficient for the above purposes, the life tenant will be entitled, when the investments are realised, to be recouped out of the proceeds of sale of the investments the amount of the deficit, so as to provide him with the full 4 per cent., less tax, for the whole period from the date of death up to the date of realisation.

As it is unwise to credit a life tenant with money not actually received, any amount by which the interest due exceeds the funds available should not be entered in the estate books, except by way of memorandum. A statement in the form shown in the following illustration is suggested:

Illustration

A. died on 1st April, 1967. The residue of his estate, £62,000, included the following unauthorised investments:

	Probate Value	Value on anniversary of death	Sale Price (net)	Date of Sale
	£	£	£	
£10,000 6% Preference Shares in A. Ltd	11,500	12,000	12,000	13/6/69
£10,000 Ordinary Shares in A. Ltd	14,100	—	14,000	25/8/67
£1,000 4% Debentures in B. Ltd	950	960	965	13/6/69
£8,000 Ordinary Stock ..	4,200	4,000	3,500	18/1/70

Interest and dividends were received as follows:

Preference Shares in A. Ltd, yearly on 30th September.

Ordinary Shares in A. Ltd, 5% less tax on 15th July, 1967, *re* year ⁂ to 31st May, 1967.

Debentures in B. Ltd, 6 months' interest on 1st October, 1967, year's interest on 1st October, 1968.

On 1st April, 1968, the executors invested £14,129 in 3½% War Loan and on 1st April, 1970, £16,196 in 2½% Consols. Write up all accounts recording these transactions so far as they concern unauthorised investments. The executors had no power to postpone the conversion of securities.

The standard rate of Income tax was 8s 3d in the £ in 1967-68, 1968-69 and 1969-70. Calculations to nearest £.

STATEMENT OF EQUITABLE APPORTIONMENTS
DATE OF DEATH, 1ST APRIL, 1967

Unauthorised Investments	Value at end of the year following death or, if sold in that year, net proceeds of Sale	Date of sale	First Year 1967/68		Second Year 1968/69		Third Year 1969/70	
			Period Days	Interest at 4% per annum	Period Days	Interest at 4% per annum	Period Days	Interest at 4% per annum
	£			£		£		£
£10,000 Preference Shares in A. Ltd..	12,000	13/6/69	365	480	365	480	73	96
£10,000 Ordinary Shares in A. Ltd ..	14,000	25/8/67	146	224	—	—	—	—
£1,000 Debentures in B. Ltd ..	960	13/6/69	365	38	365	38	73	8
£8,000 Ordinary Stock in B. Ltd ..	4,000	18/1/70	365	160	365	160	292	128
Gross 4 per cent	..	..		902		678		232
Arrears brought forward (gross) ..	..	..						36
								268
Less Income tax	..	..		372		280		110
				530		398		158
Deduct Income available (net) ..	..	..		530		377		*158
Arrears (net) c/f	..	..				21		
(gross) c/f	..	..				36		

* Payable out of proceeds of sale of investments.

Since Income tax is not deductible until the payment of the arrears out of capital, the carry-forward has been grossed up as shown above.

As investments are to be treated *en bloc*, it is advisable, in order to avoid the risk of over-paying the life tenant, to credit the income therefrom to capital until the end of the year, when it will be transferred to a special account, e.g. 'Income from Unauthorised Investments Account', from which the necessary transfers will be made to the credit of the life tenant, as per the statement. Any cash paid to the life tenant out of capital will be adjusted by a transfer in the Cash Book. Similarly, capitalised income will be adjusted.

The ledger accounts recording the transactions summarised above would then be as follows:

ORDINARY SHARES IN A. LTD

		Nominal	Income	Capital			Nominal	Income	Cap
1967 April 1	Estate Account ..	£ 10,000	£	£ 14,100	1967 July 15	Cash—Dividend *re* year to 31st May, 1966, 5%, *less* tax	£	£	£
1968 April 1	Income on Unauthorised Investments Account ..			294	Aug. 25	Cash—Sale ..	10,000		14,
					1968 April 1	Estate A/c—Loss..			
		£ 10,000		£ 14,394			£ 10,000		£ 14,

6% PREFERENCE SHARES IN A. LTD

		Nominal	Income	Capital			Nominal	Income	Capital
		£	£	£	1967		£	£	£
67 11	Estate Account ..	10,000		11,500	Sept. 30	Cash—Year's dividend, less tax ..			353
					1968				
58 11	Income on Unauthorised Investments Account ..			353	April 1	Balance c/d ..	10,000		11,500
	£	10,000	£	11,853		£	10,000	£	11,853
12	Balance b/d ..	10,000		11,500	Sept. 30	Cash—Year's dividend, less tax ..			353
					1969				
59 4 1	Income on Unauthorised Investments Account ..			353	April 1	Balance c/d ..	10,000		11,500
	£	10,000	£	11,867		£	10,000	£	11,867
59 4 1	Balance b/d ..	10,000		11,500	1969 June 13	Cash—Sale ..	10,000		12,000
70 4 1	Estate A/c—Profit			500					
	£	10,000	£	12,000		£	10,000	£	12,000

4% DEBENTURES IN B. LTD

		Nominal	Income	Capital			Nominal	Income	Capital
		£	£	£	1967	*	£	£	£
7 1	Estate Account ..	1,000		950	Oct. 1	Cash — Half-year's interest, less tax..			12
					1968				
8 1	Income on Unauthorised Investments Account ..			12	April 1	Balance c/d ..	1,000		950
		£1,000		£962			£1,000		£962
2	Balance b/d ..	1,000		950	Oct. 1	Cash—Year's interest, less tax ..			24
					1969				
9 1	Income on Unauthorised Investments Account ..			24	April 1	Balance c/d ..	1,000		950
		£1,000		·£974			£1,000		£974
9 2	Balance b/d ..	1,000		950	1969 June 13	Cash—Sale ..	1,000		965
0 1	Estate A/c—Profit			15					
		£1,000		£965			£1,000		£965

ORDINARY STOCK IN B. LTD

		Nom- inal	In- come	Capital			Nom- inal	In- come	Ca
		£	£	£			£	£	
1967 April 1	Estate Account ..	8,000		4,200	1968 April 1	Balance c/d ..	8,000		4
1968 April 2	Balance b/d ..	8,000		4,200	1969 April 1	Balance c/d ..	8,000		4
1969 April 1	Balance b/d ..	8,000		4,200	1970 Jan. 18 April 1	Cash—Sale .. Estate A/c—Loss..	8,000		3
		£8,000		£4,200			£8,000		£4

INCOME ON UNAUTHORISED INVESTMENTS

			£			
1968 April 1	Life Tenant .. .. .. Estate Account		530 129	1968 April 1	Preference Shares in A. Ltd .. Ordinary Shares in A. Ltd .. Debentures in B. Ltd	
			£659			£
1969 April 1	Life Tenant		377	1969 April 1	Preference Shares in A. Ltd .. Debentures in B. Ltd	
			£377			£

LIFE TENANT

			£			
1968 April 1	Cash		530	1968 April 1	Income on Unauthorised Invest- ments	
1969 April 1	Cash		377	1969 April 1	Income on Unauthorised Invest- ments	
1970 April 1	Cash		158	1970 April 1	Estate Account	£

ESTATE ACCOUNT

		£			£
1968 April 1	Ordinary Shares in A. Ltd— Loss on sale .. .. .. Balance c/d	100 62,029	1967 April 1 1968 April 1	Balance b/f .. .. .. Income on unauthorised invest- ments—Surplus	62,
		£62,129			£62.
April 1	Ordinary Shares in A. Ltd— Loss on sale .. .. .. Balance c/d	100 62,029			
		£62,129	1968 April 2	Balance b/d	62,
1970 April 1	Ordinary Stock in B. Ltd—Loss Life Tenant—to make good equitable apportionment of interest .. .. .. Provision for Income Tax, Sec- tion 53 .. .. .. Balance c/f	700 158 111 61,575	1969 April 2 1970 April 1	Balance b/d .. .. .. Preference Shares in A. Ltd— Profit .. .. Debentures in B. Ltd—Profit ..	62,
		£62,544			£62.

CASH BOOK

		Income £	Capital £			Income £	Capital £
1967				1968			
15	Dividend 5%, *less* tax, Ordinary Shares in A. Ltd		294	April 1	Life Tenant per statement	530	
25	Ordinary Shares in A. Ltd		14,000		Transfer to Income		530
30	Dividend 6%, *less* tax, Preference Shares in A. Ltd		353		Investment—3½% War Stock		14,129
1	Interest on 4% Debentures in B. Ltd. Half-year, *less* tax		12				
1968							
1	Transfer from Capital	530					
		£530	£14,659			£530	£14,659
1968				1969			
30	Dividend 6%, *less* tax, Preference Shares in A. Ltd		353	April 1	Transfer to Income		377
1	Interest 4%, *less* tax, Debentures in B. Ltd		24		Life Tenant per statement	377	
1969							
1	Transfer from Capital	377					
		£377	£377			£377	£377
1969				1970			
13	Preference Shares in A. Ltd		12,000	April 1	Transfer to Income		158
	Debentures, B. Ltd		965		Life Tenant per statement	158	
1970					Investment—2½% Consols		16,196
18	Ordinary Shares, B. Ltd		3,500		Balance c/f		111
1	Transfer from Capital	158			(to meet Income Tax)		
		£158	£16,465			£158	£16,465

Note to Illustration:
The £158 paid to the life tenant out of the proceeds of realisation of investments on 1st April, 1970, is the equivalent of £269, less tax at 8s 3d in £. Since this sum is not paid out of profits or gains brought into charge to Income tax, it will be assessable on the trustees under Section 53, Income and Corporation Taxes Act 1970, and the tax payable under this assessment should be provided for.

(b)   Unauthorised Investments made by the Executors

The principle which limits the income of the life tenant to 4 per cent. on investments left by the testator which ought to be converted has no application to investments made by a trustee in breach of trust. If no loss of capital results from the breach, the remainderman cannot claim to have the capital augmented by bringing in that part of the income produced which represents a return in excess of 4 per cent. If the amount of the trust fund as originally constituted is specific, and there has been no loss in consequence of the breach of trust, the remainderman has no equity to demand that the fund be appreciated at the expense of the life tenant. No question of adjustment arises as would be the case if the property settled had been speculative or wasting and so of unascertained or fluctuating value.

Where the breach of trust results in a capital loss, the tenant for life, who is not a party to the breach, cannot be called upon to refund any income already received; but he cannot claim any part of the amount realised upon sale, without bringing into account all the income he has received while the unauthorised investment subsisted. Thus, where a trustee, without the knowledge of the tenant for life or remainderman, sells out an authorised investment, and with the proceeds purchases an unauthorised investment and a loss results, the tenant for life is entitled to such a proportion of the amount realised by the unauthorised investment plus the income he received therefrom during its continuance, as the dividends he would have received from the authorised investment in the same period bear to the capital value of the authorised investment plus those dividends (*Re Bird, in re Evans, Dodd* v. *Evans*). Where there is no loss, the life tenant is entitled to the whole income even if the trustee is the tenant for life (*Re Hoyles, Row* v. *Jagg*).

Illustration

Without the knowledge of the beneficiaries, a trustee sold an authorised investment, £20,000 3% Corporation Stock at 46, purchasing with the proceeds £8,000 Ordinary Stock in A.X. Ltd. Nine months later, the Ordinary Stock was sold for £6,500, having paid 2% in the meantime. Had the Corporation Stock been retained, the life tenant would have received two half-yearly dividends. Show the apportionment of the proceeds of sale of the Ordinary Stock, ignoring Income Tax. The Corporation Stock was quoted at 45 when the Ordinary Stock was sold.

Proceeds of Sale	..	..	..	£6,500
Dividends received by life tenant		..	..	160
Apportionable fund ..		..	..	£6,660
Dividends which the life tenant would have received on Corporation Stock		..	..	£600
Capital value of Corporation Stock ..			..	9,000
Add said dividends ..		..	..	600
				£9,600

Amount apportionable to life tenant $\frac{600}{9,600}$ of £6,660 = £416

Less Dividend actually received 160

Proportion of proceeds of sale payable to life tenant £256

Although the calculation is made with a view to adjusting as between the beneficiaries the position produced by a breach of trust, it must not be overlooked that where the breach causes a loss to the trust property, those trustees who are parties to the breach may be made liable to restore to the trust property the amount which has been lost.

(c) *Re Earl of Chesterfield's Trusts*

The rule in *Re Earl of Chesterfield's Trusts* applies where part of the residue left to persons in succession consists of outstanding personal estate not in authorised investments, such as a reversionary interest or similar property (e.g., a life policy on the life of another (*Re Morley, Morley* v. *Haig*)), which is either not converted immediately or is retained until it falls into possession. It is important to bear in mind that this rule is merely an application of the *Howe* v. *Dartmouth* principle, and the terms of the will may bar it. Consequently it has no application to realty (*In re Woodhouse*) or intestacy, subject to the provisions of the will in the case of a partial intestacy (Administration of Estates Act 1925, s. 33 (1)).

The principle in *Re Earl of Chesterfield* has been applied to:

(a) the instalments paid to the estate (at a rate varying with profits) in respect of the deceased's share in a partnership (*Re Hollebone, Hollebone* v. *Hollebone*); each instalment (including the interest thereon) was apportionable at 4 per cent. compound interest;

(b) annual payments equal to the testator's share of the profits of a company, of which he had been an employee, payable under a service agreement (*In re Payne; Westminster Bank Ltd* v. *Payne*); and

(c) a debt due to the estate carrying no interest (*re Duke of Cleveland's estate, Hay* v. *Wolmer*).

The object of the rule is to place the tenant for life in exactly the same position as if the outstanding property had been sold as at the testator's death (as it could have been, subject to any contrary directions contained in the will) and the proceeds invested in authorised securities. If this had been done, the life tenant would have received the income arising from those authorised securities each year.

Under the rule in *Re Earl of Chesterfield's Trusts* the life tenant receives the income in one sum when the property falls in or is realised, and compound interest is allowed so as to compensate him for the loss of the use of the money until payment.

The apportionment between the tenant for life and the remainderman is made by ascertaining the sum which, put out at 4 per cent. per annum on the day of the testator's death, and accumulated at *compound interest*, calculated at the rate, *less* Income tax, which with yearly rests would, with the accumulations of interest, produce at the date of receipt the amount actually received. The sum so ascertained is treated as capital and the rest as income.

Illustration (1)

A. died on 5th April, 1968, and part of the residuary personal estate—which was bequeathed to B. for life, with remainder to C. – consisted of a reversionary interest, valued at £800 for Estate Duty purposes.

This was retained till 5th April, 1970, when it fell into possession; and it then consisted of £1,000 Illyria 4 per cent. stock (market value 75) and £150 cash.

Show the Reversionary Interest Account, and the apportionment of the proceeds between capital and income; the rate of Income Tax was 8s 3d in the £. Ignore Death Duties.

	£
£1,000 Illyria 4 per cent. at 75	750
Cash	150
Total Proceeds	£900

4% *less* tax at 8s 3d = 2·35% actual.

Present worth of reversionary interest of date of death = £900 × $\dfrac{100}{102\cdot35} \times \dfrac{100}{102\cdot35}$ = £857 9s 4d.

Income is therefore entitled to:

1st year, 4 per cent. *less* tax on £858	£21
2nd year, 4 per cent. *less* tax on £879	22
Amount due to Income	£43

REVERSIONARY INTEREST

		Income	Capital			Income	Capital
1968 April 5		£	£ 800	1970 April 5	Cash	£	£ 150
1970 April 5	Estate Account..				Illyria 4%, £1,000 @ 75 ..		750
	Transfer to Income under the in *Re Earl of Chesterfield's Trusts* ..		43		Transfer from Capital ..	43	
	Income Account	43					
	Estate Account: Profit on realisation		57				
		£43	£900			£43	£900

Illustration (2)

A reversionary interest was valued at the testator's death on 30th June, at £750. One year and 32 days having elapsed, it fell in, and was represented by cash and investments of the value of £825.

Apportion this under the rule in *Re Chesterfield's Trusts*, assuming Income tax at $41p$ (8s 3d) in £.

The present worth of £825, 1 year and 32 days ago, at 4 per cent. compound interest (*less* tax at $41p$ (8s 3d) is ascertained as follows:

Had there been invested on the testator's death, 1 year and 32
days ago, the sum of £1,000
At 4%, *less* tax at $41p$ (8s 3d) this would have produced in the
first year interest amounting to   23

Amount at end of first year   1,023
In a further 32 days this amount would have produced

$$£1,023 \times \frac{2 \cdot 35}{100} \times \frac{32}{365} \quad .. \quad .. \quad .. \quad .. \quad .. \quad = \quad 2$$

Amount on reversion falling in £1,025

If £1,025 would be produced by the investment of £1,000, £825 would
be produced by investing £825 $\times \dfrac{1000}{1025}$ = £805.

REVERSIONARY INTEREST

	Income	Capital		Income	Capital
	£	£ 750	Cash and Investments ..	£	£ 825
Estate Account			Transfer from Capital ..	20	
Transfer to Income under the rule in *Re Earl of Chesterfield's Trusts* ..		20			.
Income Account	20				
Estate Account: Profit on realisation ..		55			
	£20	£825		£20	£825

It would appear that, although Income tax is taken into account in arriving at the apportionment, the whole proceeds retain their impress of capital for Income tax purposes, and no tax is payable thereon to the Revenue. This is not a case of making up income out of capital, but of paying part of the capital out as compensation for there having been no income.

(d) Allhusen v. Whittell

Where a testator has bequeathed the residue of his estate so as to create a life interest with remainder over, the presumption is that he intended the life tenant to enjoy as from the date of death the interest of the pure residue, and that the life tenant should derive no advantage through delay in paying funeral expenses, debts, and legacies.

Funeral expenses, debts, and legacies cannot all conveniently be paid immediately at or after the death of the testator, so that assets which otherwise would be absorbed in the discharge of these amounts remain in the hands of the personal representative. These assets may produce income, and as the personal representative has a whole year in which to pay the funeral expenses, debts and legacies, it is clear that if he postponed payment so far as is legally proper, the income for the year succeeding death would be considerably augmented by the income on assets which were used for these payments.

The decision in *Allhusen* v. *Whittell* requires that in adjusting the accounts between the life tenant and the remainderman, the amounts paid in respect of the debts, funeral expenses and legacies, are not to be treated as payments either out of capital or income only, but are to be apportioned by *ascertaining what sum with interest for the year succeeding death would amount to the total required to pay the debts, funeral expenses and legacies.* The rate of interest to be taken depends on the ratio subsisting between the actual net income for the year succeeding death and the gross capital of the estate. In applying the rule, the income of the estate must be calculated, not on the gross amount received, but on the basis of the net amount, after the deduction of Income tax (*Re Oldham, Oldham* v. *Myles*). 'Income' includes profits of the testator's business (*Re Elford*).

Before explaining the practical application of the rule (since debts etc. are rarely paid at the end of the executor's year), illustration (1) sets out the arithmetic underlying the applicaton of the rule.

Illustration (1)

The assets of the estate of a testator were valued at £10,000, and the funeral expenses, debts and legacies amounted to £1,000.

The total income *less* tax for the year succeeding death amounted to £250, i.e. exactly 2½ per cent. of the gross estate.

Show the apportionment between the life tenant and estate capital.

	£
Gross capital	10,000
Income for year after death, equal to 2½ per cent. of gross capital	250
	£10,250

This amount of £10,250 is apportionable, under the rule in *Allhusen* v. *Whittell*, as follows:

FUNERAL EXPENSES, DEBTS, LEGACIES, ETC.:	£	£
Amount required at 2½ per cent. per annum to produce £1,000 in one year $\frac{100}{102\cdot5}$ of £1,000 ..	976	
Interest on £976 at 2½ per cent. per annum for one year $\frac{2\cdot5}{102\cdot5}$ of £1,000	24	
		1,000
CAPITAL:		
Gross Capital	10,000	
Less Apportionment of funeral expenses, debts, etc.	976	
		9,024
LIFE TENANT:		
Total Income	250	
Less Apportionment of funeral expenses, debts, etc.	24	
		226
		£10,250

A provision in a will excluding the application of the rule in *Howe* v. *Lord Dartmouth* and the rule in *Re Earl of Chesterfield's Trusts*, does not of itself exclude the rule in *Allhusen* v. *Whittell* (*In re Ullswater* (*deceased*). The *Law Times*, (Vol. 231, p. 172) recommends that the rule in *Allhusen* v. *Whittell* should not be excluded where the estate is large enough for the rate of Estate Duty to be 30 per cent. or more, as its exclusion would give the life tenant an undue benefit. Where the rule in *Allhusen* v. *Whittell* is not excluded, a direction to simplify its application would be useful.

In *Re McEuen, McEuen* v. *Phelps* the method of giving effect to the rule was considerably modified. The court directed that all the income should be credited to the life tenant, but that he should be charged with interest at 4 per cent. per annum from the date of death to the dates of the various payments in respect of funeral expenses, testamentary expenses, debts, and legacies, on such a capital sum as with interest would provide the amount required for such payments. It should be noted that the rate of interest, of 4 per cent. per annum, was agreed by the interested parties, as it was approximately the rate earned by the estate.

In *Re Wills, Wills* v. *Hamilton* [1915] it was laid down that where the payments and appropriations cannot be completed in the executor's year the income apportionment ought to be calculated on the average rate of interest earned by the estate in each year. It is clear that Income tax must be taken into account in computing the interest earned by the estate (*Re Oldham*)

The correct method is to ascertain the actual income produced by the assets sold to provide for the various payments, and to charge that amount against the life tenant. In practice, however, this would involve complicated and elaborate calculations, and therefore it is better to adopt an agreed rate. It would appear from *dicta* in the judgment in *Re McEuen*, that where non-income-producing assets are sold for the purpose of paying capital debts, no apportionment whatever should be made. This would be so also where income-producing assets are sold *cum div.*, since, following the ruling in *Scholefield* v. *Redfern* no apportionment is made in respect of the realised proceeds of such sales. If both non-income-producing assets and income producing assets are sold, consideration has to be given as to which assets have been used to pay debts. There is no case decision on this matter, but it would seem appropriate to pay debts rateably out of such assets or out of the specific asset sold for the purpose of paying the debt. Further apportionments, under the *Allhusen* v. *Whittell* rule will occur only in the case of income-producing assets. Illustration (2) shows the manner in which the *Allhusen* v. *Whittell* rule should be applied.

Illustration (2)

A. died on 31st December, leaving an estate valued gross at £40,000. On the following 1st April, Estate Duty on personalty, amounting to £5,029, was paid, and on 1st July the funeral expenses, debts and legacies amounting to £8,094 were discharged. During the year following the death the net income amounted to £1,531.

The residue being settled, state how the payments referred to are to be apportioned between capital and income under the rule in *Allhusen* v. *Whittell*, as applied in *Re McEuen*.

The capital sum at the date of death which at 4 per cent. less income tax at 41p (8s 3d) in £ would amount to £5,031 on the following 1st April, is ascertained as follows:

$$\frac{100}{100 + \left(2 \cdot 35 \times \frac{91}{365}\right)} \times £5,029 = £5,000 \text{ (to nearest £1)}$$

Therefore the capital sum is £5,000
and the amount chargeable against income equal to 4 per cent.
thereon less tax at 41p (8s 3d) for 91 days is (to nearest £1) ..   29

Total to be apportioned £5,029

The capital sum at the date of death which at 4 per cent. interest less tax would amount to £8,094 on 1st July is ascertained as follows:

$$\frac{100}{100 + \left(2 \cdot 35 \times \frac{182}{365}\right)} \times £8,094 = £8,000 \text{ (to nearest £1)}$$

Therefore the capital sum is £8,000
and the amount chargeable against income equal to 4 per cent.
thereon less tax at 41p (8s 3d) for 91 days is (to nearest £1)   ..   94

Total to be apportioned £8,094

As these payments will have been charged to capital in the first instance it will be necessary to debit Income Account and credit Estate Account with the ascertained adjustment, and to make a corresponding transfer between the capital and income columns of the Cash Book.

ESTATE ACCOUNT

	£		£
Estate duty on Personalty	5,029	Sundry Assets	40,000
Legacies, debts and funeral expenses	8,094	Income Account: Adjustment under rule in *Allhusen* v. *Whittell*, as amended by *Re McEuen*	123

INCOME ACCOUNT

	£			£
Estate Account: Adjustment under rule in *Allhusen* v. *Whittell*, as amended by *Re McEuen*	123	Sundry Dividends, etc.		1,531

In the case of small estates or estates of moderate size it is very often a good rough and ready rule to allow the interest on the Estate Duty to be paid out of income and the capital to be paid out of capital. In strictness it seems that the amount paid both for capital and interest in respect of the Estate Duty ought to be treated as being the debt or liability to be discharged and to be apportioned between income and capital.

The principle of *Allhusen* v. *Whittell* has also been applied where a testatrix left the residue of her estate in trust for persons in succession, the whole income from unconverted property to be applied as if it were income from authorised investments. The residue included two leasehold houses with only a few years to run, and nine months after the death the executors assigned the leases, which were onerous, paying to the assignees the sums of £500 and £100 as consideration for their undertaking the liabilities under the leases. The executors had already paid £353 for rent, rates, taxes and other outgoings in respect of the leases. If the leaseholds had not been sold, the life tenant could not have objected to the obligations arising from time to time under the leases being met out of income of the estate. In the view of the judge, this had not occurred, since the leaseholds had been disposed of and the liability ended within the executor's year. The onerous property had not, in fact, been put into possession of the life tenant and the court directed that the total sum of £953 be apportioned on the basis of *Allhusen* v. *Whittell*, viz.

'that a sum is to be ascertained which, when added to the interest upon it at the rate for the time being produced by the estate for the period from the death of the testatrix to the date of actual expenditure, will amount to the sum expended; the sum so ascertained will be borne by capital, and the excess of the expenditure over that sum will be borne by income' (*In re Shee, Taylor* v. *Stoger*).

The operation of the rule in *Allhusen* v. *Whittell* is commonly

excluded by express provision in the will, and in practice if not
excluded it is often disregarded because of its complexity and
the small difference it would make owing to the fact that the
debts, legacies, and so on, are usually paid long before the
expiration of the executor's year.

(e) Re Atkinson

A mortgage investment provides coincident and co-extensive
security for both principal and interest, and in consequence, if
any loss is sustained on realisation of such mortgage security,
both principal and interest must abate proportionately. This
case is not confined to residuary bequests, but would apply
equally in any trust and to authorised securities. In the case of
unauthorised investments in residue, however, it appears that
Re Fawcett (supra) would apply and not *Re Atkinson*.

The appropriate principle in such cases was defined in *Re
Atkinson, Barbers' Co.* v. *Grose-Smith*, and is to the effect that
the principal, and all arrears of interest to the date of realisation,
must be aggregated, and the amount realised divided in the
ratio that the arrears of interest and the principal respectively
bear to the aggregation. It seems clear from the decision in *Re
Morris's Will Trusts* (see below) that the gross arrears of interest
are to be taken into account in making this apportionment.

Illustration (1)

During continuance of a trust, default was made in the payment of interest
on a loan on mortgage of £1,000 at 5 per cent. Interest has been regularly
paid up to 31st December, 1966. The property was realised on 31st
December, 1969, and produced £800 net. Show the apportionment as
between income and capital, and give the ledger account, ignoring Income
tax. Calculations to the nearest £.

	£
The amount due to capital is	1,000
The amount due to income is 5 per cent. on £1,000 for three years	150
Total amount involved	£1,150

Capital is therefore entitled to $\dfrac{1,000}{1,150} \times £800$ ..   ..   =   696

Income is entitled to $\dfrac{150}{1,150} \times £800$ ..   ..   ..   =   104

£800

LOAN ON MORTGAGE

Date		Income	Capital	Date		Income	Capital
1966 Jan. 1	Balance ..	£	£ 1,000	1969 Dec. 1	Cash, proceeds of sale of property, apportioned under the rule in *Re Atkinson* ..	£	£
1969 Dec. 31	Income Account	104				104	696
					Estate Account: Loss on realisation		304
		£104	£1,000			£104	£1,000

If arrears of interest exist at the date of death of the testator, these will form part of the capital for the purpose of the apportionment so far as they are not made good prior to realisation.

It is the duty of the trustee, where he is in possession as mortgagee, to apply any rents received as follows:

(1) In discharge of any interest due or in arrear at the date of the testator's death;

(2) In payment to the life tenant to the extent of the full mortgage interest;

(3) Any surplus to be applied as capital (*Re Coaks, Coaks* v. *Bayler*).

Illustration (2)

A testator died on the 31st December, 1968. Part of the residue consisted of a loan on mortgage of £1,000 at 5 per cent. per annum.

Interest had been regularly paid half-yearly up to and including 30th June, 1968, after which default was made.

On 1st July, 1969, the property was let for six months at a rent of £90 per annum, and on the 31st December, 1969, the property was sold for £824.

Show the apportionment as between capital and income, ignoring Income tax.

Particulars	Total Involved	Amount due in in respect of Principal	Interest accrued prior to death	Interest accrued subsequent to death
	£	£	£	£
Amount due 31 December, 1969	1,075	1,000	25	50
Less Rent Received ..	45		25	20
	£1,030	£1,000	—	£30

Capital is therefore entitled to $\dfrac{1,000}{1,030} \times £824$ .. $=$ 800

Income is entitled to $\dfrac{30}{1,030} \times £824$ .. .. $=$ 24

£824

It would appear that any expenditure incurred by the personal representative in relation to the property prior to sale should be charged to capital or income according to the nature of the expenditure, and that only the net rents, viz. rents received less expenditure of a revenue nature, should be utilised in paying off arrears of interest as at the date of the testator's death and arrears of interest accruing subsequent to the date of the testator's death.

It seems, moreover, that any capital expenditure incurred, or any excess of revenue expenditure over revenue receipts, should be deducted from the realised proceeds of the property.

Illustration (3)

X. died on the 31st December, 1967. During his lifetime he had advanced £1,000 at 5 per cent. per annum on property valued at £1,600.

Interest had been paid regularly up to and including 30th June, 1967, after which default was made.

The personal representative of X. took possession of the property, which remained unlet until midsummer 1968, during which time the sum of £10 was paid in respect of general repairs and £5 ground rent.

The property was let at midsummer 1968 for £100 a year, and sold as from midsummer, 1969, for £874, the payments out in the meanwhile being:

> Commission for letting property, 5 per cent. on one year's rent.
> Advertising property for sale, £10.
> Ground rent, £10 per annum.
> Show the apportionment of the proceeds between capital and income, ignoring Income tax.

INCOME AND EXPENDITURE ON PROPERTY

		Income	Capital			Income	Capital
		£	£	1968		£	£
1968	Cash:			Sept. 29	Cash	25	
e 24	Repairs	10		Dec. 25	Cash	25	
	Ground rent	5					
. 25	Ground rent	5		1969			
	Commission on letting			Mar. 25	Cash	25	
	property	5					
1969				June 24	Cash	25	
e 24	Ground rent	5					
	Advertising property for				Mortgage Account ..		10
	sale		10				
	Mortgage Account:						
	Capital, in respect of						
	arrears of interest up to						
	date of Testator's death	25					
	Income Account ..	45					
		£100	£10			£100	£10

MORTGAGE

	Income	Capital		Income	Cap
	£	£		£	£
Estate Account		1,000	Income and Expenditure Account	45	
„ Arrears of Interest up to date of death		25	Cash: Apportionment of proceeds of sale	25	8
Income and Expenditure Account..					
Income Account	70	10	Estate Account: Loss on realisation		
	£70	£1,035		£70	£1,0

The apportionment of the sale price of the property, viz. £874, is made as follows:

CAPITAL: £   £   £

Loan 1,000

Arrears to date of testator's death 25

           —— 1,025

   Less Cash on account of arrears 25

             —— 1,000

INCOME:

Interest at 5 per cent. per annum on £1,000 for

  $1\frac{1}{2}$ years   75

   Less Cash on account of arrears 45

               ——   30

    Total amount due on capital and income   £1,030

                   £

Realised price   874

  Less Capital expenditure   10

    Net realised price £864

CAPITAL: £   £

$\dfrac{1,000}{1,030}$ × £864 ..   ..   =   839

  Add Amount charged to capital and now reimbursed   10

                ——   849

INCOME:

$\dfrac{30}{1,030}$ × £864   ..   ..   =   25

    Realised price £874

The question whether, for the purpose of the apportionment under the rule in *Re Atkinson,* Income tax should be deducted from the arrears of interest has apparently not been judicially settled. As, however, the right to deduct Income tax from annual interest does not arise until the interest is paid, it is thought that this gross interest should come into the computation. This implication appears to have been made in *Re Morris's Will Trust* where, under a series of arrangements with debenture holders the claims under the debentures were surrendered in consideration of the allotment of debenture stock in another company and a payment in cash. The sum due to the deceased's estate in respect of the debentures held by him was £4,300 for principal and £1,526 less tax for interest, and a further £1,733 less tax for interest on interest. The total value of the consideration received by the estate was £4,300 made up of debenture stock £2,580 and cash £1,720. It was remarked that the £1,720 bore approximately the same proportion to £4,300 as the interest plus interest on interest bore to the total sum due, viz. 40 per cent. It was held that the life tenant should receive such amount as bore to the whole amount received the same proportion as the arrears of interest plus interest on interest not paid on the due date bore to the total sum due. The actual figures were not mentioned, but they appear to have been £(1,526 + 1,733) : £(4,300 + 1,526 + 1,733) = 43 per cent.; and the sum awarded to the life tenant was the above mentioned £1,720; if the net figures of interest had been taken the proportion would have been approximately £1,720 : £(4,300 + 1,720), or under 30 per cent. Normally, interest on arrears of interest cannot be taken into account (*Re Moore, Moore* v. *Johnson*), but in the above case the scheme specifically provided for interest on interest.

Instead of immediately exercising their power of sale, the trustees may seek an order for foreclosure. Upon the making of such an order by the court, the mortgagor would lose any equity he possessed to redeem the mortgaged property. As from the date of the order made absolute, the mortgage ceases (the whole right of the mortgagor therein being extinguished), and no further interest can accrue. If the property is let pending sale, the tenant for life is entitled to receive, as income, the *whole* of the net rents, since foreclosed property must be regarded as

being in the same position as if it had orginally formed part of
the estate of the testator (*In re Horn's Estate, Public Trustee* v.
Garnett). Foreclosed property would fall within the definition of
'land' in the Law of Property Act 1925, and would now come
within the operation of s. 28 (2) and in consequence would not
be subject to apportionment. Interest accrued at the date of
foreclosure remains due, however, for the purposes of the rule
in *Re Atkinson*, and when the property is sold, the proceeds
must be apportioned under that rule by reference to the
amounts due at the date of foreclosure (*In re Horn's Estate*,
supra).

Illustration (4)

A. died on 1st January, 1966. Part of his residuary estate, left to persons
in succession, consisted of a mortgage for £4,000, interest at 5% per
annum being receivable on 31st March and 30th September. On 31st
March, 1966, the mortgagor defaulted. An order for foreclosure was made
absolute on 31st December, 1967. The property was let at £360 per
quarter as from Lady Day, 1968, and was sold on Lady Day, 1970, for
£3,600. Show how the sum received would be apportioned. Ignore income
and other taxes.

The apportionment would be as follows:

Principal	£4,000
Interest accrued at death, 3 months	50
Amount due to Capital	4,050
Interest accrued since death to date of foreclosure, 2 years	400
Total	£4,450

Capital $\dfrac{4,050}{4,450} \times £3,600 = £3,276.$

Income $\dfrac{400}{4,450} \times £3,600 = £324.$

The whole of the rents received since foreclosure belong to the life
tenant.

(f) *Re Perkins*

Where a testator, having made himself liable to pay an annuity
for a period which continues after his death, leaves the residue
of his estate to a person for life with remainder over, the payment of the annuity (if not the subject of a charge on some
other property) will form a debt payable out of the residue.

Applying the principle in *Allhusen* v. *Whittell*, there must be ascertained, as each payment of the annuity becomes due, what sum, invested at 4 per cent. per annum *simple interest* on the day of the testator's death, would produce the instalment of the annuity then due. The sum so found will be capital, the balance income. In the case of *Re Perkins, Brown* v. *Perkins* interest was taken at the rate of 3 per cent., because the residue was invested in Consols, but it was explicitly stated in the judgment that, except for this special circumstance, 4 per cent. was the proper rate. This case was followed in *Re Poyser, Landon* v. *Poyser*.

Illustration (1)

A. died on 1st January, 1969, having covenanted to pay an annuity of £400 per annum to B. for life. The residue of his estate is bequeathed to C. for life, with remainder to D.

Show the necessary calculations for apportioning the payments on 31st December, 1969, and 31st December, 1970, and give the Annuity Account, taking Income tax into account at 8s 3d in £.

Annuity to be paid	£400	

Apportionment for first year:

$$\frac{100}{104} \times £400 \quad .. \quad .. \quad .. \quad .. \quad .. \quad = \quad £384 \quad \text{Capital}$$

4 per cent. simple interest on £384 .. .. 16 Income

£400

Apportionment for second year:

$$\frac{100}{108} \times £400 \quad .. \quad .. \quad .. \quad .. \quad .. \quad = \quad £370 \quad \text{Capital}$$

4 per cent. on £370 for two years .. .. 30 Income

£400

ANNUITY

Date		Income	Capital	Date		Income	Capital
		£	£			£	£
1969 Dec. 31	Cash	9	225	1969 Dec. 31	Income Account ..	16	
	Income Tax	7	159		Capital Account ..		384
1970 Dec. 31	Cash	18	217	1970 Dec. 31	Income Account ..	30	
	Income Tax	12	153		Capital Account ..		370

It will be observed that under the rule in *Re Perkins*, the earlier payments consist mainly of capital, but that the amount chargeable to income increases year by year. The reason for this is that each instalment, though payable at a future date, was a liability of the testator at his death. Theoretically, a capital sum is set aside at the date of death which, with interest, will provide the amount of each payment as and when it becomes due, and therefore the more remote the payment, the greater will be the proportion thereof attributable to interest, and the smaller will be the capital sum necessary to produce the payment.

It must be noted that the rule in *Re Perkins* only applies to cases where there is a personal covenant to pay the annuity (*In re Darby; Russell* v. *McGregor*), and has no application to ordinary annuities bequeathed by will if payable out of income, for the treatment of which *see* Chap. XIV, § 19. If, however, the will directed the annuities to be paid out of capital, the rule would apply.

Income tax is, of course, deductible from each instalment of the annuity. In so far as the payment is out of capital, an assessment will be raised under Section 53, Income and Corporation Taxes Act 1970, to collect the tax from the executor. The tax deducted from the portion paid out of income will be retained by the executor, under Section 52, Income and Corporation Taxes Act 1970, being a recoupment of tax already paid on the income out of which it is paid.

(g) *Wasting or Fluctuating Assets Specifically Settled*

Where specific assets of a wasting or fluctuating nature are specifically settled, either by deed or will, *without any trust for conversion*, the life tenant is entitled to the income actually produced during his life tenancy, and this notwithstanding any power given to the trustees to vary securities (*Lord* v. *Godfrey*). If, however, such property is settled by will *by way of trust for sale*, and no provision is made as to the intermediate income, the life tenant is only entitled to an equitable apportionment, the balance of the income itself being capitalised (*Wentworth* v. *Wentworth*).

In the case of specific trust property expropriated by compulsory purchase (e.g. where specifically settled leaseholds having short terms to run are compulsorily acquired or are sold by the court in an administration action), the tenant for life is entitled to receive an annuity of such an amount that the payment of it would exhaust the fund provided by the compensation monies received for the land taken for the number of years which the leaseholds had to run (*Askew* v. *Woodhead*; *Re Lingard, Lingard* v. *Squirrell*).

(h) Settled Shares

The right, as between life tenant and remainderman, to a bonus declared on settled shares, depends on the power and intention of the company as to capitalising accumulated profits.

If the company has power either to distribute profits as dividend, or to convert them into capital, the decision of the company, in accordance with its regulations, is binding on everyone interested. What is paid by the company as dividend goes to the tenant for life, and what is paid by the company to the shareholder as capital, or appropriated as an increase of capital in the concern, enures to the benfit of all who are interested in the capital (*Bouch* v. *Sproule*). Should the constitution of a company empower it to capitalise its accumulated profits, and it actually exercises the power, giving no option except to take the bonus in the form of shares, then such shares are capital (*Bouch* v. *Sproule, supra*); *Re Evans*). This principle was also followed in the later case of *Re Speir, Holt* v. *Speir*, where, notwithstanding that the testator directed that 'dividends, bonuses and income' should be paid to the tenant for life, it was held that bonus shares distributed by a company, shares in which formed part of the estate, were to be regarded as capital.

Shares issued in pursuance of an absolute option given by a company to take the dividend either in cash or in new shares are income (*Re Despard*), unless the company's intention is, notwithstanding the option, that the dividend shall be applied in taking up new shares (*Re Evans, supra*), but only to the extent to which they are paid up by the amount of dividend (*Re Malam*). If the trustee elects to take shares which have a higher market value than the cash option, the life tenant has a charge on them for the cash offered; the balance of the value is capital (*Re Hume Nisbet's Settlement*). A bonus to be applied in the payments of calls on shares is capital (*Re Hatton*).

A trustee holding shares cannot exercise an option to take cash or shares at his absolute discretion, but is bound to take the greatest benefit offered by the company (*Re Evans, supra*).

An issue of bonus shares must be distinguished from a distribution of capital profits made by a company, which latter is to be regarded as income in the hands of the shareholder for the purposes of determining its destination (*Hill (R.A.)* v. *Permanent Trustee Co. of New South Wales*). Such a capital distribution in respect of shares held on trust belongs to the life tenant. The fact that it may not be liable to Income tax or Surtax does not prevent its having the character of income as between the beneficiaries (*Re Doughty*). A contrary decision given by the court of first instance in *Re Ward's Will Trusts* apparently based on the particular wording of the company's Articles of Association, was doubted by the Court of Appeal in *Re Doughty*. A distribution of capital profits which is satisfied by the transfer to the shareholders of stock forming part of the assets of the company, is similarly to be regarded as income in the hands of the shareholders (*Re Sechiari*).

On the declaration of a bonus issue of shares, a shareholder acquires an equitable interest in those shares until they are actually issued. Therefore a letter of renunciation constitutes a disposition for Estate Duty purposes (*Pye-Smith* v. *C.I.R.*).

Calls on settled shares are payable out of capital, unless the settlement provides otherwise (Trustee Act 1925, s. 11 (2)); if paid by the life tenant, he is entitled to a lien on the shares for the amount (*Re Malam*).

The Trustee Act 1925, s. 10 (4), empowers trustees, where rights to subscribe for any securities are offered in respect of any holding in a company, to exercise such rights and apply capital money of the trust in payment of the consideration, or to renounce such rights or assign them for the best consideration that can reasonably be obtained, to any person, including any beneficiary under the trust, without being responsible for any loss for any such act done by them in good faith.

The consideration received for the sale of such rights must be held as capital money of the trust.

Distributions of assets in a liquidation are capital, even where there are accumulated profits (*Re Armitage*). So is an authorised return of capital under sanction of the court.

(i) Settled Policies

The premiums on settled policies are a capital charge, and, if there are no funds available, must be raised by mortgage of the policies; if the trustees pay the premiums out of income, the life tenant is entitled to be recouped the amount, with interest at 4 per cent. (*Re Morley, Morley* v. *Haig*). In such a case, upon the policy falling in, the proceeds after such recoupment must be apportioned under the rule in *Re Earl of Chesterfield's Trusts* (*Re Morley, supra*).

(j) Loss of Capital and Income

Where there has been a loss of both capital and income of an authorised security bearing interest at a fixed rate and securing both capital and income, i.e., the income of the fund has fallen into arrear, and on realisation of the investment the amount received is insufficient to repay the capital and arrears of income, then the amount received must be apportioned, so as to give the life tenant the same proportion of arrears of interest as the remainderman receives of capital (*Re Moore; and see Re Atkinson, supra*). Generally, the life tenant has no claim against capital for loss of income where the investments do not carry a fixed rate. As to loss on an unauthorised investment by trustees see *Re Bird, supra.*

If, by the terms of an investment, the payment of interest depends upon profits being made, and there is no profit, then in the event of a deficiency on realisation, the life tenant is not entitled to any portion of the proceeds, which are all capital (*Re Taylor's Trust*). If income alone is lost, the loss falls on the tenant for life; thus losses incurred in carrying on a business must be made good out of subsequent profits, and not out of capital (*Upton* v. *Brown*).

The practice of the firm determines the liability as between tenant for life and remainderman where a share in a partnership is settled; if the method in prosperous years has been to divide the whole profits, and in years in which there has been a loss, to write off each partner's share of loss against his capital, this must also be done as between life tenant and remainderman (*Gow* v. *Forster*). Depreciation of machinery is a loss which, following the practice of the business, must be charged before ascertainment of the share of profits due to the life tenant (*Re Crabtree, Thomas* v. *Crabtree*).

If part of the capital of an unauthorised investment is lost without the income having previously fallen into arrear, the life tenant simply receives less income in future, and need not refund any portion of income previously received, provided he is not a party to the improper investment.

Where an unauthorised investment is made at the request of the tenant for life, and the security is insufficient, the life tenant must repay to capital the amount of income received by him (*Raby* v. *Ridehalgh*) unless he makes good the loss of capital upon the realisation of the security (*Re Hoyles*, *Row* v. *Jagg*).

§ 5. Where doubts arise

The question whether an amount should be charged or credited to capital or income in dealing with executorship accounts is continually arising and presenting difficulties, and no hard-and-fast rule can be laid down.

A good rule to follow in practice, where a doubt exists as to whether the amount is applicable to capital or income is, in the case of a receipt, to treat it as capital, and in the case of a payment, to charge it to income. By doing this the executor frees himself from the danger attaching to an over-distribution of income, and should it subsequently be ascertained that his treatment was incorrect, the error can very easily be rectified.

CHAPTER XII

POWERS AND DUTIES OF THE PERSONAL REPRESENTATIVE

§ 1. Introduction

It is the duty of the personal representatives to collect the assets of the deceased, pay the debts, liabilities and testamentary expenses and distribute the remainder of the estate to the beneficiaries. In the absence of any instruction in the will, the personal representative is not entitled to any remuneration, only his expenses. The property of the deceased rests in the personal representative at death, but the latter can only prove his title by obtaining probate of the will or letters of administration. The executor is entitled to one year's grace during which time he cannot be compelled to pay debts or distribute the estate. A personal representative is liable to account for all assets which have come into or could but for his negligence have come into his hands. He cannot purchase assets from the estate. He should be careful to avoid personal liability when dealing with assets of the estate, particularly when dealing with shares in companies and the deceased's business.

§ 2. Duties of the Personal Representative

The office of the personal representative imposes on the holder certain duties which must be strictly performed. This is true as much of an administrator as of an executor appointed by will, for it is provided that every person to whom administration of the real and personal estate of a deceased person is granted has, subject to the limitations contained in the grant, the same rights and liabilities and is accountable in like manner as if he were the executor of the deceased (A.E.A. 1925, s. 21).

The personal representative is responsible for seeing that the deceased is buried in a manner befitting his station in life; and that no undue expense is incurred (*Stackpoole* v. *Stackpoole*).

The Human Tissue Act 1961 authorised the removal of any

part of the human body of a deceased person for therapeutic purposes or for medical education or research provided:

(a) the deceased had given such authority in writing at any time or orally in the presence of two witnesses during his last illness; or

(b) such authority is given by the person lawfully in possession of the body and no objection has been made to this by

    (i) the deceased during his lifetime,
       or

    (ii) the surviving spouse or any other relative of the deceased; or

(c) if an inquest or post-mortem is to be held the consent of the coroner is given; or

(d) if the body is in a hospital the person in control and management of the hospital may authorise removal.

The executor is lawfully in possession of the body of the deceased (*Williams* v. *Williams*). The body must be removed by a registered medical practitioner who is satisfied by a personal examination that life is extinct. Authority for removal may not be given by a person who is entrusted with the body only for the purpose of burial or cremation.

The question of the funeral expenses allowed for the purposes of Estate Duty has been discussed in Chapter III. The personal representative, however, can charge against the estate the expenses he has incurred, provided these are reasonable, having regard to the deceased's position and station in life. Extravagance is only permissible if directed by the will, but each case must be decided on its merits. Executors should be prudent, as excessive expenditure might be chargeable against them personally on the grounds of devastavit. If the estate is insolvent, only *necessary* expenses may be incurred.

After the funeral, the duties of the personal representative are:

(1) to make an inventory of the deceased's estate;

(2) to seek probate or administration, as the case may be;

(3) to get in the estate;

(4) to pay the debts;

(5) to pay the legacies;

(6) to make necessary investments;

(7) to distribute the residue.

In carrying out his duties, or exercising his powers in the administration, any one of several personal representatives alone can generally bind the estate, since each has full power with regard to the administration and the acts of one of them are deemed to be the acts of all (*Owen* v. *Owen*); but he cannot effect a conveyance or assent of real estate without the concurrence of all the representatives or an order of the court (A.E.A. 1925, s. 2 (2); *see* § 5 *post*). Moreover, one executor cannot bind his fellow-executors, unless they concur, since he is not entitled to impose fresh liabilities on them (*Turner* v. *Hardey*).

A sole executor can give a valid receipt for the proceeds of sale under a settlement or trust for sale (L.P.A. 1925, s. 27) but in general not fewer than two trustees or a trust corporation can give a valid discharge for such proceeds (*See* further as to this, § 10 *post*.)

Every person becoming executor in the chain of representation to a testator has the same rights in respect of the real and personal estate of that testator as the original executor would have had, if living, and is, to the extent to which the estate, whether real or personal, of that testator has come to his hands, answerable as if he were an original executor (A.E.A. 1925, s. 7 (4)). An administrator *de bonis non* has the same powers and is subject to the same liabilities with respect to the assets he is called upon to administer as if he were the original representative.

§ 3. Vesting of Property

On the death of a person his estate, both real and personal, vests in his personal representative, who becomes endowed with full powers to deal with it for the purpose of administration. It must be remembered, that although the *title* of the executor or administrator is absolute, his interest is qualified. He takes the property upon trust to apply it in payment of the debts of the deceased and to administer it in accordance with the provisions of the will (if there be one) and with the law. If the personal representative be executor of the deceased, he derives his authority from the will of his testator (*Comber's Case*), and probate is merely legal recognition of that authority (*Smith* v. *Milles*). If he be administrator, his authority emanates solely from the court, and does not exist until letters of administration are granted (*Comber's Case, supra*).

It follows from this that an executor can, before the grant of probate, act in any way necessary to protect the estate. He may assent to a legacy, get in and receive the testator's estate, release debts, assign property, and in fact do everything except compel the payment of money, since for this, evidence of authority, viz., the production of probate, is necessary. He may commence an action but cannot carry it beyond the point where he must prove his title (*Wankford* v. *Wankford*). His acts stand even if he dies without proving the will (*Kelsey* v. *Kelsey*).

The administrator, on the other hand, has, strictly speaking, no authority till letters are granted, but, in order to allow him to protect the estate, the letters of administration, when granted, are deemed in law to relate back to the death, so that the administrator is enabled, even before the grant, to do any acts of a beneficial nature which are necessary for the protection of the estate (*Tharpe* v. *Stallwood*). This doctrine of relation back of an administrator's title to the date of the intestate's death has no application, however, to actions at law, and no action can be commenced by an administrator before the grant is made (*Ingall* v. *Moran*), with the apparent exception, under the Administration of Estates Act, s. 2, of an action in respect of a trespass against real estate (including chattels real (A.E.A., s. 3 (1)). He may obtain the appointment of a receiver to prevent a wrong to the estate (*In the goods of Pryse*) and see *Ingall* v. *Moran*).

Although the personal representative is invested with dominion over the estate of the deceased, the trusts for due administration which are impressed upon his title require him not to sell any part of the deceased's property unless realisation is directed by the will (if any) or is necessary to pay debts due from the deceased or to preserve the estate, or is in pursuance of a discretion duly exercised under a trust for sale arising by operation of law, as upon an intestacy. Notwithstanding this limitation upon the personal representative's power of sale, a purchaser for value from him will acquire a good title even though a sale of the particular property is not authorised or otherwise justifiable in the interests of the estate. A conveyance of a legal estate is not invalidated by reason only that the purchaser may have notice that all debts, liabilities, funeral and testamentary or administration expenses, duties and legacies have been discharged or provided for (so that there appears to be no occasion for the personal representative to sell at all) (A.E.A. 1925, s. 36 (8)).

A transfer to a purchaser for value will confer a good title upon him despite the fact that, prior to the conveyance, the executor has assented to a devise or bequest of the subject-matter of the transfer, provided the purchaser has obtained from the executor a written declaration that he has not given an assent in respect of the property in question, and provided further that notice of a previous assent or conveyance has not been annexed to the probate or administration (*ibid.*, s. 36 (6)).

That revocation of a grant does not prejudicially affect a purchaser for value has already been seen (Chapter II, § 5 *supra*).

§ 4. Personal Estate

An executor or administrator can sell, assign, mortgage, or pledge any portion of the personal estate. These transactions must be *bona fide* and done for the benefit of the estate; fraud or collusion may render such a transfer void (*Mead* v. *Lord Orrery*). He may also assign or sublet leasehold property (A.E.A. 1925, ss. 2 (1), 39; L.P.A. 1925, s. 28 (1) (as amended by the Law of Property (Amendment) Act 1926, Sch.); Settled Land Act 1925, s. 41).

Trust property of which the deceased was sole trustee vests in the personal representative (A.E.A. 1925, § 1), who may in writing appoint himself or some other person to be a trustee in the place of the deceased (Trustee Act 1925, s. 36 (1)). Where the deceased was not sole trustee, the vacancy would be filled according to the terms of the trust.

Partnership property, even if it includes real estate, is personalty and the personal representative has the power to make the surviving partners account for the share of the deceased partner (Partnership Act 1890, ss. 20, 22, 42).

Shares in companies are personal estate (Companies Act 1948, s. 73); the powers of the personal representative in relation thereto are dealt with in 7 (*j*) below.

The Bank of England may require all the representatives to join in a transfer of stock (National Debt Act 1870, s. 23).

§ 5. Real Estate

The *whole estate*, both real and personal, to which the deceased was entitled for an interest not ceasing on his death, vests in the executor or administrator. For the purposes of administration, or during a minority or life interest, or until distribution, the personal representative has power to sell, mortgage or charge both real and personal estate, and all the powers, discretions and duties conferred or imposed by law on trustees for sale (A.E.A. 1925, ss. 1, 2, 39). Additional powers of sale are conferred by the Trustee Act 1925, ss. 12, 16, and the Settled Land Act 1925, ss. 39, 40; of mortgaging by the Settled Land Act 1925, s. 71, and Trustee Act 1925, s. 16, and of leasing by the Settled Land Act 1925, s. 41. He may grant an option to take a lease, the option to be exercisable in a stated number of years, not exceeding ten (Settled Land Act 1925, s. 51), or accept a surrender of a lease (*ibid*. s. 52), or enter into a contract to effect a lease (*ibid*. s. 90).

At any time after the expiration of one year from the death of the owner of the land, if his personal representatives have failed, on the request of the person entitled to the land, to convey the land to that person, the court may, if it thinks fit, on the application of that person, and after notice to the personal representatives, order that the conveyance be made (A.E.A. 1925, ss. 43 (2), 44).

In granting administration, the High Court must have regard to the rights of all persons interested in the estate of the deceased or in the proceeds of sale thereof, and in particular, administration with the will annexed may be granted to a devisee or legatee. In regard to land settled otherwise than by the will of the deceased, administration may be granted to the trustees of the settlement. The appointment of trustees under a settlement as special executors in respect of the settled land (under A.E.A. 1925, s. 22) has already been considered (Chapter II, § 3, *supra*). Where the deceased died wholly intestate, administration must be granted to one or more of the persons interested in the residuary estate, if they apply, but as regards land settled previously to the death, it is granted to the trustees, if any, of the settlement, who are willing to act. If, however, by reason of the insolvency of the estate or other special circumstance, it appears to the court to be necessary or expedient to appoint as administrator some person other than the person normally entitled to a grant, the court may appoint such person as it thinks expedient (Supreme Court of Judicature (Consolidation) Act 1925, s. 162, as amended by the Administration of Justice Act 1928, s. 9).

An executor can sell the real estate, but anyone who deals with him can require the production of probate. An administrator could also sell or mortgage the real estate even before the grant of letters of administration, since the subsequent grant would make former acts valid, but in practice, a prospective purchaser or mortgagee will not accept the title offered by a representative vendor who cannot produce probate or grant of administration.

As regards real estate, where there is more than one personal representative, a conveyance cannot be made without the concurrence of all the representatives or an order of the court. Where probate is granted to one or some of a plurality of persons named as executors, conveyance of the real estate may be made by the proving executor or executors without an order of the court, and such a conveyance will be as effective as if all the persons named as executors had concurred in the conveyance (A.E.A. 1925, ss. 2 (2); 8).

Special personal representatives who have obtained a grant limited to settled land can dispose of the settled land, without reference to or concurrence of the general representatives. In the same way, the general representatives can dispose of the other property and assets without the concurrence of the special representatives (A.E.A. 1925, s. 24).

§ 6. The Executor's Year

Whilst the executor is not bound to distribute the estate before the expiration of one year, called the 'executor's year' (A.E.A. 1925, s. 44), yet he should not, if it can be avoided, so extend the period of administration. He should use all reasonable expedition (*Pearson* v. *Pearson*). The duty to exercise due diligence is owed to creditors and beneficiaries alike, though there is no rule of law that the executor must pay the debts of the testator within a year after the testator's death; but if the debts are not paid within the year, the onus of justifying the delay is on the executors (*Re Tankard; Tankard* v. *Midland Bank Executor and Trustee Co.*).

§ 7. Collecting the Assets

(a) The Inventory

When lawfully so required the personal representatives must exhibit on oath in court a true and perfect inventory and account of the real and personal estate of the deceased (A.E.A. 1925, s. 25). It is, therefore, always prudent for a personal representative to take an inventory of the assets which have come to him in that capacity.

An administrator is, by the terms of the bond, required to prepare an inventory if called upon to do so.

(b) Getting in the Estate

The personal representative should at once proceed to acquaint himself with all the details relating to the deceased's estate, getting it in, and generally exercising all proper controlling powers.

The personal representative of an occupier of land is, on the death of such occupier, entitled to *emblements*, that is, crops such as corn and other growth of the earth which are *annually* produced, not spontaneously but by labour and industry. If, however, the lands are specifically devised, the devise carries the *emblements* with it. The rule does not apply to fruit growing on trees or to planted trees, except trees, etc., grown by a nursery-man or gardener for resale; nor does it apply to ordinary grass, but it most likely applies to the grasses such as clover, sainfoin, etc., grown especially.

(c) Donationes Mortis Causa and Gifts Inter Vivos

A *donatio mortis causa* is a gift of an anomalous nature. It differs essentially from a perfect gift *inter vivos* in that it is conditional upon and revocable until the death of the donor; moreover, a disposition may be effectual as a *donatio*, notwithstanding that the mode and form of transfer which may be requisite in the case of a gift *inter vivos* have not been adopted.

To take effect as a *donatio mortis causa*, the gift must be made by the donor (*a*) in contemplation of death, (*b*) subject to the condition that it is not to take effect if the donor recovers, and (*c*) by way of delivery to the donee or to someone on his behalf, i.e., the donor must part with dominion over the subject matter.

A *donatio* will not be vitiated by reason of the fact that the donor dies from a cause other than that upon which his expectation of death was founded, so long as it was made in his last illness. Thus, where a donor made a gift prior to a proposed operation which was not, however, performed, and died two days later from another cause, the gift was held to be a valid *donatio* (*In re Richards, Jones* v. *Rebbeck*). Similarly, where a person lying ill with cancer, made a gift, but actually died a few weeks later from pneumonia, the gift was held to be a valid *donatio* (*Wilkes* v. *Allington*).

The condition that the gift is to take effect only if and when the donor dies will be implied wherever the donor has made the *donatio* in his last illness and there is nothing to establish that it was not *mortis causa* (*Gardner* v. *Parker*).

The subject matter of the *donatio* must be DELIVERED or the effective means of obtaining possession thereof transferred to the donee, e.g. in the case of bulky goods, the delivery of the key of the building where they were stored was held to be valid delivery of the goods forming the *donatio* (*Ward* v. *Turner*).

A *donatio mortis causa*, unlike a gift *inter vivos*, is necessarily revoked if the donor recovers from the illness under which death was contemplated which existed at the time the *donatio* was made; it is ambulatory until death and may be reclaimed from the donee on a deficiency of assets for the purpose of paying the testator's debts (*Drury* v. *Smith*).

The following are good *donationes*': delivery of negotiable instruments, e.g. a promissory note, bill of exchange, or cheque of a third party, payable to order, even though not indorsed; mortgage deeds; bonds; policies of assurance; a post office savings bank deposit book; banker's deposit receipts (but not a deposit account book (*Delgoffe* v. *Fader*)); and national savings certificates. A cheque given by the drawer *mortis causa*, and presented to and paid by the bank upon which it was drawn after the drawer's death, but without notice of that fact by the bank, was held to be good (*Tate* v. *Hilbert*). The following are *not* good *donationes*': the delivery of a certificate of building society shares, railway stock, or title deeds; the deceased's own cheque, unless paid or presented for payment or negotiated for value before notice of the donor's death is given to the bank (*Rolls* v. *Pearce*), in which case the gift takes the semblance of a perfected gift *inter vivos* (cf. *Re Owen*, below); a cheque of the donor presented after death where the account is overdrawn (*Re Beaumont*); and a promissory note made by the donor (*Re Leaper*), (unless, presumably, it was cashed or negotiated before the donor's death.

In *Re While*, A., in expectation of death, gave his wife a cheque equivalent to the balance of his current account at a bank. He had previously sent for the bank manager, who arrived at 11 a.m. The wife handed the cheque to him with instructions to open an account in her name. The manager departed with the cheque, the bank being only a few minutes' walk away. A. died at 12.30 p.m. It was held that the gift was valid, the manager having received the cheque from the wife in exercise of his authority, and the transaction having been completed within the lifetime of the donor. A. also drew a cheque for £200 in favour of his wife on an account at another bank, this also being handed to the bank manager. The cheque was, however, by mistake post-dated, and this gift was held to be inoperative.

If a *donatio mortis causa* is made, but the donor recovers, and the subject matter is not reclaimed or surrendered, it is presumed that the intention of the parties is to confirm the gift, and it will then assume the character and be subject to the incidents of a gift *inter vivos*.

Reference should be made to Chapter XIV, § 3 (*f*) for comparison of a *donatio mortis causa* with a legacy.

A gift *inter vivos* is an absolute gift made during the lifetime of the donor without reference to special circumstances such as accompany a *donatio mortis causa*. Whatever may be requisite to complete the title of the donee must have been accomplished. A gift of money by means of a cheque drawn by the donor is not complete until the cheque has been cashed (*Re Owen*), or negotiated for value to a third party (*Rolls* v. *Pearce*). The execution of a transfer of shares in proper form and its delivery to the transferee normally completes a gift of the shares in question; the date of registration of the transfer is irrelevant (*Re Rose*, *Rose* v. *C.I.R.*). If Treasury consent is required, however, the gift is not complete till the consent has been obtained (*re Fry*). Should a donor instruct a broker to buy shares for a donee, the gift is completed when he passes the donee's name to the broker on the Stock Exchange 'name day' (*re Smith, Bull* v. *Smith*).

A *donatio mortis causa* is ALWAYS subject to Estate Duty (F.A. 1894, s. 2); gifts *inter vivos* are subject to Estate Duty ONLY IF MADE WITHIN SEVEN YEARS (if to a charity or for public purposes, one year) OF DEATH or where they were subject to a reservation by the donor or where the donor has retained an interest in the property. In both cases the donee is liable for any duty payable (F.A. 1894, s. 9).

It has already been observed that absence of due formality of transfer which would be fatal to a gift *inter vivos* will not defeat the operation of a *donatio mortis causa*. Thus the delivery of a cheque drawn by a third party payable to the donor's order and not indorsed by him is imperfect as a gift *inter vivos* but will be effective as a *donatio*. For this reason the donee may, after the donor's death, seek to invest a gift with the character of a *mortis causa* donation.

It is not all property that can form the subject of a gift *mortis causa*, e.g. realty and leaseholds cannot, for an actual or constructive delivery must be possible.

(d) Bills of Exchange

The personal representative may indorse or assign a promissory note or bill of exchange payable to the deceased or his order but he avoids personal liability thereon by indorsing in his representative capacity (Bills of Exchange Act 1882, s. 31). If a debtor gives to his creditor a blank acceptance for a certain sum and the creditor dies before the instrument is completed, his personal representative may fill up the paper as a bill payable to drawer's order, insert his own name as drawer and enforce payment of the bill against the acceptor (*Scard* v. *Jackson*). Presentment, notice of dishonour, and payment should be made by or to the executor or administrator.

Where the drawee of a bill is dead, presentment for acceptance may be made to his personal representative; but the holder may instead treat the bill as dishonoured without presentment (Bills of Exchange Act 1882, s. 41). Presentment for payment must be made to the personal representative if with reasonable diligence he can be discovered (*ibid*, s. 45).

(e) Patents

The personal representative can apply for a patent for an invention of which the deceased died possessed, but the application must contain a declaration by the applicant that he believes the deceased was the true and first inventor (Patents Act 1949, s. 1).

(f) Contracts

Generally speaking, contracts made by the deceased are binding on the personal representative; and if a joint contract was in progress at the time of death, the representative of the deceased is entitled to a share of the profits, not estimated, but actually gained at the completion of the contract (*McLean* v. *Kennard*).

The personal representative is not liable, however, on the contracts of the deceased so far as they were of a purely personal nature, such as an agency, or where the personal care or skill of the deceased was essential for their performance (*Farrow* v. *Wilson; Wentworth* v. *Cock*). These contracts are discharged by the impossibility of performance brought about by the death of the deceased party.

(g) Rights of Action

The old rule *actio personalis moritur cum persona* (that personal rights of action die with the death of a party) now applies only where the cause of action is defamation, seduction, inducing one spouse to leave or remain apart from the other, or adultery. In all other cases causes of action subsisting against or vested in the deceased survive against or, as the case may be, for the benefit of, his estate. Where a cause of action survives for the benefit of the estate, the damages recoverable (*a*) shall not include any exemplary damages; (*b*) in the case of a breach of promise to marry shall be limited to such damage (if any) to the estate as flows from the breach; and (*c*) where the death of that person was caused by the act or omission which gives rise to the cause of action, shall be calculated without reference to any loss or gain to his estate consequent on his death, except that a sum in respect of funeral expenses may be included (Law Reform (Miscellaneous Provisions) Act 1934, s. 1).

No proceedings are maintainable in respect of a cause of action in tort which has survived *against* the estate, unless either (*a*) proceedings against the deceased in respect of that cause of action were pending at the date of his death, or (*b*) proceedings are taken in respect thereof not later than six months after his personal representative took out representation (Law Reform (Limitation of Actions, etc.) Act 1954). Such a claim would be statute-barred under the Limitation Act 1939 if made more than six years after the right of action accrued; but that Act provides that the limitation is not to apply if some other Act sets another limit (see *Airey* v. *Airey*). If proceedings were not pending at the date of death and were statute-barred at that date, however, it appears that no proceedings could be taken by the personal representative.

If a person dies before or at the same time as the damage has been suffered as a result of his wrongful act or omission, a cause of action is deemed to have subsisted against him before his death.

If the estate against which the proceedings are maintainable is insolvent, any liability in respect of the cause of action is a debt provable in the administration of the estate, notwithstanding that it is a demand in the nature of unliquidated damages arising otherwise than by a contract, promise or breach of trust (Law Reform (Miscellaneous Provisions) Act 1934, s. 1).

If the death of the deceased was caused by the wrongful act, neglect or default of some person, so that an action for damages could have been brought by the deceased if he had lived, the personal representative can commence an action for the benefit of the wife, husband, parent or child of the deceased (Fatal Accidents Act 1846, s. 1, 'Lord Campbell's Act'). The Fatal Accidents Act 1959, extended the classes of dependants for whose benefit or by whom an action may be brought under the Fatal Accidents Act 1846 to include any person who is, or is the issue of, a brother, sister, uncle or aunt of the deceased person. The relationship with the deceased for the purposes of the Act may be by adoption, by affinity, as a brother, etc., of the half blood and any step-child of any person is treated as that person's child and an illegitimate person as the legitimate child of his mother and reputed father. There are consequential amendments to the Law Reform (Married Women and Tortfeasors)

Act 1935 and the Carriage by Air Act 1932. Assessment of any damages is not to take into account any insurance money, benefit, pension or gratuity which has been or will or may be paid as a result of the death. The court may give such damages as it may think proportioned to the material damage resulting from the death to the parties for whose benefit the action is brought, and the net amount recovered must be divided among such persons in such shares as the court directs. The foundation of a claim under this enactment is the dependency of the person for whom damages are sought upon the person whose death resulted from the wrongful act of the defendant. The action must be commenced within three years after the death unless extended by leave of the Court where—

(i) the plaintiff did not know 'material facts of a decisive character' (although he had taken all reasonable steps to find out) within that period, or until less than twelve months before the end of that period, in sufficient time to commence proceedings before the expiry of the three-year period; and

(ii) that he continued to be ignorant of such facts until a date not more than twelve months before he commenced proceedings (Limitation Act 1963).

In the case of a deceased person, if the deceased could have satisfied the above conditions before he died, the elapse of the three-year period will not defeat claims providing proceedings are commenced—

(a) within twelve months of the date when the deceased first knew, or could have known, the relevant facts, or

(b) within twelve months of the death where the deceased did not know and could not have known the facts before his death.

If the executor or administrator does not bring an action within six months of the death, an action may be brought by the persons beneficially interested in the result (Fatal Accidents Act 1864, s. 1). For these purposes, the term 'parent' includes a father, mother, grandfather, grandmother, stepfather and step-mother; and the term 'child' includes a son, daughter, grand-child or stepchild (Fatal Accidents Act 1846, s. 5) and a legitimated child (Legitimacy Act 1926, s. 6 (1)). A person is deemed to be the parent or child of the deceased person notwithstanding that he was only related to him illegitimately or in consequence of adoption, any illegitimate person and any adopted person being treated as the legitimate offspring of his mother and reputed father or, as the case may be, of his adopters, provided the adoption was in pursuance of an order under what is now the Adoption Act 1958 (Law Reform (Miscellaneous Provisions) Act 1934, s. 2).

Damages under the Fatal Accidents Act may be awarded in respect of funeral expenses if the expenses were incurred by the parties for whose benefit the action is brought (*ibid.* s. 2).

Independently of, and in addition to, any action under Lord Campbell's Act, on behalf of dependants, the personal representative can claim for the benefit of the deceased's estate damages in respect of (i) the pain and suffering caused to the deceased by the circumstances which culminated in his death, and (ii) the loss of expectation of life (*Rose* v. *Ford*).

Each party to a marriage has the same right of action in tort against the other as if they were not married. The Court can stay such an action brought while the marriage subsists if it appears that no substantial benefit would accrue to either party from the proceedings, or that the question(s) in issue could be more conveniently disposed of under Section 17, Married Women's Property Act 1882.

Under the Carriage by Air Act 1932, an action against the carrier in the event of the death of a passenger is maintainable for the benefit of such of the members of the passenger's family as sustained damage by reason of his death. The term 'member of a family' means wife or husband, parent, step-parent, grandparent, brother, sister, half-brother, half-sister, child, step-child, grandchild. An illegitimate person or adopted person is treated as being, or as having been, the legitimate child of the mother and reputed father or, as the case may be, of the adopters. The action must be brought within two years from the date on which the aircraft ought to have arrived or did arrive at its destination. This is in substitution for any other liability of the carrier in respect of the death.

Assessment of damages under the Fatal Accidents Act 1846, or the Carriage by Air Act 1932, is not to take into account any insurance money (including a return of premiums), benefit, pension or gratuity (including a return of contributions and any lump sums in respect of a person's employment) which has been or will or may be paid as a result of the death. 'Benefit' here means benefit under the National Insurance Acts 1946 (as amended by any later Act) and any payment by a friendly society or trade union for the relief or maintenance of a member's dependants (Fatal Accidents Act 1959, s. 2).

Damages under the Law Reform Act form part of the deceased's estate and are liable to Estate Duty. Damages under the Fatal Accidents Act or the Carriage by Air Act do not form part of the estate and are not liable to Estate Duty. Death benefit is payable in certain circumstances under the National Insurance (Industrial Injuries) Act 1965 where the deceased was an insured person. Payment is made, as the case may be, to the widow, widower, children or other relative of the deceased person (ss. 19–24). It is not part of the estate of the deceased for the purposes of Estate Duty. A death grant is payable on the death of an insured person or his dependant provided certain contribution requirements have been fulfilled (National Insurance Act 1965, s. 39). Such a grant is not part of the estate for Estate Duty purposes and does not affect the allowance for funeral expenses.

A personal representative may sue for arrears of a rent-charge due or accruing to the deceased in his lifetime; he may distrain for such arrears on the land so affected or charged, so long as the land remains in the possession of the person liable to pay the rentcharge or of the persons deriving title under him, and in like manner as the deceased might have done had he been living. A personal representative may sue for arrears of rent accrued in the lifetime of the deceased (Law Reform (Misc. Provisions) Act 1934, s. 1). He may also distrain upon land for arrears of rent due or accruing to the deceased in the same way as the deceased might have done had he been living. Such arrears may be distrained for after the termination of the lease or tenancy, provided the distress is made:

(a) within six months after the termination of the lease or tenancy;

(b) during the continuance of the possession of the lessee or tenant from whom the arrears were due (A.E.A. 1925, s. 26).

(h) Collection of Debts

The personal representative must get in all debts due to the estate, suing for them if necessary, and if by unreasonable delay or negligence there results a detriment to the estate, e.g. by allowing a debt to become statute-barred, he will be liable in respect thereof as for a *devastavit* (*Hayward* v. *Kinsey*). He is not, however, bound to waste money by suing when there is reasonable ground for believing that recovery is hopeless (*Clack* v. *Holland*). If the representative himself owes a debt to the estate it is a rule of equity that he is deemed to have paid the debt to himself and the amount thereof is regarded as an asset of the estate in his hands. As to that amount he is considered a trustee with all a trustee's liabilities (*In re Bourne, Davey* v *Bourne*); but evidence may be produced to show that it was the intention of the testator to forgive the debt (*Freakley* v. *Fox; Leveson* v. *Beales*).

Should the executor be jointly and severally responsible with other persons in respect of a debt due to the testator (e.g. on a promissory note), the executor is deemed to have discharged the debt at probate and to have assets of the testator in his hands to that extent. As the release of one joint debtor discharges all the joint debtors, the other parties are similarly released, and the executor cannot maintain an action at law in his capacity of executor for the payment of the sum due from his co-promisors (*Jenkins* v. *Jenkins*). Since he is deemed in equity to have paid the debt, he would have a right in his personal capacity to claim contribution from his co-promisors.

The personal representative may compound, accept security for payment of, abandon, submit to arbitration, or otherwise settle any debt, account, claim or thing whatever relating to the estate of a testator or intestate, and may give releases accordingly (Trustee Act 1925, s. 15) so long as he acts *bona fide* for the benefit of the estate.

(i) Carrying on the Business of the Deceased

The general rule is, that a trade or business carried on by the deceased alone is ended by his death, and neither an executor nor an administrator has any right to buy and sell in the course of the business so as to carry it on further than may be necessary to enable him beneficially to wind it up, and, if necessary, sell it as a going concern; but so far as it is necessary to carry it on in order to sell it as a going concern, the representative is entitled to an indemnity out of the estate against all liabilities properly incurred in so doing (*Dowse* v. *Gorton*).

The executors must perform uncompleted contracts not discharged by the death of the deceased and must therefore carry on the business to that extent, e.g. where the deceased had contracted to build a house, his executors would be liable in damages if they did not complete the contract (*Marshall* v. *Broadhurst*).

If the business is carried on beyond what is necessary to wind it up or sell as a going concern, all profits belong to the estate (*Luntley* v. *Roydon*); while losses fall on the executor or administrator personally, and he has no right of indemnity against either the business assets or any other assets (*Owen* v. *Delamere*). It is therefore wise for a personal representative to obtain an indemnity from the beneficiaries.

To entitle the executor to carry on the business further than is necessary for the purpose of realisation, there must be a distinct and positive authority and direction given by the will for that purpose (*Kirkman* v. *Booth*). The executor is then, though still personally liable for debts incurred, entitled to be indemnified out of the specific assets which he is authorised to employ in the business (*ex parte Garland*). If no specific assets are mentioned, a direction to carry on the business only authorises the executor to use the capital of the business for that purpose (*McNellie* v. *Acton*). Unless authorised by the will, the executor must not enter into transactions where his personal interest would conflict with his representative duty (*Re Thompson*).

If the will gives power to postpone sale and conversion of the estate, the executors can carry on the business at their discretion, whether with a view to sale or not (*Re Ball*). The power ceases on the estate becoming divisible (*ibid.*). The personal representatives of an intestate have power to postpone sale and conversion (A.E.A. 1925, s. 23) and thus, by inference, power to carry on the business with the capital therein invested. It is, however, doubtful if the personal representatives could employ in the business other assets of the deceased.

Persons who have become creditors since the death of the

testator, are subrogated to the executor, and are entitled to stand in his place as regards his right of indemnity against the specific assets authorised to be used in carrying on the business. If it be shown that the executor was carrying on the business with the consent, and therefore as agent of, the beneficiaries, the creditors are subrogated to the executor's right against the estate generally (*ex parte Garland, supra*). This right of subrogation and indemnity will also be effectual even against creditors of the deceased, if it be shown that the executor has carried on the business with their knowledge and consent, and therefore to some extent as their agent; but only where they have definitely assented, a mere abstinence from objecting not being sufficient to make them liable (*London County and Westminister Bank* v. *East*). If the deceased's creditors have not assented, their claim against the assets of the estate, including the business, has priority over claims of those who become creditors after the death.

An executor who has carried on the business without authority has no right of indemnity to which the creditors can claim subrogation, and their rights are accordingly confined to action against the executor personally.

(*j*) Shares in Companies

These vest in the personal representative but not so as to constitute him *ipso facto* a member of the company. He is entitled to require the company to enter his name upon the register in place of that of the deceased shareholder. If he does so, the personal representative becomes a member of the company and personally liable in respect of the shares registered in his name, with a right to indemnify himself out of the assets in his hands where he is required to pay calls upon the shares. Alternatively, he may merely notify the company of his representation of the deceased shareholder without requiring entry of his name upon the register. Then the estate alone is liable for calls, while the personal representative is entitled (subject to the articles of association of the company) to deal with the shares, e.g. by transfer, in the same way that the deceased could have done. Even here, the personal representative may incur an indirect liability where he distributes the estate without making provision for the contingency that unpaid capital in respect of the shares may be called up (*Taylor* v. *Taylor*, and see Chapter XIII, *post*).

(k) Choses in Action

With regard to *choses in action* generally, i.e. intangible legal or equitable rights to which the estate is entitled (shares and debts are examples), the personal representative should investigate their character and condition. If they consist of authorised securities they should be left undisturbed unless realisation is requisite to meet claims against the estate; in other cases he should realise them, and invest the proceeds in authorised securities. Where the deceased entered into an agreement prior to his death with his nephew, under which the latter agreed to pay an annuity during the deceased's life and thereafter the deceased's widow, the widow, as administratrix of her husband's estate, could sue the nephew for specific performance of the agreement. She was thus able to receive her annuity, which she could not have sued for in her own right since she was not a party to the contract (*Beswick* v. *Beswick*).

(l) Leaseholds

Where a leasehold interest in land is created, the grant is made subject to the imposition of certain undertakings or 'covenants' upon the lessee. The legal obligations arising out of these covenants affect the lessee in two independent aspects. First, he is bound by them in virtue of his having contracted with the lessor to observe them, i.e. by reason of the contractual relationship, technically termed 'privity of contract', which exists between covenantor and covenantee; and, secondly, certain of the covenants attach themselves to the interest or estate in the land to which they relate, and bind the lessee as the person in whom that interest is vested. The covenants which so attach themselves to the leasehold interest are those 'touching and concerning' the land or, in other words, affecting it directly, such as an undertaking to keep in repair. This secondary liability is founded upon the 'privity of estate', that is to say, the relationship subsisting between the parties as the grantor and holder respectively of a particular interest in land.

So long as the lease remains with the lessee, the obligations arising from the privity of estate overlap those which fall upon him by reason of his privity of contract with the lessor. The independence of the two sets of liabilities becomes significant when the lessee assigns the whole (residue) of the lease. In such a case he remains bound to the lessor by reason of the *privity of contract* which persists between them, while the *privity of estate* (together with the obligations dependent upon it) is shifted to the lessor and the assignee who, without having made any contract whatsoever with the original lessor, may be sued by him for breach of any of the covenants created with the lease which 'touch and concern' the land.

Illustration

In 1950, A. let Whiteacre to B. for a term of years, of which 50 remain unexpired. By his covenants in the lease B. undertook *inter alia* to keep the demised premises in good and tenantable repair. He now assigns the residue to his lease to C. The obligations created by these covenants are not *contractually* enforceable by A. against C., for there is no 'privity of contract' between them—they have not been complementary parties to any contract relating to Whiteacre. But the burden of such of the covenants in the original lease as affect directly the land demised (e.g. to keep it in repair), must be borne by C. as between him and A., for C. now owns the estate in the land in respect of which the covenants were undertaken.

B. remains contractually liable to A. upon all the covenants in the original lease, for liabilities under a contract cannot be assigned and the 'privity of contract' between A. and B. is undisturbed by the assignment unless A. grants a release to B. from his obligations.

As between B. and C. there is no 'privity of estate' (for B. no longer has any interest in the land itself), but there is a 'privity of contract' by reason of the fact that on every assignment of leasehold property there is an implied covenant between assignor and assignee that the assignee will perform and observe the covenants of the lease and keep the assignor indemnified against any breach.

The devolution upon the personal representative of a leasehold interest to which the deceased was entitled involves an executor or administrator in liabilities springing from one or both of the two sources indicated. Where the deceased was the original lessee and retained the lease until his death, the representative will be bound to the lessor by privity of contract and privity of estate. If the deceased had assigned the lease in his lifetime, the personal representative is liable, as was the deceased, upon the covenants in the lease by reason of the persistence of the contractual obligations derived from privity of contract with the lessor, although there is no longer any privity of estate. If the executor or administrator should, however, be sued in this regard for a breach of covenant committed after assignment, he will be entitled to claim indemnity from the assignee, who is deemed primarily liable for breaches occurring during the subsistence of his interest.

Where, on the other hand, the deceased was himself the assignee of a lease, because there was only privity of estate between the deceased and the lessor the executor can be liable only in respect of breaches of covenant committed since that privity was established, that is to say, since the assignment to his deceased.

Moreover, an assignment by the personal representative of the deceased's interest as assignee will preclude liability to the lessor for future breaches by the tenant in possession, for there will no longer be any privity of estate between the original lessor and the personal representative (*Rowley* v. *Adams*). The personal representative will remain liable under the express or implied covenant of indemnity to the person who assigned the lease to the deceased, even for breaches committed after assignment by the personal representative (see *Butler Estates Co.* v. *Bean*), although he will have a right of indemnity against his assignee.

As a rule, the personal representative will be liable in any case only in his representative capacity, so that he cannot be made liable beyond the value of the assets which have come into his hands; but if he should enter into and assume occupation of the demised premises he would incur a personal liability.

When sued *quâ* representative, the executor can plead *plene administravit*, but this answer cannot be raised to a claim for rent accrued after he has entered (*Helier* v. *Casbert*).

Again, where the testator was the original lessee and assigned the lease during his lifetime, his executor cannot be liable as assignee, for no estate vests in him; but he will remain liable upon the *contract* between the deceased and the lessor (*Coghil* v. *Freelove*).

Upon the principle that an executor, if he accepts office, assumes *all* its attendant liabilities, he cannot waive a lease held by the deceased, although he may, if he can induce the lessor to consent, surrender the lease where the value of the land is less than the rent payable.

The difficulties arising from the fact that the personal

representative could not obviate liability in respect of leaseholds by distributing the estate (except under order of the court), were mitigated by the 1925 legislation, which permits the personal representative (after satisfying all liabilities already accrued due and claimed, and, where necessary, setting aside a sufficient fund to answer any future claims that may be made in respect of any fixed and ascertained sum covenanted by the lessee to be laid out on the property) to convey the property to the purchaser, legatee or devisee or other person entitled to call for a conveyance thereof. The representative may thereafter distribute the residuary estate without appropriating any part, or any further part, as the case may be, to meet any future liability under the lease, and, notwithstanding such distribution, he will not be personally liable in respect of any subsequent claim under the lease. The above provisions operate without prejudice to the lessor's rights to follow the assets of the deceased (Trustee Act 1925, s. 26, as amended by Law of Property (Amendment) Act 1926, s. 7). This only protects personal representatives as such; it does not protect them in the matter of personal liability which they may incur by privity of estate if they enter into possession. In such a case, they may set aside out of the estate a fund sufficient to indemnify them against liabilities in which such privity may involve them (*Re Owers; Public Trustee* v. *Death* (No. 2)).

(*m*) *Share in a Partnership*

Where the surviving partners continue the business without any final settlement of accounts between the firm and the deceased partner's estate, then, in the absence of any agreement to the contrary, the estate is entitled, at the option of the personal representatives, to such share of the profits made since the dissolution as the court may find to be attributable to the use of his share of the partnership assets, or to interest at 5 per cent. per annum on the amount of his partnership assets. If, however, an option is given by the partnership contract to the surviving partners to purchase the deceased's interest, and that option is duly exercised, the estate is not entitled to any further share of profits, but if any partner does not exercise the option exactly in accordance with the partnership contract, he must account as above (Partnership Act 1890, s. 42).

§ 8. Liability of the Executor

The personal representative is accountable for the whole estate of the deceased, in the sense that he will be required to show what has become of it and that it has been duly applied; and he is chargeable with all property which has come into his hands. This will include not only the assets which actually belonged to the deceased at the time of his death, but all property to which the executor becomes entitled by virtue of his executorship, such as money becoming due after death, the profits of a contract not completed at the death, natural accretion to the property, profits made by carrying on the business, or an increase of any kind.

He cannot purchase the assets himself, as this would give rise to a conflict of interest and duty which might cause him to neglect his duty to do all he can for the benefit of the estate. But if the executor is the surviving partner of the deceased, he can acquire the deceased's share in the business, since the deceased knew of the position (*Hordern* v. *Hordern*). And where, in an intestacy, the surviving husband or wife is one of two or more personal representatives, the rule that a trustee may not be a purchaser of trust property does not prevent the surviving husband or wife from purchasing the matrimonial home (Intestates' Estates Act 1952, s. 5 and 2nd Schedule).

For any negligence or omission in getting in or investing the estate, by which a loss is incurred, the personal representative may be liable as for a *devastavit*. This consists in any dealing with the estate, whether done wilfully or innocently, *bona fide* or *mala fide*, resulting in prejudice, where the conduct of the representative cannot be supported as according with his duty and the standard of care he is required to exercise in his administration. Whenever the assets are 'wasted' by the default, misconduct, negligence, or rashness of the representative, he is liable to make good the damage suffered directly by the estate and ultimately by those interested in it. Even if the executor acts on the best advice that he could obtain, his liability for a *devastavit* committed remains (*National Trustees Co. of Australasia* v. *General Finance Co.*).

Where a personal representative, owing to a mistake in interpreting the deceased's will, distributes assets among persons who are not entitled thereto, he is liable in respect of *devastavit*. In the case of *Re Diplock*, a testator bequeathed his residuary estate, valued at some £260,000, to such 'charitable or benevolent' objects as his executors might select. Such a bequest was invalid (see *Chichester Diocesan Fund and Board of Finance (Incorporated)* v. *Simpson*), but the executors in ignorance of that fact, proceeded to distribute the estate amongst 139 charitable institutions of their choice. Subsequently the next-of-kin, 48 in number, who were entitled on intestacy, challenged the distribution and took proceedings against the executors and the charities to whom the estate had been distributed. The claim against the executors personally was compromised by agreement, but that against the charities went forward. It was held that the claims of the next-of-kin against the executors were not statute-barred until the lapse of 12 years from the testator's death, and their next-of-kin were entitled to exercise against the charities the executors' right of tracing the money in equity, if means of identification or disentanglement from a mixed fund remained.

Where a person as personal representative (including an executor *de son tort*) of a deceased person wastes or converts to his own use any part of the real or personal estate of the deceased, and dies, his personal representative is, to the extent of the available assets of the defaulter, liable and chargeable in respect of such waste or conversion in the same manner as the defaulter would have been if living (A.E.A. 1925, s. 29).

If a will requires an executor to carry on the deceased's business, the executor will not be allowed to set up a similar business on his own account, as his interest might then conflict with the interests of the beneficiaries whom he is bound to protect (*Re Thomson, Thomson* v. *Allen*). Where the executor was already engaged in such a business, the testator presumably appointed him with this knowledge, and the right to continue that business is not prejudiced by acceptance of the appointment as executor.

Where trustees are appointed directors of a company in virtue of shares therein held by them as trustees, they must account for remuneration received by them as directors of the company (*Re Francis, Barrett* v. *Fisher*). Similarly, where the articles of a company provided that the trustees under a specified will might, so long as they held shares in the company, appoint directors, and by virtue of the shares which they held as trustees, they appointed themselves, it was held that their remuneration must be accounted for to the estate, as being received in a fiduciary capacity (*In re Macadam, Dallow* v. *Codd*). But where the trustees were directors of the company before they held any trust shares, the fees belong to them personally and need not be accounted for, even though they have the trust shares registered in their names in order to qualify them to continue as directors (*Re Dover Coalfield Extension Ltd*).

Where an executor, although not a party to a default by his co-executor, has negligently permitted or facilitated its commission, he will be liable in respect of the default. Thus, where an executor enabled his co-executor to assume entire possession of a portion of the estate without taking any steps to ensure its due destination, the innocent, but negligent, representative was held liable for its misapplication (*Macpherson* v. *Macpherson*).

The personal representative may be charged with interest at 4 per cent. per annum if he neglects to invest balances (*Robinson* v. *Robinson* [1852]; *Re Hulkes*). He may also be charged the interest on debts bearing interest which he fails to pay as soon as it is clear that assets are available for that purpose (*Hall* v. *Hallet*).

If he lends money at a low rate of interest to himself, when a higher rate might have been obtained on equally good security, he will be chargeable with the higher rate (*Forbes* v. *Ross*).

If the executor pays into his own banking account moneys belonging to the estate, so that they become mixed with his own moneys, the rule in *Clayton's Case* does not apply; he is presumed to draw on his own money and leave the estate money in the account·(*Re Hallett's Estate*), and the moneys can be followed by the persons entitled thereto. If the bank fails, the executor is liable to the estate (*Wren* v. *Kirton*).

Should the executor invest money or other assets in his own business, the beneficiaries have the option of taking any profit made, without being responsible for any losses, or of taking interest at 5 per cent. on the assets employed for the whole period (*Wedderburn* v. *Wedderburn*). The executor may even be charged compound interest (*Raphael* v. *Boehm*), as also in other cases where he ought to have accumulated money at compound interest (*Re Emmet's Estate; Emmet* v. *Emmet; Barclay* v. *Andrew*).

The rates of interest mentioned above were those taken in the cases cited. It must not be supposed that the same rate would necessarily be applied at all times, since the court takes all the contemporaneous facts into consideration.

If the executor has overpaid income to the life tenant, e.g. where the latter has received the whole income and not an equitable proportion thereof, where equitable apportionments apply (as to which see Chapter XI, §4), the executor is personally liable to the remainderman (*Dimes* v. *Scott*) even if the value of the capital passing to the remainderman has been increased by the postponement of conversion (*ibid*).

The representative will be released from liability for a *devastavit* if it has been concurred or acquiesced in by the parties injured (*Griffiths* v. *Porter*).

When an executor has fully administered an estate in accordance with law, a subsequent administrator *de bonis non* has, in that capacity, no right to recover from a beneficiary assets which have been paid to him in due course of administration (*Re Aldhous*). The Treasury Solicitor who had received the undisposed of estate as *bona vacantia* under a mistake of fact that there was no next-of-kin in the above case was willing to make the balance of the estate available for payment to the next-of-kin, but required the protection of an order of the court.

§ 9. Remuneration of Executor

An executor or administrator is not allowed to make any profit out of his office, and accordingly he is not entitled to remuneration unless the will so provides (or unless any of the exceptions relating to trustees apply—see Chapter XVI *post*).

If a solicitor or accountant be appointed executor, he is not bound to do any professional work which could not be done by a non-professional executor; but if he does any such work he can only charge out-of-pocket expenses (*Moore* v. *Frowd; Cradock* v. *Piper*), unless the will authorises him to make his usual professional charges (*Christophers* v. *White*); and even in this case he must only charge for actual professional work, and not for the ordinary work of an executor (*Newton* v. *Chapman*).

Even where the will gives authority for the executor to make the usual professional charges, if the estate should ultimately prove to be insolvent he can only charge out-of-pocket expenses, since the professional charges in excess of actual expenses are in the nature of a legacy, and legacies cannot be paid out of an insolvent estate (*Pennell* v. *Franklin*).

Where a legacy is left to an executor as such he is not entitled to the legacy if he does not act (*Slaney* v. *Watney*), but this rule does not apply to a gift of residue to an executor (*Griffiths* v. *Pruen*). If a legacy is given to a person in the character of executor, he must establish his title to it by proving the will with the intention of acting, or must take such steps as will show beyond doubt his intention to act, e.g. by arranging for the burial of the deceased. Incapacity to act will defeat his claim.

If a legacy be given to a person who is by the will appointed executor, although the legacy and the appointment are not specifically connected, there will be a presumption that the legacy was given to the executor in that character, but rebutting evidence to the contrary may be admitted (*In re Appleton*, *Barber* v. *Tebbit*).

An administrator *pendente lite* may be granted remuneration by the court, but in no other case is an individual administrator entitled to remuneration. But if a trust corporation (other than the Public Trustee) is appointed as trustee or personal representative, either solely or jointly with another person, the court may authorise the corporation to charge such remuneration for its services as the court may think fit (Trustee Act 1925, s. 42). A corporate body, entitled and qualified to act as a custodian trustee, which is appointed to that office and at the same time to that of sole managing trustee of the same trust estate, is not entitled to remuneration as a custodian trustee (*Forster* v. *Williams Deacon's Bank*).

§ 10. Personal Representatives distinguished from Trustees

A trustee is a person in whom the title to property has been vested, by declaration of trust *inter vivos* or by will, upon trust to apply the beneficial interest for the *cestuis que trustent* (or beneficiaries). The fiduciary duty of the trustee to deal with the property in accordance with the terms of the trust has always been enforceable in equity at the suit of the beneficiaries. A personal representative, on the other hand, is under a legal duty to apply the property which vests in him upon the death of the deceased in accordance with his declared testamentary intentions and the general law. This duty can be enforced in different ways, e.g. by an administration order or by application under the Rules of the Surpeme Court, Order LV, Rule 3, for determination of any question affecting the administration of the estate.

A will may appoint the same persons both executors and trustees, and in such case they will at some time cease to deal as executors with the property subject to the trusts and assume the character of trustees. This moment of time will be important in view of the provisions relating to Capital Gains tax. Even though in a strict sense the executor remains the personal representative till the whole property is actually distributed, yet he may become a trustee of certain portions of the property before this is fully accomplished. For instance, since the Land Transfer Act 1897, the personal representative is a constructive trustee of the real estate, which vests in him for the benefit of those entitled to it; and an administrator is a trustee for sale in respect of all the property, real and personal, of an intestate. Again, directly an executor has assented to a legacy, he becomes a trustee for the legatee; and in the case of a pecuniary legacy, when he has separated a specific fund from the general corpus of the estate and appropriated it to the satisfaction of the legacy, then he becomes a trustee for the amount. The mere *separation* of the sum from the corpus is not in itself sufficient thus to make the executor trustee; he must in addition have done some specific act, either by an entry in his books, or in some other way, by which he definitely indicates the appropriation of the fund to a special purpose (*Re Gompertz, Parker* v. *Gompertz*). An executor becomes trustee of the residuary estate at the date (called 'the date of retainer') when he has completed the administration and retained the residue in trust for the beneficiaries. It is a question to be answered on all the facts as to the point of time at which this occurs in any particular case.

The question as to whether an executor is acting as executor or trustee is very important as regards his powers and liabilities:

(*a*) One of several executors can, while acting as executor, bind the estate in all dealings with personalty without the concurrence of the other or others, so that he can sell or pledge any portion of the personalty and give a good title; whereas one of several trustees cannot give a good title without the assent of his co-trustees (*Attenborough* v. *Solomon*).

(*b*) A majority of trustees cannot bind a minority. If trustees are given power to sell property if they think fit, and the majority of the trustees desire to sell, but one trustee, in the *bona fide* exercise of his discretion, refuses to concur, the court will not intervene, and the property cannot be sold, even if the beneficiaries desire it (*Tempest* v. *Camoys*). But if there was a trust for sale with discretion to postpone, a dissenting trustee would be overridden by the court, as the duty to convert would prevail unless all the trustees agreed to postpone (*Re Hilton, Gibbes* v. *Hale-Hilton*).

(*c*) One of two or more executors can give an effective receipt, and the presumption is that the money is in the custody of the signatory. If, however, more than one executor signs, each is accountable for the sum acknowledged, unless it can be shown with regard to any of them that he was never in a position effectively to control the person actually receiving the money. Co-trustees, however, must all sign receipts, but where a trustee joins in a receipt for conformity only, without actually receiving the property in question, he will not, *by that circumstance alone*, be liable for a misapplication by the person actually receiving the property unless, through his own negligence, he allowed it to remain in the hands of a co-trustee for an unreasonable time (Trustee Act 1925, s. 30). The receipt of a sole trustee or personal representative for personal property is a sufficient discharge to the person paying, assigning or transferring it, but a sole *trustee*, except where the trustee is a trust corporation, cannot give a valid receipt for:

(i) proceeds of sale or other capital money arising under a trust for sale of land;

(ii) capital money arising under the Settled Land Act 1925 (Trustee Act 1925, s. 14, as amended by Law of Property (Amendment) Act 1926, s. 7). A sole personal representative, however, can give a valid receipt for the proceeds of sale of land (Law of Property Act 1925, s. 27 (2), as amended by the 1926 Act, s. 7; A.E.A. 1925, s. 2 (1)).

(*d*) Action against a personal representative founded upon a *devastavit* must be brought within six years after the misapplication or improper dealing complained of, but the right to sue an executor for a specific or residuary legacy is not barred until the lapse of twelve years from the time when 'a present right to receive the same shall have accrued to some person capable of giving a discharge for or release of the same'. This will usually mean that the legatee is statute-barred twelve years from the date of death, when his right to the legacy arises, although his title is not perfected until the executor assents (*Waddell* v. *Harshaw*). The Limitation Act 1939 does not, however, bar the claim of a residuary legatee to assets only reduced into possession by the personal representative within twelve years of the commencement of the proceedings (see *re Welch*). With regard to interest on a legacy, the right to sue is barred at the expiration of six years. Action against a trustee for breach of trust must be brought within six years of the breach, unless the claim is based on fraud or fraudulent breach of trust or is for the recovery of trust property in the trustee's possession or converted to his own use (Limitation Act 1939, s. 19).

The Trustee Act 1925 sets out, among other matters, various powers and duties of trustees, which are indicated in Chapter XVI, *post*. The Act provides that the expressions 'trust' and 'trustee' extend to the duties incident to the office of a personal representative, and that 'trustee', where the context admits, includes a personal representative. 'Trustees for sale' means the persons (including a personal representative) holding land on trust for sale. It therefore follows that the powers and duties of trustees are also powers and duties of personal representatives, except where the different nature of the offices requires otherwise. For example, investments authorised by law for the investment of trust funds are also authorised for the investment of moneys in the hands of a personal representative, although the point would not normally arise in the case of the latter, for his duty is to distribute the estate rather than invest it. A trustee can appoint agents in certain circumstances; so therefore can a personal representative. A trustee is not generally entitled to remuneration; nor is a personal representative. A trustee may be relieved from liability for breach of trust, if he has acted honestly, reasonably and excusably; so may a personal representative. These various matters, which are common to both trustees and personal representatives, are dealt with in Chapter XVI, *post*, and that chapter should be read as applying also to personal representatives, except when the context otherwise requires.

§ 11. Distribution of the Estate

When the executor has paid the funeral expenses, debts and testamentary expenses, provided for the liabilities of the deceased and collected the assets (and converted them, as far as may be necessary, into money), he must distribute the estate in the proper order. The principal points to be borne in mind in paying creditors and beneficiaries are dealt with in Chapters XIII and XIV.

CHAPTER XIII

DISTRIBUTION OF THE ESTATE – CREDITORS

§ 1. Introduction

Having collected in the assets of the estate, the personal representative must discharge the liabilities of the estate. If there is any doubt as to whether there is sufficient assets to pay all liabilities, and probably in all cases, the personal representative should discharge the liabilities in the following order:

(1) The funeral, testamentary and administration expenses,

(2) The preferred debts in bankruptcy,

(3) The unsecured debts in bankruptcy,

(4) The deferred debts in bankruptcy.

As between debts of an equal class, the personal representative (except where he is an administrator and a creditor) can 'prefer' one creditor to another, i.e. he can pay one creditor but not another if there are insufficient assets to pay both. In the same situation and subject to him not being an administrator and a creditor, he can 'retain' assets to discharge a debt due to him and not pay another creditor of the same class as himself.

The rights of beneficiaries may be affected by the method or manner of payment by the personal representative. The classes of assets and the order in which debts are to be discharged out of those assets is laid down in Part II, First Schedule, Administration of Estates Act 1925. This order is determined by a process known as 'marshalling the assets'. A fuller explanation will be found in § 8 of this Chapter but the order is:

(1) Property of the deceased undisposed of by will, subject to the retention thereout of a fund sufficient to meet any pecuniary legacies.

(2) Property of the deceased, not specifically devised or bequeathed, but included in a residuary gift, subject to the retention thereout of a fund sufficient to meet any pecuniary legacies.

(3) Property of the deceased specifically appropriated or devised or bequeathed for the payment of debts.

(4) Property of the deceased charged with or devised or bequeathed subject to a charge for the payment of debts.

(5) The fund, if any, retained to meet pecuniary legacies.

(6) Property specifically devised or bequeathed rateably according to value.

(7) Property appointed by will under a general power, including the statutory power to dispose of entailed interests rateably according to value.

§ 2. Payment of Debts

Before any legacies are satisfied, it is the duty of the personal representative to discharge the debts and other liabilities of the deceased which survive him. For this purpose the representative must have recourse to the assets of the deceased and (as a general rule) will be liable for the payment of debts only to the extent of the assets which have, or but for his default would have, come into his hands.

Subject to the rights of encumbrancers, the real and personal estate, whether legal or equitable, of a deceased person, *to the extent of his beneficial interest* therein, and the real and personal estate of which the deceased, in pursuance of any general power, disposes by his will, are assets for payment of his debts and liabilities. Any disposition by will inconsistent with this provision is void as against the creditors. The court has power, where necessary, to administer the property for the purpose of the payment of debts and liabilities (A.E.A. 1925, s. 32).

The personal representative may pay debts and claims on any sufficient evidence, or may compromise any debts due to, or claims made on behalf of, the estate (Trustee Act 1925, s.15). However, neither an executor nor an administrator may compromise a debt due to the estate from himself, though one executor may, in a proper case, compromise a debt due from his co-executor (*Re Houghton, Hawley* v. *Blake*). The court has jurisdiction to direct whether or not a compromise should be made (*Re Ezekiel*). Statute-barred debts to which the Limitation Act has not been pleaded may properly be paid and should be, if there are sufficient assets (*Williamson* v. *Naylor*). If, however, the representative pays a debt to which the Limitation Act has been successfully pleaded in an action to recover it, he commits a *devastavit* for which he will be liable (*Midgley* v. *Midgley*). On the other hand, an executor may properly pay a statute-barred debt without the consent of his co-executor, though not, it would seem, against the latter's declared wish (*Norton* v. *Frecker*). Such a debt must not, in any case, be paid after the making of a decree for administration (*Re Wenham, Hunt* v. *Wenham*).

As has been seen, liability for the debts of the deceased attaches to the executor or administrator in his representative capacity and not, as a rule, in his personal character. Personal liability may, however, be incurred by the representative in special circumstances, e.g. for breach of covenant in a lease of land, where he has entered into possession (see Chapter XII, § 7, *supra*), or by paying a debt of lower degree before one of higher degree (see § 4, *post*).

Where the deceased had undertaken a guarantee, the executors must provide for the contingent liability thereon before they divide the estate. In doing so, however, they must see that the estate is not burdened with more than is legally due. This was well illustrated in a case where the deceased had guaranteed the payment of an annuity; the person liable to pay the annuity became bankrupt, and the annuitant claimed in the bankruptcy for the capital value of the annuity receiving a dividend thereon. The deceased's executors continued to pay the annuity after the date of adjudication. On the death of the life tenant of the deceased's estate, the bankrupt became entitled to a fifth share of the residue of that estate. The executors then purchased an annuity of the full amount guaranteed and claimed to retain out of the bankrupt's share of residue the full cost of that annuity plus the periodical payments made after the date of adjudication. It was held that, if the annuitant had not proved in the bankruptcy, the executors would have had to pay the annuity under the guarantee, and could then have proved in the bankruptcy in respect of their right of indemnity as sureties; since, however, the annuitant had, of her own accord, proved for the capital value, the executors could legally pass on to her only the difference between that sum and the dividend she had received, and therefore they could only deduct that difference in paying over the share of residue to the bankrupt's trustee (*In re Lennard, Lennard's Trustee* v. *Lennard*).

At the present time, debts due to foreign creditors can only be paid subject to the current restrictions on the remittance of currency to the countries concerned.

§ 3. Advertising for Claims

The personal representative is responsible for the due payment of debts and it is therefore prudent, though not obligatory, before paying any but the most urgent claims, for him to take advantage of the Trustee Act 1925, s. 27, by giving notice, by advertisement, to all persons having claims against, or an interest in, the estate to send in their claims before a certain date, being not less than two months after the date of the notice. The advertisement is directed at creditors and beneficiaries (the latter including legatees under the will or persons entitled to benefit on an intestacy) of whose existence or interest the personal representative is unaware; the representative would naturally be expected to communicate with creditors and beneficiaries known to him without waiting for a formal claim to be submitted.

The advertisement should appear in the *London Gazette* and, if the estate includes land and/or a business, in a local newspaper circulating in the district in which the land or business is situated. Where the estate is large and/or if the personal representative believes that creditors and beneficiaries may be spread throughout the country, it is usual (and advisable) for the notice also to appear in a national daily newspaper, e.g. *The Times*. If there is reason to believe that any claimants reside in a foreign country, the notice should be inserted in a newspaper of that country.

When the stipulated period of two months (or longer) has expired, the personal representative, then being protected against creditors or beneficiaries of whose claims he has not had notice, can safely distribute the estate after satisfying, or providing for, any claims of which he is then aware. If, without receiving formal notice, the representative is by any other means advised of a superior debt, he cannot safely pay a debt of an inferior rank without first providing for the former. The advertisement does not protect the personal representative if he knows of a claim, even if the claimant fails to answer the advertisement; the protection is against unknown claims (*Markwell's Case*).

The protection given to the representative will not prevent an unpaid creditor from following the assets into the hands of beneficiaries and recovering his debt (Trustee Act 1925, s. 27, as amended by the Law of Property (Amendment) Act 1926, Sch.).

§ 4. Order for Payment of Debts

Where the estate of the deceased is solvent, the order in which the claims of creditors are paid is not of primary importance since they will all ultimately receive full satisfaction. In an insolvent estate, however, the law deems certain liabilities of the estate to be entitled to prior satisfaction out of the available assets. These 'preferred' debts must accordingly be settled before any part of the estate is applied in paying the general or 'ordinary' debts. There may be other debts which are 'deferred', in the sense that they cannot be paid at all unless and until all other claims against the estate are satisfied.

The order of payment of debts, where the estate is insolvent, is as follows (A.E.A. 1925, 1st Sch.):

(1) The funeral, testamentary and administration expenses.

(2) Other unsecured debts in the same order as in bankruptcy, which order is determined by the provisions of the Bankruptcy Act 1914, as amended by the Companies Act 1947, and qualified by the creation of certain special priorities under specific Statutes. The relevant provisions are collated in § 7 of this Chapter.

In an insolvent estate, if the personal representative pays a debt of a particular class and it subsequently transpires that the assets remaining are insufficient to satisfy a debt of a prior class of which the representative had notice, he will be personally liable to pay to the creditor entitled to priority the amount of the deficiency, or the value of the inferior debt, whichever is the lower. Therefore, if the solvency of an estate is in doubt, the personal representative should pay debts in the order prescribed for insolvent estates, until it appears certain that the assets will be sufficient to provide for all expenses and claims against the estate.

Where the personal representative is sued for a debt due from the deceased, he should plead the existence of unsatisfied claims of higher degree against the estate, unless there are sufficient assets to pay the superior debts as well as that debt. Failure to raise the plea in the action will constitute admission by the representative that the assets are adequate, so that he will be liable to satisfy a judgment in favour of the inferior creditor and in addition, to restore, for the benefit of creditors of higher degree, the amount paid away under the judgment out of the fund to which they were entitled in priority (*Rock* v. *Leighton*). This liability is not incurred where the representative has no notice of the debts ranking in priority to that claimed in the action (*Sawyer* v. *Mercer*).

Where the personal representative, having fully distributed the estate in so far as the funds have passed through his hands, is sued in respect of debts of the deceased, he should plead *plene administravit*, and so protect himself from possible personal liability upon a judgment against him in his representative capacity arising from a deficiency of assets to satisfy the judgment. By establishing this plea that the estate has been fully administered, so that no assets remain to meet the claim in the action, the representative precludes the allegation that, by resisting the claim of the plantiff creditor upon other grounds, the existence of assets is tacitly admitted. Where some assets remain in the hands of the representative, he should plead *plene administravit praeter*, that is to say, the estate has been duly disposed of, except for assets acknowledged to remain with the executor or administrator. The effect of this plea is that a judgment obtained by the creditor can be satisfied only out of assets of the deceased admitted or proved to be in the hands of the representative, or subsequently coming within his control (*Rock* v. *Leighton, supra*).

A secured creditor (i.e. one holding a mortgage, charge or lien on property of the deceased as security for his debt) has the following alternatives. He may

(1)   stand on his security and not prove against the estate; or

(2)   surrender his security and prove for the whole debt; or

(3)   realise his security and prove for the balance (if any) of the debt; or

(4) value his security and prove for the balance (if any) of the
    debt.

To the extent that a secured creditor proves against the estate
in respect of the debt, he is an unsecured creditor and subject
to the rules of priority set out above.

§ 5. Right of Preference

A personal representative is entitled, if he thinks proper, to pay
a particular creditor or creditors without making provision for
other creditors *of equal degree;* if insufficient or no assets remain
to satisfy the claims of those other creditors, the representative
will not thereby be involved in any liability.

This right to 'prefer' is exercisable both by an executor and
an administrator, but where the administrator is a creditor, the
terms of the administration bond invariably exclude the right.

Like the statutory order of payment of debts, the right of
preference is of substantial significance only where an estate is
insolvent. In such a case the representative's preference of one
creditor to another will confer an advantage upon the former
and inflict a detriment upon the latter. Protection against too
arbitrary an exercise of the rights of preference exists in that:

(*a*) the right can be asserted only as between creditors of equal
    degree;

(*b*) the right cannot be exercised after an order appointing a
    receiver, or an order for administration of the estate by the
    court, has been made,

but the right can be exercised while an order is pending (*Re
Radcliffe*), or while an order for an account has been made but
no receiver has been appointed (*Jones* v. *Jukes*).

§ 6. Right of Retainer

Analogous to the personal representative's right to prefer one
creditor to another is his right to retain out of the assets, as
against creditors of equal degree, an amount equal to the debt
due from the deceased to himself, before or without making provision for those creditors. Here again, a creditor to whom letters
of administration are granted is in practice required to forgo his
right of retainer by the terms of his administration bond.

The original justification for the right was the representative's inability in his character as creditor to sue himself as representative of his debtor; if it were not for the right of retainer he might be compelled to satisfy the claims of other creditors who had obtained judgment, being left with nothing with which to satisfy his own debt.

The right of retainer of a personal representative (like the right to prefer creditors) may be exercised out of all assets of the deceased, but only in respect of debts owing to the personal representative in his own right, whether solely or jointly with another person (A.E.A. 1925, s. 34). Where the personal representative is also trustee of a fund to which the deceased was indebted, there can be no retainer, for the personal representative has no beneficial interest in the claim (*In re Rudd; Royal Exchange Assurance* v. *Ballantine*).

The right of retainer can be exercised only by the person legally entitled to assert the claim which the retainer is intended to satisfy. Hence, an administrator who is an undischarged bankrupt has no right to retain out of the assets received by him as administrator a debt due to him from the deceased intestate, the proper person to sue being the trustee in bankruptcy (*Wilson* v. *Wilson*); nor can an executor retain a debt due from the deceased to the trustees of a settlement under which he (the executor) is sole beneficiary (*Re Sutherland, Michell* v. *Countess Bubna*).

It is doubtful if an executor *de son tort* can exercise the power of retainer, but he can reduce his liability (if any) by deducting debts, for valuable consideration and without fraud, due to him from the deceased (A.E.A. 1925, s. 28). If he subsequently obtains a grant of administration to himself (unless as a creditor) he will acquire the right of retainer (*Pyne* v. *Wooland*). He can, if sued by a creditor or a legatee, plead *plene administravit*, i.e. that the estate has been fully administered and that there is nothing left to distribute, if such is the case.

No retainer is possible in respect of an unliquidated claim unless its amount can be assessed with certainty (*Re Compton*).

The right of retainer is exercisable with regard to statute-barred debts owed to the personal representative (*Stahlschmidt* v. *Lett*).

An executor who is surety for a debt of his testator cannot exercise his right of retainer in respect of his liability as surety, unless he pays the debt (*Re Beavan, Davies* v. *Beavan*). If he has paid the principal debt, he is entitled to retain an amount equal to the debt, but only out of the assets in his hands at the time of payment (*Re Harrison*).

The right of retainer is not affected by a decree of administration by the court (*Re Rhoades; Richmond* v. *White*). It remains exercisable even after the making of an order for administration in bankruptcy; however, it is then operative only as regards assets in the hands of the personal representative at the time that he receives notice of the presentation of the petition seeking the order (*Re Williams*), and is subject to the overriding interests of claims which are preferential in bankruptcy. Costs of an administration action brought against the estate by a creditor are not given priority over the executor's right of retainer (*In re Wester Wemyss; Tilley* v. *Wester Wemyss*).

An executor cannot retain, as against a creditor of the estate who has obtained a judgment *de bonis testatoris*, if the right of retainer was not set up in the action in which the judgment was given (*Re Marvin*). This is because of the principle that failure to plead *plene administravit* or the availability of the right of retainer constitutes an admission of assets sufficient to pay the debt claimed in the action (cf. *Rock* v. *Leighton*, in § 4 above). As to an executor *de son tort* see Chapter II, § 3 (*e*).

The 'degrees' which debts occupy in bankruptcy proceedings also apply in the administration of an insolvent estate, except that funeral, testamentary and administration expenses are given priority over all the debts. The degrees, in descending order, are:

(1)   debts 'preferred' in bankruptcy, and

(2)   all other unsecured debts, except

(3)   the claims 'deferred' in bankruptcy (see § 7 of this Chapter).

This classification determines the order of payment of debts and also the limits to the exercise of the rights of preference and retainer in relation to the administration of an insolvent estate.

A personal representative can, with regard to a claim against the estate which falls within the first degree, prefer or retain it as against other creditors of the first degree. Similarly, a claim of the second degree may be preferred or retained as against other creditors of the second degree, but not as against creditors of the first degree, and so on. Where an executor *bona fide* administered the estate fully, and exercised his right of retainer in respect of a debt due to him, it was held that a creditor of higher order, of whose claim the representative had not had notice, could not follow the assets retained by the executor (*Re Fludyer*).

Thus an executor is entitled to recover out of the estate of a bankrupt, who died without obtaining his discharge, reasonable sums paid for funeral expenses, even though the estate consists exclusively of moneys earned by the deceased after his adjudication (*Re Walker, Slocock* v. *Official Receiver*).

The right of retainer, properly so called, which has been discussed here, is not to be confused with the executor's right to retain, *as against legatees*, benefits bequeathed to them under the will until debts due from them to the estate are satisfied. This right is considered in Chapter XIV.

§ 7. Administration of the Estate of a Deceased Insolvent

Where an estate is insolvent (this being a question of fact), it may be administered in one of three ways, namely:

(1) by the personal representative; or

(2) under order of the court upon decree obtained in the Chancery Division of the High Court or in the appropriate County Court having jurisdiction; or

(3) in bankruptcy under Section 130, Bankruptcy Act 1914.

A decree for administration by the court will be sought, or a petition in bankruptcy presented, where it is considered necessary or expedient to secure for creditors of the estate more stringent regulation of the conduct of the administration than is possible in an administration out of court. The theoretical result of each form of administration should be substantially the same, apart from a variation in the costs involved, but, as has been seen, secondary differences arise in that, e.g. the rights of preference and retainer disappear or are modified where the estate is administered under judicial decree. The due order of payment prescribed by statute applies uniformly to each mode of distribution.

It is necessary to consider here only the procedure under

Section 130, Bankruptcy Act 1914 (repealed by the A.E.A. 1925, but restored by the Expiring Laws Act 1925).

Any creditor of the deceased, whose debt would have supported a bankruptcy petition if the debtor had been alive, may petition in the prescribed form to have the estate administered as that of a deceased insolvent, unless proceedings have already been commenced for administration in the Chancery Division or in a County Court. The personal representative may also present the petition.

Notice of the petition served on the executor or administrator operates as notice of an act of bankruptcy, and no payment made by him after such notice is good against the Official Receiver. The personal representative should at once make up his accounts, and prepare to hand over the assets to the Official Receiver. When the order is made, the property will vest in the Official Receiver as trustee.

In the ensuing administration, subject to the priority of funeral, testamentary, and administrative expenses, the same rules prevail as to

(*a*) the respective rights of secured and unsecured creditors;

(*b*) debts and liabilities provable;

(*c*) the valuation of annuities and future contingent liabilities; and

(*d*) priorities of debts and liabilities;

as may be in force for the time being in bankruptcy with respect to the assets of persons adjudged bankrupt (A.E.A. 1925, s. 34; Schedule I, Part I). In bankruptcy, the rule is that all provable debts and liabilities, including Crown debts, judgments, specialty debts (whether contracted for value or not) and simple contract debts, rank *pari passu*, subject to the provisions as to preferential and deferred debts.

The debts PREFERENTIAL in bankruptcy, as adapted to the administration of the estate of a deceased insolvent debtor, are mostly dealt with in the Bankruptcy Act 1914, s. 33, as amended by the Companies Act 1947, s. 115. They are as follows:

(1) Money in the possession of the debtor as an officer of a Friendly Society (Friendly Societies Act 1896, s. 35), or as an officer of a Trustee Savings Bank (Trustee Savings Bank

Act 1863, s. 14; Savings Bank Act 1891, s. 13). This money, being held by the insolvent in a fiduciary capacity, is not really a 'debt' at all; it is repayable before payment of the following debts, which rank *pari passu* among themselves.

(2) Parochial and other local rates owing by the deceased at the date of death, and having become due and payable within the twelve months next before that date.

(3) All assessed taxes up to 5th April preceding the date of the death of the debtor, not exceeding one year's assessment (*ibid.*). In the case of emoluments assessable under Sch. E, all sums deducted by an employer within 12 months next before the date of death (F.A. 1952, s. 30).

(4) Wages or salary if any clerk, servant, labourer or workman in respect of services rendered to the deceased during the four months immediately preceding his death, not exceeding £200 for any one person; also all accrued holiday remuneration.

(5) Where a labourer in husbandry has contracted for a lump sum at the end of the year of hiring, such amount as the court decides to be due, proportionate to the time served before death.

(6) All contributions payable in respect of National Insurance during the 12 months prior to the death (National Insurance Acts). This applies also to Redundancy Fund contributions.

(7) Any Purchase tax owing at the date of death and having become due within twelve months next before that date (F.A. 1942, s. 20 (1)). This applies also to Selective Employment tax.

(8) Compensation not exceeding £200 ordered under the Reinstatement in Civil Employment Act 1944, or the National Service Act 1948 (Companies Act 1947, s. 115).

The debts DEFERRED in bankruptcy are as follows:

(1) A loan by a married woman to her husband for the purpose of his trade or business, or by a husband to his wife in similar circumstances (Bankruptcy Act 1914, s. 36).

(2) Advances to a person in business in return for an interest in the profits (Partnership Act 1890, s. 3).

(3) Debts due to the vendor of goodwill where he is being paid by way of an annuity, or otherwise a share of profits (*ibid.*).

(4) Interest, so far as it represents a rate in excess of 5% per annum, and also in relation to certain transactions, e.g. moneylending contracts (Bankruptcy Act 1914, ss. 42, 66; Moneylenders Act 1927, s. 9).

It has already been seen that a personal representative remains entitled to exercise his right of retainer *out of assets in his hands* at the time he becomes aware of the presentation of a petition against the estate. If, in ignorance of his right, or by mistake, he has handed over the assets to the Official Receiver, he is entitled to be repaid the amount of his debt (*Re Rhoades*).

When the debt in respect of which the right of retainer is asserted exceeds the value of the assets, the executor may retain the assets *in specie* in satisfaction of his debt, and is not bound to convert them into money (*Re Gilbert*).

§ 8. Marshalling the Assets for the Payment of Debts

All the assets of the deceased, in which he had a beneficial interest not ceasing with his death, are available for payment of debts of the estate; any testamentary disposition to the contrary is void against the creditors (A.E.A. 1925, s. 32). Such contrary disposition may, however, be operative and material as among beneficiaries of a solvent estate. In the case of an insolvent estate, the assets will be exhausted by the claims of creditors.

Where the estate of a deceased person is solvent, the rules set out in the A.E.A. 1925, ss. 34, 35, and First Schedule, Part II, for the 'discharge of the funeral, testamentary and administration expenses, debts and liabilities' will apply, unless there are specific conflicting directions in the will.

Section 35 provides that where a person dies possessed of, or entitled to, or under a general power of appointment by his will disposes of, an interest in property which at the time of his death is charged with the payment of money, whether by way of legal mortgage, equitable charge or otherwise (including a lien for unpaid purchase money), and the deceased has not by will, deed or other document signified a contrary or other intention, the interest so charged (as among persons claiming through the deceased) is primarily liable for the payment of the charge, and every part of that interest must bear a proportionate part of the charge on the whole.

A contrary intention is not deemed to be signified merely by

(a) a general direction for the payment of debts out of the testator's personal estate, or his residuary real and personal estate or his residuary real estate; or

(b) a charge of debts upon any such estate.

The right of a person, entitled to the charge, to obtain its payment or satisfaction out of the other assets of the deceased or otherwise is expressly preserved. Consequently, in the case of a testator giving a specific legacy which has been pledged or charged, the legacy will itself bear the charge unless the application of s. 35 is excluded.

Where the testator has directed by his will that debts, otherwise charged on specific property, are to be paid out of a particular fund, they must be so paid. Should the special fund prove inadequate to discharge the liability, the property charged must be called upon to bear the deficiency (*Re Fegan, Fegan* v. *Fegan*).

Where, by his will, a testator excludes the operation of s. 35, but gives no specific directions as to the way in which the estate is to be applied in satisfaction of the liabilities attaching to it, the assets must be 'marshalled' in the order prescribed by A.E.A. 1925, First Schedule, Part II. This process consists in classifying the real and personal property of the deceased in a series of notional funds to which recourse may be had in succession, for the purpose of satisfying claims against the estate, but so that no fund is resorted to until prior funds in the 'marshalled' series are exhausted. The object of this is to preserve the rights of the *beneficiaries* among themselves in cases where it is necessary, in order to meet the liabilities of the deceased, to encroach upon property bequeathed or devised by the will. The rules applied for this purpose are designed to give effect to what may properly be supposed to have been the substantial intentions of the testator in that regard. It is an equitable principle that if a claimant has two funds to which he can resort, a person having an interest in one fund only can compel the claimant to resort to the other if that is necessary to enable both claims to be satisfied (*Aldrich* v. *Cooper*), but the choice of creditors cannot determine whether legatees shall be paid or not (Lord Eldon, *ibid.* at page 395). The rules as to marshalling give effect to that principle.

If the estate is solvent, the real and personal property therein is marshalled for the discharge of the funeral, testamentary and administration expenses and debts and liabilities of the deceased in the following order:

(1) PROPERTY OF THE DECEASED UNDISPOSED OF BY WILL, SUBJECT TO THE RETENTION THEREOUT OF A FUND SUFFICIENT TO MEET ANY PECUNIARY LEGACIES.

In applying undisposed-of property in paying debts of the estate, the interest of beneficiaries under the will is not subjected to any encroachment, provided that there is retained out of the undisposed-of property, a fund earmarked for the payment of pecuniary legacies.

(2) PROPERTY OF THE DECEASED, NOT SPECIFICALLY DEVISED OR BEQUEATHED, BUT INCLUDED (EITHER BY A SPECIFIC OR GENERAL DESCRIPTION) IN A RESIDUARY GIFT, SUBJECT TO THE RETENTION OUT OF SUCH PROPERTY OF A FUND TO MEET ANY PECUNIARY LEGACIES, SO FAR AS NOT PROVIDED FOR UNDER (1).

(3) PROPERTY OF THE DECEASED SPECIFICALLY APPROPRIATED OR DEVISED OR BEQUEATHED FOR THE PAYMENT OF DEBTS.

The first two funds having been eliminated, this is the natural fund to which recourse should next be had. It will be noticed that if the obligations of the estate have been extinguished before this fund is reached, the property comprised in it will fall into and become part of residue.

(4) PROPERTY OF THE DECEASED CHARGED WITH OR DEVISED OR BEQUEATHED SUBJECT TO A CHARGE FOR THE PAYMENT OF DEBTS.

(5) THE FUND, IF ANY, RETAINED TO MEET PECUNIARY LEGACIES.

(6) PROPERTY SPECIFICALLY DEVISED OR BEQUEATHED RATEABLY ACCORDING TO VALUE.

Note: Whether the value of a demonstrative legacy will appear as part of (5) or of (6) will depend upon the existence of the 'demonstrated' fund (see Chapter XIV, § 13).

(7) PROPERTY APPOINTED BY WILL UNDER A GENERAL POWER, INCLUDING THE STATUTORY POWER TO DISPOSE OF ENTAILED INTERESTS RATEABLY ACCORDING TO VALUE.

The rules set out above are primarily for meeting debts. If there is undisposed-of property or residuary personalty, there must first be set aside thereout a fund to meet the pecuniary legacies, since in the absence of contrary provisions in the will these are a charge on personalty. Next, undisposed-of or residuary personalty and realty are used for paying the debts, liabilities and expenses. The legacies fund cannot be touched until funds (1), (2), (3) and (4) have been exhausted (*Re Anstead*) [1943].

Illustration (1)

T. died, leaving a gross estate of £45,000. By his will he bequeathed specific legacies worth £9,000 and pecuniary legacies totalling £6,000. The residue of his estate was left to his sons A. and B. in equal shares absolutely; B., who was unmarried, had predeceased his father. The debts, duty and testamentary expenses in T.'s estate were £19,000.

(*a*) Show how the estate should be distributed.

(*b*) What would have been the position if the debts, duty and testamentary expenses had totalled (i) £10,000, and (ii) £33,000?

		£
(*a*) Gross estate		45,000
Less Specific legacies		9,000
		£36,000
Lapsed share of residue arising from B.'s death		18,000
Less Appropriation to meet pecuniary legacies		6,000
		12,000
Less Debts, duty and testamentary expenses		19,000
Deficiency to be met out of the half-share of residue bequeathed to A.		£7,000

Distribution of the estate:

	£
Debts, etc., paid	19,000
Specific legacies transferred	9,000
Pecuniary legacies paid	6,000
Residuary bequest to A—£(18,000—7,000)	11,000
	£45,000

(*b*) (i):

	£
Lapsed share of residue	18,000
Less Appropriation to meet pecuniary legacies	6,000
	12,000
Less Debts, etc.	10,000
	£2,000

The balance of £2,000 would be distributed in accordance with the rules of intestate succession (*see* Chapter XIV, Section 18).

(ii)

	£
Lapsed share of residue	18,000
Less Appropriation to meet pecuniary legacies	6,000
	12,000
Less Debts, etc.	33,000
Deficiency	21,000
Share of residue bequeathed to A.	18,000
Deficiency	£3,000

Here, the final deficiency of £3,000 must be charged against the fund appropriated to meet the pecuniary legacies of £6,000. Those legacies will therefore *abate* by 10s 0d in the £. (For abatement, *see* Chapter XIV, § 14.)

It may seem strange that property included in a residuary gift (i.e. under (2) in the table shown above) should be made available for the satisfaction of liabilities *before* the fund specifically identified for that purpose, see item (3). However, the apparent anomaly can be explained by the fact that the 'residue' of an estate cannot be determined until all claims against the estate are provided for, whether of creditors or of beneficiaries whose interests are identifiable. The property under (3) above is an identifiable interest.

Nevertheless, the practical effect of applying the order laid down in Part II of the First Schedule of the Administration of Estates Act 1925 is that the funds comprised in (2) and (3) are treated as a single fund.

Illustration (2)

X. died leaving a gross estate of £45,000. Included in this figure was an investment, valued at £14,000, charged specifically with the payment of debts and other liabilities. X. left the residue of his estate to his wife, Y., absolutely. The debts, duty and testamentary expenses amounted to (i) £13,000; (ii) £33,000. Calculate the amount due to Y. depending on which of (i) or (ii) applies.

	(i) £	(ii) £
Gross estate	45,000	45,000
Less Fund specifically charged with the payment of liabilities (under (3))	14,000	14,000
'Residue' (under (2))	31,000	31,000
Less Debts, etc.	13,000	33,000
Surplus/*Deficiency*	18,000	*2,000*
Add Fund specifically charged	14,000	14,000
Residue, as finally determined, payable to Y..	£32,000	£12,000

It will be seen that the same result would have occurred if the liabilities had been deducted *directly* from the gross estate.

It is therefore considered that the only occasion when funds (2) and (3) would need to be separated is when any balance of fund (3), which is not required for the payment of debts etc, is bequeathed to somebody *other than* the residuary legatee; in that event, fund (3) would seem to be analogous to fund (4).

The order of application may be modified by the will of the deceased. Where the will indicates with reasonable clarity the intention of the testator, and charges debts, funeral and testamentary expenses and legacies primarily on a specific portion of the property, the statutory rules take effect, subject to any variation required to carry out the intention of the deceased (*Re Littlewood, Clark* v. *Littlewood*).

These rules do not affect the liability of land to answer the Estate Duty imposed thereon in exoneration of other assets.

It should be noted that these provisions affect only the rights of beneficiaries as among themselves, and do not in any way limit the right of creditors to exercise any remedies that they may possess against any of the assets of the estate (A.E.A. 1925, s. 32).

Where a residuary legatee predeceases the testator, funeral and testamentary expenses, debts and legacies are to be paid out of such lapsed share of residue as being property 'undisposed of', before fixed shares in the residue are resorted to (*Re Lamb, Vipond* v. *Lamb*), but this is subject to testamentary directions to the contrary (*Re Petty, Holliday* v. *Petty*). Thus, where the testator directed the funeral and testamentary expenses and debts to be paid out of personalty, and devised his realty to a person who, in the event, predeceased him, so that the devise lapsed, it was held that the debts were primarily payable out of personalty, although the realty was property undisposed of by will (*Re Atkinson* [1930]; *Webster* v. *Walter*); where a residuary bequest of personalty was left 'subject to and after payment of' debts, it was held that the debts were to be satisfied out of the whole of the personalty uniformly, including lapsed shares in residue, for such shares do not become 'undisposed of by will' until the debts are determined and paid (*Re Kempthorne, Charles* v. *Kempthorne*).

A share of income of the residuary estate bequeathed by will, which bequest lapses by reason of the legatee's spouse being an attesting witness of the will, is property 'undisposed of by will' (*In re Tong, Hilton* v. *Bradbury*).

Where a testator directed a particular fund to bear his debts, and *then* made a gift of residue, it was held that there was a clear intention to exonerate the residue, and the order for payment of the debts laid down by the A.E.A. Act 1925, was varied by the will (*In re James; Lloyds Bank Ltd.* v. *Atkins*). Where the will does not contain a trust for sale, pecuniary legacies are payable out of undisposed-of realty in preference to the residue of personal estate disposed of by the will (*Re Martin; Midland Bank Executor and Trustee Co.* v. *Marfleet*). Where a will included pecuniary legacies, and then a bequest to the testatrix's daughter of 'all my real estate and the residue of my personal estate', it was held that the pecuniary legacies were a first charge on the personal estate (to the exclusion of the realty), while the debts and testamentary expenses were to be charged against the real estate, which was to be regarded as a residuary devise (*Re Wilson deceased; Wilson* v. *Mackay and Others*).

An option to purchase shares is not a specific bequest of the shares. So long as the purchase price is, with the other assets, enough to meet the debts, it, and not the shares, is the fund available (*Re Eve*).

CHAPTER XIV

DISTRIBUTION OF THE ESTATE – BENEFICIARIES

§ 1. Introduction

Having discussed the rules relating to the payment of creditors in the previous chapter, it is now necessary to describe the rules for dividing the estate after the payment of all debts between those entitled to it under the will, i.e. the beneficiaries.

The personal representatives must distribute the estate in accordance with the terms of the will and his initial problem may be to decide the type of legacy involved. These may be summarised as:

(*a*) General legacy, which is a bequest of some thing or money not forming a specified part of the estate.

(*b*) Specific legacy, which is a bequest of a specified part of the estate.

(*c*) Demonstrative legacy, which is a bequest of a general nature but payable primarily out of a specified part of the estate.

(*d*) Cumulative legacy, whereby a person in the same or a subsequent instrument is entitled to a bequest in addition to the original gift.

(*e*) Substitutional legacy is a legacy given in lieu of a previous bequest.

(*f*) Vested legacy is a legacy to which a beneficiary is entitled at the present time even though possession may be deferred.

(*g*) Contingent legacy is a bequest to which the beneficiary will be entitled at a certain time.

(*h*) Conditional legacy is a bequest which will vest only on the fulfilment of a condition.

Legacies may be left to an individual, charity or other body or to a class of persons. A beneficiary can always refuse to accept a legacy.

Interest will be payable at 4 per cent. per annum usually from the end of one year after the testator's death, but where the legacy is to be paid immediately on death, or is charged on land, or is payable to an infant for whom maintenance has not been provided, or is in satisfaction of a debt carrying interest, or is a specific legacy interest will commence with the date of death.

A specific legacy is adeemed (i.e. will not be payable) if the subject matter of that legacy does not exist at the death of the testator. Legacies also lapse if the beneficiary dies before the testator (unless the beneficiary is a child of the testator and leaves children living at the testator's death) or if a condition or contingency is not performed or occurs. Where there is insufficient estate to pay all legacies left by will, the general legacies abate first, then the specific legacies. Each legacy in a class abates proportionately. Demonstrative legacies, if specific by nature, abate with the specific legacies, otherwise they abate with the general legacies.

Annuities are usually given by way of a general legacy. Depending on the terms of the will, an annuitant can elect to have the capital value of his annuity rather than annual payments. Personal representatives may appropriate specific property to form an annuity fund.

Capital Gains tax is not payable by reason of the transfer of assets to beneficiaries, who will be deemed to have acquired them at the value at the date of death or if acquired later by the personal representative at the cost to him. The beneficiary is deemed to have acquired the asset when the personal representative acquired it. Once the personal representative has assented to the legacy, any gain arising on a later disposal will be assessed on the legatee. The latter cannot be charged to tax under Schedule D, Case VII, on such disposal.

A person who is entitled under the rules of intestacy or under a will requiring him so to do, must bring into account advances made to him prior to the intestate's or testator's death in determining his share of the residue of the estate. This provision only applies to advances to children (unless the will provides otherwise), but see § 18 as to the position on a partial intestacy. To constitute an advancement, the amount must not be a casual payment but a substantial one given on marriage or intended to establish the child in life, so as to give him permanent benefit.

The cost of educating a child through school or university would not be an advancement since this is the normal duty of a parent. Such advancements are to be treated as being paid towards the satisfaction of the child's share in his parent's estate. Complications may arise where some advances have been made more than seven years before the parent's death and others within that period. Where there is a direction in the will that advancements are to be brought into account against *net* residue, then the following rule in *Re Tollemache* must not be applied. Otherwise when advancements are to be brought in and are subject to the rule in *Re Tollemache*, they are to be valued at their net benefit to the donee (i.e. where Estate Duty is payable thereon at the amount after deduction of duty; in other cases at the value of the advance). It seems that the rights of the beneficiaries must be adjusted on the basis of the values at the date of distribution. The net value of the advances is added to the value of the estate, the total divided in accordance with the beneficiaries' interests (in intestacy, equally), and by deducting the net advances from that total, each beneficiary's share in the estate is determined.

Since income will arise from the estate, this will require division between advanced and non-advanced beneficiaries. There are two bases – that in *re Hargreaves* under which income is divided in proportion to the net interests of the beneficiaries in that estate; and in *re Poyser* under which beneficiaries are charged with interest at 4 per cent. per annum for the period from the date of death to the date of distribution (but see § 18) on the amount advanced. Such interest is added to the income of the estate and divided between the beneficiaries in accordance with their gross interests in the estate.

§ 2. Distribution to Beneficiaries

When the funeral and testamentary expenses have been paid and the debts and liabilities satisfied or provided for, the balance of the estate must be distributed among the beneficiaries.

A personal representative must distribute the property according to the directions of the will. As to property of which the will makes no disposition by way of residuary gift or otherwise, a partial intestacy arises, and that property must be distributed in accordance with the intestacy rules, subject to such of the provisions of the will as remain effectual (*Re Sullivan, Dunkley* v. *Sullivan*, see Chapter I, § 8. The personal representative, subject to his rights and powers for the purpose of administration, is a trustee for the persons entitled as upon an intestacy in respect of the part of the estate not expressly disposed of, unless it appears by the will that he is intended to take such part beneficially (A.E.A. 1925, s. 49). In default, therefore, of any person taking an absolute interest, the residuary estate of the intestate will belong to the Crown or to the Duchy of Lancaster. If the residue is to be divided into shares and a share fails or is revoked by codicil, it does not, in the absence of directions to the contrary, fall to be divided between the other residuary legatees, but will be treated as undisposed of and distributed as under an intestacy (*Sykes* v. *Sykes*).

In general, any person capable of owning property is also capable of acquiring an interest under a will. An infant cannot, however, become an 'estate owner', i.e. the owner of a *legal* interest in land, and such an interest devised to him by will is held on trust by the personal representative until the infant attains his majority. Moreover, as a matter of public policy and in accord with the principle that a person should not benefit from his own wrong, anyone who is feloniously responsible for the death of the deceased is debarred from taking benefit under his will (*Re Hall*, P.1) or (*semble*) upon his intestacy. A murderer cannot benefit from his victim's estate, but his interest does not go to the Crown as *bona vacantia*; it passes to the other beneficiaries under the will or intestacy (*Re Callaway* v. *Treasury Solicitor; re Peacock, Midland Bank Executor and Trustee Co.* v. *Peacock*).

A class of persons may be the recipients of a benefit under a will, and so also may a charity, unless the benefit is of an obnoxious character, such as a gift to superstitious uses, in which case the gift will fail. A gift directly opposed to the public interest or to public policy will be bad, although the fact that a benefit conferred by will is not consonant with the best interests of the public does not necessarily vitiate it.

Again, as has been stated already, neither an attesting witness nor the husband or wife of an attesting witness to a will can take any benefit under it; but this does not apply to an informal will made by a soldier or sailor, since such a will does not require attestation (*Re Limond*). Marriage to a witness after the attestation does not, however, debar the non-attesting spouse from benefit (*Thorpe* v. *Bestwick*).

The vesting of any interest or benefit given under a will is subject to satisfaction of, or provision for, the liabilities of the estate out of the assets. The right of the legatee is therefore imperfect until it is known that the subject matter of the gift is not required to meet claims against the estate. Hence the assent of the executor is necessary to complete the title of beneficiaries under a will (*Mead* v. *Lord Orrery*). Where, therefore, the legatee is a debtor of the estate he cannot claim to set off his debt against the legacy; on the other hand, the executor is not compelled to assent to the legacy until the debt is discharged. The legatee must be regarded as having in his hands an asset of the testator's estate, and he cannot claim part of such estate without accounting for the asset in his hands, but the executor may himself deduct the amount of the debt from the legacy (*Woodcock* v. *Eames*). This is sometimes referred to as the executor's right to 'retain' a legacy against a debt. There is not, however, any real retention by the personal representative, for the legatee, who is also bound to contribute to the estate, 'is paid by holding in his own hands a part of the mass (of assets) which, if the mass were completed, he would receive back' (*Cherry* v. *Boultbee*). The principle is applicable where the debt from the legatee is statute-barred (*Courtenay* v. *Williams*), and even as against the assignee of the legacy (*Re Knapman*), but not to debts not payable till a future time (*Re Abrahams*). A debt due from a firm cannot be set off against a legacy due to a partner legatee (*Turner* v. *Turner*). So, also, where a legatee has been adjudicated bankrupt, and the executor has proved and has received a dividend in the bankruptcy, he can no longer retain but must assent to the legacy if otherwise able to do so (*Re Sewell, White* v. *Sewell*); if the bankruptcy of the legatee occurred in the lifetime of the testator, since there never was a time when the same person was entitled to receive the legacy and be liable to pay the entire debt, the executor must pay the legacy and prove for the debt, or pay the legacy less a sum equivalent to the proper dividend in the bankruptcy upon the amount of the debt. 'The right of an executor of a creditor to retain a sufficient part of a legacy given by the creditor to pay a debt due from him to the creditor's estate is rather a right to pay out of the fund in hand than a right of set-off' (*Cherry* v. *Boultbee, supra*). If, moreover, the legatee became bankrupt in the lifetime of the deceased and had obtained his discharge before the death, the debt is extinguished and cannot be set off. A composition in bankruptcy would produce the same result (*Re Sewell, supra*). If the legatee becomes bankrupt after the testator's death, the executor can still retain the whole debt out of a pecuniary legacy, since the right existed at the date of death, and the trustee in bankruptcy is in no better position than the bankrupt himself (*Re Watson, Turner* v. *Watson*). The executor loses his right if he proves in the bankruptcy (*Stammers* v. *Elliott*, and *In Re Sewell, White* v. *Sewell, supra*).

There can be no right of set-off against a specific legacy (*see below*) (*Re Akerman; Akerman* v. *Akerman*), unless it is represented by money in the executor's hands (*Re Taylor*). Where a will provides that in the event of the death of the legatee before that of the testator, the original legatee's children shall take his share, there can be no set-off against them of a debt due from their parent (*Re Binns*).

The principle, which entitled an executor to retain or set off a legacy against a debt due to the estate, is equally valid as between an administrator and a person claiming a share in the estate of an intestate (*Re Cordwell's Estate*).

Since the assent of the executor is necessary to complete the beneficiary's title to the subject matter of the legacy if the testator, by his will, releases a debt due to him, the assent of the executor is necessary to give effect to the release. To vest a legal estate in land, the assent of the executor must be in writing (A.E.A. 1925, s. 36). With the relevant consents, the personal representative is empowered to appropriate any part of the estate in its actual condition in or towards the satisfaction of any legacy, but not so as to affect prejudicially any specific devise or bequest (A.E.A. 1925, s. 41). (See § 7 of this Chapter.)

An executor can assent to a legacy before taking out probate and the assent is good even if he dies before obtaining probate. An administrator cannot assent before he has obtained letters of administration.

§ 3. Legacies

The original meaning of the word legacy, as defined in Termes de lay Ley is 'lands or goods given unto any man by the will or testament of another'. Modern usage tends to confine its application to personalty, the expression 'devise' being employed in connection with dispositions of realty. Frequently the word 'legacy' is used in the general sense of 'bequest', i.e. a gift by will.

Legacies may be either general, specific or demonstrative:

A GENERAL LEGACY is a bequest of some thing or money, not necessarily part of the testator's estate, and not distinguished from all others of the same kind; e.g. 'I give £100 to A'; or 'I give a diamond ring to B'.

A SPECIFIC LEGACY is a gift of some specific portion of the testator's personal estate which is definitely identified and distinguished from all others; examples are 'my solitaire diamond ring'; '£100 Consols now standing in my name in the Bank of England'; or '£100 Consols being part of my £5,000 Consols'.

A DEMONSTRATIVE LEGACY is a gift of a general nature, but payable primarily out of some specified portion of the testator's estate, e.g. 'a sum of £100 payable out of my £500 Consols'.

(a) General and Specific Legacies

A general legacy is usually expressed in terms of pecuniary value. It does not follow, however, that all gifts of money are general legacies, since the words under which the gift passes may be such as to give the legacy a specific character. Thus '£100 in a certain bag', or £100 in the hands of X' would constitute specific legacies (Lawson v. Stitch; Crockat v. Crockat. A debt forgiven by the will is a specific legacy (Re Wedmore).

Even though the bequest is of some specific thing, it may still be a general legacy and not a specific legacy. To be a specific legacy it must be a bequest of 'something which a testator, identifying it by a sufficient description, and manifesting an intention that it should be enjoyed in the state and condition indicated by that description, separates in favour of a particular legatee from the general mass of his personal estate' (*Robertson* v. *Broadbent*). Thus, 'the diamond ring presented to me by A.' is a specific legacy, but 'a diamond ring' is a general legacy; and a gift of 'a brooch' or 'a horse', without further description, is a general legacy even if given by a testator leaving a number of brooches or horses; and if the testator did not possess any brooches or horses, as the case may be, the executor must purchase one to satisfy the legacy. The same words of disposition may create a specific legacy where it can be specifically satisfied, and a general one where it cannot (*Fontaine* v. *Tyler*). Unless there are qualifying words to the contrary, any such gift will be ascertained as at the date of death and not as at the date of the will (*Langdale* v. *Briggs*).

A legacy of government stock, securities or shares in companies is *prima facie* general and not specific; and this is so not only where the value is expressed in a round sum of money, but also where the amount is a sum comprising pounds, shillings and pence (*In re Willcocks, Warwick* v. *Willcocks*). Wherever the words creating a gift and the general context allow, the inference is that the testator intended to confer a general rather than a specific legacy. The question is ultimately one of interpreting the language of the will, so as to arrive at the intention of the testator. Thus, 'all the stocks to which I may be entitled at the time of my decease in the public fund' has been held to be a specific bequest (*Stephenson* v. *Dowson*).

Where chattels are bequeathed by description and the testator had, at the date of his death, a number of chattels complying with the description but exceeding the quantity specified in the bequest, e.g. a gift of six horses to the legatee, where the testator died possessing twenty horses, the legatee, and not the executor, has the right to select the chattels which are to form the gift (*Jacques* v *Chambers*). Should a testator bequeath a legacy involving selection by the legatee, the legatee can select up to the whole subject-matter comprised in the gift; there is no quantitative limit except that limit (if any) imposed by the will (*In re Wavertree of Delamere*). Thus, a gift of 'such of my horses as John may desire to have', will entitle the legatee to have the whole of the testator's stable. If the legatee dies without having made the selection, the legacy fails, for the selection is a personal right and does not pass to the legatee's executors (*Re Madge, Pridie* v. *Bellamy*). If, however, there is an immediate vested interest which passes apart from the selection, e.g. a lease granted to A of forty out of sixty acres, the personal representative of A may select the forty acres (*Jones* v. *Cherney*). Where a testatrix, who owned a number of small houses, gave one house (without identification) to each of her nephews and nieces, and one to each of certain other named persons, it was held that the gifts were not void for uncertainty; if the devisees could not agree, the distribution of the various houses should be decided by lot (*In re Knapton; Knapton* v. *Hindle*).

Where, however, the testator intended to give a particular property to the legatee, but owing to the fact that he had several such properties it was impossible to determine which of such properties was intended to be the subject matter of the gift, the legacy failed for uncertainty (*Asten* v. *Asten*). The mere misdescription of a legacy will not cause it to fail if there is no doubt as to the intention of the testator. For example, a testatrix bequeathed 'my £400 5% War Loan 1929/47'. She never had any such stock, although she had had £400 5% National War Bonds which, prior to her death, had been converted into £284 3½% Conversion Stock and £211 5% Treasury Bonds. She had no other investments. It was held that these investments represented the bequest and must pass as such (*Re Price, Trumper* v. *Price*).

In the case of foreign property specifically bequeathed, foreign duty and foreign costs must be borne by such property and not by the residue (*Re Grosvenor*).

Where the will bequeathed the deceased's business (identified by description in the will) with the wish that it be carried on, it was held that the gift included the assets treated by the testator as part of the business; in that case the assets were the stock-in-trade, trade debtors and the freehold premises in which the business was carried on. The bequest of the business was subject to the payment of the trade liabilities; the bank account, which was used for both business and private purposes, was to be excluded; while Income tax was a personal debt not payable out of the assets of the business (*In re White, McCann and Anor* v. *Hall and Anor*).

A gift of personalty to the testator's widow 'and her heirs for her and their use and benefit absolutely and for ever' has been held to give an absolute interest to the widow (*Re McElligott, Grant v. McElligott*).

A gift in a will, of 'all my money' passes not only money in the strict sense of the word, but the whole of the testator's personal estate, unless there is a context which will induce the court to give the term a narrower significance (*Perrin v. Morgan*).

(b) Demonstrative Legacies

A legacy in terms of money payable primarily out of a particular fund is a demonstrative legacy, and is of the nature of a specific legacy if the fund demonstrated exists and is sufficient, or to the extent that it is sufficient (*Sellon v. Watts*), but is of the nature of a general legacy so far as the fund demonstrated does not exist or is not sufficient (A.E.A. 1925, s. 55 (1) (ix)). Thus, a legacy of '£100 payable out of my £500 Consols', is a demonstrative legacy (*Kirby v. Potter*).

If, however, a legacy is described as '£100 Consols out of my £500 Consols', or '£100, part of my £500 Consols', this is a specific legacy (*Mullins v. Smith*). Moreover, the will may show an intention to bequeath the identical asset, e.g. where certain pecuniary legacies amounting to £710 were directed by the will to be paid 'with and out of the proceeds' of the sale of the testator's investments comprising stocks and shares, and the latter realised only £487 (which was slightly more than their value at the date when the will was made), it was held that, as the fund specified for payment of the legacies was insufficient, they must abate rateably *inter se* and were not payable out of general residue (*Re Boyd, Boyd v. Boyd*).

The distinctions between general, specific and demonstrative legacies are important, particularly, as will be seen later, as regards ademption and abatement of legacies. It is, therefore, worth resummarising the rules for distinguishing between the three types of legacy:

A general legacy is a bequest of some chattel or money not forming a specified part of the deceased's estate or payable out of a specified part of that estate.

A specific legacy is a bequest of some specific part of the deceased's estate distinguishable from the remainder of the deceased's estate.

A demonstrative legacy is a general gift payable primarily out of a specified part of the testator's estate.

(c)   Cumulative and Substitutional Legacies

Legacies are said to be cumulative where, by the same or a subsequent instrument, an additional provision is made for the legatee. A substitutional legacy is a legacy given in lieu of a previous one, where the evidence shows that it was to displace the former gift (*Martin* v. *Drinkwater*).

Whether a legacy is cumulative or substitutional is a matter of interpretation, the intention of the testator being deduced from the words of the will read in relation to all the facts of the case.

If a legacy of the same amount is given by two separate testamentary instruments (e.g. a will and a codicil), *prima facie* the legatee is entitled to both the legacies (*Benyon* v. *Benyon*). The presumption that the gifts are to be cumulative and not substitutive may, however, be rebutted by evidence of a contrary intention on the part of the testator. If, for example, the same sum is given in both instruments and the same motive is expressed (*MacKinnon* v. *Peach*), or if the repetition occurs in one and the same testamentary instrument (*Garth* v. *Meyrick*), the legatee takes one legacy only. If two or more sums of unequal amount are given by the same instrument, the legatee will *prima facie* have a right to them all (*Curry* v. *Pile*).

(d)   Vested and Contingent Legacies

A beneficiary has a vested interest in a legacy if the will confers on him a present interest, not dependent on any contingency, even if his right to receive the legacy is postponed either for a certain time or until the happening of an event. An interest which depends on the occurrence of an event which may or may not happen is a contingent interest.

The difference between a vested interest and a contingent interest must not be confused with that between an absolute interest and a limited interest, or that between an interest in possession and an interest in remainder. An absolute interest is one which confers on the legatee an interest extending to the whole subject matter of the gift (i.e. an interest in both capital and income, without restriction), whereas a limited interest is one which extends to a part only of the subject-matter (for example, a life interest, which confers a right to the income and not to the capital). An interest in possession is one which confers a right to immediate possession of the interest, whatever it may be, whether absolute or limited; an interest in remainder is one, whether absolute or limited, vested or contingent, under which the right to possession is deferred.

Thus:

(1) A legacy to 'A absolutely' confers an absolute interest vested in possession.

(2) A legacy to 'A for life' confers a limited interest vested in possession.

　　NOTE: In (1) and (2), possession would take effect if and when A was 18 years of age or over.

(3) A legacy to 'A for life, and subject thereto to B absolutely' confers on B an absolute interest vested in remainder, i.e. he gets the property when A dies.

(4) A legacy to 'A for life, and after his death to B for life confers on B a limited interest vested in remainder.

(5) A legacy to 'A for life, and subject thereto to B absolutely if he shall attain the age of twenty-one years' confers on B an absolute interest in remainder which is not vested (unless B has already attained the age of twenty-one at the death of the testator), but contingent (i.e. dependent on the event of B's attaining the age of twenty-one).

(6) A legacy to 'A, until B shall marry, and then to B for life' confers on B a limited interest in remainder, which is not vested (unless B is already married at the death of the testator), but contingent (i.e. dependent on the event of B's marrying).

The vital difference between a vested interest and a contingent interest is that a vested interest belongs to the legatee immediately on the death of the testator, and will not be lost even if the legatee dies before becoming entitled in possession; whereas a contingent interest fails if the legatee dies before the occurrence of the contingency. Thus, a legacy 'to A for life, and subject thereto to B absolutely' gives B a vested interest (assuming that he is living at the death of the testator), and should B die in A's lifetime, the legacy will be payable on the death of A to B's executors to form part of his estate. Had the legacy been 'to A for life, and subject thereto to B absolutely if he shall survive A', B's contingent interest would fail if he died in A's lifetime and his executors would be entitled to nothing; the legacy would fall into the testator's residuary estate on the death of A.

A contingent interest cannot be converted into a vested one by any action on the part of the beneficiaries, unless such action constitutes the contingency stipulated in the will. Where a life tenant assigned her interest to the contingent remainderman (i.e. he was entitled to the remainder only if he survived the life tenant), it was held that the assignment did not give the assignee a vested interest in the remainder, but merely an interest in the income of the estate during the rest of the assignor's life. The assignee would be entitled to the capital of the estate only if and when he survived the assignor. (*Re Bellville's Settlement Trusts, Westminster Bank Ltd* v. *Bellville.*)

A legacy to a person 'payable' or 'to be paid' when he attains a specified age, is vested, giving the legatee an absolute interest immediately the testator dies (*Shrimpton* v. *Shrimpton*). If the legatee survives the testator but dies before the appointed age, the legacy will form part of his estate, and will go to his personal representative, but only at the date when the legatee would have attained that age had he lived (*Crickett* v. *Dolby*). Where the words 'payable' or 'to be paid' are omitted, and the legacy is so expressed that the legatee's right to it depends upon his being alive at the date fixed for the payment, the legacy is contingent, and does not vest unless and until the specified event occurs. Thus, a bequest to a person '*at* twenty-one' or 'if' or 'when' or 'provided' he shall attain the age of twenty-one, is (subject to any contrary intention to be construed from the context) contingent upon the happening of that event; should he die without attaining that age, the legacy will fail, and will not go to his personal representative (*Hanson* v. *Graham*).

Although the above words, if taken alone, will normally make the legacy contingent, a contrary intention may be inferred if they are considered in relation to other contents of the will. Where, for example, there is a gift to the legatee of the intermediate income of the legacy, this is usually taken to negative the assumption that the testator did not intend the legacy to vest in the legatee unless he reached a certain age (*Re Gossling*). Where, however, a testator bequeathed a sum of money in trust for his wife for life, and after her death to her grandson on his attaining twenty-one years of age, provided that, should the wife die before the grandson attained that age, the income from the legacy was to be paid to the grandson's mother for his advancement and education, it was held that there was no such complete gift of the income as would make the legacy vested in the grandson (*Re Rogers, Lloyd's Bank Ltd* v. *Lory*).

Where a bequest is made to a child or other issue of the testator contingent on such person attaining a specified age, and the legatee dies in the lifetime of the testator before attaining that age, the legacy does not take effect. The fact that the child may have left issue (see § 11 of this Chapter), does not apply to save a contingent interest which has failed (*In re Wolson*).

Where the time for payment of a vested legacy is postponed by the will until the legatee attains an age greater than twenty-one, e.g. twenty-five, the court will order it to be paid to him at the age of now eighteen, formerly twenty-one (*Curtis* v. *Lukin*). The reason underlying this is that the legatee can then give a valid discharge, and could raise money on the property, so that further postponement would merely inconvenience the legatee for nobody's benefit.

Accretions to the capital of a contingent legacy which accrue between the death of the testator and the happening of the contingency belong to the legatee (*Re Buxton, Buxton* v. *Buxton*).

The position of the executor in connection with contingent legacies depends upon the nature of the contingency. If the legacy is payable on the happening of a certain event, proof of its occurrence should be obtained before the legacy is handed over. In order not to delay the distribution of the estate, the executor can either set aside a fund sufficient to discharge the legacy if and when it becomes payable, or hand over the whole of the residue to the residuary legatee on his giving satisfactory security for the discharge of the legacy if it becomes payable.

(e) Conditional Legacies

A legacy is said to be conditional when its vesting is made to depend on an event in the nature of a condition precedent, the occurrence or fulfilment of which may be affected by the volition of the legatee. The condition must be such that its fulfilment is capable of ascertainment, e.g. in the case of a legacy bequeathed to a person provided that he 'shall occupy my freehold property', it was held impossible to say what would be a sufficient occupation and the condition was void (*Re Field's Will Trusts*).

The legacy may be so expressed as to confer an interest upon the beneficiary *until* some condition is fulfilled. The legatee then acquires a vested interest which will only continue to exist so long as a condition subsequent is not fulfilled; e.g. a gift of the income of 'the residue to X, but should she marry, then to Y', confers upon X an immediate interest which will, however, be defeated by her subsequent marriage.

A bequest of real property made subject to the fulfilment of an impossible condition precedent, e.g. to swim the Atlantic, is void at common law. In the case of personalty, however, where the impossibility of the condition must have been known to the testator, a conditional legacy will vest in the legatee free from the condition (*Re Thomas's Will Trusts, Powell* v. *Thomas*). The same rule applies where a condition subsequent is impossible. If the impossibility was not known to the testator the gift fails, unless the impossibility arises through an act of the testator, when it will take effect free of the condition. In the case of a devise of realty, however, the gift fails if the condition is impossible, even though the impossibility resulted from the act of the testator (*Re Turton*).

The construction of the terms of the will is in all cases important. Where a testator directed his trustees to hold the residue of his estate to pay a certain proportion of the income to his niece 'during her life, or until she shall take the veil', and she took the veil prior·to the death of the testator, it was held that the intention of the testator was that the condition should operate from the date of the will, and the gift failed. Had it operated from the date of death only, the life interest would only have failed if she had taken the veil after that date (*Re Hewitt*).

Where an interest in property (other than entailed property) is given with an executory limitation over in the event of the donee dying without issue, the gift over becomes void if and as soon as any issue of the donee attains the age of eighteen years. An executory limitation is one conferred so as to take effect upon the determination of a prior interest.

Illustration

A bequeathed to B certain property, subject to the limitation that in the event of B's death without issue, the property should go to C. B's daughter D lived to the age of 18. The gift over to C is inoperative, and the property vested absolutely in B on the date on which his daughter reached the age of 18.

A condition in total restraint of marriage is void, but a gift *until* marriage is valid (*Morley* v. *Rennoldson*), as also is a gift subject to a restraint against marriage to a person of a particular race or creed (*Re Lysaght*). A condition that a widower or widow shall lose the gift in the event of remarriage is valid (*Newton* v. *Marsden; Allen* v. *Jackson*), although a gift subject to such a condition will not be effective if the testator and his wife are subsequently divorced, even if the latter does not remarry; an ex-wife is not regarded as a widow (*Re Dawson's Settlement, Lloyds Bank* v. *Dawson*).

(f) Legacies and Donationes Mortis Causa

A legacy and a *donatio mortis causa* are similar in that:

　(i) both may be revoked during the lifetime of the donor; and

　(ii) both are liable for debts of the deceased if there is a deficiency of assets.

A *donatio mortis causa* differs from a legacy in that:

　(i) a *donatio* does not require the assent of the personal representative;

　(ii) the mode of donation need not conform to the law of the donor's domicil; and

　(iii) a *donatio* bears its own Estate Duty, whereas a legacy, normally, does not, since the Estate Duty on all personalty is payable out of residue.

(g) Disclaimer of Legacies or of a Share on Intestacy

A person entitled to a legacy or to a share on intestacy cannot be forced to take it against his will. 'It seems contrary to common sense to say that an estate should vest in a man not assenting to it; there must be the assent of the party before any interest in the property can pass to him' (*Best, J.* in *Townson* v. *Tickell*). Where the legacy or share is refused, it is said to be disclaimed, and the subject matter falls into residue, or, if it is a share of residue, becomes property undisposed of, devolving as upon intestacy. Disclaimer may even be advantageous, as in *Re Sullivan*, where the estate was thereby freed from a clause in the will requiring certain income to be capitalised, with the result that the donee acquired a greater benefit by taking the property under the law of intestacy.

Some transactions, however, are not disclaimers or renunciations, but releases or assignments. It seems that a disclaimer by a residuary legatee of part only of an estate would be an assignment in favour of the co-residuary legatees or, failing them, the testator's next of kin on intestacy. It is, however, possible, where there is a gift of distributed properties, to disclaim one property and not another, unless the will states that they are to be taken together (cf. *Re Joel*).

Moreover, a legatee may accept a smaller sum in settlement of a legacy.

Disclaimer extinguishes a right, and if it is intended, or can be taken to have been intended to benefit certain persons, the disclaimer operates as a gift *inter vivos* attracting Estate Duty if the person disclaiming dies within seven years (*Re Stratton's Disclaimer*, where a widow disclaimed specific legacies and a devise which thereupon devolved on her sons as residuary legatees). The extinguishment is 'at the expense' of the disclaimer, and is caught by the Finance Act 1940, s. 45 (2). Where, however, the surviving spouse of a deceased intestate disclaims unconditionally his or her right under English law to a net sum charged upon the intestate's residuary estate (i.e. the 'statutory legacy' of £8,750 or £30,000, as the case may be), Estate Duty is not claimed in connection with the death of the spouse, although it could be claimed under the gift *inter vivos* rules if the death was within seven years of the disclaimer. There is a similar concession regarding certain legal rights in a Scottish estate. The concessions do not cover cases where the renunciation takes place after acceptance of the right, or if the transaction is, in effect, an acceptance and assignment. If a surviving spouse disclaims chattels to which he or she is entitled, or a person

entitled under the intestacy disclaims a share of residue, it is
not the practice to claim Estate Duty on the death of the person
who made the disclaimer. Should a person, entitled to a share
of a deceased intestate's estate, die before having accepted it,
Estate Duty is claimed on the full value of the share, even if the
personal representatives of that person accept a smaller amount.
This does not, of course, apply to the life interest of a surviving
spouse, as it is settled property on which Estate Duty was paid
on the death of the deceased spouse.

(h) Refunding of Legacies

Although legacies have been assented to and paid over to the
legatees, they may be recovered from them by the executor in
order to provide for the payment of any debts of which he was
ignorant at the time he paid the legacies (*Nelthorpe* v. *Biscoe*).

The creditors may also, if necessary, follow the assets into
the hands of the legatees.

An executor, by paying a legacy, admits the existence of
assets to pay all legacies other than those which would abate
before the one which has been paid (*Orr* v. *Kaines*); legatees
may, therefore, be entitled to sue the executor in respect of their
interest. In such a case, if the executor is insolvent, the unsatisfied legatees can compel the legatee who has been paid to
refund his benefit.

(i) Claim by Legatee

A beneficiary, like a creditor, cannot bring an action against the
estate of the deceased more than twelve years from the date
when the right to receive the share or interest accrued (Limitation Act 1939, s. 20). Time begins to run from the date of death,
unless the will directs the payment on some later date. The
Limitation Act will not bar the claim of a residuary legatee to
assets duly falling into the possession of the personal representative within twelve years of the commencement of proceedings
(see *Waddell* v. *Harshaw; re Johnson; re Welch*).

§ 4. Legacies left to a Class

A testator, by will, sometimes leaves property to a class of
persons without specifically naming those who are to benefit
under the bequest. The principles upon which the persons who

are to share are determined may be stated shortly as follows:

(1) If the testator expressly fixes the time at which the class is to be determined, his wishes must be observed, subject to the rule against perpetuities (see Chapter XVI, § 7), so that a bequest to children 'now living' means the children living at the date of the will (*Viner* v. *Francis*).

(2) If no time is expressly fixed by the testator:

(*a*) If there is an immediate gift (e.g. to the children of X), and any of the class indicated are in existence at the date of the testator's death (including any *en ventre sa mère*), it vests in those only, but if none exists at the date of the testator's death, all who subsequently come into existence will share (*Harris* v. *Lloyd*).

(*b*) If there is a gift in remainder (e.g. to X for life, with remainder to his children), it vests in those of X's children living at the testator's death, subject to letting in all those born prior to the death of X (*Re Canney's Trusts*).

(*c*) If the legacy is to vest or be paid on the happening of some specified event, no member of the class born after that event happens can share; e.g. in the case of a bequest to such children of X as have attained the age of twenty-one, the class is determined when the first child is entitled to payment, and none born thereafter can participate (*Mainwaring* v. *Beevor*).

(*d*) Where the legacy is to be held in trust for such a class, living or to be born, as shall attain the age of twenty-one, each child on attaining that age is entitled to receive an aliquot part of the accumulated income as if the class interested were then closed. If another child is subsequently born, a reapportionment of income is to be made as from his birth. During the accumulation, income is apportioned over the children living from time to time, and if one child dies without having acquired a vested interest, the share provisionally apportioned to him is to be re-assigned to the survivors in accordance with their respective shares from time to time during the period of accrual (*Re King, Public Trustee* v. *Aldridge*).

§ 5. Interest on Legacies

Legacies carry interest at the rate of 4 per cent. per annum from the end of one year from the testator's death, or if any other time of payment or rate of interest is directed by the will, then according to such directions (R.S.C., Order LV, R. 64), even if payment at that date is impracticable (*Wood* v. *Penoyre*), and even if the assets have been unproductive (*Pearson* v. *Pearson*). In the following cases they carry interest from the date of death:

(1) Where the will directs the legacy to be paid 'immediately' after the testator's death (*Re Riddell; Re Pollock*).

(2) Legacies CHARGED ON LAND (*Pearson* v. *Pearson, supra; Turner* v. *Buck*).

(3) A legacy to an INFANT CHILD of the testator for whose MAINTENANCE no other provision is made (*Harvey* v. *Wynch*); or to an infant who is not the child of the testator, where there is a clear intention that the testator intended the infant to be supported out of the legacy (*In re Stokes, Bowen* v. *Davidson*).

Similarly, where a testator, who is the parent of, or *in loco parentis* to, an infant, gives a legacy to that infant contingently upon his attaining an age other than full age, and makes no provision for maintenance, the court may order the interest on the legacy to be applied in maintaining the legatee until it vests (*Re Jones, Meacock* v. *Jones*).

(4) A legacy in SATISFACTION OF A DEBT due by the testator appears to carry interest if the debt itself bore interest (*Clark* v. *Sewell; Shirt* v. *Westby*).

(5) A SPECIFIC LEGACY earning income, and also a DEMONSTRATIVE LEGACY, SO LONG AS IT REMAINS IN ITS NATURE SPECIFIC, carries with it the income earned by the subject matter between the date of death and the assent of the executor (*Sleech* v. *Thorington; Pollock* v. *Pollock*). The income arising from a specific legacy is apportionable between the testator's estate and the legatee (*Lancefield* v. *Iggulden*), the latter being entitled to the income accrued after death only.

In special circumstances, the court may order a rate of interest in excess of the customary 4 per cent., as, for example, where the assets generally are earning a higher rate. Thus, the court ordered 5 per cent. where the payment of legacies had been postponed under an order of the court for the benefit of the residuary legatees (*In re Brinton, Brinton* v. *Preen*). All interest is simple interest unless, in particular circumstances, the court thinks fit to order compound interest to be taken.

The executor is entitled to deduct, out of interest payable on legacies, Income tax at the current standard rate (*Re Ellis Jones; Hamilton* v. *Linaker*).

If there are insufficient funds to pay legacies when due, and interest thereon becomes payable, *the legatees are entitled to appropriate payments made on account* as payments, *pro tanto*, of interest due to them at the time of the payment on the unpaid legacies (*In re Prince; Hardman* v. *Willis*).

Specific legatees of live stock are entitled to any progeny thereof born after the death of the testator, even though the assent of the executor to the legacy has not yet been given when the natural accretion occurs.

§ 6. Legacy to an Infant or Person abroad

Where it is considered necessary, e.g. in the case of a legacy to a child, or to a person absent from England, an executor may pay the amount of the legacy into court, and so free himself from all responsibility in respect thereof (Trustee Act 1925, s. 63).

The proper course is to obtain from the Inland Revenue Commissioners directions to the Bank of England to receive the amount of the legacy, and to place it to the account of the Accountant-General on behalf of the infant or person absent from England.

Where an infant is absolutely entitled, under a will or on an intestacy, to a devise or legacy, or to the whole or part of residue of the estate of the deceased, and no trustees have been appointed by the will, the personal representative may either pay the legacy, etc., into court, or appoint a trust corporation or two or more individuals, not exceeding four, to be trustees for the infant. On such appointment being made, the personal representative escapes all further liability, and the legacy may either be retained in its existing form or be invested in any authorised investment (A.E.A. 1925, s. 42).

Should the infant be of foreign domicil, the money may be paid to him upon his attaining full age, as determined by the law of his country of domicil, notwithstanding the fact that he may still be an infant according to English Law (*In re Schnapper*).

§ 7. Appropriation of Property in specie in satisfaction of Legacies

The personal representative may appropriate any part of the real or personal estate, in its actual state of investment at the time of appropriation, in or towards satisfaction of any legacy, but not so as to prejudice any specific bequest or devise. The appropriation requires the consent of the beneficiary of an absolute bequest, or of the trustee or life tenant of a settled legacy. In the case of an infant, the consent is given by the parent or guardian. No consent is required of a person who cannot be found or ascertained, while for a settled legacy, if there is no trustee other than the personal representative, and the life tenant is an infant, no consent is required to the appropriation if it is of investments authorised by the will or by statute (A.E.A. 1925, s. 41).

The requirement of the beneficiary's consent introduces a sufficient contractual element to attract 1 per cent. stamp duty (*Jopling* v. *C.I.R.*), though it appears that a provision in a will providing for appropriation without consent does not. The 1 per cent. *ad valorem* stamp duty is not payable on an appropriation of the statutory legacy of a surviving spouse in an intestacy if the surviving spouse is the sole administrator, or if the estate does not exceed the amount of the legacy, nor is it payable on the appropriation of the matrimonial home; since the surviving spouse can insist on its appropriation, there is no contractual relationship. See also Chapter XVI, § 26, (*c*).

The provisions of the current Exchange Control rules should be referred to where any money accrues to a person outside the United Kingdom.

§ 8. Legacies of Shares in Companies

When partly paid shares in a company are bequeathed to a person absolutely, the executor should transfer them to the legatee as soon as possible, in order to end the liability of the testator's estate in respect of them.

If the legatee is not *sui juris*, and the shares cannot be transferred into his name, the position of the executor becomes embarrassing, but if he merely receives dividends *qua* executor he will not thereby render himself personally liable to the company, and cannot be made a contributory, except in his representative capacity (*Buchan's Case*). It may happen, however, that unless the executor transfers the shares into his own name or that of some other person, they will be forfeited; in that case, if the legatee is not *sui juris*, the executor should, for his own protection, apply to the court for directions.

When partly paid shares are bequeathed to one person for life, with remainder to others, they ought to be sold, unless it is clearly the testator's intention that they shall be retained *in specie*. If they are intended to be enjoyed *in specie*, the position of the executor may again be difficult; if he transfers the shares into the name of the tenant for life, there is nothing to prevent the latter from selling them for his own use, while if the executor should sell the shares the remainderman would naturally seek to make him responsible for their loss. If, on the other hand, the executor has the shares transferred into his own name as trustee for the legatees, and the shares are only partly paid, a personal liability in respect of these shares will be incurred by him, that liability not being limited by the amount of the assets of the testator. Unless, therefore, the executor can retain the shares as executor without transferring them, he should, for his own safety, apply for the direction of the court.

It should be remembered that if such shares are specifically settled apart from the residue of the estate, and there is no trust for conversion, the executor has no right to sell them, and the life tenant is entitled to the whole income produced (*Lord* v. *Godfrey*).

The executor should always, before distributing the estate, provide for the contingent liability for calls on shares not fully paid; otherwise he will be personally liable, unless acting on the instructions of the court. However, if it was a remotely contingent liability at the time of distribution, he can recover the amount from the legatees (*Jervis* v. *Wolferstan*); but this is not so if a call had actually been made at the date of distribution, and the executor had notice of that call (*Whittaker* v. *Kershaw*).

§ 9. Satisfaction of a Debt by a Legacy

When a debtor transfers property to his creditor, the presumption is that he does so not as a donor but in satisfaction of his debt. Accordingly, a legacy left to a creditor of the testator, if accepted by the creditor, may operate to extinguish the liability of the estate in respect of the debt. This principle of satisfaction does not, however, commend itself to the court, for it may inflict an unintended deprivation upon the creditor, and it is therefore subject to considerable limitation in its application. Consequently, a legacy will be regarded as being in satisfaction of a debt and not independent of it only if:

(i) the debt existed at the time the will was made (*Cranmer's Case*);

(ii) the legacy is equal to or greater in amount than the debt (*Leacroft* v. *Maynard*); and

(iii) the legacy is in other respects equally as favourable as the debt.

A legacy will not be in satisfaction of a debt:

(i) if there is a direction in the will for payment of debts and legacies (*Chancey's Case*); or

(ii) if the debt is a negotiable security (*Carr* v. *Eastabrooke*); or

(iii) if the legacy is contingent or uncertain (*Nicholls* v. *Judson*); or

(iv) if the legacy is of the whole or part of a residue (*Devese* v. *Pontet*); or

(v) if the debt is upon an open and running account (*Rawlins* v. *Powell*); or

(vi) if a particular motive is assigned for the legacy; or

(vii) if the legacy is a specific legacy, unless it is so expressed in the will and the creditor accepts it as such (*Byde* v. *Byde*).

§ 10. Ademption of Specific Legacies

Where a specific legacy is given by will, but before the death of the testator the subject matter thereof is disposed of by the testator, or its form is so changed as no longer to correspond with the description of the legacy, it is said to be adeemed, and the legatee loses his benefit and is not entitled to any compensation out of the general assets (*Ashburner* v. *M'Guire*). A mere direction by the testator to sell the subject matter of the specific legacy will not adeem the legacy if the sale has not been effected

(*Harrison* v. *Asher*), while generally speaking, a sale, which was not authorised by the testator, will not operate as an ademption (*Jenkins* v. *Jones*).

Notwithstanding that the will speaks from the date of death (Wills Act 1837, s. 24), if a testator, having parted with the subject matter of the specific bequest, subsequently acquires a similar thing which is in his possession at the date of death, the legatee will, unless the proper construction of the will indicates otherwise, be deprived of benefit (*Re Portal*). The testator is regarded as intending a gift of the actual subject matter corresponding with the description of the bequest at the date the will was made.

The principle of ademption does not apply to a demonstrative legacy; if the fund demonstrated has ceased to exist, the legatee is entitled to be paid out of the general estate (*Mann* v. *Copeland*).

If the testator, in contemplation of acquiring a specific article, bequeaths it by will, but never acquires it, the gift will fail (*Stephenson* v. *Dowson*).

If the legacy consists of a specific debt due to the deceased, and part of it has been paid to him in his lifetime, the legacy is adeemed *pro tanto* (*Ashburner* v. *M'Guire*).

A specific legacy of stocks or shares will be adeemed if they have been actually disposed of, or if they have changed in form, with the consequence that the testator acquired an interest in an entirely new undertaking. If, however, the shares in the original company still exist, but have been changed in form by consolidation or sub-division, or other form of capital reconstruction, there will be no ademption if they represent substantially the same interests as those given by the will (*Re Clifford*). The terms of the statute which converts the holding may be such as to avoid ademption, e.g. it would appear from the terms of the relevant statutes that bequests of securities in industries which have been nationalised are not thereby adeemed.

Illustrations

(1) A testatrix gave 'my piano' to A. She afterwards sold the piano and bought another, which was in her possession at the date of her death. It was held that A was not entitled to the piano, since the testatrix, from the terms of her will, intended to bequeath the piano in her possession at the time she executed her will (*Re Sikes, Moxon* v. *Crossley*).

(2) A testator in his will gave to his daughter 'all my interest in my present lease of No. 1 Chesterfield Street'. The lease subsequently expired but was renewed. The testator executed a codicil after the date of the renewal, not affecting this bequest but in which he stated that in all other respects he confirmed his will. It was held that as the confirmation by codicil brought the will down to the date of the codicil, the benefit of the renewed lease passed to the daughter (*In re Reeves, Reeves* v. *Pawson*).

(3) Where a testator specifically bequeathed certain shares, but subsequently, by agreement in writing, granted some other person an option to purchase all shares of that kind within one month of his death, and on his death this option was exercised, the specific bequest of the shares was adeemed, and the proceeds of sale formed part of the residuary estate (*In re Carrington, Ralphs* v. *Swithenbank*).

(4) A testator left to a legatee an interest arising from investments in the Lambeth Water Works, a concern which was afterwards taken over by the Metropolitan Water Board; as the stock in the latter undertaking was issued to the testator in compensation for the holding in the former undertaking, it was held that ademption had taken place (*Re Slater*).

(5) A testator gave 'my ten shares in the Kirkstall Brewery Co., Limited', but during his lifetime the company was reconstructed and reincorporated under a different name. For each of his ten shares in the old company, the testator received two £5 preference shares and two £5 ordinary shares in the new company, and it was held that this did not constitute an ademption of the legacy (*Turner* v. *Leeming*).

It is emphasised that the principle of ademption can only apply to *specific* legacies. Where a testator bequeaths a *general* legacy of certain stocks which, after his death, cannot be bought, or if the legatee has a choice in the matter and says he would rather not have the stock, the legacy is not adeemed and the legatee is entitled to its value (*Re Borne; Bailey* v. *Bailey*).

Since property passes subject to any charges thereon (A.E.A. 1925, s. 35), a specific legacy, the subject matter of which has been pawned, is not adeemed, but the legatee would have to bear the cost of redeeming it, unless the will contained provisions to the contrary.

A special case of ademption arises from the principle that 'equity' leans against double portions. The principle has been stated as follows: 'Where a testator gives a legacy to a child, or to any other person to whom he has taken on himself parental obligations, and *afterwards* makes a gift or enters into a binding contract in his lifetime in favour of the same legatee, then (unless there are distinctions between the nature and conditions of the two gifts), there is a presumption *prima facie* that both gifts were made to fulfil the same natural or moral obligation of providing for the legatee; consequently the gift *inter vivos* is either wholly *or in part* a substitution for, or an ademption of, the legacy' (*Re Pollock*). A gift so made to a child is termed a 'portion'; a 'marriage portion' is a familiar example. Where a legacy is given by a parent (or person standing *in loco parentis*) to a child without reference to the object of the gift, the presumption is that it is a portion, since it is natural that a parent should provide for his child. Unless a contrary intention is indicated, it is further presumed that the parent wishes to provide for all his children, and not to make double provision for some of them. Accordingly, where a general legacy is given by will to a child, and after the date of the will a gift in the nature of an advancement (e.g. a marriage settlement) is made to the child by the testator, it is presumed that the portion was intended to be in partial satisfaction of the legacy, and the general legacy is *pro tanto* adeemed by the advancement (*Re Pollock, supra*). Should the gift be made within seven years of death, and so be subject to Estate Duty, such duty will be deducted from the advancement in ascertaining the amount by which the legacy is adeemed (*Re Beddington*). The effect of the advancement will be seen below in § 18.

The presumption that a legacy is adeemed by a portion is, however, rebutted where:

(1)   there is a substantial difference in the nature of the property given; e.g. a gift *inter vivos* of land will not adeem a legacy of money: the thing given must be *ejusdem generis* (of the same kind) with the gift which it is to satisfy (*Re Jacques, Hodgson* v. *Braisby*);

(2)   there is a difference in the nature of limitation of the gifts, e.g. where one is certain, the other contingent;

(3)   different conditions attach to the gift and the legacy respectively.

The rule is not always easy to apply; for example, where a father pays his son's debts, his action may be regarded as temporary assistance and is not necessarily an advancement (*Re Scott*). Where a father made a will, giving his residuary estate to his two sons in certain shares, and subsequently let his farms to one of his sons and made him a gift of the live and dead stock (which was valued at the time), it was held that that son's share in the residuary estate was adeemed to the extent of the value of the live and dead stock (*Re George's Will Trusts*).

If the testator is neither a parent nor a person *in loco parentis*, a legacy will be adeemed by a subsequent advance only if both legacy and advance are made for the same purpose, or if the advance is evidently made for the specific purpose of adeeming the legacy (*Re Pollock, supra; re Ware*).

§ 11. Lapse of Legacies

The general rule is that where a legacy is left to a person who dies before the testator, or before any other condition precedent to the vesting of the legacy is performed, the legacy lapses and falls into residue. If a legacy charged on real estate lapses, however, it will not fall into the residue of the personalty; the lapse will operate for the benefit of the real estate. A lapsed gift of a share of RESIDUE cannot fall into residue, but must be distributed as if there were a partial intestacy as to that share. A similar position arises where a testator divides his residue among a number of persons and subsequently, by codicil, revokes the gift of a share of residue to some one or more of those persons; in the absence of an indication to give that share to the other residuary legatees, there is an intestacy in respect of the revoked share (*In re Forrest, Carr* v. *Forrest*). A beneficiary found guilty of causing the death of a testator cannot benefit from the latter's estate; the beneficiary's interest will therefore lapse, and if it was represented by a share of residue, that share will devolve as on an intestacy (*Estate of Robertson, Marsden* v. *Marsden*). Where residue is left in trust to pay the income to two life tenants in equal shares, with remainder 'from and after their decease' to a third person, and one of the life tenants predeceases the testator, the surviving life tenant is entitled to the whole income; the gift over does not take effect till the death of the survivor (*In re Ragdale, Public Trustee* v. *Tuffill*).

Even if the gift is made payable to a particular person AND his executors, administrators or assigns, it will lapse if the person named predeceases the testator (*Maybank* v. *Brooks*) since persons entitled to take by representation only cannot acquire anything to which the person they represent had no title (*Williamson* v. *Naylor*). However, an immediate bequest to a person OR his personal representatives would be sufficient to pass the legacy to the latter (*Gittings* v. *M'Dermott*). Similarly, a clear alternative gift to another in the event of the person named dying before the testator will take effect in that event (*Sibley* v. *Cook*), and a legacy to a person AND his heirs will pass direct to the heirs of that person if he predeceases the testator (*Re Porter's Trusts*).

If a will contained gifts to the children of any child who 'shall die' in the testator's lifetime, the issue of a child, who was already dead at the date of the will, are excluded, unless the context clearly showed a contrary intention (*Re Walker*, *Walker* v. *Walker*). However, there is a most important exception to the general rule above stated, in that if the legatee is a child or other issue of the testator, and the legatee dies before the testator, leaving issue living at the testator's death, the legacy may be dealt with as if the legatee had died immediately after the testator: It will, therefore, be paid or transferred to the personal representative of that legatee, unless a contrary intention appears in the will (Wills Act 1837, s. 33). Such a legacy forms part of the deceased legatee's estate, and devolves under the terms of his will in accordance with the law in force at the time of his death (*Re Hurd*). The issue thus save the legacy from lapsing, but whether they enjoy the benefit of the subject matter of the legacy will depend on the terms of the deceased legatee's will. Property will not be deemed, for Estate Duty purposes, to pass on the legatee's death because, on a later or simultaneous death, a gift to him is prevented from lapsing by his having left issue who survived the testator (Finance Act 1958, s. 29 (2)).

Similarly, if the devisee of an 'entailed interest', e.g. a limitation to 'A and the heirs of his body', dies during the lifetime of the testator, leaving issue capable of inheriting under the entail, the devise takes effect as if the devisee had died immeidately after the testator (*ibid.*, s. 32).

§ 12. Legacies for Charitable Purposes

Generally speaking, a gift for charitable purposes is legal and valid, but where the objects are left indefinite, the legacy will fail for uncertainty, unless the intention is exclusively charitable, in which event the court would direct or supervise its distribution. For example, if a bequest is made 'for such charitable *or* deserving purposes as my executor shall select', the gift will fail as all 'deserving' objects may not be charitable. Similarly, a gift for 'charitable *or* benevolent' objects will fail (*Chichester Diocesan Fund and Board of Finance (Incorporated)* v. *Simpson; Re Endecott; Re Smith's Will Trusts*). Where property is bequeathed on trust for charitable and other non-charitable purposes in such proportions as the trustees shall appoint, if the other purposes are of a 'shadowy and indefinite nature', so that the court could not execute them, then, in default of appointment, the whole gift would fail for uncertainty (*Re Sidney*). If, however, the other purposes comprise only 'definite and ascertainable objects' then, in default of appointment, the court should divide the fund equally among all the objects (*Salusbury* v. *Denton*). It should be noted that a gift may be charitable, though not made to a charity registered under the Charities Act 1960, as not all charities have to be registered (*see* Charities Act 1960, s. 4).

'Charity' in its legal sense comprises trusts for (1) the relief of poverty, (2) the advancement of education, (3) the advancement of religion, (4) other purposes beneficial to the community not falling under any of the preceding heads (*Pemsel's Case, per Lord Macnaghten*). Whether or not a gift is a valid charitable bequest will be determined by the court by reference to this definition and the precise terms in which the legacy is expressed.

§ 13. Treatment of Legacies in the Books of Account

(a) *General Legacies*
These should not be recorded in the books until payment takes place.

(b) *Specific Legacies*
Property specifically bequeathed should be brought into the books at the Estate Duty valuation; when the legacy is satisfied the asset account should be credited, and legacies account debited.

(c) *Demonstrative Legacies*
The treatment of demonstrative legacies in the books is similar to that of general legacies.

Illustration

The estate of John Smith deceased, which consisted entirely of personalty, amounted, after payment of debts and funeral expenses, Estate Duty, and administration expenses, to £35,000.

He bequeathed the following legacies:

To Mrs Smith (widow)	£10,000
„ Miss Vera Smith (daughter, aged 20)	£2,000
„ Mrs Nora Jones (daughter)	£3,000

Nora Jones, who pre-deceased her father, John Smith, left by will the whole of the residue of her estate to her first cousin, Jack Robinson, after having made ample provision for her children.

„ Samuel Jenkins (executor) .. .. .. A handsome gratuity	
„ Charles Smith (brother)	£1,000
„ Miss Phyllis Smith (daughter)	£3,000

Phyllis Smith pre-deceased her father, John Smith, and by will left the whole of the residue of her estate to her first cousin, Jack Robinson.

„ Augustus Judson (secretary)	£2,000
„ Mrs Jack Robinson (stranger)	£3,000

Mrs Robinson, who pre-deceased the testator, by her will left the whole of the residue of her estate to her husband, Jack Robinson.

„ Jack Robinson, gold watch valued for probate at £10. The testator also left to Mr Robinson '£100 Consols out of my holding of Consols'. NOTE. The testator had sold his Consols shortly before death.

„ Roscoe W. Chandler (friend) his collection of antique snuff boxes, valued for probate at £3,000.

„ Captain Spaulding (his wife's stepfather's brother), '£1,000 payable out of my holding of 3% Government Loan'. NOTE. The testator had sold his 3% Government Loan shortly before death.

The residue to the London Hospital.

Show the Legacies Account in the estate books of John Smith, deceased.

JOHN SMITH (DECEASED)
LEGACIES ACCOUNT

			£
Cash—Mrs Smith	10,000	Estate Account	35,000
Cash—Vera Smith	2,000		
Cash—Estate of Nora Jones, deceased	3,000		
Cash—Charles Smith	1,000		
Cash—A. Judson	2,000		
Gold Watch—Jack Robinson ..	10		
Snuff Boxes—Roscoe W. Chandler ..	3,000		
Cash—Captain Spaulding	1,000		
Cash—London Hospital	12,990		
	£35,000		£35,000

Notes to Illustration

(1) NORA JONES, DECEASED

Since the legatee, a child of the testator, predeceased him but left issue living at the testator's death, the bequest takes effect as if the legatee had died immediately after the death of the testator (unless a contrary intention appears by the will) (Wills Act 1837, § 33). (*See* § 10 of this chapter.)

The estate of Nora Jones will therefore benefit to the extent of £3,000. This sum will form part of the residue of Nora Jones' estate, and will, therefore, pass to her first cousin, Jack Robinson, and not to her issue, in spite of the fact that, but for the issue, her estate would not have benefited under the will of her father, John Smith, deceased.

(2) SAMUEL JENKINS, EXECUTOR

A bequest of 'a handsome gratuity to my executor' is void owing to its uncertainty (*Jubber* v. *Jubber*).

(3) PHYLLIS SMITH

As Miss Phyllis Smith pre-deceased her father and left no issue, the legacy lapses, and falls into the residue of the father's estate.

(4) MRS JACK ROBINSON

As Mrs Robinson pre-deceased the testator the legacy lapses. It is immaterial in this context whether or not she had issue who survived the testator.

(5) JACK ROBINSON

The bequest '£100 Consols out of my holding in Consols' is a specific, not a demonstrative legacy; as the testator, at the date of his death, had no Consols, the legacy fails by ademption (*see* § 10 of this chapter).

(6) CAPTAIN SPAULDING

The bequest of '£1,000 payable out of my holding of 3% Government Loan' is a demonstrative legacy; as the subject matter of the legacy is no longer there, the legacy ranks as a general pecuniary legacy.

§ 14. Abatement of Legacies

Where legacies are charged on a mixed fund of both real and personal estate, they are payable primarily out of the personal estate, the real estate being the auxiliary fund for this purpose, unless the will or Section 33 of the Administration of Estates Act 1925 (*see* Chapter XIII, § 8) imposes a different order. Williams on *Executors and Administrators* (14th edition, p. 996) says that recent decisions suggest that the courts will somewhat readily see in the will indications of an intention to treat realty and personalty as a single fund for paying legacies.

The effect of marshalling the assets in the order set out in Part II of the First Schedule to the Administration of Estates Act 1925 (*see* Chapter XIII, § 8) is that if, after payment of the debts, etc., the estate is insufficient to pay the legacies in full, the legacies must abate.

The general legacies must abate first, proportionately among themselves, unless the will expressly or by implication indicates a contrary intention. It should be noted that a gift of an annuity is a general legacy, and must abate with the other general legacies where the estate is insufficient to pay them (including the annuity) in full. The abatement in such a case will be governed by the rules indicated in the cases which are separately considered in § 18 of this Chapter. For the purpose of abatement, the valuation of an annuity will be at the date of the court order (*Re Bradberry and Re Fry*). If the fund out of which a demonstrative legacy is made payable has ceased to exist during the testator's lifetime, such legacy becomes a general legacy, and abates with other general legacies (*Mullins* v. *Smith*).

If the fund available for general legacies is exhausted because the assets not specifically bequeathed are insufficient to pay the debts, the specific legacies and those demonstrative legacies which remain specific in character must abate at the same time as, and proportionately among themselves, together (where the residue is a mixed fund) with specific devises (*Roberts* v. *Pocock; Fowler* v. *Willoughby*).

An executor has no priority for his legacy, or any right of retainer as against other legatees of the same class, even if the legacy be left to him for his trouble as executor. Should there be a deficiency of assets, his legacy must abate with others (*Duncan* v. *Watts*).

Where the will conveys a definite indication that certain legacies should rank in priority to others of a similar class, the executor must give effect to the testator's intention. The intention must, however, be clear; it will not be inferred from the fact merely that the bequests are in number order (*Lewin* v. *Lewin*).

If a specific devise of realty has been made free of Estate Duty, such duty, which is treated as a general legacy, must abate with the general legacies, the balance of the duty being recovered from the devisee.

Illustration

The estate of Henry Thompson deceased, after payment of debts, funeral expenses, Estate Duty and testamentary expenses, consisted of the following:

	£
Cash at bank	15,000
Household furniture and personal effects valued for Estate Duty at	2,000
£1,000 5½ per cent. National Development Bonds valued for Estate Duty at	1,000

No income was receivable from the date of death to the date of distribution.

By his will he bequeathed the following legacies:

To his wife	£14,500
Do.	His household furniture and effects
To his son, Percy	£3,000
To his daughter, Joan ..	£2,000
Do.	His holding of £1,000 National Development Bonds
To his brother, William ..	His freehold country cottage
To his nephew, John ..	£500 3 per cent. Savings Bonds out of his holding in 3 per cent. Savings Bonds
To his friend, Joseph Hall ..	£500 payable out of his holding of 3 per cent. Savings Bonds
To his friend, Herbert Jones..	£500.

The testator, some years prior to his death, had sold his holding of £1,000 3 per cent. Savings Bonds. He had also sold his freehold country cottage, the net proceeds of which amounted to £800. His friend, Herbert Jones, a bachelor, had pre-deceased him.

You are required to prepare a statement showing the distribution of the estate.

DISTRIBUTION STATEMENT

	Gross legacy	Sums required to meet pecuniary legacies	Specific legacies		Net legacy
	£	£	£		£
Widow—Cash	14,500	14,500		$\frac{15}{20} \times £14,500$	10,875
„ Household Effects ..	2,000		2,000		2,000
Son, Percy—Cash	3,000	3,000		$\frac{15}{20} \times £3,000$	2,250
Daughter, Joan—Cash ..	2,000	2,000		$\frac{15}{20} \times £2,000$	1,500
„ 5½% National Development Bonds ..	1,000		1,000		1,000
Friend, J. Hall—£500 payable out of Savings Bonds ..	500	500		$\frac{15}{20} \times £500$	375
	£23,000	£20,000	£3,000		£18,000

The accounts will appear as under:

CASH BOOK

	Income	Capital		Income	Capi
	£	£		£	£
Balance b/f		15,000	Legacies Account:		
			Widow		10,8
			Son, Percy		2,2
			Daughter, Joan		1,5
			J. Hall		3
	£	£15,000		£	£15,0

£1,000 5½% NATIONAL DEVELOPMENT BONDS

	Income	Capital		Income	Capi
	£	£		£	£
Estate Account		1,000	Legacies Account		1,0

HOUSEHOLD FURNITURE AND PERSONAL EFFECTS

	£		£
Estate Account	2,000	Legacies Account	2,00

LEGACIES ACCOUNT

	£		£
		Estate Account	18,0
Cash:			
Widow	10,875		
Son, Percy	2,250		
Daughter, Joan	1,500		
J. Hall	375		
National Development Bonds Account:			
Daughter, Joan	1,000		
Household Furniture Account:			
Widow	2,000		
	£18,000		£18,0

Notes to Illustration:

(1) Since the assets, other than those required for satisfaction of the specific legacies, are insufficient to pay the general legacies in full, these must all abate rateably. The sum required to pay these legacies is £20,000; the amount available is £15,000. Each legacy will therefore abate by one-fourth.

(2) The bequest to the brother of the freehold cottage is specific, and fails by ademption.

(3) The legacy to the nephew of £500 Savings Bonds out of the deceased's holding of Savings Bonds is also specific (*Mullins* v. *Smith*), and is adeemed since the deceased had sold his holdings of Savings Bonds. The legacy to Joseph Hall of £500 payable out of the holding of Savings Bonds is, however, demonstrative. It will be payable as a general legacy, and will abate accordingly.

(4) The legacy to Herbert Jones lapses, as the legatee had predeceased the testator.

§ 15. Capital Gains tax on distributions

When distributing the estate to beneficiaries, it will be advisable for the personal representatives to bear in mind the provisions of the Finance Act 1965 in respect of Capital Gains tax. At the time the personal representative assents to the legacy, the beneficiary becomes absolutely entitled to the subject-matter of the legacy. No Capital Gains tax liability will arise at that time by reason of the assent. The legatee will be treated as if the personal representative's acquisition of the asset had been his acquisition of it. If, therefore, the property devolved on the personal representative on the testator's death, the legatee will be deemed to have acquired it at that date and for the value at that date. If the personal representative acquired the property after death to satisfy the legacy, the beneficiary will be deemed to have acquired it at the same time as and at the cost to the personal representative. The personal representative and beneficiary must realise that a disposal after assent which gives rise to a liability will be the responsibility of the beneficiary. Where the latter is chargeable at less than 30 per cent. on the gain under the alternative charge basis (s. 21, F.A. 1965), it is advisable to assent before disposal.

A transfer of assets to a residuary legatee is not a disposal by the personal representatives or an acquisition by the legatee. The rules indicated above will apply. In many cases the residuary legatee will receive the assets in specie. In deciding which assets to give to each residuary legatee care should be taken since to non-residents or charities the values are unimportant; to elderly people with relatively small incomes or those likely to be charged on the alternative basis the values are not of great importance; but to young beneficiaries or those with substantial incomes, the values are of extreme importance. This is because the values at the date of death or date of acquisition, if later, by the personal representative will fix the cost to the beneficiary of the asset transferred. To assist in revising bequests of the deceased so as to give the greatest advantage to beneficiaries, it is provided that if not more than two years after death any dispositions of the deceased's property, whether under the will or the law relating to intestacies, are varied under a deed of family arrangement or similar instrument, the deceased will have been deemed to have disposed of his assets in accordance with that deed. The variations provided in the deed are not treated as disposals.

No liability can arise under Schedule D, Case VII, on a legatee in respect of a disposal by him of the subject-matter of the legacy.

Where the personal representatives are to become trustees of any part of the estate which is to be held in trust for any legatee, they should be particularly careful to record the moment of assent for the reasons indicated in the first paragraph above.

§ 16. Income from Residue

An absolute residuary legatee is not entitled to income till the residue is ascertained, when he will get the residue, including any accrued income.

If there is a life tenant of residue, then, in the absence of any contrary directions in the will, he is entitled, as from the date of the testator's death, to the income of such portion of the residue as is in authorised investments at the date of death, and to an equitable apportionment of the income arising from the remainder until conversion. However, he is not entitled to any income from such part of the estate as is required for the payment of debts, funeral and testamentary expenses and immediate legacies, for the payment of which there must be taken such portion of the capital as, with an equitable apportionment of income, will produce the required amount.

The rules as to equitable apportionments are dealt with in Chapter XI.

§ 17. Costs in respect of Legacies

Generally speaking, the costs attending the payment of pecuniary legacies fall on residue. Should the will require the legacy to be paid in a foreign country and currency, the payment must be made there, the estate bearing the cost of remittance

(*Cockerell* v. *Barber*); in other words, where a sum of money is bequeathed, the cost of raising it must be paid out of residue. However, the costs of transferring specific legacies, including the executor's costs in connection therewith (e.g. packing and delivery) must be borne by the legatees (*Re Grosvenor; Re Fitzpatrick*).

The cost of ascertaining who are the persons entitled to a legacy, or the identity of a legatee, will fall upon the legacy itself, unless the court directs otherwise (R.S.C., Order LXV, R. 14 b). If, however, the difficulty arises from ambiguity in the will, or is in respect of the application of the law, the costs fall on residue (*Re Hall-Dare*).

The cost of paying a legacy into court, or of paying a legatee abroad the amount of his legacy also falls upon residue (*Re Cawthorne, Cockerell* v. *Barbar, supra*), but the cost of paying out of court falls on the legacy (*Re Cawthorne, supra*).

The cost of the upkeep of a specific legacy, from the testator's death until the executor's assent, must be borne by the specific legatee (*Re Pearce*), as must also the cost of its preservation, etc. (*Re Rooke*).

The principle would appear to be that the costs of getting the subject matter into the executor's hands are a charge against the estate, but the expense of handing it over is a charge against the legatee.

It is appropriate here to refer to the stamp duties payable on transfers, etc. Where stamp duty is payable, a fixed duty of ten shillings is payable on a transfer for nominal consideration in any of the following categories:

(*a*) Transfers vesting the property in trustees on the appointment of a new trustee of a pre-existing trust, or on the retirement of a trustee.

(*b*) Transfer to a residuary trustee or residuary legatee of stock, etc., forming part of the residue divisible under a will.

(*c*) Transfers to a beneficiary under a will of a specific legacy of stock, etc.

(*d*) Transfers of stock, etc., forming part of an intestate's estate, to the person entitled to it.

(*e*) Transfers to a beneficiary under a settlement on distribution of the trust funds of stock, etc., forming the share or part of the share of those funds to which the beneficiary is entitled in accordance with the terms of the settlement.

Appropriate certificates setting out the facts of the transaction are required; these should be signed by a solicitor or other person (e.g. a bank acting as trustee or executor) having full knowledge of the facts. On presentation at the stamp office, with the evidence, the transfer will be certified and stamped by the marking officer's signature and office stamp. A registering officer may pass such a transfer without the marking officer's certificate, but is then liable to a penalty if the transfer is wrongly stamped.

An assent in writing (i.e. under hand only) by a personal representative (under A.E.A. 1925, s. 36) to the vesting of any estate or interest in real property in a person entitled thereto under a will or intestacy is not chargeable with stamp duty. An assent under seal attracts ten shillings duty.

An appropriation of realty or securities in satisfaction of a *pecuniary* legacy is chargeable with *ad valorem* duty, since it constitutes a sale to the legatee, the consideration being the amount of the pecuniary legacy (but see third paragraph, § 7 (*supra*) regarding appropriations in satisfaction of the statutory legacy).

§ 18. Advancement and Hotchpot

In distributing the residuary estate of an intestate, the aim of the legislature is to preserve equality among his children. Accordingly, any money or property which, by way of advancement, or on the marriage of a child of the intestate, has been paid or settled by the intestate for the child's benefit must, subject to any contrary intention appearing from the circumstances, be taken as being paid or settled in or towards satisfaction of the child's share or the share which the child would have taken if he had survived the intestate, and must be brought into account in dividing the balance of the deceased's estate (A.E.A. 1925, s. 47). This is called 'bringing advances into hotchpot'. Many wills contain provisions to a similar effect.

An advancement is a payment *inter vivos* by a parent to a child of a portion of what that child would otherwise have been given at the death of the donor. In order to constitute an advancement, the amount must not be a casual payment but a substantial one given on marriage or intended to establish the child in life (*Taylor* v. *Taylor*). It must operate for the permanent benefit of the child. Therefore, a payment for educational purposes, however large, will not be regarded as an advancement (*Boyd* v. *Boyd*). A nomination of £508 in National Savings Certificates has been held, in the case of an intestate's estate of some £1,700 net, not to constitute a fund of such size and importance, even in relation to the intestate's other assets, as to constitute an advancement. To be brought into hotchpot as an advancement, the fund must be sufficiently substantial in itself to be in the nature of a permanent provision (*Re Hayward*). The rule as to bringing advances into hotchpot applies in the case of either an intestate father or mother. The advancement must be brought into account at its value at the date of the intestate's death. If the advancement consisted of a life interest, or an interest for a term of years, it must be brought in, even if given on marriage, or to commence on the parent's death.

A child advanced is required to bring the advance into hotchpot for the benefit of other children, but not for the benefit of the widow or widower of the deceased (*Kircudbright* v. *Kircudbright*); this applies also where there is a hotchpot clause in a will (*Stewart* v. *Stewart*). If a deceased child has been advanced, his children must bring in the advancement made to their parent if they wish to share in the distribution, since the issue take the share which their parent would have taken if living at the death of the intestate (A.E.A. 1925, s. 47). Issue of the deceased remoter than his children need not, however, bring into account advances from the deceased to themselves; only advances to a CHILD of the deceased have to be brought in, that child's issue simply standing in his shoes and taking what he himself would have taken had he lived. This is not applicable to a child's indebtedness to his parent, so that, where a testator gave his residuary estate in trust for his children, and the issue of his deceased children claimed their deceased parent's share, they were not liable to bring in a debt owing by that parent to the testator (*Re Binns, Public Trustee* v. *Ingle*).

Where a will contains a hotchpot clause, it will set out the intention of the testator, and such intention must be observed. If there is a direction in the will to bring into hotchpot a debt due by a child, the hotchpot clause will still be operative notwithstanding the fact that the indebtedness of the advanced child had been released by his bankruptcy, and the father had proved therein. The release must only be held to operate to the extent of the amount received in dividend (*In re Ainsworth, Millington* v. *Ainsworth*).

If the residue is settled, it is necessary to observe the distinction between advances and loans in such a case, since advances carry interest only from the date of distribution, i.e. the date of the death of the life tenant, the date of advance, or the date of the death of the testator or intestate, whichever date is latest (*Re Rees, Rees* v. *George*), whereas loans carry interest as from the date of death of the testator or intestate (*Re Young*).

The term 'intestate' includes a person who leaves a will but dies intestate as to some beneficial interest in his real or personal estate (A.E.A. 1925, s. 55 (1) (vi)). On a partial intestacy, therefore, all the provisions as to bringing advancements into account apply. Moreover, on a PARTIAL INTESTACY, there must be brought into account (*as between issue only*) any beneficial interests acquired by any issue of the deceased UNDER HIS WILL, but not beneficial interests acquired *under the will* by other persons (A.E.A. 1925, s. 49).

In addition, *on a partial intestacy only*, the surviving spouse's statutory legacy of £8,750 or £30,000 is diminished by the value at the date of the intestate's death of any beneficial interests taken under the will, except personal chattels (Intestates' Estates Act 1952). Owing to the provision that benefits taken under the will by 'any issue' must be brought into account, it appears that the children of a deceased child of a partial intestate must bring in not only gifts under the will to themselves but also gifts under the will to their deceased parent which are prevented from lapsing because he left issue. This is to preserve equality among the children of the intestate. In some cases the benefits under the will may be such that the rights under a partial intestacy may profitably be disclaimed.

Illustration (1)

A died and the residue of his estate, amounting to £50,000, was divisible equally between his three children, B, C, and D. B had already during the lifetime of his father received the sum of £10,000, while C had received £5,000, and D £4,000. Divide the residue between the children, bringing the advances into hotchpot, and ignoring interest on advances and death duties.

Particulars	Total	B.	C.	D.
	£	£	£	£	£
Residue	50,000			
Advances	19,000			
	69,000	23,000	23,000	23,000
Less Advances	19,000	10,000	5,000	4,000
Actual distribution	£50,000	£13,000	£18,000	£19,000

It may happen that the amount advanced during the lifetime of the deceased exceeds the amount to which the person advanced is theoretically entitled out of the residue of the estate to be distributed, after taking the advances into account. The person advanced cannot be called upon to refund the excess, and in distributing the residue he is ignored.

Illustration (2)

Advances of £15,000, £5,000, £4,000 were made during the lifetime of A, to B, C, and D respectively, and the residue of the estate divisible between these amounted to £10,000.

The share of each would be one-third of £34,000 = £11,333 6s 8d. B, having received an advance in excess of this amount, is ignored, and the division is made as follows. The residue, plus the advances to C and D, amounts to £19,000, which, being divided between C and D, entitles them to £9,500 each. After deducting their respective advances, C will take £4,500, and D £5,500. (Interest and death duties have been ignored.)

In difficult cases it would be wise for the executor to apply to the court for instructions by way of originating summons.

As already pointed out, the bringing into hotchpot of advances operates for the benefit of the children of the deceased, and not for the benefit of the surviving spouse.

Illustration (3)

X died intestate, leaving a widow and three sons, A, B, and C. During his lifetime, X had advanced to his son A the sum of £1,200.

The residue, apart from the advance and the widow's appropriation, amounted to £42,000. Show the distribution thereof, ignoring interest and duties.

DISTRIBUTION STATEMENT

Particulars	Total	In trust for Widow	A	B	C
	£	£	£	£	£
Residue—Divisible ½ to Widow for life and ½ to Children	42,000	21,000			
Add Advance	1,200				
	43,200	21,000	7,400	7,400	7,400
Less Advance	1,200		1,200		
	£42,000	£21,000	£6,200	£7,400	£7,400

On the widow's death, the amount held in trust for her will be divided equally among A, B, and C

In some instances, it may happen that the amount of an advance to a child exceeds the share to which he is immediately entitled under his parent's intestacy, but is less than that share when augmented by the amount payable upon the death of the surviving spouse. As, on the first distribution, the other children would receive less than the amount properly due to them, it would appear equitable that the advancee should either pay interest on the amount of the excess of his advance over his immediate share, or pay the excess into the estate. On the other hand, it may be argued that the deceased parent gave him the advance and intended him to benefit over the others until a final settlement. The point has not yet been judicially settled.

Illustration (4)

Y died intestate, leaving a widow and three sons, K. L and M. During his lifetime, Y had advanced to his sons K and L the sums of £10,500 and £3,000 respectively.

After providing for the widow's appropriation of personal chattels and £8,750, there remained £24,000 for distribution. Show how it should be distributed, ignoring interest and duties.

DISTRIBUTION STATEMENT

Particulars	Total	In trust for Widow	K	L	M
	£	£	£	£	£
Residue—Divisible ½ to Widow for life and ½ to Children	12,000	12,000			
Add Advance L	3,000				
	15,000		—	7,500	7,500
Less Advance	3,000			3,000	
Immediate distribution	£12,000			£4,500	£7,500
Final Distribution on death of Widow: (Assuming value of property unchanged):					
Amount available	12,000				
Add Amount already distributed	12,000				
Advances K and L ..	13,500				
	37,500		12,500	12,500	12,500
Deduct advances and amount already distributed	25,500		10,500	7,500	7,500
	£12,000		£2,000	£5,000	£5,000

It will be observed that K has been advanced too much to warrant his sharing in the first distribution, but he shares in the second. Presumably some adjustment should be made as mentioned above.

It would be inequitable to allow K to take any share of the first distribution, as that would aggravate the position.

The courts have adopted two methods of dividing income between advanced and unadvanced beneficiaries of a testator's estate.

Under the first, the beneficiaries are not debited with interest on their advances, but are credited with a share of the net income proportionate to their *net* shares of the estate (*Re Hargreaves; Hargreaves* v. *Hargreaves*). Under the second, each beneficiary is credited at the date of distribution with his full share of the estate, and the advanced beneficiaries are debited with 4 per cent. interest on their advances, which interest is added to the estate income, and the total income is then credited to the beneficiaries in proportion to their *gross* shares of the estate (*Re Poyser; Landon* v. *Poyser*).

There has also been some conflict of opinion as to whether the proper date for valuation of the residuary estate, when advances are to be brought into hotchpot, should be the date of death of the testator or the date of distribution. The doubt began with the decision in *Re Hargreaves*, which was not followed in the later decision of *Re Poyser*. In *Re Gunther, Alexander* v. *Gunther* the court reverted to *Re Hargreaves* and directed that the estate must be ascertained by valuation at the date of death, unless the will indicates some other date. In a later case (*In re Hillas-Drake*) Simmonds, J., reviewing the previous decisions, said that the object of the hotchpot provision was to ensure equality between beneficiaires; if the estate were valued at the date of distribution there would be no difficulty in securing such equality. If, on the other hand, the date of the testator's death was the proper date, equality was not necessarily achieved, since, if the assets increased in value before distribution, the advanced beneficiary subsequently lost in the distribution more than he had gained by his advancement, whilst if the assets had depreciated, the advanced beneficiary was allowed to retain a substantial advantage. In his opinion, *re Gunther, supra*, was out of line with authority and inconsistent with established principle and practice. He decided that the rights of the beneficiaries must be adjusted upon the basis of the value of the assets at the date of distribution, and that with regard to income, there being no provision to the contrary in the will, he would follow *In re Wills, Dulverton* v. *MacLeod*, in which the principle, propounded in *re Poyser, supra*, was adopted, viz. that the beneficiaries should be debited, against their shares of residuary income, with interest at 4 per cent. per annum, on the advances brought into hotchpot. A life interest must be valued as such, not as an absolute interest (*Re Morton*).

Interest on advances, where applicable, is computed from the date when the advances first become entitled to income, i.e. when the beneficial interests fall into possession on the death of the life tenant, the date of the advance, the determination of a trust for accumulation, or the death of the testator or intestate, whichever is the latest date (*Re Rees, supra*).

Illustration (5)

The position of an estate at the date of distribution was that the assets had realised £40,000. Income received was £2,400 being one year's income.

The estate is left in equal shares to the deceased's three sons, A, B and C, and advances had been made to A £10,000, and B £7,000.

Show the distribution of the estate, ignoring death duties and Income tax.

(1) Applying *re Hargreaves*.

	Total	A	B	C
	£	£	£	£
Capital:				
Residue ..	40,000			
Advances	17,000			
Total	57,000	19,000	19,000	19,000
Less Advances	17,000	10,000	7,000	—
Net Shares in Capital ..	40,000	9,000	12,000	19,000
Income:				
Income, divisible on basis of net shares in estate	2,400	540	720	1,140
Distribution of estate	£42,400	£9,540	£12,720	£20,140

(2) Applying *re Poyser*.

	Total		A		B		C	
	£	£	£	£	£	£	£	£
Net Shares in Capital as above		40,000		9,000		12,000		19,000
Income ..	2,400							
Add Interest at 4% on Advances for one year ..	680							
Divisible equally ..	3,080	say	1,027		1,027		1,026	
Deduct Interest on advances ..	680		400		280		—	
		2,400		627		747		1,026
		£42,400		£9,627		£12,747		£20,026

Where a testator gives his residuary estate to his children with power to postpone conversion, and some of the children have been advanced, the trustee, for the purpose of ascertaining the income pending distribution, must bring in the gross income of the estate and the gross amount representing the interest on the advanced shares; and when the distributive shares have been ascertained, Income tax is to be deducted from each (*In re Foster, Hunt* v. *Foster*).

Where property is transferred to or settled on the child within the seven years immediately prior to the testator's death, so that the advanced beneficiary pays Estate Duty personally on the advance, because of the testator's dying within the statutory period, the amount for which the advancee is accountable for purposes of hotchpot is the advance less the Estate Duty thereon (*Re Beddington, Micholls* v. *Samuel*).

Where advancements have been made *more* than seven years before the death of the testator (so that they are not liable to assessment to Estate Duty) and they are brought into hotchpot, the following rules apply:

(1) If the beneficiaries are remaindermen entitled absolutely to the residue of the testator's estate following the cessation of an intermediate interest (e.g. the death of the life tenant), the advances must first be added to the *gross* value of the settled funds at the date of the cesser of interest. Any Estate Duty payable on the settled funds, as the result of the cesser of interest, will then be charged to the beneficiaries in proportion to their net shares. This means that each beneficiary bears duty on that proportion of the settled funds to which he is entitled. For this purpose, it has been decided that the amounts to be brought into hotchpot are

(*a*) the *gross* advances, if made more than seven years before the *testator's* death, or

(*b*) the *net* advances (i.e. after deducting the duty, if any, payable by the beneficiaries themselves as donees) if made within seven years (*Re Tollemache, Forbes* v. *Public Trustee; Re Slee, Midland Bank Executor and Trustee Co. Ltd* v. *Slee and Others*).

(2) If the will expressly directs that the residue is to be determined *after* deducting testamentary expenses, including Estate Duty, and requires that advances be brought into hotchpot, then the amounts concerned (as determined under (1) (*a*) and (*b*) above) will be brought into account against the *net* residue, after deducting the duty payable on the testator's death and/or on the cesser of the intermediate interest (*Re Slee, supra*).

Illustration (6)

A died and the residue of his estate, after charging £844 Estate Duty, amounted to £9,600. The residue was divisible equally among his three sons, B, C and D. More than seven years before A's death he had advanced C £2,000. Divide the residue between B, C and D, ignoring interest on the advance.

Particulars					Total	B	C	D
				£	£	£	£	£
Residue			..	9,600				
Add Estate Duty ..		..	..	844				
Advance		..	..	2,000				
					12,444	4,148	4,148	4,148
Less Advance		..	..	..	2,000		2,000	
					10,444	4,148	2,148	4,148
Less Estate Duty (in ratio 4,148: 2,148: 4,148)					844	335	174	335
					£9,600	£3,813	£1,974	£3,813

Illustration (7)

X died, leaving a net estate of £70,000, on which Estate Duty of £28,125 was paid. Included in the figure of £70,000 were amounts representing the dutiable proportions of advances made to his sons during his lifetime.

Details of these advances are as follows:

To son A—£3,000, 9 years before the death of X.

    £2,000, 2 ,,   ,, ,,

,, B—£3,000, 8 ,,   ,, ,,

,, C—£3,000, 6 ,,   ,, ,,

X.'s will expressly provided that advancements made by him to his sons were to be brought into hotchpot against the residue of his estate, such residue to be the amount remaining after payment of testamentary expenses and Estate Duty. The residue was bequeathed to X's three sons, A, B and C, in equal shares absolutely, and they all survived their father. Testamentary expenses amounted to £1,640.

Particulars		£	Total £	A £	B £	C £
Net free estate			65,900			
Gifts *inter vivos:*						
A		2,000				
C £3,000						
Less Reduction under Section 64, Finance Act 1960—30% ..	900					
		2,100				
			4,100			
Net estate passing, ..			70,000			
Less						
Estate duty..		26,478				
Testamentary expenses ..		1,640				
			28,118			
Net residue..			41,882			
Add Advances:						
A—£3,000+(£2,000 less £804)..		4,196				
B		3,000				
C—£3,000 less (£844) ..		2,156				
			9,352			
			51,234	17,078	17,078	17,078
Less Advances			9,352	4,196	3,000	2,156
			£41,882	£12,882	£14,078	£14,922

In an intestacy, where there is a surviving spouse and issue, and it is necessary to apply the *Tollemache* rule, it is thought that on the distribution of that half share of residue not held in trust for the surviving spouse, only half of the Estate Duty should be added back under the rule, since only one half of the estate is being divided, the surviving spouse's life interest being confined to the other half of the net residue, after deducting Estate Duty. On the death of the surviving spouse, the other half of the duty would be adjusted. However, it is felt that a judicial decision is required before the matter can be free from doubt.

§ 19. Annuities

If an annuity is given by will, the first payment does not become due until the first anniversary of the testator's death (*Gibson* v. *Bott*). If it is directed that the first year's payment shall be made before then, the second payment does not become due until the end of the second year (*Irvin* v. *Ironmonger*). However, the executor cannot be compelled to make the first payment until the anniversary of death, even if by a direction in the will it is *due* before that date (A.E.A. 1925, s. 44). If the will directs the annuity to be paid quarterly on the usual quarter days, the annuitant is only entitled to the proportional payment from the date of death to the first quarter day (*Williams* v. *Wilson*). The court is very unwilling to allow interest on arrears of annuities (*Torrie* v. *Brown*). Since a legacy is not payable until the first anniversary of death (except at the discretion of the personal representative), then a legacy for life, with remainder over, is considered as a legacy payable on that anniversary, not an annuity accruing since death. The interest on the legacy will accrue from the end of the executor's year only and will not be due until the second anniversary of death (*Gibson* v. *Bott*).

Although the first payment may not be due until the end of the executor's year, the annuity runs from the date of death of the testator.

Executors may be directed by the will:

(i) to purchase an annuity; or

(ii) to pay an annuity out of the general income of the estate; or

(iii) to pay an annuity out of the income of a fund specifically appropriated for that purpose.

Alternatively, an option may be granted to adopt any one of the above methods.

If trustees are directed to expend a definite sum in purchasing an annuity, or to purchase an annuity of a definite amount, the bequest is regarded as a legacy of the capital sum equal to the cost of such an annuity at the date of death, and the annuitant may elect to have that sum paid over to him instead of taking an annuity; if the annuitant dies before the annuity is purchased, his personal representative can claim the capital sum (*Re Brunning, Gammon* v. *Dale, In re Robbins, Robbins* v. *Legg*).

If the will charges the annuity on property specifically devised or bequeathed, the executors are not concerned with the annuity; they must in due course transfer the property to the specific legatee or devisee, who will be responsible for the payment of the annuity. But if the annuity is directed to be paid out of the rents of the real estate, any deficiency is payable out of the residuary personal estate (*Paget* v. *Huish*). If the will gives certain legacies, and then directs that the residue be held on trust to pay an annuity, the legacies have priority over the annuity (*Haynes* v. *Haynes*).

Where there is a bequest of pecuniary legacies and/or an annuity for life, with a gift over of residue, and in order to provide for the annuity the executors are directed to appropriate a fund which is to fall into residue upon the death of the annuitant; then

(i) if the estate is insufficient to pay the legacies and also to set aside the requisite fund, but these are sufficient to pay the legacies (apart from the annuity) in full, and to buy an annuity of the prescribed amount, the legacies must be paid in full and the annuitant may elect to take in cash the purchase price of the annuity (*Re Cottrell, Buckland* v. *Bedingfield. In re Cox; Public Trustee* v. *Eve; re Wilson*). If, however, the annuity is subject to a protective trust, which would have the effect of determining the annuity if and when recipient sought to assign or charge it, the executor is bound to purchase an annuity which would be subject to the protective trust (*Re Dempster*). Any surplus would then go to the residuary legatee;

(ii) if the estate is insufficient to pay the legacies and also to provide the capital value of the annuity, the capital value must abate with the other legacies, and the annuitant may elect, as before, to take the abated amount, provided again that there is no protective trust which precludes such election. An annuitant is entitled to the capital value only where the question arises between legatees and annuitants (*In re Cottrell, supra*); or between annuitants *inter se* and residuary legatees (*In re Cox, supra*).

Each annuity must normally be valued on an actuarial basis, having no regard to the health of the annuitant or occupational risks (*re Bradberry, supra*).

The Court of Appeal has held, however, that the rule, under which annuitants were entitled to the actuarial value of their annuities when the annual income was insufficient, is one of convenience rather than of law, and if it is clear that the capital of the estate will be sufficient to discharge the annuities during the lifetime of the annuitants, the annuities ought not to be valued, but should be paid out of income, with resort to capital to the extent that this might prove to be necessary (*In re Hill; Westminster Bank Ltd* v. *Wilson*). Furthermore, the rule does not apply when the fund to be set aside for answering the annuity is *not* to fall into residue on the annuitant's death, but is disposed of separately; in these circumstances, the persons entitled to the fund in remainder should be left with the hope of receiving something, should the capital of the fund not be exhausted during the annuitant's lifetime (*Re Thomas; Public Trustee* v. *Falconer*).

Where a will provided for the payment of an annuity, but made no disposition of the residue, so that a partial intestacy would arise on the death of the annuitant, and the estate was sufficient to pay the annuity, though not wholly out of income, the court directed the actuarial value of the annuity to be paid to the annuitant, under the principle of *Re Cottrell* (*supra*). During the annuitant's life the income of the residue might have to be accumulated to recoup to capital the sum paid to the annuitant out of capital (*In re Vardon*), but accumulations are not available to make up a deficiency in the annuity (*Re Cameron*). Where an annuity is bequeathed, and 'subject thereto' the residue devolves on some other person, then so long as the annuity is being paid in full, the trustees have no power to retain surplus income of a past year for the purpose of making good a possible deficiency in a future year (*Re Platt, Sykes* v. *Dawson*). The annuitant is not prejudiced, as he will be entitled to have capital sold to make good any deficiency in the annuity (*ibid*).

The term 'annuity' includes a life interest in a settled legacy which, on the death of the life tenant, will fall into residue (*In re Richardson; In re Ellis*). Where it becomes necessary for an annuity to be valued, personal representatives are entitled to act as the court would have ordered, without obtaining a court order, but they may apply for directions if in doubt or difficulty (*Re Bradberry*).

A gift of the income from a particular fund or residue is not an annuity, and the life tenant simply gets the income available. Should the will direct that the annuities are to be paid out of the income of the residuary estate, with power to resort to capital should the income prove insufficient, the annuitants are not entitled to have the value of their annuities paid to them; where there is an express power to resort to capital, that method must be followed (*In re Chassiron; Lloyds Bank* v. *Sharpe*).

An annuitant, who dies before the date of the court order (or action on similar lines by the executors), is only entitled to the arrears of annuity to the date of his death (*ibid.*).

If the estate is being administered by the court, then in the event of an annuity having to abate with other legacies (*see ante* § 14), the annuitant is entitled to the abated capital sum, unless there is a condition subsequent, in which case the court will usually order the purchase of a government annuity.

(a) Purchase of an Annuity

A purchase directed by the will may be effected through the government or an insurance company, or the annuitant may elect to have the capital sum paid over to him instead of taking an annuity. It has been held that, if the will does not specify the manner of purchase, a government annuity should be purchased, or the capital value reckoned according to government tables (*Re Castle, Nesbitt* v. *Bauph*). It is thought, however, that the rates of interest used in the government tables are now out of step with commercial rates, and the court would have regard to the latter, and agree to the amounts being based on a purchase from an insurance company. The cost price will be treated in the books in the same way as a general legacy, cash being credited and Legacies Account debited; subsequently Legacies Account will be closed by transfer to Estate Account, the payment being a capital charge.

(b) Annuity payable out of General Income

Where the annuity is payable out of residue (i.e. primarily out of the income therefrom and, in the case of a deficiency in any year, out of capital), and there is no life tenancy to keep the estate open, the courts will not force a large estate to be retained merely in order to secure a small annuity; the annuitant is entitled to security for what is to come to him, but no more (*Re Parry, Scott* v. *Leak*). The executor, to protect himself, should apply to the court for directions as to the fund to be set aside to meet the annuity. If the annuity is charged on income only, the fund must be such as to make it practically certain that the income therefrom will be sufficient, but if charged also on capital, the fund must be large enough to make it practically certain that the annuitant will be paid out of income and capital, if necessary (*Harbin* v. *Masterman*). Where there are no directions in the will the annuity is payable first out of the income of the residue and secondly out of capital (*Carmichael* v. *Gee*).

Where there is a life tenancy and the estate is kept open, a personal account will be opened for the annuitant, and all payments made to him will be debited thereto. The amount paid will be the sum after deducting Income tax from the gross amount of the annuity. The Income tax deducted will be debited to the annuitant's account and credited to Income Tax Account at the time of each payment. At the end of each period, Income Account will be debited and the Annuitant's Account credited with the amount of the annuity before deduction of Income tax.

If the annuity is directed to be paid out of income, with no resort to capital, future income must be used to make good arrears unless the surplus income has been disposed of to a life tenant.

(c) *Annuity payable out of the Income of a Fund Specifically Appropriated*

When a specific investment, producing the exact amount of income required, is bequeathed to pay the annuity or if, in accordance with an express provision in the will, part of the residue is appropriated for the same purpose (as would generally be the course adopted in the case of an estate where there was no life or other intermediate interest), it is advisable to debit the Estate Capital Account and credit an 'Annuity Fund Account' with an amount equivalent to the value of the asset in question, in order to distinguish the portion of the estate set aside for this purpose.

The income column of the Investment Account will be credited with the income (usually interest) when received, and at the end of each period the total will be transferred to the credit of the Annuitant's Personal Account, which will be debited with all amounts paid on account. On the death of the annuitant, the amount to the credit of the Annuity Fund Account will be transferred back to the Estate Capital Account.

It sometimes happens that the investment specifically be-queathed/appropriated does not produce sufficient income every year to meet the full amount of the annuity. If in any year resort has to be made to capital, the proceeds of sale of the investment will be credited to the Investment Account and debited to cash; any profit or loss on sale should be transferred to the Annuity Fund Account. There should then be debited to the Annuity Fund Account and credited to the annuitant the amount payable to him out of capital. Such amount will be the net amount (after deducting Income tax) of the deficiency. Such amount is not grossed up; the Section 170 assessment is on the amount paid (*John Morant Settlement Trustees* v. *C.I.R.*). Unless the will provides otherwise, any ultimate deficiency in the fund set aside must come out of the other residue, of which the fund was part (*May* v. *Bennet*).

It must be remembered that, although the annuity is paid *less* tax, resort to capital must be made for the difference between the *gross* annuity and the *gross* income. The tax on the difference will be accounted for to the Inland Revenue under Section 53, Income and Corporation Taxes Act 1970, while the annuitant will receive a certificate showing the gross annuity (in full) and the tax thereon.

(d) Option to Purchase or Pay Annuities out of Income
In all cases where he has an option under the will, the executor will be guided by the circumstances, with particular reference to the age and health of the annuitant, and to the wishes of the other parties interested. Where the residue of the estate is to be distributed, the usual method is to purchase, in order that the trust need not be kept open merely for the sake of the an-nuity; where, however, there is a tenant for life, and the trust must in any case be kept open, it is usual to pay the annuity out of income.

If the will gives power, without directions, to purchase an annuity of a stated amount, the annuitant cannot demand the capital sum until the executors or trustees have in their hands funds which they propose to use for the purchase of the annuity (*Re Mabbet, Pitman v. Holborrow*).

(e) Income Tax on Annuities paid out of Income

Unless the will directs to the contrary, Income tax must be deducted when paying the annuitant, for otherwise the tax would fall on the other beneficiaries. An annuity 'free of all deductions' is not free of Income tax unless there is a proviso in the will to that effect (*In re Wells' Will Trusts; Public Trustee* v. *Wells*).

Where the will directs that the annuity shall be paid 'free of Income tax', this includes Surtax, and the annuitant is entitled to be paid out of Income the amount of Surtax applicable to the annuity (*Re Reckitt, Reckitt* v. *Reckitt*). The sums paid by the trustees on account of Surtax on an annuity left free of Income tax (including Surtax) are additional annuities to which the appropriate Income tax must be added, i.e. the gross amount is such sum as will provide the net amount of the annuity after deducting Income tax and Surtax (*Lord Michelham's Trustees* v. *C.I.R.; Exors. of Lady M.* v. *C.I.R.* A testator who does not want Surtax to be included must therefore say so. This can be achieved by a statement such as 'after deduction of Income tax', as Surtax is not charged by deduction (*Re Crawshay, Crawshay* v. *Crawshay*).

Where the annuity is not given 'free of Income tax', tax at the standard rate at the date when the payment becomes due must be deducted and retained by the trustees as part of the estate, s. 52, Income and Corporation Taxes Act 1970, unless the payment is not made out of profits or gains brought into charge to tax (e.g. when it is made out of capital), in which case the tax must be accounted for to the Inland Revenue (*ibid.* s. 53) (see (*c*) *supra*).

A trustee who does not deduct tax is personally liable to account for it (*Re Sharp, Rickett* v. *Rickett*), but the court *may* allow him to deduct from future instalments (*Re Musgrave, Machell* v. *Parry; re Wooldridge, Wooldridge* v. *Coe*). On an annuity not given by will, but which forms a debt due from the estate, the court cannot give such relief (*Re Hatch, Hatch* v. *Hatch*).

If the annuity is given 'free of Income tax', the annuitant is entitled only to the annuity, and accordingly the proportion of Income tax on the annuitant's personal and similar allowances that the grossed annuity bears to the annuitant's total income is recoverable from the annuitant by the trustees (*Re Pettit, Le Fevre* v. *Pettit*; see also *in re Maclennon, Few* v. *Byrne*). The annuitant is trustee of his statutory right to recover for the benefit of the estate Income tax overpaid in respect of the annuity and is bound at the request of the trustees to sign the proper claim form (*In re Kingcombe; Hickley* v. *Kingcombe*).

In the case of any 'free of tax' annuity payable under a will or disposition made before 3rd September, 1939 (i.e. where the deceased died before that date), only the appropriate fraction of such an annuity is payable and the annuitant must refund the appropriate fraction of what he would have refunded if the 1938–39 rates and allowances had continued. The appropriate fraction is that fraction which the difference between 20 shillings in the £ and the standard rate bears to 14s 6d (*Berkeley* v. *Berkeley*).

Illustration

A died on 1st January, 1969, and by his will bequeathed an annuity of £200 per annum to be purchased for his father; an annuity of £500 per annum payable half-yearly out of the general income of the estate to his daughter (the balance of the income to go to his widow); and an annuity of £300 per annum to his son, payable half-yearly out of the income arising from £7,500 4 per cent. C.P. Ltd Debenture Stock, valued for Estate Duty at 75, interest payable half-yearly 1st January and 1st July. After payment of Estate Duty and testamentary expenses the balance of the estate, including this stock, amounted to £57,500. The estate income for the year ended 1st January, 1970 (exclusive of the interest on the 4% Debenture Stock), amounted to £2,400, all taxed by deduction. The annuity to the father was purchased on the 1st March, 1969, for £2,000. Show the ledger accounts affected by these transactions for the year ending 1st January, 1970. Take Income tax into account at 8s 0d in the £.

ESTATE CAPITAL ACCOUNT

1969		£	1969		£
Jan. 1	Annuity Fund Account: Amount transferred, representing value at £7,500 C.P. Ltd 4% Debenture Stock, valued for Estate Duty at 75, specifically appropriated for payment of son's annuity..	5,625	Jan. 1	Balance	57,500
1970					
Jan. 1	Purchase of Annuity for father	2,000			
	Balance c/f	49,875			
		£57,500			£57,500

ANNUITY FUND ACCOUNT

		£	1969 Jan. 1		£
				Estate Account: Amount transferred, representing value of £7,500 C.P. Ltd 4% Debenture Stock, valued for Estate Duty at 75, specifically appropriated for payment of son's annuity.. ..	5,625

C.P. LTD 4 PER CENT. DEBENTURE STOCK

Date		Nominal Value	Income	Capital	Date		Nominal Value	Income	Capital
		£	£	£			£	£	£
1969 Jan. 1	Estate Account, valued at 75 as per Estate Duty Account ..	7,500		5,625	1969 July 1	Cash: Interest for half-year to date, £150, less tax..		90	
1970 Jan. 1	Son: Annuity A/c ..		300		1970 Jan. 1 ,, ,,	Cash: do. .. Income Tax A/c Balance c/f ..	7,500	90 120	5,6
		£7,500	£300	£5,625			£7,500	£300	£5,6

DAUGHTER—ANNUITY ACCOUNT

1969 July 1	Cash: Half-year's Annuity less tax	£ 150	1970 Jan. 1	Estate Income Account ..	£ 500
1970 Jan. 1	Cash: do. .. .. .. Income Tax Account ..	150 200			
		£500			£500

SON—ANNUITY ACCOUNT

1969 July 1	Cash: Half-year's Annuity less tax	£ 90	1970 Jan. 1	C.P. Ltd Interest on 4% Debenture Stock	£ 300
1970 Jan. 1	Cash: do. .. .. .. Income Tax Account ..	90 120			
		£300			£300

INCOME TAX ACCOUNT

1970 Jan. 1	Estate Income, £2,400 at 8s C.P. Ltd Debenture Interest, £300 at 8s	£ 960 120	1970 Jan. 1	Son—Annuity Account .. Daughter—Annuity Account .. .. .. Estate Income Account ..	£ 120 200 760
		£1,080			£,1080

ESTATE INCOME ACCOUNT

1970 Jan. 1			£	1970 Jan. 1		£	£
	Daughter—Annuity	..	500		Income (gross):		
	Income Tax	..	760		Cash 1,440		
	Widow—Balance ..	..	1,140		Income Tax Account 960		2,400
			£2,400				£2,400

§ 20. Residue

The residue, when ascertained, will be distributed in accordance with the terms of the will, or, if there is no will, according to the rules of intestacy. Whether the residue has or has not been ascertained, and whether the executors have or have not expressly, or by conduct, assented to such ascertainment, are questions of fact; the residue may be ascertained even if there is an outstanding mortgage upon it (*Commissioners of Inland Revenue* v. *Smith*).

As was seen in Chapter XI, if the residue is left to persons in succession, the executors must, unless otherwise directed by the will, convert the residue into authorised securities. If, however, the residue is given absolutely, the executor's duty is to sell so much of the property of the deceased as is necessary to pay Estate Duty, testamentary expenses and legacies and convey the balance as it stands.

In distributing the capital to remaindermen, a trustee who has notice that one of them has mortgaged his share must pay out of such share to the mortgagee the principal, interest and costs, and hand over the balance only to the remainderman concerned (*Hockey* v. *Western*).

An executor is entitled, when he has fully wound up the estate and distributed any balance in his hands, to get a proper settlement of his accounts and a release from liability. From a pecuniary legatee he is only entitled to a receipt. From the residuary legatee(s) he is entitled to a receipt and he should have his accounts approved by the beneficiaries in writing, identifying the said accounts, and accepting the final distribution in full discharge if, as is often the case in an executorship, there have been any complicated dealings with the property, including any change of investments, payments out, and management of the property. The executor (like a trustee) cannot, as a rule, demand a release under seal. Moreover, an indemnity is usually refused by beneficiaries, except where the executors or trustees will remain, or may come, under some personal liability by reason of their having become executors or trustees, e.g. where they have granted leases of trust property which have since been sold and they, as original lessors, remain liable for the covenants under the leases.

CHAPTER XV

BOOKS AND ACCOUNTS

§ 1. Introduction

The recommended system of accounts is based on the normal double-entry system of book-keeping. There is one other principal method of preparing trust accounts, and this is followed sometimes by the legal profession. It is based purely on a cash system, i.e. it necessitates the preparation of cash accounts for both capital and income items; the balance of the assets and liabilities of the estate being recorded in memorandum form. As the assets are realised and as the liabilities are satisfied, a note is made alongside the entry in the memorandum schedule, and the appropriate receipt or payment is shown in the relevant cash account. One of the principal arguments claimed for this method is that it does not show fluctuations in value of assets over a period, thus decreasing the chances of causing confusion in the minds of the beneficiaries and other interested parties. One disadvantage of this method is the antithesis of this argument, inasmuch as the beneficiaries will be interested in knowing the value of their share in the trust, or in the estate, at any particular moment. In order to show this, values will have to be shown on the list of assets and liabilities, which becomes an incomplete balance sheet.

In preparing accounts care must be taken to differentiate at all times between the interest of any life-tenant and that of the remainderman. So far as the life-tenant is concerned, he is interested in knowing the total income to which he has been entitled during the period, the source of that income, and any reasons for fluctuations in the income. The remainderman, however, is interested in changes in assets which have taken place during the period and the value of his share of the trust funds. The Institute of Chartered Accountants in England and Wales has made certain recommendations with regard to the layout of accounts. These recommendations follow the principles which apply to the accounts of a normal trading business, necessarily adjusted for the peculiarities appertaining to trust accounts. They provide, *inter alia*, for the preparation of a Balance Sheet of the trust estate, together with supporting schedules and subsidiary accounts, and an Income Account, differentiating between the income which accrues to separate trusts. The balance on the Estate Capital Account will indicate the value of the interests of the beneficiaries in these trust funds. It is suggested that the assets be valued at their probate value (i.e. the value adopted for Estate Duty purposes), any subsequent acquisitions being shown at cost.

The principal account will be the Estate Capital Account. The primary entries which will be made in this account will consist of the assets and liabilities in existence at the date of death. Once these have been listed, it is usual to strike a balance to ascertain the net value of the estate upon which Estate Duty is chargeable. This account will be charged with the Estate Duty properly borne by the estate, together with any other charges which are properly chargeable against capital, e.g. costs of obtaining probate. When assets and liabilities are sold and there is a profit or loss on sale, the profit or loss will be entered on the appropriate side of the Estate Capital Account. Similarly any other benefit which subsequently accrues to capital will be credited to the Estate Capital Account.

The maximum information should be given to the life-tenant concerning the income to which he becomes entitled. The Income Account, together with its supporting schedules, will show the income actually received from the individual assets by the trustees or deemed to have been received by them, i.e. income in the hands of agents. Accrued income due, except in cases where it might show a completely false position if such income was omitted from the accounts, when a note should be inserted, is not included. Expenses chargeable to income, including those due but unpaid, should be provided for in the normal manner and the total charged to Income Account. All expenditure should be classified under appropriate headings. so that any fluctuations in the expenditure over the periods may be readily recognised by the beneficiaries.

The actual books of account, which need be maintained by the executors or trustees, will normally consist of a journal, a cash book, and a ledger. The former will be used to detail opening and closing entries of the estate, together with entries not originating in the cash book, according to normal accounting principles. The cash book should include three columns on each side, so as to show receipts and payments on account of income, receipts and payments on account of capital, and a total bank column. It is usual to ensure that all receipts are banked, and as many items as is practicable are paid by cheque, thus making the cash book a copy, to all intents and purposes, of the bank account. Cash expenditure will not usually necessitate the use of a petty cash book, as out-of-pocket expenses and other expenses of a small nature will be reimbursed to the executors or trustees periodically. Occasionally, transfers will be necessary between income and capital, e.g. in the case of equitable apportionments, and such transfers will warrant entries in both the income and capital columns on either side of the cash book, together with entries in the journal. So far as the ledger is concerned, the accounts to be used for the purposes of recording investments will be ruled to show changes in the nominal value of the investments and receipts, payments, and transfers on account of income and capital, i.e. there will be three columns on either side of the account. The remainder of the accounts in the ledger will follow the usual ruling, and it is suggested that separate accounts be opened for the individual types of expense, e.g. an account for testamentary expenses, and an account for funeral expenses. Separate accounts should also be opened for each life tenant and each residuary legatee.

Where investments are concerned, it is usual to ignore fluctuations in value, so that when an investment is realised any profit or loss on realisation is transferred to the Estate Capital Account. If part only of an investment has been realised, the profit or loss should be calculated only on the part so realised, and the balance of the investment should be brought down at its probate value or cost price, after adjusting for any necessary apportionment. The market value at each balance sheet date can be disclosed to the beneficiaries by a separate schedule.

Accounts should be prepared annually on the anniversary of death.

§ 2. The System of Accounts

The system of accounts which is recommended and exemplified in this work is that which takes for its basis the valuation for

Estate Duty purposes, or, in the case of a trust, the values at its inception. The opening assets and liabilities are debited and credited respectively to the various asset and liability accounts, the corresponding double entry being made through the Estate Capital Account. Assets acquired and liabilities incurred subsequent to the commencement of the administration or trust are brought in at cost price and dealt with in the usual way. Any differences arising through variations in value, as far as the capital assets and liabilities are concerned, will be adjusted through the Estate Capital Account.

In the case of settled estates, strict distinction is necessarily observed between capital and income, and the books and accounts are ruled accordingly with capital and income columns; and where there are investments, a further column is provided for the nominal value.

The system, which is explained in detail in this chapter, has advantages over any other system because of the arithmetical check on its accuracy.

There are two other methods of keeping executorship accounts.

(1) To record the details of initial assets and liabilities in memorandum books; to record capital and income cash transactions; and to record investments in terms of the nominal values only.

(2) A similar system prepared upon a double entry basis, with a special column for initial assets or liabilities which are unrealised or unpaid.

These two methods differ merely in that the latter is conducted on a double entry basis, their common object being to charge the executor or trustee only with moneys actually received by him.

The first of these alternative methods does not give the satisfactory check which is provided by books kept on a double entry basis, and both methods are more cumbrous in their working than that which is recommended in this book. It is therefore desirable to examine briefly the arguments upon which the use of those methods rests for justification, namely:

(1) That the Estate Duty valuations are merely in the nature of estimates, and do not necessarily represent the actual facts of the case.

(2) That executorship accounts are particularly affected by legal considerations, and that lawyers are in the habit of dealing with accounts from a cash point of view, and will not consider those drawn up in any other form.

(3) That in the event of assets failing to realise the estate duty valuation, the executors might be held liable if in the first instance they had incorporated such valuations in the body of the accounts.

(4) That it is important for the beneficiaries to be able to see at a glance what portion of the estate has been realised, and what assets remain unrealised, at the date of any Balance Sheet.

Dealing with these arguments *seriatim:*

(1) The term 'value' has only a relative meaning, and if 'present value' is the only proper basis upon which facts of account can be recorded, it is obviously hopeless to attempt to keep books at all. Some starting-point must be taken, and the valuations for Estate Duty, having been sworn to on oath and accepted by the Inland Revenue authorities, should be sufficient for book-keeping purposes, apart from the fact that they are the only values available at the date of death.

(2) However true this may have been in the past, at the present time the legal profession recognises more every day the inadequacy of a cash basis for the presentation of accounts.

(3) The determining factor as to whether or not the executor or trustee is personally liable for a loss in any given circumstances is not whether he has entered a transaction in the books or placed an item in one column or another, but whether he has in fact committed a *devastavit* or breach of trust. Whatever the nature of the entry he makes will not absolve him if, upon the actual facts, he has committed an impropriety in administration causing loss to the estate.

(4) It is not necessary to present a Balance Sheet dividing up the assets in an arbitrary manner in order to show which have been acquired subsequent to the death of the testator, as this can be done equally well by the insertion of the words 'at cost' or 'as per Estate Duty valuation', so that an

ordinary Balance Sheet can be prepared which is easier of comprehension by beneficiaries having no technical knowledge of accounts.

These considerations therefore justify the assertion that the system adopted in this work possesses every advantage which any other method can show; that it is comparatively at no disadvantage. It is, moreover, easier in its working, and is founded on strict double entry principles, while the final accounts give the most useful information in the simplest form.

Further details concerning trust accounts will be found in Part III of the following chapter.

The following is the text of a memorandum and recommendation issued by the Council of the Institute of Chartered Accountants in England and Wales on the form and contents of executorship and trust accounts:

The Recommendations of the Institute of Chartered Accountants in England and Wales

(The Council of the Institute of Chartered Accountants in England and Wales has made the following recommendations to members regarding the accounts of deceased persons' estates and the more general types of trusts (excluding special trusts such as pension funds and unit trusts), which while recognising the form in which accounts are prepared is a matter within the discretion of the trustees, it is hoped that trust accounts will be prepared.)

Trust Accounts

(1) The main object of trust accounts is to demonstrate that the trust funds, including the income thereof, have been applied in accordance with the provisions of the trust instrument. They should also convey to beneficiaries and other interested parties, as well as to the trustees, information about the transactions and the current state of affairs of the trust. Trust accounts may also be useful for taxation and other purposes.

(2) Special considerations, which are not necessarily dealt with in the following paragraphs, obtain in the case of trusts under the Settled Land Act 1925 and those for which prescribed forms of account exist (e.g. certain charities).

(3) Trust accounts differ from ordinary commercial accounts in a number of ways because of different underlying circumstances. For instance there are many trusts where income is separately accounted for, thus lessening the need for production of annual accounts, and, in the case of established trusts, where changes of investments are infrequent and the income is mandated to a single life tenant, the interval between accounting dates may be several years and the accounts might deal only with capital transactions. Accounts dealing with all or selected aspects of the trust will be required in the following circumstances:

(*a*) where there is a distribution or other significant change in the trust fund or in the rights in it;

(*b*) in the case of the estate of a deceased person which is settled for any period, when the initial administration of the estate has been completed, i.e. when the final Estate Duty figures have been settled, testamentary expenses paid, and the investments assembled into a fairly permanent portfolio;

(*c*) at selected intervals, to show changes in capital accounts, even when there are no other matters to be dealt with.

If accounts are prepared less frequently than annually, particular care will be necessary to ensure that the underlying records are kept up to date and that the investments come under regular review by the trustees.

(4) The following taxes have been repealed, or were operative for one year only:

special charge, imposed by the Finance Act 1968, by reference to investment income for the year to 5th April, 1968;

special contribution, imposed by the Finance Act 1948, by reference to investment income for the year to 5th April, 1948;

legacy and succession duties, repealed by the Finance Act 1949, as respects deaths occurring on or after 30th July, 1949.

Inasmuch as these taxes were chargeable to capital and, where separate funds are involved, perhaps disproportionately to those funds, their incidence may still be relevant in trust accounts. In paragraph 57, guidance is offered as to the treatment of special charge; the same general principles would have applied to special contribution and legacy and succession duties, but these are not dealt with in detail.

(5) In addition to being accountable for money and other assets actually coming into their hands, trustees are responsible for the administration of the trust. The extent of their responsibility and the way it has been discharged will, therefore, not be apparent unless the periodical accounts deal with both these aspects. This will involve the recording of all the assets and liabilities of the trust, including for example, interests in expectancy and foreign estate. The balance sheet will then show the position of the trust as a whole and not merely those assets which have come into the hands of the trustees.

(6) There is a fundamental distinction in trust accounts between income and capital. Often there are interests in income and interests in capital which conflict and the drawing of this distinction is essential to show the relative positions of those concerned.

(7) Various special aspects of the administration of trusts make it necessary to consider how to deal with:

(*a*) the three ranges of investments ('narrower', 'wider' and 'special') if the Trustee Investments Act 1961 is applied;

(*b*) investments acquired by the trustees from a testator or settlor which, but for special powers to postpone sale or to retain, would be unauthorised;

(*c*) assets which have not yet come into the trustees' hands;

(*d*) accumulations of income, and investments made therefrom;

(*e*) special legal considerations such as statutory and equitable apportionments, deeds of family arrangement, court orders;

(*f*) the linking of taxes (e.g. Estate Duty, Capital Gains tax, Betterment levy) with the particular funds out of which they are payable.

(8) Some trustees, and many beneficiaries, may know little about accounting. Trust accounts should, therefore, be as simple and clear as is consistent with the showing of sufficient detail for a proper understanding of the transactions. These requirements can be fulfilled by using schedules and subsidiary accounts for many matters of detail, cross-referencing them to the main accounts. It is desirable that the trustees should sign the accounts and that beneficiaries should formally signify agreement with their personal accounts; clarity and simplicity of presentation, by making the accounts more easily understood, will help adoption of this procedure.

(9) The accounts and their underlying records may have to be examined because of a dispute (e.g. between trustees and beneficiaries) or, in the case of a discretionary settlement, to calculate estate duty on the death of a beneficiary. In addition to emphasising the need for clarity and adequate detail, these possibilities indicate that accounts, vouchers and records generally should be kept for a longer period than if they were commercial documents.

(10) Trust accounts are the responsibility of the trustees. An accountant preparing accounts for trustees should submit with them a report reciting any instructions given to him and stating the principles adopted in presentation and any special factors, problems or outstanding matters. These recommendations do not deal with the form of either such reports or audit reports. However, the accountant should make it clear whether or not he has audited the accounts.

(11) It will usually facilitate a clear understanding of the accounts if a short history is attached showing the incidents which led up to the position displayed by the accounts, the names of the trustees and a brief explanation of the devolution of the funds. If the trust instrument(s) is complex, such explanation may be restricted to present interests in income and such indication of succeeding interests as is feasible within the compass of a short note.

(12) For quoted investments, a stock-broker's valuation of the portfolio may accompany the accounts and this valuation,

together with the accounts, should ideally give sufficient information to enable the Capital Gains tax implications of investment policy to be considered.

(13) The recommendations below may not apply fully throughout the entire field of trust accounts, but it is considered that the fundamental principles should not differ in substance from those now recommended. It must, however, be emphasised that trusts are so varied in their nature that there should be flexibility in the manner of presenting accounts and that a standard form is neither practicable nor desirable.

(14) The following paragraphs contain references to statutory and equitable apportionments, and to the operation of the Trustee Investments Act 1961. Nowadays, many wills and settlements specifically exclude the former, and, by incorporating their own wide investment powers, override those in the Act.

Recommendations

(15) It is therefore recommended that the following principles should normally be applied in connection with the records and the preparation of accounts of trusts.

General Principles

(16) Trustees should maintain records from which, in the light of the trust instrument(s) and legal considerations, periodical statements of account can be prepared. The records and/or the trust accounts should preserve all the information that may be required at future dates (possibly long deferred) for any review of the trustees' transactions and for Capital Gains tax purposes. Although traditionally it has been recommended that this should be achieved by keeping books on complete double-entry principles, less formal methods are now acceptable provided that those principles govern the preparation of the trust accounts.

(17) There should be prepared and kept with the trust documents a short history of the trust and a summary of the relevant provisions of the will or other trust instrument(s).

However, the original terms should be consulted where necessary. Other information which might be suitably recorded and kept readily available and up to date would include the trustees' names and addresses, the names and addresses of present and future beneficiaries, their dates of birth (especially where the attainment of a specified age is relevant to the will or settlement), the dates of their marriages (where this is likewise relevant), and their relationship to the testator or settlor. It may be appropriate to set out some or all of the above information in a statement attached to the accounts.

(18) The date to which accounts are made up should be decided according to the circumstances and will not necessarily be the anniversary of the creation of the trust. Having regard to the taxation liabilities of the trust and of the beneficiaries, it may frequently be convenient for accounting periods to correspond with fiscal years; but in some cases it may be necessary for accounts to be made up to the anniversary of the trust's creation if the rules of law relating to equitable apportionments are applicable or if there are other special circumstances. The nature of the trust assets, the dates on which income is receivable, the due dates of annuities, are all factors that may affect the selection of the most convenient accounting date.

(19) Income and capital transactions should be segregated clearly. This may be assisted by the use of separate columns in accounting records.

(20) Periodical accounts should normally consist of:

(*a*) balance sheet of the whole of the trust estate;

(*b*) capital account, summarising capital transactions either from the commencement of the trust or since the last account;

(*c*) income account, where appropriate;

(*d*) schedules and subsidiary accounts explaining in greater detail the major items appearing in the balance sheet, capital account and income account;

showing separately the figures for any special funds.

(21) The balance sheet, capital account and income account should be presented as simply as possible, all detail being relegated to the schedules and subsidiary accounts.

Balance Sheet

(22) The various items in the balance sheet should be grouped under appropriate headings, so that significant totals are readily apparent. Presentation becomes even more important when the Trustee Investments Act 1961 has been applied and the capital account and the assets represented by it have been divided into narrower-, wider-, and special-range parts.

(23) Where there are differing interests in the same trust the accounts will consist of two or more self-balancing sections, and can be made more understandable if the balance sheet layout is designed with this in mind. For instance, if there are few liabilities, it will probably be better to deduct them from the assets than to show them on the liabilities side. In this way, the liabilities would be confined to the various funds and beneficiaries' current account balances, and the net assets by which they are represented, would appear by sections immediately opposite them. This form of presentation is not always possible, but whenever it is, it should be adopted.

Distinction between Capital and Income

(24) Capital items should be clearly segregated from income balances, either by appropriate grouping, or possibly by the use of separate columns.

Comparative Figures

(25) Comparative figures should be included if they serve a useful purpose. Normally, however, the supporting schedules will be more informative than any comparison of total figures with those on the previous accounting date.

Capital Account

(26) Generally the capital account in the balance sheet will show the balance of the capital funds held, so far as they have been ascertained. If the Trustee Investments Act 1961 has

been applied, the division of the fund into two or three parts should be shown, but in that case it is important to show the total of the capital account and not merely the amounts of its parts. Where distributions of capital have been made to beneficiaries it is permissible, and sometimes necessary (e.g. where advancement has taken place), to show the original capital available for distribution and the amount of the distributions to date.

(27) Where the valuation of a significant part of the fund has not been agreed for probate or stamp duty purposes, the capital account should be amplified by way of note to that effect. This would also apply where the value of the assets is known to differ materially from their balance sheet amount.

Liabilities

(28) Where appropriate, liabilities on capital account (e.g. Estate Duty, Capital Gains tax, unpaid legacies) should be distinguished from those on income account which themselves should be analysed so as to segregate balances due to beneficiaries from other liabilities.

(29) Accruing liabilities on capital account are normally provided for but in special or difficult circumstances may alternatively be recorded by way of note. An example would be where the Trustee Investments Act 1961 has been applied and it is not known from which part of the fund a liability will be paid. (For treatment of accruals on income account see paragraph 67.)

(30) It is normally preferable to deal by way of note with:
  (*a*) known liabilities whose amounts cannot be determined with substantial accuracy;
  (*b*) contingent liabilities including:
  guarantees given by a deceased;
  potential Capital Gains tax on an unrealised but recorded appreciation of the trust's investments;
  Estate Duty on an *inter vivos* settlement should the settlor die within seven years of the endowment;
  Estate Duty in a discretionary settlement in the event of the death of a beneficiary;

(c) Estate Duty on the death of a life tenant (subject to the exemption under the 'surviving spouse' rule); contingent legacies.

Where it is desirable to indicate the financial effect to the beneficiaries, an amount should be set aside to meet the possible liability covered by the note, or should be dealt with in the covering report.

Tax on Capital Gains

(31) In normal cases it will be possible to quantify any outstanding liability in respect of tax on capital gains. In these cases it should be treated as a creditor and charged against the surplus which has been added to capital.

(32) Where allowable losses have been established, the cumulative total available to be carried forward should be noted.

(33) If payment of Capital Gains tax is postponed under the provisions of the Finance Act 1965, Schedule 10, paragraph 4, provision should be made for the whole of the tax, and a note added explaining the period over which the instalments are payable.

(34) If it is known that there will be a future disposal for Capital Gains tax purposes under the Finance Act 1965, section 25 (e.g. 15 year period) this should be stated in a note.

Betterment Levy

(35) The recommendations on accounting principles set out in Members' Handbook, Statement N26 (Land Commission Act 1967; accounting implications), should be followed, in so far as they are deemed applicable to trust accounts, with the following exceptions:

(a) whereas it would be prudent accounting if levy attributable to the capital value of future rents reserved by a lease should be written off to income account by way of charge against the rents receivable over the period of the lease, as recommended in paragraph 10 (c) (ii) of N26, this should not be done in trust accounts without the benefit of legal advice (particularly in the case where the life tenant is not impeachable for waste);

(*b*) whereas paragraph 13 of N26 states that levy payable need not be separately disclosed other than in exceptional circumstances, in the case of trusts the accounts or schedules attached thereto should include some details regarding levy paid or payable.

(36) In respect of trusts or deceased persons' estates holding any interest in land, it will often be necessary to make appropriate inquiries as to whether any transaction has taken place which may be a chargeable act or event under the Act. If the result of such inquiries indicates that a chargeable act or event has or may have taken place and any levy chargeable has not been assessed by the Commission or the Commission has not given assurance that no levy is payable, an appropriate note indicating the possible liability should be appended to the accounts.

(37) If the levy has been assessed but not paid at the balance sheet date or if payment is to be postponed or paid by instalments, provision should be made for the liability or possible liability in the accounts with appropriate comments.

Assets

(38) In normal circumstances investments will appear in the balance sheet under a few broad classifications with the detail appearing in schedules attached. Where, however, there are few investments, no changes having taken place during the year, it would be permissible to detail them in the balance sheet. The total market value of the quoted investments should always appear on the face of the balance sheet as well as in the schedules.

(39) Where the trustees have applied the Trustee Investments Act 1961 they should have earmarked specific investments to each part of the fund. It is most important that this allocation should be strictly maintained at all times and that the total of the investments of each part of the fund should appear, either in the balance sheet or in the investment schedules.

(40) Where the trustees of a deceased person's estate have power to postpone the sale of unauthorised investments, such

holdings may need to be distinguished in the accounts so that points of equitable apportionment or investment policy can be understood.

(41) The circumstances in which an asset is acquired by a trust will determine the value at which it is brought into the trust books. If it devolves on the trustees as part of a deceased person's estate, the probate value (normally the market value at the date of death) will be adopted. If it is a gift from a living settlor, the market value at the date of the gift will likewise become the book value. If the asset is purchased at arm's length by the trustees, cost will be the basis adopted.

(42) On the eventual disposal of an asset, its cost or its market value at the date of acquisition, as appropriate, will generally become relevant for the purpose of computing Capital Gains tax. It will be convenient if the cost or market value appearing in the accounts is made to agree with that which will govern the Capital Gains tax position on disposal. Where small realisations of investments (e.g. sales of fractional shares and rights to new shares) have taken place and where the proceeds are less than 5 per cent. of the value of the investments, the proceeds would be deducted from the cost or market value. It is not suggested, however, that assets acquired before 6th April, 1965, should be restated at their market value at that date, unless there is some circumstance or occurrence such as a part-disposal which renders it obligatory to adopt that value for Capital Gains tax purposes subsequently.

(43) The other significant departures from the general principle set out in paragraphs 41 and 42 would be:

(a) where, because of a provision in the trust instrument, the accounts would be difficult to understand or inappropriate if Capital Gains tax base values were adopted;

(b) where investments are held in unit or investment trusts and those trusts' net capital gains are apportioned among the investors. In those cases the amounts so apportioned are to be treated for Capital Gains tax purposes as representing additions to the cost of the holdings concerned. A memorandum should be kept of these amounts but it would normally be preferable to ignore them for book-keeping purposes unless they became significant, when they would probably be dealt with in accounts by way of note.

(44) The assets of a trust may become subject to Estate Duty or Capital Gains tax, or both, while remaining within the ownership of the trustees, e.g. on the cesser of a life interest, or except for deaths after 30th March, 1971, at 15 year intervals from the creation of the trust. On such an event, the current values agreed for duty or tax purposes should be adopted in the accounts. In this way not only will the duty or tax borne be shown to bear a proper relationship to the assets involved, but the base for subsequent Capital Gains tax liabilities will normally be established in the books.

(45) There may be a revaluation of trust assets for reasons unconnected with taxation, e.g. in order to effect a division of the trust funds for the purpose of applying the Trustee Investments Act 1961 or of carrying out some provision of the trust instrument. If such a revaluation is adopted in the accounts, consideration should be given to the impact of Capital Gains tax should the assets be disposed of at their new book amounts. If a material liability to tax would result, at least the position should be disclosed in a note on the accounts. It may, however, be preferable to create a provision for the potential Capital Gains tax liability out of the surplus on revaluation. In the event of a partial distribution of capital to one or more beneficiaries, the potential Capital Gains tax liability must be taken into account in order to preserve the interests of all beneficiaries. In such circumstances, a provision should be set up and, if any of the investments are realised to make the partial distribution, the tax arising should be set against the provision.

(46) Stockbrokers' valuations may be attached to trust accounts, and if they are made at the balance sheet date, they may be used as a substitute for the investment schedules. It must, however, be remembered that in many cases they will not agree with the balance sheet total for investments because the book amount will not be included as part of the information.

(47) Where statutory apportionments arise, any income apportioned to capital should be credited to trust capital account and not used to write down the investments concerned (see paragraph 66). To do otherwise would be meaningless unless accrued income were similarly dealt with on all investment transactions.

(48) The composition of cash and bank balances as between capital, income and special funds should be shown. If the grouping adopted for the balance sheet as between capital, income and special funds makes it necessary, the bank balance(s) will have to be divided so that the appropriate amounts appear under their proper headings in the balance sheet, but the aggregate bank balance should also be shown.

(49) A note should be made in respect of any known assets of which the amounts cannot be determined with substantial accuracy, for example, reversions and claims for damages.

Special Funds

(50) Where special funds arise by reason of the existence of separate trusts or settled funds within the main administration, the capital and liabilities of such special funds should be stated under separate headings and the corresponding assets should also be stated separately. The treatment of special charge on different funds will depend on the circumstances of the life tenants or annuitants (see paragraph 57). Where it is desired to show a special relationship between the funds (e.g. they are particular fractions of residue) it will be necessary to show the original capital of each fund inset, with the charge and related professional fees as deductions.

Capital Account

(51) The opening entries for any form of trust record will be derived from the cost or acquisition values of the assets concerned (see paragraph 41).

(52) For deceased persons' estates, the opening entries should show the assets and liabilities at the figures applicable for Estate Duty purposes, a balance being struck to show the net estate sub-divided, if necessary to show:

(*a*) property on which duty either has been paid or is currently payable;

(*b*) property not currently assessable to duty; and

(*c*) property exempt from duty.

(53) The capital account for any period should show, suitably classified and in adequate detail, the extent to which the trust capital account has been affected by matters such as:

(*a*) surpluses or deficits on realisations;

(*b*) taxation of capital gains;

(*c*) adjustments of book figures to Capital Gains tax base values;

(*d*) Estate Duty;

(*e*) special charge imposed by the Finance Act 1968;

(*f*) administration expenses;

(*g*) changes for Estate Duty purposes as shown in corrective affidavits;

(*h*) legacies, or appropriations to special funds; and

(*i*) statutory or equitable apportionments.

(54) Separate figures should be presented for each part of a trust which has been split in accordance with the provisions of the Trustee Investments Act 1961; this may be achieved by presenting one account with several columns.

Estate Duty

(55) Where appropriate, the capital account should show the total on which Estate Duty is payable and the amount paid; also, the information relating to Estate Duty should include matters such as the lower rate of duty applicable to agricultural property and a reference to any property which is aggregable for duty purposes though not forming part of the estate for which the trustees are accountable. Any other material matters affecting the Estate Duty should also be stated in the capital account. If the detail is considerable, it should be relegated to a supporting schedule.

(56) In some cases the agreement of valuations for Estate Duty purposes may be a protracted matter extended over several years; for example, where the estate includes interests in land, unquoted shares, or business goodwill. Where this

occurs, the fact of the Estate Duty being provisional should be stated with an indication, where appropriate and practicable, whether the outstanding amount involved may be material.

Special Charge

(57) Where special charge (see paragraph 4) is paid out of a trust it is charged to capital in the same way as Estate Duty. Where particular funds are directed by a will to be free from duty the special charge may prove to be a charge against the residuary estate but normally it will be a charge upon the funds whose income gives rise to the tax paid. Where more than one person is interested in the income of one undivided fund then the various payments of the special charge will be charged to the capital of that fund and future shares of income will be adjusted. Professional charges for dealing with special charge will be dealt with in the same way as the tax itself.

Comparative Figures

(58) Comparative figures for the preceding period will not normally serve a useful purpose in the capital account.

Special Funds

(59) Special funds, dealt with separately in the balance sheet, should have their separate capital accounts (see also paragraph 23).

Income Account

(60) The purpose of an income account is to inform those interested as to the amount, sources and division of income and, occasionally, to assist in the understanding of the taxation position. The main emphasis, according to circumstances, should be one or more of:

(a) the stewardship of the trustees, when much detail will be shown;

(b) the pattern of income, when the grouping of the figures will be used to produce significant totals, for instance, the income from fixed interest and other types of investment or possibly, the significant diversification of invest-

ments. This will help the appraisal of future requirements and budgeting;

(c) division of income, as in cases where apportionments
are made or there are several funds each with a different
life tenant;

(d) assistance to beneficiaries and trustees in adjusting or
understanding their taxation, where for example relief
is available against Surtax for Estate Duty on accrued
income (Section 19, Finance Act 1956) or there are
assessments on property income.

(61) The form of the accounts must be that which is most apt
to the trust, comprehensible to trustees and beneficiaries
(who may not be business-trained) and useful in managing
the trust. Items should be grouped in appropriate classifications; for example, interest on Government securities,
dividends, interest of mortgages, rents, business profits,
credit from realised capital on equitable apportionments. All
items involving considerable detail, such as investment
income, should be included in total only, with supporting
schedules showing the details. If appropriate, comparative
figures should be given.

Income

(62) The trustees are normally required to account for income
when it is receivable, so that the account will not generally
include accruing income. Items in the hands of agents, such
as rents collected but not handed over to the trustees,
should be regarded for accounting purposes as having been
received. Consideration should be given to the effect of any
distortion caused by the exclusion of accrued items, for
example, where a company alters its dividend-paying
timetable and, as a result, the accounts include more or less
than a normal year's income. Where material distortion
occurs, a note on the accounts or a reference in the accompanying report will be necessary in most cases. Income
received in advance of due date should be carried forward
in the balance sheet.

(63) Where a trade is carried on by trustees, the usual account
ing principles applicable to a trading concern should be

followed so far as relates to the trading profit and a note on the accounts will be necessary to indicate that this basis has been applied. The trading activity will sometimes have an accounting year which does not coincide with the trust accounting year, and the results should then be incorporated in the trust accounts on the basis of the trading year. Again an explanatory note on the accounts will be necessary.

(64) Where there are relatively few changes on capital account, an income account, not accompanied by a balance sheet, may be acceptable. There will also be cases where no formal income account is needed, for example where all income is mandated to one life tenant or where the disposal of income is so straightforward that a copy of the Inland Revenue form R59 or R59A (Trust Estate: Statement of Income for the year ending 5th April) is an acceptable substitute.

(65) Income may be received:
  (a) gross but liable to Income tax by direct assessment;
  (b) net after deduction of tax;
  (c) net under special arrangement, e.g. building society interest;
  (d) exempt from tax, e.g. National Savings Certificates interest.

It should be made clear whether the income is shown gross or net and any charge for tax should be related to the income being taxed. The form of presentation will depend largely on the circumstances of the trust, in particular the types and number of sources of income and the period(s) covered by the accounts.

Statutory Apportionments

(66) In accounting for deceased persons' estates, investments are normally shown *cum* dividend. Where, in such a case, all or part of a dividend after death is apportioned to capital, it should be added to the balance of the estate capital account. Thus the investment will continue to be accounted for at probate (and Capital Gains tax) value. Where the investment is shown *ex* dividend then the dividend apportioned to capital will usually be credited to the

account for those dividends which are separately shown in the Inland Revenue Affidavit. Ultimately any balance on this account will be written off to estate capital account.

Expenditure

(67) The income account should include all amounts payable in respect of the accounting period including, where material to a proper view of the distributable income, amounts accrued up to the accounting date but not then due for payment. Annuities payable are not normally accounted for on an accruals basis although there will be cases where an income account would give an incorrect view of the amount of the surplus income if no accrual were made.

(68) Items of expenditure and other deductions from income should be grouped in appropriate classifications; for example, administration expenses, interest on overdraft, income tax, interest on estate duty and other taxes, annuities, transfers to capital as a result of apportionments.

Tax on Income

(69) The charge for Income tax will exclude tax on short-term gains under Case VII of Schedule D, as that will be a charge against capital. As indicated in paragraph 65, the treatment of the charge for tax on income will depend upon the form of presentation of the accounts. Where tax still has to be assessed on income shown in the accounts, due provision should be made. Any adjustment to the tax of earlier years should be shown separately.

(70) There may be cases where the presentation alone cannot make clear how the tax is related to the income shown in the accounts, for instance where:

  (*a*) tax is assessed under Schedules B or D and the charge does not represent standard rate on the income for a particular accounting year;

  (*b*) the rule in *re Pettit* applies (i.e. certain annuities paid free of tax);

  (*c*) trust income is assessed to tax directly on the life tenant.

In all such cases, an appropriate explanatory note should be made in the accounts.

Balance of Income

(71) The income account should show the balance available after debiting all items chargeable against income. It should show the manner in which the net balance has been applied by the trustees; for example, amounts divided amongst the beneficiaries and transfers to accumulations accounts, indicating the bases of division in cases such as those where adjustment is required for interest on advances of capital to beneficiaries.

Schedules and Subsidiary Accounts

(72) Wherever possible, detail should be relegated to schedules and subsidiary accounts, leaving only the significant totals in the main accounts.

(73) Appropriate cross-references should be given in both the main and the subsidiary documents.

Investments

(74) The investment schedule should be so prepared as to enable totals in the main accounts to be identified readily. The grouping of the items in the schedule should therefore correspond with the grouping adopted in the balance sheet and it may be necessary to present more than one schedule. Where the trustees have applied the Trustee Investments Act 1961 the schedule(s) should show clearly to which part of the fund each investment has been allocated.

(75) Special funds dealt with separately in the balance sheet or income account should in any case have their separate investment schedules.

(76) The following information will normally be relevant in the investment schedule(s), although it may not all be necessary in every case:

(*a*) description, nominal amounts and book amounts of investments; also in the case of quoted investments, the values at 6th April, 1965, where relevant for Capital Gains tax purposes and, unless a broker's valuation is attached, the market values. In the case of investments outside the Scheduled Territories, the extent to which the premium on investment currency has been taken into account in arriving at the valuation, should be stated. In the case of unquoted investments, a valuation will not normally be available. It may, however, be helpful for the schedule to include the date of the latest valuation and the value placed on them;

(*b*) in the case of mortgages, details of the amount, security, rate of interest and due dates thereof, with particulars of any arrears of interest;

(*c*) the gross or net amount of interest and dividends (see paragraph 65);

(*d*) acquisitions, disposals and revaluations of investments during the period and resultant surpluses or deficits;

(*e*) statutory apportionments of dividends between capital and income, shown item by item. (Equitable apportionments do not usually fall to be dealt with item by item and should therefore be explained in the capital and income accounts by narration or, if appropriate, by reference to a separate schedule);

(*f*) in the case of real estate and leasehold estate, the probate value, cost or other book amount, as applicable, with such details as tenure, property expenses suitably analysed, rents receivable and particulars of any arrears;

(*g*) in the case of life assurance policies, the aggregate premiums paid to date (plus, in the case of an existing policy acquired, the value at the date of acquisition), brief detail of the sums assured and maturity dates of the policies, and if relevant, their surrender values.

Accounts with Beneficiaries

(77) Accounts with beneficiaries should generally be presented. This is particularly important where the details are complicated; for example, where there are periodical payments on account of income, accumulations accounts, maintenance accounts, or special difficulties. It is desirable that beneficiaries should be able to verify easily any amounts shown in the accounts as having been paid to them.

Capital Cash Summary Account

(78) A capital cash summary account, containing in summarised form all significant information regarding the receipts and

payments on capital account during the period covered by the accounts, may sometimes be helpful in larger estates. The information shown by such a summary account is not normally apparent in the capital account, which includes transactions other than receipts and payments. The summary account therefore provides a link between the capital cash shown in the balance sheet and that shown in the previous balance sheet.

Other Schedules

(79) Examples of other matters, for which separate schedules should be prepared where the detail involved makes it desirable, are the following:

(*a*) debtors;

(*b*) creditors;

(*c*) taxation, where the tax position of the trust is complex;

(*d*) executorship, administration or management expenses on both income and capital accounts;

(*e*) pecuniary and specific legacies, showing those paid or satisfied;

(*f*) Estate Duty where the detail is considerable, showing specifically any amounts charged to individual beneficiaries.

With regard to paragraphs 49 and 52 of the above memorandum, it is considered that it would be cumbersome and impracticable in most cases to record in the books of account each individual receipt or payment at its gross figure, debiting or crediting Income Tax Account with the tax deducted therefrom. Moreover, where apportionments are necessary of dividends or interest received on securities which are quoted on the Stock Exchange, since the *cum div.* quotation includes only the *net* amount of the accrued dividend or interest, only the *net* amount which has accrued prior to the death must be credited to the Trust Capital Account or to the capital column of the Investment Account for subsequent transfer to Trust Capital Account, in order that the balance of that column will represent the value of the security as at the date of death for both Estate Duty and Capital Gains tax purposes. Such net amount of dividend or interest accrued to the date of death actually represents the realisation of part of the probate valuation of the security, and not income on which tax has been suffered by the estate.

For practical purposes, therefore, it is considered that each individual receipt of income or payment in the nature of interest, annuities, etc., may be recorded in the books at the net amount actually received or paid. A periodical adjustment should then be made whereby Income on Investments Account is credited and Income Tax Account debited in one sum with the total amount of Income tax suffered by deduction on the aggregate amount of the dividends, etc., attributable to income, and Income Tax Account is credited and Interest, Annuities, etc. Accounts are debited with the total amount of tax recouped by deduction during the accounting period. In the Income Account, income received and interest, annuities, etc., paid under deduction of tax will thus be stated gross, and the amount of Income tax actually suffered by income will be shown, as recommended by the Council of the Institute.

§ 3. The Books of Account

The books which executors or trustees should keep are as follows:

      (1) Journal.

      (2) Cash Book.

      (3) Ledger.

      (4) Rent Roll (if necessary).

      (5) Minute Book (if necessary).

§ 4. The Journal

Modern practice tends to dispense with the use of the journal, the files of original documents being often used as the posting media. If used the journal will be in the usual form, and may record:

(*a*) a concise epitome of the will from the financial point of view, in order to avoid the necessity of repeated reference to the will in dealing with the accounts;

(*b*) the opening entries relating to the assets and liabilities at the date of death, as per the Estate Duty Account;

(c) the adjustments necessary in consequence of the apportionment of income and expenses;

(d) specific legacies and devises;

(e) adjustments in respect of profits or losses on capital account arising from the realisation of assets;

(f) transfers, closing entries, and any transactions of a special nature:

If personal accounts are kept with brokers, the purchase or sale of investments may also be journalised.

In all cases a full narrative should be shown in respect of each journal entry.

§ 5. The Cash Book

The Cash Book should be ruled with three cash columns on either side, headed respectively:

(1) Income.
(2) Capital.
(3) Bank.

The last column is necessary where separate bank accounts for capital and income are not kept; it is then possible to see a total column at a glance, what proportion of the balance as shown by the bank column relates to income, and what proportion to capital.

It is desirable that instructions be issued to the various companies and other authorities for dividends, interest, etc., to be paid direct to the bank account of the estate. A separate bank account must in all cases be opened in the name of the executors of the estate, and in no case should any executor use his own bank account for estate moneys. Where there are more than two executors it is customary for cheques to be signed by any two of the number, thus preventing any unnecessary delay.

All securities should be lodged for safe custody at the bank, or kept in a box by the bank, provided with two separate locks, the respective keys of which should be held by two of the executors.

In writing up the Cash Book, full narrative should be given for all entries, particularly when recording the apportionments as between capital and income, the deduction of Income tax and other allowances.

A voucher number column should be provided on each side'
and all vouchers, both as regards receipts and payments
(including the paid cheques, where there are no receipts),
numbered consecutively. All vouchers should be properly filed
and preserved, so that they can be readily referred to at any
future time. The term 'voucher', as regards receipts, refers
particularly to the counterfoils of dividends and interest
warrants, brokers' notes, auctioneers' accounts, etc., and
counterfoils in respect of rents received.

At the end of each balancing period, a reconciliation between
the balances of the Cash Book and Bank Statement should be
made and entered in the Cash Book.

§ 6. The Ledger

The ledger should be ruled with two columns on either side, the
first representing income and the second capital. In the case of
accounts for stocks and shares, however, an additional column
should be provided, to record the nominal amount, so that the
balance held can be seen at a glance.

At the head of each investment account should be shown the
date when dividends or interest payments fall due, so that it
can be seen by inspection whether all income from the particular
asset concerned has been received. If the testator died before
6th April, 1965, the value (where known) at that date for
Capital Gains tax purposes should be shown.

(a) The usual Ledger Accounts

The customary accounts to open in the ledger are:

(1) Estate Capital Account (otherwise termed 'Estate' or
'Corpus' Account).

(2) Estate Income Account.

(3) Funeral expenses.

(4) Testamentary expenses, including Estate Duty.

(5) A separate account for each debtor.

(6) Legacies and devises.

(7) Executorship expenses.

(8) A separate account for each investment.

(9) A separate account for each annuitant.

(10) A separate account for each life tenant.

(11) A separate account for each residuary legatee.

(12) Taxation Account.

(b) Profits and Losses on Sale of Investments

Where profits or losses on the sale of investments are transferred through the journal to the Estate Capital Account, the balance of stock remaining may be brought down at the original value as per the Estate Duty Account.

Illustration

Part of the estate of A., who died 1st May, consisted of £20,000 Government 3 per cent. stock, valued for Estate Duty at 43. £10,000 stock was sold on the 30th June for £4,305 *ex div.* Show the ledger account for the investment, bringing down a balance after the receipt of the quarter's dividend due on 5th July. Income tax is at 40p (8s.) in the £. Calculations to nearest £.

GOVERNMENT 3 PER CENT. STOCK ACCOUNT

Date		Nominal Value	Income	Capital	Date		Nominal Value	Income	Cap
19.. May 1	Estate Capital Account: £20,000 at 43	£ 20,000	£	£ 8,600	19.. June 30	Cash: Sale ..	£ 10,000	£	4,
July 5	Estate Account: Profit on sale of £5,000 stock			5	July 5	Cash: Div. on £20,000 stock for quarter to date £75 *Less* tax at 40p. 30			
	Accrued dividend in probate values			13		Capital 26 days		32	
July 5	Income Account		32			Income 65 days Balance ..	10,000		4,
		£20,000	£32	£8,618			£20,000	£32	£8,
July 6	Balance	10,000		4,300					

Notes to Illustration:

(*a*) BRINGING DOWN A BALANCE OF STOCK

Where the quotation at the date of death is *cum div.*, the net principal value will form the basis of the value on which the balance of stock should be brought down, as above, i.e. $\frac{10,000}{20,000}$ of £8,600 = £4,300.

In the case of stocks valued *ex div.* for Estate Duty purposes, the price at which the balance of stock is brought down is the similar proportion of the original valuation as increased by the whole amount of the next dividend.

The practice varies as to the method of valuing the balance of stock or shares where part has been sold. It is permissible simply to carry down the balance of the account. The conventional method, however, is to carry down the proportion of what the balance would have been if there had been no sale that the nominal value of the stock retained bears to the nominal value of the holding prior to the sale, as in the above illustration.

Where the stock has been purchased by the estate in the first instance, the brokerage, etc., will have been charged to capital as forming part of the cost, and must be allowed for when a balance is brought down at cost.

(*b*) DIVIDEND RECEIVED AFTER SALE OF STOCK *ex div.*
Where stock is sold *ex div.*, it should be remembered that the subsequent dividend will be upon the whole amount of the stock, including the proportion sold, as seen in the illustration.

(*c*) *Fluctuations in Value of Assets*

Fluctuations in the value of assets need not be taken into consideration until the ultimate result is ascertained by realisation or distribution, when the matter automatically adjusts itself.

In preparing accounts for beneficiaries it is, however, desirable to show the current market values of investments, so that they may be aware of the position of affairs, and these should be embodied in a separate schedule of investments, or shown as memorandum entries in a separate column of the Balance Sheet.

In the case of an ascertained loss, e.g. where a final dividend has been received on shares in a company which has been wound up, the balance on the investment account should be written off to Estate Capital Account.

Capital Gains tax payable on the realisation of assets should be charged to Estate Capital Account and not the account for the asset whose disposal gave rise to the charge.

(*d*) *Treatment of Income*

The income arising from each asset should be posted direct to the credit income column of the particular Asset Account, and transferred in one total therefrom at the close of each period to the credit of the Income Account of the estate.

It is important to note, in dealing with executorship accounts, that income accruing, or accrued due, but not received, should not normally be taken into account, for if this is done the executor might easily distribute more income than is subsequently received, in which case he might be held personally liable to refund to the estate the amount over-distributed. Reference should, however, be made to paragraphs 62 to 65 inclusive of the recommendations of the Council of the Institute of Chartered Accountants (*ante*, § 2).

Where beneficiaries have received from an estate advances on which they have to pay interest, and such has not been paid in cash, the above rule does not operate. In such cases the interest will be set off against the income, and only the net balance paid over to the beneficiaries. This treatment is essential in order to adjust the rights of the beneficiaries as between themselves.

On the other hand, the executor should provide in full for all accrued liabilities, in order to retain in hand the cash required to meet them.

§ 7. The Rent Roll

Where the estate includes a large number of properties yielding rents, it is necessary to keep a rent roll, ruled for half-yearly, quarterly or weekly payments, as the circumstances of the case require.

The following is a convenient ruling to adopt for quarterly rents, which can be modified where necessary.

FORM OF QUARTERLY RENTAL BOOK

No.	Property	Name of Tenant	Annual Rent	Amount due			Amount credited							Total Amount credited	Arrears carried
				Arrears brought forward	Rent for Quarter ending 19	Total Amount due	Date Received	C.B. folio	Cash	Allowances					
										Income Tax	Repairs	Other Allowances			

The executor should carry into the ledger only the actual net cash received; but care should be taken to balance the Rental Book periodically, and to carry forward arrears so that they are not lost sight of in the subsequent period.

§ 8. The Minute Book

In estates of importance, where there is more than one executor, and in the case of trust accounts, it is advisable to keep a minute book, in order to record the resolutions passed and the transactions effected. This often prevents disputes and difficulties arising between the executors or trustees, and in the cases of enforced absence from the meetings the absentee is enabled to follow the proceedings.

Minutes of each meeting should be drawn up and all the executors or trustees should sign them at the conclusion of the meeting.

§ 9. Illustrations of a Set of Executorship Books and Accounts

(a) Illustration (1)

A.B. died 31st October, 1969, and left estate as follows:	£
Household furniture	450
Cash in house	10
Cash at Bank	1,250
100 Ordinary shares of £10 each in Brown & Co. Ltd, valued at £15 per share	1,500
Mortgage at 5 per cent. on Freehold property	2,000
Interest thereon paid to 30th June, 1969.	
Share in Business of A.B. & Co., valued at date of death	6,132
Sundry Debtors	100

His liabilities amounted to £25.

Funeral expenses amounted to £50.

A legacy of £100 was bequeathed to his executor and was paid on the 28th January, 1970. The residue of the estate was left in trust for his infant son.

The household furniture was sold on 15th December, 1969, for £480; and the shares were sold on the same date at £14 10s. 0d. each *ex div.*, a dividend being received on 25th January, 1970, at 10 per cent. per annum for the year ending 31st December, 1969. Mortgage interest was received on 31st December, 1969, on which date the share in the business of A.B. & Co. was received with interest at 5 per cent. per annum.

The Estate Duty was paid on the 30th November, 1969, and the liabilities and funeral expenses were discharged on 20th December, 1969, on which date £50 of the debts due were received, the balance being unpaid at the date of preparation of the accounts.

Prepare the accounts of the estate as at 31st January, 1970.

Ignore Income tax and Capital Gains tax.

Make apportionments in months, and calculate to the nearest £.

JOURNAL

1969 Oct. 31			£	£
	Sundries: Dr.			
	Household Furniture		450	
	Cash in House		10	
	Cash at Bank		1,250	
	100 Ordinary Shares in Brown & Co., Ltd		1,500	
	Mortgage of Freehold Property		2,000	
	Interest accrued (4 months) at 5%		33	
	Share in business of A.B. & Co.		6,132	
	Sundry Debtors		100	
	To Estate Capital Account			11,475
			£11,475	£11,475
	Assets of deceased at date of death.			
	Estate Capital Account .. .. Dr.		75	
	To Sundries:			
	Liabilities			25
	Funeral Expenses			50
			£75	£75
	Deceased's liabilities at death, and funeral expenses.			
1970 Jan. 31	Estate Capital Account .. .. Dr.		350	
	To Estate Duty			350
	Being Duty on 25% of excess over £10,000.			
	Estate Capital Account .. .. Dr.		100	
	To Legacy Account			100
	Being legacy to executor.			
	Sundries: Dr.			
	Shares in Brown & Co. Ltd		17	
	Mortgage		17	
	Interest on Share in A.B. & Co.		51	
	To Estate Income Account			85
			£85	£85
	Transfer of Income.			
	Estate Income Account .. .. Dr.		1	
	To Interest on Estate Duty			1
	Transfer of Interest.			
	Sundries: Dr.			
	Household Furniture		30	
	Shares in Brown & Co., Ltd		33	
	To Estate Capital Account			63
	Transfer of Profit on Sale.		£63	£63

CASH BOOK

Date		Income	Capital	Date		Income	Capital
1969		£	£	1969		£	£
c. 31	Estate Capital Account..		1,260	Nov.30	Estate Duty　　..		350
c. 15	Household Furniture　..		480		Interest on Estate Duty		
	Share in Brown & Co.,				2% on £350 for 1 month	1	
	Ltd　..　..　..		1,450	Dec. 20	Liabilities　..　..		25
c. 20	Sundry Debtors　..		50		Funeral Expenses　..		50
c. 31	Mortgage Interest:			1970			
	Capital 4 months		33	Jan. 28	Legacy to Executor　..		100
	Income 2 months　..	17		Jan. 31	Balance c/f　..　..	84	8,963
	Share in A.B. & Co.　..		6,132				
	Interest on Share in A.B.						
	& Co. – 2 months at						
	5% p.a.　..　..	51					
1970							
, 25	Dividend on Shares in						
	Brown & Co., Ltd:						
	Capital 10 months　..		83				
	Income 2 months　..	17					
		£85	£9,488			£85	£9,488
1970							
. 31	Balance b/f　..　..	84	8,963				

ESTATE CAPITAL ACCOUNT

Date		Capital	Date		Capital
1969		£	1969		£
. 31	Sundry Creditors ..　..　..	25	Oct. 31	Household Furniture　..　..	450
	Funeral Expenses ..　..　..	50		Cash in House　..　..　..	10
	Balance carried down　..　..	11,400		Cash at Bank　..　..　..	1,250
				Shares in Brown & Co. Ltd　..	1,500
				Mortgage　..　..　..	2,000
				Interest on Mortgage (4 months)..	33
				Shares in Business of A.B.& Co.	6,132
				Sundry Debtors　..　..　..	100
		£11,475			£11,475
1970					
31	Estate Duty　..　..　..	350	Oct. 31	Balance　..　..　..　..	11,400
	Legacy Account　..	100	1970		
	Balance c/f　..　..　..	11,013	Jan. 31	Household Furniture (Profit on	
				Sale)　..　..　..　..	30
				Shares in Brown & Co. Ltd (do.)	33
		£11,463			£11,463
			1970		
			Jan. 31	Balance b/f　..　..　..	£11,013

HOUSEHOLD FURNITURE

Date		Capital	Date		Capital
1969		£	1969		£
. 31	Estate Capital Account　..　..	450	Dec. 15	Cash　..　..　..　..	480
1970					
, 31	Estate Capital Account (Profit) ..	30			
		£480			£480

SHARES IN BROWN & CO. LTD (100 SHARES £10 EACH)

Date		Nominal	Income	Capital	Date		Nominal	Income	Cap.
1969 Oct. 31	Estate Capital Account ..	£ 1,000	£	£ 1,500	1969 Dec. 15	Cash	£ 1,000	£	£ 1,4
1970 Jan. 31	Estate Capital A/c (Profit) ..			* 33	1970 Jan. 25	Cash, Dividend		17	
	Income A/c ..		17						
		£1,000	£17	£1,533			£1,000	£17	£1,5

* Alternatively, if the sale had not been in the executor's year, the figure of £83 sho
be transferred to Estate Capital Account when there will be a loss of £50. This wo
show the correct Capital Gains tax position.

MORTGAGE OF FREEHOLD PROPERTY

Date		Income	Capital	Date		Income	Capi
1969 Oct. 31	Estate Capital Account..	£	£ 2,000	1969 Dec. 31	Cash, Interest	£ 17	£
	Estate Capital Account, Interest to date of death		33				
1970 Jan. 31	Income Account ..	17		1970 Jan. 31	Balance c/f		2,0
		£17	£2,033			£17	£2,0
Jan. 31	Balance b/f		2,000				

SHARE IN BUSINESS OF A.B. & CO.

Date		Income	Capital	Date		Income	Capi
1969 Oct. 31	Estate Capital Account..	£	£ 6,132	1969 Dec. 31	Cash	£	£ 6,13
					Cash, Interest	51	
1970 Jan. 31	Income Account ..	51					
		£51	£6,132			£51	£6,13

SUNDRY DEBTORS

Date		Capital	Date		Capi
1969 Oct. 31	Estate Capital Account	£ 100	1969 Dec. 20	Cash	£ 5(
			1970 Jan. 31	Balance c/f	5(
		£100			£10(
1970 Jan. 31	Balance b/f	50			

SUNDRY CREDITORS

Date		Capital	Date		Capi
1969 Dec. 20	Cash	£ 25	1969 Oct. 31	Estate Capital Account	£ 25

FUNERAL EXPENSES

Date		Capital	Date		Capital
		£	1969		£
1969 Dec.20	Cash	50	Oct. 31	Estate Capital Account	50

ESTATE DUTY

Date		Capital	Date		Capital
		£	1970		£
1969 Nov. 30	Cash	350	Jan. 31	Estate Capital Account	350

INTEREST ON ESTATE DUTY

Date		Income	Date		Income
		£	1970		£
1969 Nov. 30	Cash	1	Jan. 31	Estate Income Account	1

LEGACY

Date		Capital	Date		Capital
		£	1970		£
1970 Jan. 28	Cash	100	Jan. 31	Estate Capital Account	100
		£100			£100

ESTATE INCOME ACCOUNT

Date		Income	Date		Income
1970 Jan. 31	Interest on Estate Duty	£ 1	1970 Jan. 31	Dividend on Shares in Brown & Co.	£
	Balance c/f	84		Ltd	17
				Interest on Mortgage	17
				Interest on share in A.B. & Co. ..	51
		£85			£85
			1970 Jan. 31	Balance b/f	£84

BALANCE SHEET OF A.B., DECEASED, 31st January, 1970

		£			£
Estate Capital Account		11,013	Mortgage on Freehold Property		2,000
			Sundry Debtors		50
			Balance at Bank: Capital		8,963
					11,013
Estate Income Account		84	Balance at Bank: Income		84
		£11,097			£11,097

(b) Illustration (2)

A. White died on the 15th November, 1968, and by his will left his household furniture valued for probate at £1,000 to his widow absolutely,
together with his motor car, valued at £450. The only other legacies were
£900 to a Charity, and £100 to his housekeeper. The residue of his estate,
both real and personal, he left to his widow for life, and at her death to
his son and daughter in equal shares.

The estate, other than the specific legacies, was as follows:

Cash in house, £124 (this was paid into the bank forthwith).

Balance at Bankers, £821.

Freehold property valued at £24,000.

£5,000 Loan on mortgage at 5 per cent. interest, payable quarterly
on 31st March, 30th June, 30th September and 31st December.

£10,000 Dominion 3 per cent. stock 1970–72 at 86½.

Share of Goodwill and Capital in the firm of A. White & Co., at
date of death, £20,000, £15,000 of which was paid on 31st December,
1968, and the balance on 30th September, 1969, in each case with
interest at 5 per cent. per annum.

Rents at £1,200 per annum, payable quarterly, were received on the due
dates.

The dividends on the Dominion 3 per cent. stock were received on the
due dates, viz. 5th January, April, July and October.

The interest on mortgage was received on the due dates, with the
exception of that payable 30th September, 1969, which had not been
received at the date of closing the books.

Sundry debts due by deceased, £567 including tax on the rents accrued
to death, and funeral expenses, £60, were paid on 28th February, 1969,
when the legacies were also paid.

Testamentary expenses (all capital), excluding Estate Duty, amounted to
£90, and were paid on 28th February, 1969, the account for Estate Duty
being brought in and the duty on personalty paid on the 20th February,
1969.

Repairs to freehold property were paid on 20th September, 1969,
amounting to £90.

Estate Duty on the realty was paid on 15th November, 1969, with the
aid of a bank overdraft. On 30th September, 1969, £1,500 was paid off
the mortgage.

The widow was paid £500 on 1st July and £350 on 1st October respectively.

Write up the books for the first year after the testator's death, and draw
up Income Account and Balance Sheet as at 15th November, 1969.

Income tax to be taken into account at 8s. in £ and calculations to
nearest £.

JOURNAL

1968				£	£
Nov. 15	Sundry Assets:	Dr.			60,227
	To Estate Capital				
	£10,000 Dominion 3% Stock @ 86 *cum div.*			8,650	
	Cash in the house			125	
	Balance at Bank			821	
	Loan on mortgage			5,000	
	Interest thereon to date of death:				
	At 5% 46 days	£31			
	Less Income Tax @ 8s.	12			
		———		19	
	Household furniture and motor car			1,450	
	A. White & Co.:				
	Share of Goodwill and Capital			20,000	
	Freehold property			24,000	
	Rent of above:				
	Quarter ending 25th December				
	To date of death—47 days			162	
				£60,227	£60,227
	Assets at date of death as per Estate Duty Account.				
	Estate Capital	Dr.		627	
	To Sundry Liabilities:				
	Debts due at death				567
	Funeral expenses				60
				£627	£627
	Liabilities at date of death as per Estate Duty Account.				
1969					
Feb. 28	Legacies	Dr.		1,450	
	To Household furniture, etc.				1,450
	Specific Legacies left to wife absolutely.				
	Estate Capital	Dr.		2,450	
	To Legacies				2,450
	Transfer.				
Nov. 15	Estate Capital	Dr.		20,950	
	To Testamentary expenses				20,950
	Transfer.				

CASH BOOK

Date		Income	Capital	Bank	Date		Income	Capital	Bank
		£	£	£			£	£	£
1968 Nov. 15	Estate Capital Account: Balance at Bank		821	821	1969 Feb. 20	Estate Duty at 35% on personalty £35,600		12,460	
	Balance in hand		125	125		Interest on duty on personalty at 2% per annum from date of death to Feb. 20— 97 days	66		12,52
Dec. 25	Freehold Property: Rent for Quarter to date, £300. Capital–47 days Income–40 days	138	162	300	Feb. 28	Testamentary expenses		90	9
Dec. 31	A. White & Co., £15,000 Capital repaid with interest at 5% per annum on £20,000 from date of death to date, 46 days, £126 less tax at 8s. in £	75	15,000			Debts due at death		567	56
	Loan on Mortgage, Interest at 5% on £5,000 for quarter to date £62 less tax at 8s. in £ Capital–46 days Income–46 days	19	19	15,113		Funeral expenses		60	6
1969 Jan. 5	Dominion 3% Stock: Interest on £10,000 for quarter to date £75 less tax at 8s. in £ Capital–41 days Income–51 days	25	20	45		Legacies: Charity Housekeeper		900 100	900 10
					July 1	Widow on account of income to date	500		50
Mar. 25	Freehold Property: Rent for quarter to date	300		300	Sept. 20	Repairs to Freehold property	90		9
Mar. 31	Loan on mortgage: Interest at 5% on £5,000 for quarter to date £62 less tax at 8s. in £	38		38	Oct. 1	Widow on account of income to date	350		35
April 5	Dominion 3% Stock: Interest on £10,000 for quarter to date £75 less tax at 8s. in £	45		45	Nov. 15	Estate Duty at 35% on realty £24,000		8,400	8,40
					Nov. 15	Balance c/f.	475	70	54
	Carried forward	£640	£16,147	£16,787		Carried forward	£1,481	£22,647	£24,128

CASH BOOK (*continued*)

Date		Income	Capital	Bank	Date		Income	Capital	Bank
		£	£	£			£	£	£
	Brought forward	640	16,147	16,787		Brought forward	1,481	22,647	24,128
une 24	Freehold property: Rent for quarter to date	300		300					
une 30	Loan on mortgage: Interest for quarter to date less tax at 8s. in £	38		38					
July 5	Dominion 3% Stock: Interest for quarter to date less tax at 8s. in £	45		45					
ept, 29	Freehold property: Rent for quarter to date	300		300					
ept. 30	Mortgage – part repayment A. White & Co., Balance of Capital Interest thereon at 5% per annum less tax at 8s. in £ from 31st Dec. 1969: 274 days	113	1,500 5,000	6,613					
Oct. 5	Dominion 3% Stock: Interest for quarter date less tax at 8s. in £	45		45					
		£1,481	£22,647	£24,128			£1,481	£22,647	£24,128
1969 Nov. 16	Balance b/f.	475	70	545					

ESTATE CAPITAL ACCOUNT

1968		£	1968		£
Nov. 15	Debts due at death ..	567	Nov. 15	Sundry Assets as per Estate Duty Account–	
	Funeral expenses ..	60		Dominion 3% Stock:	
	Balance as per Estate Duty Account:			£10,000 @ 86½% ..	8,650
	Personality £35,600			Cash in the house *cum div*	125
	Realty .. 24,000			Cash at Bank	821
		59,600		Loan on Mortgage ..	5,000
				Interest thereon to date of death at 5%, 46 days £31	
				Less Tax at 8s. 12	
					19
				Household furniture and motor car	1,450
				A. White & Co.:	
				Goodwill and Capital	20,000
				Freehold property ..	24,000
				Rents on above for quarter ending 25th December—87 days. To date of death—47 days ..	162
		£60,227			£60,227
1969			1969		
Feb. 28	Legacies	2,450	Nov. 15	Balance b/d.	59,600
Nov. 15	Testamentary expenses ..	20,950		Dominion 3%	
	Balance c/d.	36,220		Stock Account	20
		£59,620			£59,620
			1969		
			Nov. 16	Balance b/d.	36,220

DOMINION 3 PER CENT. STOCK 1970–72

Date		Nominal Value	Income	Capital	Date		Nominal Value	Income	Capital
1968		£	£	£	1969		£	£	£
Nov. 15	Estate Capital Account: Stock values at 86% *cum div* as per Estate Duty Account	10,000		8,650	Jan. 5	Cash: Dividend on £10,000 for quarter to date, £75, less tax: Capital – 41 days			20
1969						Income – 51 days		25	
Nov. 15	Income Account on Investments		160		April 5	Ditto – All Income		45	
	Estate Account: Accrued Interest to death			20	July 5	Ditto		45	
					Oct. 5	Ditto		45	
					Nov. 15	Balance c/d	10,000		8,650
		£10,000	£160	£8,670			£10,000	£160	£8,670
1969									
Nov. 16	Balance b/d	10,000		8,650					

LOAN ON MORTGAGE AT 5 PER CENT.

Date		Income	Capital	Date		Income	Capital
1968 Nov. 15	Estate Capital Account	£	£ 5,000	1968 Dec. 31	Cash: Interest at 5% on £5,000 for quarter to date, £62 10s., *less* tax	£	£
	Ditto: Interest thereon to date of death at 5% 46 days, £31, *less* tax ..		19		Capital – 46 days ..		19
1969 Nov. 15	Income on Investments Account	95		1969 Mar. 31	Income – 46 days .. Ditto – All Income ..	19 38	
				June 30	Ditto – All Income ..	38	
				Sept. 30	Cash:		1,500
				Nov. 15	Balance c/d		3,500
		£95	£5,019			£95	£5,019
1969 Nov. 16	Balance b/d		3,500				

A. WHITE & CO., CAPITAL

Date		Income	Capital	Date		Income	Capital
1968 Nov. 15	Estate Capital Account: Share of Goodwill and Capital at date of death	£	£ 20,000	1968 Dec. 31	Cash: Capital repaid with interest 5% on £20,000 from day of death to date, 46 days, £126, *less* tax	£ 75	£ 15,000
1969 Nov. 15	Income on Investments Account	188		1969 Sept. 30	Cash: Balance of Capital .. Interest at 5% per annum 274 days ..	113	5,000
		£188	£20,000			£188	£20,000

FREEHOLD PROPERTY

Date		Income	Capital	Date		Income	Capital
1968 Nov. 15	Estate Capital Account: as per Estate Duty Account	£	£ 24,000	1968 Dec. 25	Cash: Rent for quarter to date £300	£	£
	Ditto – rent for quarter ending 25th December (87 days) to date of death, 47 days ..		162	1969 Mar. 25	Capital – 47 days .. Income – 40 days .. Cash: Rent for quarter to date	138 300	162
1969 Sept. 20	Cash: Repairs	90		June 24	Ditto	300	
Nov. 15	Income Account ..	948		Sept. 29	Ditto	300	
				Nov. 15	Balance c/d		24,000
		£1,038	£24,162			£1,038	£24,162
1969 Nov. 16	Balance b/d		24,000				

HOUSEHOLD FURNITURE AND MOTOR CAR

Date		Capital	Date		Capit
1968 Nov. 15	Estate Capital Account	£ 1,450	1969 Feb. 28	Legacies – Widow	£ 1,450

INCOME TAX

Date		Income	Date		Incom
1969 Nov. 15	Income on Investments Tax deducted	£ 295	1969 Nov. 15	Estate Income Account	£ 7
Nov. 15	Balance carried down: Provision for Sch. D, Case VIII, assessment on rents 1968-69 .. .. .. 175 1969-70 .. .. .. 240 —— 	 415			
		£710			£7
			1969 Nov. 16	Balance b/d	4

LEGACIES

Date		Capital	Date		Capit
1969 Feb. 28	Household Furniture, etc.: Widow	£ 1,450	1969 Feb. 28	Estate Capital Account	£ 2,45
	Cash – Charity	900			
	Cash – Housekeeper	100			
		£2,450			£2,450

TESTAMENTARY EXPENSES

Date		Income	Capital	Date		Income	Capita
1969 Feb. 20	Cash: Estate duty at 35% on personalty, £35,600 .. Interest on personalty duty, £12,460 at 2% per annum from day after date of death to Feb. 20 =97 days	£ 66	£ 12,460	1969 Nov. 15 Nov. 15	Estate Capital Account Estate Income Account	£ 66	£ 20,95
Feb. 28	Cash		90				
Nov. 15	Cash: .. .. .. Estate duty at 35% on Realty, £24,000 ..		8,400				
		£66	£20,950			£66	£20,95

DEBTS DUE AT DEATH

1969		£	1968		£
Feb. 28	Cash	567	Nov. 15	Estate Capital Account	567
		£567			£567

FUNERAL EXPENSES

1969		£	1968		£
Feb. 28	Cash	60	Nov. 15	Estate Capital Account	60
		£60			£60

WIDOW

1969		£	1969		£
July 1	Cash	500	Nov. 15	Income Account, net income for year	910
Oct. 1	Cash	350			
Nov. 15	Balance c/d	60			
		£910			£910
			1969		
			Nov. 16	Balance b/d	£60

INCOME ON INVESTMENTS

1969		£	1969		£
Nov. 15	Income Account	738	Nov. 15	Dividends, Interest, &c. (net):	
				Dominion 3%	160
				Mortgage	95
				A. White & Co...	188
					443
				Income Tax Account:	
				Tax deducted	295
		£738			£738

ESTATE INCOME ACCOUNT

FOR THE YEAR ENDED 15TH NOVEMBER, 1969

	£				£
Interest on Estate Duty	66	Interest and Dividends			738
Income Tax on income for year	710	Rents on Freehold Properties ..	£1,038		
Balance transferred to Widow's Account ..	910	*Less* Repairs..	90		
					948
	£1,686				£1,686

THE ESTATE OF A. WHITE, DECEASED
BALANCE SHEET, AS AT 15TH NOVEMBER, 1969

	£	£		£
Estate Capital Account		36,220	Freehold Property, at probate value ..	24,00
			£10,000 Dominion 3% Stock, 1970-72 at probate value, *less* accrued interest to date of death	8,6:
			Loan on Mortgage at 5%, *less* amount re-paid	3,5(
			Balance at Bank on Capital Account ..	
				36,2:
Estate Income Account:			Balance at Bank on Income Account ..	4
Widow. Income for year ..	910			
Less Paid on Account	850			
	60			
Provision for Income Tax	415			
		475		
		£36,695		£36,6:

Notes to Illustration:

(*a*) THE APPORTIONMENT OF DIVIDEND ON DOMINION 3 PER CENT. STOCK

The quotation of this stock on the 15th November is *cum dividend*, consequently the accrued interest will be included in the price, and it is not necessary for Estate Duty purposes to bring in the accrued interest in addition. See the ledger account showing the effect of this treatment therein.

(*b*) INTEREST ON ESTATE DUTY

Interest accrued on the Estate Duty on personalty at 2 per cent. per annum during the period from the date of death to the date of payment. The interest is chargeable to income. If any part of that period had fallen after April, 1970, the rate of interest would have been 3 per cent.

(*c*) ESTATE DUTY ON REALTY

The duty on real estate is not due till one year after the testator's death; consequently interest does not run thereon until after that period has elapsed, unless the property has been sold in the meantime when interest runs from the date of sale.

(*d*) THE DIVISION OF CASH BETWEEN CAPITAL AND INCOME

One of the advantages of using the form of Cash Book shown in the illustration becomes apparent when it is desired to invest the balance of corpus realised, or to hand over to a tenant for life a definite portion of income received to date, when the correct amount can be ascertained by merely striking a balance on the respective columns of the Cash Book.

(*e*) INCOME ACCRUED BUT NOT RECEIVED AT THE DATE OF CLOSING
         ACCOUNTS

In the illustration it will be observed that the mortgage interest due on 30th September, but not received before closing the books, is not brought into account, thus observing the general rule of non-anticipation of income. In rendering accounts to beneficiaries, however, executors and trustees should attach a schedule of such income accrued due but not received at the date of the accounts, with a note explaining the circumstances in each case. This is important, as it affords to the beneficiaries information as to the cause of any fluctuation in income.

(*f*) INCOME TAX

It is a wise practice in trust accounts to provide in full for all accruing liabilities, thus retaining funds in hand to meet them. The calculation of the provision for the accrued Income tax under Schedule D, Case VIII, should be noted.

§ 10. Judgment and Accounts in Administration Action

The ordinary form of judgment in an action for administration brought by beneficiaries to have accounts taken, both of the real and personal estate, runs as follows:

Declare that the trust of the will ought to be performed and carried in execution, and order and decree the same accordingly.

Let the following accounts and enquiries be taken and made (that is to say):

(1) An account of the personal estate of the testator not specifically bequeathed come to the hands of the executors, or of any or either of them, or to the hands of any other persons by the order or for the use of the executors, or any or either of them.

(2) An account of the testator's debts.

(3) An account of the testator's funeral expenses.

(4) An account of the legacies and annuities given by the testator's will.

(5) An inquiry what parts (if any) of the testator's personal estate are outstanding or undisposed of.

And let the testator's personal estate (not specifically bequeathed) be applied in payment of his debts and funeral expenses in a due course of administration, and then in payment of the legacies and annuities (if any) given by his will. And let the following further inquiries and accounts be made and taken (that is to say):

(6) An inquiry what real estate the testator was seized of, or entitled to, at the time of his death.

(7) An account of the rents and profits of the testator's real estate received by the trustees of the testator's will, or any or either of them, or by any other person or persons, by the order or for the use of the said trustees, or any or either of them.

Then follow further enquiries as to the amounts due on any incumbrances affecting the real estate, and as to their priorities; and direction as to the sale of the real estate and the bringing the proceeds into court, and their consequential application.

The forms of accounts in an administration action are as follows:

Illustration

PERSONAL ESTATE

RECEIPTS ON ACCOUNT OF PERSONAL ESTATE					PAYMENTS AND ALLOWANCES ON ACCOUNT OF PERSONAL ALLOWANCES				
No. of Item	Date when received	Names of persons from whom received	On what account received	Amount received	No. of Item	Date when paid or allowed	Names of persons to whom paid or allowed	For what purpose paid or allowed	Amou paid allow
				£ s. d.					£ s.

REAL ESTATE

		RECEIPTS								PAYMENTS AND ALLOWANC				
No. of Item	Date when received	Tenant's Name	Description of premises	Annual rent	Arrears due at	Amount due at	Amount received	Arrears remaining due	Observations	No. of Item	Date of payment or allowance	Names of persons to whom paid or allowed	For what purpose paid or allowed	Amount
				£ s. d.	£ s. d.	£ s. d.	£ s. d.	£ s. d.						£ s.

When the account has been brought in, any party who is dissatisfied with it may produce evidence to show that the accounting party has received more than he has admitted by his account (this being known as 'surcharging'). The items of disbursements have to be proved by the accounting party – those of 40s and over by the production of the vouchers, and those under that amount by the oath of the accounting party, giving full particulars. No item for general expenses will, in any event, be allowed. The vouching of such items is, however, only evidence that those amounts have been actually paid, and any party may apply for the disallowance of any of such items upon the ground that they were not proper disbursements (this is known as 'falsifying').

In taking an account, no balance is in general struck until all the receipts and payments have been gone through, and no rest can be made unless directed by the decree, although simple interest may be charged in a proper case without any such directions in the decree. Where an account is directed to be taken, with rests as against an accounting party, a balance must be struck at each rest (e.g. yearly), which the decree requires to be made, by deducting the amount of the payments from the amount of receipts up to that time. Interest at the rate ordered is then calculated on the balances, and carried into the next account so as to charge the accounting party with compound interest.

An executor can always get the sanction and protection of the court by means of an originating summons, without having a complete administration of the estate; but parties interested are only entitled to an administration judgment where there are questions which cannot be properly determined except by an administration action. On the other hand, any party interested may by originating summons compel the trustee to account.

CHAPTER XVI

TRUSTS AND TRUSTEES
PART I – TRUSTS

§ 1. Nature and History of Trusts

A trust exists when property is held by one person, called the 'trustee', for the benefit of another person, called the *cestui que trust* or 'beneficiary'. The trustee is the nominal owner of the property, the beneficiary the real owner. The usual reason for the separation of the nominal from the real ownership in this way is that various beneficiaries have successive or partial interests in the property, so that it is not possible for any one of them to hold it as absolute owner. Thus, if property is to be held for the benefit of one person during his life, and after his death for the benefit of others, it is necessary for trustees to hold the property in order to give effect to the successive interests of the beneficiaries. Again, if property belongs to a number of people jointly or in common, trustees will hold the property for the benefit of them all, though in this case it is not unusual to find that the trustees are the same persons as the beneficiaries. Another reason for the holding of property by trustees may be that the beneficiary is an infant and unable to hold the legal title to the property or to give a valid receipt for the property if it were transferred to him. It is possible for property to be held on trust for a single beneficiary, who is *sui juris* (i.e. who has legal capacity to contract) and capable of holding the property himself; in this case the trustee is often called a bare trustee, or nominee.

Although the beneficiaries under a trust are usually persons, it is possible to create trusts for particular objects, such as the promotion of a political activity or the care of animals, without the existence of any human beneficiary. Such trusts, unless they are charitable, are said to be of imperfect obligation, because they are unenforceable. If the trustee chooses to carry them into effect, he can do so; but if he does not, the trust cannot be enforced, and the property passes to the persons entitled on failure of the trust.

470

Trusts form an interesting chapter in English legal history. The Common Law, which was enforced by the King's Courts from Norman times, regarded the owner of property as being entitled in his own right, and did not recognise any trust to which his ownership might be subject. In the eyes of the Common Law the beneficiary under a trust had no interest at all in the property. Yet the practice of putting property into trust became common by the 14th century, for various reasons. A trust, or a use, as it was called in those days, might be created, for example, to avoid dues payable to the lord of the manor – the modern settlement to avoid death duties may be an instance of history repeating itself – or to keep a beneficiary's assets out of the hands of his creditors, or to enable a man to make a will of his land, a right which was restricted by the Common Law. So long as the trustee carried out the use, all went well, but cases arose of unscrupulous trustees failing to do so and claiming the property as their own, a claim which was upheld by the Court of Common Law. This injustice led to beneficiaries petitioning the King to give them justice, and the King referred the matter to the Lord Chancellor. The Lord Chancellor dealt with such cases in accordance with his view of what was just and equitable, and gradually his jurisdiction assumed the force of law, and the principles he established became precedents for future cases and built up the rules of law known as Equity, administered by the Court of Chancery. It was in the realm of the law of trusts that Equity first arose, though its jurisdiction eventually extended to all branches of the law in order to remedy injustices which were not taken into account by the Common Law.

An attempt by statute (the Statute of Uses, 1535) to put an end to trusts failed in its purpose, and this Act was repealed by the Law of Property Act 1922. The Trustee Act 1925 contains provisions regulating the powers and duties of trustees, but much of the law of trusts and trustees still depends on the principles of Equity.

Owing to the historical development of the law of trusts, the interest of a beneficiary came to be referred to as the equitable interest in the property, whereas the interest of the trustee was the legal interest. It is, however, not strictly correct today to say that the title of the trustee is always the legal title, for it is possible for equitable interests themselves to be the subject of a trust. For example, a person who has an equitable interest in settled property, expectant on the death of a life tenant, might settle his remainder on trust, and the trustees of the derivative settlement created by him would hold an equitable interest only; the legal interest would be in the trustees of the original settlement. The interest of the beneficiary under a trust must always be equitable.

A trust must be distinguished from a contract. A contract is an agreement supported by consideration, and the remedy of one contracting party against the other for breach of contract is to claim damages, or occasionally specific performance of the contract. A contract does not of itself confer any interest in property, but merely gives one contracting party a right *in personam* (i.e. a right against a particular person) against the other party to the contract. A person on whom, by a contract, a benefit is to be conferred, has no right of action on the contract unless he is a party to it. In the case of a trust, although it is true to say that a person only becomes trustee by his so agreeing, yet his obligations do not rest in contract, but are imposed on him by the principles of equity, binding him to deal with the trust property in accordance with the trust. If he commits a breach of trust, the beneficiaries have not only a remedy against him personally for the breach, but also a right *in rem* (i.e. in property) represented by their interest in the trust property, which they may be able to enforce by following the property, quite apart from their right of action against the trustee personally. A beneficiary can compel the performance of the trust, notwithstanding that he may not have been a party to its creation. The distinction can be brought out by an example. A. makes an agreement with B. whereby, in consideration of A. paying B. £1,000, B. is to pay an annuity of £100 a year to C. B. fails to pay the annuity. C. has no right of action against him, as C. is a stranger to the contract between A. and B. A., but not C., can claim against B. for breach of contract. In contrast, A. pays £1,000 to B. to be held by him on trust to pay an annuity of £100 a year to C. If B. fails to pay the annuity, C. has a right of action against B. for breach of trust and a right to enforce the claim against the £1,000 which is held in trust or against the property into which it has been converted.

§ 2. Creation of Trusts

Trusts may be classified according to the mode of their creation as (*a*) express, (*b*) implied, (*c*) resulting, (*d*) constructive.

(*a*) *Express Trusts*

Trusts may be created expressly, either by will or by disposition *inter vivos*. Trusts may also arise on intestacy by virtue of the law as to intestacies.

On the death of a person his property passes to his personal representative. If under his will or on his intestacy all his property passes to beneficiaries who are *sui juris* and entitled absolutely, no trust will arise, for on completion of the administration the property will be transferred to them. If, however, the property is to be enjoyed by persons in succession, or if any beneficiaries are infants, the trust created by the will or intestacy will take effect on completion of the administration. Usually the same persons are both personal representatives and trustees, and in that event their capacity changes to that of trustees as soon as the administration has been completed and the property is retained in trust. Occasionally different persons are appointed trustees, and then the commencement of the trust is evidenced by the transfer of the property from the personal representatives to the trustees. The date of commencement of the trust will be important for *inter alia* the purposes of Capital Gains tax. On the administration being completed and the assets being placed in the hands of trustees, no liability will arise, but from that date the ultimate beneficiary will suffer Capital Gains tax (the trustees will pay it) on the assets being passed to him. Such assets will be transferred to him at the value at the date the assets are passed to him. If the assets had never passed to the trust the beneficiary would not suffer any liability, since he would take the assets at probate value.

A trust is created by disposition *inter vivos*, either by the person in whom property is vested declaring himself to be a trustee thereof (a declaration of trust) or by the transfer of property to some person to be held by him on trust. These are disposals for Capital Gains tax purposes by the purpose setting up the trust. The commonest examples of dispositions *inter vivos* creating trusts are marriage settlements and voluntary settlements.

(b) *Implied Trusts*

An implied trust arises when no express trusts of property are declared, but a trust is implied from the presumed intention of the parties. A common instance occurs on the purchase of property in the name of another. In such a case there is a presumption of a trust in favour of the person who provided the purchase money. This presumption may be rebutted by evidence to the contrary. If the person into whose name the property is conveyed is someone for whom the purchaser is under an obligation to provide, there is a presumption, called 'a presumption of advancement', that no trust in favour of the purchaser was created, but that the beneficial interest as well as the legal title was intended to belong to the person in whose name the property was purchased. This presumption of advancement arises in favour of the wife and child of the purchaser and in favour of any person to whom the purchaser stands in *loco parentis*. The presumption of advancement is likewise capable of being rebutted by evidence that a trust was in fact intended in favour of the purchaser. No presumption of advancement arises in favour of a husband, and it is doubtful whether it arises when a woman purchases property in the name of her child. The presumption does not arise in favour of an illegitimate child unless the father stands in *loco parentis* by having taken upon himself the duty of providing for the child.

(c) *Resulting Trusts*

A resulting trust arises when the beneficial interest in the trust property returns (or results) to the person who provided it. This occurs when the declared trusts fail to exhaust the beneficial interests in the property. For example, a father settles property, on the occasion of his son's marriage, on his son for life, then on his son's wife for life, and subject thereto, on trust for the children of the marriage. The wife dies without issue, so that there is no beneficiary to inherit on the termination of the son's life interest. There is a resulting trust, subject to the son's life interest, in favour of the father.

Some writers classify implied and resulting trusts together, on the basis that both depend on the presumed intention of the parties.

(d) Constructive Trusts

These are trusts which do not arise from the expressed or presumed intention of the parties, but from construction of Equity in order to give effect to what justice demands. The commonest example is a trust imposed on a person in a fiduciary capacity to hold any profit which he has made out of his position for the benefit of the persons to whom he owes a duty. The leading case is *Keech* v. *Sandford*, where trustees of a lease which they held for an infant were unable to obtain from the landlord a renewal of the lease for the benefit of the infant. They therefore applied for and obtained a renewal on their own behalf. It was held by the court that they were bound to hold the lease as trustees for the infant. It is to be observed that a constructive trust imposed in this way is not based on any assumption that the trustees have acted to the detriment of the beneficiary, but on the principle that a trustee or other person in a fiduciary capacity must not make any profit out of his position. Other examples of constructive trusts are a vendor's lien for unpaid purchase money, which imposes a trust on the purchaser; a purchaser's lien for prematurely paid purchase money; the obligation of an agent to account to his principal for secret profits; and the obligation of a mortgagee to account to the mortgagor for the surplus proceeds of sale of the mortgaged property.

§ 3. Formalities for the Creation of a Trust

(a) Will or Codicil

A trust which is to take effect only on death, and which is to be revocable until then, should be created by will or codicil, executed in manner laid down by the Wills Act 1837, s. 9 (*see* Chapter I, § 3, *ante*).

(b) Writing

Generally speaking, a trust can be created *inter vivos* in any manner which is sufficient to show that the person in whom the property is vested is to hold it for the benefit of another or others. 'Equity looks to the intent rather than to the form.' Although trusts are usually expressed in writing, an oral declaration of trust, if it can be proved, is sufficient. Moreover, implied and resulting trusts arise merely from the presumed

intention of the parties without either writing or oral declaration. There is an exception to the rule that writing is not
required, in the case of land. By L.P.A. 1925, s. 53, a declaration
of trust respecting land or any interest therein must be evidenced
by writing signed by the person who is able to declare such
trusts or by his will. The section does not affect the creation or
operation of resulting, implied or constructive trusts. It will be
observed that the section does not require writing to create the
trust, but only to evidence it, so that it will be sufficient if the
writing comes into existence at any time, even after the trust
was created.

The creation of trusts must be distinguished from the disposition of the interest of a beneficiary under a trust, for such a
disposition is required by the same section to be in writing,
whether the interest is in land or any other property. In that
case the requirement is not simply one of evidence, but the
disposition itself must be in writing.

(c) Secret Trusts

Secret trusts are those which are not created in accordance with
the formalities required by statute, and yet to which Equity
gives effect so as not to allow a statute to be used as an 'engine
of fraud'. The only statutory requirements as to form are
Section 53, L.P.A. 1925 (relating to trusts of land), and Section
9, Wills Act 1837 (relating to trusts created by will), both of
which are explained in the preceding paragraph.

As regards trusts of land created *inter vivos*, the usual effect
of failure to comply with Section 53, L.P.A. 1925, is that trust
is unenforceable, and the legal owner of the property is entitled
to retain it free from any trusts. Where, however, the person
appointed trustee is not the donor or settlor, but is some third
party to whom the property has been transferred on the oral
understanding that he would give effect to the trust, it would be
fraud on his part to attempt to take the property for his own
benefit, and Equity will restrain him from doing so, notwithstanding the statute. Thus, in *Rochefoucauld* v. *Boustead*, land
was conveyed to X by a document which did not indicate any
trust, but the conveyance was made on the understanding
between the settlor and X that the property should be held for
the benefit of Y. X attempted to hold the property for his own

benefit. Y brought action against him, and although he was unable to produce sufficient written evidence the court admitted oral evidence to prove the existence of the trust, and made a declaration of trust in favour of Y. It will be appreciated that where the trust property is other than land, there is no possibility of a secret trust created *inter vivos* in the sense defined above, because, even if no trust appears on the face of any document, there is no obstacle to proving its existence by oral evidence.

It is in relation to wills that secret trusts are most frequently encountered, and they take the form of a gift subject to a trust which does not appear on the face of the will. The reasons why a testator should omit the trusts from the will may be many and various. Most usually, the reason is either because he wishes to be able to alter the trusts from time to time without going through the formality of making another will, or because he wishes to conceal from the public the gift which he is making, as in the case of a man giving property to his mistress or illegitimate children. For the purpose of the law of secret trusts, two kinds of cases must be distinguished: firstly, those cases in which, on the face of the will, there is an absolute beneficial gift to the person who is to be trustee and, secondly, those cases in which the will states that the property is to be held on trust, but does not state what the trusts are.

In the first kind of case, that of an apparent beneficial gift to the trustee, the rule is that the person to whom the property is given by the will must carry out the trust if it was communicated to him at any time, whether before or after the making of the will, during the testator's life, and he either accepted the trust, or by his silence indicated that he would perform it. If he hears of the trust only after the testator's death, then he is entitled to take the property beneficially. There is no question then of his having induced the testator to make his will in that form, or to leave it unaltered, in reliance on any promise. If, however, the testator had, during his lifetime, indicated to the donee that he was to hold the property on trust, but the donee only becomes aware of what the trusts are after the testator's death, the donee will not be allowed to take the property beneficially. In that case the secret trust will not be effective, because it was not communicated during the testator's lifetime; but because the donee knew in the testator's lifetime that a trust was intended, he will be compelled to hold the property on trust for the residuary legatee, or, if the gift was one of residue, for the persons entitled on the testator's intestacy. For example, in *Re Boyes*, a testator made his will giving a legacy to his solicitor, and informed the solicitor that the legacy was to be held on trust for a person whose name would be disclosed to him subsequently. The solicitor was not told the name during the testator's lifetime, but after his death he discovered among the deceased's papers a memorandum naming the beneficiary. It was held that the trust failed and the legacy fell into residue. Had the solicitor not been told by the testator that he was to hold the legacy on trust, he would have been entitled to keep it for himself notwithstanding discovery of the memorandum.

In the case of a will which indicates a trust, but does not specify what the trust is, as in the case of a gift to X 'to be held by him on such trusts as I have indicated to him', the rule is that the trusts are validly created if they are communicated to the donee before or at the time of the making of the will. Apparently communication afterwards, even although it may be during the testator's lifetime, is ineffective. The reason for this rather curious rule, if it is indeed the law (as to which there is some doubt) is that the mention of an undisclosed trust in the will creates a trust for the residuary legatees or for the persons entitled on inestacy, and to alter that trust after the making of the will would be an alteration of the will contrary to Section 9, Wills Act 1837. If the trusts are not communicated in due time, the donee is never allowed to hold beneficially.

Secret trusts are also enforced in the cases of intestacy. This occurs when the intestate has refrained from making a will in reliance on the promise of the person entitled on intestacy to hold the property on certain trusts communicated to him during the lifetime of the intestate.

It may be asked how Equity is able to set aside the provisions of the L.P.A. 1925, as to writing, and of the Wills Act 1837, as to the execution of wills and codicils. The answer is that Equity allows the statutes to operate, as indeed it must, for the courts cannot overrule the legislature; but when the property has passed in accordance with the statute, Equity intervenes to impose a trust on any person who cannot conscientiously retain the property for himself. It will be observed that the equitable principles giving effect to secret trusts only operate in those cases where the person named as trustee has agreed, expressly or impliedly, to carry out the trusts, so that it would be against conscience to allow him to profit from the absence of requisite formalities.

(d) Completely Constituted and Incompletely Constituted Trusts

A trust may be constituted *inter vivos* by the person in whom the property is vested either declaring himself a trustee thereof or transferring the property to another person to be held on trust. Where the property is to be transferred to the trustee, the trust is said to be incompletely constituted until everything necessary for vesting the property in the trustee has been done. What is necessary in any particular case depends on the nature of the property. The legal estate in freehold land is transferred by deed of conveyance, in leasehold land by deed of assignment, in stocks and shares by deed or document (according to the company's Articles) of transfer entered in the company's register, in personal chattels by deed or by delivery. If the trust has not been completely constituted in the proper way, it will not be enforceable by volunteers, that is, by persons who have not given consideration for the creation of the trust, for 'Equity will not assist a volunteer'. Persons who have given value can enforce even an incompletely constituted trust, for 'Equity looks on that as done which ought to be done'. In the case of a marriage settlement, not only the parties to the marriage, but also the children, are regarded as having given value therefor, so that an incompletely constituted trust would be enforceable by them. A voluntary settlement would not be enforceable unless the trust were completely constituted.

The position of a volunteer is well illustrated in *Re Plumptre's Marriage Settlement*. In that case a wife, by her marriage settlement, covenanted to settle her after-acquired property on trust for herself and her husband successively for life, with remainder to the issue of the marriage, and with an ultimate trust in favour of her next-of-kin. The wife became possessed of after-acquired property, but failed to transfer it to the trustees of the settlement in accordance with her covenant. On her death, in 1909, intestate and without issue, her husband was entitled under the law then in force to the whole of her personal property,

and he claimed the after-acquired property which she had failed
to settle. Had there been children of the marriage, his claim
would have failed against them, because they would not have
been volunteers. But it was held that the wife's next-of-kin, who
were ultimate beneficiaries under the settlement, could not
claim the transfer of the after-acquired property to the trustees
of the settlement, as they were volunteers under an incompletely
constituted trust.

An attempted transfer, which fails in its effect through not
being in the proper form, will not be treated as a declaration of
trust, for the donor or settlor has shown an intention to divest
himself of the property, not to constitute himself a trustee.
Such an attempted transfer will therefore be ineffective to
create any trust in favour of a volunteer. Thus, in *Richards* v.
Dellbridge, an intending donor wrote and signed a note on his
lease 'This deed I give to E. B. Richards from this time forth.'
Had this been a declaration of trust, there would have been a
sufficient memorandum to satisfy the L.P.A. 1925, s. 53; but it was
an attempted transfer, and not being by deed of assignment, failed
to confer any interest on the donee. 'There is no equity to perfect
an imperfect gift' (per Turner, L.J., in *Milroy* v. *Lord*).

An incompletely constituted trust will, however, become
completed if the proposed trustee (or the beneficiary) takes the
office of executor of the deceased donor's will, for the legal title
is thereby vested in the trustee and the assistance of Equity is
no longer required (*Strong* v. *Bird*). And the same is true where
the proposed trustee takes out letters of administration of the
estate of the deceased (*Re James*).

(e) The Three Certainties

It has been said that for the creation of a trust three things,
called the 'three certainties', are necessary: certainty of words,
certainty of subject-matter, and certainty of beneficiaries.

'Certainty of words' means that, although no particular form
of words is required to create an express trust, the words used,
whether oral or written, must be sufficiently clear to show that
a trust was intended. In every case it is a matter of construing
the particular words, in the light of all the circumstances if the
words are oral, or from an examination of the document as a
whole if the words are written. The difficulty of deciding

whether a trust is intended arises most frequently in construing a will where the testator has expressed a desire in relation to a particular gift. Such words of desire are called 'precatory' words. If they give rise to a trust (A PRECATORY TRUST), the donee of the gift is bound to hold it on trust to give effect to the desire. If they are not sufficiently certain to create a trust, the donee takes the gift absolutely and it is left to him to give effect to the desire or not as he chooses. In *Re Adams and the Kensington Vestry*, a testator gave his estate to his wife 'in full confidence that she would do what was right as to the disposal thereof between my children'. It was held that no trust in favour of the children had been created, and that the widow took an absolute interest. Similarly, in *Re Diggles*, a gift to the testatrix's daughter, coupled with the words 'it is my desire that she allows Anne Gregory an annuity of £25 during her life', was held to be an absolute gift, creating no trust in favour of Anne Gregory. The modern trend of judicial authority is against construing precatory words as creating any trust. The well-drawn will or settlement will make the matter clear either by expressing the desire as a trust, or by saying 'without creating any trust in that behalf'.

'Certainty of subject-matter' means both that the property to which the trust is to attach must be clearly identified or identifiable and that if there is more than one beneficiary the respective interests which they are to take must be defined or ascertainable. Thus, a gift of 'sufficient of my property to enable X to live in comfort' would fail to create any gift in his favour through uncertainty of the property to which it was to attach. But a gift to X of 'such one of my horses as he may select' would be good, because the property to which the gift is to attach will become identified as soon as X makes his selection. When the property is defined, but the interests which the beneficiaries are to take is not stated, the uncertainty can sometimes be cured by applying the equitable maxim 'equality is equity' and dividing the property equally among the beneficiaries. This will be done where the gift is to 'A, B and C', simply. In other cases, however, it may be clear that a gift in equal shares was not intended, and then uncertainty will cause failure. For example, a gift to a wife 'remembering always, according to circumstances, the Church of God and the poor' failed to create any trust in favour of the Church or the poor, because their interests were neither defined nor ascertainable (*Sprange* v. *Barnard*).

'Certainty of objects' relates, not to the interests which the objects are to take, but to the identification of the beneficiaries themselves. If it is uncertain who is to benefit, the trust will fail. Thus, a gift to a son 'and his dependants' was held to create no trust in favour of the dependants, as it was uncertain who they were (*Re Ball*). A testator cannot by his will delegate to another the power of selecting the persons to benefit under his will, unless he has himself designated the class and left to his trustees the selection of objects from that class. The law will not allow a testator to appoint someone else to make a will for him after his death (*Grimond* v. *Grimond*). Thus, in *Re Wood*, deceased, a testatrix bequeathed a fund on trust to pay £2 a week to the 'week's good cause' (the objects of which were not necessarily charitable), for which an appeal should be broadcast by the British Broadcasting Corporation. It was held that the gift failed for uncertainty of objects, because the testatrix had delegated to the British Broadcasting Corporation the power of selecting beneficiaries. A charitable trust, however, is an exception to this rule, for it will not fail through uncertainty of objects if a general charitable intention is shown. For example, a bequest of property to be divided 'amongst such charitable institutions as my executors shall select' creates a valid trust in favour of the institutions selected by the executors.

The effect of failure of one of the certainties differs according to the circumstances. If the failure is that of precatory words to create a trust, then the beneficiary to whom the property is given subject to the desire takes free from any trust. If the failure is that of identifying the subject-matter, then the attempted creation of a trust is entirely ineffectual. An uncertainty as to beneficial interest will cause the property to result to the settlor, or in the case of a will to fall into residue, or if the uncertainty relates to residue, to be dealt with as property undisposed of by will. Should it be, however, that the whole beneficial interest is given to one or more beneficiaries, subject to uncertain interest of others, the beneficiaries whose interests are certain will take the entire property free from the uncertain interests. Uncertainty of objects will have the same effect as uncertainty of beneficial interest.

(f) Executed and Executory Trusts

It might be thought that the phrase 'executed trust' refers to one which has been fully carried out, whereas 'executory trust' means one which is still on foot. In fact the expressions are used in a different connection, in reference to the creation of a trust rather than to its carrying out. An executed trust is one in which the settlor has 'been his own conveyancer', that is to say, in which he has set out the detailed provisions of the trusts which he is creating. In the case of an executory trust, on the other hand, the settlor has merely indicated generally the trusts which he intends, leaving it to the parties or to the court to settle the exact details. For example, an agreement for a marriage settlement might provide for the settlement of property 'on the usual trusts for the parties to the marriage and their issue'. This is an executory trust, and when the marriage settlement comes to be drawn up, the usual trusts must be set out in detail. Such usual trusts are probably sufficiently well known to prevent any failure of the agreement for uncertainty.

§ 4. Trusts of Land

The English real property law is highly technical in character, and in this account of trusts and trustees it is not proposed to enter into details of conveyancing law and practice. The reader should, however, be aware in outline of the methods by which a trust of land is created, and the incidents attaching thereto.

A trust of land takes the form either of a settlement governed by the provisions of the Settled Land Act 1925, when the land is referred to as 'settled land', or a trust for sale governed in the main by the provisions of the Law of Property Act 1925.

(a) Settled Land

When it is desired to create a trust of settled land, the legal estate, that is to say, the freehold or the leasehold, as the case may be, is vested in the person who is to be the first tenant for life under the settlement. This tenant for life therefore occupies a dual position: in one capacity he is the legal owner of the property and able to deal with it by sale, mortgage, leasing or in any other way, as far as the outside world is concerned; in another capacity he is trustee for the other interests arising under the settlement. As legal owner he must act in a fiduciary capacity having regard not only to his own interest, but also to the interests of those who are to succeed him under the settlement. To guard against any improper dealing with the trust property by the tenant for life in his capacity of legal owner, limitations are placed by the Settled Land Act 1925 on the powers of a tenant for life, and if he exceeds these powers any person dealing with him does so at his peril. Furthermore, capital moneys, such as sale or mortgage moneys, cannot be paid to the tenant for life, since only the trustees of the settlement, who must be at least two in number or a trust corporation, can give a receipt for capital moneys (Settled Land Act 1925, s. 18). (The position of a sole trustee, who cannot give a valid receipt for capital moneys, should be contrasted with that of a personal representative, who can do so – *see* Chapter XII, § 10, *ante*.) The trustees will invest any such moneys upon the trusts of the settlement, and will only pay the tenant for life the income arising from the investments during his life.

Trustees under the Settled Land Act 1925 have all the powers of investment given to trustees by law (*see* § 13 *post*), and in addition have various other powers of investing or applying capital moneys, e.g. in discharge of incumbrances, in paying for authorised improvements, in the purchase of land, in paying road charges. Capital money arising from settled land in England or Wales cannot be applied in the purchase of land out of England and Wales unless authorised by the settlement (Settled Land Act 1925, s. 73).

On the death of a tenant for life, the legal estate passes, if the settlement still continues, to the trustees of the settlement or other persons appointed by the will of the tenant for life, as special personal representatives under a grant of probate specially limited to the settled land (A.E.A. 1925, s. 22). The special personal representatives then convey the legal estate to the next tenant for life by a vesting assent (Settled Land Act 1925, s. 7). If the settlement comes to an end on the death of a tenant for life, his general executors are entitled to a grant of probate not excluding the settled land, and they convey the property to the remainderman under the settlement (*Re Bridgett and Hayes' Contract*).

A settlement under the Settled Land Act 1925 is always created by two documents, one a vesting deed or vesting assent, and the other a trust instrument. The vesting deed, in the case of a settlement *inter vivos*, or vesting assent in the case of a settlement made by will, conveys the property to the tenant for life, states that it is settled land, names the trustees and the persons entitled to appoint new trustees, and sets out any powers, additional to or larger than the statutory powers, which may be conferred by the trust instrument on the tenant for life. This vesting deed or assent is the document by which the tenant for life proves to persons dealing with him his title to the property, and such persons will therefore know the limitations on his powers, to be found either in the Settled Land Act 1925, or in the statement of additional or larger powers, and they will know who are the trustees to whom they must pay capital money. The trust instrument, which is either a document *inter vivos* or a will, does not affect third parties dealing with the tenant for life, but concerns the beneficiaries. It sets out the trusts affecting the settled land, appoints trustees, contains power (if any) to appoint new trustees, and states any additional or larger powers conferred on the tenant for life. The powers conferred on a tenant for life by the Settled Land Act 1925 cannot be cut down in any way by the terms of the settlement.

All the powers and provisions contained in the Trustee Act 1925 with reference to the appointment of new trustees, and the discharge and retirement of trustees (*see* §§ 9 and 12, *post*), apply to and include trustees for the purposes of the Settled Land Act 1925 (Trustee Act 1925, s. 64 (1)). Where new trustees of a settlement are appointed, a memorandum of the names and addresses of the persons who are for the time being the trustees thereof for the purposes of the Settled Land Act 1925 is to be endorsed on or annexed to the last or only principal vesting instrument (*ibid.*, s. 35 (2)).

Land is settled under the Settled Land Act 1925 when it is desired to give the tenant for life as free a hand as possible in managing and dealing with the settled property. It is common in the case of large estates which are intended to descend from generation to generation in the same family.

(b) *Trust for Sale*

In the case of a trust for sale, the land is conveyed, not to the tenant for life, but to the trustees of the settlement. They are directed to hold it on trust to sell and to invest the proceeds of sale on the trusts of the settlement. In practice it is usually not intended that the trustees shall sell immediately or perhaps at all, and indeed a power to postpone sale is implied in the case of every trust for sale of land unless a contrary intention appears (L.P.A. 1925, s. 25 (1)). Although in theory it is a settlement of the proceeds of sale, in fact it generally approximates to a settlement of land. The form of a trust for sale is adopted when it is desired to give the powers of managing and dealing with the trust property to the trustees, and not to the tenant for life.

Trustees for sale have all the powers of a tenant for life and the trustees of a settlement under the Settled Land Act 1925 (L.P.A. 1925, s. 28 (1)). Proceeds of sale of land held on trust for sale or other capital moneys must be paid to two trustees or a trust corporation (L.P.A. 1925, s. 27 (2)).

The tenant for life under a trust for sale has no powers of dealing with the trust property or of management, unless the trustees, as they are entitled to do under the L.P.A. 1925, s. 29, revocably delegate to him by writing their powers of leasing, accepting surrenders of leases and management. If there is any question of selling, mortgaging or otherwise dealing with the property, except in way of letting or management, it is the trustees, and not the tenant for life, who carry through the transaction.

A trust for sale is usually created by two documents, one being a conveyance of the property to the trustees, with which alone an outsider is concerned as proof of title, and the other being the trust instrument declaring the trusts and powers relating to the proceeds of sale. Appointments of new trustees of conveyances on trust for sale on the one hand and of the settlement of the proceeds of sale on the other hand are to be effected by separate instruments, but in such manner as to secure that the same persons become trustees of the conveyance on trust for sale as become the trustees of the settlement of the proceeds of sale. Where new trustees of a conveyance on trust for sale relating to a legal estate are appointed, a memorandum of the persons who are for the time being the trustees for sale is to be endorsed on or annexed thereto (Trustee Act 1925, s. 35).

§ 5. Protective Trusts

Although a beneficiary who has a limited interest (that is, an interest which is less than an absolute interest) under a trust is unable to deal with the trust property itself, yet he is free to dispose of his beneficial interest in any way he may choose. Thus, a life tenant might sell his life interest for a capital sum; the trustees would continue to hold the trust property itself, but they would thenceforth pay the income, during the life of the life tenant, to the purchaser of the life interest. Or, a remainderman might sell his interest in remainder; in that case, the trustees would continue to hold the trust property during the continuance of the prior interests, and on the remainder falling into possession they would transfer the property to the purchaser instead of to the remainderman. Furthermore, the interest of a beneficiary is available to his creditors, and can be reached by way of equitable execution or by its passing to the beneficiary's trustee in bankruptcy.

To protect an improvident beneficiary against himself, an interest may be given to him which is to endure only so long as he does not deprive himself of the right to personal enjoyment of the interest. In that case he has nothing of which he can dispose or which can be taken in execution or by his trustee in bankruptcy. It is usual in such cases to make him one of the objects of a discretionary trust after his interest has come to an end in that way, so that he retains the possibility of some benefit under the trust notwithstanding the loss of his original interest. It may be mentioned that a settlor cannot create for himself, but only for other people, an interest which is not to be available for the beneficiary's creditors, for if created for himself it would be a fraud on the bankruptcy laws.

A convenient way of describing a trust of the nature indicated above is the use of the phrase 'PROTECTIVE TRUSTS'. This phrase is defined by the Trustee Act 1925, s. 33. This definition can be incorporated in any present-day settlement simply by directing income to be held 'on protective trusts', without setting out the detailed nature of those trusts.

Section 33 provides that where any income, including an annuity or other periodical income payment, is directed to be held on protective trusts for the benefit of any person (called 'the principal beneficiary') for the period of his life or for any less period, then, during that period (called 'the trust period') the income, without prejudice to any prior interest, is to be held on the trusts therein set out. Those trusts are as follows:

(i) Upon trust for the principal beneficiary during the trust period, or until he does or attempts to do or suffers any act or thing, or until any event happens, whereby he would, if absolutely entitled to the income, be deprived of the right to receive it or any part thereof. In such event, as well as on termination of the trust period, whichever first happens, the trust in favour of the principal beneficiary fails or determines.

(ii) On such failure or determination, the income is to be held, during the subsistence of the trust period, upon discretionary trusts for the maintenance, support or benefit of the principal beneficiary, his spouse and his children or more remote issue. If he has no spouse or issue, then the income is to be held on discretionary trusts for him and the persons who would be entitled to the trust property or income if he were dead.

DISCRETIONARY TRUSTS are trusts under which the trustees have power to apply the income in such shares and in such manner as they may think fit for the benefit of the objects of the discretion or some one or more of them.

§ 6. Charitable Trusts

Charitable trusts are those which are established for charitable purposes only. 'Charitable purposes' has been defined in *Pemsel's Case* following the Charitable Gifts Act 1601 (43 Eliz. C. 4), as comprising the following principal divisions:

(i) for the relief of poverty;

(ii) for the advancement of education;

(iii) for the advancement of religion;

(iv) for any other purposes beneficial to the community not falling under any of the preceding heads.

The first three purposes are specific, but the fourth is vague, and there has been much judicial interpretation of what is to be regarded as a purpose beneficial to the community within the meaning of Pemsel's case. Not every object of public general utility is to be included under that head; the object must come within the spirit and intention of the Statute of Elizabeth. An example of a purpose within the spirit of the Statute is a trust for aged persons, even though not limited to those who are poor (*Re Robinson*, deceased), just as a trust for the sick is charitable, whether or not the sick persons are in need of financial assistance. The court's view of what is for the public benefit changes from time to time with the differing circumstances of society; for instance, it has been held that a trust for the abolition of vivisection is not charitable, as not being for a purpose beneficial to the community (*National Anti-Vivisection Society* v. *Commissioners of Inland Revenue*). A trust whose objects include the repeal of legislation is not charitable, for it cannot be presumed to be for the benefit of the community to undo what Parliament has done. To be charitable, the objects of a trust must not be limited to a small class, such as the relatives of the donor, but must extend to a substantial section of the community, so that there is some element of public benefit. Exceptionally, it seems that a trust for relief of poverty (but not, e.g. a trust for the education) of the donor's relatives (*Isaac* v. *Defruz*), and a trust for the advancement of religion of a limited class are good charitable trusts. The inhabitants of a particular parish constitute a sufficiently wide section of the community to make a trust in their favour charitable. A trust whose objects include some purposes which are not charitable, cannot be a charitable trust. Where a testator directed his residuary estate to be applied for such 'charitable or benevolent' objects as his executors might select, it was held that the trust was not charitable, for objects which were benevolent would not necessarily be charitable within the legal meaning of the term (*Chichester Diocesan Fund and Board of Finance (Incorporated)* v. *Simpson*).

Charitable trusts differ from other trusts in a number of respects, of which the following are the most important:

(a) *No failure for uncertainty*

A gift for charitable purposes will not fail by reason of uncertainty as to the objects for which it is to be applied. It is quite in order for a settlor or testator to give property for such charitable purposes as his trustees may select.

(b) *Cy-pres doctrine*

If a general charitable intention is shown, a gift will not fail through impossibility of carrying it into effect, but the property will be applied to similar charitable purposes as nearly as possible in accordance with the intention of the settlor or testator. As a result of the Charities Act 1960, this may now be done where the trusts have become outdated through changing circumstances. The Charities Act 1960, also introduces the principle that even where no general charitable intention is expressed, property given for specific charitable purposes may be applied *cy-près* where the original donor cannot be found or the donor has executed a written disclaimer of his right to have the property returned to him.

(c) *Rule against Perpetuities does not apply*

The Rule against Perpetuities (*see* § 7, *post*) does not apply to a trust for charitable purposes. It may be provided that property is to be held on charitable trusts in perpetuity, or that at some period outside the limit allowed for other trusts the property is to go over from one charity to another. But the Rule would have to be observed if property were to pass at some date in the future from charitable to non-charitable trusts, or vice versa.

(d) *Income Tax*

The income of a body of pesons or trust established for charitable purposes only is entitled to various exemptions from Income tax and exemption from Capital Gains tax.

(e) *Trustees act by a majority*

In the case of charitable trusts the decision of a majority of the trustees binds a minority.

(f) *Number of trustees*

The number of trustees of a charitable trust of land is not limited to four (Trustee Act 1925, s. 34 (3)), as is the case with other trusts of land (*see* § 11, *post*).

§ 7. Rule against Perpetuities

The policy of the law is to curtail the power of an owner of property to direct the future devolution of property *ad infinitum*, it being deemed to be contrary to the public interest that property should never become susceptible of free alienation or transfer.

The law has accordingly contrived a rule to protect the principle that future interests in property can be effectively created only if they are so limited that they must necessarily vest in the beneficiary within a given maximum period of time, called the 'perpetuity period'. The rule itself is termed the 'Rule against Perpetuities', and it will be understood that it is directed against the creation of a perpetual succession of interests in property; it achieves its object by nullifying any future interest which does not become a vested interest within the 'perpetuity period'. An interest is said to 'vest' when the following matters are indubitably and specifically ascertained in relation to it:

(i) who is to acquire the interest;

(ii) what shall be the 'quantity' of interest he is to acquire;

(iii) the existence of any facts requisite to entitle him to enjoyment.

Thus:

A devise 'to A for life and then to B in fee simple', confers a vested interest upon B, although he is not entitled to *possession* until A's death. All three requisites to identify and establish the interest are specifically determined.

On the other hand:

A devise 'to A for life and then to B in fee simple if he should be living at A's death; but if he should predecease A, then to C in fee simple', gives a vested interest to A, and a vested interest (liable to be divested) to B, but a contingent interest to C. The fact essential to determine whether C will ever be entitled to enjoy the property, namely whether B will predecease A, cannot be ascertained until the death of A or B. If B dies before A, C's interest will become vested on B's death; otherwise it will fail.

The basis of the Rule against Perpetuities is that the grant of an estate or interest to take effect in possession at a future time must, if it is not vested at the time of its creation, vest within the period of a life in being plus 21 years after that person's death. By the Perpetuities and Accumulations Act 1964 a settlor or testator can, as an alternative to the period mentioned, specify a period of years, not exceeding eighty, as the perpetuity period. The 1964 Act affects only trust instruments coming into operation after 16th July, 1964.

It will be observed that the classic perpetuity period is measured by the duration of the life of some (specified) person, 'in being', i.e. a person who is known to be living at the date when the instrument creating the future interest becomes operative, plus 21 years after his death. The period of gestation may be added to the 21 years if, at the end of the 21 years, the beneficiary is a child *en ventre sa mère*. Where the instrument is a settlement *inter vivos* it becomes operative when executed; a will takes effect upon the death of the testator.

The 1964 Act provided that the fact that a disposition might not vest within the perpetuity period would not necessarily invalidate it and in most cases it would remain valid until it was clear that the disposition must vest outside the period. This 'wait and see' principle is excluded, however, when a fixed term of years has been specified as the perpetuity period or when the period is defined by reference to the survivor of certain named Royal lives.

Illustrations

A testator gave his residuary estate 'to A for life with remainder to the eldest son of A to become a clergyman of the Church of England'.

This disposition would remain valid until 21 years after the date of death of A. when, if none of his sons had become an Anglican clergyman, it would fail.

X, by his will, leaves property to the trustees thereof on trust to distribute the income at their discretion among a specified class of persons, some of whom may be unborn at the date of his death. He directs that the perpetuity period applicable shall be eighty years from the date of his death. This is a valid disposition and the perpetuity period will be eighty years.

Before the 1964 Perpetuities Act was passed no person, however young or old, was deemed incapable of having a child. The 1964 Act provided (s. 2) that if the ability of a person to have a child should arise in any proceedings there should be a presumption that a male person aged 14 years or over and a female aged not less than 12 years or more than 55 years could conceive or have a child. This presumption is, however, rebuttable in the case of a living person by evidence that he or she will or will not be able to conceive or have a child at the time in question.

The 1964 Act (s. 4) provides that where the vesting of property is made to depend upon the beneficiary attaining an age greater than 21 years and the trust would otherwise be void, the vesting age is to be deemed to be reduced to the age nearest the specified age consistent with the gift being valid. Thus, if a testator leaves property by will to such of the children of A as shall attain the age of 25 years and A's youngest child had not been born at the date of death of the testator A is the life in being for the purposes of the Rule. It follows that if the youngest child is two at A's death the vesting age for all A's children is reduced to 23 under s. 4 above.

S. 5 of the 1964 Act prevents a gift in trust being void because of the 'unborn widow'. Assume the will provides for a life interest to A, then a life interest to any widow who might survive A for her life, and then for the children of A living at the date of death of the survivor of A and his widow. Before 1964 the gift to the children was void if A was unmarried at the date of death of the testator because he might marry a wife who was unborn at that date. Under s. 5 the gift to the children will vest 21 years after the death of A in favour of the children living at that date but will not take effect in possession until the death of the widow.

In relation to a trust which includes a power of appointment the application of the Rule against Perpetuities varies according to whether the power is special or general. A special power is one under which the donee of the power may appoint only amongst members of a restricted class. For the purposes of the Rule against Perpetuities a power of appointment should be treated as a special power unless:

(*a*) in the instrument creating the power it is expressed to be exercisable by one person only, and

(*b*) it could at all times during its currency, when that person is of full age and capacity, be exercised by him so as immediately to transfer to himself the whole of the interest governed by the power without the consent of any other person or compliance with any other condition, not being a formal condition relating only to the mode of exercise of the power:

provided that for the purpose of determining whether a disposition made under a power of appointment exercisable by will only is void for remoteness the power shall be treated as a general power where it would have fallen to be so treated if exercisable by deed (Section 7, *ibid*).

The Rule against Perpetuities does not apply to an option to purchase the reversion of a lease expectant on the determination thereof. An option to purchase any other interest in land must be exercised with the perpetuity period, which is twenty-one years (Section 9, *ibid*).

If neither the period of twenty-one years nor the fixed period of years (not exceeding eighty) applies, the Act defines the persons who could be taken to be lives in being for the purpose of determining the perpetuity period (Section 3). In the case of a special power of appointment exercisable in favour of members of a class these persons included any member or potential member of the class. Thus, if the trustees of a will are given a special power to appoint to the issue of a testator, the lives in being include those members of the issue who are living at the date of death of the testator and an appointment is valid if it is made before the expiration of 21 years from the death of the last survivor of such persons.

Certain limitations are excepted from the application of the Rule, notably gifts to charities and limitations after entailed interests.

A gift by will of a fund, the income of which is to be used by the trustees thereof 'so far as they legally can do so' for the upkeep of certain graves, etc. (not a charitable trust), is a valid trust for a period of 21 years from the testator's death (*Re Hooper, Parker and Webb*).

§ 8. Rule against Accumulations

The principle which prohibits postponement of the vesting of an estate or interest beyond the perpetuity period, applies also to dispositions for the accumulation of income arising out of property. The Rule against Accumulations is now contained in the L.P.A. 1925, ss. 164–166 and ss. 13, 14, Perpetuities and Accumulations Act 1964, and no person may by any instrument or otherwise settle or dispose of any property in such manner that the income thereof shall be wholly or partially accumulated for any longer period than one of the following:

(*a*) The life of the grantor or settlor; or

(*b*) A term of 21 years from the death of the grantor, settlor or testator; or (*c*) The duration of the minority or respective minorities of any person or persons living or *en ventre sa mère* at the death of the grantor, settlor or testator; or

(*d*) The duration of the minority or respective minorities only of any person or persons who under the limitations of the instrument directing the accumulations would, for the time being, if of full age, be entitled to the income directed to be accumulated; or

(*e*) A term of 21 years from the date of the making of the disposition; or

(*f*) The duration of the minority or respective minorities of any person or persons in being at that date.

The difference between the third and fourth periods is that, to be within the third period, the minority of any person, *whether a beneficiary or not*, can be chosen, provided that that person is living or *en ventre sa mère* at the death of the grantor, settlor or testator; whereas for the fourth period, only the minority of a *beneficiary* can be chosen, but in that case it is immaterial whether or not he was living at the death.

Where any accumulation is directed which infringes the perpetuity rule, it is void. One which infringes the accumulation rule alone is void only as regards the excess of the period of accumulation over that allowed as above, and the income arising after the expiration of the period of valid accumulation is divisible among the persons who would have been entitled to the income if there had been no direction to accumulate.

The above provisions do not prevent accumulations:

(1) for payment of the debts of a grantor, settlor, testator or other person;

(2) for raising portions for any child or other issue of a grantor, settlor, or testator, or for any child or issue of a person taking any interest under any settlement or other disposition directing the accumulations or to whom any interest is thereby limited;

(3) of the produce of timber or wood.

The second exemption is intended to enable owners of property to make provision for their children, and, in particular their younger children, without the necessity of selling portions of the estates which they own. This power, if abused, might reproduce all the evils which Thellusson's Act sought to abolish, and hence the exemption is stringently interpreted. Thus a disposition with the object of accumulating the *whole of a testator's property* in a portions fund is void (*Wildes* v. *Davies* [1853]).

The period of accumulation by trustees of surplus income under a settlement for minors is not to be taken into account in determining the period of accumulation for the purposes of the above prohibition.

The accumulation of income for the purchase of land is prohibited for any longer period than the minority of any person or persons who under the trusts directing the accumulation would for the time being, if of full age, be entitled to receive the income.

An exception is made in respect of moneys to be accumulated for the ultimate reduction of the National Debt (Superannuation and other Trust Funds (Validation) Act 1927).

PART II – TRUSTEES

§ 9. Appointment of Trustees

(a) *Who may be a trustee*

Any individual who is capable of holding property is capable of acting as trustee. An infant cannot be appointed trustee (L.P.A. 1925, s. 20). A corporation can be appointed trustee.

There are certain persons whom the court would not appoint as trustee. There is no objection to the settlor or testator appointing any such person, for he is free to appoint whom he pleases. On the appointment of a new trustee, however, it would be inadvisable, except in special circumstances, to appoint any person whom the court would not appoint, for the appointment is liable to be set aside by the court. The persons whom the court would not appoint are (i) persons under disability, such as bankrupts, (ii) a person resident abroad, unless the trust property or all the beneficiaries are abroad, (iii) a beneficiary, or the solicitor, husband or wife of a beneficiary.

(b) First Trustees

The first trustees are appointed by the settlor or testator. If he does not so appoint, or the trustees do not accept, the settlor himself becomes trustee, in the case of a settlement *inter vivos*, and the personal representative in the case of a settlement made by will. The appointed trustees are not bound to act, but if they accept the trust, as by executing the deed in the case of a settlement *inter vivos*, or taking out probate if they are also personal representatives under the will, or if they in fact act, they are bound to carry out their duties until such time as they are released. An appointed trustee may make his refusal to act clear beyond doubt by a disclaimer in writing, although there is no legal necessity for such a document.

(c) New trustees

A new trustee may be appointed in the place of another where that other (i) is dead (including a trustee appointed by will who died before the testator), (ii) remains out of the United Kingdom for more than twelve months, (iii) desires to be discharged, (iv) refuses to act, (v) is unfit to act, (vi) is incapable of acting, or (vii) is an infant. A corporation trustee is deemed incapable of acting if it has been dissolved. A new trustee may also be appointed in the place of a trustee who has been removed under a power in the trust instrument.

The number of trustees may be increased by the appointment of an additional trustee, provided that none of the existing trustees is a trust corporation, and that the effect of the appointment is not to bring the number of trustees above four.

The appointment is made by the person or persons nominated for that purpose by the trust instrument. If there is no such person, or no such person able and willing to act, then the surviving or continuing trustee or trustees for the time being, or the personal representative of the last surviving or continuing trustee, make the appointment. A person who is appointed executor by the will of a sole or last surviving trustee may exercise the power of appointing new trustees without accepting the office of executor, if there is no other executor able and willing to prove the will. A refusing or retiring trustee can, if willing, act in the appointment of a new trustee.

The appointment is made by a document in writing. There is

no objection to the appointor appointing himself as a new trustee in place of another, but he may not appoint himself as an *additional* trustee (Trustee Act 1925, s. 36).

Whenever it is expedient to appoint a new trustee, and it is inexpedient, difficult or impracticable so to do without the assistance of the court, the court may by order appoint (*ibid.*, s. 41).

A separate set of trustees, not exceeding four, may be appointed for any part of the trust property held on trusts distinct from those relating to any other part or parts of the trust property. This may be done notwithstanding that no new trustees are to be appointed for the other parts. Any existing trustee may be appointed or remain one of such separate set of trustees (*ibid.*, s. 37).

(d) Vesting of trust property

A deed of appointment of a new trustee may contain an express declaration vesting the trust property in those who are trustees after the appointment. Even if it does not contain an express declaration, a vesting declaration is now implied on an appointment made by deed. Similarly, on the discharge of a trustee by deed under the statutory power (*see* § 12, *post*), there may be an express vesting declaration, and, if not, there is an implied declaration vesting the property in the continuing trustees.

Neither an express nor an implied vesting declaration extends to (i) mortgages (other than debentures) of land; (ii) leases containing covenants against assigning or disposing of the land without consent, where the required consent has not been obtained prior to the execution of the deed of appointment; (iii) stocks, shares, etc., which are transferable only in the books of the company, etc. (Trustee Act 1925, s. 40). In the case of property falling within those classes the appropriate form and procedure of transfer is required in order to vest the property in the new or continuing trustees. A mortgage should be transferred by transfer of mortgage; a lease by assignment with the consent of the lessor; stocks and shares by the appropriate transfer registered in the company's register.

Even in the cases of other kinds of property, the new or continuing trustees should take whatever action may be appropriate to get the property under their control. It is true that the property will have vested in them through the implied vesting declaration, but this will not be sufficient in itself to enable them to protect the trust property. For instance, deeds of freehold land should be delivered into the custody of the new or continuing trustees or held by a solicitor, bank, etc., on their behalf; a bank account should be transferred into the names of the new or continuing trustees, so that the bank knows that they and they alone have authority to operate the account; personal chattels should be delivered, actually or constructively, to the new or continuing trustees; in the case of a policy of assurance, the assurance office should be notified of the new appointment; and so on, according to the nature of the property in question.

The court has extensive power to make vesting orders (Trustee Act ₁925, ss. 44 to 56), and in particular on the appointment of a new trustee by the court, the court can make an order vesting the trust property in those who are trustees after the appointment.

§ 10. Transmission of Office

On the death of one of two or more trustees, the surviving trustee or trustees continue to act alone, unless and until a new trustee is appointed to act with him or them. On the death of a sole or last surviving or continuing trustee, his personal representative becomes trustee in his place (Trustee Act 1925, s. 18).

§ 11. Number of Trustees

The maximum number of trustees of a settlement of land, whether under the Settled Land Act 1925, or by way of trust for sale, is four. If more than four trustees are appointed of a settlement of land then only the four first-named act. These provisions do not apply to charitable trusts or to trusts of portions terms or terms for enforcing rent-charges (Trustee Act 1925, s. 34). In the case of settlements of property other than land there is no upper limit to the number of trustees, except that additional trustees must not be appointed so as to bring the number above four (*ibid.*, s. 36).

There is no minimum limit to the number of trustees, but certain provisions must be borne in mind in this connection.

One is that a sole trustee (other than a trust corporation) is unable to give a valid receipt for capital money arising under a trust for sale of land or under the Settled Land Act 1925 (Trustee Act 1925, s. 14 (2)). It will therefore be necessary to have at least two trustees or a trust corporation of a settlement of land if dispositions involving the receipt of capital money are involved. Secondly, it is to be observed that a trustee cannot retire so as to leave only one trustee (not being a trust corporation) acting, unless it is a case where the settlement is of pure personalty and only one trustee was originally appointed, or a sole trustee retiring and appointing a sole trustee in his place (*ibid.*, s. 37 (1) (*c*)).

§ 12. Retirement and Removal of Trustees

Where a trustee is desirous of being discharged from the trust, and after his discharge there will be either a trust corporation or at least two individuals to act as trustees to perform the trust, then with the consent of his co-trustees and of the persons (if any) empowered to appoint new trustees, he may by deed retire from the trust without the appointment of a new trustee (Trustee Act 1925, s. 39 (1)).

A trustee may retire or be removed on the appointment of a new trustee in his place (Trustee Act 1925, s. 36 (1)), provided that, except in the case of a pure personalty settlement of which only one trustee was originally appointed, there will remain at least two trustees or a trust corporation (*ibid.*, s. 37 (i) (*c*)). A trustee may retire on the appointment of the Public Trustee (Public Trustee Act 1906, s. 5), who is himself a trust corporation.

A trustee may also retire or be removed under any provision in that behalf contained in the trust instrument, or by consent or compulsion of all the beneficiaries, if they are *sui juris*. He may also be removed by order of the court. He cannot be removed by any number of beneficiaries short of all of them, except by order of the court.

§ 13. Powers of Investment

A trustee may invest trust funds only in authorised investments, that is to say, investments authorised by the trust instrument or by law. The investments authorised by law are indicated by the Trustee Investment Act 1961.

The trust instrument may exclude the trustee's power to invest in all or any of the investments authorised by law or may vary the power in any way (*Re Harari*).

The Trustee Investments Act 1961 considerably extended the powers of investment of trustees. In the following paragraphs references to sections are to the Trustee Investments Act 1961 unless otherwise stated.

Under the Act a trustee is empowered to invest any property (whether real or personal property) in any manner specified in Part I or II of the First Schedule to the Act ('narrower-range' investments) or, subject to what is stated below, in any manner specified in Part III of that Schedule ('wider-range' investments) and may also from time to time vary such investments. Investment in wider-range investments is limited to one half of the trust fund and cannot be effected unless and until the trust fund has been divided into two parts which must be equal in value at the time of the division (s. 2). If the trustees obtain from a person, whom the trustees reasonably believe to be qualified, a valuation in writing of any property the valuation shall be conclusive in determining whether the division of the trust fund has been duly made (s. 5).

A trustee is not liable for breach of trust by reason only of his continuing to hold an investment which has ceased to be an investment authorised by the trust instrument or by the general law.

A trustee may, unless expressly prohibited by the instrument creating the trust, retain or invest in securities payable to bearer which, if not so payable, would have been authorised investments; but such SECURITIES TO BEARER must, unless the trustee is a trust corporation BE DEPOSITED for safe custody and collection of income WITH A BANKER or banking company. A direction that investments shall be retained or made in the name of a trustee is not deemed to be such an express prohibition. A trustee is not responsible for any loss incurred by reason of such deposit, and any sum payable in respect of such deposit and collection can be paid out of the income of the trust property.

In regard to the investment of trust monies in mortgages of real and leasehold property, the Trustee Act 1925 provides that a trustee lending money on the security of any property on which he can properly lend, is not chargeable with breach of trust by reason only of the proportion borne by the amount of the loan to the value of the property at the time when the loan was made, if it appears to the court:

(*a*) that in making the loan the trustee was acting upon a report as to the value of the property made by a person whom he reasonably believed to be an able practical surveyor or valuer, instructed and employed independently of any owner of the property; and

(*b*) that the amount of the LOAN DOES NOT EXCEED TWO-THIRDS OF THE VALUE OF THE PROPERTY as stated in the report; and

(*c*) that the loan was made under the advice of the surveyor or valuer.

Section 6 (7) provides that without prejudice to Section 8 of the Trustee Act 1925 (which relates to valuation and the proportion of the value to be lent, where a trustee lends on the security of property) the advice required by the Section shall not include in the case of a loan on the security of freehold or leasehold property, advice on the suitability of the particular loan.

A trustee lending money on the security of any leasehold property is not chargeable with breach of trust only upon the ground that in making such loan he dispensed either wholly or partly with the production or investigation of the lessor's title. A trustee is not chargeable with breach of trust only upon the ground that in effecting the purchase, or in lending money upon the security, of any property he has accepted a shorter title than the title which a purchaser is, in the absence of a special contract, entitled to require, if in the opinion of the court the title accepted be such as a person acting with prudence and caution would have accepted (Trustee Act, s. 8).

After division the two parts of the fund are to be kept separate and no transfer is to be made between them unless authorised or required by the Act, or a compensating transfer of assets is made at the same time. The effect is, therefore, that after division of the trust fund into two equal parts in this way funds belonging to the narrower-range part can only be invested in narrower-range investments while funds belonging to the wider-range part may be invested in either wider-range or narrower-range investments. The proportion of the fund which may be invested in wider-range securities may be increased by Treasury Order

to not more than three-quarters (s. 13). The powers of investment may also be extended by Order in Council (s. 12).

Trustees must have regard to the need for diversification of
investments of the trust in so far as is appropriate to the
circumstances of the trust. Before investing in certain of the
narrower-range investments, or in any of the wider-range
investments, a trustee must obtain and consider written advice
from a person who is reasonably believed by the trustee to be
qualified by his ability and practical experience of financial
matters to give it, as to whether the proposed investment is
satisfactory (s. 6).

(*a*) *Narrower-range investments not requiring advice* (First
Schedule, Part I) are:

Defence Bonds; National Savings Certificates; National
Development Bonds; Ulster Savings Certificates; deposits
in the Post Office Savings Bank; ordinary deposits in a
Trustee Savings Bank and deposits in a bank or department
thereof certified under the Finance Act 1956, s. 9 (3).

(*b*) *Investments requiring advice are:*

(i) *Narrower-range Investments* (First Schedule, Part II)

(1) British Government Securities (other than those
included in Part I), Treasury Bills and Tax Reserve
Certificates.

(2) Securities the interest on which is guaranteed by the
British Government.

(3) Fixed interest securities of any nationalised undertaking in the United Kingdom.

(4) Fixed interest securities issued and registered in the
United Kingdom by the Government or any public
or local authority in the Commonwealth.

(5) Fixed interest securities issued and registered in the
United Kingdom by the International Bank for
Reconstruction and Development.

(6) Debentures issued in the United Kingdom by a
United Kingdom company having a paid-up capital
of not less than one million pounds, and which has
paid dividends on all its issued capital in each of the
immediately preceding five years.

(7) Stock of the Bank of Ireland.

(8) Debentures of the Agricultural Mortgage Corporation Ltd or the Scottish Agricultural Corporation
Ltd.

(9) Loans to and fixed-interest securities issued by any
local authority in the United Kingdom and charged
on all or any of the revenues of the authority, and
in deposits with any such authority by way of
temporary loan.

(10) Debentures or guaranteed or preference stock in
statutory water undertakers within the meaning of
the Water Act 1945, and having during each of the
immediately preceding ten years paid a dividend of
not less than 5 per cent. on its ordinary shares.

(11) Deposits by way of special investment in a Trustee
Savings Bank (other than one certified under
Section 9 (3) of the Finance Act 1956).

(12) Deposits in a building society designated under
Section 1 of the House Purchase and Housing Act
1959.

(13) Mortgages of freehold property in England and
Wales or Northern Ireland and of leasehold property
in those countries having an unexpired term of not
less than sixty years; and loans on heritable security
in Scotland.

(14) Perpetual rent-charges on land in England and
Wales or Northern Ireland and feu duties, etc., in
Scotland.

(ii) *Wider-range Investments* (First Schedule, Part III)

(1) Stocks and Shares quoted on a recognised stock
exchange, issued in the United Kingdom by a
company incorporated therein, having a paid-up
capital of not less than one million pounds and which
has paid dividends on all its issued capital in each of
the immediately preceding five years.

(2) Shares in any building society designated under Section 1 of the House Purchase and Housing Act 1959.

(3) Units or other shares of any authorised unit trust.

Where any property (other than dividends or interest) accrues to a trust fund after it has been divided, it shall be treated as belonging to that part of the fund out of the property of which it accrued. Thus, a profit on the sale of an investment will be credited to the part of the fund to which the investment belonged prior to the sale. In the case of accrued property which is not attributable to the property comprised in either part of the fund, the value of each part must be increased by the same amount, any necessary transfer being made from one part to the other to achieve this result (s. 2). Where property is acquired in consideration of a money payment (e.g. the taking up of shares under a 'rights' issue) the acquisition shall be treated as an investment and not as the accrual of property to the fund, notwithstanding that the amount of the consideration is less than the value of the property acquired (s. 2).

Where, in the exercise of any power or duty of a trustee, property has to be taken out of a trust fund (e.g. where it becomes necessary to pay out a beneficiary on his becoming absolutely entitled to his share) the withdrawal may be made from either part of the fund, at the trustee's discretion, without any compensating transfers of assets being necessary from one part of the fund to the other (s. 2). Where property is appropriated out of a trust fund so as to form a separate fund, and the fund has been divided into two parts, then, if the separate fund is so divided, the narrower-range and wider-range parts thereof may be constituted so as either to be equal, or to bear to each other the same proportion as the two corresponding parts of the fund out of which it was so appropriated (the values of those parts being ascertained as at the time of appropriation) or some intermediate proportion (s. 4 (3)).

The powers conferred by the Act are in addition to and not in derogation from any powers conferred otherwise than by the Act (e.g. powers of investment or of postponing conversion conferred by the trust instrument, or by the Court). Property held under such special powers is defined as 'special-range property' and must be carried to a separate part of the fund. Such property does not have to be taken into account when dividing the trust fund into the narrower-range and the wider-range parts. Where special-range property is sold and converted into property other than special-range property it may be transferred to either the narrower-range part or the wider-range part, or apportioned between them. Such transfer of property from one of those parts to the other must then be made as may be necessary to secure that the value of each of those parts is increased by the same amount (s. 3 and Second Schedule).

Illustrations

(1) On 1st January, 1969, the residue of the estate of A.B. deceased, which was held in trust, was valued at:

		£
£20,000 3 per cent. Savings Bonds 1965–75	.. .. ..	14,000
£5,000 5 per cent. Defence Bonds ..	.. ..	5,000
£50,000 3½ per cent. War Loan ..	.. ..	21,000
Freehold house	.. ..	5,000
		£45,000

The will authorised the retention of the freehold house. The trustees decided, after obtaining the requisite advice, to sell the War Loan, and to invest the proceeds as follows:

			£
2,000 Ordinary Shares in M.N. Ltd	.. .. ..	..	6,000
5,000 ,, ,, P.Q. Ltd	.. .. ..	..	7,500
4,000 ,, ,, S.T. Ltd	.. .. ..	..	6,500
Loans to local authorities ..	.. .. ..	..	1,000
			£21,000

On completion of the above transactions the Balance Sheet of the trust will appear as follows:

ESTATE OF A.B. DECEASED

BALANCE SHEET AS AT 1ST JANUARY, 1969

Estate Capital Account:	£	Narrower-range Investments:	£	£
Narrower-range part	20,000	£20,000 3% Savings Bonds 1965–75	14,000	
Wider-range part	20,000	£5,000 5% Defence Bonds ..	5,000	
Special-range part	5,000	Loans to local authorities ..	1,000	
				20,000
		Wider-range Investments:		
		2,000 Ordinary Shares in M.N. Ltd	6,000	
		5,000 Ordinary Shares in P.Q. Ltd	7,500	
		4,000 Ordinary Shares in S.T. Ltd	6,500	
				20,000
		Special-range Investment:		
		Freehold Property		5,000
	£45,000			£45,000

(2) At a later date the freehold property in Illustration (1) was sold for £7,500 and the whole amount was invested in wider-range investments (3,000 ordinary shares in O.K. Ltd). To enable the compensating transfer to be made to the narrower-range part 1,000 of the ordinary shares in M.N. Ltd were sold for £4,000, and £3,750 was invested in local authority loans.

The Balance Sheet of the trust will then appear as under:

State Capital Account:	£	£	Narrower-range Investments:	£	£
Narrower-range part	20,000		£20,000 3% Savings Bonds 1965–75	14,000	
Add Transfer from special-range part	3,750		£5,000 5% Defence Bonds ..	5,000	
		23,750	Loans to local authorities ..	4,750	
					23,750
Wider-range part..	20,000		Wider-range Investments:		
Add Transfer from special-range part	3,750		1,000 Ordinary Shares in M.N. Ltd	3,000	
Profit on sale of 1,000 shares in M.N. Ltd	1,000		5,000 Ordinary Shares in P.Q. Ltd	7,500	
		24,750	4,000 Ordinary Shares in S.T. Ltd	6,500	
Special-range part	5,000		3,000 Ordinary Shares in O.K. Ltd	7,500	
Add Profit on sale of freehold property	2,500		Cash at Bank	250	
		7,500			24,750
Deduct Transfer to:					
Narrower-range part £3,750					
Wider-range part 3,750					
		7,500			
		£48,500			£48,500

Note: The Cash at Bank (which is available for investment in wider-range investments) is represented by:

					£
Proceeds of freehold property	..	..	..	..	7,500
Proceeds of shares in M.N. Ltd	..	..	..	..	4,000
					11,500
Deduct: Cost of: Shares in O.K. Ltd	..	..	£7,500		
Loans to local authorities	..	3,750			
					11,250
					£250

(3) Assume that the property comprised in Illustration (1) is held on trust for A. during his lifetime, and on his death one-half of the property is to be appropriated to be held on a separate trust for B.

At the date of A.'s death the narrower-range investments were valued at £25,000 and the wider-range investments at £30,000. The value to be appropriated to the separate trust for B. is therefore $\frac{1}{2}$(£30,000 + £25,000) = £27,500. Under Section 2 (4) of the Act the trustee may, in the exercise of his discretion, take the whole £27,500 out of the wider-range invest-ments, or part out of the wider-range investments and part out of the narrower-range investments, without any compensating transfer of assets from one part to the other. Under Section 4 (3) of the Act if it is desired to apply the Act to the new trust for B. this trust may be divided in either of the following proportions:

(a) Equally, i.e. narrower-range $\frac{1}{2}$ × £27,500   ..   .. £13,750
               wider-range $\frac{1}{2}$ × £27,500   ..   .. £13,750

(b) Proportionally, i.e. narrower-range $\frac{25,000}{55,000}$ × £27,500   .. £12,500

               wider-range $\frac{30,000}{55,000}$ × £27,500   .. £15,000

(c) Any proportion falling between the limits in (a) and (b).

Where a trustee improperly advances trust money on a mortgage security which would at the time of the investment be a proper investment in all respects for a smaller sum than is actually advanced thereon, the security is deemed an authorised investment for the smaller sum, and the trustee is only liable to make good the sum advanced in excess thereof with interest (§ 9).

Where any shares of or debentures in a company are subject to a trust, the trustees may concur in any scheme or arrangement:

(a) for the reconstruction of the company;

(b) for the sale of all or any part of the property and under-taking of the company to another company;

(c) for the amalgamation of the company with another company;

(d) for the release, modification, or variation of any rights, privileges or liabilities attached to the securities or any of them;

in like manner as if they were entitled to such securities bene-ficially, with power to accept any securities of any denomination or description of the reconstructed or purchasing or new com-pany in lieu of or in exchange for all or any of the first-mentioned securities; and the trustees are not responsible for any loss occasioned by any act or thing so done in good faith, and may retain any securities so accepted for any period for which they could have properly retained the original securities.

If any conditional or preferential right to subscribe for any securities in any company is offered to trustees in respect of any holding in such company, they may as to all or any of such securities, either exercise such right and apply capital money subject to the trust in payment of the consideration, or renounce such right, or assign, for the best consideration that can be reasonably obtained the benefit of such right or the title thereto to any person, including any beneficiary under the trust, without being responsible for any loss occasioned by any act or thing so done by them in good faith. The consideration for any such assignment must be held as capital money of the trust.

These powers are exercisable subject to the consent of any person whose consent to a change of investment is required by law or by the instrument, if any, creating the trust (*ibid.*, s. 10). By Section 9 (1) trustees can concur in any scheme or arrangement for the acquisition by another company of the securities or the control of a company in whose shares or debentures the trust funds are invested. Section 9 (2) declares that the power to subscribe for securities under a 'rights' issue includes power to retain such securities for any period for which the trustee has power to retain the holding in respect of which the right to subscribe was offered, but subject to any conditions under which the trustee has that power.

Land is not a trustee investment, and trustees of a settlement of personalty are not entitled to invest therein, unless the trust instrument authorises it. Ground rents are interests in land. Freehold ground rents are simply freehold land which has been let, usually on long leases, at rents appropriate to the land, with covenants by the lessees to erect buildings on the land. At the end of the lease the land, together with the buildings thereon, revert to the ground landlord. Accordingly ground rents are not investments which are authorised for trustees.

Trustees of a settlement of land under the Settled Land Act 1925 are authorised to invest capital money in the purchase of land (Settled Land Act 1925, s. 73). Trustees for sale of land have all the powers of a tenant for life and the trustees under the Settled Land Act 1925 (L.P.A., 1925, s. 28 (1)); and they are therefore authorised to invest the proceeds of sale of land in the purchase of other land so long as the proceeds are identifiable (*Re Wellsted's Will Trusts*).

A clause in a settlement giving trustees power to invest in land does not authorise them to purchase a dwelling-house for

occupation by beneficiaries under the settlement, where part of
the purchase price is paid for the advantage of vacant possession
(*Re Power's Will Trusts*).

If a will contains a list of authorised securities, a trustee is
still entitled to invest in trustee investments unless expressly
forbidden to do so (*Re Warren*). Moreover, specific investments
which are settled may be realised and the proceeds invested in
trustee securities (*Re Pratt*).

§ 14. Powers of Delegation

The general rule is that a trustee must personally carry out the
powers, duties and discretions conferred on him, and must not
delegate to any other person. This rule is subject to the following
exceptions:

(a) *Power to employ agents*

Trustees may, instead of acting personally, employ and pay an
agent, whether a solicitor, banker, stockbroker, or other person,
to transact any business or do any act required in the execution
of the trusts, including the receipt and payment of money. The
trustees are entitled to be allowed and paid all charges and
expenses so incurred. They are not responsible for the default
of any such agent if employed in good faith.

Trustees may appoint any person to act as their agent or
attorney for the purpose of selling, managing or otherwise
dealing with or administering any property outside the United
Kingdom, including the execution or exercise of any discretion,
trust or power in relation to any such property. They are not,
by reason only of their having made such appointment, responsible for any loss arising thereby.

Without prejudice to the general power of appointing agents,
referred to in the preceding paragraph, a trustee may appoint
a solicitor to be his agent to receive and give a discharge for
any money, property, etc., receivable by the trustee under the
trust, by permitting the solicitor to have the custody of a deed
containing a signed receipt therefor, and is not liable for breach
of trust by reason only of making or concurring in the appointment. Likewise, a trustee may appoint a banker or solicitor to
be his agent to receive insurance money, by permitting such agent
to have the custody of the policy with a receipt signed by the

trustee. Any such money, property, etc., must not be allowed to remain in the hands or under the control of the solicitor or banker longer than is reasonably necessary for him to transfer it to the trustee (Trustee Act 1925, s. 23).

(b) Power to delegate during absence abroad

A trustee intending to remain out of the United Kingdom for a period exceeding one month may delegate his trusts, powers and discretions to any person, including a trust corporation. Delegation to an individual co-trustee is allowed only if there is at least one other trustee. The power of attorney does not come into operation unless and until the donor is out of the United Kingdom, and is revoked by his return. The trustee so delegating his powers remains liable for the acts or defaults of the attorney as though they were his own.

The power of attorney must be attested by at least one witness, and filed at the Central Office of the Supreme Court (there is no time limit – Admin. of Justice Act 1956, s. 18). There must also be filed a statutory declaration by the trustee that he intends to remain out of the United Kingdom for a period exceeding one month from the date of such declaration or from a date therein mentioned. If the power of attorney relates to land the title to which is registered under the Land Registration Act 1925, an office copy must be filed at the Land Registry before dealing with the land or land charges (Trustee Act 1925, s. 25).

(c) Power to delegate management of land

Trustees for sale of land may by writing revocably delegate their powers of leasing, accepting surrenders of leases, and management, to the tenant for life if of full age, without being liable for his acts or defaults (L.P.A. 1925, s. 29).

§ 15. Power of Maintenance and Accumulation

(a) Out of capital

An adult beneficiary who is *sui juris* is entitled to call for the payment to him of any trust capital to which he is absolutely entitled, so that no question of whether the trustees are entitled to maintain him out of the capital can arise. But if the beneficiary is an infant, he cannot call on the trustees to pay the capital over to him, for, being an infant, he could not give a good receipt. It has been held that in appropriate circumstances trustees may apply, for the maintenance of an infant, capital to which he is absolutely entitled (*Re Howarth*), but they would be ill-advised to do so without an order of the court. With a view to the application of capital to which an infant is beneficially entitled for his maintenance, education or benefit, the court may make an order appointing a person to convey the property, to transfer stock, and so forth according to the nature of the property in question (Trustee Act 1925, s. 53). It has been held that the power of the court extends to authorising a mortgage of an infant's interest in remainder so as to raise capital money or his maintenance (*Re Gower's Settlement*).

(*b*) *Out of income*

This is governed by the Trustee Act 1925, s. 31, unless its operation is excluded by contrary intention expressed in the trust instrument (*ibid.*, s. 69 (2)).

Under s. 31 trustees are empowered at their sole discretion to apply for or towards the maintenance, education or benefit of infant beneficiaries the whole or such part of the income of any property, real or personal, as may in the circumstances be reasonable:

(1) whether the infant's interest is *vested* or *contingent*, but subject to any prior interests or charges affecting the property; and

(2) whether or not there is:

    (*a*) any other fund applicable to the same purpose;

    (*b*) any person bound by law to maintain and educate the infant.

The amounts expended on maintenance must be reasonable and consistent with the infant's age and station in life, and proportionate to amounts paid from other available funds (if any).

Accumulations from previous years may be applied, and not only income for the current year.

A married infant has power to give valid receipts for all income (including statutory accumulations made during the minority) as if the infant were of full age (L.P.A. 1925, s. 21).

(c) *Payment of income to adult beneficiaries*

Where a person on reaching majority does not then acquire a vested interest in the income, but the limitation or trust carries the intermediate income of the property, the trustees must pay to him the income from the property and the income from any accumulations, until he attains a vested interest or dies, or the interest fails (Trustee Act 1925, s. 31 (1) (ii)). This direction to the trustees confers upon them power to pay the income in such cases only where no contrary intention is indicated in the instrument creating the trust (*ibid.*, s. 69 (2)). Accordingly, a direction to accumulate the intermediate income between the majority of the beneficiary and the acquisition by him of a vested interest will operate to displace the power of the trustees to pay the income over to him, for such a direction shows a 'contrary intention' (*Re Turner's Will Trusts*). Any such direction, to be valid, must be within the limits prescribed by the Rule against Accumulations (*see* § 9, *ante*).

(d) *Destination of accumulations*

Income not spent on maintenance during minority must be invested by the trustees in authorised securities.

Where the interest is a vested one or the property becomes his on reaching majority or prior marriage, such unspent income must be held on trust for the beneficiary personally as an absolute interest.

In other cases, e.g. where the infant has only a contingent interest in the income, such unspent income must be added to the capital of the fund.

(e) *Limitation must carry intermediate income*

The power given to trustees by Section 31 applies to all interests vested in possession where they produce income or carry interest, if the income or interest becomes the beneficiary's property absolutely as it accrues.

In the case of a contingent interest, Section 31, Trustee Act 1925, applies only if the limitation or trust carries the intermediate income of the property (s. 31 (3)). Section 175, Law of Property Act 1925, provides that in the case of a contingent or future specific devise or bequest of property, or of a contingent residuary devise of freehold land, or of a specific or residuary devise of freehold land to trustees upon trust for persons whose interests are contingent, the contingent or future beneficiary is entitled to the intermediate income of that property from the death of the testator, except so far as dispositions of such income, or any part thereof, have been made. It will be seen that Section 175 only applies to interests created by will. Furthermore, it does not apply to a future or contingent *pecuniary* legacy (*Re Raine*), or to a future legacy of residue (*Re Gillett's Will Trusts*).

The power of maintenance given by Section 31 does, however, apply to certain legacies to which Section 175, Law of Property Act 1925, does not apply. These are future or contingent legacies (including pecuniary legacies) by the parent of (or a person standing *in loco parentis* to) the legatee, if and for such period as, under the general law, the legacy carries interest for the maintenance of the legatee, in which case the rate of interest is 5 per cent. per annum if the income available is sufficient. Such a legacy does not carry interest under the general law if other adequate provision has been made for the legatee's maintenance. These provisions apply to a vested annuity as if the annuity were the income of property held by trustees in trust to pay the income to the annuitant, save that accumulations during the infancy of the annuitant must be held in trust for him or his personal representatives absolutely (Trustee Act 1925, s. 31 (4)).

§ 16. Power of Advancement

The powers already discussed to provide for the maintenance of infants must be distinguished from the powers conferred by the Trustee Act 1925, s. 32, as to *advancement*. An advancement is a substantial capital payment made with the object of establishing the donee in life or of making provision for him or in some way advancing his interests (*Taylor* v. *Taylor*). Maintenance on the other hand involves the application of funds to preserve or secure the well-being of the person maintained. Under s. 32, trustees may at any time or times pay or supply any capital money which is subject to a trust, for the advancement or benefit, in such manner as they may, in their absolute discretion, think fit, of ANY PERSON (not necessarily an infant) ENTITLED TO THE CAPITAL of the trust property or of any share thereof.

It appears that the term 'benefit' includes maintenance (*Re Breed's Will*).

This power exists whether the interest of the person so entitled is:

(i) absolute or contingent on his attaining any specified age or on the occurrence of any other event, or subject to a gift over on his death under any specified age or on the occurrence of any other event; or

(ii) in possession or in remainder or reversion; or

(iii) liable to be defeated by the exercise of a power of appointment or revocation, or to be diminished by the increase of the class to which he belongs.

Provided that:

(*a*) the money so paid or applied for the advancement or benefit of any person *shall not exceed altogether in amount one-half of the presumptive or vested share* or interest of that person in the trust property; and

(*b*) if that person is or becomes absolutely and indefeasibly entitled to a share in the trust property, *the money so paid or applied shall be brought into account as part of such share*; and

(*c*) no such payment or application shall be made so as to prejudice any person entitled to any prior life or other interest, whether vested or contingent, in the money paid or applied, unless such person is in existence and of full age and consents in writing to such payment or application.

Section 32 applies only where the trust property consists of money or securities, or of property held upon trust for sale, calling in and conversion; and such money or securities or the proceeds of such sale, calling in and conversion are not 'by statute or in equity considered as land', or applicable as capital money for the purposes of the Settled Land Act 1925.

The equitable doctrine of conversion is worth stating here in the terms of the judgment in *Fletcher* v. *Ashburner*, where it was said that 'money directed to be employed in the purchase of lands, and land directed to be sold and turned into money, are to be considered as that species of property into which they are directed to be converted; and this in whatever manner the direction is given, whether by will, by way of contract, marriage articles, settlement or otherwise; and whether the money is actually deposited, or only covenanted to be paid, whether the land is actually conveyed or only agreed to be conveyed, the owner of the fund, or the contracting parties may make land money, and money land'.

The provisions of Section 32 apply to the statutory trusts arising on intestacy (A.E.A. 1925, s. 47). The Instrument creating the trust may exclude or modify the application of Section 32 (Trustee Act 1925, s. 69 (2)).

It has been held that the words in Section 32 'on the occurrence of any other event' must be construed as including any event, whether single or compound, other than the single event of attaining a specified age, and that the power of advancement may be exercised notwithstanding that the interest of an infant is contingent on the double event of survivorship and the attainment of a specified age (*In re Garrett, Croft* v. *Brick*).

§ 17. Power to Insure

Although it is not legally certain that trustees are bound to insure buildings and other insurable property comprised in the trust against loss or damage by fire, it is thought that as they are given statutory power (Trustee Act 1925, s. 19 (1) and Settled Land Act 1925, s. 102 (2) (*e*)) to insure to any amount not exceeding three-fourths of the full value of the building or property (the premiums being payable out of the income of the property or of other property subject to the same trusts) that they might commit a devastavit if they did not do so and a fire ensued. This power does not extend to any building or property which a trustee is bound forthwith to convey absolutely to any beneficiary upon being requested to do so (*ibid.*, s. 19 (2)). In such a case he should obtain the authority of the beneficiary to insure. It is curious that the statutory power of insurance is limited to three-fourths of the value of the property, as this would result in under-insurance, and a consequent reduction in the amount payable by the insurers in the event of a loss. Trustees would be well advised to obtain the authority of the person entitled to the income to insure up to full value and to charge the whole of the premiums against income. Failing such authority, the trustees might be justified in applying capital in payment of the balance of the insurance premium to bring the amount insured up to full value, but it would be advisable to apply to the court for directions. Trustees lending money on mortgage of buildings should see that there is a covenant by the mortgagor to insure, and that the insurance is, in fact, kept on foot.

Insurance money receivable under a policy kept up under any trust, power, covenant or obligation is capital money and is to be held upon trusts corresponding as nearly as may be with the trusts affecting the property in respect of which it was payable. The money may be applied, with the consent of any person whose consent is required to investment, in reinstating the property lost or damaged. The rules that the insurance money is to be treated as capital money, and that consent may be required to reinstatement, are without prejudice to the right of any person (such as a tenant) interested in the premises to require, under the Fires Prevention (Metropolis) Act 1774, s. 83, that the insurance office shall spend the money in rebuilding the premises (Trustee Act 1925, s. 20).

§ 18. Miscellaneous Powers

The Trustee Act 1925 sets out various miscellaneous powers of trustees, of which the following may be mentioned.

A trustee of a trust for sale or having a power of sale may sell or concur with any other person in selling the trust property, either together or in lots, by public auction or by private contract, subject to such conditions as he thinks fit (Trustee Act 1925, s. 12).

A trustee has power to compound liabilities, being able to accept any property before the time at which it is transferable or payable, sever and apportion any blended trust funds or property, pay or allow any debt or claim on any evidence that he thinks sufficient, accept any composition or security for any debt or property claimed, allow time for payment of any debt, and compromise, etc., any debt, account, claim or thing whatever (*ibid.*, s. 15).

Where trustees are authorised to pay or apply capital money subject to the trust for any purpose or in any manner, they have power to raise the money required by sale, conversion, calling in or mortgage of all or any part of the trust property for the time being in possession. This does not apply to trustees of property held for charitable purposes, or to trustees under the Settled Land Act 1925 where the legal estate is not vested in them (Trustee Act 1925, s. 16).

Trustees may deposit any documents held by them relating to the trust, or to the trust property, with any banker or banking company or any other company whose business includes the undertaking of the safe custody of documents. Any sum payable in respect of such deposit is to be paid out of the income of the trust property (*ibid.*, s. 21).

Where the trust property includes any reversionary interest, the trustees cannot call for the transfer of the property to them until the reversionary interest falls into possession. In the meantime they are not bound to place a notice of distringas on the securities, or to take any similar steps for the protection of their interest, unless and until required in writing so to do by some beneficiary, due provision being made for payment of the cost of any proceedings required to be taken. On the reversionary interest falling into possession, the trustees should take the necessary steps to get the property under their control. They are authorised to agree its value, to accept authorised investments in or towards satisfaction, to allow deductions for expenses, etc., which they may think proper or reasonable, and to execute any release to discharge accountable parties.

Trustees may, for the purposes of the trust, from time to time (by duly qualified agents) ascertain and fix the value of any trust property in such manner as they think proper, and any valuation so made in good faith shall be binding upon all persons interested under the trust (*ibid.*, s. 22). Such a valuation might be made, for example, where the trust property was being divided in specie amongst the beneficiaries, in accordance with a power contained in the trust instrument.

In accordance with the principles of Equity, the trustees have power to do all acts which are reasonable and proper for the protection of the trust property and of the interests of the beneficiaries, subject to any restrictions contained in the trust instrument or imposed by law. The court will not interfere with the *bona fide* exercise of a trustee's power, but he must act honestly and must not benefit one beneficiary at the expense of another. Although in general beneficiaries are entitled to inspect trust documents, this right does not extend to:

(*a*) documents relating to the deliberations of the trustees leading to decisions taken in good faith as to the exercise of discretionary powers, as these are decisions taken in a confidential role and the trustees are not bound to disclose their motives and reasons; and

(*b*) communications between individual trustees, or between a trustee and an individual beneficiary, as these are not trust documents (*Re Londonderry's Settlement*).

§ 19. Unanimity of Trustees

The duties imposed on trustees whether by law or by the trust instrument, must be carried out, and any one trustee can require the others to concur in doing so, and if necessary apply to the court to compel compliance.

Powers and discretions must be distinguished from duties. For the exercise of a power or discretion, not imposing a duty on the trustees, the consent of all trustees is required (except in the case of charitable trusts (*see* § 6, *ante*)), and if any one refuses to exercise a power or discretion, it cannot be exercised. This is subject to the right of any trustee or beneficiary to apply to the court for an order, if the court thinks fit, that a particular power or discretion should be exercised. If, however, a power or discretion must be exercised in one way or another, it becomes a *duty*, and the trustees are *bound* to exercise it. When there is a disagreement between the trustees as to the manner in which such a power or discretion should be exercised, the only course is to apply to the court for directions, unless all the beneficiaries, being *sui juris*, agree in instructing the trustees to exercise it in a particular manner.

The line between duties on the one hand, and powers or discretions on the other, is sometimes finely drawn, and in a case of dispute between trustees it is essential to discover into which category the subject-matter of dispute falls. The following are examples:

(i) Trustees for sale of property have a duty to sell, subject to a power to postpone sale. If, therefore, one trustee wishes to sell and the others do not, the property must be sold, since there is a duty to sell and unanimity would be required for the exercise of the discretion to postpone sale.

(ii) The application of income for the maintenance of an infant is a power and not a duty, so that income can only be so applied if all the trustees agree, unless the court otherwise orders. On the other hand, the payment of income to a person on attaining majority, under the Trustee Act 1925, s. 31 (1) (ii) (*see* § 15 (*c*), *ante*), is a duty which the trustees are bound to perform, notwithstanding that some or all of them may not wish to do so.

(iii) Insurance under the Trustee Act 1925, s. 19 (*see* § 17, *ante*), is a power and not a duty, and if one of the trustees does not agree to insure, his co-trustees cannot do so (*Re McEacharn*).

(iv) Investment of trust moneys is a power, and if there is a disagreement among the trustees as to whether an investment should be changed, nothing can be done unless the court or all beneficiaries, being *sui juris*, direct a change. But if trust money is lying idle awaiting investment, there is a duty to invest it, and if the trustees disagree as to the manner of investment, application must be made to the court, failing instructions from all beneficiaries, being *sui juris*.

§ 20. Control of Trust Funds

It is the duty of a trustee to get and keep the trust funds under his control, or if he is one of two or more trustees, under the control of himself and his co-trustees.

On the creation of a trust *inter vivos*, the trust instrument will set out a list of the trust investments. Each trustee must see that all these investments are transferred into the names of himself and his co-trustees by whatever means are appropriate to the particular property in question, and he must effect any necessary registration and give any necessary notices. He must also see that the deeds and documents of title are brought under the control of himself and his co-trustees. Stock and share certificates and other securities should be deposited for safe custody with a bank or any company whose business includes the undertaking of safety of documents. Title deeds of land which are constantly required for such matters as sales, mortgages or leasing may properly be left with the trustees' solicitors. In all cases deeds and documents must be deposited or left with the bank, solicitor, etc., in the names of all the trustees. It is specifically provided in the Trustee Act 1925, s. 7, that bearer securities are to be deposited by a trustee, not being a trust corporation, for safe custody and collection of income with a banker or banking company, and that a trustee shall not be responsible for any loss incurred by reason of such deposit.

A trustee appointed by will is usually also appointed executor, and in that case he will first carry out his executorship duties and then assume the position of trustee. In those cases where the trustee is a different person from the executor, he must take over from the executor when the administration is completed, and in doing so must check the executorship account to see that the trust fund which he takes over is in order. He must take the steps indicated above to get the whole of the trust property into his name and under his control.

A new trustee, on his appointment, should check the capital accounts of the trust from its inception, so as to ensure that he is receiving the whole of the trust property and that no loss has occurred through any prior breach of trust. He should take steps, as indicated above, to get the whole of the trust property into the names and under the control of himself and his co-trustees. The implied vesting of property on the appointment of a new trustee is dealt with in § 19 (c), *ante*.

When the time comes for a distribution of trust funds to a particular or among all beneficiaries, the trustees should bear in mind that there may be a liability for Capital Gains tax and reserve sufficient funds to meet this (for Capital Gains tax see Chapter V and § 31 *post*).

§ 21. Remuneration of Trustee

A trustee is entitled to re-imburse himself all expenses incurred in or about the execution of the trusts or powers (Trustee Act 1925, s. 30 (2)), and he has a lien on the trust property for expenses so incurred. Any costs of litigation in which he may be involved as trustee will be ordered to be paid out of the trust property, unless he has been guilty of misconduct.

A trustee is not allowed to make any profit out of his office, and accordingly as a general rule he is not entitled to any remuneration for his services. This rule excludes any payment in the nature of fees to a business or professional trustee. The rule excluding any right to remuneration is subject to the following exceptions:

(a) Remuneration is allowed if authorised by the trust instrument. Such a clause is commonly found in a will of which a professional man is appointed trustee, and it usually extends specifically to allowing him to charge, not only for professional services, but also for matters which a trustee could have done without professional assistance. Remuneration payable to an executor under a clause in the will is regarded as a legacy; it would not be payable if the estate were insolvent or if the executor had witnessed the will, and it would abate if necessary with other pecuniary legacies.

(b) Remuneration can be paid out of income or capital belonging to any beneficiary who, being *sui juris*, consents thereto.

(c) The court has a general power to sanction the payment of remuneration to a trustee, and in particular the Trustee Act 1925, s. 42, provides that the court, on appointing a corporation other than the Public Trustee to be a trustee, may authorise the corporation to charge such remuneration for its services as trustee as the court thinks fit.

(d) A solicitor-trustee is entitled to costs out of pocket when he acts as solicitor in an action on behalf of himself and his co-trustee jointly, except in so far as the costs have been increased by his being one of the parties (*Cradock* v. *Piper*). Thus, profit costs were disallowed where a solicitor-trustee appointed his firm (including himself) to act as solicitors to the trust, although there was an agreement that the solicitor-trustee should not share in the profit costs (*Re Gates*, approved in *Re Hill*); he should have appointed his partner as independent solicitor (*Re Hill, ante*).

(e) Remuneration is allowed for administering a trust of property abroad if customary in the local courts (*Chambers* v. *Goldwin*).

(*f*) The Public Trustee is allowed to charge for acting as trustee such fees as may be fixed by the Treasury (Public Trustee Act 1906, s. 9).

§ 22. Personal Dealings of Trustee with Trust Property

A trustee is not allowed to purchase or otherwise deal with the trust property for his own benefit. Even if he makes full disclosure to the beneficiaries of all matters within his knowledge and pays a fair price, the beneficiaries can still set aside the sale without proving any fraud by the trustee or loss to them (*Ex parte James*). The trustee would be liable to repay to the beneficiaries the income produced by such property from the date of his purchase (*Silkstone and Haigh Moor Coal Co.* v. *Edey*). If a trustee who has purchased trust property resells at a profit, the beneficiaries can adopt the resale and claim the profit (*Baker* v. *Carter*). A sale to a trustee's agent or nominee could similarly be set aside at the instance of a beneficiary. Even a sale to the trustee's wife or child could probably be set aside on the presumption that the trustee obtained some benefit therefrom. A sale to a company in which the trustee was a shareholder would not be invalid in itself, but if the transaction were challenged by a beneficiary, the onus would be on the company to prove that the price was the best obtainable and not inadequate at the time (*Farrar* v. *Farrar Ltd*). If, however, the company were one of which the trustee was beneficial owner of all or substantially all the shares, the sale would be regarded as a sale to him and would be voidable (*Silkstone and Haigh Moor Coal Co.* v. *Edey* (*supra*)). A trustee cannot purchase trust property from a person to whom it has been sold by the trustees, if he purchases before completion of the sale to that person (*Williams* v. *Scott*), but if the purchase has been completed, the trustee is not necessarily debarred from himself buying the property from the purchaser at some future date, though he may be required to show that the original sale by the trustees was *bona fide*. A former trustee may not purchase the trust property if he has retired from the trust for the purpose of enabling him to do so; but if his retirement has no connection with any intention to purchase, he would not be prevented from purchasing at a later date. It has been held that the trustees of a person's marriage settlement are not precluded from purchasing property of which that person is trustee (*Hickley* v. *Hickley*).

A tenant for life under the Settled Land Act 1925, who stands in the position of a trustee in the exercise of his legal powers, is nevertheless enabled to purchase the settled property for his own benefit (Settled Land Act 1925, s. 68).

A purchase by a trustee of the trust property is a case in which the purchaser is buying from himself or from himself and others. The case of a purchase by a trustee of a beneficiary's interest in the trust property is different, for here the trustee is not purchasing from himself but from the beneficiary, and a transaction of that nature is not subject to such stringent rules. A trustee is at liberty to purchase the interest of a beneficiary, provided that he makes full disclosure of all facts within his knowledge and pays a fair price, and that the beneficiary was *sui juris* and independently advised (*Thomson* v. *Eastwood*). In one case where a trustee bargained at arm's length with a beneficiary who was separately advised, but did not disclose a valuation which he had had made for himself, the sale was set aside (*Dougan* v. *Macpherson*).

§ 23. Breach of Trust

(a) *What constitutes a breach*

A breach of trust occurs when a trustee fails to carry out any of the duties imposed on him by the trust instrument or by law, or when he exercises any of his powers or discretions improperly. He is responsible for his own acts or defaults, but not generally for those of others.

A trustee is not as a rule responsible for the conduct of his agents if appointed in good faith, but exceptionally he *is* responsible for the acts or defaults of an attorney whom he appoints to act for him during his absence abroad (*see* § 14, Powers of Delegation, *ante*). The Trustee Act 1925, specifically provides that a trustee is not answerable for the acts, receipts, neglects or defaults of any banker, broker or other person with whom any trust money or securities are deposited, or for the insufficiency or deficiency of any securities, unless the same happens through his own wilful default.

A trustee is not accountable or answerable for the acts, receipts, neglects or defaults of any other trustee, or for any other loss, unless the same happens through his own wilful default.

A trustee sometimes signs a receipt, as is said, 'for conformity'; that is, he signs it in order to supply one of the necessary signatures, though he has not actually received the money or property to which it relates. For example, in selling stocks and shares it is customary for the trustees to sign the form of transfer, which embodies a receipt for the sale moneys, and to send it to their broker to enable him to deliver the stocks or shares and collect the sale moneys. A trustee is not answerable for loss occasioned by his signing for conformity, unless it happens through his own wilful default (Trustee Act 1925, s. 30).

It will be observed from the preceding paragraphs that in several cases a trustee is not liable for loss unless it occurs through his own 'wilful default'. A trustee is guilty of wilful default only if he knows that he is committing and intends to commit a breach of trust, or commits a breach by acting recklessly, not caring whether it is a breach or not (*Re City Equitable Fire Insurance Co. Ltd*). If a trustee facilitates a breach of trust on the part of his agent or co-trustee by allowing trust money or property to remain in the hands of or under the control of that other for an undue length of time, without seeing to the application thereof, he is guilty of wilful default and liable accordingly.

A new trustee is not liable for breaches of trust committed by his predecessors, but it is his duty to do his best to compel any former or continuing trustee to make good a prior breach which comes to his knowledge. A trustee is not liable for breaches of trust committed after he has retired, unless he retired for the purpose of enabling a breach of trust to be committed.

It must not be supposed that a trustee is never liable for breach of trust unless it occurs through his own wilful default. In general, he is liable whether the breach was conscious or careless or not; it is only in the specific cases of liability for acts and defaults of agents, etc., detailed in the Trustee Act 1925, s. 30 (1), that his liability is limited to cases of wilful default (*Re Vickery*). In some other cases his liability is specifically limited in a particular way, e.g. he is not liable for the default of agents if employed in good faith (Trustee Act 1925, s. 23 (1)). Apart from any such exemptions, he is liable if a

breach of trust occurs, however careful he may have been. For
example, if he invests trust money in an unauthorised investment, believing on reasonable grounds that it was authorised,
he would nevertheless have committed a breach of trust.

The court has power to relieve a trustee wholly or partly
from personal liability, if he has acted honestly and reasonably
and ought fairly to be excused both for the breach of trust and
for omitting to obtain the directions of the court in the matter
(*ibid.*, s. 61).

(b) *Measure of trustee's liability for breach of trust*

A trustee who commits a breach of trust is liable to make good
any capital loss, and to pay interest in respect of any loss of
income. The rate of interest is 4 per cent. per annum, unless
the trustee has used the trust property for his own purposes or
has been guilty of fraud or serious misconduct, in which cases
the court may order a higher rate of interest, usually 5 per cent.,
and sometimes compound interest. If the trustee has made a
profit out of the use of trust money for his own purposes, as by
using it in his business, he is liable to pay over the profit, if
greater than 5 per cent.

A breach consisting in investing trust money in unauthorised
investments renders the trustee liable both to replace the money,
if any loss has occurred, and to make up the income to 4 per
cent. Any capital profit or excess income, of course, belongs to
the beneficiaries. A trustee wrongfully retaining an unauthorised
investment is liable for the difference between the price obtained
when it is in fact realised and the price which he would have
obtained if he had sold at the correct time. A trustee selling an
authorised investment in order to purchase one which is unauthorised is liable, not only for any loss arising out of the
unauthorised investment, but also for any increased cost of
replacing the authorised investment sold.

A trustee cannot set off a loss arising from one breach of
trust against a profit accruing from another, so that if one
unauthorised investment is successful and another is not, the
trustee will not be allowed to credit the profit on the one against
the loss on the other, but will be required to make up the loss
on the one in full.

(c) *Limitation of liability*

A trustee is usually protected against personal liability for breach of trust by lapse of time. The period prescribed by the Limitation Act 1939 (s. 19 (2)), is six years from the date at which the right of action against the trustee accrued. Generally, the right of action accrues when the breach is committed, whether the beneficiary knows of it or not. But if the beneficiary is under a disability, such as infancy, or is a remainderman, the right accrues when the disability ceases or the remainder falls into possession, as the case may be. A beneficiary whose right of action against the trustee is barred cannot take advantage of the right of a beneficiary not barred. Thus, in *Re Fountaine*, a trustee had committed a breach of trust in relation to a fund settled on a life tenant and a remainderman; when the breach was discovered, the right of action of the life tenant was barred by lapse of time; the remainderman, whose right was not barred, compelled the trustee to make good the capital loss out of his own resources; it was held by the court that the income arising from the money replaced was not to be paid to the life tenant, but could be retained by the trustee personally until the remainder fell into possession.

There is no time limit for suing a trustee when (i) the trustee has been party or privy to any fraud or fraudulent breach of trust; or (ii) the trustee is in possession of the trust property or the proceeds thereof, or has converted trust property to his own use, even though innocently.

(d) *Following and tracing the trust property*

Apart from his right of action against the trustee personally, a beneficiary may be able to obtain satisfaction by following or tracing the trust property.

'Following' consists in claiming the trust property itself so long as it remains identifiable. The right will not avail against a purchaser for value without notice of the beneficial interests. The basis of the right of following is that the property belongs to the beneficiaries and can be claimed by them as their own property.

'Tracing' is resorted to when the trust property has become mixed with other property, but a means of identification or disentanglement exists. Equity will permit tracing when the person who owns the mixed fund is a volunteer or otherwise stands under a fiduciary obligation to replace the trust property. Tracing does not depend on the subsistence of any right of action against the trustee.

Where a trustee pays trust money into his own bank account, and subsequently draws out money for his personal use, it is presumed that he has drawn out his own money and not the trust money, so that the trust money can be traced in the bank account (*Re Hallett's Estate*). On the other hand if he draws out for his own purposes more than the amount of his own money, so that he must have used part of the trust money, it is not to be presumed that a subsequent payment-in of his own money is in replacement of the trust money (*Roscoe* v. *Winder*). In consequence, trust money mixed with personal money in a bank account can only be traced to the extent of the lowest figure at which the account stood at any time since the mixing. Where more than one trust fund is blended in the same account, the Rule in *Clayton's Case* applies, and the trustee is presumed to have drawn out money of the trust fund which was first paid in (*Re Stenning*).

In *Re Diplock* affirmed by the House of Lords *sub-nom.; Minister of Health* v. *Simpson and Others*, the executors of the will of the deceased distributed most of the estate, amounting to about a quarter of a million pounds, amongst one hundred-and thirty-nine charitable institutions, in pursuance of directions in the will to apply the estate for 'charitable or benevolent objects'. The direction in the will was invalid. Forty-eight persons, who were entitled on intestacy as next-of-kin, started proceedings against the executors, but they agreed to a compromise under which the executors paid them a certain sum of money. They thereby lost their right of action against the executors personally. This did not, however, debar them from tracing the property into the hands of the charitable institutions as volunteers, and they were held entitled to recover so long as, in each particular case, a means of identification or disentanglement from a mixed fund remained.

(e) *Indemnity and contribution*

A trustee who is chargeable with breach of trust may have a right of indemnity against his co-trustees or against a beneficiary in certain circumstances. A right of indemnity means a right to require another person to make good a loss suffered. It must be distinguished from a right of contribution, which is the right of one person, who has been compelled to make good a loss, to require others to pay to him their proper share of the loss by way of contribution.

A trustee has a right of indemnity against a co-trustee in the following circumstances:

  (i) against a co-trustee who has profited from the breach of trust to the extent of that profit;

 (ii) against a co-trustee who has been guilty of fraud, if the trustee claiming indemnity is innocent;

(iii) against a co-trustee who acted as solicitor to the trust and who advised the breach;

(iv) against a co-trustee who was a party to the breach and who is also a beneficiary to the extent of his beneficial interest.

A trustee who is also a beneficiary is not entitled to any share of the trust fund until he has made good any breach of trust for which he is liable. The assignee of a trustee-beneficiary, other than an assignee for value (such as a mortgagee) who took his assignment before the breach of trust, is in no better position. Thus in *Re Dacre* the interest of a deceased trustee-beneficiary, who had been guilty of breach of trust, had passed to innocent beneficiaries under his will; it was held that those latter beneficiaries could not claim his interest without first making good the breach of trust.

A beneficiary who, being *sui juris* and having full knowledge of the facts, consents, whether in writing or not, to a breach of trust, cannot hold a trustee liable therefor. Other beneficiaries may, however, do so, and if the consenting beneficiary has instigated, requested or consented *in writing* to the breach, the trustee may apply to the court for an order impounding all or any part of the interest of that beneficiary in the trust estate, by way of indemnity to the trustee or persons claiming through him. The making of an order is in the court's discretion (Trustee Act 1925, s. 62 (1)). 'In writing' applies to 'consent' only: it is not necessary that an instigation or request should be written for the section to operate (*Griffiths* v. *Hughes*). The order of

indemnity will take priority over a claim by an assignee (such
as a mortgagee) of the beneficiary's interest (*Bolton* v. *Curre*),
unless the assignee is an assignee for value before the occurrence
of the breach of trust.

A trustee who has been compelled to make good a breach of
trust may have a right of contribution against his co-trustees,
even though he cannot claim indemnity. Towards the beneficiaries each trustee is fully liable for breach of trust, and can be
compelled to make good the whole of the loss. But as between
themselves they are liable in equal shares, except when a right
of indemnity can be claimed by one against another. If there is
no right of indemnity, any trustee who has paid more than his
share of the loss can claim contribution from the others.
Contribution applies when all are equally innocent, and probably (under the Law Reform (Married Women and Tortfeasors)
Act 1935, s. 6), which allows contribution between joint tortfeasors, when all are guilty of fraud.

(*f*) *Release of trustee*

A trustee may be released by the beneficiaries from liability for
breach of trust. Such a release will operate only against those
beneficiaries who were parties to the release, and only if they
were *sui juris* at the time of the release and had full knowledge
of the facts. On the termination of a trust, it is customary for a
trustee to obtain a deed or document of release from the beneficiaries to whom he is handing over the fund, but this will only
extend to releasing him from liability for breaches of trust
which were referred to in the release or otherwise brought to
the notice of the beneficiaries.

§ 24 Powers of the Court

The court has a general supervision over trusts and over the
exercise of their duties, powers and discretions by trustees.
Accordingly it is always open to any trustee or beneficiary to
apply to the court for an order as to any matter which cannot,
or cannot conveniently, be dealt with otherwise. Apart from
this general power of the court, Trustee Act 1925, Part IV, sets
out specific powers of the court. Certain of these specific powers
have already been mentioned in the text in their appropriate
place (such as the power of the court to appoint and remove

trustees, and the power to relieve a trustee from personal liability for breach of trust). Amongst the specific powers of the court not previously dealt with may be mentioned the power of the court to give judgment in the absence of a trustee who cannot be found (s. 59); to charge costs against capital or income or against such persons as to the court seems just (s. 60); to order dealings with money paid into court (s. 63). The court in question is the High Court (Chancery Division), or in cases arising in Lancashire or Durham, the Chancery Court of Lancaster or the Palatine Court of Durham. The county court has jurisdiction in small cases, usually when the value of the trust property does not exceed £500.

The Variation of Trusts Act 1958 was passed to put beneficiaries who are infants or under some form of disability in the same position, as nearly as may be, as beneficiaries who are of full age and capacity. It enables the Court to assent to any variation or revocation of trusts or to any alteration of the administrative powers of the trustees which the Court considers would be for the benefit of any of the following:

(*a*)   A beneficiary who is incapable of assenting by reason of infancy or other incapacity;

(*b*)   A person, whether ascertained or not, who may become entitled to an interest under the trust at a future date or on the happening of a future event;

(*c*)   An unborn beneficiary;

(*d*)   A person in respect of any discretionary interest of his under protective trusts where the interest of the principal beneficiary has not failed or determined. It also provides that, in considering whether a proposed variation of trusts is for the benefit of any beneficiary, the court is not required to have regard to the interest of persons entitled under a discretionary trust which has not yet come into operation.

The provisions of the Act have been used, with the consent of the Court, to bring to an end trusts or re-arrange the interests of beneficiaries for the purposes of saving Estate Duty. The Court will take into consideration not only the financial benefits to the beneficiaries but also the social and educational benefits which may arise from the variation (*In re Weston's Settlements*).

The Variation of Trusts Act 1958 extends the jurisdiction of the court to vary trusts in the interests of beneficiaries who by reason of some disability are unable to give their consent. The arrangement must be for the benefit of the person on whose behalf the approval is given.

If there is a dispute as to the construction of a settlement, the court may sanction a compromise which will result in saving Estate Duty (*Re Lord Hylton's Settlement, Barclays Bank* v. *Jolliffe*). The Divorce Court may vary settlements so as to avoid taxation (*Thomson* v. *Thomson and Whitmee*).

PART III – ACCOUNTS

§ 25. Introduction

The recommendations of the Institute of Chartered Accountants in England and Wales concerning the accounts of an Executor (see Chapter XV, § 2) are appropriate to the preparation of trust accounts. Accounts can be prepared annually on the anniversary of the inception of the trust, but the need to prepare trust returns and certificates of income for taxation purposes makes the 5th April a convenient date. When preparing accounts, the provisions of the Trustee Investments Act 1961 must be borne in mind. Entries will be made in the books of account on the usual double-entry principles. When legal personal representatives have completed the administration of the estate but continue to hold the assets to pay the income therefrom to the life tenant, they will become trustees. From that date, trust accounts will be prepared. On the inception of a trust, the value of the assets for Capital Gains tax purposes should be entered at the head of each asset account.

§ 26. Trust Accounts for Minors

(a) *Accumulations of income*

When property is left in trust for minors, the balance of income will be divided equally or in accordance with the terms contained in the will, and credited to the separate accounts of the minors, usually called Income Accumulations Accounts. Any amounts paid by way of maintenance for the children will be debited to their respective accounts, and not to the Estate Income

Account, since such payments may vary with the ages of the children.

The accumulations must be invested from time to time, and the investments so made ear-marked accordingly as being on Accumulations Account. The income arising therefrom must be credited to a special Accumulations Income Account, and divided between the children in proportion to the balances on their separate Accumulations Accounts at the commencement of the year in question.

Repayments of Income tax upon accumulations of income during a minority are the property of the beneficiary and not capital (*Re Fulford, Fulford* v. *Hyslop*). Such repayments will not occur in respect of income arising after 5th April, 1969.

Illustration

The following is a Trial Balance of the Adams Trust at 23rd October, 1970:

	Dr.	Cr.
	£	£
Estate Capital Account		30,000
Beneficiaries' Accumulations Accounts as at 23rd October, 1969:		
Fanny		1,100
John		800
Charles		1,100
Investments on Estate Capital Account at cost	30,000	
Investments on Accumulations Accounts at cost	3,000	
Cash at Bank on Accumulations Account	870	
Balance of Estate Income Account, 23rd October, 1970		1,200
Balance of Accumulations Income Account, 23rd October, 1970		120
Beneficiaries' Maintenance Accounts:		
Fanny	Nil	
John	230	
Charles	220	
	£34,320	£34,320

The beneficiaries are all minors, and share the general income equally. Draw up a Balance Sheet as at 23rd October, 1970, and prepare in a concise form each beneficiary's Accumulation Account for the year.

BALANCE SHEET, 23RD OCTOBER, 1970

	£	£		£	£
Estate Capital Account		30,000	Investment on Estate Capital Account at cost		30,000
Beneficiaries' Accumulations Accounts:			Investments on Accumulations Accounts at cost	3,000	
Fanny	1,544				
John	1,002				
Charles	1,324		Cash at Bank on Accumulations Accounts	870	
		3,870			3,870
		£33,870			£33,870

BENEFICIARIES' ACCUMULATIONS ACCOUNTS
FOR THE YEAR ENDED 23RD OCTOBER, 1970

		Fanny	John	Charles			Fanny	John	Charle
		£	£	£			£	£	£
Oct. 23	Maintenance ..	—	230	220	Oct. 2	Balance b/f ..	1,100	800	1,100
	Balance b/f ..	1,544	1,002	1,324	Oct. 2	Estate Income ..	400	400	400
						Accumulations Income ..	44	32	44
		£1,544	£1,232	£1,544			£1,544	£1,232	£1,544

(b) Schedules of investments

In trust accounts of any size it is common for the trustees to render schedules of the investments on Estate Capital Account to the various beneficiaries under the will, showing at a glance what investments there were at the commencement of the year under review, the dealings during the year, and the amount held at the end of the year, with additional columns showing the market prices at the close of the period, and the consequent appreciation or depreciation on the book values.

It is advisable that such a schedule be examined by the auditors, and it is not uncommon to find the market values certified by a stockbroker.

Even if it is not necessary for schedules to be rendered to the beneficiaries, as in the case of minors, it is desirable that such be drawn up so that each trustee may see the position clearly.

The following is a convenient ruling, but this can be modified to suit the particular circumstances. A similar schedule would be prepared showing the investments on Accumulations Accounts where necessary.

SCHEDULE OF INVESTMENTS IN ESTATE CAPITAL ACCOUNT

Nominal Amount of investment	Particulars of investment	Folio in Ledger	Amount at commencement of year at cost or Probate valuation	Subsequent Dealings	Amount at end of year at cost or Probate valuation	Market value at end of year	Appreciation in value*	Depreciation in value*	Rate % on Nominal Amount	Date dividends are payable	Paid to	Amount of dividend received	Rate % on valuation in books

* Before adjusting for any liability to or relief from Capital Gains tax.

(c) *Appropriation of share upon distribution in specie*

On a beneficiary becoming entitled to be paid his share of the estate of a deceased person or of a settled trust, such share may be satisfied in one of the following ways:

(1) If each of the investments of the trust is capable of precise division, by transferring to the beneficiary his exact proportion of the nominal amount of each investment. For example, if the beneficiary's share of the estate were one-third, where practicable the simplest and most equitable method of satisfaction would be to transfer to him one-third in nominal value of each of the investments held, irrespective of the market value, and one-third of the cash. He would thereby receive his proper share of the estate, whatever the market value of the assets may be. If, at the date of transfer, any of the investments so transferred are quoted *ex div.*, on the subsequent receipt of the dividends the trustees would have to pay to the beneficiary the amount applicable to his share.

(2) All the assets may be converted into cash, and the beneficiary's exact proportion thereof paid over to him.

(3) Where any of the securities or other assets of the trust are not capable of exact division, e.g. where some of the assets consist of land and buildings or of investments which cannot be transferred in fractional amounts, and it is not desired to realise them, it will be necessary to revalue each asset in order to ascertain the total value of the beneficiary's share of the estate as at the date of distribution.

The amount of any appreciation in the value of an asset will be debited to the particular Asset Account and credited to the Estate Capital Account, whilst the amount of any depreciation in value will be credited to the Asset Account and debited to Estate Capital Account. The balance of the Estate Capital Account will then represent the value of the estate as at the date of distribution, and the beneficiary's proportion thereof will be debited to Estate Capital Account and credited to the beneficiary's Distribution Account. The trustees must calculate the Capital Gains tax due as a result of the distribution and debit the beneficiary's Distribution Account accordingly. This latter account will then be debited, and the appropriate Asset

Accounts credited, with the value, as at the date of distribution, of each asset transferred to him. The calculation of the Capital Gains tax liability is described fully in Chapter XI of *Capital Gains Tax* by the author.

Where the distribution becomes necessary owing to the coming of age of an infant beneficiary, and the trustees also hold investments representing accumulations of income, any profit or loss arising from the revaluation of these investments must be divided between the beneficiaries in proportion to the balances standing on their respective Accumulation Accounts in exactly the same way as the income on accumulations investments, and not in the proportion in which they are entitled to share in the estate capital.

The balance thus ascertained will represent the amount due to the beneficiary under this heading, and a scheme of appropriation must be prepared showing how it is proposed to discharge it. The nominal value of each investment may be divided in the ratio that the balance standing to the credit of the beneficiary's Accumulations Account, as at the date of the last Balance Sheet, bears to the total amount standing to the credit of all the beneficiaries on Accumulations Account at that date, or an agreement may be arrived at as to the assets which shall be transferred.

Where any of the assets consist of mortgages or other assets which cannot be called in or divided, it is sometimes arranged for these to be retained by the trustees on behalf of all the parties, the share of income applicable to the one coming of age being paid over to him as and when received, and the capital divided when realisation ultimately takes place.

In cases of difficulty, any scheme of appropriation should be submitted to the court and made under an order of the court, and this is particularly important where the respective values of the assets which cannot be exactly divided are uncertain.

Any income received after the appropriation has been made relating to the share of the beneficiary, and not, therefore, included in the scheme of appropriation, must be handed over to him when received.

Where investments are appropriated to meet a legacy, the rules in *Re Henderson* (*see* Chap. XI, § 2, (*b*)) are to be followed. A transfer of stock to meet a *pecuniary* legacy is a conveyance on sale chargeable with *ad valorem* stamp duty as the transaction is analogous to the purchase of a security with the amount of the legacy (*Joping* v. *C.I.R.*). Only ten shillings stamp duty is chargeable on a transfer of stock, etc., in satisfaction of a share of *residue*. (See also Chap. XIV, § 7.)

Illustration

A, B and C are minors and each is entitled to one-third of the capital of a trust. A comes of age on 21st May, 1970, and it is desired to prepare a scheme of appropriation of capital and income accumulations. The accounts have been taken yearly on 12th September; and at 12th September, 1969, the Trial Balance was as follows:

TRIAL BALANCE, 12TH SEPTEMBER, 1969

	Nominal Value	Dr	Cr
	£	£	£
Investments on Capital Account:			
Consols, 2½%	30,000	13,500	
Dominion, 5%	12,000	9,500	
Ilyria Power and Light Co., 1,000 shares	1,000	1,680	
XY & Co., Ltd, 10% debentures	400	400	
Estate Capital Account			25,080
Investments on Accumulations Account:			
Government Short-term Loans, 5%	3,300	3,102	
Corporation 1975–77 Stock, 5%	4,000	3,000	
XY & Co., Ltd, 73 shares of £10 each	730	730	
Wicksted Corp.: Loan on Mortgage	1,500	1,500	
Cash on Deposit Account		1,000	
Cash on Current Account		268	
A – Accumulations Account			2,400
B – „ „			3,600
C – „ „			3,600
		£34,680	£34,680

The values of the stocks at 12st May, 1970, are to be taken as follows:

Consols 28, Dominion 5 per cent. 89, Ilyria Power & Light Co. 37s., XY Debentures 100 Shares, Government Loans 98, Corporation 5 per cent. 76. The shares in XY Ltd were valued at £1,098. A agreed to take £3,707 5 per cent. Dominion Stock, 350 shares in Ilyria Power at £200, Ilyria Power XY debentures. He took his porportion of the Accumulations investments, except the preference shares, of which he is to take 18. The Wicksted Corporation mortgage is repayable in two years and is to be retained by the trustees on behalf of B and C.

In the case of capital the difference is to be adjusted in the Consols, and in the case of accumulations in cash.

The amount standing to the credit of the Estate Income Account at 21st May, 1970, amounted to £360, and £200 stood to the credit of the Accumulations Income Account at the same date in respect of income received.

Maintenance in respect of A, B and C at the rate of £20 per month each had been paid from 12th September, 1969, on the 15th of each month.

The Capital Gains tax payable on the transfer of assets to A was £40.

APPROPRIATION OF FUNDS REPRESENTING CAPITAL TO A AT 21ST MAY, 1970

Security	Nominal Amount	Book Value at 12th Sept. 1969	Market Value at 21st May, 1970		Stock to be transferred	
			Price	Amount	Nominal Amount	Market Value at 21st May, 1970
	£	£		£	£	£
Consols, 2½%	30,000	13,500	£28	8,400	10,582	2,963
Dominion, 5%	12,000	9,500	£89	10,680	3,797	3,300
Ilyria Power and Light ..	1,000	1,680	37/-	1,850	350 shares	647
X.Y & Co., Ltd, 10% debentures	400	400	£100	400	£200	200
	—	£25,080	—	£21,330	—	£7,110

APPROPRIATION OF FUNDS REPRESENTING INCOME ACCUMULATIONS TO A AT 21ST MAY, 1970

Security	Nominal Amount	Book Value at 12th Sept., 1969	Market Value at 21st May, 1970		Stock to be transferred	
			Price	Amount	Nominal Amount	Market Value at 21st May, 1970
	£	£	£	£	£	£
Government Short-term Loans, 5%	3,300	3,102	98	3,234	825	808
Corporation, 1975–77 5% ..	4,000	3,000	76	3,040	1,000	760
X.Y & Co., Ltd, preference shares of £10 each	73 shares	730		1,098	18 shares	271
						1,839
Wicksted Corporation loan on mortgage	1,500	1,500	Par	1,500	Nil	
Cash as at 12th Sept., 1969 ..		1,268		1,268		696
	—	£9,600	—	£10,140	—	£2,535

The total amount standing to the credit of the Beneficiaries' Accumulations Accounts at 12th September, 1969, is £9,600, of which A is entitled to £2,400, which is exactly one quarter.

The amount finally due to him is, therefore, as follows:

	£
Balance of A's Accumulations Account as at 12th September, 1969..	2,400

Add $\frac{2,400}{9,600}$ = ¼ of £540, being net appreciation of market values of investments at 21st May, 1970, as compared with book values at 12th September, 1969, as per schedule .. 　　135

2,535

Add 　　⅓ of Estate Income Account as at 21st May, 1970, £360 .. 　　120

$\frac{2,400}{9,600}$ = ¼ of Accumulations Income Account as at 21st May, 1970, £200 .. 　　50

2,705

Deduct 　Maintenance from 12th September, 1969, to 21st May, 1970, 9 months at £20 .. 　180
Capital Gains tax .. 　　40
　　　　　220

£2,485

This will be discharged as follows:

	£
Securities at market value 21st May, 1970, as per schedule ..	1,839
Cash (£696 + £120 + £50 — £220) ..	646

£2,485

Assuming the above transactions and adjustments to be fully recorded in the books, the relevant accounts will appear as follows:

ESTATE CAPITAL

1970 May 21		£	1969 Sept. 12		£
	Loss on revaluation of Investments:			Balance b/f	25,080
	Consols	5,100	1970 May 21	Profit on revaluation of investments:	
	A. Distribution:			Dominion 5%	1,180
	One-third of £21,330	7,110		Ilyria Power	170
	Balance c/f	14,220			
					£26,430
		£26,430			
			1970 May 22	Balance b/f	£14,220

ACCUMULATIONS

1970		A. £	B. £	C. £	1969		A. £	B. £	C. £
May 21	Cash:				Sept. 12	Balances b/f ..	2,400	3,600	3,60
	Maintenance	180	180	180	1970				
	A. Distribution Account ..	2,485			May 21	Estate Income	120	120	12
	Capital Gains tax	40				Accumulations Income ..	50	75	7
	Balance b/f ..		3,818	3,817		Net profit on re-valuation of investments ..	135	203	20
		£2,705	£3,998	£3,997			£2,705	£3,998	£3,99
					1970				
					May 22	Balance c/f ..		£3,818	£3,81

DISTRIBUTION TO A.

1970		£	1970		£
May 21	£10,582, Consols..	2,963	May 21	Transfer from:	
	£3,333, Dominion Stock ..	3,300		Estate Capital	7,11
	350 Shares – Ilyria Power ..	647		Accumulations..	2,48
	£200 X.Y Debentures	200			
	£825 Government Loan.. ..	808			
	£1,000 Corporation 1975–77 Stock	760			
	18 X.Y & Co. Preference Shares	271			
	Cash	646			
		£9,595			£9,59

After paying out A., the Balance Sheet of the trust will appear as follows:

BALANCE SHEET AS AT 21ST MAY, 1970

	£		£	£
Estate Capital Account	14,220	Investments on Capital Account:		
		£19,418 2½% Consols	5,437	
Accumulations Accounts:		£8,293 5% Dominion Stock ..	7,380	
B. £3,818		650 £1 shares, Ilyria Power and Light	1,203	
C. 3,817		200 X.Y.Z Debentures	200	
	7,635			14,22
Capital Gains tax due	40	Investments and Cash on Accumulations Accounts:		
		£2,475 5% Government Loans..	2,426	
		£3,000 Corporation 1975–77 3% Stock	2,280	
		55 £10 Preference Shares X.Y & Co. Ltd	827	
		£1,500 Wicksted Corporation Loan on Mortgage	1,500	
		Cash	642	
				7,67
	£21,895			£21,89

Notes

(1) It has not been considered necessary to show the investment accounts.

(2) The cash balance is computed as follows:

	£		£
Balance at 12th September, 1969—		Payments for maintenance to 21st May, 1970—	
Deposit	1,000	A	180
Current Account ..	268	B	180
		C	180
	1,268	Distribution Account A	646
Estate Income to 21st May, 1970	360	Balance c/f	642
Accumulations Income to 21st May, 1970	200		
	£1,828		£1,828

(3) The method of procedure in the first table (Capital appropriation) is as follows:

   (i) Prepare the Book Value Column from the Trial Balance.

   (ii) Work out the market value and complete this column.

   (iii) Divide the total by 3, inserting the result as total of the Stock to be transferred (market value) column. Insert items in the latter column, adjusting Consols (market value) to balance; work out nominal amount of Consols.

   (iv) Prepare accumulations appropriation in similar manner.

(4) It is no offence against principles to adjust to market value in the books, and this method is often simpler to employ.

§ 27. Accounts

It is the duty of a trustee to keep true and accurate accounts of all transactions for which he is responsible as trustee. No particular form is required by law for trust accounts, but they must include full particulars of all receipts and payments, and those receipts and payments must be substantiated by vouchers. Separate accounts must be kept for separate trusts.

A trustee may, instead of keeping accounts personally, employ an accountant to do it for him, and the cost thereof will be a charge against the estate. The trustee will not be responsible for the default of an accountant if employed in good faith (Trustee Act 1925, § 23). A trustee can demand to be paid or guaranteed the costs of furnishing accounts in an administration action (*Re Bosworth*).

The beneficiaries are entitled to examine the accounts, and the trustee must have them ready for inspection at any time. Trust accounts should be rendered to the beneficiaries periodically, and in particular on the termination of the interest of any beneficiary. On termination of the trust itself an account should be rendered to the remainderman, showing the capital falling into his possession.

If the trustee neglects to keep proper accounts or to give explanations to beneficiaries, he may have to bear personally the costs of an action which may be instituted against him, and in a case of gross neglect these may include the costs of taking and vouching the accounts (*In re Skinner*, *Cooper* v. *Skinner*).

Trustees may, in their absolute discretion from time to time, but not more than once in every three years, unless the nature of the trust or any special dealings with the trust property make a more frequent exercise of the right reasonable, cause the accounts of the trust property to be examined or audited by an independent accountant. For that purpose they must produce such vouchers and give such information as the accountant may require. The costs of the examination or audit, including the fee of the auditor, are to be paid out of the capital or income of the trust property, or partly in one way and partly in the other, as the trustees in their absolute discretion think fit. In default of any direction by the trustees to the contrary in any special case, costs attributable to capital shall be borne by capital and those attributable to income by income (Trustee Act 1925, s. 22 (4)).

Under the Public Trustee Act 1906 any trustee or beneficiary is entitled to apply to the Public Trustee for investigation and audit of the accounts (Public Trustee Act 1906, s. 13) (*see* § 28 and 29 *post*)

§ 28. The Trustee Investments Act 1961

In the examples in § 26 of this chapter, the provisions of the Trustee Investments Act were ignored. In many cases, the will or trust instrument will provide for the trustees to have wider powers of investment than that permitted under the Act. A common form giving such wider powers would be:

'Power to apply or invest any money under the trusts hereof in the purchase of or at interest upon the security of such stocks funds shares securities or other investments or property of whatever nature and wherever situate (including the purchase or improvement of a freehold or leasehold dwellinghouse situate in the United Kingdom) and whether providing income or not and whether involving liabilities or not or upon such personal credit with or without security as the Trustees in their absolute discretion shall think fit and to the intent that the Trustees shall have the same powers in all respects as if they were absolute owners beneficially entitled.'

'Power to change any investments or property for the time being forming part of the Trust Fund for others is hereby authorised.'

In such cases the trustees do not need to concern themselves with the provisions of the Act. In those cases where the Act applies, the Accounts must distinguish between wider-range, narrow-range and special range investments. Reference should be made to the recommendations of the Institute of Chartered Accountants in England and Wales concerning the accounting entries relating to trust accounts. Where the Act applies and the trustee of a trust fund has decided to apply the powers granted by the Act to invest in wider-range investments, it will be necessary to divide the trust fund capital account into a special-range part (if applicable), a narrower-range part and a wider-range part.

All assets (less liabilities attached thereto) coming within the special range should be earmarked and an amount equivalent to the total book value thereof transferred from the existing general capital account to an account for the special-range part. The Act does not require special-range property to be revalued but it may be decided to do so on the grounds of consistency of treatment between the three parts.

The remaining assets (for example, investments, mortgage loans and bank balances, but excluding any held on account of accumulated income) should be valued by a person qualified to do so and the book values adjusted accordingly. The balance remaining on the original capital account, after adjusting any differences on revaluation, will require to be divided equally between the narrower-range part and the wider-range part of the fund.

This division must be reflected by an allocation to the two

parts of the fund of all the revalued assets less liabilities. In making this allocation the following points should be borne in mind:

(*a*) those narrower-range investments which are intended to be retained should be allocated to the narrower-range part;

(*b*) liabilities should be allocated to that part which contains the assets from which they will be met or to which they are attached;

(*c*) it may be necessary to split a single holding or balance in order to achieve equality in value between the two parts, and

(*d*) the assets and liabilities should be clearly designated in the accounting records.

The following is an example of the capital account of a trust fund showing the effect of making the division:

		£
Balance immediately prior to division	..	45,000
Less Transfer to special-range part (representing book value of special-range property)		10,000
		35,000
Add Net difference on revaluation of remaining property		5,000
		40,000
Less Transfer to:	£	
Narrower-range part	20,000	
Wider-range part	20,000	
		£40,000

There will now be three parts as follows:

Capital Account					£
Special-range part					10,000
Narrower-range part					20,000
Wider-range part					20,000
					£50,000

Examples of net assets which might compose the various parts are as follows:

Special-range part	£	£
Freehold property at cost	7,000	
Household furniture at probate value ..	1,000	
Shares in a private company at probate value	4,000	
	12,000	
Less mortgage on freehold property ..	2,000	
		10,000
Narrower-range part		
Investments at the revaluation	16,000	
Loans on mortgage at the revaluation ..	3,500	
Balance at bank	500	
		20,000
Wider-range part		
Investments at the revaluation	17,000	
Debt due from brokers	1,000	
Balance at bank	2,500	
	20,500	
Less Creditors for expenses chargeable to capital	500	
		20,000
		£50,000

(a) Transactions after division

Once the division has been made between narrower-range and wider-range parts, the assets allocated to these parts remain separate and a transfer may only be made between the parts if compensated by a reverse transfer. This principle of segregation must be borne in mind in recording all capital transactions after the division; the use of separate columns in cash-books and ledgers may be appropriate.

Sales

Since the object of making the division will usually be to enable the trustee to invest in wider-range investments, the first transactions to be expected after division are the sale of some or all of the assets allocated to the wider-range part and re-investment in wider-range investments. The proceeds of any such sales however reinvested must remain in the wider-range part of the fund. Similarly, the proceeds of any subsequent sales of property in either part must remain in the part concerned. The balance on the capital account of that part should be adjusted for any difference between the net proceeds and the book value of the assets sold.

Purchases

Purchases of investments in either the narrower- or wider-range parts can only be made with funds available in the same part, although funds can sometimes be made available from the other part by means of a compensating transfer.

Accretions (*other than special-range property*)

Where property (other than dividends or interest) accruing to a trust fund arises from property in either the narrower- or wider-range parts, it must be treated as belonging to the part of the fund from which it arises. Examples are a free scrip issue and a cash bonus on conversion of a government security.

In the case of a rights issue, the proceeds of sale of the 'rights' belong to the same part of the fund as the original holding. Where the 'rights' are taken up, the transaction is treated as a purchase by the part of the fund from which the payment is made.

Accruals to a trust fund which do not arise from assets in any part must be apportioned between the narrower- and wider-range parts so that each is increased by the same amount. It may be necessary to make realisations or transfers to achieve this. One example is the capital portion of a reversionary interest falling into possession.

Where dividends or interest are required to be added to the capital of a trust fund they must be apportioned equally between the narrower- and wider-range parts irrespective of the part of the fund from which the income arose.

Balances of income retained by a trustee may be invested in narrower-range investments, but if wider-range investments are to be held it will be necessary to form a separate income fund to be divided equally into narrower- and wider-range parts. It is important that an income fund should not be merged with the original capital fund unless it is held on identical trusts, but that a separate fund should be opened, the investments of which will require to be segregated from the remainder of the trust property.

Withdrawals

When the trustee has exercised his discretion under Section 2 (4) of the Act as to the part or parts of the fund out of which property is to be taken, the capital accounts will be debited accordingly. There is no necessity for compensating transfers in such cases.

Compensating transfers

In some circumstances it may be necessary or desirable to make a transfer between the narrower- and wider-range parts. This can be done only if compensated by a transfer in the reverse direction of equal value at the time of transfer. The transfer will be recorded at the revised value and any difference adjusted on the capital account of the part of the fund from which the transfer is made.

Examples are:

(a) narrower-range investments may be held in the wider-range part which the trustee wishes to transfer to the narrower-range part in exchange for other investments held in the narrower-range part;

(b) investments in the narrower-range part may change their nature so as no longer to qualify as narrower-range investments, in which case they should be sold, or transferred to the wider-range part in exchange for cash or narrower-range investments held in the wider-range part of the fund;

(c) a narrower-range investment in the wider-range part may be exchanged for cash in the narrower-range part in order to allow the purchase of a wider-range investment in the wider-range part.

Special range

It should be borne in mind that the special-range part should not hold narrower-range investments. It is, however, possible to hold wider-range investments in the special-range part if they are held under special powers (including a power to postpone conversion).

Where special-range property is realised the proceeds, unless reinvested in the special range (if so permitted), must be transferred to the narrower- and wider-range parts in equal portions. Where the special powers permit the trustee to invest in special-range property, the capital required to make any such investment may be taken from either the narrower- or wider-range parts in such proportions as the trustee thinks fit, subject to the general need for diversification and suitability of investments. In all these cases the consequent entries will have to be made in the capital, asset and other accounts as appropriate.

(b) Presentation of accounts

For the period in which the division takes place the trust accounts should show details of the revaluations of the assets, the adjustment of book values and the division into the various parts.

Thereafter the trust accounts should show separately the balance on each part of the capital account (any movement in the balance thereon being explained) and appropriate details of the assets comprising each part.

In the following illustrations, the provisions of the Act are complied with in two cases. The first, on the occasion of the setting up of the trust, and the second, in connection with a trust for minors.

Illustration (1)

Hardcastle died on 30th November, 1969, possessed of the following property:

	Value for Estate Duty £
His freehold residence	10,000
Life Policies	21,000
Cash and Bank balance	10,905
Household furniture and effects	3,000
5,000 £1 Ordinary shares in Marlow & Diggory Ltd ..	15,000
20,000 5s. Ordinary shares in Holly and the Ivy Ltd ..	40,000
£10,000 3½% War Loan	4,420
	ex interest

Debts due at death amounted to £305 (including all taxation liabilities) and funeral expenses amounted to £90.

Hardcastle made the following bequests in his will, which contained no special powers as to investment, but specifically barred equitable apportionments:

(i) To his wife, his freehold residence, free of duty, together with the household furniture and effects.

(ii) To his son, Tony, and his daughter, Kate, £2,500 each.

(iii) To his executors and trustees, Sir Charles Marlow and Roger Lumpkin, £250 each.

He directed the residue to be held in trust for his wife during her lifetime, with remainder to Tony and Kate in equal shares.

The following transactions took place in the year ended 30th November, 1970:

1969

Dec.   1   Received half-year interest on £10,000 3½% War Loan.

1970

Feb. 28   Paid Estate Duty on realty and personalty.

Mar.   1   Paid debts due at death and funeral expenses.

     2   Received proceeds of life policies.

   29   Received dividend of 12%, less tax, for the year ended 31st January, 1970, on 5,000 shares in Marlow & Diggory Ltd.

Apr.   1   Sold shares in Marlow & Diggory Ltd for £23,000.

  30   Received final dividend for the year ended 31st December, 1969, of 40% less tax on the 20,000 shares in Holly and the Ivy Ltd, making with an interim dividend paid on 5th November, 1969, 60% for the year.

June   1   Received half-year's interest on £10,000 3½% War Loan.

July   1   The executors and trustees gave their assent to the specific bequests and paid the pecuniary legacies.

  15   The executors and trustees consulted you in order to enable them to take advantage of the powers of investment contained in the Trustee Investments Act 1961. Following your advice they divided the trust fund as required by the Act. For this purpose the following valuations were obtained:

20,000 5s. Ordinary shares in Holly and the Ivy
Ltd £48,000
£10,000 3½% War Loan £4,395

The Trustees sold 8,000 of the shares in Holly and the Ivy Ltd for £23,300 and then purchased the following narrower-range investments:

£10,000 3% Savings Bonds 1965–75   .. £18,080
£4,000 3% British Transport Guaranteed Stock
1968–73   ..   .. £3,000

They also placed £850 on deposit account with the Albo Bank Ltd, and invested £1,150 in the purchase of 500 £1 Ordinary shares in Gibberne Ltd.

Aug. 15 Received half-year's interest less tax on £10,000 3% Savings Bonds.

Oct. 1 Received half-year's interest less tax on £4,000 3% British Transport Stock.

Received interim dividend of 6% less tax on 12,000 Ordinary shares in Holly and the Ivy Ltd in respect of the year ended 31st December, 1970.

Paid to widow £400 on account of income.

The following accounts only have been written up since they explain the entries relating to the above transactions:

(a) the Capital Account;

(b) the Cash Book.

An Income Account for the year ended 30th November, 1970, and a Balance Sheet as at that date have been shown.

Capital Gains tax and expenses on the purchases and sales of investments are to be ignored. The standard rate of income tax is taken at 10s. in the £.

ESTATE CAPITAL ACCOUNT

1969		£	£	1969		£
Nov. 30	Debts due at death ..		305	Nov. 30	Freehold Residence	10,00
	Funeral expenses ..		90		Life Policies	21,00
	Balance c/d:				Cash and Bank Balances	10,90
	Realty	10,000			Household Furniture and Effects	3,00
	Personalty	94,000			5,000 £1 Ordinary Shares in Marlow & Diggory Ltd	15,00
			104,000		20,000 5s. Ordinary Shares in Holly and the Ivy Ltd	40,00
					£10,000 3½% War Loan ex interest	4,42
					Add half-year's interest less tax..	7
			£104,395			£104,39
1970			£	1969		£
Feb. 28	Estate Duty:			Nov. 30	Balance b/d	104,00
	Personalty	4,763		1970		
	Realty	44,963		April 1	Profit on sale of shares in Marlow & Diggory Ltd	8,25
July 1	Specific bequests to Widow:			July 15	Profit on revaluation of shares in Holly and the Ivy Ltd for purposes of Trustee Investments Act, 1961	8,87
	Freehold Residence ..	10,000				
	Household Furniture ..	3,000				
	Legacies:					
	Tony	2,500				
	Kate	2,500				
	Executors	500				
July 15	Loss on revaluation of War Loan for purposes of Trustee Investments Act, 1961	7				
	Balance c/f:					
	Narrower-range Part ..	26,446				
	Wider-range Part ..	26,446				
			£121,125			£121,12

CASH BOOK

		Income	Capital			Income	Capital
		£	£			£	£
1969 Nov. 30	Estate Capital A/c ..		10,905	1969 Feb. 28	Estate Duty on: Realty £10,000.. .. Personalty £94,000 ..		4,763 44,963
Dec. 1	½-year's Interest (gross) on £10,000 3½% War Loan		175		Interest on Personality 2% × £44,963 for 3 months	221	
1970 Mar. 2	Life Policies		21,000	Mar. 1	Debts		305
29	Dividend on 5,000 £1 shares in Marlow and Diggory Ltd for year ended 31.1.70, 12% less tax £300—				Funeral expenses ..		90
	Capital 10 months ..		250	July 1	Legacies: Tony .. .. .. Kate .. .. .. Executors		2,500 2,500 500
	Income 2 months ..	50		July 15	Balance c/d	129	584
April 1	Sale of shares in Marlow and Diggory Ltd ..		23,000				
30	Final dividend for year to 31.12.69 on 20,000 5s. shares in Holly and the Ivy Ltd, less tax £1,000 *Add* interim dividend received 5.11.69 .. 500						
	£1,500						
	Capital 11 months .. £1,375 *Less* interim .. 500		875				
	Income 1 month ..	125					
June 1	½-year's Interest (gross) on £10,000 3½% War Loan	175					
		£350	£56,205			£350	£56,205

		Income	Capital			Income	Capital
		£	£			£	£
1970 July 15	Balance b/d	129	584	1970 July 15	Purchase of: £10,000 3% Savings Bonds		18,080
	Sale of 8,000 shares in Holly and the Ivy Ltd		23,300		£4,000 3% British Transport Stock ..		3,000
Aug. 15	½-year's interest, less tax on £10,000 3% Savings Bonds	75			Transfer to Deposit Account		850
					500 shares in Gibberne Ltd		1,150
Oct. 1	½-year's interest, less tax on £4,000 3% British Transport	30		Oct. 1	Widow, on account ..	400	
	Interim Dividend on 12,000 5s. shares in Holly and the Ivy Ltd, less tax	360			Balance c/f	194	804
		£594	£23,884			£594	£23,884

ESTATE OF HARDCASTLE DECEASED
BALANCE SHEET AT 30TH NOVEMBER, 1970

	£	£		£	£
ESTATE CAPITAL ACCOUNT			INVESTMENT AND CASH ON CAPITAL ACCOUNT		
Narrower-range Part	26,446		Narrower-range Part:		
Wider-range Part	26,446		£10,000 3½% War Loan at		
		52,892	valuation on 15.7.68 ..	4,395	
			£10,000 3% Savings Bonds		
ESTATE INCOME ACCOUNT	594		1965 – 75 at cost	18,080	
Less Provision for Income Tax			£4,000 3% British Transport		
on War Loan Interest ..	87		Guaranteed Stock 1968 – 73		
			at cost	3,000	
	507		Balance on Deposit with Albo		
Less Payment to Widow on Ac-			Bank Ltd	850	
count	400		Cash	121	26,446
		107			
Income Tax payable		175	Wider-range Part:		
			12,000 5s. Ordinary shares in		
			Holly and the Ivy Ltd at		
			balance of valuation on		
			15.7.70	24,700	
			500 £1 Ordinary shares in Gib-		
			berne Ltd at cost	1,150	
			Cash	596	
					26,446
					52,892
			Cash on Income Account ..	107	
			Cash retained to meet income		
			tax liability:		
			Capital £87		
			Income £88		
			—	175	
					282
		£53,174			£53,174

Notes:

(1) The valuation of the estate at 15th July, 1970, was: £

    Cash on Capital Account 584

        Less retained for Schedule D, Case III, liability on
£140 3½% War Loan interest apportioned to
capital 87

                                        497

£10,000 3½% War Loan 4,395

£20,000 5s. Ordinary shares in Holly and the Ivy Ltd .. 48,000

                                        £52,892

            Narrower-range £26,446
            Wider-range £26,446

Subsequent profit on sale of shares ignored, but could credit wider-range Capital Account.

(2) The cash remaining on capital account after the purchase and sale of investments for the purpose of the division under the Trustee Investments Act, 1961, and the Schedule D, Case III, liability of £87 amounts to £717. Of this, £121 is attributable to the Narrower-range Investments and £596 to the Wider-range Investments.

(3) The profits and loss on sale or revaluation of investments are:

		3½% War Loan £		Shares in Marlow & Diggory Ltd £		Shares in Holly and the Ivy Ltd £
Value for Estate Duty ..	£4,420			15,000		40,000
Add ½-year's interest ..	70	4,490				
Interest on dividends credited to capital	175			250		875
Less Provision for income tax	87	88				
		4,402		14,750		39,125
Proceeds or valuation ..		4,395		23,000		48,000
	(Loss)	£7	(Profit)	£8,250	(Profit)	£8,875

(4) Since the War Loan was quoted ex-interest at the date of death, the full half-year's interest due on 1st December must be brought into account for Estate Duty purposes.

(5) Under the Trustee Investments Act 1961, not more than one-half of the trust fund may be invested in the Wider-range Investments, and before any such investment is made, the fund must be divided into two parts of equal value at the date of the division. If necessary, a compensating transfer must then be made to give effect to the division of the fund into Narrower-range and Wider-range Investments.

(6) Of the £360 interim dividend on the shares in Holly and the Ivy Ltd on 1st October, only eleven-twelfths thereof, £330, has accrued to the date of the Balance Sheet. However, in view of the accrued income on the other securities, the trustees would appear to have been justified in paying the life tenant £400 on account of income generally.

Illustration (2)

George and Henry, both minors, are the beneficiaries of a trust established by their father's will. The will directed the trustees to retain the two freehold properties until such time as, in their absolute discretion, they could advantageously sell them. The trust fund has been divided into identifiable parts under the provisions of Section 2 of the Trustee Investments Act 1961. The Balance Sheet of the trust as on 31st December, includes the following figures relating to capital:

Investments and Property at cost or probate value:

	£	£
Narrower-range:		
U.K. Government Stocks	18,000	
Local Authority Loan	2,000	
		20,000
Wider-range:		
8,000 Ordinary shares of £1 each in Orion Ltd..		20,000
Special-range:		
Freehold property – Bath	15,000	
Freehold property – Bristol	15,000	
		30,000
		£70,000

During the half-year ended subsequent 30th June, the trustees' transactions on capital account comprised, in order of date:

(1) Realisation of freehold property at Bristol: net proceeds of sale £18,000.

(2) Purchase of 2,000 new shares in Orion Ltd for £3,500 under 'rights' issue.

(3) Receipt of £1,500 on sale of bonus issue in respect of holding of shares in Orion Ltd.

(4) Subscription of £16,000 for new U.K. Government Stock issue.

You are required:

(a) to write up the trust Capital Account for the half-year ended 30th June, in separate columns representing the three ranges of capital; and

(b) to list the book amounts of the assets as on 30th June, under the headings of the three ranges of investments.

The following entries are made on the basis of the principles set out in (1) to (3) below:

(1) By Section 3 of the Trustee Investments Act 1961, on the conversion of special-range property into other property, transfers must be made so that the narrower-range part and the wider-range part are each increased by the same amount.

(2) The profits arising from the sales are treated as belonging to the parts of the fund out of the property of which they have respectively accrued, viz. the profit on the property to the special-range part and the sale of bonus shares to the wider-range part.

(3) The shares acquired in consideration of a money payment is treated as an investment, not as an accrual of property to the fund.

(a)   TRUST CAPITAL ACCOUNT

		Narrower-range Part	Wider-range Part	Special-range Part			Narrower-range Part	Wider-range Part	Special-range Part
		£	£	£			£	£	£
June 30	Narrow-range and Wider-range parts – transfer ..			18,000	Jan. 1	Balance b/f ..	20,000	20,000	30,000
	Balance c/f ..	29,000	30,500	15,000	June 30	Freehold property, Bristol – book surplus on sale ..			3,000
						Orion Ltd – Ordinary shares account – sale of bonus shares..		1,500	
						Special-range part, transfer..	9,000	9,000	
		£29,000	£30,500	£33,000			£29,000	£30,500	£33,000

(b) ASSETS AS ON 30TH JUNE

		Narrower-range £	PARTS Wider-range £	Special-range £
U.K. Government Stocks	.. ..	27,000	7,000	
Local Authority Loan ..	.. ..	2,000		
Orion Ltd Ordinary shares	.. ..		23,500	
Freehold property – Bath	.. ..			15,000
		£29,000	£30,500	£15,000

WORKINGS

				£
Proceeds of Sale of Bristol Property ..	..	..	..	18,000
Proceeds of Sale of Bonus Shares	..	..	..	1,500
				£19,500

	Application: £	Narrower-range £	Wider-range £
Purchase of 1,000 Shares in Orion Ltd	3,500		3,500
Subscription for new U.K. Government Stock	16,000	9,000	7,000
	£19,500	£9,000	£10,500

INVESTIGATION AND AUDIT OF EXECUTORS AND TRUSTEES ACCOUNTS

§ 29. Investigation under the Public Trustee Act 1906

(a) The Public Trustee and his powers

The object of the legislature in creating the office of public trustee was to establish a public department of the state to which the administration of trusts could be committed by those persons who were not desirous of appointing private individuals as trustees or executors.

The public trustee is a corporation sole with perpetual succession and a common seal (Public Trustee Act 1906, s. 1);

and the Consolidated Fund of the United Kingdom is liable to make good any liability which the public trustee, if he were a private trustee, would be liable to discharge (*ibid*. s. 7).

The powers of the public trustee under the Public Trustee Act 1906 are very wide, and he may *inter alia* act as executor, administrator, trustee or custodian trustee (*ibid*. ss. 3–6, 15); and he can also upon application order an investigation of the accounts of any trust (*ibid*. s. 13). He is also constituted a trust corporation (Judicature Act 1925, s. 175 (1)) which enables him to act as a sole trustee or jointly with other trustees. In the case of an estate of less value than £1,000, the public trustee, on the application by any person who is entitled to an order for administration must, in the absence of good reason for refusing, administer the estate.

(b) Administration by the Public Trustee

Before the passing of the Public Trustee Act 1906, the only method by which it was possible to obtain an investigation of a trust was by taking legal action against the trustees, in the course of which the taking of an account could be ordered. This method is still available, and is conducted by the master or registrar of the court in the presence of the parties. Upon the completion of the taking of the account, payment of any sum certified by the master or registrar to be due to the estate can be immediately enforced.

Under the Public Trustee Act 1906 it is provided that any person who could apply to the court for the administration of the estate by the court, can apply to the public trustee if the gross capital value of the estate is less than £1,000; and if application is made to the court for administration of a small estate, the court may order that it shall be administered by the public trustee (*ibid*. § 3). For the purposes of such administration the public trustee has the power and authorities exercisable by a master of the Supreme Court acting in the administration of an estate (Public Trustee Rules 1912, R. 14).

(c) Audit under the Act

The Public Trustee Act 1906, however, affords machinery for the investigation and audit of the accounts of any trust on the application of any trustee or beneficiary, and its provisions can be applied to any trust, and not only to trusts in connection with which the public trustee may be acting. The Act does not make an audit compulsory, but it enables interested parties to obtain an investigation or audit in a proper case without taking the matter into court for administration.

Section 13 of the Act contains the regulations as to the appointment, duties, and remuneration of the auditor, and is as follows:

13. (1) Subject to rules under this Act, and unless the court otherwise orders, the condition and accounts of any trust shall on an application being made and notice thereof given in the prescribed manner by any trustee or beneficiary, be investigated and audited by such solicitor or public accountant as may be agreed on by the applicant and the trustees, or, in default of agreement, by the public trustee or some person appointed by him: provided that (except with the leave of the court) such an investigation or audit shall not be required within twelve months after any such previous investigation or audit, and that a trustee or beneficiary shall not be appointed under this section to make an investigation or audit.

(2) The person making the investigation or audit (hereinafter called the auditor) shall have a right of access to the books, accounts, and vouchers of the trustees, and to any securities and documents of title held by them on account of the trust, and may require from them such information and explanation as may be necessary for the performance of his duties: and upon the completion of the investigation and audit shall forward to the applicant and to every trustee a copy of the accounts, together with a report thereon, and a certificate signed by him to the effect that the accounts exhibit a true view of the state of the affairs of the trust, and that he has had the securities of the trust fund investments produced to and verified by him, or (as the case may be) that such accounts are deficient in such respects as may be specified in such certificate.

(3) Every beneficiary under the trust shall, subject to rules under this Act, be entitled at all reasonable times to inspect and take copies of the accounts, report, and certificate, and, at his own expense, to be furnished with copies thereof, or extracts therefrom.

(4) The auditor may be removed by the order of the court, and if any auditor is removed, or resigns, or dies, or becomes bankrupt, or incapable of acting before the investigation and audit is completed, a new auditor may be appointed in his place in like manner as the original auditor.

(5) The remuneration of the auditor and the other expenses of the investigation and audit shall be such as may be prescribed by rules under this Act, and shall, unless the public trustee otherwise directs, be borne by the estate: and, in the event of the public trustee so directing, he may order that such expenses be borne by the applicant or by the trustees personally, or partly by them and partly by the applicant.

(6) If any person having the custody of any documents to which the auditor has a right of access under this section fails or refuses to allow him to have access thereto, or in any wise obstructs the investigation or audit, the auditor may apply to the court, and thereupon the court shall make such order as it thinks just.

(7) Subject to rules of court, applications under or for the purposes of this section to the High Court shall be made to a judge of the Chancery Division in chambers.

(8) If any person in any statement of accounts, report, or certificate required for the purposes of this section wilfully makes a statement false in any material particular, he shall be liable on conviction on indictment to imprisonment for a term not exceeding two years, and on summary conviction to imprisonment for a term not exceeding six months, with or without hard labour, and in either case to a fine in lieu of or in addition to such imprisonment.

The following are the provisions contained in the Public Trustee Rules 1912:

31. Any application under Section 13 (1) of the Act shall be made to the public trustee, and notice thereof shall (unless the public trustee otherwise directs) be given by the applicant to every other person being a trustee or beneficiary under the trust.

32. (1) Upon receiving any such application the public trustee may in his absolute discretion by notice to the applicant require that before a day to be specified in the notice such security (by deposit of a sum of money) as he shall deem sufficient shall be given to him by the applicant for the payment of any expenses of the investigation and audit which may be ordered by the public trustee to be paid by the applicant personally.

(2) Where any such requirement is made no further proceedings shall be taken upon the application until the security has been given and if the same is not given before the day specified in the notice the application shall be disallowed unless under special circumstances the public trustee thinks fit to extend the time for giving the security or to dispense therewith.

(3) Any sum so deposited shall be kept by the public trustee on deposit in his name and to a separate account at a bank until all proceedings in connection with the investigation and audit have been concluded, and thereupon the deposited sum and the interest (if any) allowed thereon by the bank shall be applied in or towards payment of any expenses of the investigation and audit which may be so ordered to be paid by the applicant personally and the balance (if any) shall be paid to the applicant.

33. The public trustee may in his absolute discretion upon the application of any trustee or beneficiary direct that the investigation and audit shall extend only to a specified period of time or to a specified part of the trust property or shall be otherwise restricted.

34. If within one month from the date of the application under Section 13 (1) of the Act no solicitor or public accountant shall have been appointed by the applicant and the trustees to conduct the investigation and audit, there shall be deemed to be a default of agreement within the meaning of the said Section 13 (1) and the applicant may apply to the public trustee accordingly.

35. The remuneration of the auditor and the other expenses of the investigation and audit shall be such as may be determined by the public trustee. Provided that the public trustee may refer the costs of any solicitor (being part of such expenses) for taxation to a taxing master of the Supreme Court, and in such case the amount of the said costs when taxed shall be included in such expenses.

36. (1) Where any investigation or audit has been made, copies of the report and certificate of the auditor under Section 13 (2) of the Act and such copies of accounts and other documents as the public trustee may require shall be forwarded to him by the auditor, and shall be considered by the public trustee before giving any direction or making any order under Section 13 (5) of the Act.

(2) The expense of making and forwarding any such copies as aforesaid and the fee of the public trustee (within the limits prescribed by or in pursuance of any order relating to the fees of the public trustee for the time being in force) shall for the purpose of Section 13 (5) of the Act be part of the expenses of the investigation and audit.

37. (1) Before making any order under Section 13 (5) of the Act the public trustee shall, if any of the parties interested so desire, hear the said parties in such manner as he shall think fit.

(2) Any such order shall specify the person by or to whom any sum is to be paid and the amount of such sum provided that such an order may direct payment of the taxed costs of any solicitor employed in connection with the investigation and audit, and such costs shall be taxed by a taxing master of the Supreme Court, and the amount of such costs when taxed shall be paid as if such amount had been specified in the order.

(3) Any such order may be enforced in the same manner as a judgment or order of the court to the same effect.

A trustee required to produce books or documents to the person appointed to make an investigation cannot make terms before doing so (*Re Williams*).

An appeal lies to the court from any order of the public trustee given in non-administrative matters (*Re Oddy* (1911)).

Trustees may in their absolute discretion, from time to time, but not more than once in every three years, unless the nature of the trust or any special dealings with the trust property make a more frequent exercise of the right reasonable, cause the account of the trust property to be examined or audited by an independent accountant. They must, for that purpose, produce such vouchers and give such information to him as he may require. The costs of the examination or audit, including the fee of the auditor, are to be paid out of capital or income, or partly in one way and partly in the other, as the trustees in their absolute discretion think fit, but in default of any directions by the trustees to the contrary in any special case, costs attributable to capital are to be borne by capital, and those attributable to income by income (Trustee Act 1925, s. 22 (4)).

The limitation of the trustees' power to have the accounts audited, except in special circumstances, at more frequent intervals than once in every three years, does not appear in any way to prevent a beneficiary applying to the court or to the public trustee (when the latter is not himself the trustee) for an audit to be conducted, in accordance with the existing practice, when the circumstances justify the application.

§ 30. Programme of the Audit of Trust Accounts

The audit of trust accounts on behalf of executors and trustees or beneficiaries, or either of them, will vary according to the particular circumstances of the case; but the following programme, with such modifications as may be necessary, will be found sufficient in most instances for an audit made either under the Public Trustee Act 1906, under the Trustee Act 1925, s. 22 (4), or voluntarily by consent of the parties:

(1) Examine the will, and carefully note the instructions of the deceased with relation to:

(*a*) any property specifically mentioned;

(*b*) directions as to general, specific, or demonstrative legacies;

(*c*) distribution of residue (if any);

(*d*) authority of executors to invest in other than trustee investments, or to retain or postpone conversion of existing investments;

(*e*) general directions as to carrying on the business (if any) of the deceased;

(*f*) directions as to any debts of the deceased not legally enforceable;

    (g) instructions as to how annuities (if any) are to be treated, whether by purchase or by payment out of income;

    (h) creation of special trusts for minors or others, and investments to be made thereunder;

    (i) the allocation of specific property for payment of debts (if any).

If there is an epitome of the will entered in the books, see that it is a proper extract thereof.

(2) Examine the private books of account belonging to the deceased, together with all papers and documents relating to the estate.

(3) Examine the Estate Duty Account and Corrective Accounts (if any) for Estate Duty, seeing that all assets and liabilities the existence of which is known are properly included.

(4) Vouch the opening entries relating to the original assets and liabilities, with the Estate Duty Account.

(5) When investments at the date of death are quoted *cum div.*, see that the accruing dividend is not brought into the Estate Duty Account in addition to the price.

(6) Vouch the Cash Book.

Receipts: Verify by reference to the following documents:

    (a) For sale of investments, brokers' sold notes.

    (b) For sale or property by auction or private treaty, auctioneers' accounts, solicitors' letters, etc.

    (c) Dividends, interest, etc., from counterfoils of dividend and interest warrants, reference to documents of title, etc.

    (d) Rents, from the counterfoils of the Rents Receipt Book (*see* also (10) below).

    (e) Debts due to testator, from the correspondence, and any other evidence available.

Payments: Verify by reference to the following documents:

    (a) For purchase of investments, brokers' bought notes.

    (b) For Estate Duty, the probate of the will.

    (c) For other payments, the usual vouchers.

(*d*) For payments to annuitants and beneficiaries, legal receipts or paid cheques.

(7) See that all income that ought to have been received has been received, and enquire into outstandings (if any).

(8) See that all apportionments necessary under the Apportionment Act 1870, or by case law, have been properly made.

(9) Cast the Cash Book, check in detail and reconcile with bank statements.

(10) If a Rent Roll is kept, examine it with the counterparts of tenants' leases and agreements. Check:

(*a*) particulars of property;

(*b*) annual rental;

(*c*) dates of payments thereof;

(*d*) treatment of repairs.

Check allowances for repairs, etc. See copy of the authority given by the deceased or his executor for the execution of repairs, etc. Enquire carefully into arrears, as to whether they are genuine, and will be received in due course.

(11) If the business of the deceased is being carried on by the executors, either in accordance with the instructions in the will, or for the purpose of being wound up, accounts will have been taken at date of death, which will be examined by the auditors, and the accounts of the executors in relation to carrying on the business will be subjected to the usual audit.

(12) See that all investments are in accordance with the terms of the will, or are trustee investments and have been appropriated, if relevant, as narrow-, wider- or special-range investments, and that all bonus shares receivable, rights issues and similar matters arising from the investments have been properly dealt with.

(13) See that no *devastavit* has been committed in respect of capital.

(14) See that the distribution of the estate follows the will.

(15) If any specific trusts are created under the will, see that these are properly recorded in the books, and the specific investments made in respect thereof duly ear-marked. If

the trust is on behalf of minors, see that the income arising therefrom is dealt with in accordance with either the will, or the directions of the court, as the case may be.

(16) Obtain certificate from the bank as to bank balances, and verify the existence of the investments, title deeds, etc., taking care that these are all produced at the same time. Where investments are registered in the name of the sole executor, obtain written acknowledgment from him that he holds on behalf of the estate or trust free of charge or encumbrance.

(17) Check all casts and postings in Journal, Cash Book, and Ledger.

(18) Check Income Account, seeing that no income has been brought into account that has not been received.

(19) Check the Balance Sheet and Schedule of Investments, etc.

(20) If appointed under Section 13 of the Public Trustee Act 1906, the auditor must forward to the party applying for his appointment, and to every trustee, a copy of the accounts, duly certified by him, together with a report thereon. The form of the certificate will be as follows:

'I hereby certify that the above accounts exhibit a true and fair view of the state of the affairs of the.... Trust, and that I have had the securities of the trust fund investments produced to me, and that I have verified the same',

or will give particulars of any matters in respect of which the accounts are incorrect, or the production of securities deficient.

Copies of the report and certificate of the auditor must be forwarded to the Public Trustee, together with such copies of the accounts and other documents as he may require.

§ 31. Capital Gains tax and Trustees

The provisions relating to Capital Gains tax on trustees have been briefly dealt with in an earlier part of this work. In so far as trustees are concerned, the setting up of a trust is an acquisition and the cessation of the trust is a disposal. In the interim period between those dates the trustees will be liable at 30 per cent. on any capital gains and at normal Income tax rates on any short-term gains assessable under Schedule D, Case VII. The alternative charge basis appropriate to an individual and set out in Section 21, Finance Act 1965, does not apply to trustees.

Changes in trustees do not give rise to either Capital Gains tax or Schedule D, Case VII, liabilities, since the trustees of a settlement are treated as a continuing body of persons.

As already mentioned, the provisions of Schedule D, Case VII, will apply on any chargeable gain which arises where the acquisition and disposal are within twelve months of each other and where the provisions of that Case do not specifically exempt the transaction from liability. Such liability will arise regardless of whether there are life interests or discretionary interests and whether or not the income is accumulated. For Capital Gains tax purposes, however, the distinction is of importance since in the case of accumulating and discretionary trusts the assets of the trusts have to be re-valued every fifteen years and Capital Gains tax paid on the deemed gain.

For Capital Gains tax purposes a life interest in relation to a settlement:

(a) includes a right under the settlement to the income of or the use or occupation of, settled property for the life of a person other than the person entitled to the right or for lives;

(b) does not include any right which is contingent on the exercise of the discretion of the trustee or the discretion of some other person; and

(c) does not include an annuity notwithstanding that the annuity is payable out of or charged on settled property or the income of settled property.

This work is not the place in which to discuss the many complicated provisions relating to Capital Gains tax and trusts. Full details will be found in Chapter 11 of *Capital Gains Tax* by the author. Two points do arise, however, in connection with Estate Duty and Capital Gains tax in so far as they affect trustees. Where the trust comes to an end on the death of a beneficiary due to some other person becoming absolutely entitled to the assets of the trust, the trustees are deemed to have disposed of and immediately re-acquired all the assets forming part of the settled property for a consideration equal to their market value. Consequently there will be chargeable gains assessable on the trustees by reason of the death before 31st March, 1971. In such cases the trustees may claim relief against the chargeable gains so arising if the executors of the deceased person do not need to claim the whole of the exemption of £5,000 to which a person becomes entitled on his death. Section 24, Finance Act 1965, provides that the gains arising on a deemed disposal on death shall only be assessed to the extent that the gains exceed £5,000 and then only on the excess. Section 25 provides that, to the extent that relief cannot be given on £5,000 of gain in computing the tax on the deceased's free estate, the trustee of any settled property by reason of the death. Where there is more than one trust the amount of the relief is to be apportioned according to the respective aggregates of the chargeable gains (less allowable losses) which accrue to those trustees respectively on the death. This latter provision applies in respect of deaths after 5th April, 1969. For deaths before that date the apportionment is according to the respective values of the settled property. If the deceased had obtained retirement relief so that the relief under Section 24 was lower than £5,000 then the amount available to the trustees is similarly reduced.

APPENDIX I

LEGACY DUTY AND SUCCESSION DUTY

(a) Former charge of Legacy Duty and Succession Duty

In connection with deaths and certain other events occurring before 30th July, 1949, legacy duty or succession duty was chargeable (with exceptions) on the value of benefits received by legatees and successors, at rates depending on their relationship to the testator, intestate or predecessor.

Legacy duty was chargeable on pure personalty and leaseholds given on trust for sale, devolving under a will or on an intestacy or as a donation *mortis causa*. It was chargeable not only on immediate benefits so derived, but also on benefits in remainder, such as those falling into possession on the death of a life tenant under the will or intestacy. It applied not only to specific, pecuniary and demonstrative legacies, but also to gifts of residue and property undisposed of by will. Life and other limited interests, as well as absolute interests, attracted the duty.

Succession duty was chargeable on land, both freehold and leasehold (except leaseholds given by will on trust for sale) devolving under a will or on an intestacy. It was also chargeable on all benefits derived otherwise than under a will or on an intestacy, such as benefits under a settlement *inter vivos*, whether of land or pure personalty. No benefit arising in respect of any one death was chargeable with both legacy and succession duty; only one of the two duties was payable. While there were numerous differences in detail between the two duties, they were similar in general principle and can be considered together.

(b) Rates of Legacy Duty and Succession Duty

The rate of legacy duty was determined by the relationship of the beneficiary to the testator or intestate. The relationship of the beneficiary to a deceased life tenant or anyone else was immaterial, if that deceased was a different person from the testator or intestate. For example, if a testator by will bequeathed pure personalty to his brother for life and then to his brother's son, the duty to be borne by the brother's son on his remainder would be at the rate applying to his relationship of nephew to the testator, not of son to the life tenant.

The rate of succession duty was determined by the relationship of the successor to the predecessor. The 'successor' was the person whose interest attracted the duty; the 'predecessor' was the person from whom the interest of the successor was derived. Thus, in the case of land devolving under a will or on an intestacy, the predecessor was the testator or intestate; in the case of property devolving under a settlement *inter vivos*, the settlor. Relationship of the successor to a life tenant (who was not also the predecessor) or any one else was immaterial, as in the case of legacy duty.

566

The scale of rates of duty in force in relation to any particular legacy or succession depended, in the case of legacy duty, or of succession duty on land devolving under a will or on an intestacy, on the date when the testator or intestate died; in the case of succession duty on benefits derived otherwise than under a will or on an intestacy, on the date when the first succession arose, i.e. usually on the date of death of the first life tenant under the settlement. When those events occurred on or before 29th April, 1909, the scale was that fixed for legacy duty by the Stamp Act 1815, and for succession duty by the Succession Duty Act 1853. The old scale is not considered of sufficient importance to be shown here, but it may still come into point, as will appear hereafter, in those increasingly rare cases in which the death of the testator or intestate, or the first death under the settlement, occurred in those early days, and the next death in relation to the settled property occurred in the nineteen-forties.

When the events above referred to occurred after 29th April, 1909, but before 16th April, 1947, the scale shown below in the second column applied.

When the events occurred on or after 16th April, 1947, but before 30th July, 1949, the scale shown below in the third column applied. It will be seen that the rates during that period were doubled, except in the case of legacies or successions for charitable or public purposes. The Finance Act 1947 not only doubled the rates for testators or intestates dying, or first successions arising, on or after 16th April, 1947, for it also doubled the rates if legacy duty or succession duty became payable by reason of the death of a life tenant or annuitant (or for certain other reasons) between those dates, notwithstanding that the testator or intestate had died, or the first succession had arisen, earlier. This matter is dealt with further in paragraph (d) of this Appendix.

Relationship of beneficiary to testator, intestate or predecessor	Testator or intestate died, or first succession arose, between 30th April, 1909, and 15th April, 1947 (inclusive)	Testator or intestate died, or first succession arose, between 16th April, 1947, and 29th July, 1949 (inclusive)
Husband, wife, lineal descendants (i.e. children, etc.) or lineal ancestors (i.e. parents, etc.)	1%	2%
Brothers and sisters and their descendants (i.e. nephews, nieces, etc.)	5%	10%
Beneficiaries for public or charitable purposes	10%	10%
Any other relations (e.g. uncles, aunts, and more remote relations) and strangers in blood	10%	20%

Relations of the half blood counted as relations of the whole blood.

A beneficiary such as a son-in-law who had married a relation of the testator, intestate or predecessor was liable at the rate for that relation, but there was no reduction for a beneficiary such as a step-child who was related to a person whom the testator, etc., had married. A divorced wife or husband of the testator, etc., was treated as a stranger in blood, but not so a divorced spouse of a relation. Legitimate and legitimated children and persons adopted under the Adoption of Children Act 1926 paid at the lowest rates; an illegitimate child was treated as related to his mother (as from 13th July, 1944), but to no one else.

Higher rates of succession duty were payable in cases where the property had escaped Estate Duty, but such cases were too rare to merit attention now.

(c)   Exemptions from Legacy Duty and Succession Duty

There were numerous exemptions from legacy duty and succession duty, most of which related to legacies or successions of small value. There was, however, one important exemption of frequent occurrence, which should be carefully borne in mind.

Where the principal value of the property passing on the death of the deceased in respect of which estate duty was payable (other than property in which the deceased never had an interest, and property of which the deceased never was competent to dispose and which on his death passed to persons other than the husband or wife or a lineal ancestor or descendant of the deceased) did not exceed £15,000, whatever might have been the value of the legacy or succession, no legacy or succession duty was payable by husband, wife, lineal descendants or lineal ancestors (Finance (1909–10) Act 1910, s. 58 (2) (a)). The 'deceased' referred to was the testator, intestate, or the person on whose death the first succession arose.

It is to be observed that this exemption applied only to beneficiaries liable at the lowest rate (the 1% or 2% rate). It depended, not on the beneficiary's legacy or succession not exceeding £15,000 in value, but on the property attracting Estate Duty (with certain exceptions) not exceeding that figure.

Illustration (1)

A died in 1928, having by his will bequeathed an annuity of £100 a year to his brother for life, and subject thereto the whole of his estate to his wife for life and after her death to his children. His free estate was valued for Estate Duty at £14,000. The only other property attracting Estate Duty on his death was a fund of £10,000 of which he had been life tenant and which passed on his death to his nephew.

A's brother would pay legacy duty at 5 per cent. on the value of his annuity. A's wife and children would be exempt from legacy and succession duty, as the total value liable to Estate Duty (excluding the £10,000 fund of which A was never competent to dispose and which on his death did not pass to his wife or lineal ancestors or descendants) did not exceed £15,000.

Illustration (2)

The facts were as stated above, except that the £10,000 fund passed to A.'s children on his death. In this case his wife and children are not exempt from legacy duty (on pure personalty) and succession duty (on land) in respect of his free estate, because the dutiable property to be taken into account was valued at £24,000. Whether the children pay legacy duty or succession duty on the £10,000 fund depends upon whether their relationship to the testator, intestate or predecessor who settled the fund was a '1 per cent. rate', and if so whether the property passing on the death of the testator, intestate or first life tenant under a settlement *inter vivos* exceeded £15,000.

(d) Settled property

Where property was settled on persons in succession, and a charge to legacy duty or succession duty arose before 30th July, 1949, the rules as to payment of the duty depended on whether all the possible beneficiaries of the settled property were or were not liable at the same rate.

In the case of beneficiaries liable at different rates, or some liable and others not, each beneficiary was chargeable with duty on the value of his benefit as and when he became entitled to it. Thus, a life tenant would pay on the value of an annuity equal to the annual income from the property (calculated according to his age) and a remainderman would pay on the value of the capital when it fell in on the death of the life tenant.

In the case of beneficiaries liable at the same rate, duty was payable immediately at the appropriate rate on the capital value of the settled property and it was payable out of the capital. This payment covered the interests of all successive beneficiaries, and no more duty was payable so long as the property devolved under the settlement. An exception to this rule that no more duty was payable was created by the Finance Act 1947, for that Act provided that if any death or other event occurred on or after 16th April 1947 which would have given rise to a charge for duty on settled property but for the fact that it had previously been paid to cover the successive interests of beneficiaries all liable at the same rate, additional duty would be payable equal to the pre-existing rate (except in the case of beneficiaries for public or charitable purposes). For example, if a testator who died in 1936 had settled property on trust for his wife for life and after her death for his children, duty would have been paid in 1936 at 1 per cent. on the capital (assuming that the '£15,000 exemption' did not apply). On the death of the wife in 1948, an additional 1 per cent. would have been payable by the children on the capital coming to them, to make the rate up to the increased figure of 2 per cent. These provisions ceased to have effect in respect of deaths occurring on or after 30th July, 1949, when legacy and succession duties were abolished.

(e) Abolition of Legacy Duty and Succession Duty

No legacy duty or succession duty is payable on a legacy derived from a testator or intestate dying on or after 30th July, 1949, or on a succession conferred on or after that date. Moreover, no duty is payable on the death of a life tenant or an annuitant, or on any other event formerly attracting duty, occurring on or after that date, notwithstanding that the testator or intestate, or the first life tenant under a settlement *inter vivos*, may have died before that date (Finance Act 1949, s. 27). For example, if a testator, who died in 1936, bequeathed the residue of his estate to a cousin for life, and subject thereto to a nephew absolutely, the cousin would have paid legacy duty (on pure personalty) or sucession duty (on land) at 10 per cent. on the value of his life interest, but on the death of the cousin today, no legacy duty or succession duty would be payable by the nephew. He thus escaped the 5 per cent. duty which he would have been liable to pay had the cousin's death occurred before 16th April, 1947, or 10 per cent. if it had occurred between that date and 29th July, 1949. If the testator instead died to-day, no legacy duty or succession duty would be payable either by the cousin or by the nephew.

(*f*)   *Allowance for and Repayment of Legacy and Succession Duty*
Where legacy duty or succession duty has been paid in connection with a death before 30th July, 1949, on the capital of settled property to cover the successive interests of beneficiaries all liable at the same rate, and the interest of a beneficiary falls into possession by reason of a death or other event occurring on or after that date, no legacy duty or succession duty is payable on his interest. For one reason, the duty has already been satisfied by payment out of the capital; for another, the duties have been abolished. But it is apparent that, if no special provision were made, the beneficiary whose capital had borne duty in advance would find himself prejudiced, as compared with a beneficiary whose capital had not borne duty, for the former would gain no advantage by the abolition of the duties.

It is accordingly provided (Finance Act 1949, s. 29) that where legacy duty or succession duty has been so satisfied by payment on the capital, the *rate* of duty so paid shall be set in reduction of the *rate* of Estate Duty payable on the settled property on the death on or after 30th July, 1949, of a person not competent to dispose of the property. If the rate of legacy duty or succession duty so paid is higher than the rate of Estate Duty which would otherwise be payable, the Estate Duty is cancelled altogether, and the difference between the *amount* of legacy duty or succession duty paid and the *amount* of the Estate Duty which would otherwise be payable is to be repaid by the Commissioners of Inland Revenue.

Illustration (1)

A died in 1938, having by his will left all his property to his brother for life and then to his brother's son absolutely. The estate (after payment of debts, funeral and testamentary expenses and Estate Duty) amounted to £20,000. Legacy duty was paid thereon at 5 per cent. to satisfy the duty in respect of the interests of the brother and the nephew, both of whom were liable at the same rate. The brother died on 30th November, 1967, the fund then being worth £22,000. Assuming no aggregation on the brother's death, the rate of Estate Duty would be 15 per cent., but this was reduced to 10 per cent. by reason of the prior payment of legacy duty. The Estate Duty payable was therefore £2,200.

Illustration (2)

The facts are the same as illustrated above, except that the fund was valued at £5,000 at A's death (the legacy duty being £250) and at £6,500 at the brother's death. The rate of Estate Duty on the brother's death (assuming no aggregation) would be 2 per cent. (£130). Since the rate of 5 per cent. is greater than the rate of 2 per cent., no Estate Duty is payable, and a repayment of £120 (the difference between £250 and £130) is due.

The death which attracts the allowance or repayment is the first death on or after 30th July, 1949, on which Estate Duty becomes payable on the settled property. If the property is exempt from Estate Duty on that first death, no allowance is called for, nor will any repayment be made. Thus, if a testator died in 1938, having left all his property (exceeding £15,000 in value) to his wife for life and then to the children, legacy duty or succession duty would have been paid on the capital, but there would be no allowance or repayment on the death of the wife today, because the property is exempt from Estate Duty on her death.

A repayment of legacy duty or succession duty under the foregoing provisions is to be deemed an accretion to the fund out of which the duty was paid. Normally a settled fund used to bear its own legacy duty or succession duty, so that the repayment would be added to and devolve with the settled property. If, however, a settled legacy had been given by will free of duty, the duty would have been paid out of the residue of the testator's estate; in that event the repayment would belong to residue and not to the settled fund. A claim to repayment has to be made by the persons entitled; those persons will be the trustees of the fund to which the repayment is to an accretion, or if the fund has been vested in the beneficiaries, the beneficiaries or any of them or their executors may claim.

The principles explained above apply when the first death on or after 30th July, 1949, is that of an annuitant instead of a life tenant, and in that case it is the 'slice' of capital referable to the annuity which obtains the allowance of estate duty.

Illustration (3)

A died in 1938, having by his will left all his property to his nephew absolutely, subject to the payment of an annuity of £100 a year to his brother for life. The estate amounted to £20,000. Legacy duty was paid at 5 per cent. on £20,000 (£1,000) to satisfy the duty in respect of the interests of both brother and nephew. The brother died on 30th November, 1968, the fund being then worth £22,000 and producing an income of £700 a year. The 'slice' of capital set free by the cesser of the annuity is one-seventh of £22,000 = £3,143. Assuming that £10,000, the brother's free estate, is the only property aggregable, the rate of duty on the £3,143 would be 8 per cent., but it is to be reduced to 3 per cent. The rate of duty on the other property, the free estate of the brother, of course remains at 8 per cent.

If in the illustration shown above there had been no aggregation, so that the rate of duty on the brother's death was nil, a repayment of legacy duty would have been due. The position in that case is one of some doubt.

It would appear that only that part of the legacy duty of £1,000 paid which was proportionate to the slice of capital supporting the annuity would qualify for repayment.

A case for allowance or repayment of legacy duty or succession duty may arise whenever the duty has been paid on the capital to cover successive interests. The usual reason for such payment on the capital was liability of all beneficiaries at the same rate, as shown in the foregoing explanation, but it must be borne in mind that the same rules apply even if the payment on the capital was for other reasons. Other reasons are rare, but an instance would be where the duty had been commuted by arrangement with the Estate Duty Office in a case where the law did not call for payment on the capital.

APPENDIX II

DOUBLE TAXATION RELIEF AGREEMENTS – ESTATE DUTY

At the time of printing, June 1970, the following agreements are in force:

Canada ..	..	The Double Taxation Relief (Estate Duty) (Canada) Order 1946, S.R. & O. 1946	No. 1884
France ..	..	,, ,, ,, (France) Order 1963, S.I. 1963	No. 1319
India ..	..	,, ,, ,, (India) Order 1956, S.I. 1956	No. 998
Italy ..	..	,, ,, ,, (Italy) Order 1968, S.I. 1968	No. 304
Netherlands	..	,, ,, ,, (Netherlands) Order 1950, S.I. 1950	No. 1197
Pakistan	..	,, ,, ,, (Pakistan) Order 1957, S.I. 1957	No. 1522
South Africa	..	,, ,, ,, (South Africa) Order 1947, S.R. & O. 1947	No. 314
South Africa	..	,, ,, ,, (South Africa) Order, 1955 S.I. 1955	No. 424
Sweden ..	..	,, ,, ,, (Sweden) Order 1961, S.I. 1961	No. 578
Sweden ..	..	,, ,, ,, (Sweden) Order 1965, S.I. 1965	No. 599
Switzerland	..	,, ,, ,, (Switzerland) Order 1957, S.I. 1957	No. 426
United States of America	..	,, ,, ,, (U.S.A.) Order 1946, S.R. & O. 1946	No. 1351

There are also reciprocal arrangements with the Republic of Ireland – The Relief in respect of Double Taxation (Irish Free State) Declaration 1923 (S.R. & O. 1923, No. 406).

APPENDIX III
GLOSSARY
OF
TERMS, TRANSLATIONS AND DEFINITIONS

Abatement. A *pro rata* diminution of benefits, claims, rights or liabilities.

Accumulation. The continual increase of principal by the re-investment of interest. By s. 31, Trustee Act 1925, the income attributable to an infant beneficiary and not expended on his maintenance must be accumulated.

Ad Colligenda Bona Defuncti. For the purpose of collecting the property of the deceased. A form of grant of letters of administration made where the estate is of a perishable or precarious nature and a general grant cannot be made at once.

Ademption. The complete or partial failure of a specific legacy by some act or with the knowledge of the testator during his lifetime, whereby the subject matter of the legacy has ceased to exist or is fundamentally transformed, so that it no longer exists *in specie* as described in the will, e.g. the sale of the object specifically bequeathed; or its conversion into some other object, unless the thing is changed in name or form only and remains substantially the same.

Ademption by portion. The presumption that a portion (*q.v.*) advanced, e.g. on marriage, is intended to satisfy to the extent of the value of the portion a legacy left to the child by his parent.

Ad Litem. For the purposes of the action (litigation).

Administration. Dealing with the estate of a deceased person, i.e. collecting assets, paying the debts, and distributing any surplus amongst the persons entitled.

Administrator. An administrator is a person appointed by the court to administer the estate of an intestate, or of a testator where an executor has not been appointed, or if appointed, does not act.

Advancement. Advancement is a payment by a parent, during his lifetime, to a child of a portion of what that child would have been entitled to receive at the parent's death. It is also the term applied to a payment by trustees out of the capital of an estate to set up a beneficiary in life in accordance with the Trustee Act 1925, s. 32.

Ad Valorem. According to the value.

Advowson. The right of presentment to a church or an ecclesiastical benefice.

Affidavit. A sworn statement supported by oath administered by a Commissioner for Oaths, or a Registrar or certain other persons authorised to receive affidavits.

574

Aggregation. The conception of different parcels of property as forming one composite estate for the purpose of computing the rate of estate duty payable.

Agnati. Kindred by the father's side.

Ancillary Probate. A subordinate or ancillary grant, e.g. the re-sealing by the High Court of a grant made in a foreign country.

Animus Revocandi. The intention of revoking.

Animus Testandi. The intention of making a will.

Annuity. A sum certain payable annually. An annuity may be payable either for a given number of years or until the happening of a contingency, e.g. the death of the annuitant. It is called a rent charge if its payment is charged on real estate.

Apportionment. The process of dividing the benefit accruing out of property for the purpose of adjusting the rights of the persons concerned therein according to their interests.

Appointment. See Power of Appointment.

Appropriation. Making a thing the property of a person. The application of a particular fund or asset to satisfy a particular debt or legacy.

Assets. Rights and benefits in or over property, tangible or intangible, capable of pecuniary assessment and of legal assertion.

Attorn. To turn over, i.e. to transfer subjection from one person to another, e.g. to 'attorn tenant' is to agree to consider oneself as the tenant of one person where one was previously tenant of another.

Bequest. A gift by will.

Blood. Persons connected by blood relationship, i.e. descended from one or more common ancestors. Whole blood: descended from the same pair of ancestors; half-blood: descended from one common ancestor only.

Bona Vacantia. Property to which no person can claim title. Such property if susceptible of being owned, will vest in the Crown, Duchy of Lancaster, or Duke of Cornwall, according to its situation, e.g. property of an intestate who leaves no issue, spouse or next-of-kin.

Caeterorum. Of the remainder.

Capital. Capital, as used in connection with executorship matters, means the *corpus* of the estate.

Caveat. 'Let him beware.' A warning or notice entered in official records, e.g. the books of the offices of a registry or court, by an interested party to prevent a step being taken without previous notice to the person entering the *caveat*.

Cesser of Interest. The cessation or determination of an interest in property, annuity, etc., by the happening of the event by reference to which it was to come to an end.

Cestui que Trust. 'For whom is the trust.' A beneficiary under a trust. The person who has an equitable or beneficial interest in or ownership of property, the legal estate whereof is in the trustee.

Cestui que Vie. 'For whose life.' A person for the duration of whose life property is granted to another person.

Chattels. Any property other than freehold land.

Chattels Personal. The name given to movable, tangible articles of property which in the eye of the law are deemed to be personal property.

Chattels Real. Interests in land less than freehold (e.g. leaseholds) devolving on the personal representative save as provided in Part IV, Administration of Estates Act 1925. The term 'chattels real' is to be distinguished from 'chattels personal', the former being immovable personalty and the latter movable personalty.

Chose in Action. Property which cannot be the subject of physical possession, such as a debt or other right of action, e.g. stocks and shares, but which the owner can enforce by action at law.

Chose in Possession. A legal right capable of physical assertion, e.g. ownership of a personal chattel.

Citation. A notice to participate in legal proceedings. If the person cited fails to appear in the proceedings he cannot thereafter challenge them.

Codicil. A codicil is an instrument made by a testator subsequently to the will, annexed to and to be taken as part of it, being for its explanation or alteration, or to make some addition to or some subtraction from the former disposition of the testator. It must be executed with the same formalities as a will.

Cognati. Kindred by the mother's side.

Committee of Lunatic. A person or persons appointed to administer the estate of a person of unsound mind.

Consanguinity. Relationship by blood, either lineally, i.e. in direct line as in the case of father and son, or collaterally, by descent from a common ancestor.

Constructive Trust. A trust inferred by law without reference to the presumed intention of any party, in order to preserve the equities between persons interested in the property subjected to the trust.

Coverture. The status of a wife during marriage.

Cum Testamento Annexo. With the will annexed.

Custodian Trustee. A trustee who has the custody and care of trust property but not its management.

Cy-pres. 'Near thereto.' A doctrine under which a charitable trust may be carried out for a purpose similar to that specified by the settlor where the specific charitable object has failed.

Death Duty. A duty leviable in respect of property passing on death.

De bonis non administratis. 'Of goods not yet administered.' A grant of letters of administration as regards property not yet distributed.

De son tort. 'Of his own wrong.' (*See* Executor de son tort.)

Devastavit. 'He has wasted (the assets).' A devastavit is the wasting or misapplication of the assets by an executor or administrator.

Devise. A gift of real property by a will.

Discretionary Trust. A trust under which the trustees have power to apply the income in such shares and in such manner as they think fit for the benefit of the objects of the discretion or some one or more of them.

Domicil. A person's fixed and permanent legal home. Domicil depends primarily on the physical fact of residence plus intention to remain or return. It may be a domicil of origin or birth, by operation of law, or of choice. The question of domicil may affect the validity of a marriage, or the descent of property, the incidence of death duties, etc.

Donatio Mortis Causa. 'Gift on account of death.' A gift of personal property intended to become effective only on his death made by a person who apprehends that he is in danger of death.

Durante Absentia. During absence. A limited grant of administration during absence of the rightful representative.

Durante Dementia. So long as insanity lasts. A limited grant of administration for the period of insanity of the rightful representative.

Durante Mino Ætate. During infancy. A limited grant of administration during the minority of the rightful representative.

Durante Viduitate. During widowhood.

Easement. A right enjoyed by the owner of land over the lands of another, e.g. a right of way.

Emblements. Growing crops (e.g. corn) produced annually by human industry.

Encumbrance. A charge or liability attached to property, e.g. a mortgage. The person entitled or to whom the liability is owed is the 'encumbrancer'.

Entail. A limitation of property in successive interests to be enjoyed in lineal descent, e.g. a grant to X and the heirs of his body, or to X and Y and the heirs of their body, or to X and the heirs male of his body (*see* Fee Tail).

Equity of Redemption. The right of a mortgagor to redeem mortgaged property by paying off the principal and interest.

Estate. This term is used in executorship as meaning the property of the deceased person.

Estate Duty. Estate duty is a graduated stamp duty payable on the principal value of all property, real and personal, settled or not settled, passing at death, after deducting funeral expenses, debts and encumbrances.

Estate pur autre vie. An estate lasting for the lifetime of another person.

Executor. A representative appointed by the will or codicil of a deceased person to administer his estate after his death.

Executor de son tort. An unauthorised person intermeddling with the estate.

Executorship. Executorship is the office of a person authorised to administer the estate of a deceased.

Executorship Expenses. (*See* Testamentary expenses.)

Falsify. Showing proof that an item has been wrongly inserted in an account stated. (*See* 'Surcharge'.)

Fee Simple. Freehold ownership of land.

Fee Tail. An estate in land limited to a man and the heirs of his body or particular heirs of his body. Generally called an estate tail.

A tenant-in-tail of full age has power to dispose by will, by means of a devise or bequest referring specifically either to the property, or to the instrument under which it was acquired, or to entailed property generally, of all property of which he was tenant-in-tail in possession at his death, unless the entail is a Statutory one, in which case the entail cannot be so barred (Law of Property Act 1925, s. 176).

Foreclosure. An order for foreclosure is an order made by the court, which puts an end to the equity of redemption of a mortgagor who has defaulted in payment of principal or interest, when due, and vests the legal estate in the mortgagee.

Funeral Expenses. Funeral expenses are the costs of the funeral, the grave and the like, suitable to the rank and position the deceased held during his lifetime.

Heir. The person succeeding to the real estate of a deceased person upon intestacy. (Descent to the heir-at-law was abolished by s. 45, Administration of Estates Act 1925.)

Heirloom. Chattels accruing to the heir as real estate by custom, or settled with real estate to follow the limitations thereof, and which would otherwise pass to the executors as personalty. A tenant for life can sell heirlooms, the proceeds being capital money, but not without an order of the court (Settled Land Act 1925, s. 67).

Holograph Will. A will entirely in the hand-writing of the testator.

Hotchpot. Bringing into account sums already received by a claimant before fixing his share of a larger fund. In executorship, hotchpot is the bringing into account by a child or his issue, where the child has been advanced in the parent's lifetime, of the sum so advanced, if he or they wish to share with the brothers and sisters of the child in the distribution of the parent's estate. See Chap. XIV, § 18, as to hotchpot in a partial intestacy.

Impeachment for Waste. Liability for committing waste upon lands. The liability incurred by a life tenant in wasting the settled property, e.g. cutting down timber, working and disposing of minerals, allowing houses to fall into disrepair, etc. (*See* 'Waste.')

Implied Trust. A trust to be implied from the unexpressed but presumed, intention of a party.

Income. The receipts arising from the investment of capital.

In Loco Parentis. In place of a parent. A person is *in loco parentis* when he means to put himself in the situation of the lawful father of the child, with reference to the father's office and duty of making a provision for the child (*ex parte Pye* (1811)).

In re. In the matter of.

Interest in Possession. A right in or over property entitling the owner of that right to the immediate enjoyment of the benefit or advantage to which the right gives rise.

Intestate. An intestate is a person who has died without making a valid will; also a person who leaves a will but has not disposed of all his property thereby.

Issue. The term 'issue' includes children, grandchildren and all other lineal descendants of a person.

Joint Tenancy. The estate of two or more persons in the same land, each of such persons having acquired his interest at the same time by the same title with unity of interest and possession – the only legal-co-ownership as regards legal estates now recognised.

On the death of one of the parties, the other takes his share by survivorship. Trustees are always joint tenants.

Lapse. Lapse is the failure of a legacy or devise by reason of the death of the legatee or devisee in the testator's lifetime. An exception arises in the case of issue of the testator who leaves issue surviving the testator. A lapsed share of residue forms an intestacy, but a lapsed legacy (other than of residue) falls into residue.

Leasehold. Land held under a lease for a term of years. Chattels Real.

Legacy. A legacy is a gift of personal property by will.

Legacy Duty. Legacy Duty was duty payable on personal property (with the exception of leasehold property) bequeathed by will, or passing under an intestacy. It was abolished by the Finance Act 1949.

Letters of Administration. The term applied to the document given by the court under its seal to a person, authorising him to administer the estate of an intestate or of a testator where there is no executor capable of acting.

Lex Situs. The law of the place where the property is situated.

Life Tenant. A life tenant is one who is entitled to receive the income from property either during the term of his own life or that of another person (i.e. *pur autre vie*).

NOTE: The expression properly applies only to an interest in land, but is normally used also with regard to personalty.

Next-of-Kin. Next-of-kin is the term applied to those who are lineally or collaterally related in the nearest degree to a given person.

Nuncupative Will. A will made verbally before witnesses.

The only nuncupative wills now valid are those of sailors at sea or soldiers or airmen on active service.

Originating Summons. (*See* Summons.)

Para rationabilis. A reasonable portion.

Pendente Lite. While the suit is pending.

Per Capita. *Per capita* (literally 'by the heads') means that if a man dies intestate leaving children, they share his estate equally between them. Where applicable, brothers and sisters, or uncles and aunts, also take *per capita*.

Per my et per tout. 'By the half and by all.' An expression used to indicate the interests of joint tenants.

Per Stirpes. Literally 'by the stems', e.g. if a man dies intestate leaving children, and children of a deceased child, then the children of the deceased child take the share their parent would have taken. Where applicable, the issue of brothers and sisters, or of uncles and aunts, also take *per stirpes*.

Perpetuities. Executory or future interests in land so limited that they may vest at a time more remote than permitted by law, viz. after 21 years from the death of a person in being at the date when the instrument purporting to confer the future interest comes into question.

Personal Representative. The person, whether executor or administrator, who is charged with the administration of the estate of a deceased person, and in whom the estate is vested for the purpose of distribution.

Personalty. Personalty is all movable property and chattels real, i.e. all property other than freehold interests in land. Pure personalty is personal property unconnected with land. Mixed personalty inclu des interests in land such as leaseholds.

Per Testes. By witnesses.
Proving a will in solemn form is known as proving *per testes*.

Plene Administravit. 'He has fully administered' (that is, in accordance with the rules of law). The defence set up by a personal representative, when sued upon a debt of the deceased which he has no asset to satisfy.

Plene Administravit Praeter. He has fully administered except to the extent of the assets acknowledged to be in his hands.

Portion. The provision made for a child by a parent or a person in *loco parentis*.

Power of Appointment. A power given by will or deed, by one person to another, to appoint the person or persons to whom property shall pass on some future event.

The person exercising the power is called the donee of the power, and the person in whose favour it is exercised is called the appointee.

A general power of appointment gives the donee a right to appoint in favour of any one (including himself), whereas a limited power gives the right to appoint only to some or all of certain persons, or classes of persons.

Power of Attorney. A formal instrument by which one person authorises another to act for him.

Precatory Trust. A trust implied from the use of words advising or recommending money bequeathed to be applied in a particular manner. A trust is not always implied by the use of precatory words, i.e. words of wish, hope, desire or entreaty accompanying a gift, that the donee will dispose of the property in a particular way. The presumption today is against construing such words as a trust.

Pre-emption. The right of purchasing property in priority to other persons.

Preference. Preference is the right of the executor to pay one creditor before another of equal degree.

Probate. Probate is the proving of the will.

NOTE: The document usually spoken of as 'Probate' consists of the probate copy of the will, together with a smaller parchment bearing the seal of the court, and properly called the 'Probate Act'.

Realty. Freehold property and certain exceptional choses in action. Chattels Real are now deemed to be included under this heading, but not for Estate Duty purposes.

Remainderman. A remainderman is one who takes the real estate after the death of the life tenant. He is also called the 'reversioner'; and both expressions are frequently used with reference to personal property.

Rent Charge. An annual sum charged upon land by deed or statute, payable to a person who is not the landlord and to whom an express power of distress is given.

Residuary Devisee. A residuary devisee is one who takes the residue of the real property after the payment of all debts and legacies charged on the realty.

Residuary Legatee. A residuary legatee is one who takes the remainder of the personal property after the payment of all debts and legacies.

Resulting Trust. An implied trust arising in favour of the person creating the trust, where e.g. the trusts for the original beneficiaries have been exhausted.

Retainer. The right of the executor to retain a debt due to himself as against other creditors of equal degree.

Reversion, Reversionary Interest. A right in property the enjoyment of which is deferred, but which will revert to the owner on the expiration of the time of deferment.

Satisfaction. Satisfaction is the extinguishment of a creditor's claim by means of a legacy. Also, the ademption of a legacy in certain circumstances by a gift made to the proposed legatee during the lifetime of the testator.

Settlement. Every device by which the enjoyment of estate under the same deed or will may be had by different persons in succession.

Settled Land. Land limited to persons in succession, so that the person for the time being in the possession or enjoyment of it has no power to deprive the others of their right of future enjoyment.

Succession Duty. Succession duty was a duty payable by one who becomes entitled to real estate or leaseholds under a will or intestacy, or to any property devolving on death otherwise than by will or intestacy. Abolished by the Finance Act 1949.

Sui Juris. A person is said to be *sui juris* when he is under no contractual disability and can bind himself without reference to or control by others.

Summons. A citation to appear before the court, communicated to the party by means of a document called a writ. In some circumstances the issue of a writ is not required, in which case the summons is termed an originating summons.

Surcharge. Proof of an omission of an item in an account stated, for which credit ought to have been given. (Also *see* 'Falsify'.)

Tenant-in-Tail. The life tenant of an entailed estate. (*See* 'Fee Tail'.)

Tenant pur autre vie. A tenant for the life of another.

Testamentary Expenses. Testamentary expenses are the expenses of proving a will, including the expenses of an action, if an action has been necessary, the Estate Duty on the free personal estate in Great Britain, costs of administration, broker's fees, expenses of sales, etc.

Testator. The person making a will.

Trust. A disposition of property whereby the title thereto is vested in one or more 'trustees' who are required from the terms of the disposition (the 'trust instrument' or 'settlement') to apply the benefits arising out of the property for the advantage of the 'beneficiaries' or 'cestuis que trustent'.

Trust Corporation. The public trustee or a corporation appointed by the court in any particular case to be a trustee or entitled by rules made under Section 4 (3) of the Public Trustee Act 1906, to act as custodian trustee.

Trustee. One to whom is committed the administration of a trust. A person who holds property on trust for another.

Ultra vires. 'Beyond the power.' An act outside the power conferred by law, and therefore invalid.

Vested. A present as distinguished from a contingent right. An estate is said to be vested in possession when it gives a present right to immediate possession of the property. An estate which gives a present right to the future possession of property is said to be vested in interest.

Waste. The destruction or damage of property by a life tenant or other limited owner. It may be voluntary or active waste, e.g. the improper cutting of timber; or permissive waste, e.g. allowing property to go to ruin; or equitable waste, e.g. the wanton destruction of property.

Will. A testamentary declaration by which a person signifies his wishes as to the devolution of his property after his death.

APPENDIX IV

ESTATE DUTY – DISCRETIONARY TRUSTS

1. The Board of Inland Revenue have had representations that trustees and their professional advisers are uncertain about the kind of records that trustees will need to maintain in the light of the legislation imposing a charge on discretionary trusts (Sections 36 and 37, Finance Act 1969, as amended by Section 31, Finance Act 1970). This statement indicates the practice of the Estate Duty Office in relation to some aspects of the legislation which affect the matter.

2. Broadly, Estate Duty is payable on the death of a beneficiary under a discretionary trust on the same proportion of the trust property as the proportion that the deceased received of the trust income arising during a specified period of up to seven years (the 'relevant period' as defined in Section 37, running to the date of death, or the date of advance out of the settled funds etc.).

3. In the context, 'income' is considered to be income determined on ordinary trust principles. It is not, e.g. income as ascertained for Income tax purposes. The Revenue view is that it is income net of Income tax which the trustees are liable to pay, and net of any income which trustees must properly retain as a provision against future or contingent liabilities falling upon income, such as Surtax which is levied on the settler and which he can reclaim from the trustees.

Under Section 36 (6) (d), Finance Act 1969, costs, expenses and fees properly payable out of income are to be deducted from the income. They are considered to be payable at the time when they become due and payable even if they are not in fact paid until later.

4. The term 'arising' (during the relevant period) is considered, in the case of income consisting of dividends, interest, rent etc., to mean 'received by the trustees'. This means that neither dividends nor other income received in respect of a period spanning the beginning or end of a relevant period need be apportioned. In some cases, e.g. an unincorporated business or a landed estate, it will be sufficient to use the normal periodical accounts of the business or estate; income for broken periods at the beginning and end of the relevant period may be estimated by a time apportionment or such other method as seems reasonable in the particular circumstances.

5. Section 37 (3) (b), Finance Act 1969, provides the test for deciding once and for all whether, and to what extent, a payment made to a discretionary beneficiary is a payment of income or capital. If it is an income payment it may become part of the numerator of the fraction which determines how much of the trust fund is dutiable on his death. If it is a capital payment and was made after 15th April, 1969, parts of it may become

liable to Estate Duty on the deaths within the next seven years of any of the other discretionary beneficiaries, and the trustees, who will be accountable for any such Estate Duty, may wish to obtain from the Estate Duty Office a certificate under Section 44 (3), Finance Act 1950, which quantifies their liability.

The test requires regard to be had to all income subject to the discretionary trust arising since 15th April, 1963, up to the time of the particular payment in question and provides that the payment is to be treated as income to the extent that there was a balance of income at that time sufficient to cover it after allowing for all previous payments since 15th April, 1963, treated as income payments. For the purpose of the test, all income available during the period for distribution under the discretion is included whether it derives from the original trust fund or from accumulations or accretions subsequently added to it; there is no need to separate the income according to its sources.

Trustees need therefore to analyse their past accounts on this basis and keep a note of any income payments made to discretionary beneficiaries during the period 15th April, 1963, to 15th April, 1969, and of any unexhausted balance of income available for future distribution at the end of that period.

Beginning with 16th April, 1969, a similar analysis should in strictness be made whenever a payment is made. In practice it may be sufficient to make a formal analysis only when there is any uncertainty as to the status of a payment under the test. The figures required by such an analysis are:

1. Any unexhausted balance of income brought forward from the last analysis;
2. The income received during the intervening period; and
3. All payments made during that period.

BOARD OF INLAND REVENUE
PRESS NOTICE

11th September, 1970

APPENDIX V

REDEMPTION OF SURVIVING SPOUSE'S LIFE INTEREST ON INTESTACY

Where on an intestacy, a surviving husband or wife is entitled to a life interest in part of the residuary estate, the surviving spouse may elect that the life interest shall be redeemed by paying its capital value to the surviving spouse. The personal representative can purchase or redeem the life interest but in addition to paying the capital value will have to pay the costs of the transaction. This will mean that the residuary estate of the intestate may be dealt with and distributed free from the life interest.

The capital value of the life interest is to be reckoned in accordance with the following rules:

(i) ascertain the annual value of the life interest to which the surviving husband or wife would be entitled if the said part of the residuary estate (whether or not yielding income) were on the date of the redemption of the life interest re-invested in $2\frac{1}{2}\%$ Consols;

(ii) ascertain the amount which, if invested on the said date in the purchase of an immediate life annuity from the National Debt Commissioners, through the Post Office Savings Bank, would purchase an annuity for the surviving spouse of the annual value ascertained under (i) above;

(iii) deduct from the amount so ascertained five per cent. of that amount;

(iv) if the age of the tenant for life on the said date exceeds eighty years, deduct a further five per cent. of the amount ascertained under (ii) above for each complete year by which the age exceeds eighty.

The balance is the capital value, with the proviso that it is not to be reduced below one and a half times the annual value calculated in (i) above.

An election under this provision is only exercisable if at the time of the election the whole of the said part of the residuary estate consists of property in possession, but for this purpose a life interest in property partly in possession and partly not in possession may be treated as consisting of two separate life interests for those respective parts of the property.

If the tenant for life dies after the exercise of the election but before effect is given to it, the date of redemption is to be taken to be the date immediately before the death of the tenant for life.

The election is exercisable only within the period of twelve months from the date on which representation with respect of the estate of the intestate is first taken out; but the Court may extend the period if the surviving husband or wife satisfies the Court that the limitation to twelve months will operate unfairly:

(a) in consequence of the representation first taken out being probate of a will subsequently revoked on the grounds that the will was invalid; or

(b) in consequence of a question where a person had an interest in the estate, or as to the nature of the interest in the estate, not having been determined at the time when representation was first taken out; or

(c) in consequence of some other circumstances affecting the administration or distribution of the estate.

An election is exercisable, except where the tenant for life is the sole personal representative, by notifying the personal representative, or, where there are several of whom one is the tenant for life, all of them, except for the tenant for life, in writing.

Where the tenant for life is the sole personal representative, an election is not effective unless written notice thereof is given to the Principal Probate Registrar within the period within which it must be made. A record must be kept of such notices and the record made available to the Public.

In considering for the purposes of the foregoing provision when representation was first taken out, a grant limited to settled land or to trust property is left out of account and a grant limited to real estate or personal estate is left out of account unless the grant limited to the remainder of the estate has previously been made or is made at the same time (Intestates' Estates Act 1952, s. 2). The personal representatives may raise:

(a) the net sum of £8,750 or £30,000 (as appropriate) or any part thereof and the interest thereon payable to the surviving spouse of the intestate on a security of the whole or any part of the residuary estate of the intestate (other than the personal chattels), so far as that estate may be sufficient for the purpose or the said sum and interest may not have been satisfied by an appropriation under the statutory power; and

(b) in like manner, the capital sum, if any, required for the purchase or redemption of the life interest of the surviving spouse of the intestate or any part thereof not satisfied by the application for that purpose of any part of the residuary estate of the intestate;

and in either case, the amount, if any, properly required for the costs of the transaction.

Where the residuary estate of an intestate comprises an interest in a dwelling house (which term includes the garden and amenity land) in which the surviving spouse was resident at the intestate's death, the surviving spouse may require the personal representative to appropriate that interest in or towards satisfaction of any absolute interest of the surviving spouse in the estate of the intestate or towards redeeming the life interest of the surviving spouse.

This right is not exercisable where the interest is:

(i) a tenancy which at the date of death would determine within two years; or

(ii) a tenancy which the landlord by notice given after the death could be determined within two years of the death.

The part of a building occupied as a separate dwelling is treated as a dwelling house for this purpose; where:

(iii) the dwelling house is part of a building, an interest in the whole of which is comprised in the residue; or

(iv) the house is held with agricultural land, an interest in which is comprised in the residue; or

(v) the whole or part of the house was at the time of death used as an hotel or lodging house; or

(vi) a part of the house was used for purposes other than domestic purposes;

the right to require appropriation cannot be exercised unless the Courts so order after being satisfied that the result will not be the diminishment in value of assets in the residue other than the said house, or make them more difficult to dispose of for the benefit of the other beneficiaries. An application can be made in such a case by the surviving spouse or by the personal representative(s).

The right is only exercisable within twelve months from the first taking out of representation, unless the Court extends the period because it would operate unfairly. It cannot be exercised after the death of the surviving spouse. Notice must be given to all personal representatives. With the consent of the personal representative(s) a notice may be revoked before the property is actually appropriated. The surviving spouse can require the personal representative to have the house valued and to inform him or her before he or she decides to exercise the right.

During the twelve months (or extended period ordered by the Court) the personal representative must not sell the house without the consent of the surviving spouse except where money is required to pay debts and this can only be found by selling the house. If, however, on an application by the personal representative where the house is part of the other property ((i) to (vi) above), the Court does not order that the surviving spouse may exercise the right of appropriation, the Court may authorise the personal representative to dispose of the interest in the house within twelve months (or the extended period). This provision does not apply where the surviving spouse is the sole personal representative or one of two or more personal representatives. It does not confer on the surviving spouse any right as against a purchaser from the personal representative. Where the surviving spouse is one of two or more personal representatives, the rule that a trustee may not purchase trust property does not prevent the surviving spouse from purchasing out of the estate an interest in a dwelling house in which he or she was resident at the time of the intestate's death. Any excess of the value of the interest in the house over the value of the interest of the surviving spouse in the estate can be satisfied by a payment in cash by the surviving spouse.

If the surviving spouse is of unsound mind or a defective, the requirement or consent may be given by the Committee or Receiver, or if there is no Committee or Receiver, by the Court. An infant can make the requirement or consent himself. A sane murderer cannot benefit under his victim's will and this rule extends to preventing him taking any share under his victim's intestacy (*in re Sigsworth; Bedford* v. *Bedford*), nor can any person claiming through him benefit (*in re Pollock; Pollock* v. *Pollock*). In the absence of evidence as to the state of mind of the person who did the killing, the Court will proceed on the assumption that the assault was felonious; if the killing was done while of unsound mind, this disqualification does not apply (*re Petts*).

APPENDIX VI

Estate Duty Rates for deaths between 16th April, 1969 and 21st March, 1972 inclusive.

(1) Rates for deaths on or after 16th April, 1969 and before 31st March, 1971:

Slice		Rate per cent.	Aggregate	Estate Duty on Aggregate
On the first	£10,000	Nil	£10,000	Nil
On the next	£7,500	25	£17,500	£1,875
,, ,, ,,	£12,500	30	£30,000	£5,625
,, ,, ,,	£10,000	45	£40,000	£10,125
,, ,, ,,	£40,000	60	£80,000	£34,125
,, ,, ,,	£70,000	65	£150,000	£79,625
,, ,, ,,	£150,000	70	£300,000	£184,625
,, ,, ,,	£200,000	75	£500,000	£334,625
,, ,, ,,	£250,000	80	£750,000	£534,625
,, ,, ,,	£1,307,500	85	£2,057,500	£1,646,000

In no case could the amount of duty exceed 80 per cent. of the aggregate value and this limit applied where the net principal value of the estate exceeded £2,057,500.

(2) Rates for deaths after 30th March, 1971 and before 22nd March, 1972, there will be no liability on the first £12,500 of principal value of assets. As a result, the table will become:

Slice		Rate per cent.	Aggregate	Estate duty on Aggregate
On the first	£12,500	Nil	£12,500	Nil
On the next	£5,000	25	£17,500	£1,250
,, ,, ,,	£12,500	30	£30,000	£5,000
,, ,, ,,	£10,000	45	£40,000	£9,500
,, ,, ,,	£40,000	60	£80,000	£33,500
,, ,, ,,	£70,000	65	£150,000	£79,000
,, ,, ,,	£150,000	70	£300,000	£184,000
,, ,, ,,	£200,000	75	£500,000	£334,000
,, ,, ,,	£250,000	80	£750,000	£534,000
,, ,, ,,	£1,307,500	85	£2,057,500	£1,645,325

In no case can the effective rate exceed 80 per cent. which applies to estates exceeding £2,070,000.

Illustration:

P died on 31st March, 1971, having made the following gifts as wedding presents (i.e. gifts in consideration of marriage) during his lifetime:

589

(*a*) On the marriage of his son Q in August, 1967, £10,000 to Q absolutely.
This will be exempt from duty on P's death as it was made before
20th March, 1968, and complies with Section 53, Finance Act 1963.

(*b*) On the marriage of his nephew and godson R, in June 1970, in cash
£2,500.
As this gift was made after 19th March, 1968, and R was not a
descendant of P, the exemption limit is £1,000 and the sum of £1,500
will be liable to Estate Duty. The date of death being less than four
years after the date of the gift, there is no reduction under Section 64,
Finance Act 1960.

(*c*) On the marriage of his daughter S in August 1970:

(i) £2,000 in cash to S absolutely;

(ii) Investments then worth £6,000 to Trustees to pay the income to S
for life and on her death to hold the capital in trust for the children
of the marriage absolutely.

On 31st March, 1971, the settled investments had a market value of
£8,000. The total of the two gifts on P's death is £10,000 in value, of which
£5,000 is the limit of exemption under Section 36, Finance Act 1968
and the sum of £5,000 is liable to Estate Duty. The exemption fraction
$\frac{£5,000}{£10,000}$ is applied rateably to each gift. His daughter S will therefore be
personally liable to pay Estate Duty on 5/10ths of £2,000 = £1,000 and the
trustees will pay duty on 5/10ths of £8,000 = £4,000 out of the capital of
the settlement.

APPENDIX VII

PROVISIONS OF THE FINANCE ACT 1972

RATES

The rates of estate duty for deaths on or after 22nd March, 1972 are set out on p.86.

EXEMPTIONS

Section 121 has introduced a further exemption in respect of property passing on a death on or after 22nd March, 1972. This exemption does not relate to a specific form of property, but to the value of property left to certain persons.

In determining the principal value of the estate, subject to certain exemptions in respect of gifts dealt with later, there is disregarded:

(i) **property given to:**

The National Gallery	British Museum	The National
Science Museum	(Natural History)	Museum of Wales
Victoria & Albert	London Museum	Wallace Collection
Museum	National Maritime	National Galleries of
Imperial War Museum	Museum	Scotland
National Portrait	Tate Gallery	National Museum of
Gallery	Ulster Museum	Antiquities of
Geological Museum	Ulster Folk	Scotland
National Library of	Museum	National Library of
Wales	The Royal Scottish	Scotland
The British Museum	Museum	

Apart from the above specific bodies the Treasury may approve any other similar national institution which exists wholly or mainly for the purpose of preserving for the public benefit a collection of scientific, historic or artistic interest. Further bodies to which bequests will reduce the principal value of the estate include:

Any museum or art gallery in the United Kingdom which exists wholly or mainly for that purpose and is maintained by a local authority or university in the United Kingdom.

Any library the main function of which is to serve the needs of teaching and research at a university in the United Kingdom.

The National Art Collections Fund.

The National Trust for Places of Historic Interest or Natural Beauty.

The National Trust for Scotland for Places of Historic Interest or Natural Beauty.

591

(ii) **property given to charities, up to a limit of £50,000:**

'Charity' in its legal sense comprises four principal divisions:

trusts for the relief of poverty;

trusts for the advancement of education;

trusts for the advancement of religion; and

trusts for any other purposes beneficial to the community not falling under any of the preceding heads (Lord Macnaghten in *Commissioners for Special Purposes of Iucome Tax* v. *Pemsel* [1891], 3 T.C. 53).

(iii) **property given to or devolving on the deceased's widow or widower, up to a limit of £15,000:**

This exemption covers not only bequests by will but also gifts prior to death and which are subject to estate duty (see Chapter VI). The effect of the exemption is:

(*a*) to exempt from duty an estate of £30,000, providing the wife receives an outright bequest of £15,000 since the remaining sum is below the minimum amount on which duty is payable;

(*b*) to ensure that a husband should make gifts to his wife during his lifetime of up to £15,000 and as the value of the gifts reduces for estate duty purposes (see p.191) to make further gifts.

Illustration (1)

A man makes a gift of £15,000 to his wife. After four years, the value of that gift for estate duty purposes will fall by 15 per cent. In that year, the husband can make a further gift of £2,250. After five years, the value of the original gift for estate duty purposes falls by another 15 per cent. so that a further gift of £2,250 can be made. After six years, the value of the original gift for estate duty purposes has fallen to £6,000. Having made further gifts of £4,500, the husband can make a further gift of £4,500 in that year and £6,000 in the following year. A similar process can be carried out with each gift.

It is advisable to make gifts in a lifetime since with inflation the value of the husband's estate may be increasing. By this means and either by his living more than seven years after the gift or by making gifts of cash, the husband will pass part of that inflationary increase to his wife.

The Government were not anxious for the foregoing provisions to give rise to limited period gifts to avoid duty on a death but with the property later reverting to the family to the detriment of the Institution. Consequently certain gifts of property within (i) to (iii) above do *not* give rise to any reduction in the principal value of an estate. These are:

(*a*) A gift which takes effect on the termination of any interest or the determination of any period, other than an interest or period terminating on or before the death;

(*b*) A gift which is dependent on a condition which is not satisfied within twelve months after the death;

(c) A gift within (i) and (ii) which is less than the donor's full interest in the property given;

(d) A gift within (i) and (ii) which is for a limited period;

(e) A gift within (i) and (ii) which is defeasible or of which any part is or may become applicable for other than charitable purposes or for the purposes of those bodies listed in (i) above.

In determining the exclusions in (c), (d) and (e):

any question whether a gift is less than the donor's full interest in the property given is decided at a time twelve months after the death and any gift which has not been defeated at that time and is not defeasible after that time is treated as not being defeasible (whether or not it was capable of being defeated before that time).

The foregoing rules might have required the re-writing of many wills since it is usual to provide that bequests to spouses do not take effect if the spouse does not survive the deceased by a defined period, often 28 days. It is specifically provided in paragraph 1, Schedule 26, that the exclusion in (a) above does not apply in such cases.

COMPUTATION OF DUTY

The effect of the foregoing exemption on the estate duty liability on a death is easily seen.

Illustration (2)

Assume a man dies on 30th June, 1972. His estate consisted of:

A freehold house, valued at	£20,000
Investments, valued at	50,000
Personal chattels, valued at	6,000
Cash at bank	4,000
	£80,000

If that man left his estate to his son, the duty would be £26,250. If he left £15,000 to his widow outright, duty would be levied on £65,000, so that the amount payable would be £18,750. If he left £15,000 to his widow and £50,000 to a charity, the duty would be:

Aggregate value of assets		£80,000
Less: bequest to widow	£15,000	
bequest to charity	50,000	
		65,000
Value of estate for purposes of duty		£15,000

Duty payable – nil.

ALLOCATION OF RELIEF

If in Illustration (2), the residue of the property is left to the wife, there is no problem. But if the residue is left to anybody other than the widow or the charity on what basis is the benefit for the relief from duty apportioned? This matter is dealt with in Part II of Schedule 26.

The amount of the reduction referred to in the following paragraphs is the reduction in estate duty after allowing for:

any reduction in the estate rate (e.g. on agricultural property); and

any reduction due to the free estate being of a value of £15,000 or less while the settled estate exceeds that figure (s. 16 (3). F.A. 1894).

The Act uses two terms:

'exempt property' which is so much of any property as corresponds to the value to be disregarded; and

'chargeable property' which is the remainder of the property forming part of the estate.

In apportioning the benefit of the reduction:

(A) no part of the reduction is to reduce the duty on the chargeable property, except in so far as the duty would be attributable to property specifically given but would fall on residue.

Illustration (3)

The deceased died with an estate valued at £80,000. He left a house valued at £15,000 to his widow free of duty and gave the residue to his son. Since the reduction in duty is caused by the gift to the widow, it would be correct to give the full amount of the reduction effectively to her, but the gift was free of duty so that she is not interested. The residue would find a smaller amount of duty.

(B) Where property given as a share in residue or in a fund is exempt property the reduction resulting from that property being exempt property does not reduce the duty on the remainder.

Illustration (4)

The deceased's estate consisted of free residue given to his widow of £120,000 and a vested reversionary interest in his father's will trust left to his children of £80,000.

$$\text{The duty payable on £185,000 is} \qquad \text{£90,000}$$

This sum is divided as follows:

$$\text{Payable by executors } \frac{105}{185} \times \text{£90,000} \quad = \quad \text{£51,081}$$

$$\text{Payable by trustees } \frac{80}{185} \times \text{£90,000} \quad = \quad 38,919$$

$$\text{£90,000}$$

(C) The reduction is to be made as is most favourable to the widow or widower.

(D) Subject to (A) to (C) above, the reduction is treated as reducing duty on property bearing its own duty (whether or not specifically given) before duty on property not bearing its own duty.

ASCERTAINMENT OF EXEMPT AND CHARGEABLE PROPERTY

It will be realised from the foregoing that the benefit of the reduction in duty is to be given to the widow, widower, charity or body listed in (i). It is not intended to benefit other persons, except indirectly. In certain circumstances a decision may be needed to decide which of two or more possible assets are to constitute exempt property. In general, since the allocation is to be on the basis most favourable to the widow or widower, any agreement between either and the Commissioners is to be conclusive. Furthermore as already indicated property bearing its own duty (see p.98) is to be exempt property before other property. Finally there is a sweeping up provision whereby each asset is to be taken as exempt or chargeable to the extent proportionate to its value.

(E) Where there is a free estate of not more than £15,000 and settled property passing on death, the free estate is not included in the property passing on death.

Illustration (5)
Assume in Illustration (4) that the free estate had been £12,000 and the deceased had a vested life interest in a settlement of £200,000 and that he had left one-third of that interest to his wife and two-thirds to his children.
Duty on free estate – nil
Duty on settled property of £200,000—£15,000=£185,000=£90,000.
Proportion of duty applicable to widow: $\dfrac{51,667}{185,000}$
Proportion of duty applicable to children: $\dfrac{133,333}{185,000}$

(F) To determine the value of an annuity (since the bequest or gift to the widow may be by way of an annuity) it is necessary to determine the sum needed to produce an income equal to the amount of the annuity.

(G) Bequests may need to be abated (see p.393). Paragraphs 14 to 17 inclusive of Part III of Schedule 26 deal with relief in these circumstances.

In the following the words 'appropriate value' mean:
(a) in the case of property which bears its own duty, the principal value (i.e. the value for estate duty purposes) of that property;
(b) in the case of other property:
if it is property given to a charity, the widow or widower, the aggregate of the principal value (so far as it does not exceed £50,000 or £15,000 respectively (but these sums are reduced by the amount of property specifically given)) and the grossed-up equivalent of the remainder;
if it is property not given to a listed body in (i), charity, widow or widower, the appropriate value is the grossed-up equivalent of the remainder.

The 'grossed-up equivalent' is the amount, as would after deduction of estate duty at the appropriate rate, be equal to the principal value. The appropriate rate for this purpose in relation to any property (which is not included in a free estate not exceeding £15,000) is the estate rate if the exemptions in (i), (ii) and (iii) did not apply. In relation to any free estate which may exceed £15,000 in value but where marginal relief applies (see p.87) the appropriate rate is found by taking the duty which would be payable on that property if no relief were given other than exempting the initial £15,000 in value and dividing such duty by the principal value of the property.

Initially it is necessary to compute the aggregate of the following specific gifts:

(a) the principal value of any property given to the bodies listed in (i).

(b) the appropriate value of any property given to a charity, the widow or widower; and

(c) the appropriate value of any property not falling within (b) or (c).

In the case of the widow or widower it is necessary to include also sums to which she or he are specifically entitled. Debts created by the deceased otherwise than for full consideration and for which no deduction can be made in computing estate duty under s. 7 (1), F.A. 1894, are deemed to be property specifically given.

If this aggregate exceeds the principal value of the estate, it is to be reduced by such proportion thereof as would result in such aggregate being equal to the principal value.

If the aggregate is less than the principal value, so much of the remainder shall be exempt property as consists of gifts to bodies in (i) above and as consists of the limits in (ii) and (iii) after deducting the amounts in (b) and (c) taken into account in determining the aggregate.

(H) Where amounts are payable out of different funds, such as could occur in connection with the problems discussed in Marshalling the Assets (see p.357), the calculations in (G) have to be made separately for each of those funds.

EVENTS AFTER DEATH

Where after death property previously treated as exempt because it is bequeathed to a charity ceases to be used for charitable purposes and other property is not substituted, duty becomes chargeable on such property and the persons entitled thereto become accountable for the duty. The extra duty is determined by calculating the duty which would have been payable if the property had not been exempt on the earlier death and comparing that sum with the amount actually paid. The difference is the duty payable now.

Property which would have been exempt from duty anyway because it consists of works of art etc. will remain exempt property even if sold after death. But if the property had been given to the widow or widower, the exemption only continues if sold in their lifetime. Similar rules apply where the undertaking required under section 48 (1) Finance Act 1950 is broken or timber is sold.

DEEDS OF FAMILY ARRANGEMENT

Providing the deed of arrangement is entered into not more than two years after death, the terms of the deed are deemed to have been made by the deceased.

INLAND REVENUE ANNOUNCEMENTS

Live Animals

It has previously been the view of the Board of Inland Revenue that live animals were not capable of attracting the 45 per cent. reduction of duty which has been allowable under certain provisions of the estate duty law. These provisions include section 23 of the Finance Act 1925, section 28 Finance Act 1949, section 28 Finance Act 1954, section 35 and Schedule 17, Part III, paragraphs 8 and 19 of the Finance Act 1969. The Board have now been advised, however, that the relief is allowable in respect to working animals and 'production livestock' kept for the purposes of a business.

'Production livestock' for this purpose comprises, broadly, live animals which are kept for permanent employment in farming and comparable businesses and the function of which is the production of saleable products (e.g. the young of the animal). Animals which are kept primarily in order to be sold, live or dead, or in order to provide a saleable product after slaughter are not considered to fall under this description. Whether the relief is allowable in any given case will depend on the purposes for which the particular animals are kept.

Having regard to section 35 of the Finance Act 1951, which restricts the re-opening of cases on the ground of legal mistake where duty has been paid and its payment and acceptance were regarded as satisfying the claim for duty on a view of the law which at the time is generally received or adopted in practice, the benefit of the new practice cannot be accorded to any case where the duty has already been settled and paid.

Pecuniary Legacies

Where a testator has bequeathed a pecuniary legacy which is payable to the legatee at an age not exceeding 25 years, and pending payment of the legacy a residuary legatee is entitled to income from property held to provide the legacy, such property (up to the amount of the pecuniary legacy) will be disregarded for the purposes of any liability to duty under section 2 (1) (b) (i) of the Finance Act 1894, as substituted by section 36 (2) of the Finance Act 1969, on the death of the residuary legatee or a successor to his interest. This extra-statutory concession does not apply to a legacy or legacies which amount to more than £2,000 in the case of any one pecuniary legatee.

Works of Art Concession

Where on a death occurring on or before 30th March, 1971, exemption from estate duty under section 40 of Finance Act 1930 and relief from capital gains tax have been allowed on an object as being of national, scientific, historic or artistic interest and it is subsequently sold within three years of the death, section 39 (2) of Finance Act 1969 has the effect that there is no deduction for the relevant capital gains tax in arriving at the amount on which estate duty is then chargeable. Notwithstanding section 39 (2) a deduction may in practice be allowed in respect of the smaller of

(i) the extra capital gains tax which would have been chargeable at the death if the relief had not been allowed, or (ii) the capital gains tax actually charged as a consequence of the sale.

A similar deduction may be allowed where the liability to estate duty arises because of a disposal (otherwise than by sale) within a period of three years from the death or because of the non-observance within that period of an undertaking given when the exemption was allowed.

Estate Duty on Benefits under Superannuation Schemes

These notes explain in general terms the practice of the Estate Duty Office regarding liability to estate duty on lump sums and annuities payable on death under the rules of employees' retirement benefits schemes and superannuation funds and under retirement annuity contracts and trust schemes approved under section 22 of the Finance Act 1956.

A. *Payments to the deceased's legal personal representatives*

1. Payments that are legally due to the legal personal representatives and cannot be withheld from them at the discretion of any person exercisable after the death are liable to duty as part of the deceased's free estate. The legal personal representatives are accountable for the duty under section 8(3) of the Finance Act 1894.

2. Amounts liable to duty under this head are subject to normal aggregation with other property passing on the death for the purpose of determining the rate of duty.

B. *Where the deceased had a general power of nomination*

3. Where the deceased had a general power to nominate a benefit to anyone he wished and he had not exerciesed his power irrevocably in his lifetime, the benefit is liable to duty under section 2 (1) (a) of the Finance Act 1894, and the legal personal representatives are accountable for the duty under section 8 (3).

4. The case where the deceased had at the time of his death an option to have a sum of money paid to his legal personal representatives normally falls under this head. Where, however, an annuity is payable to the deceased's widow, widower or dependant under a contract or trust scheme approved under section 22 of the Finance Act 1956, and the deceased had an option to have a sum of money paid instead to his legal personal representatives, duty is not charged under this head (section 39 (2) of the Finance Act 1957).

5. Amounts liable to duty under this head are subject to normal aggregation with other property passing on the death.

C. *Annuities which continue to be payable after the deceased's death*

No duty is payable on deaths on or after 16th April, 1969, where the annuity continues as a separate item, but if the annuity after death is payable to the deceased's legal personal representatives it becomes liable under A above.

D. *Interests provided by the deceased*

For deaths on or after 16th April, 1969, no duty arises in respect of an annuity or other interest purchased or provided by the deceased to the extent that a beneficial interest accrues or arises on his death.

E. *Death of Pensioner or Annuitant*

It has never been the official practice to claim duty under section 2 (1) (b) of the Finance Act 1894 on the cesser of a pension or annuity payable under approved superannuation arrangements, even where the benefit was charged on the assets of a Fund. Paragraph 10 (c) of Part II of Schedule 17 to the Finance Act 1969 now expressly exempts pensions and annuities of this kind from any liability under the substituted section 2 (1) (b) of the 1894 Act (which imposes the new charge of estate duty on settled property). The sub-paragraph provides that the new charge is not to apply by reason of an interest of the deceased under such a scheme or in such a fund as is described in section 387 (1) or (2) of the Income Tax Act 1952, being an interest by way of pension or annuity. The exemption covers not only statutory superannuation schemes and schemes and funds approved by the Inland Revenue but also certain schemes and funds which, because of the date when they were set up or of the level of remuneration of the employees concerned, did not require formal approval.

The concluding part of paragraph 10 (c) makes it clear that the exemption does not extend to the death of a person who had an interest under a trust (or who benefited under a discretionary trust) of a *lump sum* benefit payable under a scheme or fund. If a lump sum benefit is settled (for example, in the exercise of discretionary powers as to the disposal of a death benefit), a claim for duty may arise on the death of any beneficiary under the settlement.

F. *Payments made in exercise of a discretion*

Where a lump sum benefit payable under a scheme or fund is not settled but is distributed in exercise of a discretion exercisable after the death, the death of a person to whom a payment is made will not give rise to any liability under the substituted Section 2 (1) (b).

G. *Gifts Inter Vivos*

It is not the official practice to claim estate duty under section 2 (1) (c) of the Finance Act 1894, as a gift *inter vivos*, on any benefit payable under superannuation arrangements such as are referred to in paragraph 10 (c) of Part II of Schedule 17 to the 1969 Act (see E above) or under an approved retirement annuity contract or trust scheme. This is so even if the benefit arises as a result of the surrender by the deceased, within seven years of his death, of part of a benefit to which he would have been entitled, as where an employee gives up part of his retirement pension in exchange for an annuity for his widow to begin on his death.

This practice does not extend to any *separate* provision made by an employee for his dependants or others, for example under a group life insurance scheme operated in conjunction with superannuation arrangements. Premiums paid by the deceased on a policy on his life effected under a scheme of this kind may be chargeable to duty as gifts *inter vivos*, although the gifts will commonly qualify for exemption under Section 37 of the Finance Act 1968 as normal income gifts.

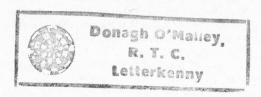

INDEX

601